NE능률 영어교과서

대한민국 고등학생 **10명 중 4.7명**이 보는 교과서

영어 고등 교과서 점유율 1위
[7차, 2007 개정, 2009 개정, 2015 개정]

KB124441

능률보카

그동안 판매된
능률VOCA 1,100만 부

대한민국 박스오피스
**천만명을 넘은 영화
단 28개**

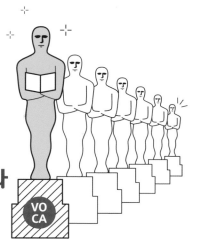

VOCA

그동안 판매된
리딩튜터 1,800만 부
차곡차곡 쌓으면 18만 미터

에베레스트 20배 높이

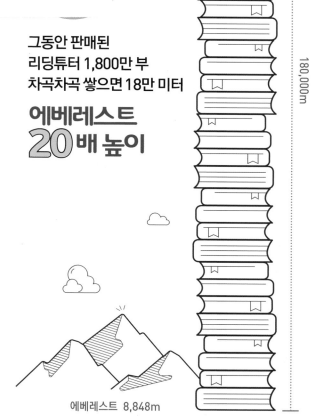

READING TUTOR

180,000m

에베레스트 8,848m

그래머존

그동안 판매된 400만 부의 그래머존을 바닥에 쭉~ 깔면

1000km 서울 - 부산 왕복가능

서울

부산

능률
EBS 수능특강

• • •

변형 문제
영어(상)

612제

지은이	NE능률 영어교육연구소
선임 연구원	김지현
외주연구원	콘텐츠 인앤아웃
영문 교열	Angela Lan
맥편집	하이테크컴
디자인	민유화, 김연주
영업	한기영, 이경구, 박인규, 정철교, 하진수, 김남준, 이우현
마케팅	박혜선, 남경진, 이지원, 김여진

Copyright©2023 by NE Neungyule, Inc.

All rights reserved. No part of this publication may be reproduced, stored in a retrieval system, or transmitted in any form or by any means, electronic, mechanical, photocopying, recording, or otherwise, without the prior permission of the copyright owner.

✖ 본 교재의 독창적인 내용에 대한 일체의 무단 전재 · 모방은 법률로 금지되어 있습니다.

✚ 파본은 구매처에서 교환 가능합니다.

Let's grow together

NE능률이
미래를
창조합니다.

건강한 배움의 고객가치를 제공하겠다는 꿈을 실현하기 위해
42년 동안 열심히 달려왔습니다.

앞으로도 끊임없는 연구와 노력을 통해
당연한 것을 멈추지 않고

고객, 기업, 직원 모두가 함께 성장하는 NE능률이 되겠습니다.

NE 능률

NE능률의 모든 교재가 한 곳에 - 엔이 북스

NE_Books

www.nebooks.co.kr ▼

NE능률의 유초등 교재부터 중고생 참고서,
토익·토플 수험서와 일반 영어까지!
PC는 물론 태블릿 PC, 스마트폰으로 언제 어디서나
NE능률의 교재와 다양한 학습 자료를 만나보세요.

✓ 필요한 부가 학습 자료 바로 찾기
✓ 주요 인기 교재들을 한눈에 확인
✓ 나에게 딱 맞는 교재를 찾아주는 스마트 검색
✓ 함께 보면 좋은 교재와 다음 단계 교재 추천
✓ 회원 가입, 교재 후기 작성 등 사이트 활동 시 NE Point 적립

건강한
배움의 즐거움

NE 능률

영어교과서 리딩튜터 능률보카 빠른독해 바른독해 수능만만 월등한 개념 수학 유형 더블 토마토 토익 NE 클래스
NE_Build & Grow   NE_Times   NE_Kids(굿잡, 상상수프)   NE_능률 주니어랩 아이챌린지

·2024학년도 수능 및 내신 대비·

능률
EBS 수능특강

변형 문제
영어(상)

612제

Structure & Features

1

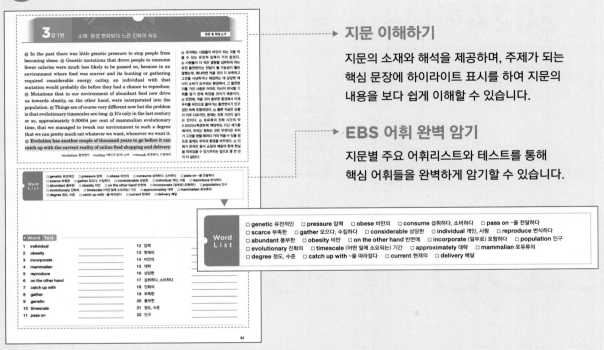

지문 이해하기

지문의 소재와 해석을 제공하며, 주제가 되는
핵심 문장에 하이라이트 표시를 하여 지문의
내용을 보다 쉽게 이해할 수 있습니다.

EBS 어휘 완벽 암기

지문별 주요 어휘리스트와 테스트를 통해
핵심 어휘들을 완벽하게 암기할 수 있습니다.

2

내신 빈출 유형 집중 훈련하기

올바른 어법 및 어휘 고르기, 동사를 알맞은 형태로 고
쳐 쓰기, 우리말에 맞게 영작하기 등 학교 시험에 자주
출제되는 3가지 유형을 집중 훈련할 수 있습니다.

`2강 4번`

At my high school, two students were ___(A)___ to Tufts University. However, the editor of our newspaper, who had w career for a Tufts ad hearing that news, I wa about my own chanc That morning, all I cou University. At about 1 front office came to ge ③ hands me a note to it. My heart pounded. of breath. I had no rig wanted it more than a our number. It rang Laughing with happi You got into Tufts!!" I j ⑤ attracted the attent office. A thrill ran thr that I will never, ever

`고난도`

15 윗글의 밑줄 친 부분 번호를 쓰고 고쳐 쓰

(1) _____ → ___
(2) _____ → ___
(3) _____ → ___

16 윗글의 빈칸 (A), (B)에 공통으로 들어갈 단어를 영영 뜻풀이를 참고하여 쓰시오. (단, 주어진 글자로 시작하여 어법에 알맞은 형태로 쓸 것)

to allow someone to join an organization

a _____

고난도 문항으로 수능·내신 완벽 대비

엄선된 고난도 문항을 통해 3점짜리 킬러 문항에 완벽하게 대비할 수 있습니다.

`04` `2강 4번`

다음 글의 내용과 일치하지 않는 것은?

At my high school, two students wer to Tufts University. However, the edi newspaper, who had worked his w school career for a Tufts admission, wa Upon hearing that news, I was overwhe anxiety about my own chances of gettin That morning, all I could think about University. At about 10:30, an assistan front office came to get me out of math handed me a note to call home. I knew My heart pounded. My hands shook. I of breath. I had no right to expect a " wanted it more than anything in my li our number. It rang twice. My mom Laughing with happiness, she said, "Y You got into Tufts!!" I jumped up and ye attracting the attention of everyone i office. A thrill ran through me. It was that I will never, ever forget.

① Tufts 대학 신문 편집장은 고교 내내 Tufts 입 한 게 드러나 사퇴해야 했다.
② 다른 학생의 Tufts 대학교 입학 결과를 들은 나 성에 대한 불안에 휩싸였다.
③ 오전 10시 30분경 행정 보조 사무원이 나를 찾 는 수학 수업을 듣던 중이었다.
④ 내가 집으로 전화를 했을 때 벨이 두 번 울리자 를 받았다.
⑤ 합격 소식을 들은 나는 뛰어오르며 소리 질렀 람들의 주의를 끌게 되었다.

전 지문 변형 문제 풀기

한 지문당 3~4문제의 변형 문제로 지문을 완전히 숙지하고 다양한 유형의 변형 문제에 대비할 수 있습니다.

`08` `2강 4번`

주어진 글 다음에 이어질 글의 순서로 가장 적절한 것은?

At my high school, two students were accepted to Tufts University. However, the editor of our newspaper, who had worked his whole high-school career for a Tufts admission, was rejected.

(A) I knew this was it. My heart pounded. My hands shook. I was short of breath. I had no right to expect a "yes," but I wanted it more than anything in my life. I dialed our number. It rang twice. My mom picked up.

(B) Laughing with happiness, she said, "You got in! You got into Tufts!!" I jumped up and yelled, "Yes!" attracting the attention of everyone in the front office. A thrill ran through me. It was a moment that I will never, ever forget.

(C) Upon hearing that news, I was overwhelmed with anxiety about my own chances of getting accepted. That morning, all I could think about was Tufts University. At about 10:30, an assistant from the front office came to get me out of math class and handed me a note to call home.

`내신 만점` `서술형`

`9강 1번`

Southern sea lions are seals with small, clearly visible external ears. They are much more mobile on land than true seals, being able to rotate their rear flippers sideways to propel their bodies forward. Sea lions can move quite fast in this manner. A fully grown southern sea lion bull is much larger and more impressive than his northern cousin, the California sea lion. This massive animal (A) measuring well over 2 m long and weighs up to half a tonne. His enormous neck is decorated with a shaggy mane; hence the name 'sea lion', which also (B) referred his roar. The elegant, nearly yellowish females that make up his harem weigh roughly half the average weight of an adult male, but then they expend less energy. From the time he comes ashore in December (C) to which he leaves in March, the bull sea lion neither eats nor sleeps for more than a few minutes at a time: guarding his harem is a full-time job.

*harem 하렘(번식기 때 바다사자 수컷 한 마리가 거느리는 암컷의 무리) *mane 갈기

`9강 2번`

Thomas Hopkins Gallaudet was born in Philadelphia on December 10, 1787. His family moved to Hartford, Connecticut, (A) which he attended the Hartford Grammar School. He entered Yale College in 1802 and graduated the youngest in his class. Gallaudet became interesting in the education of deaf people after meeting Alice Cogswell, the deaf daughter of a neighbor. With funding from Cogswell's father and others, Gallaudet went to Europe in 1815 to learn how to teach deaf children. 영국의 청각 장애인 학교들에서 본 것에 만족하지 못해서, Gallaudet visited a school in Paris. There, he received training from deaf teachers Jean Massieu and Laurent Clerc. Gallaudet accompanied Laurent Clerc back to Hartford in 1816 and established the first school for the deaf in the United States in 1817, now (B) knew as the American School for the Deaf. Gallaudet served as the institution's principal until 1830. He (C) married with one of his former students, Sofia Fowler, and had eight children.

`09` 윗글에서 다음 질문에 대한 답을 찾아 우리말로 쓰시오. (35자 내외)

Q: What gives southern sea lions the ability to move faster on land than true seals?

A: _____

`고난도`

`10` 윗글의 밑줄 친 부분을 어법상 알맞은 형태로 고쳐 쓰시오.

(A) measuring → _____
(B) referred → _____
(C) to which → _____

`고난도`

`11` 윗글의 밑줄 친 부분을 어법상 알맞은 형태로 고쳐 쓰시오.

(A) which → _____
(B) knew → _____
(C) married with → _____

`12` 윗글의 밑줄 친 우리말 의미와 일치하도록 `보기` 의 단어를 활용하여 `조건` 에 맞게 영작하시오.

`보기` British / he / saw / deaf people / by / dissatisfy / in / what / for / schools

`조건` · 분사구문을 활용할 것
· 필요시 어형을 바꿔 쓸 것
· 총 12단어로 쓸 것

_____

130

내신 만점 서술형

시험에 자주 등장하는 서술형 문제를 통해 까다로운 내신 유형에 대비할 수 있습니다.

Contents

❶ Every year the Modern Art Association holds an awards night to honor accomplished artists in our state. ❷ For this year's program, we are featuring new and progressive artistic groups like yours.

❸ In a matter of one year, your vocal group has become well known for its unique style and fantastic range. ❹ We will be honored if you help us celebrate this year's accomplishments in modern art by performing two selections for us on the evening of October 6.

❺ If you accept our invitation, your travel and lodging expenses will be entirely covered. ❻ We must finalize our schedule by August 18, so we would appreciate it if you could let us know as early as possible if you are able to accept our invitation.

❶ 매년 현대 미술 협회는 우리 주의 뛰어난 미술가들을 기리기 위해 시상식의 밤을 개최합니다. ❷ 올해의 프로그램을 위해 저희는 귀 그룹 같은 새롭고 현대적인 예술 그룹들을 특별히 출연시키고자 합니다. ❸ 불과 1년 만에, 귀 보컬 그룹은 독특한 스타일과 환상적인 음역으로 유명해졌습니다. ❹ 여러분이 10월 6일 저녁에 저희를 위해 선곡하신 두 곡을 공연함으로써 저희가 현대 미술에서의 올해의 업적을 축하하도록 도와주신다면 저희에게 영광일 것입니다. ❺ 만약 여러분이 저희의 초청을 받아들이신다면, 여러분의 이동 경비와 숙박비는 (저희가) 전부 부담하겠습니다. ❻ 저희가 8월 18일까지 저희 일정 계획을 마무리해야 하므로, 여러분이 저희의 초청을 받아들이실 수 있는지 가능한 한 일찍 저희에게 알려 주실 수 있다면 감사하겠습니다.

Word List

□ award 상; 상을 주다　□ honor 경의를 표하다, 영예를 주다　□ accomplished 뛰어난　□ state (미국의) 주
□ feature 특별히 출연시키다　□ progressive 현대적인, 진보적인　□ in a matter of 불과 ~ 만에　□ vocal 목소리의, 가창의
□ range 음역, 범위　□ celebrate 축하하다　□ accomplishment 업적, 공적　□ perform 공연하다　□ selection 선곡, 발췌곡
□ invitation 초대(장)　□ lodging 숙박　□ entirely 완전히, 전적으로　□ cover (비용을) 부담하다　□ finalize 마무리하다
□ appreciate 감사하다　□ accept 받아들이다

• Word Test

1	lodging		11	(미국의) 주	
2	entirely		12	축하하다	
3	honor		13	받아들이다	
4	accomplished		14	(비용을) 부담하다	
5	perform		15	초대(장)	
6	range		16	목소리의, 가창의	
7	feature		17	현대적인, 진보적인	
8	in a matter of		18	마무리하다	
9	award		19	감사하다	
10	selection		20	업적, 공적	

Every year the Modern Art Association holds an awards night to honor ❶ accomplished / accomplishing artists in our state. For this year's program, we are featuring new and progressive artistic groups like ❷ you / yours .

In a matter of one year, your vocal group has become well known for its unique style and fantastic range. We will be honored if you help us celebrate this year's accomplishments in modern art by ❸ performing / performance two selections for us on the evening of October 6.

If you accept our invitation, your travel and lodging expenses will be entirely ❹ covered / concealed . We must finalize our schedule by August 18, so we would appreciate it if you ❺ can / could let us know as early as possible if you are able to accept our invitation.

Every year the Modern Art Association ❶ _____ (hold) an awards night to honor accomplished artists in our state. For this year's program, we are featuring new and progressive artistic groups like yours.

In a matter of one year, your vocal group ❷ _____ (become) well known for its unique style and fantastic range. We will ❸ _____ (honor) if you help us celebrate this year's accomplishments in modern art by performing two selections for us on the evening of October 6.

If you accept our invitation, your travel and lodging expenses will be entirely covered. We must finalize our schedule by August 18, so we would appreciate it if you could let us ❹ _____ (know) as early as possible if you are able to accept our invitation.

Every year the Modern Art Association holds an awards night to honor accomplished artists in our state. For this year's program, we are featuring ❶ _____ _____ _____ _____ _____ (새롭고 현대적인 예술 그룹들) like yours.

❷ _____ _____ _____ _____ _____ _____ (불과 1년 만에), your vocal group has become well known for its unique style and fantastic range. We will be honored if you help us celebrate this year's accomplishments in modern art by performing two selections for us on the evening of October 6.

If you accept our invitation, ❸ _____ _____ _____ _____ _____ (여러분의 이동 경비와 숙박비) will be entirely covered. We must finalize our schedule by August 18, so we would appreciate it if you could let us know ❹ _____ _____ _____ _____ (가능한 한 일찍) if you are able to accept our invitation.

❶ Thank you for the interest you have shown in the FC Rainbow City 50 Year Anniversary products. ❷ The reason I'm writing this email is to provide you with an update on your recent order. ❸ We regret to inform you that due to unprecedented levels of demand in an extremely short space of time we're unable to fulfil your order for the FC Rainbow City 50 Year Anniversary Shirt 2XL. ❹ We are processing a refund for your original purchase. ❺ You will receive a refund back to the original form of payment within 2-7 business days. ❻ If you have any further questions, please feel free to write to me and I will be happy to assist you. ❼ We always appreciate your support and love as a loyal FC Rainbow City fan. ❽ Once again, we apologize for this inconvenience.

*unprecedented 전례가 없는

❶ FC Rainbow City 50주년 기념상품에 귀하께서 보여 주신 관심에 감사드립니다. ❷ 제가 이 이메일을 쓰고 있는 이유는 귀하의 최근 주문에 대한 최신 정보를 제공하기 위해서입니다. ❸ 매우 짧은 시간 동안 전례 없는 수준의 수요로 인해 FC Rainbow City 50주년 기념 셔츠 2XL에 대한 귀하의 주문을 이행할 수 없음을 귀하께 알려 드리게 되어 유감입니다. ❹ 저희는 귀하께서 원래 구매하신 상품에 대한 환불을 처리하고 있습니다. ❺ 귀하께서는 영업일 기준 2~7일 이내에 원래 지불하신 방식으로 환불금을 되돌려 받게 될 것입니다. ❻ 추가 질문이 있으신 경우에, 개의치 마시고 저에게 메일을 보내 주시면 기꺼이 귀하께 도움을 드리겠습니다. ❼ FC Rainbow City의 열렬한 팬으로서의 귀하의 지지와 사랑에 항상 감사드립니다. ❽ 다시 한번 이번 불편에 대해 사과드립니다.

Word List

□ **anniversary** 기념일, 기념행사　□ **provide** 제공하다　□ **update** 최신 정보　□ **recent** 최근의　□ **regret to** *do* ~하게 되어 유감이다
□ **inform** 알리다　□ **demand** 수요　□ **extremely** 매우, 극도로　□ **fulfil(l)** 이행하다, 충족하다　□ **process** 처리하다
□ **refund** 환불, 환불금　□ **original** 원래의　□ **purchase** 구매, 구매품　□ **form** 방식, 종류　□ **payment** 지불, 납입
□ **business day** 영업일　□ **further** 추가의, 그 이상의　□ **appreciate** 감사하다　□ **support** 지지, 성원　□ **loyal** 열렬한, 충성스러운
□ **apologize** 사과하다　□ **inconvenience** 불편

• Word Test

1	update		12	제공하다	
2	purchase		13	불편	
3	fulfil(l)		14	감사하다	
4	inform		15	열렬한, 충성스러운	
5	extremely		16	원래의	
6	form		17	지지, 성원	
7	process		18	사과하다	
8	further		19	지불, 납입	
9	anniversary		20	환불, 환불금	
10	recent		21	수요	
11	regret to *do*		22	영업일	

네모 안에서 옳은 어법·어휘를 고르시오.

Thank you for the ❶ interest/advantage you have shown in the FC Rainbow City 50 Year Anniversary products. The reason I'm writing this email is to provide you ❷ for/with an update on your recent order. We regret to inform you that ❸ due to/in spite of unprecedented levels of demand in an extremely short space of time we're unable to ❹ fulfil/neglect your order for the FC Rainbow City 50 Year Anniversary Shirt 2XL. We are processing a refund for your original purchase. You will receive a refund back to the original form of payment within 2-7 business days. If you have any further questions, please feel free ❺ writing/to write to me and I will be happy to assist you. We always appreciate your support and love as a loyal FC Rainbow City fan. Once again, we apologize for this inconvenience.

*unprecedented 전례가 없는

● 유형 2 괄호 안의 동사를 알맞은 형태로 쓰시오.

Thank you for the interest you ❶ _____ (show) in the FC Rainbow City 50 Year Anniversary products. The reason I'm writing this email is ❷ _____ (provide) you with an update on your recent order. We regret to inform you that due to unprecedented levels of demand in an extremely short space of time we're unable to fulfil your order for the FC Rainbow City 50 Year Anniversary Shirt 2XL. We ❸ _____ (process) a refund for your original purchase. You will receive a refund back to the original form of payment within 2-7 business days. If you have any further questions, please feel free to write to me and I will be happy to assist you. We always ❹ _____ (appreciate) your support and love as a loyal FC Rainbow City fan. Once again, we apologize for this inconvenience.

*unprecedented 전례가 없는

● 유형 3 우리말에 맞게 빈칸에 알맞은 말을 쓰시오.

Thank you for the interest you have shown in the FC Rainbow City 50 Year Anniversary products. The reason I'm writing this email is to provide you with an update on your recent order. We regret to inform you that due to unprecedented levels of demand ❶ _____ _____ _____ _____ _____ _____ _____ (매우 짧은 시간 동안) we're unable to fulfil your order for the FC Rainbow City 50 Year Anniversary Shirt 2XL. We are processing a refund for your original purchase. You will receive a refund back to the original form of payment ❷ _____ _____ _____ _____ (영업일 기준 2~7일 이내에). If you have any further questions, please ❸ _____ _____ _____ (개의치 말고 쓰다) to me and I will be happy to assist you. We always appreciate your support and love as a loyal FC Rainbow City fan. Once again, we apologize ❹ _____ _____ _____ (이번 불편에 대해).

*unprecedented 전례가 없는

9

❶ Thank you for sending your work samples and discussing your views about the editor's position we have opened. ❷ I have reviewed your work and reflected at length on our last conversation, particularly your hesitancy to demonstrate your editorial approach to analytical topics. ❸ Since we talked I have interviewed several other candidates with substantial editorial credentials and have become convinced that analytical skills and technical knowledge are an important prerequisite for the job. ❹ My conclusion is that your background is not appropriate for the position and, frankly, that you would not enjoy the job during a necessary period of training. ❺ I regret that we must make this decision. ❻ Again, thank you for your interest in the job.

*credentials 자격, 자격 증명서 **prerequisite 필수 조건

❶ 귀하의 작업 샘플을 보내 주시고 우리가 공개 채용하기로 한 편집자직에 대한 귀하의 견해를 논해 주셔서 감사합니다. ❷ 귀하의 작업 결과물을 살펴보았고, 우리의 지난번 대화, 특히 분석적인 주제에 대해 귀하의 편집 방식을 보여 주기를 주저하셨던 것에 대해 오랫동안 생각했습니다. ❸ 우리가 대화를 나눈 이후로, 저는 상당한 편집 자격을 갖춘 몇몇 다른 지원자를 면접했고, 분석 능력과 전문 지식이 이 일에 대한 중요한 필수 조건임을 확신하게 되었습니다. ❹ 제 결론은 귀하의 배경이 이 직책에 적합하지 않으며, 솔직히 말해, 귀하가 필수 연수 기간 동안 이 일을 즐기지 않으리라는 것입니다. ❺ 이러한 결정을 내려야 해서 유감입니다. ❻ 거듭 이 일에 대한 귀하의 관심에 감사드립니다.

Word List

□ view 견해 □ editor 편집자 □ reflect 생각하다, 숙고하다 □ at length 오랫동안, 상세히 □ hesitancy 주저, 망설임 □ demonstrate 보여 주다, 입증하다 □ editorial 편집의 □ analytical 분석적인 □ candidate 지원자, 후보자 □ substantial 상당한 □ convince 확신시키다 □ technical 전문적인, 기술적인 □ conclusion 결론 □ background 배경 □ appropriate 적합한 □ frankly 솔직히 □ regret 유감스럽게 생각하다

• Word Test

1	reflect	9	편집의
2	substantial	10	배경
3	analytical	11	지원자, 후보자
4	technical	12	적합한
5	editor	13	결론
6	frankly	14	보여 주다, 입증하다
7	at length	15	주저, 망설임
8	view	16	확신시키다

Thank you for sending your work samples and discussing your views about the editor's position we have opened. I have reviewed your work and reflected at length on our last conversation, particularly your ❶ hesitancy/consistency to demonstrate your editorial approach to analytical topics. ❷ Since / While we talked I have interviewed several other candidates with ❸ substantial/substantially editorial credentials and have become convinced that analytical skills and technical knowledge are an important prerequisite for the job. My conclusion is ❹ that / why your background is not appropriate for the position and, frankly, that you would not enjoy the job during a necessary period of training. I ❺ refuse / regret that we must make this decision. Again, thank you for your interest in the job.

*credentials 자격, 자격 증명서   **prerequisite 필수 조건

Thank you for sending your work samples and ❶ _____ (discuss) your views about the editor's position we have opened. I ❷ _____ (review) your work and reflected at length on our last conversation, particularly your hesitancy ❸ _____ (demonstrate) your editorial approach to analytical topics. Since we talked I ❹ _____ (interview) several other candidates with substantial editorial credentials and have become convinced that analytical skills and technical knowledge ❺ _____ (be) an important prerequisite for the job. My conclusion is that your background is not appropriate for the position and, frankly, that you would not enjoy the job during a necessary period of training. I regret that we must make this decision. Again, thank you for your interest in the job.

*credentials 자격, 자격 증명서   **prerequisite 필수 조건

Thank you for sending your work samples and discussing your views about the editor's position we have opened. I have reviewed your work and ❶ _____ _____ _____ (오랫동안 생각했습니다) on our last conversation, particularly your hesitancy to demonstrate your editorial approach to analytical topics. Since we talked I have interviewed ❷ _____ _____ _____ (몇몇 다른 지원자들) with substantial editorial credentials and have become convinced that analytical skills and technical knowledge are an important prerequisite for the job. My conclusion is that your background is not appropriate for the position and, frankly, that you would not enjoy the job ❸ _____ _____ _____ _____ (필수 기간 동안) of training. I regret that we must ❹ _____ _____ _____ (이러한 결정을 내리다). Again, thank you for your interest in the job.

*credentials 자격, 자격 증명서   **prerequisite 필수 조건

❶ I feel sincerely honored and privileged that you have invited me to be the guest speaker at the upcoming regional conference of the Personnel Management Association. ❷ I am fully aware that this will be a prestigious event, considering that you have invited a few senators to this gathering.

❸ Regrettably, as much as I would like to speak at the conference, I will not be able to do so because I will be out of the country on that day due to a family event.

❹ With that, I would like to suggest Ms. Julia Spencer to take my place as guest speaker. ❺ Ms. Spencer has been working in the field of human resources for 30 years, she is an expert in human and social organization, and she has done many speaking engagements throughout her career. ❻ Please let me know if you decide to invite her as my alternate so that I can give her advanced notice.

❼ Once again, thank you for your invitation. ❽ I hope your event is a great success.

*senator 상원 의원

❶ 곧 있을 인사관리협회의 지역 회의에 초청 연사로 저를 청해 주셔서 진심으로 명예롭고 영광스럽게 생각합니다. ❷ 이 모임에 상원 의원 몇 분을 초대하셨다는 점을 고려하면, 저는 이 행사가 훌륭한 행사가 될 것임을 충분히 알고 있습니다. ❸ 유감스럽게도, 회의에서 연설하고 싶지만, 저는 가족 행사로 인해 그날 외국에 나가 있을 것이기 때문에 그렇게 할 수 없을 것 입니다. ❹ 이에 저는 제 자리를 대신할 초청 연사로 Julia Spencer 씨를 추천하고 싶습니다. ❺ Spencer 씨는 30년 동안 인사 분야에서 일해 오고 있고, 인적 조직 및 사회 조직 전문가이며, 경력 내내 많은 연설 업무를 해 왔습니다. ❻ 제 대체 연사로 그녀를 초대하기로 결정하시면 그녀에게 사전 고지할 수 있도록 제게 알려 주십시오.

❼ 다시 한번, 귀하의 초대에 감사드립니다. ❽ 저는 귀하의 행사가 큰 성공을 거두기를 바랍니다.

Word List

□ sincerely 진심으로 □ honored 영광스러운 □ privileged 영광스러운, 특권을 가진 □ upcoming 곧 있을, 다가오는
□ regional 지역의 □ conference 회의 □ association 협회 □ be aware that ~라는 것을 알다 □ prestigious 훌륭한, 명망 있는
□ gathering 모임 □ regrettably 유감스럽게도 □ in the field of ~의 분야에서 □ human resources 인사부, 인적 자원
□ expert 전문가 □ organization 조직 □ engagement 업무, 참여, 고용 (계약) □ career 경력
□ alternate 대체[대신] 할 사람, 대리인 □ advanced 사전의 □ notice 고지, 통지

• Word Test

1	be aware that		11	전문가
2	conference		12	업무, 참여, 고용 (계약)
3	upcoming		13	진심으로
4	privileged		14	고지, 통지
5	in the field of		15	모임
6	honored		16	지역의
7	association		17	조직
8	career		18	인사부, 인적 자원
9	prestigious		19	유감스럽게도
10	alternate		20	사전의

I feel sincerely honored and ❶ privileged / underprivileged that you have invited me to be the guest speaker at the upcoming regional conference of the Personnel Management Association. I am ❷ full / fully aware that this will be a prestigious event, considering that you have invited a few senators to this ❸ collecting / gathering .

Regrettably, as much as I would like to speak at the conference, I will not be able to do so ❹ why / because I will be out of the country on that day due to a family event.

With that, I would like to suggest Ms. Julia Spencer to take my place as guest speaker. Ms. Spencer has been working in the field of human resources for 30 years, she is an expert in human and social organization, and she has done many speaking engagements throughout her career. Please let me know ❺ if / unless you decide to invite her as my alternate so that I can give her advanced notice.

Once again, thank you for your invitation. I hope your event is a great success.

*senator 상원 의원

I feel sincerely honored and privileged that you ❶ _____ (invite) me to be the guest speaker at the upcoming regional conference of the Personnel Management Association. I am fully aware that this will be a prestigious event, ❷ _____ (consider) that you have invited a few senators to this gathering.

Regrettably, as much as I would like to speak at the conference, I will not be able to do so because I will be out of the country on that day due to a family event.

With that, I would like to suggest Ms. Julia Spencer to take my place as guest speaker. Ms. Spencer has ❸ _____ (work) in the field of human resources for 30 years, she is an expert in human and social organization, and she ❹ _____ (do) many speaking engagements throughout her career. Please let me know if you decide ❺ _____ (invite) her as my alternate so that I can give her advanced notice.

Once again, thank you for your invitation. I hope your event is a great success.

*senator 상원 의원

I feel sincerely honored and privileged that you have invited me to be the guest speaker at the upcoming regional conference of the Personnel Management Association. I am fully aware that this will be a prestigious event, considering that you have invited a few senators to this gathering.

Regrettably, as much as I would like to speak at the conference, I will not be able to do so because I will be ❶ _____ _____ _____ _____ (외국에 나가 있는) on that day due to a family event.

With that, I would like to suggest Ms. Julia Spencer ❷ _____ _____ _____ _____ (제 자리를 대신할) as guest speaker. Ms. Spencer has been working in the field of human resources for 30 years, she is an expert in human and social organization, and she has done many speaking engagements ❸ _____ _____ _____ (그녀의 경력 내내). Please let me know if you decide to invite her as my alternate so that I can give her ❹ _____ _____ (사전 고지).

Once again, thank you for your invitation. I hope your event is a great success.

*senator 상원 의원

01 1강 1번

다음 글의 밑줄친 부분 중, 어법상 틀린 것은?

Every year the Modern Art Association holds an awards night to honor ① accomplished artists in our state. For this year's program, we are featuring new and progressive artistic groups like ② yours. In a matter of one year, your vocal group has become well known for its unique style and fantastic range. We will be honored if you help us celebrate this year's accomplishments in modern art by ③ performing two selections for us on the evening of October 6.

If you accept our invitation, your travel and lodging expenses will be ④ entire covered. We must finalize our schedule by August 18, so we would appreciate it if you could let us know as early as possible ⑤ if you are able to accept our invitation.

02 1강 2번

다음 빈칸에 들어갈 말로 가장 적절한 것은?

Thank you for the interest you have shown in the FC Rainbow City 50 Year Anniversary products. The reason I'm writing this email is _____. We regret to inform you that due to unprecedented levels of demand in an extremely short space of time we're unable to fulfil your order for the FC Rainbow City 50 Year Anniversary Shirt 2XL. We are processing a refund for your original purchase. You will receive a refund back to the original form of payment within 2-7 business days. If you have any further questions, please feel free to write to me and I will be happy to assist you. We always appreciate your support and love as a loyal FC Rainbow City fan. Once again, we apologize for this inconvenience.

*unprecedented 전례가 없는

① to apologize for the delivery of the wrong item
② to inform you that there is a delay in your delivery
③ to explain our decision to deny your refund request
④ to provide you with an update on your recent order
⑤ to explain how to request a size, style, or color exchange

03 1강 3번

밑줄 친 this decision이 다음 글에서 의미하는 바로 가장 적절한 것은?

Thank you for sending your work samples and discussing your views about the editor's position we have opened. I have reviewed your work and reflected at length on our last conversation, particularly your hesitancy to demonstrate your editorial approach to analytical topics. Since we talked I have interviewed several other candidates with substantial editorial credentials and have become convinced that analytical skills and technical knowledge are an important prerequisite for the job. My conclusion is that your background is not appropriate for the position and, frankly, that you would not enjoy the job during a necessary period of training. I regret that we must make this decision. Again, thank you for your interest in the job.

*credentials 자격, 자격 증명서 **prerequisite 필수 조건

① sending your work samples to another editor
② asking for credentials in analytical skills and technical knowledge
③ announcing you that you are not appropriate for the position
④ interviewing several other candidates before making the final decision
⑤ providing the candidates with training on editorial approach to analytical topics

04 [1강 4번]

주어진 글 다음에 이어질 글의 순서로 가장 적절한 것은?

I feel sincerely honored and privileged that you have invited me to be the guest speaker at the upcoming regional conference of the Personnel Management Association. I am fully aware that this will be a prestigious event, considering that you have invited a few senators to this gathering.

(A) Regrettably, as much as I would like to speak at the conference, I will not be able to do so because I will be out of the country on that day due to a family event.

(B) Please let me know if you decide to invite her as my alternate so that I can give her advanced notice. Once again, thank you for your invitation. I hope your event is a great success.

(C) With that, I would like to suggest Ms. Julia Spencer to take my place as guest speaker. Ms. Spencer has been working in the field of human resources for 30 years, she is an expert in human and social organization, and she has done many speaking engagements throughout her career.

*senator 상원 의원

① (A) – (C) – (B) 　② (B) – (A) – (C)
③ (B) – (C) – (A) 　④ (C) – (A) – (B)
⑤ (C) – (B) – (A)

05 [1강 1번]

다음 글의 내용과 일치하지 않는 것은?

Every year the Modern Art Association holds an awards night to honor accomplished artists in our state. For this year's program, we are featuring new and progressive artistic groups like yours.

In a matter of one year, your vocal group has become well known for its unique style and fantastic range. We will be honored if you help us celebrate this year's accomplishments in modern art by performing two selections for us on the evening of October 6.

If you accept our invitation, your travel and lodging expenses will be entirely covered. We must finalize our schedule by August 18, so we would appreciate it if you could let us know as early as possible if you are able to accept our invitation.

① 현대 미술 협회는 뛰어난 미술가들을 기리기 위한 시상식의 밤을 매년 개최한다.
② 이 글을 수신하는 그룹은 불과 1년 만에 독특한 스타일과 환상적인 음역으로 유명해졌다.
③ 글쓴이는 수신인에게 10월 6일 축하 공연에 전시할 작품 두 점을 출품할 것을 요청했다.
④ 수신인이 초대에 응할 경우, 이동 경비와 숙박비는 주최 측에서 전액 부담한다.
⑤ 추최 측은 일정 계획을 8월 18일까지 마무리해야 하므로 가능한 한 일찍 초청 수락 여부를 알려달라고 한다.

06 [1강] [2번]

다음 글의 내용과 일치하지 <u>않는</u> 것은?

Thank you for the interest you have shown in the FC Rainbow City 50 Year Anniversary products. The reason I'm writing this email is to provide you with an update on your recent order. We regret to inform you that due to unprecedented levels of demand in an extremely short space of time we're unable to fulfil your order for the FC Rainbow City 50 Year Anniversary Shirt 2XL. We are processing a refund for your original purchase. You will receive a refund back to the original form of payment within 2-7 business days. If you have any further questions, please feel free to write to me and I will be happy to assist you. We always appreciate your support and love as a loyal FC Rainbow City fan. Once again, we apologize for this inconvenience.

*unprecedented 전례가 없는

① FC Rainbow City가 50주년을 맞아 기념상품을 출시하였다.
② FC Rainbow City는 편지 수신인에게 제품의 전 사이즈 매진을 알리고 있다.
③ FC Rainbow City는 편지 수신인이 원래 구매한 상품에 대한 환불 처리를 하고 있다.
④ 편지 수신인은 원래 지불한 방식으로 환불금을 되돌려받게 된다.
⑤ 편지 수신인은 추가 질문이 있을 경우, 이메일을 통해 문의를 하도록 안내받았다.

07 [1강] [3번]

다음 글에서 전체 흐름과 관계 <u>없는</u> 문장은?

Thank you for sending your work samples and discussing your views about the editor's position we have opened. ① I have reviewed your work and reflected at length on our last conversation, particularly your hesitancy to demonstrate your editorial approach to analytical topics. ② Since we talked I have interviewed several other candidates with substantial editorial credentials and have become convinced that analytical skills and technical knowledge are an important prerequisite for the job. ③ In addition, some credentials may serve as prerequisites for jobs in the industry, so obtaining qualifications can improve your job prospects. ④ My conclusion is that your background is not appropriate for the position and, frankly, that you would not enjoy the job during a necessary period of training. ⑤ I regret that we must make this decision. Again, thank you for your interest in the job.

*credentials 자격, 자격 증명서   **prerequisite 필수 조건

08 [1강] [4번]

(A), (B), (C)의 각 네모 안에서 문맥에 맞는 낱말로 가장 적절한 것은?

I feel sincerely honored and privileged that you have invited me to be the guest speaker at the upcoming regional conference of the Personnel Management Association. I am fully aware that this will be a (A) prestigious / pretentious event, considering that you have invited a few senators to this gathering.

(B) Respectably / Regrettably, as much as I would like to speak at the conference, I will not be able to do so because I will be out of the country on that day due to a family event.

With that, I would like to suggest Ms. Julia Spencer to take my place as guest speaker. Ms. Spencer has been working in the field of human resources for 30 years, she is an expert in human and social organization, and she has done many speaking engagements throughout her career. Please let me know if you decide to invite her as my (C) administrate / alternate so that I can give her advanced notice.

Once again, thank you for your invitation. I hope your event is a great success.

*senator 상원 의원

	(A)	(B)	(C)
①	prestigious	Respectably	administrate
②	prestigious	Regrettably	alternate
③	prestigious	Regrettably	administrate
④	pretentious	Respectably	alternate
⑤	pretentious	Respectably	administrate

● 내신 만점 서술형

1강 1번

Every year the Modern Art Association holds an awards night to honor ① accomplished artists in our state. For this year's program, we are ② featuring new and progressive artistic groups like yours.

In a matter of one year, your vocal group has become well known for its unique style and fantastic ③ range. We will be honored if you help us celebrate this year's accomplishments in modern art by performing two ④ selections for us on the evening of October 6.

If you accept our invitation, your travel and lodging expenses will be entirely ⑤ charged. We must finalize our schedule by August 18, so we would appreciate it if you could let us know as early as possible if you are able to accept our invitation.

09 윗글의 밑줄 친 부분 중, 문맥상 어색한 것을 1개 찾아 그 번호를 쓰고 고쳐 쓰시오.

_____ → _____

10 윗글의 밑줄 친 yours가 가리키는 것을 본문에서 찾아 쓰시오. (3단어)

_____

1강 2번

Thank you for the interest you have shown in the FC Rainbow City 50 Year Anniversary products. The reason I'm writing this email is to provide you with an update on your recent order. We regret to inform you that 매우 짧은 시간 동안 전례 없는 수준의 수요로 인해 (~에 대한) 귀하의 주문을 이행할 수 없다 for the FC Rainbow City 50 Year Anniversary Shirt 2XL. We are processing a ___(A)___ for your original purchase. You will receive a ___(B)___ back to the original form of payment within 2-7 business days. If you have any further questions, please feel free to write to me and I will be happy to assist you. We always appreciate your support and love as a loyal FC Rainbow City fan. Once again, we apologize for this inconvenience.

*unprecedented 전례가 없는

11 윗글의 밑줄 친 우리말 의미와 일치하도록 보기 의 단어를 활용하여 조건 에 맞게 문장을 완성하시오.

> 보기 fulfil / unprecedented levels of / unable to / demand / we're / due to

> 조건 · 필요시 어형을 바꿔 쓸 것
> · 〈보기〉의 단어를 반드시 모두 사용할 것

_____ in an extremely short space of time _____

12 윗글의 빈칸 (A), (B)에 공통으로 들어갈 단어를 영영 뜻풀이를 참고하여 쓰시오. (단, 주어진 글자로 시작할 것)

> money that was yours that you get again, especially because you have paid too much for something or have decided you do not want it

r_____

Thank you for sending your work samples and ① discuss your views about the editor's position we have opened. I have reviewed your work and reflected at length on our last conversation, particularly your hesitancy to demonstrate your editorial approach to analytical topics. Since we talked ② I have interviewed several other candidates with substantial editorial credentials and have become ③ convincing that analytical skills and technical knowledge ④ are an important prerequisite for the job. My conclusion is that your background is not appropriate for the position and, frankly, ⑤ what you would not enjoy the job during a necessary period of training. I regret that we must make this decision. Again, thank you for your interest in the job.

*credentials 자격, 자격 증명서 **prerequisite 필수 조건

고난도

13 윗글의 밑줄 친 부분 중, 어법상 틀린 것을 3개 찾아 그 번호를 쓰고 고쳐 쓰시오.

(1) _____ → _____

(2) _____ → _____

(3) _____ → _____

14 윗글에서 다음 질문에 대한 답을 찾아 우리말로 쓰시오. (35자 내외)

Q: In the last conversation made between the writer and the addressee, what was the addressee hesitant to do?

A: _____

I feel sincerely honored and privileged that you have invited me to be the guest speaker at the upcoming regional conference of the Personnel Management Association. I am fully aware that this will be a prestigious event, considering that you have invited a few senators to this gathering. Regrettably, 회의에서 연설하고 싶지만, I will not be able to do so because I will be out of the country on that day due to a family event.

With that, I would like to suggest Ms. Julia Spencer to take my place as guest speaker. Ms. Spencer has been working in the field of human resources for 30 years, she is an _____ in human and social organization, and she has done many speaking engagements throughout her career. Please let me know if you decide to invite her as my alternate so that I can give her advanced notice.

Once again, thank you for your invitation. I hope your event is a great success.

*senator 상원 의원

15 윗글의 밑줄 친 우리말 의미와 일치하도록 보기 의 단어를 순서대로 배열하여 영작하시오.

보기   I / like / would / speak / as / as / at / to / the conference / much

_____

_____

16 윗글의 빈칸에 들어갈 단어를 영영 뜻풀이를 참고하여 쓰시오. (단, 주어진 글자로 시작할 것)

someone who has a particular skill or who knows a lot about a particular subject

e _____

❶ The phone rang late at night, and Sam sat up with a jolt. ❷ It felt to him as though his life was going to change after he picked up the flashing piece of metal that was vibrating on the end table. ❸ He couldn't shake the feeling that whatever he was about to learn would have an impact on the rest of his life. ❹ Sam's hand shook slightly as he answered the phone. ❺ It was from a number he didn't recognize. ❻ "Hey, Sam speaking." ❼ His voice was gruff and hesitant. ❽ "Hey there, friend, long time no see! It's John Havisham here. Hope that the last party Joe had over at the cottage wasn't too boring?" ❾ Sam felt relief flood over him. ❿ John would call occasionally to catch up on local news, ask whether Patty's art gallery had any exceptional pieces of art for sale, and order a few kegs of beer to be shipped to his home in Halifax.

*jolt 놀람　**gruff 걸걸한　***keg (맥주 저장용의 작은) 통

❶ 늦은 밤에 전화벨이 울렸고, Sam은 깜짝 놀라 일어나 앉았다. ❷ 그는 작은 탁자 위에서 진동하고 있는 그 번쩍이는 금속 조각을 집어 들고 나면 자신의 인생이 바뀔 것 같은 느낌이 들었다. ❸ 그는 자신이 막 알게 될 것이 무엇이든지 간에 자신의 남은 인생에 영향을 미칠 것 같다는 느낌을 떨칠 수 없었다. ❹ 전화를 받을 때 Sam의 손이 약간 떨렸다. ❺ 그가 모르는 번호로부터 걸려 온 전화였다. ❻ "여보세요, Sam입니다." ❼ 그의 목소리는 걸걸하고 머뭇거렸다. ❽ "어이, 친구, 오랜만이야! John Havisham이야. Joe가 오두막으로 초대했던 지난 파티가 너무 지루하지는 않았겠지?" ❾ Sam은 자신에게 안도의 물결이 밀려드는 것을 느꼈다. ❿ John은 가끔 전화해서 지역 소식을 알아내고, Patty의 화랑에 팔려고 내놓은 특별한 예술품이라도 있는지 물어보고, Halifax에 있는 자신의 집으로 맥주 몇 통을 배달해 달라고 하곤 했다.

Word List

□ **flashing** 번쩍이는　□ **piece** 조각, 작품　□ **vibrate** 진동하다　□ **end table** (소파 옆에 붙여 놓는) 작은 탁자　□ **shake** 떨쳐버리다, 흔들다
□ **impact** 영향　□ **slightly** 약간　□ **recognize** 알다, 인식하다　□ **hesitant** 머뭇거리는, 망설이는　□ **have over** ~으로 초대하다
□ **cottage** 오두막　□ **relief** 안도　□ **flood** 밀려들다　□ **occasionally** 가끔　□ **catch up on** (소식·정보를) 알아내다
□ **art gallery** 미술관, 화랑　□ **exceptional** 특별한, 이례적인　□ **ship** 배송하다, 배달하다

• Word Test

1	shake		10	특별한, 이례적인
2	flood		11	조각, 작품
3	ship		12	미술관, 화랑
4	flashing		13	(소파 옆에 붙여 놓는) 작은 탁자
5	cottage		14	약간
6	have over		15	알다, 인식하다
7	vibrate		16	가끔
8	catch up on		17	영향
9	hesitant		18	안도

The phone rang late at night, and Sam sat up with a jolt. It felt to him as though his life was going to change after he picked up the flashing piece of metal ❶ that / when was vibrating on the end table. He couldn't shake the feeling that ❷ however / whatever he was about to learn would have an impact on the rest of his life. Sam's hand shook slightly as he answered the phone. It was from a number he didn't ❸ recognize / appreciate . "Hey, Sam speaking." His voice was gruff and ❹ reliant / hesitant . "Hey there, friend, long time no see! It's John Havisham here. Hope that the last party Joe had over at the cottage wasn't too boring?" Sam felt relief flood over him. John would call occasionally to catch up on local news, ask ❺ whether / although Patty's art gallery had any exceptional pieces of art for sale, and order a few kegs of beer to be shipped to his home in Halifax.

*jolt 놀람   **gruff 걸걸한   ***keg (맥주 저장용의 작은) 통

The phone rang late at night, and Sam sat up with a jolt. It felt to him as though his life was going to change after he ❶ _____ (pick) up the flashing piece of metal that was vibrating on the end table. He couldn't shake the feeling that whatever he was about to learn would have an impact on the rest of his life. Sam's hand ❷ _____ (shake) slightly as he answered the phone. It was from a number he didn't recognize. "Hey, Sam speaking." His voice was gruff and hesitant. "Hey there, friend, long time no see! It's John Havisham here. Hope that the last party Joe ❸ _____ (have) over at the cottage wasn't too boring?" Sam felt relief flood over him. John would call occasionally to catch up on local news, ask whether Patty's art gallery had any exceptional pieces of art for sale, and order a few kegs of beer to ❹ _____ (ship) to his home in Halifax.

*jolt 놀람   **gruff 걸걸한   ***keg (맥주 저장용의 작은) 통

The phone rang late at night, and Sam sat up with a jolt. It felt to him as though his life was going to change after he picked up the flashing piece of metal that was vibrating on the end table. He ❶ _____ _____ _____ (느낌을 떨칠 수 없었다) that whatever he was about to learn would ❷ _____ _____ _____ _____ (~에 영향을 미치다) the rest of his life. Sam's hand shook slightly as he answered the phone. It was from a number he didn't recognize. "Hey, Sam speaking." His voice was gruff and hesitant. "Hey there, friend, long time no see! It's John Havisham here. Hope that the last party Joe had over at the cottage wasn't too boring?" Sam ❸ _____ _____ _____ (안도의 물결을 느꼈다) over him. John would call occasionally to ❹ _____ _____ _____ _____ _____ (지역 소식을 알아내다), ask whether Patty's art gallery had any exceptional pieces of art for sale, and order a few kegs of beer to be shipped to his home in Halifax.

*jolt 놀람   **gruff 걸걸한   ***keg (맥주 저장용의 작은) 통

❶ One day we were asked to write a whole composition about some birds in Gaelic. ❷ I knew I could do it easily in English so it shouldn't be too difficult in Gaelic. ❸ The words came very easily and although I wasn't sure I'd got all the past, present and future tenses perfectly correct, overall I decided I'd made a really good job of it. ❹ Sister Cecilia then came towards me, and said, "Now, Kathleen O'Malley, let me see what you've done." ❺ She read my essay. ❻ I sat there patiently waiting for the praise I felt sure would be forthcoming. ❼ I did notice that her colour was getting more and more ruddy, and suddenly she said, "Kathleen O'Malley, do you expect to pass?" ❽ Without hesitation, I replied, "Yes, sister." ❾ She then continued, "I've never read anything like this before." ❿ I realized she had been anything other than blown away by my Gaelic masterpiece. ⓫ As a horrible sense of self-pity started slowly to descend on me, she went over to one of the girls and said, "Now I'm sure you've got a better composition." ⓬ She read that girl's work and a big smile spread across her face.

*Gaelic 게일어

❶ 어느 날 우리는 게일어로 어떤 새들에 관해 완전히 갖추어진 짧은 글을 쓰라는 요구를 받았다. ❷ 나는 영어로 그것을 쉽게 할 수 있어서 게일어로도 그다지 어렵지 않으리라는 것을 알고 있었다. ❸ 단어들이 아주 쉽게 떠올랐고 모든 과거, 현재, 미래 시제를 완벽하게 정확히 했는지는 확신할 수 없었지만, 전반적으로 그것을 정말 잘 해냈다고 판단했다. ❹ Cecilia 수녀님이 그때 나에게 다가와서 "자, Kathleen O'Malley, 네가 한 것을 내게 보여 주렴."이라고 말씀하셨다. ❺ 그녀는 내 에세이를 읽었다. ❻ 나는 곧 나오리라고 확신하는 칭찬을 참을성 있게 기다리며 거기 앉아 있었다. ❼ 나는 그녀의 안색이 점점 더 붉어지고 있는 것을 정말 알아차렸는데, 그녀는 갑자기 "Kathleen O'Malley, 네가 통과할 거라고 생각하니?"라고 말했다. ❽ "네, 수녀님." 이라고 나는 주저 없이 대답했다. ❾ 그러자 그녀는 "나는 이런 것을 전에 결코 읽어 본 적이 없다."라고 말을 계속했다. ❿ 나는 그녀가 게일어로 된 나의 명작에 감동한 것이 전혀 아니라는 것을 깨달았다. ⓫ 끔찍한 자기 연민감이 나에게 천천히 내려앉기 시작했을 때, 그녀는 여자아이 중 한 명에게 가서 "자, 분명히 네가 더 나은 작문을 했을 거야."라고 말했다. ⓬ 그녀는 그 여자아이의 글을 읽었고 환한 미소가 그녀의 얼굴에 퍼졌다.

Word List

□ whole 완전한　□ composition 짧은 글, 작문　□ tense 시제　□ overall 전반적으로　□ make a good job 잘 해내다
□ patiently 참을성 있게　□ forthcoming 곧 오려고 하는, 다가오는　□ notice 알아차리다　□ ruddy 붉은　□ hesitation 망설임
□ blow away ~을 감동시키다　□ masterpiece 걸작, 명작　□ horrible 끔찍한　□ self-pity 자기 연민　□ descend 내려앉다, 다가오다
□ spread 번지다, 퍼지다

● Word Test

1	patiently	_____	9	잘 해내다	_____
2	masterpiece	_____	10	알아차리다	_____
3	overall	_____	11	끔찍한	_____
4	blow away	_____	12	완전한	_____
5	composition	_____	13	번지다, 퍼지다	_____
6	self-pity	_____	14	망설임	_____
7	forthcoming	_____	15	시제	_____
8	ruddy	_____	16	내려앉다, 다가오다	_____

One day we were asked to write a whole ❶ component/composition about some birds in Gaelic. I knew I could do it easily in English so it shouldn't be too difficult in Gaelic. The words came very easily and although I wasn't sure I'd got all the past, present and future tenses perfectly correct, overall I decided I'd made a really good job of ❷ it/them. Sister Cecilia then came towards me, and said, "Now, Kathleen O'Malley, let me see what you've done." She read my essay. I sat there patiently waiting for the praise I felt sure would be forthcoming. I did notice that her colour was getting more and more ruddy, and suddenly she said, "Kathleen O'Malley, do you expect to pass?" ❸ With/Without hesitation, I replied, "Yes, sister." She then continued, "I've never read ❹ nothing/anything like this before." I realized she had been anything other than blown away by my Gaelic masterpiece. As a horrible sense of self-pity started slowly to descend on me, she went over to one of the girls and said, "Now I'm sure you've got a ❺ worse/better composition." She read that girl's work and a big smile spread across her face.

*Gaelic 게일어

One day we ❶ _____ (ask) to write a whole composition about some birds in Gaelic. I knew I could do it easily in English so it shouldn't be too difficult in Gaelic. The words came very easily and although I wasn't sure I'd got all the past, present and future tenses perfectly correct, overall I decided I'd made a really good job of it. Sister Cecilia then came towards me, and said, "Now, Kathleen O'Malley, let me see what you've done." She ❷ _____ (read) my essay. I sat there patiently waiting for the praise I felt sure would be forthcoming. I did notice that her colour ❸ _____ (get) more and more ruddy, and suddenly she said, "Kathleen O'Malley, do you expect ❹ _____ (pass)?" Without hesitation, I replied, "Yes, sister." She then continued, "I've never read anything like this before." I realized she had been anything other than blown away by my Gaelic masterpiece. As a horrible sense of self-pity started slowly to descend on me, she went over to one of the girls and said, "Now I'm sure you've got a better composition." She read that girl's work and a big smile ❺ _____ (spread) across her face.

*Gaelic 게일어

One day we were asked to write a whole composition about some birds in Gaelic. I knew I could do it easily in English so it shouldn't be too difficult in Gaelic. The words came very easily and although I wasn't sure I'd got all the past, present and future tenses perfectly correct, overall I decided I'd made a really good job of it. Sister Cecilia then came towards me, and said, "Now, Kathleen O'Malley, let me see what you've done." She read my essay. I sat there ❶ _____ _____ _____ _____ _____ (칭찬을 참을성 있게 기다리며) I felt sure would be forthcoming. I did notice that her colour was getting ❷ _____ _____ _____ _____ (점점 더 붉은), and suddenly she said, "Kathleen O'Malley, do you expect to pass?" Without hesitation, I replied, "Yes, sister." She then continued, "I've never read anything like this before." I realized she had been anything other than ❸ _____ _____ _____ (~에 감동한) my Gaelic masterpiece. As a horrible sense of self-pity ❹ _____ _____ _____ _____ (천천히 내려앉기 시작했다) on me, she went over to one of the girls and said, "Now I'm sure you've got a better composition." She read that girl's work and a big smile spread across her face.

*Gaelic 게일어

22

❶ Spring is in bloom and the park wears a new green coat. ❷ There are the tennis courts, a garden, and a small hill with an old house that used to be a manor and is now used for events and a food stand selling ice cream and snacks to sticky-fingered children. ❸ Two sets of train tracks loop around the park: the real one and the miniature one that is only for the summer and very small children. ❹ The sun is just starting to set, and while listening to the calming songs of the birds, Rosemary can see people enjoying the lengthening days. ❺ Runners make their way up the hill and down again. ❻ And on the edge of the park closest to her balcony a low redbrick building wraps its arms around a perfect blue rectangle of water. ❼ A place to spend the day without disturbance, the pool is striped with ropes that split the lanes and she can see bright towels on the deckchairs. ❽ Swimmers float in the water like petals. ❾ It is a place she knows well. ❿ It is the lido, her lido.

*lido 야외 풀장

❶ 봄이 한창이고 공원은 새로운 녹색 코트를 입고 있다. ❷ 테니스 코트와 정원, 그리고 한때는 저택이었다가 지금은 행사용으로 사용되고 있는 오래된 집과 (군것질을 하여) 손가락이 끈끈한 아이들에게 아이스크림과 간식을 파는 음식 가판대가 있는 작은 언덕이 있다. ❸ 두 개의 기차선로가 공원을 따라 고리 모양으로 나있는데, 실제 선로와 여름철과 아주 어린 아이들만을 위한 축소 모형선로이다. ❹ 이제 막 해가 지기 시작하고 있는데, Rosemary가 새들의 잔잔한 노래에 귀를 기울이는 동안 사람들이 점점 길어지는 낮을 즐기는 모습이 보인다. ❺ (운동 삼아) 달리는 사람들이 언덕을 올라갔다가 다시 내려간다. ❻ 그리고 그녀의 발코니에서 가장 가까운 공원 가장자리에는 낮은 붉은 벽돌 건물이 더할 나위 없이 푸른 직사각형의 물을 감싸고 있다. ❼ 하루를 방해받지 않고 보낼 수 있는 장소인 수영장에는 레인을 나누는 밧줄이 줄무늬를 만들고 있는데, 그녀에게 접의자 위의 밝은 색 수건이 보인다. ❽ 수영하는 사람들이 꽃잎처럼 물에 떠 있다. ❾ 그것은 바로 그녀가 잘 아는 곳이다. ❿ 그것은 야외풀장, 그녀의 야외풀장이다.

Word List	
□ **bloom** 한창, 최고점 □ **manor** 저택, 장원(莊園) □ **food stand** 음식 가판대 □ **sticky-fingered** (군것질을 하여) 손가락이 끈끈한 □ **track** 선로 □ **loop** 고리 모양으로 이동하다[움직이다] □ **calming** 진정시키는 □ **lengthen** 길어지다 □ **edge** 가장자리, 모서리 □ **redbrick** 붉은 벽돌을 쓴 □ **wrap** 감싸다, 둘러싸다 □ **rectangle** 직사각형 □ **disturbance** 방해, 소란 □ **stripe** 줄무늬를 넣다 □ **split** 나누다, 쪼개다 □ **deckchair** 접의자 □ **float** 뜨다 □ **petal** 꽃잎	

• Word Test

1	bloom		10	길어지다	
2	deckchair		11	감싸다, 둘러싸다	
3	stripe		12	진정시키는	
4	sticky-fingered		13	직사각형	
5	manor		14	선로	
6	disturbance		15	꽃잎	
7	loop		16	나누다, 쪼개다	
8	redbrick		17	음식 가판대	
9	float		18	가장자리, 모서리	

Spring is in bloom and the park wears a new green coat. There are the tennis courts, a garden, and a small hill with an old house ❶ | that / what | used to be a manor and is now used for events and a food stand selling ice cream and snacks to sticky-fingered children. Two sets of train tracks loop around the park: the real one and the miniature one that is only for the summer and very small children. The sun is just starting to set, and ❷ | during / while | listening to the calming songs of the birds, Rosemary can see people enjoying the lengthening days. Runners make their way up the hill and down again. And on the edge of the park closest to her balcony a low redbrick building wraps ❸ | its / their | arms around a perfect blue rectangle of water. A place to spend the day without ❹ | incidence / disturbance |, the pool is striped with ropes ❺ | what / that | split the lanes and she can see bright towels on the deckchairs. Swimmers float in the water like petals. It is a place she knows well. It is the lido, her lido.

*lido 야외 풀장

Spring is in bloom and the park wears a new green coat. There are the tennis courts, a garden, and a small hill with an old house that ❶ _____ (use) to be a manor and is now used for events and a food stand ❷ _____ (sell) ice cream and snacks to sticky-fingered children. Two sets of train tracks loop around the park: the real one and the miniature one that ❸ _____ (be) only for the summer and very small children. The sun is just starting to set, and while listening to the calming songs of the birds, Rosemary can see people ❹ _____ (enjoy) the lengthening days. Runners make their way up the hill and down again. And on the edge of the park closest to her balcony a low redbrick building ❺ _____ (wrap) its arms around a perfect blue rectangle of water. A place to spend the day without disturbance, the pool is striped with ropes that split the lanes and she can see bright towels on the deckchairs. Swimmers float in the water like petals. It is a place she knows well. It is the lido, her lido.

*lido 야외 풀장

❶ _____ _____ _____ _____ (봄이 한창이다) and the park wears a new green coat. There are the tennis courts, a garden, and a small hill with an old house that used to be a manor and is now used for events and a food stand selling ice cream and snacks to sticky-fingered children. ❷ _____ _____ _____ _____ _____ (두 개의 기차선로들) loop around the park: the real one and the miniature one that is only for the summer and very small children. The sun is just starting to set, and while listening to the calming songs of the birds, Rosemary can see people enjoying the lengthening days. Runners make their way up the hill and down again. And ❸ _____ _____ _____ _____ (~의 가장자리에는) the park closest to her balcony a low redbrick building wraps its arms around a perfect blue rectangle of water. A(n) ❹ _____ _____ _____ _____ _____ (하루를 보낼 수 있는 장소) without disturbance, the pool is striped with ropes that split the lanes and she can see bright towels on the deckchairs. Swimmers float in the water like petals. It is a place she knows well. It is the lido, her lido.

*lido 야외 풀장

❶ At my high school, two students were accepted to Tufts University. ❷ However, the editor of our newspaper, who had worked his whole high-school career for a Tufts admission, was rejected. ❸ Upon hearing that news, I was overwhelmed with anxiety about my own chances of getting accepted. ❹ That morning, all I could think about was Tufts University. ❺ At about 10:30, an assistant from the front office came to get me out of math class and handed me a note to call home. ❻ I knew this was it. ❼ My heart pounded. ❽ My hands shook. ❾ I was short of breath. ❿ I had no right to expect a "yes," but I wanted it more than anything in my life. ⓫ I dialed our number. ⓬ It rang twice. ⓭ My mom picked up. ⓮ Laughing with happiness, she said, "You got in! You got into Tufts!!" ⓯ I jumped up and yelled, "Yes!" attracting the attention of everyone in the front office. ⓰ A thrill ran through me. ⓱ It was a moment that I will never, ever forget.

❶ 내가 다니는 고등학교에서 학생 두 명이 Tufts 대학교에 합격했다. ❷ 하지만 우리 (학교) 신문 편집장은, Tufts 대학교 입학을 위해 고등학교 생활 내내 노력했는데도, 불합격했다. ❸ 그 소식을 듣자마자, 나는 나 자신이 합격할 가능성에 대한 불안감에 휩싸였다. ❹ 그날 아침, 나는 생각이 온통 Tufts 대학교에 가 있었다. ❺ 10시 30분경에 행정실의 보조 사무원이 와서 나를 수학 수업에서 나오게 하고 집으로 전화하라는 쪽지를 내게 건네주었다. ❻ 나는 올 것이 왔다는 것을 알았다. ❼ 나는 가슴이 두근거렸다. ❽ 나는 두 손이 떨렸다. ❾ 나는 숨이 가빴다. ❿ 내게 '입학 허가'를 기대할 권리는 없었지만, 나는 내 인생에서 그 어떤 것보다도 더 그것을 원했다. ⓫ 나는 우리 집 전화번호로 전화를 걸었다. ⓬ 전화가 두 번 울렸다. ⓭ 엄마가 받았다. ⓮ 엄마는 즐겁게 웃으면서 "너 합격했어! 너 Tufts 대학교에 합격했어!!"라고 말했다. ⓯ 나는 뛰어오르며 "좋았어!"라고 소리 질렀고, 행정실에 있던 모든 사람의 주의를 끌게 되었다. ⓰ 전율이 나를 엄습했다. ⓱ 그것은 내가 결코 한시도 잊지 못할 순간이었다.

Word List

□ editor 편집장   □ career 경력   □ admission 입학   □ reject 불합격시키다, 거부하다   □ overwhelmed (감정에) 휩싸인
□ anxiety 불안감   □ chance 가능성, 확률   □ assistant 조수, 보조원   □ front office 행정실, (사업체의) 본부   □ hand 건네주다
□ pound (심장이) 두근거리다   □ short of breath 숨이 가쁜   □ expect 기대하다   □ dial 전화를 걸다, 다이얼을 돌리다
□ pick up (전화기를) 들다   □ yell 소리 지르다   □ attract (주의·흥미 등을) 끌다   □ thrill 전율

• Word Test

1	reject	_____	10	경력	_____
2	pick up	_____	11	가능성, 확률	_____
3	dial	_____	12	입학	_____
4	short of breath	_____	13	건네주다	_____
5	yell	_____	14	기대하다	_____
6	assistant	_____	15	전율	_____
7	front office	_____	16	편집장	_____
8	attract	_____	17	(감정에) 휩싸인	_____
9	pound	_____	18	불안감	_____

At my high school, two students were accepted to Tufts University. ❶ |However/Therefore|, the editor of our newspaper, ❷ |who / that| had worked his whole high-school career for a Tufts admission, was rejected. Upon ❸ |hearing / to hear| that news, I was ❹ |delighted/overwhelmed| with anxiety about my own chances of getting accepted. That morning, all I could think about was Tufts University. At about 10:30, an assistant from the front office came to get me out of math class and handed me a note to call home. I knew this was it. My heart pounded. My hands shook. I was short of breath. I had no right to expect a "yes," but I wanted it more than anything in my life. I dialed our number. It rang twice. My mom picked up. Laughing with happiness, she said, "You got in! You got into Tufts!!" I jumped up and yelled, "Yes!" attracting the ❺ |attention/attraction| of everyone in the front office. A thrill ran through me. It was a moment that I will never, ever forget.

At my high school, two students ❶ _____ (accept) to Tufts University. However, the editor of our newspaper, who ❷ _____ (work) his whole high-school career for a Tufts admission, was rejected. Upon hearing that news, I was overwhelmed with anxiety about my own chances of getting accepted. That morning, all I could think about ❸ _____ (be) Tufts University. At about 10:30, an assistant from the front office came to get me out of math class and ❹ _____ (hand) me a note to call home. I knew this was it. My heart pounded. My hands shook. I was short of breath. I had no right to expect a "yes," but I wanted it more than anything in my life. I dialed our number. It rang twice. My mom picked up. Laughing with happiness, she said, "You got in! You got into Tufts!!" I jumped up and yelled, "Yes!" ❺ _____ (attract) the attention of everyone in the front office. A thrill ran through me. It was a moment that I will never, ever forget.

At my high school, two students were accepted to Tufts University. However, the editor of our newspaper, who had worked his whole high-school career for a Tufts admission, was rejected. Upon hearing that news, I was overwhelmed with anxiety about ❶ _____ _____ _____ _____ _____ _____ (나 자신이 합격할 가능성). That morning, all I could think about was Tufts University. At about 10:30, an assistant from the front office came to get me out of math class and handed me a note to call home. I knew this was it. My heart pounded. My hands shook. ❷ _____ _____ _____ _____ _____ (나는 숨이 가빴다). I had no right to expect a "yes," but I wanted it ❸ _____ _____ _____ _____ (그 어떤 것보다도 더) in my life. I dialed our number. It rang twice. My mom picked up. Laughing with happiness, she said, "You got in! You got into Tufts!!" I jumped up and yelled, "Yes!" attracting the attention of everyone in the front office. ❹ _____ _____ _____ _____ _____ (전율이 나를 엄습했다). It was a moment that I will never, ever forget.

01 2강 1번

주어진 글 다음에 이어질 글의 순서로 가장 적절한 것은?

> The phone rang late at night, and Sam sat up with a jolt. It felt to him as though his life was going to change after he picked up the flashing piece of metal that was vibrating on the end table.

(A) "Hey, Sam speaking." His voice was gruff and hesitant. "Hey there, friend, long time no see! It's John Havisham here. Hope that the last party Joe had over at the cottage wasn't too boring?"

(B) He couldn't shake the feeling that whatever he was about to learn would have an impact on the rest of his life. Sam's hand shook slightly as he answered the phone. It was from a number he didn't recognize.

(C) Sam felt relief flood over him. John would call occasionally to catch up on local news, ask whether Patty's art gallery had any exceptional pieces of art for sale, and order a few kegs of beer to be shipped to his home in Halifax.

*jolt 놀람 **gruff 걸걸한 ***keg (맥주 저장용의 작은) 통

① (A) – (C) – (B)
② (B) – (A) – (C)
③ (B) – (C) – (A)
④ (C) – (A) – (B)
⑤ (C) – (B) – (A)

02 2강 2번

밑줄 친 she had been anything other than blown away by my Gaelic masterpiece가 다음 글에서 의미하는 바로 가장 적절한 것은?

One day we were asked to write a whole composition about some birds in Gaelic. I knew I could do it easily in English so it shouldn't be too difficult in Gaelic. The words came very easily and although I wasn't sure I'd got all the past, present and future tenses perfectly correct, overall I decided I'd made a really good job of it. Sister Cecilia then came towards me, and said, "Now, Kathleen O'Malley, let me see what you've done." She read my essay. I sat there patiently waiting for the praise I felt sure would be forthcoming. I did notice that her colour was getting more and more ruddy, and suddenly she said, "Kathleen O'Malley, do you expect to pass?" Without hesitation, I replied, "Yes, sister." She then continued, "I've never read anything like this before." I realized she had been anything other than blown away by my Gaelic masterpiece. As a horrible sense of self-pity started slowly to descend on me, she went over to one of the girls and said, "Now I'm sure you've got a better composition." She read that girl's work and a big smile spread across her face.

*Gaelic 게일어

① my Gaelic masterpiece had failed to impress her
② she had been completely blown away by my Gaelic composition
③ she had never seen any other Gaelic masterpiece in her life
④ she had tried to protect my Gaelic masterpiece from being blown away
⑤ she had never seen a better Gaelic composition than mine

다음 글의 밑줄 친 부분 중, 어법상 틀린 것은?

Spring is in bloom and the park wears a new green coat. There are the tennis courts, a garden, and a small hill with an old house that ① used to be a manor and is now used for events and a food stand selling ice cream and snacks to sticky-fingered children. Two sets of train tracks loop around the park: the real one and the miniature one ② that is only for the summer and very small children. The sun is just starting to set, and while listening to the calming songs of the birds, Rosemary can see people ③ to enjoy the lengthening days. Runners make their way up the hill and down again. And on the edge of the park closest to her balcony a low redbrick building ④ wraps its arms around a perfect blue rectangle of water. A place to spend the day without disturbance, the pool is striped with ropes that ⑤ split the lanes and she can see bright towels on the deckchairs. Swimmers float in the water like petals. It is a place she knows well. It is the lido, her lido.

* lido 야외 풀장

다음 글의 내용과 일치하지 않는 것은?

At my high school, two students were accepted to Tufts University. However, the editor of our newspaper, who had worked his whole high-school career for a Tufts admission, was rejected. Upon hearing that news, I was overwhelmed with anxiety about my own chances of getting accepted. That morning, all I could think about was Tufts University. At about 10:30, an assistant from the front office came to get me out of math class and handed me a note to call home. I knew this was it. My heart pounded. My hands shook. I was short of breath. I had no right to expect a "yes," but I wanted it more than anything in my life. I dialed our number. It rang twice. My mom picked up. Laughing with happiness, she said, "You got in! You got into Tufts!!" I jumped up and yelled, "Yes!" attracting the attention of everyone in the front office. A thrill ran through me. It was a moment that I will never, ever forget.

① Tufts 대학 신문 편집장은 고교 내내 Tufts 입학을 위해 일한 게 드러나 사퇴해야 했다.
② 다른 학생의 Tufts 대학교 입학 결과를 들은 나는 입학 가능성에 대한 불안에 휩싸였다.
③ 오전 10시 30분경 행정 보조 사무원이 나를 찾아 왔을 때 나는 수학 수업을 듣던 중이었다.
④ 내가 집으로 전화를 했을 때 벨이 두 번 울리자 엄마가 전화를 받았다.
⑤ 합격 소식을 들은 나는 뛰어오르며 소리 질렀고, 행정실 사람들의 주의를 끌게 되었다.

(A), (B), (C)의 각 네모 안에서 문맥에 맞는 낱말로 가장 적절한 것은?

The phone rang late at night, and Sam sat up with a jolt. It felt to him as though his life was going to change after he (A) hung up / picked up the flashing piece of metal that was vibrating on the end table. He couldn't shake the feeling that whatever he was about to learn would have an impact on the rest of his life. Sam's hand shook slightly as he answered the phone. It was from a number he didn't recognize. "Hey, Sam speaking." His voice was gruff and (B) confident / hesitant. "Hey there, friend, long time no see! It's John Havisham here. Hope that the last party Joe had over at the cottage wasn't too boring?" Sam felt (C) grief / relief flood over him. John would call occasionally to catch up on local news, ask whether Patty's art gallery had any exceptional pieces of art for sale, and order a few kegs of beer to be shipped to his home in Halifax.

*jolt 놀람 **gruff 걸걸한 ***keg (맥주 저장용의 작은) 통

(A)	(B)	(C)
① hung up	...... confident	...... grief
② hung up	...... hesitant	...... relief
③ picked up	...... hesitant	...... grief
④ picked up	...... hesitant	...... relief
⑤ picked up	...... confident	...... grief

다음 빈칸에 들어갈 말로 가장 적절한 것은?

One day we were asked to write a whole composition about some birds in Gaelic. I knew I could do it easily in English so it shouldn't be too difficult in Gaelic. The words came very easily and although I wasn't sure I'd got all the past, present and future tenses perfectly correct, overall I decided I'd made a really good job of it. Sister Cecilia then came towards me, and said, "Now, Kathleen O'Malley, let me see what you've done." She read my essay. I sat there patiently waiting for the praise I felt sure would be forthcoming. I did notice that her colour was getting more and more ruddy, and suddenly she said, "Kathleen O'Malley, do you expect to pass?" Without hesitation, I replied, "Yes, sister." She then continued, "I've never read anything like this before." I realized she had been anything other than blown away by my Gaelic masterpiece. As _____ started slowly to descend on me, she went over to one of the girls and said, "Now I'm sure you've got a better composition." She read that girl's work and a big smile spread across her face.

*Gaelic 게일어

① a huge wave of relief
② a clear feeling of jealousy
③ a horrible sense of self-pity
④ a strong sense of belonging
⑤ a growing sense of confidence

2강 3번

다음 글의 내용과 일치하지 <u>않는</u> 것은?

Spring is in bloom and the park wears a new green coat. There are the tennis courts, a garden, and a small hill with an old house that used to be a manor and is now used for events and a food stand selling ice cream and snacks to sticky-fingered children. Two sets of train tracks loop around the park: the real one and the miniature one that is only for the summer and very small children. The sun is just starting to set, and while listening to the calming songs of the birds, Rosemary can see people enjoying the lengthening days. Runners make their way up the hill and down again. And on the edge of the park closest to her balcony a low redbrick building wraps its arms around a perfect blue rectangle of water. A place to spend the day without disturbance, the pool is striped with ropes that split the lanes and she can see bright towels on the deckchairs. Swimmers float in the water like petals. It is a place she knows well. It is the lido, her lido.

* lido 야외 풀장

① 언덕에 있는 집은 전에는 저택이었다가 지금은 행사용으로 사용되고 있다.
② 음식 가판대는 아이스크림과 간식을 어린이들에게 판매한다.
③ 고리 모양으로 난 두 개의 기차선로는 각각 여름용과 아주 어린 아이용이다.
④ 발코니에서 가장 가까운 공원 가장자리에는 붉은 벽돌 건물이 푸른 물을 감싸고 있다.
⑤ 수영장에는 레인을 나누는 밧줄이 줄무늬를 만들고 있고 수영하는 사람들이 물에 떠 있다.

2강 4번

주어진 글 다음에 이어질 글의 순서로 가장 적절한 것은?

At my high school, two students were accepted to Tufts University. However, the editor of our newspaper, who had worked his whole high-school career for a Tufts admission, was rejected.

(A) I knew this was it. My heart pounded. My hands shook. I was short of breath. I had no right to expect a "yes," but I wanted it more than anything in my life. I dialed our number. It rang twice. My mom picked up.

(B) Laughing with happiness, she said, "You got in! You got into Tufts!!" I jumped up and yelled, "Yes!" attracting the attention of everyone in the front office. A thrill ran through me. It was a moment that I will never, ever forget.

(C) Upon hearing that news, I was overwhelmed with anxiety about my own chances of getting accepted. That morning, all I could think about was Tufts University. At about 10:30, an assistant from the front office came to get me out of math class and handed me a note to call home.

① (A) – (C) – (B)
② (B) – (A) – (C)
③ (B) – (C) – (A)
④ (C) – (A) – (B)
⑤ (C) – (B) – (A)

The phone rang late at night, and Sam sat up with a jolt. It felt to him as though his life was going to change after he picked up the flashing piece of metal that was vibrating on the end table. He couldn't shake the feeling that (A) however he was about to learn would have an impact on the rest of his life. Sam's hand shook slightly as he answered the phone. It was from a number he didn't recognize. "Hey, Sam speaking." His voice was gruff and hesitant. "Hey there, friend, long time no see! It's John Havisham here. Hope that the last party Joe had over at the cottage wasn't too (B) bored?" Sam felt relief flood over him. John would call occasionally to catch up on local news, ask whether Patty's art gallery had any exceptional pieces of art for sale, and (C) ordering a few kegs of beer to be shipped to his home in Halifax.

*jolt 놀람   **gruff 걸걸한   ***keg (맥주 저장용의 작은) 통

09 윗글의 밑줄 친 the flashing piece of metal이 가리키는 것을 본문에서 찾아 쓰시오. (2단어)

_____

10 윗글의 밑줄 친 부분을 어법상 알맞은 형태로 고쳐 쓰시오.

(A) however → _____

(B) bored → _____

(C) ordering → _____

One day 우리는 게일어로 어떤 새들에 관해 완전히 갖추어진 짧은 글을 쓰라는 요구를 받았다. I knew I could do it easily in English so it shouldn't be too difficult in Gaelic. The words came very ① laboriously and although I wasn't sure I'd got all the past, present and future tenses perfectly correct, overall I decided I'd made a really good job of it. Sister Cecilia then came towards me, and said, "Now, Kathleen O'Malley, let me see what you've done." She read my essay. I sat there patiently waiting for the ② praise I felt sure would be forthcoming. I did notice that her colour was getting more and more ③ ruddy, and suddenly she said, "Kathleen O'Malley, do you expect to pass?" Without hesitation, I replied, "Yes, sister." She then continued, "I've never read anything like this before." I realized she had been anything other than blown away by my Gaelic masterpiece. As a horrible sense of ④ self-pity started slowly to descend on me, she went over to one of the girls and said, "Now I'm sure you've got a ⑤ better composition." She read that girl's work and a big smile spread across her face.

*Gaelic 게일어

11 윗글의 밑줄 친 우리말 의미와 일치하도록 보기 의 단어를 활용하여 문장을 완성하시오 (단, 필요시 단어를 추가하고, 어형을 바꿔 쓸 것)

보기   composition / in Gaelic / ask / a whole /

_____

_____

12 윗글의 밑줄 친 부분 중, 문맥상 어색한 것을 1개 찾아 그 번호를 쓰고 고쳐 쓰시오.

_____ → _____

Spring is in bloom and the park wears a new green coat. There are the tennis courts, a garden, and a small hill with 한때는 저택이었다가 지금은 행사용으로 사용되고 있는 오래된 집 and a food stand selling ice cream and snacks to sticky-fingered children. Two sets of train tracks loop around the park: the real one and the miniature one that is only for the summer and very small children. The sun is just starting to set, and while listening to the calming songs of the birds, Rosemary can see people enjoying the lengthening days. Runners make their way up the hill and down again. And on the edge of the park closest to her balcony a low redbrick building wrapping its arms around a perfect blue rectangle of water. A place to spend the day without disturbance, the pool is striped with ropes that split the lanes and she can see bright towels on the deckchairs. Swimmers float in the water like petals. It is a place she knows well. It is the lido, her lido.

*lido 야외 풀장

13 윗글의 밑줄 친 우리말 의미와 일치하도록 보기 의 단어를 순서대로 배열하여 영작하시오.

> 보기   a manor / for / to / used / be / used / that / events

an old house _____

and is now _____

14 윗글에서 다음 질문에 대한 답을 찾아 우리말로 쓰시오. (30자 내외)

Q: When the sun is just starting to set, what can Rosemary see listening to the songs of the birds?

A: _____

At my high school, two students were ___(A)___ to Tufts University. However, the editor of our newspaper, who had worked his whole high-school career for a Tufts admission, ① rejected. Upon hearing that news, I was overwhelmed with anxiety about my own chances of getting ___(B)___. That morning, all I could think about ② was Tufts University. At about 10:30, an assistant from the front office came to get me out of math class and ③ hands me a note to call home. I knew this was it. My heart pounded. My hands shook. I was short of breath. I had no right ④ to expect a "yes," but I wanted it more than anything in my life. I dialed our number. It rang twice. My mom picked up. Laughing with happiness, she said, "You got in! You got into Tufts!!" I jumped up and yelled, "Yes!" ⑤ attracted the attention of everyone in the front office. A thrill ran through me. It was a moment that I will never, ever forget.

고난도

15 윗글의 밑줄 친 부분 중, 어법상 틀린 것을 3개 찾아 그 번호를 쓰고 고쳐 쓰시오.

(1) _____ → _____
(2) _____ → _____
(3) _____ → _____

16 윗글의 빈칸 (A), (B)에 공통으로 들어갈 단어를 영영 뜻풀이를 참고하여 쓰시오. (단, 주어진 글자로 시작하여 어법에 알맞은 형태로 쓸 것)

> to allow someone to join an organization

a_____

❶ In the past there was little genetic pressure to stop people from becoming obese. ❷ Genetic mutations that drove people to consume fewer calories were much less likely to be passed on, because in an environment where food was scarcer and its hunting or gathering required considerable energy outlay, an individual with that mutation would probably die before they had a chance to reproduce. ❸ Mutations that in our environment of abundant food now drive us towards obesity, on the other hand, were incorporated into the population. ❹ Things are of course very different now but the problem is that evolutionary timescales are long. ❺ It's only in the last century or so, approximately 0.00004 per cent of mammalian evolutionary time, that we managed to tweak our environment to such a degree that we can pretty much eat whatever we want, whenever we want it. ❻ Evolution has another couple of thousand years to go before it can catch up with the current reality of online food shopping and delivery.

*mutation 돌연변이   **outlay (에너지 등의) 소비   ***tweak 변경하다, 수정하다

❶ 과거에는 사람들이 비만이 되는 것을 막을 수 있는 유전적 압력이 거의 없었다. ❷ 사람들이 더 적은 열량을 섭취하게 하는 유전 돌연변이는 전달이 될 가능성이 훨씬 덜했는데, 왜냐하면 먹을 것이 더 부족하고 그것을 사냥하거나 채집하는 데 상당한 에너지 소비가 요구되는 환경에서, 그 돌연변이를 가진 사람은 아마도 자신이 번식할 기회를 얻기 전에 죽었을 것이기 때문이다. ❸ 반면에, 먹을 것이 풍부한 환경에서 이제 우리를 비만으로 몰아가는 돌연변이가 인구 집단 속에 포함되었다. ❹ 물론 지금은 상황이 아주 다르지만, 문제는 진화 기간이 길다는 것이다. ❺ 포유류의 진화 시간의 약 0.00004퍼센트에 해당하는 지난 세기쯤에서야, 우리는 원하는 것은 무엇이든 우리가 그것을 원할 때마다 거의 먹을 수 있을 정도로 용케도 우리의 환경을 바꾸었다. ❻ 진화가 온라인 음식 쇼핑과 배달의 현재 현실을 따라잡을 수 있기까지는 앞으로 몇 천 년이 더 걸린다.

Word List

□ **genetic** 유전적인   □ **pressure** 압력   □ **obese** 비만의   □ **consume** 섭취하다, 소비하다   □ **pass on** ~을 전달하다
□ **scarce** 부족한   □ **gather** 모으다, 수집하다   □ **considerable** 상당한   □ **individual** 개인, 사람   □ **reproduce** 번식하다
□ **abundant** 풍부한   □ **obesity** 비만   □ **on the other hand** 반면에   □ **incorporate** (일부로) 포함하다   □ **population** 인구
□ **evolutionary** 진화의   □ **timescale** (어떤 일에 소요되는) 기간   □ **approximately** 대략   □ **mammalian** 포유류의
□ **degree** 정도, 수준   □ **catch up with** ~을 따라잡다   □ **current** 현재의   □ **delivery** 배달

• Word Test

1	individual		12	압력
2	obesity		13	현재의
3	incorporate		14	비만의
4	mammalian		15	대략
5	reproduce		16	상당한
6	on the other hand		17	섭취하다, 소비하다
7	catch up with		18	진화의
8	gather		19	부족한
9	genetic		20	풍부한
10	timescale		21	정도, 수준
11	pass on		22	인구

In the past there was ❶ little / few genetic pressure to stop people from becoming obese. Genetic mutations that drove people to consume fewer calories were ❷ more / much less likely to be passed on, because in an environment ❸ when / where food was scarcer and its hunting or gathering required considerable energy outlay, an individual with that mutation would probably die before they had a chance to reproduce. Mutations that in our environment of ❹ abundant / apparent food now drive us towards obesity, on the other hand, were incorporated into the population. Things are of course very different now but the problem is that evolutionary timescales are long. It's only in the last century or so, approximately 0.00004 per cent of mammalian evolutionary time, that we managed to tweak our environment to such a degree that we can pretty much eat ❺ whatever / wherever we want, whenever we want it. Evolution has another couple of thousand years to go before it can catch up with the current reality of online food shopping and delivery.

*mutation 돌연변이   **outlay (에너지 등의) 소비   ***tweak 변경하다, 수정하다

In the past there ❶ _____ (be) little genetic pressure to stop people from becoming obese. Genetic mutations that drove people ❷ _____ (consume) fewer calories were much less likely to ❸ _____ (pass) on, because in an environment where food was scarcer and its hunting or gathering ❹ _____ (require) considerable energy outlay, an individual with that mutation would probably die before they had a chance to reproduce. Mutations that in our environment of abundant food now drive us towards obesity, on the other hand, ❺ _____ (incorporate) into the population. Things are of course very different now but the problem is that evolutionary timescales are long. It's only in the last century or so, approximately 0.00004 per cent of mammalian evolutionary time, that we managed to tweak our environment to such a degree that we can pretty much eat whatever we want, whenever we want it. Evolution has another couple of thousand years to go before it can catch up with the current reality of online food shopping and delivery.

*mutation 돌연변이   **outlay (에너지 등의) 소비   ***tweak 변경하다, 수정하다

In the past there was little genetic pressure to ❶ _____ _____ _____ _____ _____ (사람들이 비만이 되는 것을 막다). Genetic mutations that drove people to consume fewer calories were much less likely to be passed on, because in an environment where food was scarcer and its hunting or gathering required considerable energy outlay, an individual with that mutation would probably die before they had a chance to reproduce. Mutations that in our environment of abundant food now drive us towards obesity, ❷ _____ _____ _____ _____ (반면에), were incorporated into the population. Things are of course very different now but the problem is that evolutionary timescales are long. It's only in the last century or so, approximately 0.00004 per cent of mammalian evolutionary time, that we managed to tweak our environment to such a degree that we can pretty much eat whatever we want, ❸ _____ _____ _____ _____ (우리가 그것을 원할 때마다). Evolution has another couple of thousand years to go before it can ❹ _____ _____ _____ (~을 따라잡다) the current reality of online food shopping and delivery.

*mutation 돌연변이   **outlay (에너지 등의) 소비   ***tweak 변경하다, 수정하다

34

❶ The idea of family support, suggested as one of the preconditions of any child's success, is far from being faultless. ❷ Thus, for example, the well-known musical psychologist Jane Davidson and her colleagues state that all the parents of children who later become successful musicians were, in fact, their charges' great friends and allies from earliest childhood. ❸ If the great jazz musician Sidney Bechet were to hear of such a conclusion he would be surprised indeed. ❹ His altogether respectable parents, who dreamed of something rather more substantial and reliable than a career in music for their son, actually hid his clarinet from him. ❺ Robert Schumann's mother, the widow of a publisher and literary translator, reconciled herself only with difficulty to her son's choice of music as a profession; while Christoph W. Gluck, the great reformer of opera, was forced to roam about Italy and Bohemia after being expelled from home by his father. ❻ Even some of the great musical geniuses, it is clear, were given switches and coal by an unkind Fate instead of the presents other youngsters received. ❼ The 'universal support' given by parents to beginning musicians turns out, upon closer examination, to be a myth.

*charge 보살펴야 하는 사람　**reconcile oneself to ~을 감수하다　***switch 회초리

❶ 가족 성원에 대한 생각은, 어떤 아이든 그 아이의 성공의 전제 조건의 하나라고 제안되는데, 결코 결점이 없는 것은 아니다. ❷ 따라서, 예컨대 유명한 음악 심리학자인 Jane Davidson과 그녀의 동료들은 나중에 성공한 음악가가 된 아이들의 모든 부모가 사실은 그들이 유년기부터 보살펴야 하는 아이들의 훌륭한 친구이며 협력자였다고 말한다. ❸ 만약 위대한 재즈 음악가인 Sidney Bechet가 그런 결론을 듣는다면, 그는 정말 놀랄 것이다. ❹ 아들을 위해 음악에서의 직업보다는 다소 더 실질적이고 믿음직한 것을 꿈꿨던, 전적으로 존경할 만한 그의 부모는 실제로 그의 클라리넷을 그에게서 감췄다. ❺ 출판업자이자 문학 번역가의 미망인이었던 Robert Schumann의 어머니는 자기 아들이 직업으로 음악을 선택한 것을 겨우 간신히 감수했으며, 한편, 훌륭한 오페라 개혁가였던 Christoph W. Gluck는 자기 아버지에 의해 집에서 쫓겨난 후 Italy와 Bohemia를 여기저기 떠돌아야 했다. ❻ 심지어 위대한 음악 천재 중 몇몇은 다른 아이들이 받았던 선물이 아니라 냉혹한 운명에 의해 회초리와 석탄을 받았던 것이 분명하다. ❼ 초보 음악가에게 부모가 주는 '보편적 성원'은 더 자세히 조사해 보면 근거 없는 믿음으로 판명된다.

Word List

□ precondition 전제 조건　□ faultless 결점이 없는, 완전한　□ psychologist 심리학자　□ colleague 동료　□ state 말하다
□ ally 협력자, 동맹국　□ conclusion 결론　□ indeed 정말로　□ respectable 존경할 만한　□ substantial 실질적인
□ reliable 믿음직한, 신뢰할 만한　□ widow 미망인　□ literary 문학의　□ profession 직업　□ reformer 개혁가
□ roam 떠돌다, 헤매다　□ expel 쫓아내다, 추방하다　□ genius 천재　□ coal 석탄　□ myth 신화, 근거 없는 믿음

• Word Test

1	faultless	11	천재
2	ally	12	결론
3	roam	13	미망인
4	myth	14	석탄
5	expel	15	존경할 만한
6	precondition	16	개혁가
7	profession	17	믿음직한, 신뢰할 만한
8	state	18	문학의
9	substantial	19	심리학자
10	indeed	20	동료

The idea of family support, suggested as one of the ❶ contradictions/preconditions of any child's success, is far from being faultless. Thus, for example, the well-known musical psychologist Jane Davidson and her colleagues state ❷ that/what all the parents of children who later become successful musicians were, in fact, their charges' great friends and allies from earliest childhood. If the great jazz musician Sidney Bechet were to hear of such a conclusion he would be surprised indeed. His altogether respectable parents, ❸ who/that dreamed of something rather more substantial and ❹ reliable/unreliable than a career in music for their son, actually hid his clarinet from him. Robert Schumann's mother, the widow of a publisher and literary translator, reconciled herself only with difficulty to her son's choice of music as a profession; ❺ while/since Christoph W. Gluck, the great reformer of opera, was forced to roam about Italy and Bohemia after being expelled from home by his father. Even some of the great musical geniuses, it is clear, were given switches and coal by an unkind Fate instead of the presents other youngsters received. The 'universal support' given by parents to beginning musicians turns out, upon closer examination, to be a myth.

*charge 보살펴야 하는 사람   **reconcile oneself to ~을 감수하다   ***switch 회초리

The idea of family support, ❶ _____ (suggest) as one of the preconditions of any child's success, ❷ _____ (be) far from being faultless. Thus, for example, the well-known musical psychologist Jane Davidson and her colleagues state that all the parents of children who later become successful musicians were, in fact, their charges' great friends and allies from earliest childhood. If the great jazz musician Sidney Bechet were to hear of such a conclusion he would be surprised indeed. His altogether respectable parents, who ❸ _____ (dream) of something rather more substantial and reliable than a career in music for their son, actually hid his clarinet from him. Robert Schumann's mother, the widow of a publisher and literary translator, reconciled herself only with difficulty to her son's choice of music as a profession; while Christoph W. Gluck, the great reformer of opera, ❹ _____ (force) to roam about Italy and Bohemia after being expelled from home by his father. Even some of the great musical geniuses, it is clear, were given switches and coal by an unkind Fate instead of the presents other youngsters received. The 'universal support' given by parents to beginning musicians ❺ _____ (turn) out, upon closer examination, to be a myth.

*charge 보살펴야 하는 사람   **reconcile oneself to ~을 감수하다   ***switch 회초리

The idea of family support, suggested as one of the preconditions of any child's success, ❶ _____ _____ _____ _____ _____ (결코 결점이 없는 것은 아니다). Thus, for example, the well-known musical psychologist Jane Davidson and her colleagues state that all the parents of children who later become successful musicians were, in fact, their charges' great friends and allies from earliest childhood. If the great jazz musician Sidney Bechet were to hear of such a conclusion he would be surprised indeed. His altogether respectable parents, who dreamed of something rather more substantial and reliable than a career in music for their son, actually ❷ _____ _____ _____ _____ _____ (그의 클라리넷을 그에게서 감췄다). Robert Schumann's mother, the widow of a publisher and literary translator, reconciled herself only with difficulty to her son's choice of music as a profession; while Christoph W. Gluck, the great reformer of opera, was forced to roam about Italy and Bohemia ❸ _____ _____ _____ _____ _____ (집에서 쫓겨난 후) by his father. Even some of the great musical geniuses, it is clear, were given switches and coal by an unkind Fate instead of the presents other youngsters received. The 'universal support' given by parents to beginning musicians turns out, ❹ _____ _____ _____ (더 자세히 조사해 보면), to be a myth.

*charge 보살펴야 하는 사람   **reconcile oneself to ~을 감수하다   ***switch 회초리

37

❶ A key feature particular to stories is that they have the ability to transport the reader. ❷ While experiencing stories, one can feel emotionally involved and as if being swept away as a participant. ❸ There is some evidence that being transported into a story requires a suspension of disbelief; enjoying *Jurassic Park* or a Harry Potter tale may involve putting aside what one knows about the world that contradicts the story. ❹ A story that suggests an unexpected outcome ("George Washington declined the nomination to become the first president of the United States") results in readers being slower to verify well-known facts ("George Washington was elected first president of the United States"). ❺ This suspension of disbelief may make one less likely to spot problems in a narrative, as illustrated by a study in which participants read a story and circled any "false notes" or parts that did not make sense. ❻ Green and Brock refer to this method as "Pinocchio circling": just as the puppet's nose signaled when he told a falsehood, authors also leave clues when they are being untruthful. ❼ But readers who were more transported by the story spotted fewer "Pinocchios."

*verify 확인하다

❶ 이야기 특유의 한 가지 중요한 특징은 이야기에는 독자를 다른 세상에 있는 것처럼 느끼게 하는 능력이 있다는 것이다. ❷ 이야기를 경험하는 동안, 감정적으로 몰입되어 참여자로서 정신없이 빠져드는 듯한 기분을 느낄 수 있다. ❸ 이야기 속 다른 세상에 있는 것처럼 느껴지는 것에는 불신의 유예가 필요하다는 몇 가지 증거가 있는데, *Jurassic Park*나 Harry Potter 이야기를 즐기는 것은 이야기와 모순되는 세상에 대해 알고 있는 바를 제쳐 두는 것을 수반할 수도 있다. ❹ 예상치 못한 결과('George Washington은 미국의 초대 대통령에 지명되는 것을 거부했다')를 말하는 이야기는 독자들이 잘 알려진 사실('George Washington은 미국의 초대 대통령으로 당선되었다')을 확인하는 데 더 느려지게 만든다. ❺ 이러한 불신의 유예는, (연구의) 참가자들이 이야기를 읽고 말이 되지 않는 '거짓 정보'나 부분이라면 어느 것이나 동그라미를 쳤던 한 연구가 예증하듯이, 이야기 속에서 문제를 발견할 가능성을 더 적게 만들 수도 있다. ❻ Green과 Brock은 이 방법을 '피노키오 동그라미 치기'라고 부르는데, 꼭두각시가 거짓말을 했을 때 그 꼭두각시의 코가 신호를 보낸 것과 꼭 마찬가지로, 작가들 역시 자신들이 거짓말을 하고 있을 때는 단서를 남긴다. ❼ 하지만 이야기에 의해 더욱 다른 세상에 있는 것처럼 느낀 독자는 더 적은 '피노키오'를 발견했다.

Word List

□ **feature** 특징　□ **transport** 다른 세상에 있는 것처럼 느끼게 하다　□ **emotionally** 감정적으로　□ **involved** 몰두하는, 관여하는
□ **sweep away** ~을 정신없이 빠져들게 만들다　□ **suspension** 유예, 중지　□ **disbelief** 불신　□ **put aside** ~을 제쳐 두다
□ **contradict** ~과 모순되다, 반박하다　□ **outcome** 결과　□ **decline** 거부하다, 거절하다　□ **nomination** 지명, 임명
□ **result in** ~한 결과를 낳다　□ **elect** 당선시키다, 선출하다　□ **spot** 발견하다　□ **narrative** 이야기　□ **illustrate** 예증하다, 설명하다
□ **make sense** 타당하다, 의미가 통하다　□ **circle** ~에 동그라미를 치다　□ **signal** 신호하다　□ **falsehood** 거짓말, 거짓임
□ **clue** 단서　□ **untruthful** 거짓말을 하는

1	sweep away	12	당선시키다, 선출하다
2	feature	13	거짓말, 거짓임
3	put aside	14	지명, 임명
4	contradict	15	유예, 중지
5	spot	16	결과
6	decline	17	단서
7	result in	18	불신
8	illustrate	19	이야기
9	transport	20	몰두하는, 관여하는
10	circle	21	감정적으로
11	untruthful	22	타당하다, 의미가 통하다

• 유형 1 네모 안에서 옳은 어법·어휘를 고르시오.

A key feature particular to stories is that they have the ability to ❶ transport/translate the reader. While experiencing stories, one can feel emotionally involved and as if being swept away as a participant. There is some evidence that being transported into a story requires a suspension of disbelief; enjoying *Jurassic Park* or a Harry Potter tale may involve putting aside ❷ that/what one knows about the world that ❸ contradicts/corresponds the story. A story that suggests an unexpected outcome ("George Washington declined the nomination to become the first president of the United States") results in readers being slower to verify well-known facts ("George Washington was elected first president of the United States"). This suspension of disbelief may make one less likely to spot problems in a narrative, as illustrated by a study ❹ in which/that participants read a story and circled any "false notes" or parts that did not make sense. Green and Brock refer to this method as "Pinocchio circling": just as the puppet's nose signaled when he told a falsehood, authors also leave clues when they are being untruthful. But readers who were more transported by the story spotted ❺ less/fewer "Pinocchios."

*verify 확인하다

A key feature particular to stories is that they have the ability to transport the reader. While ❶ _____ (experience) stories, one can feel emotionally involved and as if being swept away as a participant. There is some evidence that being transported into a story ❷ _____ (require) a suspension of disbelief; enjoying *Jurassic Park* or a Harry Potter tale may involve putting aside what one knows about the world that contradicts the story. A story that ❸ _____ (suggest) an unexpected outcome ("George Washington declined the nomination to become the first president of the United States") results in readers being slower to verify well-known facts ("George Washington ❹ _____ (elect) first president of the United States"). This suspension of disbelief may make one less likely to spot problems in a narrative, as ❺ _____ (illustrate) by a study in which participants read a story and circled any "false notes" or parts that did not make sense. Green and Brock refer to this method as "Pinocchio circling": just as the puppet's nose signaled when he told a falsehood, authors also leave clues when they are being untruthful. But readers who were more transported by the story spotted fewer "Pinocchios."

*verify 확인하다

A key feature particular to stories is that they have the ability to transport the reader. While experiencing stories, one can feel emotionally involved and ❶ _____ _____ _____ _____ _____ (마치 정신없이 빠져드는 듯한) as a participant. There is some evidence that being transported into a story requires a suspension of disbelief; enjoying *Jurassic Park* or a Harry Potter tale may involve ❷ _____ _____ (제쳐 두는 것) what one knows about the world that contradicts the story. A story that suggests an unexpected outcome ("George Washington declined the nomination to become the first president of the United States") results in readers being slower to verify well-known facts ("George Washington was elected first president of the United States"). This suspension of disbelief may make one ❸ _____ _____ _____ (~할 가능성을 더 적게) spot problems in a narrative, as illustrated by a study in which participants read a story and circled any "false notes" or parts that did not ❹ _____ _____ (말이 되다). Green and Brock refer to this method as "Pinocchio circling": just as the puppet's nose signaled when he told a falsehood, authors also leave clues when they are being untruthful. But readers who were more transported by the story spotted fewer "Pinocchios."

*verify 확인하다

❶ Marketing is based on notions that are 20 years out of date. ❷ The notion that if you put enough messages out there some of them will be heard. ❸ The notion that 'building the brand' is money well spent. ❹ The notion that people believe what they see and read. ❺ Recent initiatives to take advantage of Web 2.0 technologies are merely reactions that apply old techniques to new media. ❻ Marketing needs to rethink the messages it is communicating, to whom it's communicated and the methods being used. ❼ Many companies are disappointed at the lack of tangible return on their multi-million pounds marketing activities. ❽ Advertising remains the largest budget item on most firms' marketing plans. ❾ Advertising may be a fixture in a company's annual spend, but management boards are increasingly questioning why this is. ❿ The most recent Brandchannel survey illustrates this point well. ⓫ Four of the world's five largest brands have never conducted any advertising, and the same is true for seven out of the 10 fastest-growing brands. ⓬ There is no proven causal relationship between advertising and financial performance. ⓭ And advertising is just the tip of the melting marketing iceberg.

*tangible return 유형 수익

❶ 마케팅은 시대에 20년 뒤떨어진 개념들에 기반을 두고 있다. ❷ 곧 충분히 많은 메시지를 밖으로 내보내면 그중 일부는 사람들이 들을 것이라는 개념, ❸ '브랜드 구축'은 돈이 잘 사용되는 것이라는 개념, ❹ 그리고 사람들은 보고 읽는 것을 믿는다는 개념이다. ❺ 웹 2.0 기술을 활용하려는 최근의 주창은 그저 낡은 기술을 새로운 매체에 적용하는 반응에 불과하다. ❻ 마케팅은 그것이 전달하고 있는 메시지, 그것이 전달되는 대상, 사용되고 있는 방법을 재고해야 한다. ❼ 많은 회사가 수백만 파운드의 마케팅 활동에 대한 유형 수익의 부족에 실망하고 있다. ❽ 광고는 대부분의 기업 마케팅 계획에서 여전히 가장 큰 예산 항목이다. ❾ 광고는 회사의 연간 지출에서 고정적인 요소일 수 있지만, (회사의) 이사회는 점점 더 왜 그런지에 대해 의문을 제기하고 있다. ❿ 가장 최근의 Brandchannel 설문 조사가 이 점을 잘 보여 준다. ⓫ 세계 5대 브랜드 중 4개는 광고를 한 번도 한 적이 없으며, 이는 최고속 성장 10대 브랜드 중 7개도 마찬가지이다. ⓬ 광고와 재무 성과 사이에는 입증된 인과 관계가 없다. ⓭ 그래서 광고는 마케팅이라는 녹고 있는 빙산의 일각일 뿐이다.

Word List

□ **based on** ~에 기반한   □ **notion** 개념, 생각   □ **out of date** 시대에 뒤떨어진, 구식의   □ **initiative** 주창, 계획, 진취성
□ **take advantage of** ~을 활용하다   □ **merely** 그저, 단지   □ **reaction** 반응   □ **apply** 적용하다   □ **method** 방법
□ **lack** 부족   □ **budget** 예산   □ **fixture** 고정적인 요소   □ **annual** 연간의   □ **management board** 이사회   □ **survey** 설문 조사
□ **illustrate** 잘 보여 주다   □ **conduct** (특정한 활동을) 수행하다   □ **causal** 원인이 되는   □ **performance** 성과   □ **iceberg** 빙산

• Word Test

1	illustrate		11	빙산	
2	take advantage of		12	그저, 단지	
3	fixture		13	성과	
4	conduct		14	방법	
5	notion		15	설문 조사	
6	out of date		16	~에 기반한	
7	initiative		17	반응	
8	causal		18	예산	
9	lack		19	적용하다	
10	management board		20	연간의	

Marketing is based on notions that are 20 years out of date. The notion that if you put enough messages out there some of them will be heard. The notion that 'building the brand' is money well spent. The notion that people believe ❶ that / what they see and read. Recent ❷ initiatives / competitors to take advantage of Web 2.0 technologies are merely reactions that apply old techniques to new media. Marketing needs to rethink the messages it is communicating, to ❸ whom / whose it's communicated and the methods being used. Many companies are disappointed at the lack of tangible return on their multi-million pounds marketing activities. Advertising remains the largest budget item on most firms' marketing plans. Advertising may be a ❹ fixture / fixation in a company's annual spend, but management boards are ❺ increasing / increasingly questioning why this is. The most recent Brandchannel survey illustrates this point well. Four of the world's five largest brands have never conducted any advertising, and the same is true for seven out of the 10 fastest-growing brands. There is no proven causal relationship between advertising and financial performance. And advertising is just the tip of the melting marketing iceberg.

*tangible return 유형 수익

Marketing is based on notions that are 20 years out of date. The notion that if you put enough messages out there some of them will ❶ _____ (hear). The notion that 'building the brand' is money well spent. The notion that people believe what they see and read. Recent initiatives to take advantage of Web 2.0 technologies ❷ _____ (be) merely reactions that apply old techniques to new media. Marketing needs to rethink the messages it is communicating, to whom it's ❸ _____ (communicate) and the methods being used. Many companies are disappointed at the lack of tangible return on their multi-million pounds marketing activities. Advertising ❹ _____ (remain) the largest budget item on most firms' marketing plans. Advertising may be a fixture in a company's annual spend, but management boards are increasingly questioning why this is. The most recent Brandchannel survey illustrates this point well. Four of the world's five largest brands have never conducted any advertising, and the same ❺ _____ (be) true for seven out of the 10 fastest-growing brands. There is no proven causal relationship between advertising and financial performance. And advertising is just the tip of the melting marketing iceberg.

*tangible return 유형 수익

Marketing is based on notions that are ❶ _____ _____ _____ _____ _____ (시대에 20년 뒤떨어진). The notion that if you put enough messages out there some of them will be heard. The notion that 'building the brand' is money well spent. The notion that people believe ❷ _____ _____ _____ _____ _____ (그들이 보고 읽는 것). Recent initiatives to take advantage of Web 2.0 technologies are merely reactions that apply old techniques to new media. Marketing needs to rethink the messages it is communicating, to whom it's communicated and ❸ _____ _____ _____ _____ (사용되고 있는 방법). Many companies are disappointed at the lack of tangible return on their multi-million pounds marketing activities. Advertising remains the largest budget item on most firms' marketing plans. Advertising may be a fixture in a company's annual spend, but management boards are increasingly questioning why this is. The most recent Brandchannel survey illustrates this point well. Four of the world's five largest brands have never conducted any advertising, and the same is true for seven out of the 10 fastest-growing brands. There is no ❹ _____ _____ _____ (입증된 인과 관계) between advertising and financial performance. And advertising is just the tip of the melting marketing iceberg.

*tangible return 유형 수익

01 3강 1번

다음 글의 밑줄 친 부분 중, 어법상 틀린 것은?

In the past there was little genetic pressure to stop people from ① becoming obese. Genetic mutations that drove people to consume fewer calories were much less likely to be passed on, because in an environment ② which food was scarcer and its hunting or gathering required considerable energy outlay, an individual with that mutation would probably die before they had a chance to reproduce. Mutations that in our environment of abundant food now drive us towards obesity, on the other hand, ③ were incorporated into the population. Things are of course very different now but the problem is that evolutionary timescales are long. It's only in the last century or so, approximately 0.00004 per cent of mammalian evolutionary time, ④ that we managed to tweak our environment to such a degree that we can pretty much eat whatever we want, whenever we want it. Evolution has another couple of thousand years to go before ⑤ it can catch up with the current reality of online food shopping and delivery.

*mutation 돌연변이   **outlay (에너지 등의) 소비
***tweak 변경하다, 수정하다

02 3강 2번

다음 빈칸에 들어갈 말로 가장 적절한 것은?

The idea of family support, suggested as one of the preconditions of any child's success, is far from being faultless. Thus, for example, the well-known musical psychologist Jane Davidson and her colleagues state that all the parents of children who later become successful musicians were, in fact, their charges' great friends and allies from earliest childhood. If the great jazz musician Sidney Bechet were to hear of such a conclusion he would be surprised indeed. His altogether respectable parents, who dreamed of something rather more substantial and reliable than a career in music for their son, actually hid his clarinet from him. Robert Schumann's mother, the widow of a publisher and literary translator, reconciled herself only with difficulty to her son's choice of music as a profession; while Christoph W. Gluck, the great reformer of opera, was forced to roam about Italy and Bohemia after being expelled from home by his father. Even some of the great musical geniuses, it is clear, were given switches and coal by an unkind Fate instead of the presents other youngsters received. _____ turns out, upon closer examination, to be a myth.

*charge 보살펴야 하는 사람   **reconcile oneself to ~을 감수하다
***switch 회초리

① The universal support given by parents to beginning musicians
② The strong emphasis on the preconditions of any child's success
③ The significance of indifferent parents for a child's musical career
④ The importance of financial support for musical geniuses and their families
⑤ The belief that the pursuit of a dream despite all the odds will pay off someday

03 3강 3번

(A), (B), (C)의 각 네모 안에서 문맥에 맞는 낱말로 가장 적절한 것은?

A key feature particular to stories is that they have the ability to transport the reader. While experiencing stories, one can feel emotionally (A) detached/involved and as if being swept away as a participant. There is some evidence that being transported into a story requires a suspension of disbelief; enjoying *Jurassic Park* or a Harry Potter tale may involve putting aside what one knows about the world that contradicts the story. A story that suggests an unexpected outcome ("George Washington declined the nomination to become the first president of the United States") results in readers being (B) quicker/slower to verify well-known facts ("George Washington was elected first president of the United States"). This suspension of disbelief may make one less likely to spot problems in a narrative, as illustrated by a study in which participants read a story and circled any "false notes" or parts that did not make sense. Green and Brock refer to this method as "Pinocchio circling": just as the puppet's nose signaled when he told a falsehood, authors also leave clues when they are being untruthful. But readers who were more transported by the story spotted (C) fewer / more "Pinocchios."

*verify 확인하다

(A)	(B)	(C)
① detached	⋯⋯ quicker	⋯⋯ fewer
② detached	⋯⋯ slower	⋯⋯ fewer
③ involved	⋯⋯ slower	⋯⋯ fewer
④ involved	⋯⋯ slower	⋯⋯ more
⑤ involved	⋯⋯ quicker	⋯⋯ more

04 3강 4번

글의 흐름으로 보아, 주어진 문장이 들어가기에 가장 적절한 곳은?

Four of the world's five largest brands have never conducted any advertising, and the same is true for seven out of the 10 fastest-growing brands.

Marketing is based on notions that are 20 years out of date. The notion that if you put enough messages out there some of them will be heard. The notion that 'building the brand' is money well spent. The notion that people believe what they see and read. Recent initiatives to take advantage of Web 2.0 technologies are merely reactions that apply old techniques to new media. Marketing needs to rethink the messages it is communicating, to whom it's communicated and the methods being used. (①) Many companies are disappointed at the lack of tangible return on their multi-million pounds marketing activities. (②) Advertising remains the largest budget item on most firms' marketing plans. (③) Advertising may be a fixture in a company's annual spend, but management boards are increasingly questioning why this is. (④) The most recent Brandchannel survey illustrates this point well. (⑤) There is no proven causal relationship between advertising and financial performance. And advertising is just the tip of the melting marketing iceberg.

*tangible return 유형 수익

05 3강 1번

다음 글의 밑줄 친 부분 중, 문맥상 낱말의 쓰임이 적절하지 <u>않은</u> 것은?

In the past there was little genetic pressure to stop people from becoming obese. Genetic mutations that drove people to consume fewer calories were much ① <u>less</u> likely to be passed on, because in an environment where food was scarcer and its hunting or gathering required considerable energy outlay, an individual with that mutation would probably die before they had a chance to reproduce. Mutations that in our environment of ② <u>abundant</u> food now drive us towards obesity, on the other hand, were incorporated into the population. Things are of course very different now but the problem is that evolutionary timescales are ③ <u>short</u>. It's only in the last century or so, approximately 0.00004 per cent of mammalian evolutionary time, that we managed to tweak our environment to such a degree that we ④ <u>can</u> pretty much eat whatever we want, whenever we want it. Evolution has another couple of thousand years to go before it can ⑤ <u>catch</u> up with the current reality of online food shopping and delivery.

*mutation 돌연변이 **outlay (에너지 등의) 소비
***tweak 변경하다, 수정하다

다음 글의 내용과 일치하지 <u>않는</u> 것은?

The idea of family support, suggested as one of the preconditions of any child's success, is far from being faultless. Thus, for example, the well-known musical psychologist Jane Davidson and her colleagues state that all the parents of children who later become successful musicians were, in fact, their charges' great friends and allies from earliest childhood. If the great jazz musician Sidney Bechet were to hear of such a conclusion he would be surprised indeed. His altogether respectable parents, who dreamed of something rather more substantial and reliable than a career in music for their son, actually hid his clarinet from him. Robert Schumann's mother, the widow of a publisher and literary translator, reconciled herself only with difficulty to her son's choice of music as a profession; while Christoph W. Gluck, the great reformer of opera, was forced to roam about Italy and Bohemia after being expelled from home by his father. Even some of the great musical geniuses, it is clear, were given switches and coal by an unkind Fate instead of the presents other youngsters received. The 'universal support' given by parents to beginning musicians turns out, upon closer examination, to be a myth.

*charge 보살펴야 하는 사람 **reconcile oneself to ~을 감수하다
***switch 회초리

① Jane Davidson 연구팀은 성공한 음악가들이 유년기에 부모의 성원을 받았다고 주장했다.
② Sidney Bechet의 부모는 자녀의 다른 직업을 꿈꾼 나머지 클라리넷을 감추기도 했다.
③ Robert Schumann의 어머니는 아들이 음악가 대신 출판업자나 번역자가 되기를 바랐다.
④ 오페라 개혁가 Christoph W. Gluck의 아버지는 아들을 집에서 쫓아내기까지 했다.
⑤ 위대한 음악 천재 중 몇몇은 다른 아이들이 받았던 선물은커녕 부모의 반대에 부딪혔다.

다음 글의 내용을 한 문장으로 요약하고자 한다. 빈칸 (A), (B)에 들어갈 말로 가장 적절한 것은?

A key feature particular to stories is that they have the ability to transport the reader. While experiencing stories, one can feel emotionally involved and as if being swept away as a participant. There is some evidence that being transported into a story requires a suspension of disbelief; enjoying *Jurassic Park* or a Harry Potter tale may involve putting aside what one knows about the world that contradicts the story. A story that suggests an unexpected outcome ("George Washington declined the nomination to become the first president of the United States") results in readers being slower to verify well-known facts ("George Washington was elected first president of the United States"). This suspension of disbelief may make one less likely to spot problems in a narrative, as illustrated by a study in which participants read a story and circled any "false notes" or parts that did not make sense. Green and Brock refer to this method as "Pinocchio circling": just as the puppet's nose signaled when he told a falsehood, authors also leave clues when they are being untruthful. But readers who were more transported by the story spotted fewer "Pinocchios."

*verify 확인하다

↓

Enjoying a story may require putting aside what one understands about the world that ___(A)___ the story, and this suspension of disbelief may make it more difficult to notice ___(B)___ in it.

(A)	(B)
① controverts	...... flaws
② explains	...... lessons
③ confirms	...... probability
④ refuses	...... truths
⑤ supports	...... lies

08 3강 4번

다음 글의 요지로 가장 적절한 것은?

Marketing is based on notions that are 20 years out of date. The notion that if you put enough messages out there some of them will be heard. The notion that 'building the brand' is money well spent. The notion that people believe what they see and read. Recent initiatives to take advantage of Web 2.0 technologies are merely reactions that apply old techniques to new media. Marketing needs to rethink the messages it is communicating, to whom it's communicated and the methods being used. Many companies are disappointed at the lack of tangible return on their multi-million pounds marketing activities. Advertising remains the largest budget item on most firms' marketing plans. Advertising may be a fixture in a company's annual spend, but management boards are increasingly questioning why this is. The most recent Brandchannel survey illustrates this point well. Four of the world's five largest brands have never conducted any advertising, and the same is true for seven out of the 10 fastest-growing brands. There is no proven causal relationship between advertising and financial performance. And advertising is just the tip of the melting marketing iceberg.

*tangible return 유형 수익

① 웹 활용 등 새로운 매체를 활용한 마케팅을 더욱 확장해야 한다.
② 기업의 규모에 맞는 광고 및 마케팅 투자 계획을 수립하는 것이 중요하다.
③ 광고를 포함한 현재의 마케팅 전략이 재무 성과에 큰 효과를 주지 못하고 있다.
④ 마케팅 활동에 많은 자금을 투자한 기업들이 확실한 성과를 보는 데는 시간이 필요하다.
⑤ 세계의 큰 브랜드나 빠르게 성장하고 있는 대다수 브랜드의 마케팅 전략을 배워야 한다.

3강 1번

과거에는 사람들이 비만이 되는 것을 막을 수 있는 유전적 압력이 거의 없었다. Genetic mutations that drove people to consume fewer calories were much less likely to be passed on, because in an environment where food was scarcer and its hunting or gathering required considerable energy outlay, an individual with <u>that mutation</u> would probably die before they had a chance to reproduce. Mutations that in our environment of abundant food now drive us towards obesity, on the other hand, were incorporated into the population. Things are of course very different now but the problem is that evolutionary timescales are long. It's only in the last century or so, approximately 0.00004 per cent of mammalian evolutionary time, that we managed to tweak our environment to such a degree that we can pretty much eat whatever we want, whenever we want it. Evolution has another couple of thousand years to go before it can catch up with the current reality of online food shopping and delivery.

*mutation 돌연변이 **outlay (에너지 등의) 소비
***tweak 변경하다, 수정하다

09 윗글의 밑줄 친 우리말 의미와 일치하도록 보기의 단어를 활용하여 조건에 맞게 문장을 완성하시오.

보기	there / be / little / from / to / become / stop / people / pressure / obese / genetic

조건	· 필요시 어형을 바꿔 쓸 것 · 〈보기〉의 단어를 반드시 모두 사용할 것

In the past _____.

10 윗글의 밑줄 친 that mutation이 가리키는 것을 본문에서 찾아 우리말로 쓰시오. (25자 내외)

_____

_____

The idea of family support, ① suggests as one of the preconditions of any child's success, is far from being faultless. Thus, for example, the well-known musical psychologist Jane Davidson and her colleagues state that all the parents of children who later become successful musicians were, in fact, their charges' great friends and allies from earliest childhood. If the great jazz musician Sidney Bechet ② is to hear of such a conclusion he would be surprised indeed. His altogether respectable parents, who dreamed of something rather more substantial and reliable than a career in music for their son, actually ③ hid his clarinet from him. Robert Schumann's mother, the widow of a publisher and literary translator, reconciled herself only with difficulty to her son's choice of music as a _____; while Christoph W. Gluck, the great reformer of opera, was forced to roam about Italy and Bohemia after ④ expelling from home by his father. Even some of the great musical geniuses, it is clear, ⑤ were given switches and coal by an unkind Fate instead of the presents other youngsters received. The 'universal support' given by parents to beginning musicians turns out, upon closer examination, to be a myth.

*charge 보살펴야 하는 사람 **reconcile oneself to ~을 감수하다
***switch 회초리

11 윗글의 밑줄 친 부분 중, 어법상 틀린 것을 3개 찾아 그 번호를 쓰고 고쳐 쓰시오.

(1) _____ → _____

(2) _____ → _____

(3) _____ → _____

12 윗글의 빈칸에 들어갈 단어를 영영 뜻풀이를 참고하여 쓰시오. (단, 주어진 글자로 시작할 것)

a job that you need special skills and qualifications to do, especially one with high social status

p_____

A key feature particular to stories is that they have the ability to transport the reader. While experiencing stories, one can feel emotionally involved and as if being swept away as a participant. There is some evidence that being transported into a story requires a suspension of disbelief; enjoying *Jurassic Park* or a Harry Potter tale may involve 이야기와 모순되는 세상에 대해 알고 있는 바를 제쳐 두는 것. A story that suggests an unexpected outcome ("George Washington declined the nomination to become the first president of the United States") results in readers being slower to verify well-known facts ("George Washington was elected first president of the United States"). This suspension of disbelief may make one less likely to spot problems in a narrative, as illustrated by a study in which participants read a story and circled any "false notes" or parts that did not make sense. Green and Brock refer to this method as "Pinocchio circling": just as the puppet's nose signaled when he told a falsehood, authors also leave clues when they are being untruthful. But readers who were more transported by the story spotted fewer "Pinocchios."

*verify 확인하다

13 윗글의 밑줄 친 우리말 의미와 일치하도록 보기 의 단어를 활용하여 영작하시오. (단, 필요시 어형을 바꿔 쓸 것)

보기 putting / that / what / one / know / about / aside / the story / the world / contradict

_____

_____

14 윗글의 밑줄 친 This suspension of disbelief가 문맥적으로 의미하는 바를 찾아 우리말로 쓰시오. (40자 내외)

_____

Marketing is based on notions that are 20 years out of date. The notion that if you put enough messages out there some of them will be heard. The notion that 'building the brand' is money well spent. The notion that people believe what they see and read. Recent initiatives to take advantage of Web 2.0 technologies are merely reactions that apply old techniques to new media. Marketing needs to rethink the messages it is communicating, to whom it's communicated and the methods being used. Many companies are disappointed at the lack of tangible return on their multi-million pounds marketing activities. Advertising remains the largest budget item on most firms' marketing plans. Advertising may be a fixture in a company's annual spend, but management boards are increasingly questioning why <u>this</u> is. The most recent Brandchannel survey illustrates this point well. Four of the world's five largest brands have never conducted any advertising, and the same is true for seven out of the 10 fastest-growing brands. There is no proven ＿＿＿＿＿＿＿＿＿ relationship between advertising and financial performance. And advertising is just the tip of the melting marketing iceberg.

*tangible return 유형 수익

15 윗글의 밑줄 친 this가 가리키는 것을 본문에서 찾아 우리말로 쓰시오. (25자 내외)

＿＿＿＿＿＿＿＿＿＿＿＿＿＿＿＿＿＿＿＿

＿＿＿＿＿＿＿＿＿＿＿＿＿＿＿＿＿＿＿＿

16 윗글의 빈칸에 들어갈 단어를 영영 뜻풀이를 참고하여 쓰시오. (단, 주어진 글자로 시작할 것)

being a connection or relationship between two events, where one event causes the other

c＿＿＿＿＿＿＿＿

❶ A key assumption in consumer societies has been the idea that "money buys happiness." ❷ Historically, there is a good reason for this assumption — until the last few generations, a majority of people have lived close to subsistence, so an increase in income brought genuine increases in material well-being (e.g., food, shelter, health care) and this has produced more happiness. ❸ However, in a number of developed nations, levels of material well-being have moved beyond subsistence to unprecedented abundance. ❹ Developed nations have had several generations of unparalleled material prosperity, and a clear understanding is emerging: More money does bring more happiness when we are living on a very low income. ❺ However, as a global average, when per capita income reaches the range of $13,000 per year, additional income adds relatively little to our happiness, while other factors such as personal freedom, meaningful work, and social tolerance add much more. ❻ Often, a doubling or tripling of income in developed nations has not led to an increase in perceived well-being.

*subsistence 최저 생계

❶ 소비 사회의 핵심 가정은 '돈으로 행복을 얻는다'는 생각이었다. ❷ 역사적으로, 이러한 가정에는 충분한 이유가 있다. 즉, 지난 몇 세대 전까지 대다수 사람이 최저 생계에 가깝게 살아왔기 때문에, 소득 증가는 물질적 복지(예를 들어, 음식, 주거, 의료)의 진정한 향상을 가져왔으며, 이는 더 많은 행복을 낳았다. ❸ 그러나 많은 선진국에서 물질적 복지의 수준이 최저 생계를 넘어 전례 없는 풍요로 옮겨갔다. ❹ 선진국은 여러 세대에 걸쳐 비할 데 없는 물질적 번영을 누려 왔고, 명확한 이해가 부상하고 있는데, 우리가 매우 낮은 수입으로 생활할 때는 더 많은 돈이 더 많은 행복을 가져온다는 것이다. ❺ 그러나 세계 평균으로서, 1인당 소득이 연간 13,000달러 범위에 이르면, 추가 소득이 우리의 행복을 상대적으로 거의 늘리지 않지만, 개인의 자유, 의미 있는 일, 그리고 사회적 관용과 같은 다른 요소들이 훨씬 더 많이 보탬이 된다. ❻ 흔히 선진국에서는 소득이 두 배 또는 세 배로 증가해도 체감되는 행복의 증대를 가져오지는 않았다.

Word List

□ assumption 가정　□ consumer society 소비 사회　□ generation 세대　□ a majority of 대다수의　□ income 소득
□ genuine 진정한, 진짜의　□ material 물질의　□ well-being 복지, 행복, 안녕　□ shelter 주거, 주거지　□ unprecedented 전례 없는
□ abundance 풍요. 풍부　□ unparalleled 비할 데 없는　□ prosperity 번영, 번성　□ emerge 부상하다, 나타나다
□ per capita income 1인당 소득　□ range 범위　□ factor 요인, 요소　□ tolerance 용인, 관용　□ triple 3배가 되다
□ perceive 감지하다, 인지하다

Word Test

1	consumer society		11	진정한, 진짜의	
2	a majority of		12	요인, 요소	
3	emerge		13	범위	
4	abundance		14	가정	
5	triple		15	용인, 관용	
6	shelter		16	소득	
7	well-being		17	세대	
8	unparalleled		18	번영, 번성	
9	per capita income		19	물질의	
10	perceive		20	전례 없는	

네모 안에서 옳은 어법·어휘를 고르시오.

A key assumption in consumer societies ❶ has / have been the idea that "money buys happiness." Historically, there is a good reason for this assumption — until the last few generations, a majority of people have lived close to subsistence, so an increase in income brought genuine increases in ❷ material / emotional well-being (e.g., food, shelter, health care) and this has produced more happiness. However, in a number of developed nations, levels of material well-being have moved beyond subsistence to unprecedented ❸ allowance / abundance . Developed nations have had several generations of unparalleled material prosperity, and a clear understanding is emerging: More money does bring more happiness when we are living on a very low income. ❹ Finally / However , as a global average, when per capita income reaches the range of $13,000 per year, additional income adds relatively ❺ little / a little to our happiness, while other factors such as personal freedom, meaningful work, and social tolerance add much more. Often, a doubling or tripling of income in developed nations has not led to an increase in perceived well-being.

*subsistence 최저 생계

• 유형 2 괄호 안의 동사를 알맞은 형태로 쓰시오.

A key assumption in consumer societies has been the idea that "money buys happiness." Historically, there is a good reason for this assumption — until the last few generations, a majority of people ❶ _____ (live) close to subsistence, so an increase in income brought genuine increases in material well-being (e.g., food, shelter, health care) and this ❷ _____ (produce) more happiness. However, in a number of developed nations, levels of material well-being ❸ _____ (move) beyond subsistence to unprecedented abundance. Developed nations ❹ _____ (have) several generations of unparalleled material prosperity, and a clear understanding is emerging: More money does bring more happiness when we are living on a very low income. However, as a global average, when per capita income ❺ _____ (reach) the range of $13,000 per year, additional income adds relatively little to our happiness, while other factors such as personal freedom, meaningful work, and social tolerance add much more. Often, a doubling or tripling of income in developed nations has not led to an increase in perceived well-being.

*subsistence 최저 생계

• 유형 3 우리말에 맞게 빈칸에 알맞은 말을 쓰시오.

A key assumption in consumer societies has been the idea that "money buys happiness." Historically, there is a good reason for this assumption — ❶ _____ _____ _____ _____ _____ (지난 몇 세대들 전까지), a majority of people have lived close to subsistence, so an increase in income brought genuine increases in material well-being (e.g., food, shelter, health care) and this has produced more happiness. However, ❷ _____ _____ _____ _____ _____ _____ (많은 선진국들에서), levels of material well-being have moved beyond subsistence to unprecedented abundance. Developed nations have had several generations of unparalleled material prosperity, and a clear understanding is emerging: More money does bring more happiness when we are living ❸ _____ _____ _____ _____ _____ (매우 낮은 수입으로). However, ❹ _____ _____ _____ (세계 평균으로서), when per capita income reaches the range of $13,000 per year, additional income adds relatively little to our happiness, while other factors such as personal freedom, meaningful work, and social tolerance add much more. Often, a doubling or tripling of income in developed nations has not led to an increase in perceived well-being.

*subsistence 최저 생계

❶ We are wired more for the struggle for survival on the savannah than we are for urban life. ❷ As a result, "Situations are constantly evaluated as good or bad, requiring escape or permitting approach." ❸ In everyday life, this means that our aversion to losses is naturally greater than our attraction to gain (by a factor of two). ❹ We have an inbuilt mechanism to give priority to bad news. ❺ Our brains are set up to *detect* a predator in a fraction of a second, much quicker than the part of the brain that *acknowledge* one has been seen. ❻ That is why we can act before we even "know" we are acting. ❼ "Threats are privileged above opportunities," Kahneman says. ❽ This natural tendency means that we "overweight" unlikely events, such as being caught in a terrorist attack. ❾ It also leads to us overestimating our chances of winning the lottery.

*savannah 초원, 사바나　**aversion 혐오

❶ 우리는 도시생활보다는 초원에서의 생존투쟁에 맞게 타고났다. ❷ 그 결과, "상황은 끊임없이 좋거나 나쁘다고 평가되어 도피를 요구하거나 접근을 허용한다." ❸ 일상생활에서, 이것은 손실에 대한 우리의 혐오가 당연히 이득에 대한 우리의 끌림보다 (두 배) 더 크다는 것을 의미한다. ❹ 우리는 나쁜 소식에 우선순위를 부여하는 내재된 기제를 가지고 있다. ❺ 우리의 뇌는 몇 분의 1초 만에 포식자를 '감지'하도록 설정되어 있는데, 포식자가 목격되었다는 것을 '인지'하는 뇌 부위보다 훨씬 더 빠르다. ❻ 그런 이유로 우리는 우리가 행동하고 있다는 것을 '알기'도 전에 행동할 수 있다. ❼ "기회에 앞서 위협에 특전이 주어진다"라고 Kahneman은 말한다. ❽ 이런 타고난 성향은 우리가 테러리스트 공격에 처하는 것 같은 일어날 것 같지 않은 사건들을 '지나치게 중시한다'는 것을 의미한다. ❾ 그것은 또한 우리가 우리 자신이 복권에 당첨될 가능성을 과대평가하게 만든다.

Word List

□ **wired** 타고나는, 천성의　□ **struggle** 투쟁　□ **survival** 생존　□ **urban** 도시의　□ **constantly** 끊임없이　□ **evaluate** 평가하다　□ **permit** 허용하다　□ **attraction** 끌림, 매력　□ **gain** 이득, 이익　□ **by a factor of** ~ 배로　□ **inbuilt** 내재된　□ **mechanism** 기제　□ **priority** 우선순위　□ **detect** 감지하다, 발견하다　□ **predator** 포식자　□ **in a fraction of a second** 몇 분의 1초 만에, 순식간에　□ **acknowledge** 인지하다　□ **privilege** 특전[특권]을 주다　□ **tendency** 성향, 경향　□ **overweight** 지나치게 중시하다　□ **overestimate** 과대평가하다　□ **lottery** 복권

• Word Test

1	overestimate	_____	12	성향, 경향	_____
2	in a fraction of a second	_____	13	포식자	_____
3	wired	_____	14	허용하다	_____
4	gain	_____	15	복권	_____
5	by a factor of	_____	16	생존	_____
6	attraction	_____	17	평가하다	_____
7	overweight	_____	18	우선순위	_____
8	privilege	_____	19	도시의	_____
9	inbuilt	_____	20	인지하다	_____
10	mechanism	_____	21	끊임없이	_____
11	detect	_____	22	투쟁	_____

We are wired more for the struggle for survival on the savannah than we are for urban life. As a result, "Situations are ❶ constant/constantly evaluated as good or bad, requiring escape or permitting approach." In everyday life, this means that our aversion to losses is naturally greater than our attraction to gain (by a factor of two). We have an inbuilt mechanism to give priority to bad news. Our brains are set up to *detect* a predator in a fraction of a second, much ❷ quick/quicker than the part of the brain that *acknowledge* one has ❸ seen/been seen . That is ❹ how/why we can act before we even "know" we are acting. "Threats are privileged above opportunities" Kahneman says. This natural tendency means that we "overweight" ❺ likely/unlikely events, such as being caught in a terrorist attack. It also leads to us overestimating our chances of winning the lottery.

*savannah 초원, 사바나 **aversion 혐오

We are wired more for the struggle for survival on the savannah than we are for urban life. As a result, "Situations are constantly evaluated as good or bad, ❶ _____ (require) escape or permitting approach." In everyday life, this means that our aversion to losses ❷ _____ (be) naturally greater than our attraction to gain (by a factor of two). We have an inbuilt mechanism to give priority to bad news. Our brains ❸ _____ (set) up to *detect* a predator in a fraction of a second, much quicker than the part of the brain that *acknowledge* one has been seen. That is why we can act before we even "know" we are acting. "Threats are privileged above opportunities" Kahneman says. This natural tendency ❹ _____ (mean) that we "overweight" unlikely events, such as ❺ _____ (catch) in a terrorist attack. It also leads to us overestimating our chances of winning the lottery.

*savannah 초원, 사바나 **aversion 혐오

We are wired more for the struggle for survival on the savannah than we are for urban life. As a result, "Situations are constantly ❶ _____ _____ _____ _____ _____ (좋거나 나쁘다고 평가되어), requiring escape or permitting approach." In everyday life, this means that our aversion to losses is naturally greater than our attraction to gain (by a factor of two). We have an inbuilt mechanism to ❷ _____ _____ _____ (~에 우선순위를 부여하다) bad news. Our brains are set up to *detect* a predator ❸ _____ _____ _____ _____ _____ _____ (몇 분의 1초만에), much quicker than the part of the brain that *acknowledge* one has been seen. That is why we can act before we even "know" we are acting. "❹ _____ _____ _____ (위협에 특전이 주어진다) above opportunities" Kahneman says. This natural tendency means that we "overweight" unlikely events, such as being caught in a terrorist attack. It also leads to us overestimating our chances of winning the lottery.

*savannah 초원, 사바나 **aversion 혐오

❶ It is not only through our actions that we can give life meaning — insofar as we can answer life's specific questions responsibly — ❷ we can fulfill the demands of existence not only as active agents but also as loving human beings: in our loving dedication to the beautiful, the great, the good. ❸ Should I perhaps try to explain for you with some hackneyed phrase how and why experiencing beauty can make life meaningful? ❹ I prefer to confine myself to the following thought experiment: ❺ imagine that you are sitting in a concert hall and listening to your favorite symphony, and your favorite bars of the symphony resound in your ears, and you are so moved by the music that it sends shivers down your spine; and now imagine that it would be possible for someone to ask you in this moment whether your life has meaning. ❻ I believe you would agree with me if I declared that in this case you would only be able to give one answer, and it would go something like: "It would have been worth it to have lived for this moment alone!"

*hackneyed 진부한

❶ 우리가 삶의 특정한 질문에 책임감 있게 대답할 수 있는 한 우리가 삶에 의미를 부여할 수 있는 것은 우리의 행동을 통해서 뿐만이 아니다. ❷ 우리는 능동적인 행위자로서 뿐만 아니라 애정 어린 인간으로서 존재의 요구를 충족시킬 수 있는데, 그것은 아름다운 것, 위대한 것, 선한 것에 대한 우리의 애정 어린 전념을 통해서이다. ❸ 아름다움을 경험하는 것이 어떻게 그리고 왜 삶을 의미 있게 만들 수 있는지를 여러분을 위해 혹시 진부한 말로 설명하도록 애써야 하겠는가? ❹ 나는 차라리 다음과 같은 사고 실험에만 국한해 보겠다. ❺ 여러분이 콘서트홀에 앉아 여러분이 가장 좋아하는 교향곡을 듣고 있고, 여러분이 가장 좋아하는 교향곡의 마디가 여러분의 귓가에 울려 퍼지며, 여러분이 그 음악에 너무 감동하여 여러분의 등골이 전율할 정도라고 상상해 보라. 그리고 이제 아마도 누군가가 여러분에게 이 순간 여러분의 삶이 의미가 있는지를 묻는 것이 가능할 것이라고 상상해 보라. ❻ 만약 여러분이 이 경우에 단지 한 가지 대답을 할 수 있고, 그 대답이 "오직 이 순간만을 위해 살아왔더라도 그럴 만한 가치가 있었을 거야!"와 같은 것일 것이라고 내가 언명한다면, 여러분은 내게 동의할 것이라고 나는 믿는다.

Word List

□ **insofar as** ~하는 한은, ~하는 정도까지는   □ **specific** 특정한   □ **responsibly** 책임감 있게   □ **fulfill** 충족하다   □ **demand** 요구
□ **existence** 존재   □ **agent** 행위자, 동인   □ **loving** 애정 어린, 사랑스러운   □ **dedication** 전념, 헌신   □ **phrase** 구절, 관용구
□ **confine oneself to** ~에 국한하다   □ **symphony** 교향곡   □ **bar** (악곡의) 마디   □ **resound** 울려 퍼지다   □ **shiver** 전율, 오싹한 느낌
□ **spine** 등골, 척추   □ **declare** 언명하다, (분명히) 말하다   □ **worth it** (시간·수고 따위를 들일 만한) 그럴 만한 가치가 있는

• Word Test

1	fulfill	10	구절, 관용구
2	bar	11	교향곡
3	worth it	12	존재
4	agent	13	요구
5	confine oneself to	14	특정한
6	insofar as	15	등골, 척추
7	dedication	16	애정 어린, 사랑스러운
8	resound	17	책임감 있게
9	declare	18	전율, 오싹한 느낌

It is not only through our actions that we can give life meaning — insofar as we can answer life's specific questions ❶ responsible/responsibly — we can fulfill the demands of existence not only as active agents but also as loving human beings: in our loving ❷ dedication/indifference to the beautiful, the great, the good. Should I perhaps try to explain for you with some hackneyed phrase how and why experiencing beauty can make life meaningful? I prefer to ❸ confine/confront myself to the following thought experiment: imagine that you are sitting in a concert hall and listening to your favorite symphony, and your favorite bars of the symphony resound in your ears, and you are ❹ so/very moved by the music that it sends shivers down your spine; and now imagine that it would be possible for someone to ask you in this moment ❺ which/whether your life has meaning. I believe you would agree with me if I declared that in this case you would only be able to give one answer, and it would go something like: "It would have been worth it to have lived for this moment alone!"

*hackneyed 진부한

It is not only through our actions that we can give life meaning — insofar as we can answer life's specific questions responsibly — we can fulfill the demands of existence not only as active agents but also as loving human beings: in our loving dedication to the beautiful, the great, the good. Should I perhaps try to explain for you with some hackneyed phrase how and why ❶ _____ (experience) beauty can make life meaningful? I prefer to confine myself to the following thought experiment: imagine that you are sitting in a concert hall and ❷ _____ (listen) to your favorite symphony, and your favorite bars of the symphony resound in your ears, and you are so moved by the music that it sends shivers down your spine; and now imagine that it would be possible for someone to ask you in this moment whether your life has meaning. I believe you would agree with me if I ❸ _____ (declare) that in this case you would only be able to give one answer, and it would go something like: "It would have been worth it to ❹ _____ (live) for this moment alone!"

*hackneyed 진부한

It is not only ❶ _____ _____ _____ (우리의 행동들을 통해서) that we can give life meaning — insofar as we can answer life's specific questions responsibly — we can ❷ _____ _____ _____ (요구들을 충족시키다) of existence not only as active agents but also as loving human beings: in our loving dedication to the beautiful, the great, the good. Should I perhaps try to explain for you with some hackneyed phrase how and why experiencing beauty can make life meaningful? I prefer to confine myself to the following thought experiment: imagine that you are sitting in a concert hall and listening to your favorite symphony, and your favorite bars of the symphony ❸ _____ _____ _____ _____ (여러분의 귓가에 울려 퍼지다), and you are so moved by the music that it sends shivers down your spine; and now imagine that it would be possible for someone to ask you in this moment whether your life has meaning. I believe you would agree with me if I declared that in this case you would only be able to give one answer, and it would go something like: "❹ _____ _____ _____ _____ _____ _____ (그럴 만한 가치가 있었을 거야) to have lived for this moment alone!"

*hackneyed 진부한

❶ The process of research is often not entirely rational. ❷ In the classical application of the 'scientific method', the researcher is supposed to develop a hypothesis, then design a crucial experiment to test it. ❸ If the hypothesis withstands this test a generalization is then argued for, and an advance in understanding has been made. ❹ But where did the hypothesis come from in the first place? ❺ I have a colleague whose favourite question is 'Why is this so?', and I've seen this innocent question spawn brilliant research projects on quite a few occasions. ❻ Research is a mixture of inspiration (hypothesis generation, musing over the odd and surprising, finding lines of attack on difficult problems) and rational thinking (design and execution of crucial experiments, analysis of results in terms of existing theory). ❼ Most of the books on research methods and design of experiments — there are hundreds of them — are concerned with the rational part, and fail to deal with the creative part, yet without the creative part no real research would be done, no new insights would be gained, and no new theories would be formulated.

*withstand 잘 견디다 **spawn 탄생시키다, 낳다 ***muse over ~에 대해 숙고하다

❶ 흔히 연구 과정은 전적으로 합리적이지는 않다. ❷ '과학적 방법'의 전형적인 적용에서, 연구자는 가설을 세우고, 그런 다음 그것을 검증하기 위한 결정적 실험을 설계해야 한다. ❸ 만약 그 가설이 이 검증을 잘 견디면 그 후 일반화에 대한 지지를 얻게 되고 이해의 진전이 이루어진 것이다. ❹ 하지만 그 가설은 애초에 어디서 나온 것인가? ❺ 나에게는 '이것은 왜 그렇지?'라는 질문을 가장 좋아하는 동료가 있으며, 나는 이러한 순수한 질문이 상당히 많은 경우에 훌륭한 연구 프로젝트를 탄생시키는 것을 보아왔다. ❻ 연구는 영감 (가설 생성, 이상하고 놀라운 것에 대해 숙고하기, 난제에 대한 대처 방안 찾기)과 합리적 사고 (결정적 실험의 설계와 실행, 기존 이론의 관점에서의 결과 분석)의 혼합이다. ❼ 연구 방법과 실험 설계에 관한 대부분의 책은―그런 책이 수백 권 있지만―합리적인 부분과 관련이 있으며 창의적인 부분은 다루지 않지만, 창의적인 부분이 없다면 어떤 진정한 연구도 이루어지지 않을 것이고, 어떤 새로운 통찰력도 얻지 못할 것이며, 어떤 새로운 이론도 정립되지 않을 것이다.

Word List

□ entirely 전적으로, 완전히 □ rational 합리적인, 이성적인 □ application 적용 □ be supposed to ~하기로 되어 있다
□ hypothesis 가설 (*pl.* hypotheses) □ crucial experiment 결정적 실험 □ generalization 일반화 □ argue for ~에 찬성을 말하다
□ in the first place 우선, 첫째로 □ innocent 순수한, 무고한 □ brilliant 훌륭한, 화려한 □ occasion 경우 □ inspiration 영감
□ odd 이상한 □ line of attack 대처 방안 □ execution 실행, 집행 □ deal with ~을 다루다 □ insight 통찰력
□ formulate 정립하다, 공식화하다

• **Word Test**

1	be supposed to	_____	10	통찰력	_____
2	line of attack	_____	11	정립하다, 공식화하다	_____
3	crucial experiment	_____	12	~에 찬성을 말하다	_____
4	occasion	_____	13	~을 다루다	_____
5	brilliant	_____	14	순수한, 무고한	_____
6	execution	_____	15	이상한	_____
7	application	_____	16	전적으로, 완전히	_____
8	hypothesis	_____	17	영감	_____
9	in the first place	_____	18	합리적인, 이성적인	_____

The process of research is often not ❶ entire/entirely rational. In the classical application of the 'scientific method', the researcher is supposed to develop a hypothesis, then design a crucial experiment to test it. If the hypothesis withstands this test a ❷ generation/generalization is then argued for, and an advance in understanding has been made. But where did the hypothesis come from in the first place? I have a colleague ❸ whom/whose favourite question is 'Why is this so?', and I've seen this innocent question spawn brilliant research projects on quite a few occasions. Research is a mixture of ❹ implication/inspiration (hypothesis generation, musing over the odd and surprising, finding lines of attack on difficult problems) and rational thinking (design and execution of crucial experiments, analysis of results in terms of existing theory). Most of the books on research methods and design of experiments — there are hundreds of them — are concerned with the rational part, and fail to deal with the creative part, yet without the creative part no real research would be done, no new ❺ blindness/insights would be gained, and no new theories would be formulated.

*withstand 잘 견디다   **spawn 탄생시키다, 낳다   ***muse over ~에 대해 숙고하다

The process of research is often not entirely rational. In the classical application of the 'scientific method', the researcher is supposed to develop a hypothesis, then design a crucial experiment to test it. If the hypothesis withstands this test a generalization is then ❶ _____ (argue) for, and an advance in understanding has ❷ _____ (make). But where did the hypothesis come from in the first place? I have a colleague whose favourite question is 'Why is this so?', and I've seen this innocent question spawn brilliant research projects on quite a few occasions. Research is a mixture of inspiration (hypothesis generation, musing over the odd and surprising, finding lines of attack on difficult problems) and rational thinking (design and execution of crucial experiments, analysis of results in terms of existing theory). Most of the books on research methods and design of experiments — there are hundreds of them — ❸ _____ (be) concerned with the rational part, and fail ❹ _____ (deal) with the creative part, yet without the creative part no real research would ❺ _____ (do), no new insights would be gained, and no new theories would be formulated.

*withstand 잘 견디다   **spawn 탄생시키다, 낳다   ***muse over ~에 대해 숙고하다

The process of research is often not entirely rational. In the classical application of the 'scientific method', the researcher ❶ _____ _____ _____ (~해야 한다) develop a hypothesis, then design a crucial experiment to test it. If the hypothesis withstands this test a generalization is then argued for, and an advance in understanding has been made. But where did the hypothesis come from ❷ _____ _____ _____ _____ (애초에)? I have a colleague whose favourite question is 'Why is this so?', and I've seen this innocent question spawn brilliant research projects ❸ _____ _____ _____ _____ _____ (상당히 많은 경우들에). Research is a mixture of inspiration (hypothesis generation, musing over the odd and surprising, finding lines of attack on difficult problems) and rational thinking (design and execution of crucial experiments, analysis of results ❹ _____ _____ _____ (~의 관점에서) existing theory). Most of the books on research methods and design of experiments — there are hundreds of them — are concerned with the rational part, and fail to deal with the creative part, yet without the creative part no real research would be done, no new insights would be gained, and no new theories would be formulated.

*withstand 잘 견디다   **spawn 탄생시키다, 낳다   ***muse over ~에 대해 숙고하다

01 [4강 1번]

(A), (B), (C)의 각 네모 안에서 문맥에 맞는 낱말로 가장 적절한 것은?

A key assumption in consumer societies has been the idea that "money buys happiness." Historically, there is a good reason for this assumption — until the last few generations, a majority of people have lived close to subsistence, so an increase in income brought genuine (A) | increases/decreases | in material well-being (e.g., food, shelter, health care) and this has produced more happiness. However, in a number of developed nations, levels of material well-being have moved beyond subsistence to unprecedented abundance. Developed nations have had several generations of unparalleled material prosperity, and a clear understanding is emerging: More money does bring more happiness when we are living on a very (B) | low/high | income. However, as a global average, when per capita income reaches the range of $13,000 per year, additional income adds relatively little to our happiness, while other factors such as personal freedom, meaningful work, and social tolerance add much more. Often, a doubling or tripling of income in developed nations has not led to an increase in (C) | material/perceived | well-being.

*subsistence 최저 생계

	(A)		(B)		(C)
①	increases	⋯⋯	low	⋯⋯	material
②	increases	⋯⋯	low	⋯⋯	perceived
③	increases	⋯⋯	high	⋯⋯	perceived
④	decreases	⋯⋯	high	⋯⋯	material
⑤	decreases	⋯⋯	high	⋯⋯	perceived

02 [4강 2번]

글의 흐름으로 보아, 주어진 문장이 들어가기에 가장 적절한 곳은?

> That is why we can act before we even "know" we are acting.

We are wired more for the struggle for survival on the savannah than we are for urban life. As a result, "Situations are constantly evaluated as good or bad, requiring escape or permitting approach." (①) In everyday life, this means that our aversion to losses is naturally greater than our attraction to gain (by a factor of two). (②) We have an inbuilt mechanism to give priority to bad news. (③) Our brains are set up to *detect* a predator in a fraction of a second, much quicker than the part of the brain that *acknowledges* one has been seen. (④) "Threats are privileged above opportunities," Kahneman says. (⑤) This natural tendency means that we "overweight" unlikely events, such as being caught in a terrorist attack. It also leads to us overestimating our chances of winning the lottery.

*savannah 초원, 사바나 **aversion 혐오

03 [4강 3번]

다음 빈칸에 들어갈 말로 가장 적절한 것은?

It is not only through our actions that we can give life meaning — insofar as we can answer life's specific questions responsibly — we can fulfill the demands of existence not only as active agents but also as loving human beings: in our loving dedication to the beautiful, the great, the good. Should I perhaps try to explain for you with some hackneyed phrase how and why _____ can make life meaningful? I prefer to confine myself to the following thought experiment: imagine that you are sitting in a concert hall and listening to your favorite symphony, and your favorite bars of the symphony resound in your ears, and you are so moved by the music that it sends shivers down your spine; and now imagine that it would be possible for someone to ask you in this moment whether your life has meaning. I believe you would agree with me if I declared that in this case you would only be able to give one answer, and it would go something like: "It would have been worth it to have lived for this moment alone!"

*hackneyed 진부한

① loving the others
② experiencing beauty
③ achieving personal goals
④ pursuing a greater cause
⑤ playing a musical masterpiece

04 [4강] [4번]

(A), (B), (C)의 각 네모 안에서 어법에 맞는 표현으로 가장 적절한 것은?

The process of research is often not entirely rational. In the classical application of the 'scientific method', the researcher is supposed to develop a hypothesis, then design a crucial experiment to test it. If the hypothesis withstands this test a generalization is then (A) argued / arguing for, and an advance in understanding has been made. But where did the hypothesis come from in the first place? I have a colleague (B) that / whose favourite question is 'Why is this so?', and I've seen this innocent question spawn brilliant research projects on quite a few occasions. Research is a mixture of inspiration (hypothesis generation, musing over the odd and surprising, finding lines of attack on difficult problems) and rational thinking (design and execution of crucial experiments, analysis of results in terms of existing theory). Most of the books on research methods and design of experiments — there are hundreds of them — are concerned with the rational part, and (C) fail / fails to deal with the creative part, yet without the creative part no real research would

be done, no new insights would be gained, and no new theories would be formulated.

*withstand 잘 견디다 **spawn 탄생시키다, 낳다
***muse over ~에 대해 숙고하다

	(A)		(B)		(C)
①	argued	……	that	……	fail
②	argued	……	whose	……	fail
③	argued	……	whose	……	fails
④	arguing	……	that	……	fails
⑤	arguing	……	whose	……	fail

05 [4강] [1번]

다음 글에서 전체 흐름과 관계 <u>없는</u> 문장은?

A key assumption in consumer societies has been the idea that "money buys happiness." Historically, there is a good reason for this assumption — until the last few generations, a majority of people have lived close to subsistence, so an increase in income brought genuine increases in material well-being (e.g., food, shelter, health care) and this has produced more happiness. ① However, in a number of developed nations, levels of material well-being have moved beyond subsistence to unprecedented abundance. ② Developed nations have had several generations of unparalleled material prosperity, and a clear understanding is emerging: More money does bring more happiness when we are living on a very low income. ③ Couples with children and a low income, and single parents, are more vulnerable to poverty-related problems. ④ However, as a global average, when per capita income reaches the range of $13,000 per year, additional income adds relatively little to our happiness, while other factors such as personal freedom, meaningful work, and social tolerance add much more. ⑤ Often, a doubling or tripling of income in developed nations has not led to an increase in perceived well-being.

*subsistence 최저 생계

06 4강 2번

(A), (B), (C)의 각 네모 안에서 문맥에 맞는 낱말로 가장 적절한 것은?

We are wired more for the struggle for survival on the savannah than we are for urban life. As a result, "Situations are constantly evaluated as good or bad, requiring escape or permitting approach." In everyday life, this means that our aversion to losses is naturally (A) smaller / greater than our attraction to gain (by a factor of two). We have an inbuilt mechanism to give priority to bad news. Our brains are set up to *detect* a predator in a fraction of a second, much (B) slower / quicker than the part of the brain that *acknowledges* one has been seen. That is why we can act before we even "know" we are acting. "Threats are privileged above opportunities," Kahneman says. This natural tendency means that we (C) overweight / underestimate unlikely events, such as being caught in a terrorist attack. It also leads to us overestimating our chances of winning the lottery.

*savannah 초원, 사바나   **aversion 혐오

	(A)	(B)	(C)
①	smaller	slower	overweight
②	smaller	quicker	underestimate
③	greater	slower	overweight
④	greater	quicker	overweight
⑤	greater	quicker	underestimate

07 4강 3번

주어진 글 다음에 이어질 글의 순서로 가장 적절한 것은?

It is not only through our actions that we can give life meaning — insofar as we can answer life's specific questions responsibly — we can fulfill the demands of existence not only as active agents but also as loving human beings: in our loving dedication to the beautiful, the great, the good.

(A) Imagine that you are sitting in a concert hall and listening to your favorite symphony, and your favorite bars of the symphony resound in your ears, and you are so moved by the music that it sends shivers down your spine; and now imagine that it would be possible for someone to ask you in this moment whether your life has meaning.

(B) Should I perhaps try to explain for you with some hackneyed phrase how and why experiencing beauty can make life meaningful? I prefer to confine myself to the following thought experiment.

(C) I believe you would agree with me if I declared that in this case you would only be able to give one answer, and it would go something like: "It would have been worth it to have lived for this moment alone!"

① (A) – (C) – (B)
② (B) – (A) – (C)
③ (B) – (C) – (A)
④ (C) – (A) – (B)
⑤ (C) – (B) – (A)

다음 빈칸에 들어갈 말로 가장 적절한 것은?

The process of research is often not entirely rational. In the classical application of the 'scientific method', the researcher is supposed to develop a hypothesis, then design a crucial experiment to test it. If the hypothesis withstands this test a generalization is then argued for, and an advance in understanding has been made. But where did the hypothesis come from in the first place? I have a colleague whose favourite question is 'Why is this so?', and I've seen this innocent question spawn brilliant research projects on quite a few occasions. Research is a mixture of inspiration (hypothesis generation, musing over the odd and surprising, finding lines of attack on difficult problems) and rational thinking (design and execution of crucial experiments, analysis of results in terms of existing theory). Most of the books on research methods and design of experiments — there are hundreds of them — are _____, yet without the creative part no real research would be done, no new insights would be gained, and no new theories would be formulated.

*withstand 잘 견디다 **spawn 탄생시키다, 낳다
***muse over ~에 대해 숙고하다

① leaving out what research ethics is and why it is important
② enlightening researchers about the importance of creativity
③ involved in balancing between the rational part and the creative part
④ addressing inspirational perspectives of new research methods
⑤ concerned with the rational part, and fail to deal with the creative part

A key assumption in consumer societies has been the idea that "money buys happiness." Historically, there is a good reason for this assumption — until the last few generations, a majority of people have lived close to subsistence, so an increase in income brought genuine increases in material well-being (e.g., food, shelter, health care) and this has produced more happiness. However, in a number of developed nations, levels of material well-being have moved beyond subsistence to unprecedented abundance. Developed nations have had several generations of unparalleled material prosperity, and a clear understanding is emerging: More money does bring more happiness when we are living on a very low income. However, as a global average, when per capita income reaches the range of $13,000 per year, additional income adds relatively little to our happiness, while other factors such as personal freedom, meaningful work, and social tolerance add much more. Often, a doubling or tripling of income in developed nations has not led to an increase in perceived well-being.

*subsistence 최저 생계

09 윗글을 읽고 다음 질문에 영어로 답하시오. (10단어 내외)

Q: When per capita income reaches the range of $13,000 per year, what elements contribute more to happiness than income?

A: _____

10 윗글의 내용을 한 문장으로 요약하려고 한다. 빈칸 (A)와 (B)에 들어갈 알맞은 말을 본문에서 찾아 쓰시오.

When most people lived near the subsistence ___(A)___ well-being brought more happiness but as per capita income reaches $13,000 a year, it doesn't lead to a(n) ___(B)___ in perceived happiness.

(A) _____ (B) _____

We are wired more for the struggle for survival on the savannah than we are for urban life. As a result, "Situations are constantly evaluated as good or bad, requiring escape or permitting approach." In everyday life, this means that our aversion to losses is naturally greater than our attraction to gain (by a factor of two). We have an ___(A)___ mechanism to give priority to bad news. Our brains are set up to *detect* a ___(B)___ in a fraction of a second, much quicker than the part of the brain that *acknowledges* one has been seen. That is why we can act before we even "know" we are acting. "Threats are privileged above opportunities," Kahneman says. This natural tendency means that we "overweight" unlikely events, such as being caught in a terrorist attack. It also leads to us overestimating our chances of winning the lottery.

*savannah 초원, 사바나 **aversion 혐오

11 윗글의 빈칸 (A)와 (B)에 들어갈 단어를 영영 뜻풀이를 참고하여 쓰시오. (단, 주어진 글자로 시작하여 쓸 것)

> (A) existing as a natural or basic part of something
> (B) an animal that kills and eats other animals

(A) i_____ (B) p_____

12 윗글의 내용을 한 문장으로 요약하려고 한다. 빈칸 (A), (B)에 들어갈 알맞은 말을 보기 에서 찾아 쓰시오.

> 보기   ignoring / prioritizing / favorable / unlikely

> We have innate mechanisms to survive by ___(A)___ bad news and ___(B)___ situations over good opportunities.

(A) _____ (B) _____

It is not only through our actions that we can give life meaning — insofar as we can answer life's specific questions responsibly — we can fulfill the demands of existence not only as active agents but also as loving human beings: in our loving dedication to the beautiful, the great, the good. Should I perhaps try to explain for you with some hackneyed phrase how and why experiencing beauty can make life meaningful? I prefer to confine myself to the following thought experiment: imagine that you are sitting in a concert hall and listening to your favorite symphony, and your favorite bars of the symphony resound in your ears, and you are so moved by the music that it sends shivers down your spine; and now imagine that it would be possible for someone to ask you in this moment whether your life has meaning. I believe you would agree with me if I declared that in this case you would only be able to give <u>one answer</u>, and it would go something like: "It would have been worth it to have lived for this moment alone!"

*hackneyed 진부한

13 밑줄 친 <u>one answer</u>에 해당하는 말을 본문에서 찾아 우리말로 쓰시오. (30자 내외)

_____

_____

고난도

14 윗글의 요지를 본문에서 찾아 완전한 문장으로 쓰시오. (6단어)

_____

The process of research is often not entirely rational. In the classical application of the 'scientific method', the researcher is supposed to develop a hypothesis, then design a crucial experiment to test it. If the hypothesis withstands this test a generalization is then argued for, and an advance in understanding has been made. But where did the hypothesis come from in the first place? I have a colleague whose favourite question is 'Why is this so?', and 나는 이러한 순수한 질문이 훌륭한 연구 프로젝트를 탄생시키는 것을 보아 왔다 on quite a few occasions. Research is a mixture of inspiration (hypothesis generation, musing over the odd and surprising, finding lines of attack on difficult problems) and rational thinking (design and execution of crucial experiments, analysis of results in terms of existing theory). Most of the books on research methods and design of experiments — there are hundreds of them — are concerned with the rational part, and fail to deal with the creative part, yet without the creative part no real research would be done, no new insights would be gained, and no new theories would be formulated.

*withstand 잘 견디다   **spawn 탄생시키다, 낳다
***muse over ~에 대해 숙고하다

15 윗글의 밑줄 친 우리말 의미와 일치하도록 보기 의 단어를 활용하여 조건 에 맞게 문장을 완성하시오.

보기   see / spawn / brilliant / innocent / research / projects

조건   · 5형식(SVOC) 문장을 사용할 것
· 필요시 어형을 바꿔 쓸 것
· 필요시 단어를 추가하고, 총 9단어로 쓸 것

_____

_____

16 윗글의 내용을 한 문장으로 요약하려고 한다. 빈칸에 들어갈 알맞은 말을 보기 에서 찾아 쓰시오. (대·소문자 구별하여 쓸 것)

보기   innocent / inspiration / rational / research

_____ questions can produce great _____ projects, showing that research is a mixture of _____ and rational thinking in that it requires not only the creative part, but also the _____ part.

❶ Consumers usually attempt to spend as little as possible. ❷ However, it is often the case that people become too concerned with spending as little as possible in the short term, while ignoring the long-term cost of their expenditures. ❸ Homebuilders are keenly aware that most homebuyers are trying to buy a home for the lowest price possible. ❹ However, in the case of the new home, this is not the most important issue for a wise consumer. ❺ Most homes are purchased through a mortgage, and a wise homebuyer should be interested not just in the price of the mortgage, but also in the total price of owning and maintaining a home. ❻ Besides maintenance and insurance costs, this would include the mortgage and utility payments. ❼ It is usually the case that a more energy-efficient home costs more to build, and therefore has a higher mortgage payment. ❽ However, a more energy-efficient home also will result in smaller utility payments.

*mortgage 주택 융자(금)

❶ 소비자는 대개 가능한 한 적게 돈을 쓰려고 한다. ❷ 하지만 사람들이 지출의 장기적인 비용을 무시하면서 단기적으로 가능한 한 적게 쓰는 데 지나치게 신경을 쓰게 되는 경우가 흔하다. ❸ 주택 건설업자는 대부분의 주택 구매자가 가능한 한 가장 낮은 가격에 주택을 구매하고자 한다는 것을 잘 알고 있다. ❹ 하지만 새 주택의 경우, 현명한 소비자에게 이것은 가장 중요한 문제는 아니다. ❺ 대부분의 주택은 주택 융자를 통해 구매되는데, 현명한 주택 구매자는 주택 융자 가격뿐만 아니라 주택을 소유하고 유지하는 데 드는 총액에도 관심을 가져야 한다. ❻ 유지비와 보험료 이외에도 이것은 주택 융자 상환금과 공공요금 납입금을 포함할 것이다. ❼ 에너지 효율성이 더 높은 주택은 짓는 데 비용이 더 많이 들고 따라서 주택 융자 상환금이 더 높은 것이 대개 사실이다. ❽ 하지만 에너지 효율성이 더 높은 주택은 또한 공공요금 납입금이 더 적을 것이다.

Word List

☐ **consumer** 소비자　☐ **attempt** 시도하다　☐ **concerned** 신경을 쓰는, 관심을 가진　☐ **term** 기간　☐ **expenditure** 지출
☐ **homebuilder** 주택 건설업자　☐ **keenly** 빈틈없이　☐ **aware** 알고 있는　☐ **issue** 문제　☐ **maintain** 유지하다
☐ **insurance** 보험　☐ **utility** 공공요금　☐ **energy-efficient** 에너지 효율성이 높은　☐ **result in** ~한 결과를 낳다

• Word Test

1	homebuilder	_____	8	소비자	_____
2	utility	_____	9	시도하다	_____
3	concerned	_____	10	유지하다	_____
4	expenditure	_____	11	알고 있는	_____
5	energy-efficient	_____	12	기간	_____
6	keenly	_____	13	문제	_____
7	result in	_____	14	보험	_____

Consumers usually attempt to spend as little as possible. However, it is often the case that people become too concerned with spending as little as possible in the short term, ❶ while / after ignoring the long-term cost of their expenditures. Homebuilders are keenly aware that most homebuyers are trying to buy a home for the lowest price possible. ❷ However / Therefore , in the case of the new home, this is not the most important issue for a wise consumer. Most homes are purchased through a mortgage, and a wise homebuyer should be interested not just in the price of the mortgage, but also in the total price of owning and maintaining a home. ❸ Beside / Besides maintenance and insurance costs, this would include the mortgage and utility payments. It is usually the case that a more energy-efficient home costs more to build, and therefore has a ❹ higher / lower mortgage payment. However, a more energy-efficient home also will result in ❺ bigger / smaller utility payments.

*mortgage 주택 융자(금)

Consumers usually attempt to spend as little as possible. However, it is often the case that people become too concerned with spending as little as possible in the short term, while ❶ _____ (ignore) the long-term cost of their expenditures. Homebuilders are keenly aware that most homebuyers are trying to buy a home for the lowest price possible. However, in the case of the new home, this is not the most important issue for a wise consumer. Most homes ❷ _____ (purchase) through a mortgage, and a wise homebuyer should be interested not just in the price of the mortgage, but also in the total price of owning and maintaining a home. Besides maintenance and insurance costs, this would include the mortgage and utility payments. It is usually the case that a more energy-efficient home ❸ _____ (cost) more to build, and therefore ❹ _____ (have) a higher mortgage payment. However, a more energy-efficient home also will result in smaller utility payments.

*mortgage 주택 융자(금)

Consumers usually attempt to spend ❶ _____ _____ _____ _____ (가능한 한 적게). However, it is often the case that people become too concerned with spending as little as possible ❷ _____ _____ _____ _____ (단기적으로), while ignoring the long-term cost of their expenditures. Homebuilders are keenly aware that most homebuyers are trying to buy a home for the lowest price possible. However, ❸ _____ _____ _____ _____ (~의 경우에) the new home, this is not the most important issue for a wise consumer. Most homes are purchased through a mortgage, and a wise homebuyer should be interested not just in the price of the mortgage, but also ❹ _____ _____ _____ _____ _____ (~의 총액에) owning and maintaining a home. Besides maintenance and insurance costs, this would include the mortgage and utility payments. It is usually the case that a more energy-efficient home costs more to build, and therefore has a higher mortgage payment. However, a more energy-efficient home also will result in smaller utility payments.

*mortgage 주택 융자(금)

❶ It is obvious that organized party spirit is one of the greatest dangers of our time. ❷ In the form of nationalism it leads to wars between nations, and in other forms it leads to civil war. ❸ It should be the business of teachers to stand outside the strife of parties and endeavour to instill into the young the habit of impartial inquiry, leading them to judge issues on their merits and to be on their guard against accepting one-sided statements at their face value. ❹ The teacher should not be expected to flatter the prejudices either of the mob or of officials. ❺ His professional virtue should consist in a readiness to do justice to all sides, and in an endeavour to rise above controversy into a region of dispassionate scientific investigation. ❻ If there are people to whom the results of his investigation are inconvenient, he should be protected against their resentment, unless it can be shown that he has lent himself to dishonest propaganda by the dissemination of demonstrable untruths.

*dispassionate 공정한 ** propaganda 선전 *** dissemination 유포

❶ 조직화된 당파심(黨派心)이 우리 시대의 가장 큰 위험 중 하나임은 분명하다. ❷ 민족주의의 형태로 그것은 국가 간의 전쟁으로 이어지고, 다른 형태로 그것은 내전을 초래한다. ❸ 당파 싸움 밖에 서서 젊은이들에게 치우치지 않는 탐구의 습관을 주입하려고 노력하여, 그들이 문제를 시비곡직에 따라 판단하여 일방적인 진술을 액면 그대로 받아들이지 않도록 경계하게 하는 것이 교사가 하는 일이어야 한다. ❹ 교사가 군중이나 관리들의 편견에 아첨하도록 요구되어서는 안 된다. ❺ 그의 직업 덕목은 기꺼이 모든 편에 공평하게 대하려는 마음과, 논쟁을 넘어 공정한 과학적 조사 영역으로 들어가려는 노력에 있어야 한다. ❻ 그의 조사 결과가 불편한 사람들이 있다고 하더라도, 그가 입증 가능한 거짓의 유포로 부정한 선전에 가담했다는 것을 보여 줄 수 없는 한, 그는 그들의 분노로부터 보호되어야 한다.

Word List

□ obvious 분명한   □ party 당, 정당   □ nationalism 민족주의   □ civil war 내전   □ strife 싸움, 다툼   □ endeavour 노력하다; 노력
□ instill 주입하다   □ impartial 치우치지 않는, 공정한   □ judge ~ on one's merits ~을 시비곡직에 따라 판단하다
□ be on one's guard against ~ 하지 않도록 경계하다   □ statement 진술   □ at one's face value 액면 그대로   □ flatter 아첨하다
□ prejudice 편견   □ mob 군중   □ official 관리, 공무원   □ virtue 덕목   □ consist in ~에 있다   □ readiness 기꺼이 하는 마음
□ do justice to ~에게 공평하게 대하다   □ controversy 논쟁   □ resentment 분노   □ lend oneself to ~에 가담하다
□ demonstrable 입증 가능한

• Word Test

1	judge ~ on one's merits	13	치우치지 않는, 공정한
2	demonstrable	14	분노
3	at one's face value	15	덕목
4	lend oneself to	16	편견
5	consist in	17	진술
6	do justice to	18	싸움, 다툼
7	mob	19	아첨하다
8	readiness	20	논쟁
9	be on one's guard against	21	내전
10	instill	22	관리, 공무원
11	endeavour	23	당, 정당
12	nationalism	24	분명한

It is ❶ obvious/ambiguous that organized party spirit is one of the greatest dangers of our time. In the form of nationalism it leads to wars between nations, and in other forms it leads to civil war. It should be the business of teachers to stand outside the ❷ strife/dignity of parties and endeavour to instill into the young the habit of impartial inquiry, leading them to judge issues on their merits and to be on their guard against accepting one-sided statements at their face value. The teacher should not be expected to flatter the prejudices either of the mob or of officials. His professional virtue should consist in a readiness to do justice to all sides, and in an endeavour to rise above controversy into a region of dispassionate scientific investigation. If there are people ❸ to/at whom the results of his investigation are inconvenient, he should be protected against their resentment, ❹ unless/as if it can be shown that he has lent himself to ❺ honest/dishonest propaganda by the dissemination of demonstrable untruths.

*dispassionate 공정한   **propaganda 선전   ***dissemination 유포

It is obvious that organized party spirit is one of the greatest dangers of our time. In the form of nationalism it leads to wars between nations, and in other forms it leads to civil war. It should be the business of teachers ❶ _____ (stand) outside the strife of parties and endeavour to instill into the young the habit of impartial inquiry, ❷ _____ (lead) them to judge issues on their merits and to be on their guard against accepting one-sided statements at their face value. The teacher should not ❸ _____ (expect) to flatter the prejudices either of the mob or of officials. His professional virtue should consist in a readiness to do justice to all sides, and in an endeavour to rise above controversy into a region of dispassionate scientific investigation. If there are people to whom the results of his investigation ❹ _____ (be) inconvenient, he should be protected against their resentment, unless it can ❺ _____ (show) that he has lent himself to dishonest propaganda by the dissemination of demonstrable untruths.

*dispassionate 공정한   **propaganda 선전   ***dissemination 유포

It is obvious that organized party spirit is one of the greatest dangers of our time. In the form of nationalism it leads to wars between nations, and ❶ _____ _____ _____ (다른 형태들로) it leads to civil war. It should be the business of teachers to stand outside the strife of parties and endeavour to ❷ _____ _____ (~에게 심어주다) the young the habit of impartial inquiry, leading them to judge issues on their merits and to be on their guard against accepting one-sided statements ❸ _____ _____ _____ _____ (액면 그대로). The teacher should not be expected to flatter the prejudices either of the mob or of officials. His professional virtue should ❹ _____ _____ (~에 있다) a readiness to do justice to all sides, and in an endeavour to rise above controversy into a region of dispassionate scientific investigation. If there are people to whom the results of his investigation are inconvenient, he should be protected against their resentment, unless it can be shown that he has lent himself to dishonest propaganda by the dissemination of demonstrable untruths.

*dispassionate 공정한   **propaganda 선전   ***dissemination 유포

❶ What urgent tasks are you facing this week? ❷ Make a list. ❸ Then compare that list of urgent tasks to your list of critical and enabling goals. ❹ Do you see anything resembling a match? ❺ Don't be surprised if most of the "urgent" issues on your list have nothing to do with your critical and enabling goals. ❻ In the absence of serious time management, it's easy for your days to fill up with urgent but unimportant activities. ❼ The same applies to many of the commitments we all make to others in the spirit of helpfulness. ❽ "Yes, I'll help you with that report," you tell a colleague. ❾ "Yes, I'll volunteer to sell raffle tickets for the school fund-raiser." ❿ Commitments like these keep us busy without necessarily bringing us closer to our higher goals. ⓫ To be an effective time manager, you must discipline yourself to differentiate between what is urgent *and* important and what is simply urgent. ⓬ When you recognize the difference, you'll know best how to allocate your time.

*raffle ticket 경품 응모권

❶ 여러분은 이번 주에 어떤 긴급한 일에 직면해있는가? ❷ 목록을 만들라. ❸ 그런 다음 그 긴급한 일 목록을 여러분의 중대 목표 및 실행 목표 목록과 비교해 보라. ❹ 비슷하게 일치하는 어떤 것이 보이는가? ❺ 여러분의 목록에 있는 '긴급한' 문제 대부분이 여러분의 중대 목표 및 실행 목표와 아무런 관련이 없다고 해도 놀라지 말라. ❻ 진지한 시간 관리가 없을 경우, 여러분의 하루하루는 긴급하지만 중요하지 않은 활동으로 채워지기 쉽다. ❼ 우리 모두가 도움이 된다는 마음으로 다른 사람들에게 하는 많은 약속에서도 똑같이 적용된다. ❽ "네, 제가 그 보고서를 작성하는 것을 도와줄게요."라고 여러분은 동료에게 말한다. ❾ "네, 학교 기금 모금 행사를 위한 경품 응모권 판매를 자원할게요." ❿ 이와 같은 약속은 반드시 우리를 우리의 더 높은 목표에 더 가까이 가게 하지도 않으면서 우리를 계속 바쁘게 한다. ⓫ 효과적인 시간 관리자가 되기 위해서, 여러분은 긴급하'면서도' 중요한 것과 그저 긴급한 것을 구별하도록 자신을 훈련해야 한다. ⓬ 여러분이 그 차이를 깨달을 때 자신의 시간을 할당하는 방법을 가장 잘 알게 될 것이다.

Word List

□ urgent 긴급한　　□ task 일, 과제　　□ critical goal 중대 목표　　□ enabling goal 실행 목표　　□ resemble 닮다, 비슷하다
□ have nothing to do with ~와 관련이 없다　　□ in the absence of ~이 없을 경우[때]　　□ serious 진지한　　□ apply 적용되다
□ commitment 약속　　□ spirit 마음, 정신　　□ colleague 동료　　□ volunteer 자원하다
□ fund-raiser (자선 단체·조직 등을 위한) 기금 모금 행사　　□ necessarily 필연적으로, 어쩔 수 없이　　□ discipline 훈련시키다
□ differentiate 구별하다, 식별하다　　□ allocate 할당하다

• Word Test

1	task	10	진지한
2	enabling goal	11	긴급한
3	in the absence of	12	자원하다
4	fund-raiser	13	중대 목표
5	commitment	14	적용되다
6	necessarily	15	마음, 정신
7	have nothing to do with	16	닮다, 비슷하다
8	allocate	17	동료
9	discipline	18	구별하다, 식별하다

네모 안에서 옳은 어법·어휘를 고르시오.

What urgent tasks are you facing this week? Make a list. Then compare that list of urgent tasks to your list of critical and enabling goals. Do you see anything resembling a match? Don't be surprised if most of the "urgent"issues on your list have nothing to do with your critical and enabling goals. In the absence of serious time ❶ management/performance , it's easy for your days to fill up with urgent but ❷ important/unimportant activities. The same applies to many of the commitments we all make to others in the spirit of helpfulness. "Yes, I'll help you with that report,"you tell a colleague. "Yes, I'll volunteer to sell raffle tickets for the school fund-raiser."Commitments like these keep us busy without ❸ necessary/necessarily bringing us closer to our higher goals. To be an effective time manager, you must discipline ❹ you/yourself to differentiate between what is urgent *and* important and what is simply urgent. When you recognize the difference, you'll know best how to ❺ allocate/alleviate your time.

*raffle ticket 경품 응모권

• 유형 2 괄호 안의 동사를 알맞은 형태로 쓰시오.

What urgent tasks are you facing this week? Make a list. Then compare that list of urgent tasks to your list of critical and enabling goals. Do you see anything ❶ _____ (resemble) a match? Don't be surprised if most of the "urgent"issues on your list have nothing to do with your critical and enabling goals. In the absence of serious time management, it's easy for your days to fill up with urgent but unimportant activities. The same ❷ _____ (apply) to many of the commitments we all make to others in the spirit of helpfulness. "Yes, I'll help you with that report,"you tell a colleague. "Yes, I'll volunteer to sell raffle tickets for the school fund-raiser."Commitments like these keep us busy without necessarily ❸ _____ (bring) us closer to our higher goals. To be an effective time manager, you must discipline yourself ❹ _____ (differentiate) between what is urgent *and* important and what is simply urgent. When you recognize the difference, you'll know best how to allocate your time.

*raffle ticket 경품 응모권

• 유형 3 우리말에 맞게 빈칸에 알맞은 말을 쓰시오.

What urgent tasks are you facing this week? Make a list. Then compare that list of urgent tasks to your list of critical and enabling goals. Do you see anything resembling a match? Don't be surprised if most of the "urgent"issues on your list ❶ _____ _____ _____ _____ _____ (~와 아무런 관련이 없다) your critical and enabling goals. ❷ _____ _____ _____ _____ (~가 없을 경우에) serious time management, it's easy for your days to ❸ _____ _____ _____ (~로 채워지다) urgent but unimportant activities. The same applies to many of the commitments we all make to others ❹ _____ _____ _____ _____ _____ (도움이 된다는 마음으로). "Yes, I'll help you with that report,"you tell a colleague. "Yes, I'll volunteer to sell raffle tickets for the school fund-raiser."Commitments like these keep us busy without necessarily bringing us closer to our higher goals. To be an effective time manager, you must discipline yourself to differentiate between what is urgent *and* important and what is simply urgent. When you recognize the difference, you'll know best how to allocate your time.

*raffle ticket 경품 응모권

❶ We can safely argue that nearly all aspects of modern human life owe their existence to science. ❷ Electric lights, mass food production, transport, air conditioning, medicine, heating, clothing manufacture, etc. are all the products of scientific research. ❸ If we therefore convinced ourselves that our scientific endeavours were merely of interest to other scientists, then we would not only be incorrect, we would be selfish, short-sighted, and historically ignorant. ❹ Even the most theoretical and 'blue skies' research can be useful and interesting to non-scientists. ❺ We are therefore compelled to extend our science results and their implications to as many people as possible. ❻ As if we needed more jobs to do and expertise to acquire! ❼ Unfortunately, effective public engagement is something that most scientists have done poorly since the advent of modern communication technologies, so mastering a good communication strategy should be something every developing scientist should try to improve.

*blue skies 비현실적인

❶ 우리는 현대 인간 생활의 거의 모든 면이 과학 덕분에 존재한다고 주장해도 별로 틀리지 않을 수 있다. ❷ 전등, 대량 식품 생산, 운송, 에어컨, 의약품, 난방, 의류 제조 등은 모두 과학 연구의 산물이다. ❸ 그러므로 만약 우리의 과학적 노력이 단지 다른 과학자들의 관심사일 뿐이라고 확신한다면, 우리는 단지 틀린 것일 뿐만 아니라, 이기적이고 근시안적이며 역사적으로 무지한 것일 것이다. ❹ 심지어 가장 이론적이고 '현실 세계에서의 적용이 즉각적으로 분명하지 않은' 연구도 비과학자들에게 유용하고 흥미로울 수 있다. ❺ 따라서 우리는 우리가 이룬 과학의 결과와 그것의 영향이 가능한 한 많은 사람에게 미치도록 해야 한다. ❻ 마치 우리에게는 해야 할 일이 더 많이 필요하고, 습득해야 할 전문 지식이 더 많이 필요한 것처럼 말이다! ❼ 불행히도, 효과적인 대중적 관여는 현대 통신 기술의 출현 이후 대부분의 과학자가 잘하지 못했던 일이라 훌륭한 소통 전략을 숙달하는 것은 발전해 가는 모든 과학자가 향상시키도록 노력해야 하는 일일 것이다.

Word List

□ safely 별로 틀리지 않게, 무난하게   □ argue 주장하다   □ aspect 양상, 측면   □ owe ~ to ... ~은 … 덕분이다   □ existence 존재
□ mass 대량의, 대중의   □ transport 운송; 운송하다   □ convince 확신시키다   □ endeavour 노력, 시도   □ merely 단지
□ short-sighted 근시안적인, 근시의   □ ignorant 무지한   □ theoretical 이론적인
□ be compelled to do (어쩔 수 없이) ~해야만 하다   □ extend 미치다, 뻗다   □ implication 영향, 함축   □ expertise 전문 지식
□ acquire 습득하다, 얻다   □ effective 효과적인   □ engagement 관여, 참여   □ advent 출현, 도래   □ strategy 전략

• Word Test

1	engagement		12	존재	
2	mass		13	별로 틀리지 않게, 무난하게	
3	advent		14	전략	
4	owe ~ to ...		15	양상, 측면	
5	be compelled to do		16	운송; 운송하다	
6	extend		17	효과적인	
7	short-sighted		18	단지	
8	ignorant		19	전문 지식	
9	implication		20	확신시키다	
10	endeavour		21	주장하다	
11	acquire		22	이론적인	

We can safely argue that nearly all aspects of modern human life owe their existence to science. Electric lights, mass food production, transport, air conditioning, medicine, heating, clothing manufacture, etc. are all the products of scientific research. If we therefore convinced ourselves that our scientific endeavours were merely of interest to other scientists, then we would not only be ❶ correct /incorrect , we would be selfish, short-sighted, and historically ❷ ignorant/ignorance . Even the most ❸ practical/theoretical and 'blue skies'research can be useful and interesting to non-scientists. We are therefore compelled to extend our science results and their implications to as many people as possible. As if we needed more jobs to do and expertise to acquire! Unfortunately, effective public engagement is something ❹ that / what most scientists have done poorly since the advent of modern communication technologies, so mastering a good communication strategy should be something every developing ❺ scientist / scientists should try to improve.

*blue skies 비현실적인

We can safely argue that nearly all aspects of modern human life owe their existence to science. Electric lights, mass food production, transport, air conditioning, medicine, heating, clothing manufacture, etc. ❶ _____(be) all the products of scientific research. If we therefore convinced ourselves that our scientific endeavours ❷ _____(be) merely of interest to other scientists, then we would not only be incorrect, we would be selfish, short-sighted, and historically ignorant. Even the most theoretical and 'blue skies'research can be useful and interesting to non-scientists. We are therefore ❸ _____(compel) to extend our science results and their implications to as many people as possible. As if we needed more jobs to do and expertise to acquire! Unfortunately, effective public engagement is something that most scientists ❹ _____(do) poorly since the advent of modern communication technologies, so ❺ _____(master) a good communication strategy should be something every developing scientist should try to improve.

*blue skies 비현실적인

We can safely argue that ❶ _____ _____ _____ _____ (~의 거의 모든 면들) modern human life owe their existence to science. Electric lights, mass food production, transport, air conditioning, medicine, heating, clothing manufacture, etc. are all the products of scientific research. If we therefore convinced ourselves that our scientific endeavours were ❷ _____ _____ _____ _____ (단지 ~의 관심사일 뿐) other scientists, then we would not only be incorrect, we would be selfish, short-sighted, and historically ignorant. Even the most theoretical and 'blue skies'research can be useful and interesting to non-scientists. We are therefore compelled to extend our science results and their implications to ❸ _____ _____ _____ _____ _____ (가능한 한 많은 사람들). As if we needed more jobs to do and expertise to acquire! Unfortunately, ❹ _____ _____ _____ (효과적인 대중적 관여) is something that most scientists have done poorly since the advent of modern communication technologies, so mastering a good communication strategy should be something every developing scientist should try to improve.

*blue skies 비현실적인

01 5강 1번

글의 흐름으로 보아, 주어진 문장이 들어가기에 가장 적절한 곳은?

> However, in the case of the new home, this is not the most important issue for a wise consumer.

Consumers usually attempt to spend as little as possible. However, it is often the case that people become too concerned with spending as little as possible in the short term, while ignoring the long-term cost of their expenditures. (①) Homebuilders are keenly aware that most homebuyers are trying to buy a home for the lowest price possible. (②) Most homes are purchased through a mortgage, and a wise homebuyer should be interested not just in the price of the mortgage, but also in the total price of owning and maintaining a home. (③) Besides maintenance and insurance costs, this would include the mortgage and utility payments. (④) It is usually the case that a more energy-efficient home costs more to build, and therefore has a higher mortgage payment. (⑤) However, a more energy-efficient home also will result in smaller utility payments.

*mortgage 주택 융자(금)

02 5강 2번

다음 글의 내용을 한 문장으로 요약하고자 한다. 빈칸 (A), (B)에 들어갈 말로 가장 적절한 것은?

It is obvious that organized party spirit is one of the greatest dangers of our time. In the form of nationalism it leads to wars between nations, and in other forms it leads to civil war. It should be the business of teachers to stand outside the strife of parties and endeavour to instill into the young the habit of impartial inquiry, leading them to judge issues on their merits and to be on their guard against accepting one-sided statements at their face value. The teacher should not be expected to flatter the prejudices either of the mob or of officials. His professional virtue should consist in a readiness to do justice to all sides, and in an endeavour to rise above controversy into a region of dispassionate scientific investigation. If there are people to whom the results of his investigation are inconvenient, he should be protected against their resentment, unless it can be shown that he has lent himself to dishonest propaganda by the dissemination of demonstrable untruths.

*dispassionate 공정한 **propaganda 선전 ***dissemination 유포

↓

> Teachers should be unaffected by political bias, leading the young not to be ___(A)___ against any particular person, group, or point of view and conducting scientific ___(B)___ without fear of unjustified resentment

	(A)		(B)
①	impartial	……	judgement
②	impartial	……	examination
③	arguing	……	judgement
④	prejudiced	……	punishment
⑤	prejudiced	……	examination

03 5강 3번

주어진 글 다음에 이어질 글의 순서로 가장 적절한 것은?

> What urgent tasks are you facing this week? Make a list. Then compare that list of urgent tasks to your list of critical and enabling goals. Do you see anything resembling a match?

(A) The same applies to many of the commitments we all make to others in the spirit of helpfulness. "Yes, I'll help you with that report," you tell a colleague. "Yes, I'll volunteer to sell raffle tickets for the school fund-raiser." Commitments like these keep us busy without necessarily bringing us closer to our higher goals.

(B) To be an effective time manager, you must discipline yourself to differentiate between what is urgent *and* important and what is simply urgent. When you recognize the difference, you'll know best how to allocate your time.

(C) Don't be surprised if most of the "urgent" issues on your list have nothing to do with your critical and enabling goals. In the absence of serious time management, it's easy for your days to fill up with urgent but unimportant activities.

*raffle ticket 경품 응모권

① (A) – (C) – (B)　　② (B) – (A) – (C)
③ (B) – (C) – (A)　　④ (C) – (A) – (B)
⑤ (C) – (B) – (A)

04　5강 4번

밑줄 친 effective public engagement가 다음 글에서 의미하는 바로 가장 적절한 것은?

We can safely argue that nearly all aspects of modern human life owe their existence to science. Electric lights, mass food production, transport, air conditioning, medicine, heating, clothing manufacture, etc. are all the products of scientific research. If we therefore convinced ourselves that our scientific endeavours were merely of interest to other scientists, then we would not only be incorrect, we would be selfish, short-sighted, and historically ignorant. Even the most theoretical and 'blue skies' research can be useful and interesting to non-scientists. We are therefore compelled to extend our science results and their implications to as many people as possible. As if we needed more jobs to do and expertise to acquire! Unfortunately, effective public engagement is something that most scientists have done poorly since the advent of modern communication technologies, so mastering a good communication strategy should be something every developing scientist should try to improve.

*blue skies 비현실적인

① communicating with people to enhance modern human life
② reorganizing all the products of scientific research in a user-friendly manner
③ enhancing a communication strategy for close collaboration between scientists
④ spreading the outcomes of science to everyone in a more active and open way
⑤ displaying the achievement of science to public by developing communication technologies

05　5강 1번

다음 글의 밑줄 친 부분 중, 어법상 틀린 것은?

Consumers usually attempt to spend as little as possible. However, it is often the case that people become too concerned with spending as little as possible in the short term, while ① ignored the long-term cost of their expenditures. Homebuilders are keenly aware ② that most homebuyers are trying to buy a home for the lowest price possible. However, in the case of the new home, this is not the most important issue for a wise consumer. Most homes are ③ purchased through a mortgage, and a wise homebuyer should be interested not just in the price of the mortgage, but also in the total price of owning and maintaining a home. ④ Besides maintenance and insurance costs, this would include the mortgage and utility payments. It is usually the case that a more energy-efficient home costs more ⑤ to build, and therefore has a higher mortgage payment. However, a more energy-efficient home also will result in smaller utility payments.

*mortgage 주택 융자(금)

다음 빈칸에 들어갈 말로 가장 적절한 것은?

It is obvious that organized party spirit is one of the greatest dangers of our time. In the form of nationalism it leads to wars between nations, and in other forms it leads to civil war. It should be the business of teachers to stand outside the strife of parties and endeavour to instill into the young the habit of _____ inquiry, leading them to judge issues on their merits and to be on their guard against accepting one-sided statements at their face value. The teacher should not be expected to flatter the prejudices either of the mob or of officials. His professional virtue should consist in a readiness to do justice to all sides, and in an endeavour to rise above controversy into a region of dispassionate scientific investigation. If there are people to whom the results of his investigation are inconvenient, he should be protected against their resentment, unless it can be shown that he has lent himself to dishonest propaganda by the dissemination of demonstrable untruths.

*dispassionate 공정한 **propaganda 선전 ***dissemination 유포

① formal
② biased
③ detailed
④ impartial
⑤ preliminary

다음 글의 밑줄 친 부분 중, 문맥상 낱말의 쓰임이 적절하지 않은 것은?

What urgent tasks are you facing this week? Make a list. Then compare that list of urgent tasks to your list of critical and enabling goals. Do you see anything resembling a match? Don't be surprised if most of the "urgent" issues on your list have ① nothing to do with your critical and enabling goals. In the absence of serious time management, it's easy for your days to fill up with urgent but unimportant activities. The same applies to many of the commitments we all make to others in the spirit of ② helpfulness. "Yes, I'll help you with that report," you tell a colleague. "Yes, I'll volunteer to sell raffle tickets for the school fund-raiser." Commitments like these keep us busy without necessarily bringing us ③ closer to our higher goals. To be an effective time manager, you must discipline yourself to differentiate between what is urgent *and* ④ unimportant and what is simply urgent. When you recognize the difference, you'll know best how to ⑤ allocate your time.

*raffle ticket 경품 응모권

다음 글에서 전체 흐름과 관계 <u>없는</u> 문장은?

We can safely argue that nearly all aspects of modern human life owe their existence to science. Electric lights, mass food production, transport, air conditioning, medicine, heating, clothing manufacture, etc. are all the products of scientific research. ① If we therefore convinced ourselves that our scientific endeavours were merely of interest to other scientists, then we would not only be incorrect, we would be selfish, short-sighted, and historically ignorant. ② Even the most theoretical and 'blue skies' research can be useful and interesting to non-scientists. ③ We are therefore compelled to extend our science results and their implications to as many people as possible as if we needed more jobs to do and expertise to acquire! ④ Science can never offer a universal truth or an objective representation of the world even though it can question the conditions of validity and trigger reflection. ⑤ Unfortunately, effective public engagement is something that most scientists have done poorly since the advent of modern communication technologies, so mastering a good communication strategy should be something every developing scientist should try to improve.

*blue skies 비현실적인

Consumers usually attempt to spend as little as possible. However, it is often the case that people become too concerned with spending as little as possible in the short term, while ignoring the long-term cost of their expenditures. Homebuilders are keenly aware that most homebuyers are trying to buy a home for the lowest price possible. However, in the case of the new home, <u>this</u> is not the most important issue for a wise consumer. Most homes are purchased through a mortgage, and a wise homebuyer should be interested not just in the price of the mortgage, but also in the total price of owning and maintaining a home. Besides maintenance and insurance costs, this would include the mortgage and utility payments. It is usually the case that a more energy-efficient home costs more to build, and therefore has a higher mortgage payment. However, a more energy-efficient home also will result in smaller utility payments.

*mortgage 주택 융자(금)

고난도

09 윗글의 밑줄 친 <u>this</u>가 가리키는 것을 본문에서 찾아 우리말로 쓰시오. (25자 내외)

_____

_____

10 윗글에서 다음 질문에 대한 답을 찾아 우리말로 쓰시오. (15자 내외)

Q: What is the advantage of a more energy-efficient home?

A: _____

It is obvious that organized party spirit is one of the greatest dangers of our time. In the form of nationalism it leads to wars between nations, and in other forms it leads to civil war. It should be the business of teachers to stand outside the strife of parties and endeavour to instill into the young the habit of impartial inquiry, leading them to judge issues on their merits and to be on their guard against accepting one-sided statements at their face value. 교사가 군중이나 관리들의 편견에 아첨하도록 요구되어서는 안 된다. His professional virtue should consist in a readiness to do justice to all sides, and in an endeavour to rise above _____ into a region of dispassionate scientific investigation. If there are people to whom the results of his investigation are inconvenient, he should be protected against their resentment, unless it can be shown that he has lent himself to dishonest propaganda by the dissemination of demonstrable untruths.

*dispassionate 공정한 **propaganda 선전 ***dissemination 유포

11 윗글의 밑줄 친 우리말 의미와 일치하도록 보기 의 단어를 활용하여 조건 에 맞게 문장을 완성하시오.

보기 officials / flatter / expect / should / mob / prejudices / not

조건
· 수동태를 사용할 것
· 〈either A or B〉 구문을 사용할 것
· 필요시 단어를 추가하고, 총 17단어로 쓸 것

_____

_____

12 윗글의 빈칸에 들어갈 단어를 영영 뜻풀이를 참고하여 쓰시오. (단, 주어진 글자로 시작할 것)

a disagreement, especially about a public policy or a moral issue that a lot of people have strong feelings about

c_____

What urgent tasks are you facing this week? Make a list. Then compare that list of urgent tasks to your list of critical and enabling goals. Do you see anything (A) resemble a match? Don't be surprised if most of the "urgent" issues on your list have nothing to do with your critical and enabling goals. In the absence of serious time management, it's easy for your days (B) filling up with urgent but unimportant activities. The same applies to many of the commitments we all make to others in the spirit of helpfulness. "Yes, I'll help you with that report," you tell a colleague. "Yes, I'll volunteer to sell raffle tickets for the school fund-raiser." Commitments like these keep us busy without (C) necessary bringing us closer to our higher goals. 효과적인 시간 관리자가 되기 위해서, 여러분은 긴급하'면서도' 중요한 것과 그저 긴급한 것을 구별하도록 자신을 훈련해야 한다. When you recognize the difference, you'll know best how to allocate your time.

*raffle ticket 경품 응모권

13 윗글의 밑줄 친 부분을 어법상 알맞은 형태로 고쳐 쓰시오.

(A) resemble → _____

(B) filling → _____

(C) necessary → _____

14 윗글의 밑줄 친 우리말 의미와 일치하도록 보기 의 단어를 활용하여 조건 에 맞게 문장을 완성하시오.

보기 simply / discipline / between / urgent / differentiate

조건
· 관계대명사 what을 사용할 것
· 총 15단어로 쓸 것

To be an effective time manager, you must _____

_____.

We can safely argue that nearly all aspects of modern human life owe their existence to science. Electric lights, mass food production, transport, air conditioning, medicine, heating, clothing manufacture, etc. are all the products of scientific research. 그러므로 만약 우리의 과학적 노력이 단지 다른 과학자들의 관심사일 뿐이라고 확신한다면, then we would not only be incorrect, we would be selfish, short-sighted, and historically ignorant. Even the most theoretical and 'blue skies' research can be useful and interesting to non-scientists. We are therefore compelled to extend our science results and their implications to as many people as possible. As if we needed more jobs to do and expertise to acquire! Unfortunately, effective public engagement is something that most scientists have done poorly since the advent of modern communication technologies, so mastering a good communication strategy should be something every developing scientist should try to improve.

*blue skies 비현실적인

15 윗글의 밑줄 친 우리말 의미와 일치하도록 보기 의 단어를 활용하여 영작하시오. (단, 필요시 단어를 추가하고, 어형을 바꿔 쓸 것)

> 보기   to other scientists / therefore convince us / if / merely of interest / endeavours

If we _____

_____,

16 윗글의 내용을 한 문장으로 요약하려고 한다. 빈칸 (A)와 (B)에 들어갈 알맞은 말을 본문에서 찾아 쓰시오. (단, 필요시 어형을 바꿔 쓸 것)

> In the belief that people can lead their modern lives thanks to science, all the scientists should master the method of ____(A)____ with the public effectively to spread scientific results to many ____(B)____ other than scientists.

(A) _____   (B) _____

❶ Nobody has to teach a child to demand fair treatment; children protest unfairness vigorously and as soon as they can communicate. ❷ Nobody has to teach us to admire a person who sacrifices for a group; the admiration for duty is universal. ❸ Nobody has to teach us to disdain someone who betrays a friend or is disloyal to a family or tribe. ❹ Nobody has to teach a child the difference between rules that are moral — "Don't hit"— and rules that are not — "Don't chew gum in school." ❺ These preferences also emerge from somewhere deep inside us. ❻ Just as we have a natural suite of emotions to help us love and be loved, so, too, we have a natural suite of moral emotions to make us disapprove of people who violate social commitments, and approve of people who reinforce them. ❼ There is no society on earth where people are praised for running away in battle.

*vigorously 격렬하게 ** disdain 경멸하다

❶ 누구도 아이에게 공정한 대우를 요구하도록 가르칠 필요가 없다. 아이들은 격렬하게 그리고 의사소통을 할 수 있게 되자마자 불공정함에 항의하기 때문이다. ❷ 누구도 우리에게 집단을 위해 희생하는 사람을 존경하라고 가르칠 필요가 없다. (도덕적) 의무에 대한 존경은 보편적이기 때문이다. ❸ 누구도 우리에게 친구를 배신하거나 가족이나 부족에 불충한 사람을 경멸하라고 가르칠 필요가 없다. ❹ 누구도 아이에게 "때리지 마라."와 같은 도덕에 관한 규칙과 "학교에서 껌을 씹지 마라."와 같은 도덕과 무관한 규칙 사이의 차이를 가르칠 필요가 없다. ❺ 이러한 선호는 또한 우리 내면의 깊은 곳 어딘가에서 나온다. ❻ 우리가 사랑하고 사랑받도록 도울 선천적인 감정의 묶음을 가지고 있는 것처럼, 또한, 우리는 사회적 약속을 어기는 사람들을 못마땅하게 여기고 그것을 강화하는 사람들을 인정하게 만들 선천적인 도덕적 감정의 묶음을 가지고 있다. ❼ 사람들이 전투에서 도망치는 것에 대해 칭찬받는 사회는 전혀 없다.

Word List

□ demand 요구하다   □ fair 공정한   □ treatment 대우   □ protest 항의하다   □ sacrifice 희생하다   □ admiration 존경
□ universal 보편적인   □ betray 배신하다   □ disloyal 불충한   □ tribe 부족   □ moral 도덕적인   □ chew 씹다
□ preference 선호, 선호되는 것   □ emerge 나오다, 모습을 드러내다   □ suite 묶음, (한) 벌   □ disapprove of ~을 못마땅하게 여기다
□ violate 어기다   □ commitment 약속   □ reinforce 강화하다   □ on earth (부정어 뒤에서) 전혀, 도무지

• Word Test

1	disapprove of		11	요구하다	
2	suite		12	도덕적인	
3	sacrifice		13	공정한	
4	disloyal		14	씹다	
5	universal		15	대우	
6	betray		16	부족	
7	on earth		17	강화하다	
8	protest		18	선호, 선호되는 것	
9	emerge		19	존경	
10	commitment		20	어기다	

Nobody has to teach a child to demand fair treatment; children protest unfairness vigorously and as soon as they can communicate. Nobody has to teach us to admire a person who sacrifices for a group; the admiration for duty is ❶ abnormal/universal . Nobody has to teach us to disdain someone who betrays a friend or is disloyal to a family or tribe. Nobody has to teach a child the difference between rules that are moral — "Don't hit"— and rules that are not — "Don't chew gum in school." These preferences also emerge from ❷ somehow/somewhere deep inside us. Just as we have a natural suite of emotions to help us love and be loved, so, too, we have a natural suite of moral emotions to make us disapprove of people who ❸ comply/violate social commitments, and approve of people who reinforce ❹ it/them . There is no society on earth ❺ when/where people are praised for running away in battle.

*vigorously 격렬하게   **disdain 경멸하다

Nobody has to teach a child to demand fair treatment; children protest unfairness vigorously and as soon as they can communicate. Nobody has to teach us ❶ _____(admire) a person who ❷ _____ (sacrifice) for a group; the admiration for duty is universal. Nobody has to teach us to disdain someone who betrays a friend or ❸ _____ (be) disloyal to a family or tribe. Nobody has to teach a child the difference between rules that are moral — "Don't hit"— and rules that are not — "Don't chew gum in school." These preferences also emerge from somewhere deep inside us. Just as we have a natural suite of emotions to help us love and be loved, so, too, we have a natural suite of moral emotions to make us ❹ _____ (disapprove) of people who violate social commitments, and approve of people who reinforce them. There is no society on earth where people ❺ _____ (praise) for running away in battle.

*vigorously 격렬하게   **disdain 경멸하다

Nobody has to teach a child to ❶ _____ _____ _____ (공정한 대우를 요구하다); children protest unfairness vigorously and as soon as they can communicate. Nobody has to teach us to admire a person who sacrifices for a group; ❷ _____ _____ _____ _____ (의무에 대한 존경) is universal. Nobody has to teach us to disdain someone who betrays a friend or is ❸ _____ _____ (~에 불충한) a family or tribe. Nobody has to teach a child the difference between rules that are moral — "Don't hit"— and rules that are not — "Don't chew gum in school." These preferences also ❹ _____ _____ (~에서 나온다) somewhere deep inside us. Just as we have a natural suite of emotions to help us love and be loved, so, too, we have a natural suite of moral emotions to make us disapprove of people who ❺ _____ _____ _____ (사회적 약속들을 어기다), and approve of people who reinforce them. There is no society on earth where people are praised for running away in battle.

*vigorously 격렬하게   **disdain 경멸하다

79

❶ In a recent presidential election, one of our local comedians compiled a list of all the recommendations being made by both the Democratic and Republican candidates for the presidency. ❷ He then switched them, and asked committed Democratic and Republican supporters about them. ❸ Democratic voters were told their candidate thought the American military needed to be strengthened, the national borders more tightly controlled, and voter identification efforts strengthened. ❹ As for those committed to the Republican candidate, he questioned them about their support of their candidate's (supposed) statements underscoring the need to expand national health care, create a more equitable tax system, and increase the minimum wage. ❺ In every case, the supporters did not question the veracity of the list. ❻ Instead, they began justifying their candidate's positions. ❼ It was as if it did not matter what the facts were; once they had made up their minds who they were voting for, their job was to support him, not question him.

*equitable 공정한 **veracity 진실성

❶ 최근의 대통령 선거에서, 우리 지역의 코미디언 중 한 명이 민주당과 공화당의 대통령 후보 두 명 모두가 만들고 있던 모든 제안 사항을 엮어서 목록을 만들었다. ❷ 그리고 나서 그는 그것들을 맞바꾸고 그것들에 대해 열성적인 민주당과 공화당의 지지자들에게 물었다. ❸ 민주당 투표자들은 자기 후보가 미군이 강화되어야 하고, 국경이 더 엄격하게 통제되어야 하며, 투표자 신원 확인 노력이 강화되어야 한다고 생각한다는 말을 들었다. ❹ 공화당 후보에게 열성적인 사람들에 관해 말하자면, 그는 그들에게 국민 건강 보험을 확대해야 하고, 더 공정한 조세 제도를 마련해야 하고, 최저 임금을 인상해야 할 필요성을 강조하는 그들의 후보의(가상의) 주장에 대한 그들의 지지에 대해 물었다. ❺ 모든 경우에, 지지자들은 그 목록의 진실성을 의심하지 않았다. ❻ 그 대신에, 그들은 자기 후보의 입장을 정당화하기 시작했다. ❼ 마치 사실이 무엇인지는 중요하지 않은 것 같았는데, 일단 자신이 누구에게 투표할지 결심하면, 그들의 임무는 그를 지지하는 것이지, 그를 심문하는 것이 아니었기 때문이다.

Word List

☐ **presidential election** 대통령 선거 ☐ **local** 지역의 ☐ **compile** 엮어서 만들다 ☐ **recommendation** 제안 (사항), 추천
☐ **candidate** 후보 ☐ **presidency** 대통령직 ☐ **switch** 맞바꾸다 ☐ **committed** 열성적인, 헌신적인 ☐ **voter** 투표자
☐ **strengthen** 강화하다 ☐ **national border** 국경 ☐ **tightly** 엄격하게 ☐ **identification** 신원 확인
☐ **supposed** 가상의, 소위[이른바] ~이라고 하는 ☐ **statement** 주장, 의견, 진술 ☐ **underscore** 강조하다 ☐ **expand** 확대하다
☐ **health care** 의료 서비스, 보건 ☐ **minimum wage** 최저임금 ☐ **justify** 정당화하다

• Word Test

1	compile		11	맞바꾸다	
2	candidate		12	대통령 선거	
3	minimum wage		13	주장, 의견, 진술	
4	committed		14	강화하다	
5	health care		15	투표자	
6	national border		16	신원 확인	
7	presidency		17	엄격하게	
8	recommendation		18	정당화하다	
9	supposed		19	확대하다	
10	underscore		20	지역의	

In a recent presidential election, one of our local comedians ❶ compiled/consented a list of all the recommendations being made by both the Democratic and Republican candidates for the presidency. He then switched them, and asked ❷ committed/uncommitted Democratic and Republican supporters about them. Democratic voters were told their candidate thought the American military needed to be strengthened, the national borders more tightly controlled, and voter identification efforts strengthened. As for ❸ that/those committed to the Republican candidate, he questioned them about their support of their candidate's (supposed) statements underscoring the need to expand national health care, create a more equitable tax system, and increase the minimum wage. In every case, the supporters did not question the veracity of the list. Instead, they began ❹ justifying/offending their candidate's positions. It was as if it did not matter what the facts were; once they had made up their minds who they were voting for, their job was to support him, not ❺ question/questioning him.

*equitable 공정한 **veracity 진실성

In a recent presidential election, one of our local comedians compiled a list of all the recommendations being made by both the Democratic and Republican candidates for the presidency. He then switched them, and asked committed Democratic and Republican supporters about them. Democratic voters ❶ _____ (tell) their candidate thought the American military needed to be strengthened, the national borders more tightly ❷ _____ (control), and voter identification efforts strengthened. As for those committed to the Republican candidate, he questioned them about their support of their candidate's (supposed) statements ❸ _____ (underscore) the need to expand national health care, create a more equitable tax system, and increase the minimum wage. In every case, the supporters did not question the veracity of the list. Instead, they began justifying their candidate's positions. It was as if it did not matter what the facts ❹ _____ (be); once they had made up their minds who they were voting for, their job was to support him, not question him.

*equitable 공정한 **veracity 진실성

In a recent presidential election, one of our local comedians compiled a list of all the recommendations being made by both the Democratic and Republican candidates for the presidency. He then switched them, and asked committed Democratic and Republican supporters about them. Democratic voters were told their candidate thought the American military needed to be strengthened, the national borders more tightly controlled, and voter identification efforts strengthened. ❶ _____ _____ (~에 관해 말하자면) those committed to the Republican candidate, he questioned them about their support of their candidate's (supposed) statements underscoring the need to expand national health care, create a more equitable tax system, and increase the minimum wage. ❷ _____ _____ _____ (모든 경우에), the supporters did not question the veracity of the list. Instead, they began justifying their candidate's positions. It was ❸ _____ _____ _____ _____ _____ _____ (마치 ~가 중요하지 않은 것 같았던) what the facts were; ❹ _____ _____ _____ _____ (일단 그들이 결심했다면) who they were voting for, their job was to support him, not question him.

*equitable 공정한 **veracity 진실성

❶ You may believe that all forms of negative thinking are unnecessary, extreme, and irrational. ❷ Nothing could be further from the truth. ❸ Quite often, you might experience unpleasant, tragic, and upsetting events in your life that you believe to be negative. ❹ As a result of these beliefs, you experience unpleasant emotions. ❺ If you are perceiving a situation accurately, your distressing emotions will serve a useful function for you. ❻ For example, if a close friend has died and you are extremely sad because you miss your close relationship, crying, grieving, and sadness will allow you to work through the difficult situation and incorporate it into your experience so that you can move on with your life. ❼ Only when the thoughts take on an unrealistically negative and distorted quality (e.g., "my life is over because my friend is gone; the same fate will soon befall me; I have nothing left to look forward to in my life") is it likely that you will experience emotions and behavioral reactions that are dysfunctional and self-defeating.

*befall (안 좋은 일이)닥치다　**dysfunctional 역기능적인

❶ 여러분은 모든 형태의 부정적인 생각이 불필요하고, 극단적이며, 비이성적이라고 믿을지도 모른다. ❷ 그보다 사실과 더 거리가 먼 것은 없을 것이다. ❸ 꽤 자주, 여러분은 부정적이라고 믿는 불쾌하고, 비극적이고, 속상하게 하는 사건들을 여러분의 삶에서 경험할지도 모른다. ❹ 이러한 믿음의 결과로, 여러분은 불쾌한 감정을 경험하게 된다. ❺ 만약 여러분이 상황을 정확하게 인식하고 있다면, 여러분의 괴로운 감정은 여러분에게 유용한 기능을 제공할 것이다. ❻ 예를 들어, 친한 친구가 죽어 친밀한 관계가 그리워 극도로 슬프다면, 여러분은 삶을 이어 나갈 수 있도록 울고, 비통해 하고, 슬퍼함으로써 어려운 상황을 이겨 내고 그것을 여러분의 경험의 일부로 포함할 수 있을 것이다. ❼ 생각이 비현실적으로 부정적이고 왜곡된 특성을 띨 때만(예를 들면, "내 친구가 사라졌기 때문에 내 인생은 끝났어. 같은 운명이 곧 내게 닥칠 거야. 내 인생에서 기대할 것이 아무것도 없어."와 같이) 여러분은 역기능적이고 자멸적인 감정과 행동 반응을 경험할 가능성이 있다.

Word List

□ **extreme** 극단적인　□ **irrational** 비이성적인　□ **further** 더 먼　□ **tragic** 비극적인　□ **upsetting** 속상하게 하는
□ **as a result of** ~의 결과로　□ **perceive** 인식하다, 감지하다　□ **accurately** 정확하게　□ **distressing** 괴로움을 주는, 고통스러운
□ **function** 기능　□ **grieve** 슬퍼하다　□ **incorporate** 포함하다, 결합하다　□ **take on** ~을 띠다, ~을 얻다
□ **unrealistically** 비현실적으로　□ **distort** 왜곡하다　□ **self-defeating** 자멸적인, 문제를 오히려 키우는

• Word Test

1	distressing	_____	9	기능	_____
2	irrational	_____	10	왜곡하다	_____
3	grieve	_____	11	정확하게	_____
4	self-defeating	_____	12	~의 결과로	_____
5	upsetting	_____	13	비현실적으로	_____
6	take on	_____	14	더 먼	_____
7	incorporate	_____	15	극단적인	_____
8	perceive	_____	16	비극적인	_____

You may believe that all forms of ❶ positive / negative thinking are unnecessary, extreme, and irrational. Nothing could be further from the truth. Quite often, you might experience unpleasant, tragic, and upsetting events in your life that you believe ❷ being / to be negative. As a result of these beliefs, you experience unpleasant emotions. If you are perceiving a situation accurately, your ❸ distressed / distressing emotions will serve a useful function for you. For example, if a close friend has died and you are extremely sad because you miss your close relationship, crying, grieving, and sadness will allow you to work through the difficult situation and ❹ compose / incorporate it into your experience so that you can move on with your life. Only when the thoughts take on an unrealistically negative and distorted quality (e.g., "my life is over because my friend is gone; the same fate will soon befall me; I have nothing left to look forward to in my life") is it likely ❺ that / which you will experience emotions and behavioral reactions that are dysfunctional and self-defeating.

*befall (안 좋은 일이) 닥치다   **dysfunctional 역기능적인

You may believe that all forms of negative thinking ❶ _____ (be) unnecessary, extreme, and irrational. Nothing could be further from the truth. Quite often, you might experience unpleasant, tragic, and upsetting events in your life that you believe to be negative. As a result of these beliefs, you experience unpleasant emotions. If you are perceiving a situation accurately, your distressing emotions will serve a useful function for you. For example, if a close friend ❷ _____ (die) and you are extremely sad because you miss your close relationship, crying, grieving, and sadness will allow you ❸ _____ (work) through the difficult situation and incorporate it into your experience so that you can move on with your life. Only when the thoughts take on an unrealistically negative and distorted quality (e.g., "my life is over because my friend ❹ _____ (go); the same fate will soon befall me; I have nothing left to look forward to in my life") is it likely that you will experience emotions and behavioral reactions that are dysfunctional and self-defeating.

*befall (안 좋은 일이) 닥치다   **dysfunctional 역기능적인

You may believe that all forms of negative thinking are unnecessary, extreme, and irrational. Nothing could be ❶ _____ _____ _____ _____ (사실과 더 거리가 먼). Quite often, you might experience unpleasant, tragic, and upsetting events in your life that you believe to be negative. As a result of these beliefs, you experience unpleasant emotions. If you are perceiving a situation accurately, your distressing emotions will ❷ _____ _____ _____ _____ (유용한 기능을 제공하다) for you. For example, if a close friend has died and you are extremely sad because you miss your close relationship, crying, grieving, and sadness will allow you to work through the difficult situation and incorporate it into your experience so that you can ❸ _____ _____ _____ _____ _____ (여러분의 삶을 이어 나가다). Only when the thoughts take on an unrealistically negative and distorted quality (e.g., "my life is over because my friend is gone; the same fate will soon befall me; I have nothing left to ❹ _____ _____ _____ (기대하다) in my life") is it likely that you will experience emotions and behavioral reactions that are dysfunctional and self-defeating.

*befall (안 좋은 일이) 닥치다   **dysfunctional 역기능적인

❶ Evolution theory is being challenged. ❷ Darwin saw evolution as a gradual process of natural selection and survival of the fittest as the most likely phenomenon. ❸ Now evolutionists such as paleontologists Niles Eldredge and Stephen Jay Gould argue that evolution is characterized by long periods of relative stability that are punctuated by sudden changes, followed by more stability, followed by more changes, and so on. ❹ One hypothesis on why this occurs is that changes in environment cause species to diversify and specialize into several new niches, creating new lineages. ❺ In Gould's theory, a species will be unchanged for thousands or hundreds of thousands of years and then suddenly something will happen that will change it (perhaps gene-splicing?) or even wipe it out. ❻ Gould's theory can be thought of as macroevolution — periodic sudden large changes, and the normal concept of gradual evolution can be thought of as microevolution — a continuous, almost unnoticeable succession of small changes.

*paleontologist 고생물학자　**niche (특정 종류의 생물이 살기에) 적합한 환경

❶ 진화론이 도전을 받고 있다. ❷ Darwin은 진화를 자연 선택의 점진적인 과정으로, 적자생존을 가장 있을 법한 현상으로 보았다. ❸ 그런데 고생물학자인 Niles Eldredge와 Stephen Jay Gould와 같은 진화론자는 진화는 갑작스러운 변화로 중단되는 상대적 안정의 긴 기간 다음에 더 큰 안정이 따르고 다시 더 많은 변화가 따르는 것 등이 특징이라고 주장한다. ❹ 이러한 일이 왜 발생하는지에 관한 한 가지 가설은 환경 변화로 인해 종이 다양해지고 몇 가지의 새로운 적합한 환경에 특화돼 새로운 계통이 만들어진다는 것이다. ❺ Gould의 이론에서는, 종은 수천 년, 혹은 수십만 년 동안 변하지 않을 것이며, 그러다 갑자기 그것을 변화시키거나(아마도 유전자 접합?) 심지어 멸종시킬 어떤 일이 발생할 것이다. ❻ Gould의 이론은 대진화, 즉 주기적이고 갑작스러운 큰 변화로 생각될 수 있고, 점진적 진화라는 일반적인 개념은 소진화, 즉 지속적이고 거의 눈에 띄지 않는 작은 변화의 연속으로 생각될 수 있다.

Word List

□ evolution 진화　□ challenge 도전하다　□ gradual 점진적인　□ natural selection 자연선택　□ survival of the fittest 적자생존
□ phenomenon 현상　□ characterize 특징을 나타내다　□ stability 안정　□ punctuate 중단시키다　□ hypothesis 가설
□ species (생물의) 종　□ diversify 다양해지다　□ specialize 특화하다　□ lineage 계통, 혈통　□ gene-splicing 유전자 접합
□ wipe out 멸종시키다　□ macroevolution 대진화　□ periodic 주기적인　□ microevolution 소진화　□ continuous 연속적인
□ unnoticeable 눈에 띄지 않는　□ succession 연속, 계속

• Word Test

1　unnoticeable _____
2　specialize _____
3　characterize _____
4　microevolution _____
5　hypothesis _____
6　periodic _____
7　survival of the fittest _____
8　gene-splicing _____
9　lineage _____
10　punctuate _____
11　macroevolution _____

12　현상 _____
13　자연선택 _____
14　연속, 계속 _____
15　점진적인 _____
16　연속적인 _____
17　멸종시키다 _____
18　(생물의) 종 _____
19　안정 _____
20　도전하다 _____
21　진화 _____
22　다양해지다 _____

Evolution theory is being challenged. Darwin saw evolution as a gradual process of natural selection and survival of the ❶ fit / fittest as the most likely phenomenon. Now evolutionists such as paleontologists Niles Eldredge and Stephen Jay Gould argue that evolution is characterized by long periods of relative stability that are punctuated by sudden changes, followed by more stability, followed by more changes, and so on. One hypothesis on why this occurs is ❷ that / what changes in environment cause species to diversify and specialize into several new niches, creating new lineages. In Gould's theory, a species will be unchanged for thousands or hundreds of thousands of years and then suddenly something will happen that will change it (perhaps gene-splicing?) or even wipe ❸ out it / it out . Gould's theory can be thought of as macroevolution — periodic sudden large changes, and the normal concept of ❹ abrupt / gradual evolution can be thought of as microevolution — a continuous, almost unnoticeable ❺ success / succession of small changes.

*paleontologist 고생물학자   **niche (특정 종류의 생물이 살기에) 적합한 환경

Evolution theory is being challenged. Darwin saw evolution as a gradual process of natural selection and survival of the fittest as the most likely phenomenon. Now evolutionists such as paleontologists Niles Eldredge and Stephen Jay Gould argue that evolution ❶ _____(characterize) by long periods of relative stability that ❷ _____(be) punctuated by sudden changes, followed by more stability, followed by more changes, and so on. One hypothesis on why this ❸ _____(occur) is that changes in environment cause species to diversify and specialize into several new niches, ❹ _____(create) new lineages. In Gould's theory, a species will be unchanged for thousands or hundreds of thousands of years and then suddenly something will happen that will change it (perhaps gene-splicing?) or even ❺ _____(wipe) it out. Gould's theory can be thought of as macroevolution — periodic sudden large changes, and the normal concept of gradual evolution can be thought of as microevolution — a continuous, almost unnoticeable succession of small changes.

*paleontologist 고생물학자   **niche (특정 종류의 생물이 살기에) 적합한 환경

Evolution theory ❶ _____ _____ _____ (도전을 받고 있다). Darwin saw evolution as a gradual process of natural selection and survival of the fittest ❷ _____ _____ _____ _____ _____ (가장 있을 법한 현상으로). Now evolutionists such as paleontologists Niles Eldredge and Stephen Jay Gould argue that evolution is characterized by long periods of relative stability that are punctuated by sudden changes, followed by more stability, followed by more changes, and so on. One hypothesis on why this occurs is that changes in environment cause species to diversify and specialize into several new niches, creating new lineages. In Gould's theory, a species will be unchanged for thousands or ❸ _____ _____ _____ _____ _____ (수십만 년) and then suddenly something will happen that will change it (perhaps gene-splicing?) or ❹ _____ _____ _____ _____ (심지어 그것을 멸종시키다). Gould's theory can be thought of as macroevolution — periodic sudden large changes, and the normal concept of gradual evolution can be thought of as microevolution — a continuous, almost unnoticeable succession of small changes.

*paleontologist 고생물학자   **niche (특정 종류의 생물이 살기에) 적합한 환경

밑줄 친 There is no society on earth where people are praised for running away in battle.이 다음 글에서 의미하는 바로 가장 적절한 것은?

Nobody has to teach a child to demand fair treatment; children protest unfairness vigorously and as soon as they can communicate. Nobody has to teach us to admire a person who sacrifices for a group; the admiration for duty is universal. Nobody has to teach us to disdain someone who betrays a friend or is disloyal to a family or tribe. Nobody has to teach a child the difference between rules that are moral — "Don't hit" — and rules that are not — "Don't chew gum in school." These preferences also emerge from somewhere deep inside us. Just as we have a natural suite of emotions to help us love and be loved, so, too, we have a natural suite of moral emotions to make us disapprove of people who violate social commitments, and approve of people who reinforce them. There is no society on earth where people are praised for running away in battle.

*vigorously 격렬하게 **disdain 경멸하다

① Moral sense is not naturally gained, so constant education is needed.
② The sense of morality is something inherent rather than acquired.
③ Moral emotions can be strengthened by doing our duties.
④ Nobody is accused of their being immoral in a life-threatening situation.
⑤ Betrayal is not an innate human trait, but something learned from our environment.

다음 글의 내용과 일치하지 <u>않는</u> 것은?

In a recent presidential election, one of our local comedians compiled a list of all the recommendations being made by both the Democratic and Republican candidates for the presidency. He then switched them, and asked committed Democratic and Republican supporters about them. Democratic voters were told their candidate thought the American military needed to be strengthened, the national borders more tightly controlled, and voter identification efforts strengthened. As for those committed to the Republican candidate, he questioned them about their support of their candidate's (supposed) statements underscoring the need to expand national health care, create a more equitable tax system, and increase the minimum wage. In every case, the supporters did not question the veracity of the list. Instead, they began justifying their candidate's positions. It was as if it did not matter what the facts were; once they had made up their minds who they were voting for, their job was to support him, not question him.

*equitable 공정한 **veracity 진실성

① 한 코미디언이 민주당과 공화당 대통령 후보의 제안 사항을 목록으로 만들었다.
② 민주당 지지자들은 민주당 대통령 후보가 제안한 사항에 대해 질문을 받았다.
③ 민주당 지지자들은 자신의 후보가 미군이 강화되어야 한다고 생각한다는 말을 들었다.
④ 공화당 지지자들은 자신의 후보가 더 공정한 조세 제도를 마련해야 한다고 주장하는 것에 대해 지지하는지 질문을 받았다.
⑤ 지지자들은 자신이 지지하는 후보에 대해 심문하려 하지 않고 지지하는 것이 임무라고 여긴다.

03 6강 3번

다음 글의 밑줄 친 부분 중, 어법상 틀린 것은?

You may believe that all forms of negative thinking ① are unnecessary, extreme, and irrational. Nothing could be further from the truth. Quite often, you might experience unpleasant, tragic, and upsetting events in your life that you believe ② to be negative. As a result of these beliefs, you experience unpleasant emotions. If you are perceiving a situation ③ accurately, your distressing emotions will serve a useful function for you. For example, if a close friend has died and you are extremely sad because you miss your close relationship, crying, grieving, and sadness will allow you to work through the difficult situation and ④ incorporate it into your experience so that you can move on with your life. Only when the thoughts take on an unrealistically negative and distorted quality (e.g., "my life is over because my friend is gone; the same fate will soon befall me; I have nothing left to look forward to in my life") is it likely that you will experience emotions and behavioral reactions ⑤ what are dysfunctional and self-defeating.

*befall (안 좋은 일이) 닥치다 **dysfunctional 역기능적인

04 6강 4번

주어진 글 다음에 이어질 글의 순서로 가장 적절한 것은?

Evolution theory is being challenged. Darwin saw evolution as a gradual process of natural selection and survival of the fittest as the most likely phenomenon.

(A) One hypothesis on why this occurs is that changes in environment cause species to diversify and specialize into several new niches, creating new lineages. In Gould's theory, a species will be unchanged for thousands or hundreds of thousands of years and then suddenly something will happen that will change it (perhaps gene-splicing?) or even wipe it out.

(B) Now evolutionists such as paleontologists Niles Eldredge and Stephen Jay Gould argue that evolution is characterized by long periods of relative stability that are punctuated by sudden changes, followed by more stability, followed by more changes, and so on.

(C) Gould's theory can be thought of as macroevolution — periodic sudden large changes, and the normal concept of gradual evolution can be thought of as microevolution — a continuous, almost unnoticeable succession of small changes.

*paleontologist 고생물학자 **niche (특정 종류의 생물이 살기에) 적합한 환경

① (A) – (C) – (B)　　　② (B) – (A) – (C)
③ (B) – (C) – (A)　　　④ (C) – (A) – (B)
⑤ (C) – (B) – (A)

05 6강 1번

다음 빈칸에 들어갈 말로 가장 적절한 것은?

Nobody has to teach a child to demand fair treatment; children protest unfairness vigorously and as soon as they can communicate. Nobody has to teach us to admire a person who sacrifices for a group; the admiration for duty is universal. Nobody has to teach us to disdain someone who betrays a friend or is disloyal to a family or tribe. Nobody has to teach a child the difference between rules that are moral — "Don't hit"— and rules that are not — "Don't chew gum in school." These preferences also emerge from somewhere deep inside us. Just as we have a natural suite of emotions to help us love and be loved, so, too, we have a natural suite of _____ emotions to make us disapprove of people who violate social commitments, and approve of people who reinforce them. There is no society on earth where people are praised for running away in battle.

* vigorously 격렬하게 **disdain 경멸하다

① guilty   ② moral
③ extreme   ④ suppressed
⑤ contradictory

06 6강 2번

글의 흐름으로 보아, 주어진 문장이 들어가기에 가장 적절한 곳은?

> Instead, they began justifying their candidate's positions.

In a recent presidential election, one of our local comedians compiled a list of all the recommendations being made by both the Democratic and Republican candidates for the presidency. (①) He then switched them, and asked committed Democratic and Republican supporters about them. (②) Democratic voters were told their candidate thought the American military needed to be strengthened, the national borders more tightly controlled, and voter identification efforts strengthened. (③) As for those committed to the Republican candidate, he questioned them about their support of their candidate's (supposed) statements underscoring the need to expand national health care, create a more equitable tax system, and increase the minimum wage. (④) In every case, the supporters did not question the veracity of the list. (⑤) It was as if it did not matter what the facts were; once they had made up their minds who they were voting for, their job was to support him, not question him.

*equitable 공정한 **veracity 진실성

07 6강 3번

다음 글의 내용을 한 문장으로 요약하고자 한다. 빈칸 (A), (B)에 들어갈 말로 가장 적절한 것은?

You may believe that all forms of negative thinking are unnecessary, extreme, and irrational. Nothing could be further from the truth. Quite often, you might experience unpleasant, tragic, and upsetting events in your life that you believe to be negative. As a result of these beliefs, you experience unpleasant emotions. If you are perceiving a situation accurately, your distressing emotions will serve a useful function for you. For example, if a close friend has died and you are extremely sad because you miss your close relationship, crying, grieving, and sadness will allow you to work through the difficult situation and incorporate it into your experience so that you can move on with your life. Only when the thoughts take on an unrealistically negative and distorted quality (e.g., "my life is over because my friend is gone; the same fate will soon befall me; I have nothing left to look forward to in my life") is it likely that you will experience emotions and behavioral reactions that are dysfunctional and self-defeating.

*befall (안 좋은 일이) 닥치다　**dysfunctional 역기능적인

⬇

Although it is commonly believed that negative thinking has a ____(A)____ effect on people, negative thinking can be helpful for personal growth unless it is overly ____(B)____.

	(A)		(B)
①	harmful	……	enriching
②	harmful	……	destructive
③	damaging	……	enriching
④	beneficial	……	destructive
⑤	beneficial	……	reassuring

08 6강 4번

다음 글에서 전체 흐름과 관계 <u>없는</u> 문장은?

Evolution theory is being challenged. Darwin saw evolution as a gradual process of natural selection and survival of the fittest as the most likely phenomenon. ① Now evolutionists such as paleontologists Niles Eldredge and Stephen Jay Gould argue that evolution is characterized by long periods of relative stability that are punctuated by sudden changes, followed by more stability, followed by more changes, and so on. ② One hypothesis on why this occurs is that changes in environment cause species to diversify and specialize into several new niches, creating new lineages. ③ This has led to the controversial issue of covering the strengths and weaknesses of the theory of evolution in public schools. ④ In Gould's theory, a species will be unchanged for thousands or hundreds of thousands of years and then suddenly something will happen that will change it (perhaps gene-splicing?) or even wipe it out. ⑤ Gould's theory can be thought of as macroevolution — periodic sudden large changes, and the normal concept of gradual evolution can be thought of as microevolution — a continuous, almost unnoticeable succession of small changes.

*paleontologist 고생물학자　**niche (특정 종류의 생물이 살기에) 적합한 환경

Nobody has to teach a child to demand fair treatment; children protest unfairness vigorously and as soon as they can communicate. Nobody has to teach us to admire a person who sacrifices for a group; the admiration for duty is universal. Nobody has to teach us to disdain someone who betrays a friend or is disloyal to a family or tribe. Nobody has to teach a child the difference between rules that are moral — "Don't hit"— and rules that are not — "Don't chew gum in school." These preferences also emerge from somewhere deep inside us. Just as we have a natural suite of emotions to help us love and be loved, so, too, we have a natural suite of moral emotions to make us disapprove of people who violate social commitments, and _____ of people who reinforce them. There is no society on earth where people are praised for running away in battle.

*vigorously 격렬하게 **disdain 경멸하다

09 윗글에서 다음 질문에 대한 답을 찾아 우리말로 쓰시오. (20자 내외)

Q: Why don't people have to be taught to admire a person who sacrifices for a group?

A: _____

10 윗글의 빈칸에 들어갈 단어를 영영 뜻풀이를 참고하여 쓰시오. (단, 주어진 글자로 시작할 것)

> to have a positive feeling towards someone or something that you consider to be good or suitable

a _____

In a recent presidential election, one of our local comedians compiled a list of all the recommendations ① being made by both the Democratic and Republican candidates for the presidency. He then switched them, and asked committed Democratic and Republican supporters about them. Democratic voters were told their candidate thought the American military needed ② to strengthen, the national borders more tightly controlled, and voter identification efforts strengthened. As for ③ those committed to the Republican candidate, he questioned them about their support of their candidate's (supposed) statements underscoring the need to expand national health care, create a more equitable tax system, and ④ increase the minimum wage. In every case, the supporters did not question the veracity of the list. Instead, they began justifying their candidate's positions. It was as if it did not matter ⑤ that the facts were; once they had made up their minds who they were voting for, their job was to support him, not question him.

*equitable 공정한 **veracity 진실성

11 윗글의 밑줄 친 부분 중, 어법상 틀린 것을 2개 찾아 그 번호를 쓰고 고쳐 쓰시오.

(1) _____ → _____

(2) _____ → _____

12 윗글의 내용을 한 문장으로 요약하려고 한다. 보기 의 단어를 순서대로 배열하여 문장을 완성하시오.

> 보기   their / made / supported / them / unconditionally / what / have / candidates / suggestions

> The supporters of each party, regardless of
> _____ _____ _____ _____ _____, _____
> _____ _____ _____ since the moment when the supporters chose them.

You may believe that all forms of negative thinking are unnecessary, extreme, and ① irrational. Nothing could be further from the truth. Quite often, you might experience unpleasant, tragic, and upsetting events in your life that you believe to be ② negative. As a result of these beliefs, you experience unpleasant emotions. If you are perceiving a situation accurately, your distressing emotions will serve a ③ useless function for you. For example, if a close friend has died and you are extremely sad because you miss your close relationship, crying, grieving, and sadness will allow you to work through the difficult situation and ④ incorporate it into your experience so that you can move on with your life. Only when the thoughts take on an unrealistically negative and distorted quality (e.g., "my life is over because my friend is gone; the ⑤ same fate will soon befall me; I have nothing left to look forward to in my life") 여러분은 역기능적이고 자멸적인 감정과 행동 반응을 경험할 가능성이 있다.

*befall (안 좋은 일이) 닥치다 **dysfunctional 역기능적인

13 윗글의 밑줄 친 부분 중, 문맥상 어색한 것을 1개 찾아 그 번호를 쓰고 고쳐 쓰시오.

_____ → _____

14 윗글의 밑줄 친 우리말 의미와 일치하도록 보기 의 단어를 활용하여 조건 에 맞게 문장을 완성하시오.

> 보기 self-defeating/emotions/dysfunctional / behavioral reactions / will experience

> 조건 · be likely that 구문을 사용할 것
> · 관계대명사 that을 사용할 것
> · 총 16단어로 쓸 것

_____ .

Evolution theory is being challenged. Darwin saw evolution as a gradual process of natural selection and survival of the fittest as the most likely phenomenon. Now evolutionists such as paleontologists Niles Eldredge and Stephen Jay Gould argue that evolution is characterized by long periods of relative stability that are punctuated by sudden changes, followed by more stability, followed by more changes, and so on. One hypothesis on why this occurs is that changes in environment cause species to diversify and specialize into several new niches, creating new lineages. In Gould's theory, a species will be unchanged for thousands or hundreds of thousands of years and then suddenly something will happen that will change it (perhaps gene-splicing?) or even wipe it out. Gould's theory can be thought of as macroevolution — periodic sudden large changes, and the normal concept of gradual evolution can be thought of as microevolution — a continuous, almost unnoticeable succession of small changes.

*paleontologist 고생물학자 **niche (특정 종류의 생물이 살기에) 적합한 환경

15 윗글의 밑줄 친 this가 가리키는 것을 본문에서 찾아 우리말로 쓰시오. (50자 내외)

_____

_____

16 윗글의 내용을 한 문장으로 요약하려고 한다. 빈칸 (A)와 (B)에 들어갈 알맞은 말을 보기 에서 찾아 쓰시오.

> 보기 proper /steady / complicated / expected / subtle / abrupt

> Whereas Darwin's theory of evolution can be regarded as microevolution, a(n) ____(A)____ process of natural selection, that of Gould can be regarded as macroevolution, defined by periodic ____(B)____ large changes.

(A) _____   (B) _____

❶ If you're stuck developing an idea or even thinking of one, get unstuck by literally getting away from your desk. ❷ Go for a walk. ❸ Exercise. ❹ Bring your work somewhere else. ❺ Physical movement has been shown to have a positive effect on creative thinking. ❻ The philosopher and author Henry Thoreau claimed that his thoughts began to flow "the moment my legs began to move." ❼ Now scientists have discovered that taking part in regular exercise such as going for a walk or riding a bike really does improve creative thought. ❽ Professor Lorenza Colzato, a cognitive psychologist at Leiden University in the Netherlands, found in her 2013 study that people who exercised four times a week were able to think more creatively than those with a more sedentary lifestyle. ❾ One of my course sessions, an observation lab, is held outdoors, and the students love the walk and change in environment as they brainstorm possible solutions while moving across our campus.

*sedentary 주로 앉아서 지내는

❶ 만약 여러분이 아이디어 하나를 개발하거나 심지어 머리에 떠올리거나 할 때 막힌다면, 말 그대로 책상에서 벗어남으로써 빠져나가라. ❷ 산책하러 가라. ❸ 운동하라. ❹ 여러분의 일을 다른 곳으로 가져가라. ❺ 신체적인 움직임이 창의적인 사고에 긍정적인 영향을 미치는 것으로 밝혀졌다. ❻ 철학자이자 작가인 Henry Thoreau는 '내 다리가 움직이기 시작하는 순간' 생각이 흘러나오기 시작했다고 주장했다. ❼ 이제 과학자들은 산책하러 가거나 자전거를 타는 것과 같은 규칙적인 운동에 참여하는 것이 창의적인 사고를 실제로 정말 향상시킨다는 것을 발견했다. ❽ 네덜란드의 Leiden 대학교의 인지 심리학자인 Lorenza Colzato 교수는 자신의 2013년 연구에서, 일주일에 4번 운동한 사람들이 주로 앉아서 지내는 시간이 더 많은 생활 방식을 가진 사람들보다 창의적으로 생각할 수 있다는 것을 알아냈다. ❾ 내 과목 수업 중 하나인 관찰 실험은 야외에서 열리는데, 학생들은 교정을 가로질러 이동하는 동안 가능한 해결책을 브레인스토밍하면서 산책과 환경의 변화를 매우 좋아한다.

Word List

□ stuck 막힌, 꼼짝하지 못하는   □ get unstuck 빠져나가다   □ literally 말 그대로   □ effect 영향   □ philosopher 철학자
□ claim 주장하다   □ cognitive 인지의   □ session (수업) 시간   □ observation 관찰   □ lab (= laboratory) 실험, 실험실
□ outdoors 야외에서   □ solution 해결책

• Word Test

1	cognitive		7	해결책	
2	effect		8	주장하다	
3	outdoors		9	관찰	
4	get unstuck		10	철학자	
5	session		11	말 그대로	
6	lab (= laboratory)		12	막힌, 꼼짝하지 못하는	

If you're stuck developing an idea or even thinking of one, get unstuck by ❶ literary/literally getting away from your desk. Go for a walk. Exercise. Bring your work somewhere else. ❷ Physical / Psychological movement has been shown to have a positive effect on creative thinking. The philosopher and author Henry Thoreau claimed that his thoughts began to flow "the moment my legs began to move." Now scientists have discovered that taking part in regular exercise such as going for a walk or riding a bike really ❸ do / does improve creative thought. Professor Lorenza Colzato, a cognitive psychologist at Leiden University in the Netherlands, found in her 2013 study ❹ that / when people who exercised four times a week were able to think more creatively than ❺ that / those with a more sedentary lifestyle. One of my course sessions, an observation lab, is held outdoors, and the students love the walk and change in environment as they brainstorm possible solutions while moving across our campus.

*sedentary 주로 앉아서 지내는

If you're stuck ❶ _____ (develop) an idea or even thinking of one, get unstuck by literally getting away from your desk. Go for a walk. Exercise. Bring your work somewhere else. Physical movement ❷ _____ (show) to have a positive effect on creative thinking. The philosopher and author Henry Thoreau claimed that his thoughts began to flow "the moment my legs began to move." Now scientists have discovered that taking part in regular exercise such as going for a walk or riding a bike really does improve creative thought. Professor Lorenza Colzato, a cognitive psychologist at Leiden University in the Netherlands, found in her 2013 study that people who exercised four times a week ❸ _____ (be) able to think more creatively than those with a more sedentary lifestyle. One of my course sessions, an observation lab, ❹ _____ (hold) outdoors, and the students love the walk and change in environment as they brainstorm possible solutions while ❺ _____ (move) across our campus.

*sedentary 주로 앉아서 지내는

If you're stuck developing an idea or even thinking of one, ❶ _____ _____ (빠져나가라) by literally getting away from your desk. Go for a walk. Exercise. Bring your work somewhere else. Physical movement has been shown to ❷ _____ _____ _____ _____ _____ (~에 긍정적인 영향을 미친다) creative thinking. The philosopher and author Henry Thoreau claimed that his thoughts began to flow "the moment my legs began to move." Now scientists have discovered that ❸ _____ _____ _____ (~에 참여하는 것) regular exercise such as going for a walk or riding a bike really does improve creative thought. Professor Lorenza Colzato, a cognitive psychologist at Leiden University in the Netherlands, found in her 2013 study that people who exercised ❹ _____ _____ _____ _____ (일주일에 4번) were able to think more creatively than those with a more sedentary lifestyle. One of my course sessions, an observation lab, is held outdoors, and the students love the walk and change in environment as they brainstorm possible solutions while moving across our campus.

*sedentary 주로 앉아서 지내는

❶ Cosmology would not exist as a subject unless there were such a thing as "the universe" to explain. ❷ Instead of finding that space is filled with a dog's breakfast of unrelated bric-a-brac, astronomers see an orchestrated and coherent unity. ❸ On the largest scale of size there is order and uniformity. ❹ Stars and galaxies billions of light-years away closely resemble those in our astronomical backyard and are distributed in much the same way everywhere. ❺ Their compositions and motions are similar. ❻ The laws of physics appear to be identical as far out in space as our instruments can penetrate. ❼ In short, there is cosmos rather than chaos. ❽ This basic fact is crucial for our existence: life could not emerge, still less evolve to the point of intelligence, in chaos. ❾ It is also — or at least it was until recently — deeply mysterious. ❿ Why should the totality of things be organized so systematically? ⓫ To find the answer to this intriguing question, we need to understand how the universe began and work out how it evolved over billions of years to attain its present orderly and life-encouraging form.

*cosmology 우주론 **bric-a-brac 장식품 ***penetrate 침투하다

❶ 설명해야 할 '우주'와 같은 것이 있지 않다면 우주론은 하나의 학과목으로서 존재하지 않을 것이다. ❷ 우주 공간이 관련이 없는 장식품의 쓰레기 더미로 채워져 있다는 것을 발견하는 대신, 천문학자들은 체계적이고 일관적인 통일성을 본다. ❸ 최대 규모의 크기로 질서와 균일성이 존재한다. ❹ 수십억 광년 떨어진 별과 은하가 우리의 천문학적 뒷마당에 있는 것들과 매우 유사하며 모든 곳에서 매우 동일한 방식으로 분포되어 있다. ❺ 그들의 구성과 움직임은 비슷하다. ❻ 물리학의 법칙은 우리의 도구가 침투할 수 있는 한 우주 바깥 멀리에서도 동일한 것 같다. ❼ 요컨대 혼돈보다는 질서가 있다. ❽ 이 기본적인 사실은 우리의 존재에 매우 중요한데, 혼돈 속에서는 생명체가 출현할 수 없고, 더구나 지능이라고 할 정도로 진화할 수 없는 것이다. ❾ 그것은 또한 매우 신비로우며, 적어도 최근까지는 그랬다. ❿ 왜 모든 것이 그렇게 체계적으로 구성되어야 할까? ⓫ 이 흥미로운 질문에 대한 답을 찾기 위해서, 우리는 우주가 어떻게 시작되었는지 이해하고 그것이 어떻게 수십억 년에 걸쳐 진화하여 현재의 질서 있고 생명을 촉진하는 형태를 이루게 되었는지 알아낼 필요가 있다.

Word List

□ a dog's breakfast 쓰레기 더미, 더러운 것   □ unrelated 관련이 없는   □ astronomer 천문학자   □ orchestrated 체계적인, 조직화된
□ coherent 일관적인   □ unity 통일성   □ scale 규모, 눈금, 척도   □ uniformity 균일성   □ galaxy 은하   □ distribute 분포시키다
□ composition 구성   □ cosmos 질서, 우주   □ chaos 혼돈   □ crucial 매우 중요한   □ emerge 출현하다
□ still less 더구나[하물며] ~은 아닌   □ to the point of ~이라고 할 정도로   □ totality 전체, 총수   □ systematically 체계적으로
□ intriguing 흥미로운   □ work out 알아내다, 해결하다   □ attain 이루다, 도달하다

• Word Test

1 still less	12 일관적인	
2 to the point of	13 질서, 우주	
3 crucial	14 통일성	
4 intriguing	15 이루다, 도달하다	
5 orchestrated	16 관련이 없는	
6 uniformity	17 혼돈	
7 composition	18 출현하다	
8 a dog's breakfast	19 전체, 총수	
9 galaxy	20 천문학자	
10 distribute	21 체계적으로	
11 work out	22 규모, 눈금, 척도	

Cosmology would not exist as a subject ❶ [if / unless] there were such a thing as "the universe" to explain. ❷ [Instead of / In spite of] finding that space is filled with a dog's breakfast of unrelated bric-a-brac, astronomers see an orchestrated and coherent unity. On the largest scale of size there is order and uniformity. Stars and galaxies billions of light-years away closely resemble those in our astronomical backyard and are distributed in much the same way everywhere. Their compositions and motions are similar. The laws of physics appear to be identical as far out in space ❸ [to / as] our instruments can penetrate. In short, there is cosmos rather than chaos. This basic fact is ❹ [cruel / crucial] for our existence: life could not emerge, still less evolve to the point of intelligence, in chaos. It is also — or at least it was until recently — deeply mysterious. Why should the totality of things be organized so systematically? To find the answer to this intriguing question, we need to understand how the universe began and work out how it evolved over billions of years to attain ❺ [its / their] present orderly and life-encouraging form.

*cosmology 우주론 **bric-a-brac 장식품 ***penetrate 침투하다

Cosmology would not exist as a subject unless there were such a thing as "the universe" ❶ _____ (explain). Instead of finding that space is filled with a dog's breakfast of unrelated bric-a-brac, astronomers see an orchestrated and coherent unity. On the largest scale of size there is order and uniformity. Stars and galaxies billions of light-years away closely ❷ _____ (resemble) those in our astronomical backyard and ❸ _____ (distribute) in much the same way everywhere. Their compositions and motions are similar. The laws of physics appear to be identical as far out in space as our instruments can penetrate. In short, there is cosmos rather than chaos. This basic fact is crucial for our existence: life could not emerge, still less ❹ _____ (evolve) to the point of intelligence, in chaos. It is also — or at least it was until recently — deeply mysterious. Why should the totality of things be organized so systematically? To find the answer to this intriguing question, we need to understand how the universe began and work out how it evolved over billions of years ❺ _____ (attain) its present orderly and life-encouraging form.

*cosmology 우주론 **bric-a-brac 장식품 ***penetrate 침투하다

Cosmology would not exist as a subject unless there were ❶ _____ _____ _____ _____ (~와 같은 것) "the universe" to explain. Instead of finding that space is filled with a dog's breakfast of unrelated bric-a-brac, astronomers see an orchestrated and coherent unity. ❷ _____ _____ _____ _____ _____ _____ (최대 규모의 크기로) there is order and uniformity. Stars and galaxies billions of light-years away closely resemble those in our astronomical backyard and are distributed ❸ _____ _____ _____ _____ _____ (매우 동일한 방식으로) everywhere. Their compositions and motions are similar. The laws of physics appear to be identical as far out in space as our instruments can penetrate. In short, there is cosmos ❹ _____ _____ (~보다는) chaos. This basic fact is crucial for our existence: life could not emerge, still less evolve to the point of intelligence, in chaos. It is also — or at least it was until recently — deeply mysterious. Why should the totality of things be organized so systematically? To find the answer to this intriguing question, we need to understand how the universe began and work out how it evolved over billions of years to attain its present orderly and life-encouraging form.

*cosmology 우주론 **bric-a-brac 장식품 ***penetrate 침투하다

❶ Ideally, business requires a stable environment within which to operate. ❷ Yet, the framework of law which governs business activities is subject to constant change. ❸ The burden of keeping up to date may be eased slightly by making use of professional people such as an accountant or solicitor to advise on the latest developments in such areas as tax or company law. ❹ Nevertheless, the businessman will still need to keep himself informed of general legal changes which will affect his day-to-day running of the business. ❺ If he employs others in his business, he will need to keep up to date on such matters as health and safety at work, the rights of his employees and his duties as an employer. ❻ If he sells goods direct to the consumer, he must be aware of changes in consumer protection law. ❼ Almost every aspect of his business will be subject to legal regulation and the law could always change.

*solicitor 사무 변호사

❶ 이상적으로 말해, 사업은 운영될 수 있는 안정적인 환경이 필요하다. ❷ 하지만 사업 활동을 통제하는 법률 체계는 끊임없는 변화에 영향을 받는다. ❸ 세법이나 회사법과 같은 분야에서의 최근의 진전 상황들에 대해 자문을 해 줄 회계사나 사무 변호사와 같은 전문직 종사자를 활용함으로써 최신 정보를 계속 알아야 하는 부담이 조금 완화될 수도 있다. ❹ 그럼에도 불구하고, 사업가는 여전히 매일매일의 사업 운영에 영향을 미칠 전반적인 법률의 변화에 대해 스스로 계속 알아야 할 필요가 있을 것이다. ❺ 만약 그가 자신의 회사에 다른 이들을 고용 한다면, 그는 직장에서의 보건과 안전, 피고용인의 권리, 그리고 고용주로서의 자신의 의무와 같은 문제들에 관한 최신 정보를 계속 알아야 할 필요가 있을 것이다. ❻ 그가 소비자에게 직접 상품을 판매하는 경우에는 그는 소비자 보호법에서의 변화를 인지해야 한다. ❼ 그가 하는 사업의 거의 모든 측면이 법 규정의 영향을 받을 것이며 그 법은 항상 바뀔 수 있다.

Word List

□ **stable** 안정적인　□ **operate** 운영되다, 운영하다　□ **framework** 체계, 틀　□ **govern** 통제하다, 지배하다
□ **be subject to** ~에[의] 영향을 받다　□ **constant** 끊임없는, 지속적인　□ **burden** 부담
□ **keep up to date** 최신 정보를 계속 알다[유지하다]　□ **ease** 완화하다, 덜다　□ **slightly** 조금, 약간　□ **make use of** ~을 활용하다
□ **accountant** 회계사　□ **informed** 잘 아는　□ **legal** 법률(상)의, 법의, 합법적인　□ **affect** 영향을 미치다　□ **regulation** 규정, 규제

• Word Test

1	constant		9	체계, 틀
2	make use of		10	법률(상)의, 법의, 합법적인
3	informed		11	규정, 규제
4	operate		12	완화하다, 덜다
5	keep up to date		13	회계사
6	govern		14	안정적인
7	be subject to		15	조금, 약간
8	affect		16	부담

Ideally, business requires a stable environment within ❶ that / which to operate. Yet, the framework of law which governs business activities is subject to constant change. The burden of keeping up to date may be eased slightly by making use of professional people such as an accountant or solicitor to advise on the latest developments in such areas as tax or company law. ❷ Nevertheless/Consequently , the businessman will still need to keep himself ❸ inform / informed of general legal changes ❹ what / which will affect his day-to-day running of the business. If he employs others in his business, he will need to keep up to date on such matters as health and safety at work, the rights of his employees and his duties as an employer. If he sells goods ❺ direct / indirect to the consumer, he must be aware of changes in consumer protection law. Almost every aspect of his business will be subject to legal regulation and the law could always change.

*solicitor 사무 변호사

Ideally, business ❶ _____ (require) a stable environment within which to operate. Yet, the framework of law which governs business activities ❷ _____ (be) subject to constant change. The burden of keeping up to date may ❸ _____ (ease) slightly by making use of professional people such as an accountant or solicitor to advise on the latest developments in such areas as tax or company law. Nevertheless, the businessman will still need to keep himself informed of general legal changes which will affect his day-to-day running of the business. If he ❹ _____ (employ) others in his business, he will need to keep up to date on such matters as health and safety at work, the rights of his employees and his duties as an employer. If he ❺ _____ (sell) goods direct to the consumer, he must be aware of changes in consumer protection law. Almost every aspect of his business will be subject to legal regulation and the law could always change.

*solicitor 사무 변호사

Ideally, business requires a stable environment within which to operate. Yet, the framework of law which governs business activities ❶ _____ _____ _____ (~에 영향을 받는다) constant change. The burden of keeping up to date may be eased slightly ❷ _____ _____ _____ _____ (~을 활용함으로써) professional people such as an accountant or solicitor to advise on the latest developments in such areas as tax or company law. Nevertheless, the businessman will still need to keep himself informed of general legal changes which will affect his day-to-day running of the business. If he employs others in his business, he will need to ❸ _____ _____ _____ _____ (최신 정보를 계속 알다) on such matters as health and safety at work, the rights of his employees and his duties as an employer. If he sells goods direct to the consumer, he must ❹ _____ _____ _____ (~을 인지하다) changes in consumer protection law. Almost every aspect of his business will be subject to legal regulation and the law could always change.

*solicitor 사무 변호사

❶ In absolute terms, the overall demand for doctors and teachers is much larger than that for professional athletes. ❷ Education and health care make up huge chunks of the US economy — health care, measured as a percentage of GDP, is in the double digits and growing. ❸ By contrast, despite the attention paid to it, professional sports is nowhere near as big. ❹ In relation to the number of practitioners in each field, however, the demand for athletes' services is much larger than in either health care or education. ❺ The source of that demand is that hundreds of millions of people enjoy watching these sports, whether in person or on television. ❻ Fans will pay as much as hundreds of dollars per ticket to attend, while advertisers will pay literally billions of dollars to broadcasters that can deliver mass audiences for sports. ❼ The world might well be a better place if people paid less attention to spectator sports and more to reading, hiking, declaiming poetry, or practising Zen meditation, but the fact is that at the current stage of human development large numbers of people do enjoy pro sports, and that creates significant income for the industry.

*chunk 부분, 상당한 양 **declaim 낭독하다 ***Zen meditation 참선

❶ 절대적 관점에서 보면, 의사와 교사에 대한 전반적인 수요는 프로 운동선수에 대한 전반적인 수요보다 훨씬 더 많다. ❷ 교육과 의료 서비스는 미국 경제의 거대한 부분을 차지하고 있는데, GDP 비율로 측정된 의료 서비스는 두 자릿수이며 증가하고 있다. ❸ 반면에, 프로 스포츠는, 그것에 집중된 관심에도 불구하고, 크기가 그에 훨씬 미치지 못한다. ❹ 그러나 각 분야의 종사자 수와 비교하여, 운동선수의 서비스에 대한 수요는 의료 서비스나 교육에 있어서보다 훨씬 더 많다. ❺ 그러한 수요의 원천은 직접 가서든 텔레비전을 통해서든, 수억 명의 사람들이 이러한 스포츠를 보는 것을 즐긴다는 것이다. ❻ 팬은 입장을 위해 티켓당 수백 달러나 되는 돈을 지불하는 한편, 광고주는 스포츠에 대규모의 시청자를 넘겨줄 수 있는 방송사에 말 그대로 수십억 달러를 지불할 것이다. ❼ 만약 사람들이 관중 스포츠에 관심을 덜 두고 독서, 하이킹, 시낭독, 또는 참선 수행에 더 많은 관심을 둔다면, 당연히 세상은 더 좋은 곳이 되겠지만 실제는 인류 발달의 현 단계에서는 많은 수의 사람들이 진정 프로 스포츠를 즐기고, 그것이 그 산업에 상당한 수입을 창출한다.

Word List

□ absolute 절대적인 □ overall 전반적인 □ athlete 운동선수 □ make up 차지하다 □ measure 측정하다 □ digit 숫자, 자릿수
□ by contrast 반면에, 대조적으로 □ in relation to ~과 비교하여, ~과 관련하여 □ practitioner 종사자, 개업자, 개업 의사
□ source 원천 □ literally 말[문자] 그대로, 그야말로 □ broadcaster 방송사 □ might well ~하는 것도 당연한 일이다
□ spectator 관중 □ significant 상당한 □ income 수입

• Word Test

1	significant		9	측정하다
2	make up		10	반면에, 대조적으로
3	might well		11	~과 비교하여, ~과 관련하여
4	literally		12	절대적인
5	digit		13	관중
6	athlete		14	전반적인
7	income		15	방송사
8	practitioner		16	원천

In absolute terms, the overall demand for doctors and teachers is much larger than ❶ [one / that] for professional athletes. Education and health care make up huge chunks of the US economy — health care, measured as a percentage of GDP, is in the double digits and growing. By contrast, ❷ [due to / despite] the attention paid to it, professional sports is nowhere near as big. In relation to ❸ [a / the] number of practitioners in each field, however, the demand for athletes'services is much larger than in either health care or education. The source of that demand is that hundreds of millions of people enjoy watching these sports, whether in person or on television. Fans will pay as much as hundreds of dollars per ticket to attend, ❹ [while / when] advertisers will pay literally billions of dollars to broadcasters that can deliver mass audiences for sports. The world might well be a better place if people paid less attention to spectator sports and more to reading, hiking, declaiming poetry, or practising Zen meditation, but the fact is that at the current stage of human development large numbers of people do enjoy pro sports, and ❺ [it / that] creates significant income for the industry.

*chunk 부분, 상당한 양 **declaim 낭독하다 ***Zen meditation 참선

In absolute terms, the overall demand for doctors and teachers ❶ _____ (be) much larger than that for professional athletes. Education and health care make up huge chunks of the US economy — health care, measured as a percentage of GDP, ❷ _____ (be) in the double digits and growing. By contrast, despite the attention ❸ _____ (pay) to it, professional sports is nowhere near as big. In relation to the number of practitioners in each field, however, the demand for athletes'services is much larger than in either health care or education. The source of that demand is that hundreds of millions of people enjoy ❹ _____ (watch) these sports, whether in person or on television. Fans will pay as much as hundreds of dollars per ticket to attend, while advertisers will pay literally billions of dollars to broadcasters that can deliver mass audiences for sports. The world might well be a better place if people paid less attention to spectator sports and more to reading, hiking, declaiming poetry, or practising Zen meditation, but the fact is that at the current stage of human development large numbers of people do enjoy pro sports, and that ❺ _____ (create) significant income for the industry.

*chunk 부분, 상당한 양 **declaim 낭독하다 ***Zen meditation 참선

❶ _____ _____ _____ (절대적 관점에서 보면), the overall demand for doctors and teachers is much larger than that for professional athletes. Education and health care ❷ _____ _____ (~을 차지하다) huge chunks of the US economy — health care, measured as a percentage of GDP, is in the double digits and growing. By contrast, despite the attention paid to it, professional sports is nowhere near as big. ❸ _____ _____ _____ (~와 비교하여) the number of practitioners in each field, however, the demand for athletes'services is much larger than in either health care or education. The source of that demand is that hundreds of millions of people enjoy watching these sports, whether in person or on television. Fans will pay as much as hundreds of dollars per ticket to attend, while advertisers will pay literally billions of dollars to broadcasters that can deliver mass audiences for sports. The world might well be a better place if people paid less attention to spectator sports and more to reading, hiking, declaiming poetry, or practising Zen meditation, but the fact is that ❹ _____ _____ _____ _____ (현 단계에서는) of human development large numbers of people do enjoy pro sports, and that creates significant income for the industry.

*chunk 부분, 상당한 양   **declaim 낭독하다   ***Zen meditation 참선

01 7강 1번

다음 빈칸에 들어갈 말로 가장 적절한 것은?

If you're stuck developing an idea or even thinking of one, get unstuck by _____.
Go for a walk. Exercise. Bring your work somewhere else. Physical movement has been shown to have a positive effect on creative thinking. The philosopher and author Henry Thoreau claimed that his thoughts began to flow "the moment my legs began to move." Now scientists have discovered that taking part in regular exercise such as going for a walk or riding a bike really does improve creative thought. Professor Lorenza Colzato, a cognitive psychologist at Leiden University in the Netherlands, found in her 2013 study that people who exercised four times a week were able to think more creatively than those with a more sedentary lifestyle. One of my course sessions, an observation lab, is held outdoors, and the students love the walk and change in environment as they brainstorm possible solutions while moving across our campus.

*sedentary 주로 앉아서 지내는

① physically moving your furniture
② actually thinking about exercising
③ mentally readjusting your life goals
④ literally getting away from your desk
⑤ meditating positively about nature walks

02 7강 2번

(A), (B), (C)의 각 네모 안에서 어법에 맞는 표현으로 가장 적절한 것은?

Cosmology would not exist as a subject unless there were such a thing as "the universe" to explain. Instead of finding (A) what / that space is filled with a dog's breakfast of unrelated bric-a-brac, astronomers see an orchestrated and coherent unity. On the largest scale of size there is order and uniformity. Stars and galaxies billions of light-years away closely resemble those in our astronomical backyard and are (B) distributed / distributing in much the same way everywhere. Their compositions and motions are similar. The laws of physics appear to be identical as far out in space as our instruments can penetrate. In short, there is cosmos rather than chaos. This basic fact is crucial for our existence: life could not emerge, still less evolve to the point of intelligence, in chaos. It is also — or at least it was until recently — deeply mysterious. Why should the totality of things be organized so systematically? (C) Finding / To find the answer to this intriguing question, we need to understand how the universe began and work out how it evolved over billions of years to attain its present orderly and life-encouraging form.

*cosmology 우주론 **bric-a-brac 장식품 ***penetrate 침투하다

	(A)	(B)	(C)
①	what	distributed	Finding
②	what	distributing	Finding
③	that	distributing	To find
④	that	distributed	To find
⑤	that	distributed	Finding

글의 흐름으로 보아, 주어진 문장이 들어가기에 가장 적절한 곳은?

> Nevertheless, the businessman will still need to keep himself informed of general legal changes which will affect his day-to-day running of the business.

Ideally, business requires a stable environment within which to operate. (①) Yet, the framework of law which governs business activities is subject to constant change. (②) The burden of keeping up to date may be eased slightly by making use of professional people such as an accountant or solicitor to advise on the latest developments in such areas as tax or company law. (③) If he employs others in his business, he will need to keep up to date on such matters as health and safety at work, the rights of his employees and his duties as an employer. (④) If he sells goods direct to the consumer, he must be aware of changes in consumer protection law. (⑤) Almost every aspect of his business will be subject to legal regulation and the law could always change.

*solicitor 사무 변호사

다음 글의 밑줄 친 부분 중, 문맥상 낱말의 쓰임이 적절하지 <u>않은</u> 것은?

In absolute terms, the overall demand for doctors and teachers is much larger than that for professional athletes. Education and health care make up ① huge chunks of the US economy — health care, measured as a percentage of GDP, is in the double digits and growing. By contrast, despite the ② attention paid to it, professional sports is nowhere near as big. In relation to the number of practitioners in each field, however, the demand for athletes' services is much ③ larger than in either health care or education. The source of that demand is that hundreds of millions of people ④ enjoy watching these sports, whether in person or on television. Fans will pay as much as hundreds of dollars per ticket to attend, while advertisers will pay literally billions of dollars to broadcasters that can deliver mass audiences for sports. The world might well be a better place if people paid less attention to spectator sports and more to reading, hiking, declaiming poetry, or practising Zen meditation, but the fact is that at the current stage of human development large numbers of people do enjoy pro sports, and that creates ⑤ insignificant income for the industry.

*chunk 부분, 상당한 양 **declaim 낭독하다 ***Zen meditation 참선

05 7강 1번

다음 글의 내용을 한 문장으로 요약하고자 한다. 빈칸 (A), (B)에 들어갈 말로 가장 적절한 것은?

If you're stuck developing an idea or even thinking of one, get unstuck by literally getting away from your desk. Go for a walk. Exercise. Bring your work somewhere else. Physical movement has been shown to have a positive effect on creative thinking. The philosopher and author Henry Thoreau claimed that his thoughts began to flow "the moment my legs began to move." Now scientists have discovered that taking part in regular exercise such as going for a walk or riding a bike really does improve creative thought. Professor Lorenza Colzato, a cognitive psychologist at Leiden University in the Netherlands, found in her 2013 study that people who exercised four times a week were able to think more creatively than those with a more sedentary lifestyle. One of my course sessions, an observation lab, is held outdoors, and the students love the walk and change in environment as they brainstorm possible solutions while moving across our campus.

*sedentary 주로 앉아서 지내는

↓

Studies on the link between physical activity and creativity found that physical movement is the catalyst that _____(A)_____ a person who is creatively stuck and also suggested that physically active people are able to think outside the box _____(B)_____ than those who sit for prolonged periods.

	(A)		(B)
①	distracts	······	more
②	fosters	······	less
③	motivates	······	more
④	boosts	······	less
⑤	suppresses	······	more

06 7강 2번

다음 빈칸에 들어갈 말로 가장 적절한 것은?

Cosmology would not exist as a subject unless there were such a thing as "the universe" to explain. Instead of finding that space is filled with a dog's breakfast of unrelated bric-a-brac, astronomers see an orchestrated and coherent unity. On the largest scale of size there is order and uniformity. Stars and galaxies billions of light-years away closely resemble those in our astronomical backyard and are distributed in much the same way everywhere. Their compositions and motions are similar. The laws of physics appear to be identical as far out in space as our instruments can penetrate. In short, _____. This basic fact is crucial for our existence: life could not emerge, still less evolve to the point of intelligence, in chaos. It is also — or at least it was until recently — deeply mysterious. Why should the totality of things be organized so systematically? To find the answer to this intriguing question, we need to understand how the universe began and work out how it evolved over billions of years to attain its present orderly and life-encouraging form.

*cosmology 우주론 **bric-a-brac 장식품 ***penetrate 침투하다

① cosmology gave rise to life forms
② there is cosmos rather than chaos
③ chaos finds order in human existence
④ the universe is always subject to time
⑤ nothing is ever the same in our universe

07 〔7강 3번〕

다음 글의 밑줄 친 부분 중, 어법상 틀린 것은?

Ideally, business requires a stable environment within ① <u>which</u> to operate. Yet, the framework of law which governs business activities ② <u>is</u> subject to constant change. The burden of keeping up to date may be eased ③ <u>slightly</u> by making use of professional people such as an accountant or solicitor to advise on the latest developments in such areas as tax or company law. Nevertheless, the businessman will still need to keep ④ <u>him</u> informed of general legal changes which will affect his day-to-day running of the business. If he ⑤ <u>employs</u> others in his business, he will need to keep up to date on such matters as health and safety at work, the rights of his employees and his duties as an employer. If he sells goods direct to the consumer, he must be aware of changes in consumer protection law. Almost every aspect of his business will be subject to legal regulation and the law could always change.

*solicitor 사무 변호사

08 〔7강 4번〕 고난도

글의 흐름으로 보아, 주어진 문장이 들어가기에 가장 적절한 곳은?

> The source of that demand is that hundreds of millions of people enjoy watching these sports, whether in person or on television.

In absolute terms, the overall demand for doctors and teachers is much larger than that for professional athletes. (①) Education and health care make up huge chunks of the US economy — health care, measured as a percentage of GDP, is in the double digits and growing. (②) By contrast, despite the attention paid to it, professional sports is nowhere near as big. (③) In relation to the number of practitioners in each field, however, the demand for athletes' services is much larger than in either health care or education. (④) Fans will pay as much as hundreds of dollars per ticket to attend, while advertisers will pay literally billions of dollars to broadcasters that can deliver mass audiences for sports. (⑤) The world might well be a better place if people paid less attention to spectator sports and more to reading, hiking, declaiming poetry, or practising Zen meditation, but the fact is that at the current stage of human development large numbers of people do enjoy pro sports, and that creates significant income for the industry.

*chunk 부분, 상당한 양   **declaim 낭독하다   ***Zen meditation 참선

If you're stuck developing an idea or even thinking of one, get unstuck by literally getting away from your desk. Go for a walk. ____(A)____ . Bring your work somewhere else. 신체적 움직임이 창의적인 사고에 긍정적인 영향을 미치는 것으로 밝혀졌다. The philosopher and author Henry Thoreau claimed that his thoughts began to flow "the moment my legs began to move." Now scientists have discovered that taking part in regular ____(B)____ such as going for a walk or riding a bike really does improve creative thought. Professor Lorenza Colzato, a cognitive psychologist at Leiden University in the Netherlands, found in her 2013 study that people who ____(C)____(e)d four times a week were able to think more creatively than those with a more sedentary lifestyle. One of my course sessions, an observation lab, is held outdoors, and the students love the walk and change in environment as they brainstorm possible solutions while moving across our campus.

*sedentary 주로 앉아서 지내는

09 윗글의 빈칸 (A)~(C)에 공통으로 들어갈 한 단어를 쓰시오. (반드시 주어진 철자로 시작할 것, 대·소문자 구분 없음)

e_____

10 윗글의 밑줄 친 우리말 의미와 일치하도록 보기 의 단어를 순서대로 배열하여 문장을 완성하시오.

보기 to / a / thinking / physical / effect / has / have / creative / positive / been shown / movement / on

_____

_____

Cosmology would not exist as a subject 설명해야 할 우주와 같은 것이 있지 않다면. Instead of finding that space is filled with a dog's breakfast of unrelated bric-a-brac, astronomers see an orchestrated and ① coherent unity. On the largest scale of size there is order and uniformity. Stars and galaxies billions of light-years away closely ② resemble those in our astronomical backyard and are distributed in much the same way everywhere. Their compositions and motions are similar. The laws of physics appear to be ③ identical as far out in space as our instruments can penetrate. In short, there is cosmos rather than chaos. This basic fact is crucial for our existence: life could not emerge, still less evolve to the point of intelligence, in chaos. It is also — or at least it was until recently — deeply mysterious. Why should the totality of things be organized so ④ unsystematically? To find the answer to this intriguing question, we need to understand how the universe began and work out how it evolved over billions of years to attain its present ⑤ orderly and life-encouraging form.

*cosmology 우주론 **bric-a-brac 장식품 ***penetrate 침투하다

11 윗글의 밑줄 친 우리말 의미와 일치하도록 보기 의 단어를 순서대로 배열하여 문장을 완성하시오.

보기 a thing / to explain / the universe / there / as / unless / were / such

_____

_____

12 윗글의 밑줄 친 부분 중, 문맥상 어색한 것을 1개 찾아 그 번호를 쓰고 고쳐 쓰시오.

_____ → _____

Ideally, business requires a stable environment within which to operate. Yet, the framework of law which governs business activities is subject to constant ____(A)____. The burden of keeping up to date may be eased slightly by making use of professional people such as an accountant or solicitor to advise on the latest developments in such areas as tax or company law. Nevertheless, the businessman will still need to keep himself informed of general legal ____(B)____(e)s which will affect his day-to-day running of the business. If he employs others in his business, he will need to keep up to date on such matters as health and safety at work, the rights of his employees and his duties as an employer. If he sells goods direct to the consumer, he must be aware of ____(C)____(e)s in consumer protection law. Almost every aspect of his business will be subject to legal regulation and the law could always ____(D)____.

*solicitor 사무 변호사

13 윗 글의 빈칸 (A)~(D)에 공통으로 들어갈 한 단어를 쓰시오. (반드시 주어진 철자로 시작할 것, 대·소문자 구분 없음)

c_____

14 윗글에서 다음 질문에 대한 대답을 찾아 우리말로 쓰시오. (30자 내외)

Q: If a businessman hires people, on what issues does he need up-to-date information?

A: _____

In absolute terms, the overall demand for doctors and teachers is much larger than ① those for professional athletes. Education and health care make up huge chunks of the US economy — health care, measured as a percentage of GDP, is in the double digits and growing. By contrast, ② despite the attention paid to it, professional sports is nowhere near as big. In relation to the number of practitioners in each field, however, the demand for athletes' services ③ are much larger than in either health care or education. The source of that demand is that hundreds of millions of people enjoy watching these sports, whether in person or on television. Fans will pay as much as hundreds of dollars per ticket ④ to attend, while 광고주는 스포츠에 대규모의 시청자를 넘겨 줄 수 있는 방송사에 말 그대로 수십억 달러를 지불할 것이다. The world might well be a better place if people paid less attention to spectator sports and more to reading, hiking, declaiming poetry, or practising Zen meditation, but the fact is that at the current stage of human development large numbers of people ⑤ do enjoy pro sports, and that creates significant income for the industry.

*chunk 부분, 상당한 양   **declaim 낭독하다   ***Zen meditation 참선

15 윗글의 밑줄 친 부분 중, 어법상 틀린 것을 2개 찾아 그 번호를 쓰고 고쳐 쓰시오.

(1) _____ → _____

(2) _____ → _____

16 윗글의 밑줄 친 우리말 의미와 일치하도록 보기 의 단어를 순서대로 배열하여 문장을 완성하시오.

보기   billions of / sports / will pay / can deliver / advertisers / broadcasters / mass / for / dollars / literally / that / to / audiences

Number of Living Languages Spoken per Country in 2021

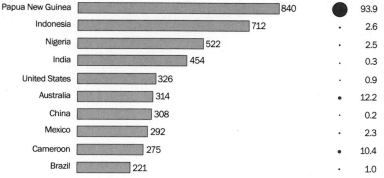

Number of languages spoken per one million inhabitants

Country		Number
Papua New Guinea	840	93.9
Indonesia	712	2.6
Nigeria	522	2.5
India	454	0.3
United States	326	0.9
Australia	314	12.2
China	308	0.2
Mexico	292	2.3
Cameroon	275	10.4
Brazil	221	1.0

❶ The above graph shows the number of living languages spoken per country in 2021, including the number of languages spoken per one million inhabitants. ❷ Papua New Guinea is the most linguistically diverse country in the world, with 840 languages spoken. ❸ Second on the list is Indonesia, with 712 different languages spoken throughout the country, immediately followed by Nigeria with 522 living languages. ❹ Among the ten countries, there are only three where the number of living languages is less than 300. ❺ In terms of the number of languages spoken per one million inhabitants, Papua New Guinea also tops the list, with 93.9 languages spoken, immediately followed by Australia with 12.2 languages. ❻ China has the smallest number of languages spoken per one million inhabitants among the ten countries.

❶ 위 도표는 거주자 100만 명당 사용되는 언어의 수를 포함하여 2021년에 국가당 현재 사용되는 언어의 수를 보여 준다. ❷ 파푸아 뉴기니는 840개의 언어가 사용되어 세계에서 언어적으로 가장 다양한 나라이다. ❸ 712개의 서로 다른 언어가 전국에서 사용되어 인도네시아가 목록에서 2위를 차지하고, 522개의 현재 사용되는 언어를 가진 나이지리아가 바로 그 뒤를 잇는다. ❹ 10개국 중에서 현재 사용되는 언어의 수가 300개 미만인 나라는 3개국뿐이다. ❺ 거주자 100만 명당 사용되는 언어의 수 면에서는 93.9개의 언어가 사용되어 파푸아 뉴기니가 역시 1위를 차지하고, 12.2개의 언어를 가진 오스트레일리아가 바로 그 뒤를 잇는다. ❻ 중국은 10개국 중에서 거주자 100만 명당 사용되는 언어의 수가 가장 적다

Word List

□ language 언어 □ per ~ 당 □ inhabitant 거주자, 주민 □ linguistically 언어적으로 □ diverse 다양한 □ list 목록
□ throughout the country 전국적으로 □ immediately 바로, 즉각 □ in terms of ~의 면에서, ~과 관련하여
□ top the list 1위를 차지하다

• Word Test

1 in terms of _____

2 throughout the country _____

3 linguistically _____

4 per _____

5 top the list _____

6 목록 _____

7 다양한 _____

8 거주자, 주민 _____

9 바로, 즉각 _____

10 언어 _____

The above graph shows the number of living languages spoken per country in 2021, including the number of languages spoken per one million inhabitants. Papua New Guinea is the most ❶ logistically/linguistically diverse country in the world, with 840 languages spoken. Second on the list is Indonesia, with 712 different languages spoken throughout the country, immediately ❷ following/followed by Nigeria with 522 living languages. Among the ten countries, there are only three ❸ where/which the number of living languages is less than 300. In terms of the number of languages spoken per one million ❹ inhabitants/immigrants, Papua New Guinea also tops the list, with 93.9 languages spoken, immediately followed by Australia with 12.2 languages. China has the smallest number of languages spoken per one million inhabitants among the ten countries.

The above graph shows the number of living languages spoken per country in 2021, ❶ _____ (include) the number of languages spoken per one million inhabitants. Papua New Guinea is the most linguistically diverse country in the world, with 840 languages ❷ _____ (speak). Second on the list is Indonesia, with 712 different languages spoken throughout the country, immediately ❸ _____ (follow) by Nigeria with 522 living languages. Among the ten countries, there are only three where the number of living languages is less than 300. In terms of the number of languages spoken per one million inhabitants, Papua New Guinea also ❹ _____ (top) the list, with 93.9 languages spoken, immediately followed by Australia with 12.2 languages. China has the smallest number of languages spoken per one million inhabitants among the ten countries.

The above graph shows the number of living languages spoken per country in 2021, including the number of languages spoken ❶ _____ _____ _____ _____ (거주자들 백만 명당). Papua New Guinea is the most linguistically diverse country in the world, with 840 languages spoken. Second on the list is Indonesia, with 712 different languages spoken ❷ _____ _____ _____ (전국적으로), immediately followed by Nigeria with 522 living languages. Among the ten countries, there are only three where the number of living languages is ❸ _____ _____ (~ 미만인) 300. ❹ _____ _____ _____ (~의 측면에서) the number of languages spoken per one million inhabitants, Papua New Guinea also tops the list, with 93.9 languages spoken, immediately followed by Australia with 12.2 languages. China has the smallest number of languages spoken per one million inhabitants among the ten countries.

U.S. College Enrollment Rates of 18- to 24-year-olds, by Race/Ethnicity: 2000, 2010 and 2018

Race/Ethnicity ╲ Year	2000	2010	2018
White	39%	43%	42%
Black	31%	38%	37%
Hispanic	22%	32%	36%
Asian	56%	64%	59%
American Indian / Alaska Native	16%	41%	24%

❶ The above table shows the college enrollment rates of 18- to 24-year-olds by race/ethnicity in 2000, 2010, and 2018 in the U.S. ❷ Among all the racial and ethnic groups listed in the table, Asians showed the highest college enrollment rate in all three years. ❸ The college enrollment rates in 2010 were higher than in 2000 for both Whites (43 vs. 39 percent) and Blacks (38 vs. 31 percent). ❹ But compared to 2010, in 2018, the college enrollment rates marked a decrease for both White and Black 18- to 24-year-olds. ❺ For Hispanics, the college enrollment rate was 10 percentage points higher in 2010 than in 2000 and 4 percentage points higher in 2018 than in 2010. ❻ Among all the groups in the table, American Indians / Alaska Natives showed the highest increase in the college enrollment rate from 2000 to 2010, but showed the highest decrease from 2010 to 2018.

❶ 위 표는 미국에서 2000년, 2010년 및 2018년의 18세에서 24세의 대학 등록률을 인종별/민족별로 보여 준다. ❷ 표에 나와 있는 모든 인종 및 민족 집단 중, 아시아인은 세 개 연도 모두에서 가장 높은 대학 등록률을 보였다. ❸ 2010년의 대학 등록률은 백인 (43퍼센트 대 39퍼센트) 과 흑인 (38퍼센트 대 31퍼센트) 둘 다 2000년보다 더 높았다. ❹ 그러나 2010년에 비해, 2018년에는 18세에서 24세의 백인과 흑인 둘 다 대학 등록률이 감소를 나타냈다. ❺ 히스패닉의 경우, 대학 등록률이 2000년보다 2010년에 10퍼센트포인트 더 높았고, 2010년보다 2018년에 4퍼센트포인트 더 높았다. ❻ 표에 있는 모든 집단 중, 아메리칸 인디언 / 알래스카 원주민이 2000년부터 2010년까지 대학 진학률이 가장 높은 증가율을 보였지만 2010년부터 2018년까지 가장 높은 감소율을 보였다.

Word List
□ **table** 표　□ **enrollment rate** 등록률　□ **race** 인종　□ **ethnicity** 민족(집단)　□ **racial** 인종의　□ **ethnic** 민족의
□ **compared to** ~에 비해　□ **mark** 나타내다　□ **decrease** 감소　□ **Hispanic** (특히 미국이나 캐나다에 사는)히스패닉[라틴 아메리카](계의)

● Word Test

1 Hispanic _____
2 enrollment rate _____
3 ethnic _____
4 race _____
5 mark _____

6 인종의 _____
7 ~에 비해 _____
8 표 _____
9 민족(집단) _____
10 감소 _____

The above table shows the college enrollment rates of 18- to 24-year-olds by race/ethnicity in 2000, 2010, and 2018 in the U.S. Among all the racial and ❶ ethnic/ethnological groups listed in the table, Asians showed the highest college enrollment rate in all three years. The college enrollment rates in 2010 were higher than in 2000 for ❷ either/both Whites (43 vs. 39 percent) and Blacks (38 vs. 31 percent). But ❸ comparing/compared to 2010, in 2018, the college enrollment rates marked a decrease for both White and Black 18- to 24-year-olds. For Hispanics, the college enrollment rate was 10 percentage points higher in 2010 than in 2000 and 4 percentage points higher in 2018 than in 2010. Among all the groups in the table, American Indians / Alaska Natives showed the highest increase in the college enrollment rate from 2000 to 2010, but showed the highest ❹ increase/decrease from 2010 to 2018.

The above table shows the college enrollment rates of 18- to 24-year-olds by race/ethnicity in 2000, 2010, and 2018 in the U.S. Among all the racial and ethnic groups ❶ _____ (list) in the table, Asians showed the highest college enrollment rate in all three years. The college enrollment rates in 2010 ❷ _____ (be) higher than in 2000 for both Whites (43 vs. 39 percent) and Blacks (38 vs. 31 percent). But compared to 2010, in 2018, the college enrollment rates marked a decrease for both White and Black 18- to 24-year-olds. For Hispanics, the college enrollment rate ❸ _____ (be) 10 percentage points higher in 2010 than in 2000 and 4 percentage points higher in 2018 than in 2010. Among all the groups in the table, American Indians / Alaska Natives ❹ _____ (show) the highest increase in the college enrollment rate from 2000 to 2010, but showed the highest decrease from 2010 to 2018.

The above table shows the college enrollment rates of 18- to 24-year-olds by race/ethnicity in 2000, 2010, and 2018 in the U.S. Among all the racial and ethnic groups ❶ _____ _____ _____ _____ (표에 나와 있는), Asians showed the highest college enrollment rate in all three years. The college enrollment rates in 2010 were higher than in 2000 for both Whites (43 vs. 39 percent) and Blacks (38 vs. 31 percent). But compared to 2010, in 2018, the college enrollment rates ❷ _____ _____ _____ (감소를 나타냈다) for both White and Black 18- to 24-year-olds. ❸ _____ _____ (히스패닉의 경우에), the college enrollment rate was 10 percentage points higher in 2010 than in 2000 and 4 percentage points higher in 2018 than in 2010. ❹ _____ _____ _____ _____ (모든 집단들 중에서) in the table, American Indians / Alaska Natives showed the highest increase in the college enrollment rate from 2000 to 2010, but showed the highest decrease from 2010 to 2018.

The Share of Women Across STEM Job Types in the U.S.

% of employed in each occupational group who are women

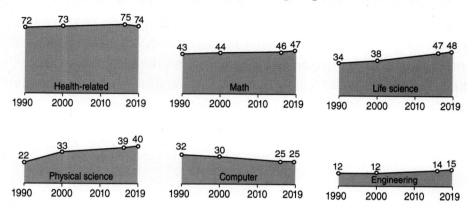

❶ 위 도표는 미국에서 1990년과 2019년 사이의 STEM(과학, 기술, 공학, 수학) 분야의 직업군에서 여성 근로자의 점유율을 보여준다. ❷ 2019년에 여성은 건강 관련 직업의 약 3/4을 차지했는데, 이것은 가장 큰 여성 직종이며, 생명 과학과 수학이 차례로 그 뒤를 이었다. ❸ 1990년에 생명 과학 직업에서 여성 근로자의 점유율은 수학 직업의 여성 근로자의 그것보다 낮았으나, 이것은 2019년에 1퍼센트포인트 차이로 역전되었다. ❹ 여성은 생명 과학과 자연 과학 직업에서 상당한 진전을 보였는데, 1990년과 2019년 사이에 각각 14퍼센트포인트와 18퍼센트포인트의 증가를 나타냈다. ❺ 1990년에, 컴퓨터 직업에서의 여성근로자의 점유율은 공학 직업의 여성 근로자 점유율의 두 배가 넘었다. ❻ 공학 직업의 여성 근로자 점유율은 1990년 12퍼센트로 STEM 직업군에서 가장 낮았으며, 2019년 15퍼센트로 소폭 상승했다.

❶ The above graphs show the share of women employees in STEM (science, technology, engineering and math) job types between 1990 and 2019 in the U.S. ❷ In 2019, women comprised about three-quarters of health-related jobs, which was the largest occupational type for women, followed by life science and math in that order. ❸ In 1990, the share of women employees in life science jobs was lower than that of women employees in math jobs, but this was reversed in 2019 by one percentage point. ❹ Women have made significant gains in life science and physical science jobs, which showed a 14- and 18-percentage-point increase, respectively, between 1990 and 2019. ❺ In 1990, the share of women employees in computer jobs was more than double that of women employees in engineering jobs. ❻ The share of women employees in engineering jobs was the lowest among STEM job types, at 12 percent, in 1990, slightly inching up to 15 percent in 2019.

Word List
□ share 점유율　□ employee 근로자　□ engineering 공학　□ comprise 차지하다, 구성하다　□ occupational 직업의
□ reverse 역전시키다　□ significant 상당한　□ gain 진전, 증가　□ physical science 자연 과학　□ respectively 각각
□ double 두 배　□ inch 조금씩 움직이다

• Word Test

1	occupational	7	공학
2	inch	8	자연 과학
3	employee	9	두 배
4	gain	10	상당한
5	comprise	11	각각
6	reverse	12	점유율

The above graphs show the share of women employees in STEM (science, technology, engineering and math) job types between 1990 and 2019 in the U.S. In 2019, women comprised about three-quarters of health-related jobs, ❶ [in which / which] was the largest occupational type for women, followed by life science and math in that order. In 1990, the share of women employees in life science jobs was ❷ [higher / lower] than that of women employees in math jobs, but this was reversed in 2019 by one percentage point. Women have made ❸ [significant / insignificant] gains in life science and physical science jobs, which showed a 14- and 18-percentage-point increase, respectively, between 1990 and 2019. In 1990, the share of women employees in computer jobs was more than double ❹ [that / those] of women employees in engineering jobs. The share of women employees in engineering jobs was the lowest among STEM job types, at 12 percent, in 1990, slightly inching up to 15 percent in 2019.

The above graphs show the share of women employees in STEM (science, technology, engineering and math) job types between 1990 and 2019 in the U.S. In 2019, women ❶ _____ (comprise) about three-quarters of health-related jobs, which was the largest occupational type for women, followed by life science and math in that order. In 1990, the share of women employees in life science jobs was lower than that of women employees in math jobs, but this ❷ _____ (reverse) in 2019 by one percentage point. Women ❸ _____ (make) significant gains in life science and physical science jobs, which showed a 14- and 18-percentage-point increase, respectively, between 1990 and 2019. In 1990, the share of women employees in computer jobs ❹ _____ (be) more than double that of women employees in engineering jobs. The share of women employees in engineering jobs was the lowest among STEM job types, at 12 percent, in 1990, slightly ❺ _____ (inch) up to 15 percent in 2019.

The above graphs show the share of women employees in STEM (science, technology, engineering and math) job types between 1990 and 2019 in the U.S. In 2019, women comprised ❶ _____ _____ (약 3/4) of health-related jobs, which was the largest occupational type for women, followed by life science and math in that order. In 1990, the share of women employees in life science jobs was lower than that of women employees in math jobs, but this was reversed in 2019 ❷ _____ _____ _____ _____ (1퍼센트 포인트 차이로). Women have made ❸ _____ _____ (상당한 진전들) in life science and physical science jobs, which showed a 14- and 18-percentage-point increase, respectively, between 1990 and 2019. In 1990, the share of women employees in computer jobs was more than double that of women employees in engineering jobs. The share of women employees in engineering jobs was the lowest among STEM job types, at 12 percent, in 1990, slightly inching ❹ _____ _____ (~까지) 15 percent in 2019.

112

The Top 8 African Countries with the Highest GDP in 1990, 2005, and 2020

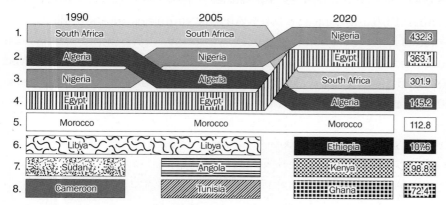

Note: The figures, in billion U.S. dollars, belong to 2020.

❶ The graph above shows the top 8 African countries with the highest GDP in 1990, 2005, and 2020. ❷ South Africa maintained its status as the African country with the highest GDP both in 1990 and 2005, but it fell to third with a GDP of $301.9 billion in 2020. ❸ In 2020, Algeria, which ranked second in 1990 and third in 2005, ranked fourth, while Nigeria and Egypt ranked first and second, respectively. ❹ Morocco ranked fifth among the top 8 African countries in 1990, 2005, and 2020, with its GDP reaching $112.8 billion in 2020. ❺ Libya ranked sixth in the listing both in 1990 and 2005, but dropped out of the top 8 African countries in 2020. ❻ Angola and Tunisia entered the top 8 African countries in 2005, and Kenya and Ghana did so in 2020, despite those countries having GDPs below $100 billion.

❶ 위 도표는 1990년, 2005년, 2020년에 가장 높은 국내 총생산(GDP)을 가진 상위 8개 아프리카 국가를 보여 준다. ❷ 남아프리카 공화국은 1990년과 2005년 둘 다 GDP가 가장 높은 아프리카 국가로서의 지위를 유지했지만, 2020년에는 GDP가 3,019억 달러로 3위로 떨어졌다. ❸ 2020년에는 1990년에 2위, 2005년에 3위였던 알제리가 4위를 차지했던 반면에, 나이지리아와 이집트는 각각 1위와 2위를 차지했다. ❹ 모로코는 1990년, 2005년, 2020년에 상위 아프리카 8개국 중 5위를 차지했는데, 2020년 모로코의 GDP는 1,128억 달러에 달했다. ❺ 리비아는 1990년과 2005년에 둘 다 목록에서 6위를 차지했지만, 2020년에는 아프리카 상위 8개 국가에서 탈락했다. ❻ 앙골라와 튀니지는 2005년에 아프리카 상위 8개국에 진입했고, 케냐, 가나는 모두 GDP가 1,000억 달러 미만이었음에도 불구하고, 2020년에 그렇게 되었다[아프리카 상위 8개 국가에 진입했다].

Word List
□ GDP (= gross ck)mestic product) 국내 총산생 □ maintain 유지하다 □ status 지위 □ rank (등급·등위·순위를) 차지하다
□ respectively 각각 □ reach 도달하다 □ listing 목록 □ drop out of ~에서 중도하차하다 □ enter 진입하다, 들어가다
□ despite ~에도 불구하고

• Word Test

1 respectively _____
2 rank _____
3 GDP (= gross domestic product) _____
4 drop out of _____
5 listing _____

6 도달하다 _____
7 지위 _____
8 ~에도 불구하고 _____
9 진입하다, 들어가다 _____
10 유지하다 _____

The graph above shows the top 8 African countries with the highest GDP in 1990, 2005, and 2020. South Africa ❶ | abandoned/maintained | its status as the African country with the highest GDP both in 1990 and 2005, but it fell to third with a GDP of $301.9 billion in 2020. In 2020, Algeria, which ranked second in 1990 and third in 2005, ranked fourth, ❷ | so/while | Nigeria and Egypt ranked first and second, respectively. Morocco ranked fifth among the top 8 African countries in 1990, 2005, and 2020, with its GDP ❸ | reaching/to reach | $112.8 billion in 2020. Libya ranked sixth in the listing both in 1990 and 2005, but dropped out of the top 8 African countries in 2020. Angola and Tunisia entered the top 8 African countries in 2005, and Kenya and Ghana ❹ | did/were | so in 2020, despite those countries having GDPs below $100 billion.

The graph above shows the top 8 African countries with the highest GDP in 1990, 2005, and 2020. South Africa ❶ _____ (maintain) its status as the African country with the highest GDP both in 1990 and 2005, but it fell to third with a GDP of $301.9 billion in 2020. In 2020, Algeria, which ranked second in 1990 and third in 2005, ranked fourth, while Nigeria and Egypt ranked first and second, respectively. Morocco ranked fifth among the top 8 African countries in 1990, 2005, and 2020, with its GDP ❷ _____ (reach) $112.8 billion in 2020. Libya ranked sixth in the listing both in 1990 and 2005, but ❸ _____ (drop) out of the top 8 African countries in 2020. Angola and Tunisia entered the top 8 African countries in 2005, and Kenya and Ghana did so in 2020, despite those countries ❹ _____ (have) GDPs below $100 billion.

The graph above shows the top 8 African countries with the highest GDP in 1990, 2005, and 2020. South Africa ❶ _____ _____ _____ (그것의 지위를 유지했다) as the African country with the highest GDP both in 1990 and 2005, but it ❷ _____ _____ _____ (3위로 떨어졌다) with a GDP of $301.9 billion in 2020. In 2020, Algeria, which ranked second in 1990 and third in 2005, ranked fourth, while Nigeria and Egypt ranked first and second, respectively. Morocco ranked fifth among the top 8 African countries in 1990, 2005, and 2020, with its GDP reaching $112.8 billion in 2020. Libya ranked sixth in the listing both in 1990 and 2005, but ❸ _____ _____ _____ (~에서 탈락했다) the top 8 African countries in 2020. Angola and Tunisia entered the top 8 African countries in 2005, and Kenya and Ghana ❹ _____ _____ (그렇게 되었다) in 2020, despite those countries having GDPs below $100 billion.

01 8강 1번

다음 도표의 내용과 일치하지 <u>않는</u> 것은?

Number of Living Languages Spoken per Country in 2021

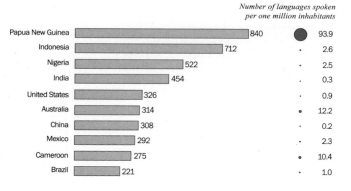

Number of languages spoken per one million inhabitants

Country	Languages	Per million
Papua New Guinea	840	93.9
Indonesia	712	2.6
Nigeria	522	2.5
India	454	0.3
United States	326	0.9
Australia	314	12.2
China	308	0.2
Mexico	292	2.3
Cameroon	275	10.4
Brazil	221	1.0

The above graph shows the number of living languages spoken per country in 2021, including the number of languages spoken per one million inhabitants. ① Papua New Guinea is the most linguistically diverse country in the world, with 840 languages spoken. ② Second on the list is Indonesia, with 712 different languages spoken throughout the country, immediately followed by India with 454 living languages. ③ Among the ten countries, there are only three where the number of living languages is less than 300. ④ In terms of the number of languages spoken per one million inhabitants, Papua New Guinea also tops the list, with 93.9 languages spoken, immediately followed by Australia with 12.2 languages. ⑤ China has the smallest number of languages spoken per one million inhabitants among the ten countries.

02 8강 2번

다음 도표의 내용과 일치하지 <u>않는</u> 것은?

U.S. College Enrollment Rates of 18- to 24-year-olds, by Race/Ethnicity: 2000, 2010 and 2018

Race/Ethnicity \ Year	2000	2010	2018
White	39%	43%	42%
Black	31%	38%	37%
Hispanic	22%	32%	36%
Asian	56%	64%	59%
American Indian / Alaska Native	16%	41%	24%

The above table shows the college enrollment rates of 18- to 24-year-olds by race/ethnicity in 2000, 2010, and 2018 in the U.S. ① Among all the racial and ethnic groups listed in the table, Asians showed the highest college enrollment rate in all three years. ② The college enrollment rates in 2010 were higher than in 2000 for both Whites (43 vs. 39 percent) and Blacks (38 vs. 31 percent). ③ But compared to 2010, in 2018, the college enrollment rates marked a decrease for both White and Black 18- to 24-year-olds. ④ For Hispanics, the college enrollment rate was 10 percentage points higher in 2010 than in 2000 and 4 percentage points lower in 2018 than in 2010. ⑤ Among all the groups in the table, American Indians / Alaska Natives showed the highest increase in the college enrollment rate from 2000 to 2010, but showed the highest decrease from 2010 to 2018.

다음 도표의 내용과 일치하지 <u>않는</u> 것은?

The Share of Women Across STEM Job Types in the U.S.

% of employed in each occupational group who are women

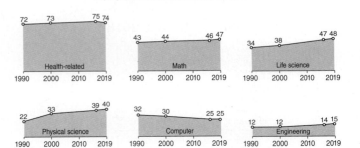

The above graphs show the share of women employees in STEM (science, technology, engineering and math) job types between 1990 and 2019 in the U.S. ① In 2019, women comprised about three-quarters of health-related jobs, which was the largest occupational type for women, followed by life science and math in that order. ② In 1990, the share of women employees in life science jobs was lower than that of women employees in math jobs, but this was reversed in 2019 by one percentage point. ③ Women have made significant gains in life science and physical science jobs, which showed a 14- and 17-percentage-point increase, respectively, between 1990 and 2019. ④ In 1990, the share of women employees in computer jobs was more than double that of women employees in engineering jobs. ⑤ The share of women employees in engineering jobs was the lowest among STEM job types, at 12 percent, in 1990, slightly inching up to 15 percent in 2019.

다음 도표의 내용과 일치하지 <u>않는</u> 것은?

The Top 8 African Countries with the Highest GDP in 1990, 2005, and 2020

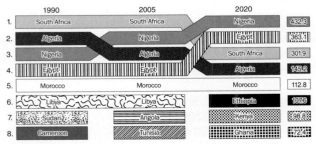

Note: The figures, in billion U.S. dollars, belong to 2020.

The graph above shows the top 8 African countries with the highest GDP in 1990, 2005, and 2020. ① South Africa maintained its status as the African country with the highest GDP both in 1990 and 2005, but it fell to third with a GDP of $301.9 billion in 2020. ② In 2020, Algeria, which ranked second in 1990 and third in 2005, ranked fourth, while Nigeria and Egypt ranked first and second, respectively. ③ Morocco ranked fifth among the top 8 African countries in 1990, 2005, and 2020, with its GDP reaching more than $115 billion in 2020. ④ Libya ranked sixth in the listing both in 1990 and 2005, but dropped out of the top 8 African countries in 2020. ⑤ Angola and Tunisia entered the top 8 African countries in 2005, and Kenya and Ghana did so in 2020, despite two of the countries having GDPs below $100 billion.

8강 1번

Number of Living Languages Spoken per Country in 2021

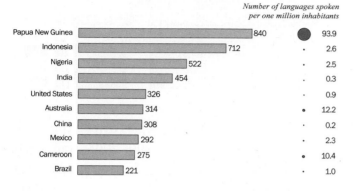

Number of languages spoken per one million inhabitants

Country	Languages	·	Per million
Papua New Guinea	840	●	93.9
Indonesia	712	·	2.6
Nigeria	522	·	2.5
India	454	·	0.3
United States	326	·	0.9
Australia	314	·	12.2
China	308	·	0.2
Mexico	292	·	2.3
Cameroon	275	●	10.4
Brazil	221	·	1.0

The above graph shows the number of living languages spoken per country in 2021, including the number of languages spoken per one million inhabitants. Papua New Guinea is 세계에서 언어적으로 가장 다양한 나라, with 840 languages spoken. Second on the list is Indonesia, with 712 different languages spoken throughout the country, immediately followed by Nigeria with 522 living languages. Among the ten countries, there are only three where the number of living languages is less than 300. In terms of the number of languages spoken per one million inhabitants, Papua New Guinea also tops the list, with 93.9 languages spoken, immediately followed by Australia with 12.2 languages. China has the smallest number of languages spoken per one million inhabitants among the ten countries.

05 윗글의 밑줄 친 우리말 의미와 일치하도록 보기 의 단어를 활용하여 문장을 완성하시오. (단, 필요시 어형을 바꿔 쓸 것)

> 보기 country / diverse / linguistic / world

8강 2번

U.S. College Enrollment Rates of 18- to 24-year-olds, by Race/Ethnicity: 2000, 2010 and 2018

Race/Ethnicity \ Year	2000	2010	2018
White	39%	43%	42%
Black	31%	38%	37%
Hispanic	22%	32%	36%
Asian	56%	64%	59%
American Indian / Alaska Native	16%	41%	24%

The above table shows the college enrollment rates of 18- to 24-year-olds by race/ethnicity in 2000, 2010, and 2018 in the U.S. Among all the racial and ethnic groups listed in the table, Asians showed the ① highest college enrollment rate in all three years. The college enrollment rates in 2010 were ② lower than in 2000 for both Whites (43 vs. 39 percent) and Blacks (38 vs. 31 percent). But compared to 2010, in 2018, the college enrollment rates marked a ③ decrease for both White and Black 18- to 24-year-olds. For Hispanics, the college enrollment rate was 10 percentage points ④ higher in 2010 than in 2000 and 4 percentage points higher in 2018 than in 2010. Among all the groups in the table, American Indians / Alaska Natives showed the highest ⑤ decrease in the college enrollment rate from 2000 to 2010, but showed the highest decrease from 2010 to 2018.

06 윗글의 밑줄 친 부분 중, 문맥상 어색한 것을 2개 찾아 그 번호를 쓰고 고쳐 쓰시오.

(1) _____ → _____

(2) _____ → _____

The Share of Women Across STEM Job Types in the U.S.
% of employed in each occupational group who are women

72 73 75 74
Health-related
1990 2000 2010 2019

43 44 46 47
Math
1990 2000 2010 2019

34 38 47 48
Life science
1990 2000 2010 2019

22 33 39 40
Physical science
1990 2000 2010 2019

32 30 25 25
Computer
1990 2000 2010 2019

12 12 14 15
Engineering
1990 2000 2010 2019

The above graphs show the share of women employees in STEM (science, technology, engineering and math) job types between 1990 and 2019 in the U.S. In 2019, women comprised about three-quarters of health-related jobs, which was the largest occupational type for women, followed by life science and math in that order. In 1990, the share of women employees in life science jobs was lower than that of women employees in math jobs, but this was _____ in 2019 by one percentage point. Women have made significant gains in life science and physical science jobs, which showed a 14- and 18-percentage-point increase, espectively, between 1990 and 2019. In 1990, the share of women employees in computer jobs was more than double that of women employees in engineering jobs. The share of women employees in engineering jobs was the lowest among STEM job types, at 12 percent, in 1990, slightly inching up to 15 percent in 2019.

07 윗글의 빈칸에 들어갈 단어를 영영 뜻풀이를 참고하여 쓰시오. (단, 주어진 글자로 시작하여 어법에 알맞은 형태로 쓸 것)

to change the order or development of events, a process, or a situation to be the opposite of what it was

r _____

The Top 8 African Countries with the Highest GDP in 1990, 2005, and 2020

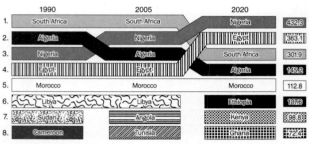

Note: The figures, in billion U.S. dollars, belong to 2020.

The graph above shows the top 8 African countries with the highest GDP in 1990, 2005, and 2020. South Africa GDP가 가장 높은 아프리카 국가로서 지위를 유지했다 both in 1990 and 2005, but it fell to third with a GDP of $301.9 billion in 2020. In 2020, Algeria, which ranked second in 1990 and third in 2005, ranked fourth, while Nigeria and Egypt ranked first and second, respectively. Morocco ranked fifth among the top 8 African countries in 1990, 2005, and 2020, with its GDP reaching $112.8 billion in 2020. Libya ranked sixth in the listing both in 1990 and 2005, but dropped out of the top 8 African countries in 2020. Angola and Tunisia entered the top 8 African countries in 2005, and Kenya and Ghana did so in 2020, despite two of the countries having GDPs below $100 billion.

08 윗글의 밑줄 친 우리말의 의미와 일치하도록 보기 의 단어를 활용하여 조건 에 맞게 문장을 완성하시오.

보기 as / GDP / its / African / the / country / status / the / with / maintain / high

조건 · 〈보기〉의 단어들을 반드시 모두 사용할 것
· 필요시 어형을 바꿔 쓸 것

_____

_____

❶ Southern sea lions are seals with small, clearly visible external ears. ❷ They are much more mobile on land than true seals, being able to rotate their rear flippers sideways to propel their bodies forward. ❸ Sea lions can move quite fast in this manner. ❹ A fully grown southern sea lion bull is much larger and more impressive than his northern cousin, the California sea lion. ❺ This massive animal measures well over 2 m long and weighs up to half a tonne. ❻ His enormous neck is decorated with a shaggy mane; hence the name 'sea lion', which also refers to his roar. ❼ The elegant, nearly yellowish females that make up his harem weigh roughly half the average weight of an adult male, but then they expend less energy. ❽ From the time he comes ashore in December to when he leaves in March, the bull sea lion neither eats nor sleeps for more than a few minutes at a time: guarding his harem is a full-time job.

*shaggy 텁수룩한　**mane 갈기　***harem 하렘(번식을 위해 한 마리의 수컷을 공유하는 암컷의 무리)

❶ 남방바다사자는 작고 뚜렷하게 보이는 외부 귀를 가진 물개다. ❷ 그것들은 참물범보다 육지에서 훨씬 더 기동성이 있는데, 몸을 앞으로 나아가게 하기 위해 뒷지느러미 발을 옆으로 둥글게 움직일 수 있기 때문이다. ❸ 바다사자는 이런 식으로 꽤 빠르게 움직일 수 있다. ❹ 완전히 자란 남방바다사자 수컷은 그것의 북방 사촌인 캘리포니아바다사자보다 훨씬 더 크고 더 인상적이다. ❺ 이 육중한 동물은 길이가 2미터가 훨씬 넘고 무게가 0.5톤까지 나간다. ❻ 그것의 거대한 목은 텁수룩한 갈기로 장식되어 있어서 '바다사자'라는 이름이 붙었고, 또한 그 이름은 그것의 포효와도 관련이 있다. ❼ 그것의 하렘을 구성하는 우아하고 거의 누르스름한 암컷들은 성체 수컷의 평균 체중의 대략 절반 정도 나가는데, 하기야 그래서 그것들은 에너지를 덜 소비한다. ❽ 12월에 뭍으로 올라올 때부터 3월에 떠날 때까지, 수컷 바다사자는 먹지도 않고 한 번에 몇 분 넘게는 잠을 자지도 않는데, 왜냐하면 자기 하렘을 지키는 일은 한순간도 쉬지 않고 해야 하는 일이기 때문이다.

Word List

□ **sea lion** 바다사자　□ **seal** 물개, 바다표범　□ **visible** 보이는　□ **external** 외부의　□ **mobile** 기동성 있는　□ **true seal** 참물범
□ **rotate** 둥글게 움직이다, 회전시키다　□ **rear flipper** 뒷지느러미발　□ **sideways** 옆으로　□ **propel** 나아가게 하다　□ **manner** 방식
□ **bull** (큰 짐승의) 수컷　□ **massive** 육중한, 거대한　□ **enormous** 거대한　□ **decorate** 장식하다　□ **hence** 따라서, 그러므로
□ **refer to** ~과 관련이 있다　□ **roar** 포효　□ **elegant** 우아한　□ **but then** 하기야 그래서　□ **expend** 소비하다　□ **ashore** 뭍으로

• Word Test

1	hence		12	방식	
2	rotate		13	바다사자	
3	true seal		14	옆으로	
4	roar		15	뭍으로	
5	propel		16	거대한	
6	refer to		17	보이는	
7	mobile		18	소비하다	
8	rear flipper		19	육중한, 거대한	
9	but then		20	장식하다	
10	seal		21	우아한	
11	bull		22	외부의	

Southern sea lions are seals with small, clearly visible external ears. They are much more mobile on land than true seals, being able to rotate their rear flippers sideways to propel their bodies ❶ backward / forward . Sea lions can move quite fast in this manner. A fully grown southern sea lion bull is ❷ more / much larger and more impressive than his northern cousin, the California sea lion. This massive animal measures well over 2 m long and weighs up to half a tonne. His enormous neck is decorated with a shaggy mane; hence the name 'sea lion', ❸ which / what also refers to his roar. The elegant, nearly yellowish females that make up his harem weigh roughly half the average weight of an adult male, but then they ❹ expend / save less energy. From the time he comes ashore in December to when he leaves in March, the bull sea lion ❺ either / neither eats nor sleeps for more than a few minutes at a time: guarding his harem is a full-time job.

*shaggy 텁수룩한 **mane 갈기 ***harem 하렘(번식을 위해 한 마리의 수컷을 공유하는 암컷의 무리)

Southern sea lions are seals with small, clearly visible external ears. They are much more mobile on land than true seals, ❶ _____ (be) able to rotate their rear flippers sideways to propel their bodies forward. Sea lions can move quite fast in this manner. A fully grown southern sea lion bull is much larger and more impressive than his northern cousin, the California sea lion. This massive animal measures well over 2 m long and ❷ _____ (weigh) up to half a tonne. His enormous neck ❸ _____ (decorate) with a shaggy mane; hence the name 'sea lion', which also refers to his roar. The elegant, nearly yellowish females that ❹ _____ (make) up his harem weigh roughly half the average weight of an adult male, but then they expend less energy. From the time he comes ashore in December to when he leaves in March, the bull sea lion neither eats nor ❺ _____ (sleep) for more than a few minutes at a time: guarding his harem is a full-time job.

*shaggy 텁수룩한 **mane 갈기 ***harem 하렘(번식을 위해 한 마리의 수컷을 공유하는 암컷의 무리)

Southern sea lions are seals with small, ❶ _____ _____ _____ _____ (뚜렷하게 보이는 외부 귀들). They are ❷ _____ _____ _____ _____ _____ (육지에서 훨씬 더 기동성이 있는) than true seals, being able to rotate their rear flippers sideways to propel their bodies forward. Sea lions can move quite fast in this manner. A fully grown southern sea lion bull is much larger and more impressive than his northern cousin, the California sea lion. ❸ _____ _____ _____ (이 육중한 동물) measures well over 2 m long and weighs up to half a tonne. His enormous neck is decorated with a shaggy mane; hence the name 'sea lion', which also ❹ _____ _____ _____ _____ (그의 포효와 관련이 있다). The elegant, nearly yellowish females that make up his harem weigh roughly half the average weight of an adult male, but then they expend less energy. From the time he comes ashore in December to when he leaves in March, the bull sea lion neither eats nor sleeps for more than a few minutes at a time: guarding his harem is ❺ _____ _____ _____ (한 순간도 쉬지 않고 하는 일).

*shaggy 텁수룩한 **mane 갈기 ***harem 하렘(번식을 위해 한 마리의 수컷을 공유하는 암컷의 무리)

120

❶ Thomas Hopkins Gallaudet was born in Philadelphia on December 10, 1787. ❷ His family moved to Hartford, Connecticut, where he attended the Hartford Grammar School. ❸ He entered Yale College in 1802 and graduated the youngest in his class. ❹ Gallaudet became interested in the education of deaf people after meeting Alice Cogswell, the deaf daughter of a neighbor. ❺ With funding from Cogswell's father and others, Gallaudet went to Europe in 1815 to learn how to teach deaf children. ❻ Dissatisfied by what he saw in British schools for deaf people, Gallaudet visited a school in Paris. ❼ There, he received training from deaf teachers Jean Massieu and Laurent Clerc. ❽ Gallaudet accompanied Laurent Clerc back to Hartford in 1816 and established the first school for the deaf in the United States in 1817, now known as the American School for the Deaf. ❾ Gallaudet served as the institution's principal until 1830. ❿ He married one of his former students, Sofia Fowler, and had eight children.

❶ Thomas Hopkins Gallaudet는 1787년 12월 10일 필라델피아에서 태어났다. ❷ 그의 가족은 코네티컷주에 있는 Hartford로 이주했고, 그곳에서 그는 Hartford Grammar School에 다녔다. ❸ 1802년 그는 Yale College에 입학하여 반에서 가장 어린 나이에 졸업했다. ❹ Gallaudet는 이웃 사람의 청각장애인 딸 Alice Cogswell을 만난 후 청각 장애인 교육에 관심을 갖게 되었다. ❺ Cogswell의 아버지와 다른 이들로부터의 자금 제공으로, Gallaudet는 청각 장애 아동을 가르치는 법을 배우기 위해 1815년 유럽으로 갔다. ❻ 영국의 청각 장애인 학교에서 본 것에 만족하지 못해, Gallaudet는 파리의 한 학교를 방문했다. ❼ 그 곳에서 그는 청각 장애인 교사 Jean Massieu와 Laurent Clerc로부터 교육을 받았다. ❽ Gallaudet는 1816년 Laurent Clerc와 함께 Hartford로 돌아왔고, 현재 American School for the Deaf로 알려진 미국 최초의 청각 장애인 학교를 1817년에 설립했다. ❾ Gallaudet는 1830년까지 그 기관의 교장으로 근무했다. ❿ 그는 자신의 이전 학생 중 한 명인 Sofia Fowler와 결혼했고, 여덟 명의 자녀를 두었다.

Word List

□ **attend** 출석하다, 다니다   □ **deaf** 청각 장애가 있는   □ **neighbor** 이웃   □ **funding** 자금(제공), 재정 지원   □ **dissatisfied** 만족하지 못한
□ **accompany** 함께 가다, 동반하다   □ **establish** 설립하다   □ **serve as** ~으로 근무하다, ~의 역할을 하다   □ **institution** 기관
□ **principal** 교장

• Word Test

1	serve as		6	설립하다	
2	neighbor		7	만족하지 못한	
3	accompany		8	교장	
4	institution		9	자금(제공), 재정 지원	
5	deaf		10	출석하다, 다니다	

Thomas Hopkins Gallaudet was born in Philadelphia on December 10, 1787. His family moved to Hartford, Connecticut, ❶ where / which he attended the Hartford Grammar School. He entered Yale College in 1802 and graduated the youngest in his class. Gallaudet became interested in the education of deaf people after meeting Alice Cogswell, the deaf daughter of a neighbor. With funding from Cogswell's father and others, Gallaudet went to Europe in 1815 to learn how to teach deaf children. Dissatisfied by ❷ what / which he saw in British schools for deaf people, Gallaudet visited a school in Paris. There, he received training from deaf teachers Jean Massieu and Laurent Clerc. Gallaudet ❸ abandoned / accompanied Laurent Clerc back to Hartford in 1816 and established the first school for the deaf in the United States in 1817, now known ❹ as / for the American School for the Deaf. Gallaudet served as the institution's principal until 1830. He married one of his former students, Sofia Fowler, and had eight children.

Thomas Hopkins Gallaudet was born in Philadelphia on December 10, 1787. His family moved to Hartford, Connecticut, where he attended the Hartford Grammar School. He entered Yale College in 1802 and graduated the youngest in his class. Gallaudet became interested in the education of deaf people after ❶ _____ (meet) Alice Cogswell, the deaf daughter of a neighbor. With funding from Cogswell's father and others, Gallaudet went to Europe in 1815 to learn how ❷ _____ (teach) deaf children. Dissatisfied by what he saw in British schools for deaf people, Gallaudet visited a school in Paris. There, he received ❸ _____ (train) from deaf teachers Jean Massieu and Laurent Clerc. Gallaudet accompanied Laurent Clerc back to Hartford in 1816 and established the first school for the deaf in the United States in 1817, now ❹ _____ (know) as the American School for the Deaf. Gallaudet served as the institution's principal until 1830. He married one of his former students, Sofia Fowler, and had eight children.

Thomas Hopkins Gallaudet was born in Philadelphia on December 10, 1787. His family moved to Hartford, Connecticut, where he attended the Hartford Grammar School. He entered Yale College in 1802 and graduated ❶ _____ _____ _____ _____ _____ (그의 반에서 가장 나이 어린). Gallaudet ❷ _____ _____ _____ (~에 관심을 갖게 되었다) the education of deaf people after meeting Alice Cogswell, the deaf daughter of a neighbor. ❸ _____ _____ _____ (~부터 자금 제공으로) Cogswell's father and others, Gallaudet went to Europe in 1815 to learn how to teach deaf children. Dissatisfied by what he saw in British schools for deaf people, Gallaudet visited a school in Paris. There, ❹ _____ _____ _____ (그는 훈련을 받았다) from deaf teachers Jean Massieu and Laurent Clerc. Gallaudet accompanied Laurent Clerc back to Hartford in 1816 and established the first school for the deaf in the United States in 1817, now known as the American School for the Deaf. Gallaudet ❺ _____ _____ _____ _____ _____ (그 기관의 교장으로 근무했다) until 1830. He married one of his former students, Sofia Fowler, and had eight children.

❶ William Black was born in Glasgow, Scotland. ❷ His father, a successful merchant, sent him to the School of Art at Glasgow, but Black pursued journalism instead of painting. ❸ As a teenager he began writing essays for the local Glasgow newspapers. ❹ Some of Black's early articles were on well-known 19th-century English writers and thinkers such as Thomas Carlyle and John Ruskin. ❺ His early novel *James Merle* (1864) made little impression. ❻ Black eventually left Glasgow for London, where he began to write for another paper, the *Morning Star*. ❼ In 1865, he married Augusta Wenzel, who died in childbirth the following year. ❽ Black then went to Europe as a foreign correspondent to cover the so-called Seven Weeks' War, a conflict between Austria and Prussia. ❾ After returning to London, he continued to work as a journalist but also began to have success as a novelist. ❿ Black set his novels in the Scottish countryside and used a great deal of local color, traditions, and dialect, often setting up a dramatic tension between his rural and his city-bred characters.

❶ William Black은 스코틀랜드의 Glasgow에서 태어났다. ❷ 성공한 상인이었던 그의 아버지는 그를 Glasgow에 있는 예술 학교에 보냈지만, Black은 그림 대신 저널리즘을 추구했다. ❸ 십 대에 그는 Glasgow 지역 신문에 에세이를 쓰기 시작했다. ❹ Black의 초기 기사들 중 일부는 Thomas Carlyle과 John Ruskin과 같은 유명한 19세기 영국 작가들과 사상가들에 관한 것이었다. ❺ 그의 초기 소설 *James Merle* (1864년)은 별다른 인상을 주지 못했다. ❻ Black은 결국 Glasgow를 떠나 런던으로 향했고, 그곳에서 그는 또 다른 신문인 *Morning Star*에 글을 쓰기 시작했다. ❼ 1865년에 그는 Augusta Wenzel과 결혼했고, 그녀는 이듬해 출산 중 사망했다. ❽ 그 후 Black은 오스트리아와 프러시아 사이의 분쟁인 소위 Seven Weeks' War를 취재하기 위해 해외 특파원으로 유럽에 갔다. ❾ 런던으로 돌아온 후, 그는 저널리스트로서 계속 일했지만, 소설가로서도 성공을 거두기 시작했다. ❿ Black은 자신의 소설 배경을 스코틀랜드의 시골로 정하고, 많은 지방색, 전통, 그리고 방언을 사용했는데, 이는 자주 그의 시골과 도시에서 자란 캐릭터들 간의 극적인 긴장을 조성했다.

Word List

□ merchant 상인　□ pursue 추구하다　□ journalism 저널리즘, 언론계　□ thinker 사상가　□ impression 인상, 감명
□ eventually 결국　□ childbirth 출산　□ correspondent 특파원　□ cover 취재하다　□ so-called 소위　□ conflict 분쟁, 갈등
□ countryside 시골, 지방　□ dialect 방언, 지방어　□ set up 조성하다, 만들다　□ tension 긴장　□ rural 시골의, 지방의
□ city-bred 도시에서 자란　□ character 등장인물

• Word Test

1	impression	_____	10	결국	_____
2	set up	_____	11	추구하다	_____
3	conflict	_____	12	방언, 지방어	_____
4	journalism	_____	13	시골, 지방	_____
5	childbirth	_____	14	사상가	_____
6	rural	_____	15	등장인물	_____
7	city-bred	_____	16	특파원	_____
8	merchant	_____	17	소위	_____
9	cover	_____	18	긴장	_____

● 유형 1 네모 안에서 옳은 어법·어휘를 고르시오.

William Black was born in Glasgow, Scotland. His father, a successful merchant, sent him to the School of Art at Glasgow, but Black pursued journalism instead of painting. As a teenager he began writing essays for the local Glasgow newspapers. Some of Black's early articles were ❶ for / on well-known 19th-century English writers and thinkers such as Thomas Carlyle and John Ruskin. His early novel *James Merle* (1864) made little impression. Black eventually left Glasgow for London, ❷ which / where he began to write for another paper, the *Morning Star*. In 1865, he married Augusta Wenzel, ❸ who / when died in childbirth the following year. Black then went to Europe as a foreign correspondent to cover the so-called Seven Weeks' War, a conflict between Austria and Prussia. After returning to London, he continued to work as a journalist but also began to have success as a novelist. Black set his novels in the Scottish countryside and used a great deal of local color, traditions, and dialect, often setting up a dramatic tension between his ❹ rural / urban and his city-bred characters.

● 유형 2 괄호 안의 동사를 알맞은 형태로 쓰시오.

William Black was born in Glasgow, Scotland. His father, a successful merchant, sent him to the School of Art at Glasgow, but Black pursued journalism instead of painting. As a teenager he began writing essays for the local Glasgow newspapers. Some of Black's early articles ❶ _____ (be) on well-known 19th-century English writers and thinkers such as Thomas Carlyle and John Ruskin. His early novel *James Merle* (1864) made little impression. Black eventually left Glasgow for London, where he began to write for another paper, the *Morning Star*. In 1865, he married Augusta Wenzel, who died in childbirth the ❷ _____ (follow) year. Black then went to Europe as a foreign correspondent ❸ _____ (cover) the so-called Seven Weeks' War, a conflict between Austria and Prussia. After returning to London, he continued to work as a journalist but also began to have success as a novelist. Black ❹ _____ (set) his novels in the Scottish countryside and used a great deal of local color, traditions, and dialect, often ❺ _____ (set) up a dramatic tension between his rural and his city-bred characters.

● 유형 3 우리말에 맞게 빈칸에 알맞은 말을 쓰시오.

William Black was born in Glasgow, Scotland. His father, a successful merchant, sent him to the School of Art at Glasgow, but Black pursued journalism ❶ _____ _____ _____ (그림 대신에). As a teenager he began writing essays for the local Glasgow newspapers. Some of Black's early articles were on well-known 19th-century English writers and thinkers such as Thomas Carlyle and John Ruskin. His early novel *James Merle* (1864) ❷ _____ _____ _____ (별다른 인상을 주지 못했다). Black eventually left Glasgow for London, where he began to write for another paper, the *Morning Star*. In 1865, he married Augusta Wenzel, who ❸ _____ _____ _____ (출산 중 사망했다) the following year. Black then went to Europe as a foreign correspondent to cover the so-called Seven Weeks' War, a conflict between Austria and Prussia. After returning to London, he continued to work as a journalist but also began to ❹ _____ _____ _____ _____ _____ (소설가로서 성공을 거두다). Black set his novels in the Scottish countryside and used a great deal of local color, traditions, and dialect, often setting up ❺ _____ _____ _____ (극적인 긴장) between his rural and his city-bred characters.

❶ Pi Day has been celebrated annually on 14 March since 1988. ❷ The brainchild of Larry Shaw, a physicist at the San Francisco Exploratorium, the date 14 March was chosen because the American pattern of writing dates is to put the month before the day, so that 14 March is written as 3/14, corresponding to the pattern of the first three digits of π, 3.14 (three point one four). ❸ In 2009, the US House of Representatives passed a resolution recognising 14 March as National Pi Day. ❹ The date has attracted increasing worldwide publicity and is celebrated in a vast variety of ways, particularly in schools and colleges, and involves the inevitable consumption of all kinds of pies as well as competitions to memorise and recite as many of the digits of π as possible. ❺ Pi Day in 2015 was particularly significant because the date corresponded to the first five digits of π, 3.1415.

*brainchild 아이디어, 두뇌의 소산　**US House of Representatives 미국 하원　*** recite 암송하다

❶ '파이의 날'은 1988년부터 해마다 3월 14일에 기념되어 왔다. ❷ San Francisco Exploratorium의 물리학자였던 Larry Shaw의 아이디어로 3월 14일이라는 날짜가 선택되었는데, 월일을 표기하는 미국 방식이 월을 일 앞에 놓는 것이어서, 3월 14일이 3/14로 표기되어 π값의 처음 세 자리 숫자의 양식, 즉 3.14와 일치하기 때문이다. ❸ 2009년에 미국 하원이 3월 14일을 '전국 파이의 날'로 인정하는 결의안을 통과시켰다. ❹ 그 날짜는 점점 더 많은 전 세계적인 매스컴의 관심을 끌어 왔고, 특히 학교와 대학에서 매우 다양한 방법으로 기념되고 있으며, π값의 자리 숫자를 가능한 한 많이 암기해서 암송하는 대회뿐만 아니라 온갖 종류의 파이의 필연적인 섭취도 또한 수반한다. ❺ 2015년의 '파이의 날'은 특히 그 날짜가 π값의 처음 다섯 자리 숫자인 3.1415와 일치했기 때문에 의미가 있었다.

Word List

□ **celebrate** 기념하다　□ **annually** 해마다　□ **physicist** 물리학자　□ **correspond to** ~과 일치하다
□ **digit** (0부터 9까지의) 아라비아 숫자　□ **resolution** 결의안　□ **recognise** 인정하다, 인식하다　□ **attract** (주의·흥미 등을) 끌다
□ **worldwide** 전 세계적인　□ **publicity** 매스컴[언론]의 관심[주목], 명성　□ **a variety of** 다양한　□ **involve** 수반하다
□ **inevitable** 필연적인, 불가피한　□ **consumption** 섭취, 소비　□ **memorise** 암기하다　□ **significant** 의미가 있는, 중요한

• Word Test

1	resolution	_____	9	필연적인, 불가피한	_____
2	publicity	_____	10	인정하다, 인식하다	_____
3	significant	_____	11	해마다	_____
4	consumption	_____	12	암기하다	_____
5	physicist	_____	13	(주의·흥미 등을) 끌다	_____
6	correspond to	_____	14	수반하다	_____
7	digit	_____	15	전 세계적인	_____
8	a variety of	_____	16	기념하다	_____

Pi Day ❶ |was / has been| celebrated annually on 14 March since 1988. The brainchild of Larry Shaw, a physicist at the San Francisco Exploratorium, the date 14 March was chosen because the American pattern of writing dates is to put the month before the day, so ❷ |that / which| 14 March is written as 3/14, corresponding to the pattern of the first three digits of π, 3.14 (three point one four). In 2009, the US House of Representatives passed a resolution recognising 14 March as National Pi Day. The date has attracted increasing worldwide publicity and is celebrated in a vast variety of ways, particularly in schools and colleges, and involves the ❸ |avoidable / inevitable| consumption of all kinds of pies as well as competitions to memorise and recite as many of the digits of π as possible. Pi Day in 2015 was particularly significant because the date ❹ |mismatched / corresponded| to the first five digits of π, 3.1415.

*brainchild 아이디어, 두뇌의 소산   **US House of Representatives 미국 하원   *** recite 암송하다

Pi Day has been celebrated annually on 14 March since 1988. The brainchild of Larry Shaw, a physicist at the San Francisco Exploratorium, the date 14 March ❶ _____ (choose) because the American pattern of writing dates is to put the month before the day, so that 14 March is written as 3/14, ❷ _____ (correspond) to the pattern of the first three digits of π, 3.14 (three point one four). In 2009, the US House of Representatives passed a resolution ❸ _____ (recognise) 14 March as National Pi Day. The date has attracted ❹ _____ (increase) worldwide publicity and is celebrated in a vast variety of ways, particularly in schools and colleges, and involves the inevitable consumption of all kinds of pies as well as competitions ❺ _____ (memorise) and recite as many of the digits of π as possible. Pi Day in 2015 was particularly significant because the date corresponded to the first five digits of π, 3.1415.

*brainchild 아이디어, 두뇌의 소산   **US House of Representatives 미국 하원   *** recite 암송하다

Pi Day has been ❶ _____ _____ (해마다 기념된) on 14 March since 1988. The brainchild of Larry Shaw, a physicist at the San Francisco Exploratorium, the date 14 March was chosen because the American pattern of writing dates is to put the month before the day, so that 14 March is written as 3/14, corresponding to the pattern of ❷ _____ _____ _____ _____ (처음 세 자리 숫자들) of π, 3.14 (three point one four). In 2009, the US House of Representatives ❸ _____ _____ _____ (결의안을 통과시켰다) recognising 14 March as National Pi Day. The date has attracted increasing worldwide publicity and is celebrated ❹ _____ _____ _____ _____ _____ _____ (매우 다양한 방법들로), particularly in schools and colleges, and involves the inevitable consumption of all kinds of pies as well as competitions to memorise and recite as many of the digits of π ❺ _____ _____ (가능한 한). Pi Day in 2015 was particularly significant because the date corresponded to the first five digits of π, 3.1415.

*brainchild 아이디어, 두뇌의 소산   **US House of Representatives 미국 하원   *** recite 암송하다

01 9강 1번

다음 글의 밑줄 친 부분 중, 어법상 틀린 것은?

Southern sea lions are seals with small, ① clearly visible external ears. They are much more mobile on land than true seals, ② being able to rotate their rear flippers sideways to propel their bodies forward. Sea lions can move quite fast in this manner. A fully grown southern sea lion bull is much larger and more impressive than his northern cousin, the California sea lion. This massive animal measures well over 2 m long and weighs up to half a tonne. His enormous neck is decorated with a shaggy mane; hence the name 'sea lion', ③ which also refers to his roar. The elegant, nearly yellowish females that make up his harem ④ weighs roughly half the average weight of an adult male, but then they expend less energy. From the time he comes ashore in December to when he leaves in March, the bull sea lion neither eats nor ⑤ sleeps for more than a few minutes at a time: guarding his harem is a full-time job.

*shaggy 텁수룩한 **mane 갈기
***harem 하렘(번식을 위해 한 마리의 수컷을 공유하는 암컷의 무리)

02 9강 2번

글의 흐름으로 보아, 주어진 문장이 들어가기에 가장 적절한 곳은?

There, he received training from deaf teachers Jean Massieu and Laurent Clerc.

Thomas Hopkins Gallaudet was born in Philadelphia on December 10, 1787. His family moved to Hartford, Connecticut, where he attended the Hartford Grammar School. He entered Yale College in 1802 and graduated the youngest in his class. (①) Gallaudet became interested in the education of deaf people after meeting Alice Cogswell, the deaf daughter of a neighbor. (②) With funding from Cogswell's father and others, Gallaudet went to Europe in 1815 to learn how to teach deaf children. (③) Dissatisfied by what he saw in British schools for deaf people, Gallaudet visited a school in Paris. (④) Gallaudet accompanied Laurent Clerc back to Hartford in 1816 and established the first school for the deaf in the United States in 1817, now known as the American School for the Deaf. (⑤) Gallaudet served as the institution's principal until 1830. He married one of his former students, Sofia Fowler, and had eight children.

03 9강 3번

다음 글의 제목으로 가장 적절한 것은?

William Black was born in Glasgow, Scotland. His father, a successful merchant, sent him to the School of Art at Glasgow, but Black pursued journalism instead of painting. As a teenager he began writing essays for the local Glasgow newspapers. Some of Black's early articles were on well-known 19th-century English writers and thinkers such as Thomas Carlyle and John Ruskin. His early novel *James Merle* (1864) made little impression. Black eventually left Glasgow for London, where he began to write for another paper, the *Morning Star*. In 1865, he married Augusta Wenzel, who died in childbirth the following year. Black then went to Europe as a foreign correspondent to cover the so-called Seven Weeks' War, a conflict between Austria and Prussia. After returning to London, he continued to work as a journalist but also began to have success as a novelist. Black set his novels in the Scottish countryside and used a great deal of local color, traditions, and dialect, often setting up a dramatic tension between his rural and his city-bred characters.

① Black's Successful Career as a Painter
② The Different Career Paths of Writers
③ William Black: A Novelist and Journalist
④ Why Black Left Art to Pursue Journalism
⑤ How Did the Countryside Affect Black's Life?

04 9강 4번

(A), (B), (C)의 각 네모 안에서 어법에 맞는 표현으로 가장 적절한 것은?

Pi Day has been celebrated annually on 14 March since 1988. The brainchild of Larry Shaw, a physicist at the San Francisco Exploratorium, the date 14 March was chosen because the American pattern of writing dates (A) $\boxed{\text{is / are}}$ to put the month before the day, so that 14 March is written as 3/14, corresponding to the pattern of the first three digits of π, 3.14 (three point one four). In 2009, the US House of Representatives passed a resolution (B) $\boxed{\text{recognised / recognising}}$ 14 March as National Pi Day. The date has attracted increasing worldwide publicity and is celebrated in a vast variety of ways, particularly in schools and colleges, and involves the inevitable consumption of all kinds of pies as well as competitions (C) $\boxed{\text{memorise / to memorise}}$ and recite as many of the digits of π as possible. Pi Day in 2015 was particularly significant because the date corresponded to the first five digits of π, 3.1415.

*brainchild 아이디어, 두뇌의 소산
US House of Representatives 미국 하원 * recite 암송하다

	(A)		(B)		(C)
①	is	……	recognised	……	memorise
②	is	……	recognising	……	memorise
③	is	……	recognising	……	to memorise
④	are	……	recognising	……	to memorise
⑤	are	……	recognised	……	to memorise

05 9강 1번

(A), (B), (C)의 각 네모 안에서 문맥에 맞는 낱말로 가장 적절한 것은?

Southern sea lions are seals with small, clearly visible external ears. They are much more (A) $\boxed{\text{mobile / immobile}}$ on land than true seals, being able to rotate their rear flippers sideways to propel their bodies forward. Sea lions can move quite fast in this manner. A fully grown southern sea lion bull is much larger and more impressive than his northern cousin, the California sea lion. This (B) $\boxed{\text{modest / massive}}$ animal measures well over 2 m long and weighs up to half a tonne. His enormous neck is decorated with a shaggy mane; hence the name 'sea lion', which also refers to his roar. The elegant, nearly yellowish females that make up his harem weigh roughly half the average weight of an adult male, but then they expend less energy. From the time he comes ashore in December to when he leaves in March, the bull sea lion neither eats nor sleeps for more than a few minutes at a time: guarding his harem is a (C) $\boxed{\text{part-time / full-time}}$ job.

*shaggy 덥수룩한 **mane 갈기
***harem 하렘(번식을 위해 한 마리의 수컷을 공유하는 암컷의 무리)

	(A)		(B)		(C)
①	mobile	……	modest	……	part-time
②	mobile	……	massive	……	part-time
③	mobile	……	massive	……	full-time
④	immobile	……	massive	……	full-time
⑤	immobile	……	modest	……	full-time

06 9강 2번

다음 글의 제목으로 가장 적절한 것은?

Thomas Hopkins Gallaudet was born in Philadelphia on December 10, 1787. His family moved to Hartford, Connecticut, where he attended the Hartford Grammar School. He entered Yale College in 1802 and graduated the youngest in his class. Gallaudet became interested in the education of deaf people after meeting Alice Cogswell, the deaf daughter of a neighbor. With funding from Cogswell's father and others, Gallaudet went to Europe in 1815 to learn how to teach deaf children. Dissatisfied by what he saw in British schools for deaf people, Gallaudet visited a school in Paris. There, he received training from deaf teachers Jean Massieu and Laurent Clerc. Gallaudet accompanied Laurent Clerc back to Hartford in 1816 and established the first school for the deaf in the United States in 1817, now known as the American School for the Deaf. Gallaudet served as the institution's principal until 1830. He married one of his former students, Sofia Fowler, and had eight children.

① Understanding the Values of Deaf Culture
② Gallaudet's Great Efforts in Deaf Education
③ Hardships in Funding Schools for the Deaf
④ Pioneering the Rights of the Deaf in the US
⑤ The Creation of Schools for the Disabled in the EU

07 9강 3번

다음 글의 밑줄 친 부분 중, 문맥상 낱말의 쓰임이 적절하지 <u>않은</u> 것은?

William Black was born in Glasgow, Scotland. His father, a successful merchant, sent him to the School of Art at Glasgow, but Black ① pursued journalism instead of painting. As a teenager he began writing essays for the local Glasgow newspapers. Some of Black's early articles were on well-known 19th-century English writers and thinkers such as Thomas Carlyle and John Ruskin. His early novel *James Merle* (1864) made little ② impression. Black eventually left Glasgow for London, where he began to write for another paper, the *Morning Star*. In 1865, he married Augusta Wenzel, who died in childbirth the following year. Black then went to Europe as a foreign correspondent to ③ cover the so-called Seven Weeks' War, a conflict between Austria and Prussia. After returning to London, he continued to work as a journalist but also began to have ④ hardship as a novelist. Black set his novels in the Scottish countryside and used a great deal of local color, traditions, and dialect, often setting up a dramatic ⑤ tension between his rural and his city-bred characters.

08 9강 4번

다음 글의 제목으로 가장 적절한 것은?

Pi Day has been celebrated annually on 14 March since 1988. The brainchild of Larry Shaw, a physicist at the San Francisco Exploratorium, the date 14 March was chosen because the American pattern of writing dates is to put the month before the day, so that 14 March is written as 3/14, corresponding to the pattern of the first three digits of π, 3.14 (three point one four). In 2009, the US House of Representatives passed a resolution recognising 14 March as National Pi Day. The date has attracted increasing worldwide publicity and is celebrated in a vast variety of ways, particularly in schools and colleges, and involves the inevitable consumption of all kinds of pies as well as competitions to memorise and recite as many of the digits of π as possible. Pi Day in 2015 was particularly significant because the date corresponded to the first five digits of π, 3.1415.

*brainchild 아이디어, 두뇌의 소산
US House of Representatives 미국 하원 * recite 암송하다

① Larry Shaw: An Icon of Mathematics
② How Mathematicians Observe Pi Day
③ The Significance of the Date of Pi Day
④ The Best Attractions to Enjoy on Pi Day
⑤ The Tradition of Consuming Pies on Pi Day

9강 1번

Southern sea lions are seals with small, clearly visible external ears. They are much more mobile on land than true seals, being able to rotate their rear flippers sideways to propel their bodies forward. Sea lions can move quite fast in this manner. A fully grown southern sea lion bull is much larger and more impressive than his northern cousin, the California sea lion. This massive animal (A) measuring well over 2 m long and weighs up to half a tonne. His enormous neck is decorated with a shaggy mane; hence the name 'sea lion', which also (B) referred his roar. The elegant, nearly yellowish females that make up his harem weigh roughly half the average weight of an adult male, but then they expend less energy. From the time he comes ashore in December (C) to which he leaves in March, the bull sea lion neither eats nor sleeps for more than a few minutes at a time: guarding his harem is a full-time job.

*shaggy 텁수룩한 **mane 갈기
***harem 하렘(번식을 위해 한 마리의 수컷을 공유하는 암컷의 무리)

09 윗글에서 다음 질문에 대한 답을 찾아 우리말로 쓰시오.
(35자 내외)

Q: What gives southern sea lions the ability to move faster on land than true seals?

A: _____

_____

고난도

10 윗글의 밑줄 친 부분을 어법상 알맞은 형태로 고쳐 쓰시오.

(A) measuring → _____

(B) referred → _____

(C) to which → _____

9강 2번

Thomas Hopkins Gallaudet was born in Philadelphia on December 10, 1787. His family moved to Hartford, Connecticut, (A) which he attended the Hartford Grammar School. He entered Yale College in 1802 and graduated the youngest in his class. Gallaudet became interesting in the education of deaf people after meeting Alice Cogswell, the deaf daughter of a neighbor. With funding from Cogswell's father and others, Gallaudet went to Europe in 1815 to learn how to teach deaf children. 영국의 청각 장애인 학교들에서 본 것에 만족하지 못해서, Gallaudet visited a school in Paris. There, he received training from deaf teachers Jean Massieu and Laurent Clerc. Gallaudet accompanied Laurent Clerc back to Hartford in 1816 and established the first school for the deaf in the United States in 1817, now (B) knew as the American School for the Deaf. Gallaudet served as the institution's principal until 1830. He (C) married with one of his former students, Sofia Fowler, and had eight children.

고난도

11 윗글의 밑줄 친 부분을 어법상 알맞은 형태로 고쳐 쓰시오.

(A) which → _____

(B) knew → _____

(C) married with → _____

12 윗글의 밑줄 친 우리말 의미와 일치하도록 **보기** 의 단어를 활용하여 **조건** 에 맞게 영작하시오.

보기 British / he / saw / deaf people / by / dissatisfy / in / what / for / schools

조건 · 분사구문을 활용할 것
· 필요시 어형을 바꿔 쓸 것
· 총 12단어로 쓸 것

_____

_____

William Black was born in Glasgow, Scotland. His father, a successful merchant, sent him to the School of Art at Glasgow, but Black _____(A)_____ journalism instead of painting. As a teenager he began writing essays for the local Glasgow newspapers. Some of Black's early articles were on well-known 19th-century English writers and thinkers such as Thomas Carlyle and John Ruskin. His early novel *James Merle* (1864) 별다른 인상을 주지 못했다. Black eventually left Glasgow for London, where he began to write for another paper, the *Morning Star*. In 1865, he married Augusta Wenzel, who died in childbirth the following year. Black then went to Europe as a foreign correspondent to _____(B)_____ the so-called Seven Weeks' War, a conflict between Austria and Prussia. After returning to London, he continued to work as a journalist but also began to have success as a novelist. Black set his novels in the Scottish countryside and used a great deal of local color, traditions, and dialect, often setting up a dramatic tension between his rural and his city-bred characters.

13 윗글의 빈칸 (A), (B)에 들어갈 단어를 영영 뜻풀이를 참고하여 쓰시오. (단 주어진 글자로 시작하여 어법에 알맞은 형태로 쓸 것)

> to try to achieve something

(A) p_____

> to give a report or description of an event on television or radio, or in a newspaper

(B) c_____

14 윗글의 밑줄 친 우리말 의미와 일치하도록 조건 에 맞게 영작하시오.

> 조건
> · 3단어로 쓸 것
> · 동사 make와 적절한 수량형용사를 활용할 것

_____

Pi Day has been celebrated annually on 14 March since 1988. The brainchild of Larry Shaw, a physicist at the San Francisco Exploratorium, the date 14 March was chosen because the American pattern of writing dates is to put the month before the day, so that 14 March is written as 3/14, corresponding to the pattern of the first three digits of π, 3.14 (three point one four). In 2009, the US House of Representatives 전국 파이의 날로 인정하는 결의안을 통과시켰다. The date has attracted increasing worldwide publicity and is celebrated in a vast variety of ways, particularly in schools and colleges, and involves the inevitable consumption of all kinds of pies as well as competitions to memorise and recite as many of the digits of π as possible. Pi Day in 2015 was particularly significant because the date corresponded to the first five digits of π, 3.1415.

*brainchild 아이디어, 두뇌의 소산
**US House of Representatives 미국 하원 ***recite 암송하다

15 윗글에서 다음 질문에 대한 답을 찾아 우리말로 쓰시오. (30자 내외)

Q: What are the two ways in which Pi Day is celebrated in the article above?

A: _____

_____

16 윗글의 밑줄 친 우리말 의미와 일치하도록 보기 의 단어를 활용하여 영작하시오. (단, 필요시 어형을 바꿔 쓸 것)

> 보기   14 March / a resolution / recognise /
> National Pi Day / pass / as

_____

_____

❶ Central Square Summer Youth T-ball Camp

❷ Enroll your child in a fun summer camp to learn T-ball and make friends. ❸ The camp focuses on teaching kids the fundamentals of throwing, catching, and batting skills.

❹ General information:

- ❺ The camp meets twice per week, on Mondays and Wednesdays.
- ❻ There will be 4 teams, and each team will have a maximum of 13 players.
- ❼ Each participant will receive a camp T-shirt and a hat.
- ❽ Lunch will be provided along with snacks.

❾ **When**: J:une 5th – July 12th, Monday/Wednesday, 10:00 a.m. – 2:00 p.m.

❿ **Where**: Central Square Park. In case of bad weather, the camp will be held in an indoor arena at Central Square.

⓫ **Registration**: Registration opens May 15th, in person at the Central Square Community Center or online at www.centralsquare.org. ⓬ Due to limited spaces, register early!

⓭ **Cost**: $45 per child

⓮ Our camp needs parent volunteer coaches. ⓯ Please contact the community center if you are able to volunteer. ⓰ Training will be provided.

❶ Central Square 여름 청소년 티볼 캠프

❷ 여러분의 자녀를 티볼을 배우고 친구를 사귈 수 있는 재미있는 여름 캠프에 등록하세요. ❸ 캠프는 아이들에게 던지기, 잡기, 치기 기술의 기초를 가르치는 데 초점을 맞추고 있습니다.

❹ 일반 정보:

❺ 캠프는 일주일에 두 번, 월요일과 수요일마다 모입니다.

❻ 4팀이 있을 것이고 팀마다 최대 13명의 선수가 있게 됩니다.

❼ 각 참가자는 캠프 티셔츠와 모자를 받게 됩니다.

❽ 간식과 함께 점심이 제공됩니다.

❾ **시간**: 6월 5일~7월 12일, 월요일/수요일, 오전 10시~오후 2시

❿ **장소**: Central Square 공원. 날씨가 좋지 않은 경우, 캠프는 Central Square의 실내 경기장에서 개최됩니다.

⓫ **등록**: 등록은 5월 15일에 시작하는데, Central Square 주민 센터에서 직접 하거나, www.centralsquare.org에서 온라인으로 할 수 있습니다. ⓬ 자리가 한정되어 있으니, 서둘러 등록하십시오!

⓭ **비용**: 어린이 한 명당 45달러

⓮ 저희 캠프에는 부모 자원봉사 코치가 필요합니다. ⓯ 자원봉사가 가능하면, 주민 센터로 연락해 주십시오. ⓰ 교육이 제공됩니다.

Word List

□ enroll 등록하다　□ fun 재미있는　□ focus on ~에 초점을 맞추다　□ fundamental (주로 복수로) 기초, 기본　□ general 일반적인　□ twice 두 번　□ per ~당　□ maximum 최대　□ provide 주다, 제공하다　□ along with ~과 함께　□ in case of ~의 경우에　□ indoor 실내의　□ arena 경기장　□ registration 등록　□ in person 직접　□ due to ~ 때문에　□ limited 제한된　□ contact 연락하다

• Word Test

1	indoor		10	연락하다
2	fundamental		11	등록
3	in case of		12	주다, 제공하다
4	twice		13	~에 초점을 맞추다
5	per		14	제한된
6	in person		15	등록하다
7	fun		16	일반적인
8	along with		17	최대
9	arena		18	~ 때문에

Central Square Summer Youth T-ball Camp

Enroll your child in a fun summer camp to learn T-ball and make friends. The camp focuses ❶ about / on teaching kids the fundamentals of throwing, catching, and batting skills.

General information:
- The camp meets twice per week, on Mondays and Wednesdays.
- There will be 4 teams, and each team will have a ❷ maximum / minimum of 13 players.
- Each participant will receive a camp T-shirt and a hat.
- Lunch will be provided along with snacks.

When: June 5th–July 12th, Monday/Wednesday, 10:00 a.m.–2:00 p.m.

Where: Central Square Park. In case of bad weather, the camp will be held in an indoor arena at Central Square.

Registration: Registration opens May 15th, in person at the Central Square Community Center or online at www.centralsquare.org. ❸ Due / Thanks to limited spaces, register early!

Cost: $45 per child

Our camp needs parent volunteer coaches. Please contact the community center ❹ if / unless you are able to volunteer. Training will be provided.

Central Square Summer Youth T-ball Camp

Enroll your child in a fun summer camp ❶ _____(learn) T-ball and make friends. The camp focuses on ❷ _____ (teach) kids the fundamentals of throwing, catching, and batting skills.

General information:
- The camp meets twice per week, on Mondays and Wednesdays.
- There will be 4 teams, and each team will have a maximum of 13 players.
- Each participant will receive a camp T-shirt and a hat.
- Lunch will ❸ _____ (provide) along with snacks.

When: June 5th–July 12th, Monday/Wednesday, 10:00 a.m.–2:00 p.m.

Where: Central Square Park. In case of bad weather, the camp will be held in an indoor arena at Central Square.

Registration: Registration opens May 15th, in person at the Central Square Community Center or online at www.centralsquare.org. Due to limited spaces, register early!

Cost: $45 per child

Our camp needs parent volunteer coaches. Please contact the community center if you ❹ _____ (be) able to volunteer. Training will be provided.

Central Square Summer Youth T-ball Camp

Enroll your child in a fun summer camp to learn T-ball and ❶ _____ _____ (친구들을 사귀다). The camp focuses on teaching kids the fundamentals of throwing, catching, and batting skills.

General information:

• The camp meets ❷ _____ _____ _____ (일주일마다 두 번), on Mondays and Wednesdays.

• There will be 4 teams, and each team will have a maximum of 13 players.

• Each participant will receive a camp T-shirt and a hat.

• Lunch will be provided along with snacks.

When: June 5th−July 12th, Monday/Wednesday, 10:00 a.m.−2:00 p.m.

Where: Central Square Park. ❸ _____ _____ _____ _____ _____ (날씨가 좋지 않은 경우에), the camp will be held in an indoor arena at Central Square.

Registration: Registration opens May 15th, ❹ _____ _____ (본인이 직접) at the Central Square Community Center or online at www.centralsquare.org. Due to limited spaces, register early!

Cost: $45 per child

Our camp needs parent volunteer coaches. Please contact the community center if you are able to volunteer. Training will be provided.

❶ **Future Scientists Program**

❷ We are now inviting applicants for
the 2023 Future Scientists Program!

❸ The Future Scientists Program provides opportunities for those interested in science and research to participate as research assistants (RA) with our institute. ❹ Research assistant positions will last for three months.

❺ **Eligibility Requirements**
- ❻ Current university or community college students, or recent graduates
- ❼ Those who are able to dedicate at least 5 hours per week for the duration of the program

❽ **Important Dates**
- ❾ March 1: application period opens.
- ❿ April 15: application period closes.
- ⓫ May 3: results of application process will be announced.
- ⓬ June 1: program begins.
- ⓭ August 31: program ends.

⓮ **Application Requirements**
- ⓯ Complete the online application form.
- ⓰ Send two letters of recommendation to fsp23_letters@institute. org.
- ⓱ There is a $20 USD application fee.

*eligibility 자격, 적격(성)

❶ 미래 과학자 프로그램

❷ 지금 2023년 미래 과학자 프로그램 지원자를 초대합니다!

❸ 미래 과학자 프로그램은 과학과 연구에 관심 있는 사람이 우리 기관에서 연구 조교로 참여할 기회를 제공합니다. ❹ 연구 조교직은 3개월 동안 지속될 것입니다.

❺ 자격 요건
- ❻ 현재 대학이나 지역 전문 대학의 학생, 또는 최근 대학 졸업자
- ❼ 프로그램 기간에 적어도 1주일에 5시간을 근무할 수 있는 사람

❽ 중요 날짜
- ❾ 3월 1일: 지원 기간이 시작됩니다.
- ❿ 4월 15일: 지원 기간이 종료됩니다.
- ⓫ 5월 3일: 지원 처리 결과가 발표될 것입니다.
- ⓬ 6월 1일: 프로그램이 시작됩니다.
- ⓭ 8월 31일: 프로그램이 종료됩니다.

⓮ 지원요건
- ⓯ 온라인 지원서를 작성하세요.
- ⓰ 추천서 2장을 fsp23_letters@institute. org로 보내세요.
- ⓱ 지원 비용은 미화 20달러입니다.

Word List

□ applicant 지원자 □ participate 참여하다 □ research assistant 연구 조교 □ institute 기관 □ last 지속되다, 계속되다
□ requirement 요건 □ current 현재의 □ community college 지역 전문 대학 □ recent 최근의 □ graduate 대학 졸업자
□ dedicate (시간·노력을) 쓰다, 바치다 □ for the duration of ~의 기간 중에 □ application 지원 □ period 기간
□ process 절차, 과정 □ complete 완료하다 □ letter of recommendation 추천서 □ fee 요금

1	period	_____	
2	community college	_____	
3	requirement	_____	
4	dedicate	_____	
5	letter of recommendation	_____	
6	participate	_____	
7	for the duration of	_____	
8	complete	_____	
9	research assistant	_____	

10	지원자	_____
11	요금	_____
12	지원	_____
13	절차, 과정	_____
14	대학 졸업자	_____
15	지속되다, 계속되다	_____
16	기관	_____
17	현재의	_____
18	최근의	_____

• 유형 1 네모 안에서 옳은 어법·어휘를 고르시오.

Future Scientists Program

We are now inviting applicants for the 2023 Future Scientists Program!

The Future Scientists Program provides opportunities ❶ for / of those interested in science and research to participate as research assistants (RA) with our institute. Research assistant positions will last for three months.

Eligibility Requirements
- Current university or community college students, or ❷ past / recent graduates
- Those ❸ that / who are able to dedicate at least 5 hours per week for the duration of the program

Important Dates
- March 1: application period opens.
- April 15: application period closes.
- May 3: results of application process will be announced.
- June 1: program begins.
- August 31: program ends.

Application Requirements
- Complete the online application form.
- Send two letters of ❹ recommendation/disapproval to fsp23_letters@institute.org.
- There is a $20 USD application fee.

*eligibility 자격, 적격(성)

Future Scientists Program

We are now inviting applicants for the 2023 Future Scientists Program!

The Future Scientists Program provides opportunities for those ❶ _____ (interest) in science and research to participate as research assistants (RA) with our institute. Research assistant positions ❷ _____ (last) for three months.

Eligibility Requirements

- Current university or community college students, or recent graduates
- Those who are able ❸ _____ (dedicate) at least 5 hours per week for the duration of the program

Important Dates

- March 1: application period opens.
- April 15: application period closes.
- May 3: results of application process will ❹ _____ (announce).
- June 1: program begins.
- August 31: program ends.

Application Requirements

- Complete the online application form.
- Send two letters of recommendation to fsp23_letters@institute.org.
- There is a $20 USD application fee.

*eligibility 자격, 적격(성)

Future Scientists Program

We are now inviting applicants for the 2023 Future Scientists Program!

The Future Scientists Program provides opportunities for ❶ _____ _____ _____ (~에 관심이 있는 사람들) science and research to participate as research assistants (RA) with our institute. Research assistant positions will last for three months.

Eligibility Requirements
- Current university or community college students, or ❷ _____ _____ (최근 대학 졸업자들)
- Those who are able to dedicate at least 5 hours per week for ❸ _____ _____ _____ _____ _____ (프로그램의 기간 동안)

Important Dates
- March 1: application period opens.
- April 15: application period closes.
- May 3: results of application process will be announced.
- June 1: program begins.
- August 31: program ends.

Application Requirements
- Complete the online application form.
- Send two letters of recommendation to fsp23_letters@institute.org.
- There is a $20 USD ❹ _____ _____ (지원 비용).

*eligibility 자격, 적격(성)

❶ Jericho Vet Hospital Canine Therapeutic Massage Class

❷ Therapeutic massage is very beneficial because it helps dogs release their physical and emotional stress. ❸ Come join our class to learn ten basic massage techniques that you can use on your dogs to help them relax.

❹ Class Information
- ❺ The class is conducted by a certified canine massage therapist.
- ❻ Participants will observe a therapeutic massage session and learn about the ten techniques applied.
- ❼ Date & Time: Saturday, March 25, 9 a.m.–11 a.m.
- ❽ Cost: $30 per person
- ❾ Only 10 spaces are available on a first-come-first-served basis.

❿ To reserve your spot, email us at jerichovethospitalctmc@abd.com or give us a call at 999–12–5210.

*canine 개의

❶ Jericho 동물 병원 개 치료 마사지 수업
❷ 치료 마사지는 개가 신체와 감정의 스트레스를 해소하는 데 도움을 주기 때문에 매우 유익합니다. ❸ 오셔서 저희 수업에 참여해 여러분의 개가 긴장을 풀도록 돕는 데 여러분의 개에게 사용할 수 있는 10가지 기본적인 마사지 기술을 배우세요.

❹ 수업 정보
- ❺ 수업은 자격증이 있는 개 마사지 치료사에 의해 진행됩니다.
- ❻ 참가자는 치료 마사지 수업을 참관하고 10가지 적용된 기술에 대해 배울 것입니다.
- ❼ 일시 : 3월 25일 토요일, 오전 9시~오전 11시
- ❽ 비용: 1인당 30달러
- ❾ 선착순으로 10명 자리만 가능합니다.

❿ 자리를 예약하시려면, jerichovethospitalctmc@abd.com 으로 이메일을 보내시거나 999-123-5210으로 전화주십시오.

Word List

□ vet hospital 동물 병원　□ therapeutic 치료의　□ beneficial 유익한　□ release 풀어 주다, 방출하다　□ emotional 감정의
□ relax 긴장을 풀다　□ conduct (특정 활동을) 하다　□ certified 자격증이 있는　□ observe 관찰하다, 보다　□ apply 적용하다
□ available 이용 가능한　□ on a first-come-first-served basis 선착순으로　□ reserve 예약하다　□ spot 자리, 곳

• Word Test

1	therapeutic		8	유익한
2	relax		9	자격증이 있는
3	conduct		10	자리, 곳
4	available		11	감정의
5	vet hospital		12	적용하다
6	release		13	예약하다
7	observe		14	선착순으로

Jericho Vet Hospital Canine Therapeutic Massage Class

Therapeutic massage is very ❶ beneficial / harmful because it helps dogs release their physical and emotional stress. Come join our class to learn ten basic massage techniques ❷ that / what you can use on your dogs to help them relax.

Class Information
- The class is conducted by a certified canine massage therapist.
- Participants will observe a therapeutic massage session and learn about the ten techniques applied.
- Date & Time: Saturday, March 25, 9 a.m.–11 a.m.
- Cost: $30 per person
- Only 10 spaces are ❸ available / unavailable on a first-come-first-served basis.

❹ Reserving / To reserve your spot, email us at jerichovethospitalctmc@abd.com or give us a call at 999-123-5210.

*canine 개의

Jericho Vet Hospital Canine Therapeutic Massage Class

Therapeutic massage is very beneficial because it helps dogs release their physical and emotional stress. Come join our class to learn ten basic massage techniques that you can use on your dogs ❶ _____ (help) them relax.

Class Information
- The class ❷ _____ (conduct) by a certified canine massage therapist.
- Participants will observe a therapeutic massage session and learn about the ten techniques ❸ _____ (apply).
- Date & Time: Saturday, March 25, 9 a.m.–11 a.m.
- Cost: $30 per person
- Only 10 spaces are available on a first-come-first-served basis.

To reserve your spot, email us at jerichovethospitalctmc@abd.com or give us a call at 999–123–5210.

*canine 개의

Jericho Vet Hospital Canine Therapeutic Massage Class

Therapeutic massage is very beneficial because it helps dogs release their physical and emotional stress. ❶ _____ _____ (와서 참여하라) our class to learn ten basic massage techniques that you can use on your dogs to help them relax.

Class Information
- ❷ _____ _____ _____ _____ (수업이 진행된다) by a certified canine massage therapist.
- Participants will observe a therapeutic massage session and learn about the ten techniques applied.
- Date & Time: Saturday, March 25, 9 a.m. – 11 a.m.
- Cost: $30 ❸ _____ _____ (1인당)
- Only 10 spaces are available ❹ _____ _____ _____ _____ (선착순으로).

To reserve your spot, email us at jerichovethospitalctmc@abd.com or give us a call at 999 – 123 – 5210.

*canine 개의

❶ **2023 Farmers' Market Scavenger Hunt**

❷ Bring your kids to the 2023 Farmers' Market Scavenger Hunt for a fun day at the farmers' market!

❸ **Date and time**: Saturday, June 3rd (9 a.m. – 12:30 p.m.)
❹ **Place**: Hillsdale County Farmers' Market outdoor parking lot

❺ Participants should be children ages 5 to 12.

❻ **General information**:
- ❼ Arrive at the market, get instructions and a list of items to find from any vendor, and start looking.
- ❽ The first ten scavenger hunt finishers each receive a $5 coupon to anything at the market.
- ❾ All participants will be entered into a drawing for another chance to win a prize at 1:00 p.m.

❿ For more information, email hcfm@freshhillsdale.com or call 375–288–0761.

*scavenger hunt 보물찾기 게임   **vendor 노점

---

❶ 2023년 Farmers' Market 보물찾기 게임

❷ 2023년 Farmers' Market 보물찾기 게임에 아이들을 데리고 와서 농산물 시장에서 즐거운 하루를 보내세요!

❸ **일시**: 6월 3일 토요일 (오전 9시~오후 12시 30분)
❹ **장소**: Hillsdale County Farmers' Market 야외 주차장

❺ 참가자는 5세에서 12세 사이의 어린이여야 합니다.

❻ **일반 정보**:
- ❼ 시장에 도착하여 어떤 노점으로부터든 지침과 찾아야 하는 품목의 목록을 받은 후 찾기 시작하세요.
- ❽ 보물찾기를 가장 먼저 끝낸 10명은 각각 시장에 있는 어떤 물건에도 쓸 수 있는 5달러 쿠폰을 받습니다.
- ❾ 모든 참가자가 오후 1시에 상품을 탈 수 있는 또 한 번의 기회를 위한 추첨 대상에 들어가게 될 것입니다.

❿ 더 많은 정보를 원하시면, hcfm@freshhillsdale.com으로 이메일을 보내시거나 375—288-0761로 전화하세요.

Word List

□ outdoor 야외의   □ parking lot 주차장   □ participant 참가자   □ instruction (보통 복수로) 지침   □ list 목록
□ item 물품, 품목   □ drawing 추첨   □ win a prize 상품을 받다

• Word Test

1 parking lot _____
2 win a prize _____
3 item _____
4 instruction _____
5 야외의 _____
6 추첨 _____
7 참가자 _____
8 목록 _____

2023 Farmers' Market Scavenger Hunt

Bring your kids ❶ at / to the 2023 Farmers' Market Scavenger Hunt for a fun day
at the farmers' market!

Date and time: Saturday, June 3rd (9 a.m. – 12:30 p.m.)
Place: Hillsdale County Farmers' Market outdoor parking lot

Participants should be children ages 5 to 12.

General information:
- Arrive at the market, get ❷ instructions/questions and a list of items to find from any vendor, and start looking.
- The first ten scavenger hunt finishers each receive a $5 coupon to ❸ nothing/anything at the market.
- All participants will be entered into a drawing for ❹ one/another chance to win a prize at 1:00 p.m.

For more information, email hcfm@freshhillsdale.com or call 375−288−0761.

*scavenger hunt 보물찾기 게임   **vendor 노점

2023 Farmers' Market Scavenger Hunt

Bring your kids to the 2023 Farmers' Market Scavenger Hunt for a fun day
at the farmers' market!

Date and time: Saturday, June 3rd (9 a.m. – 12:30 p.m.)
Place: Hillsdale County Farmers' Market outdoor parking lot

Participants should be children ages 5 to 12.

General information:
- Arrive at the market, get instructions and a list of items ❶ _____ (find) from any vendor, and start looking.
- The first ten scavenger hunt finishers each ❷ _____ (receive) a $5 coupon to anything at the market.
- All participants will ❸ _____ (enter) into a drawing for another chance to win a prize at 1:00 p.m.

For more information, email hcfm@freshhillsdale.com or call 375−288−0761.

*scavenger hunt 보물찾기 게임   **vendor 노점

2023 Farmers' Market Scavenger Hunt

❶ _____ _____ _____ (여러분의 아이들을 데리고 오라) to the 2023 Farmers' Market Scavenger Hunt for a fun day at the farmers' market!

Date and time: Saturday, June 3rd (9 a.m.−12:30 p.m.)
Place: Hillsdale County Farmers' Market outdoor parking lot

Participants should be children ages 5 to 12.

General information:
- Arrive at the market, get instructions and a(n) ❷ _____ _____ _____ (품목들의 목록) to find from any vendor, and start looking.
- The first ten scavenger hunt finishers each receive a $5 ❸ _____ _____ _____ (어떤 물건에도 쓸 수 있는 쿠폰) at the market.
- All participants will be entered into a(n) ❹ _____ _____ _____ _____ (또 한번의 기회를 위한 추첨) to win a prize at 1:00 p.m.

For more information, email hcfm@freshhillsdale.com or call 375−288−0761.

*scavenger hunt 보물찾기 게임   **vendor 노점

01 [10강 1번]

다음 안내문의 목적으로 가장 적절한 것은?

Central Square Summer Youth T-ball Camp

Enroll your child in a fun summer camp to learn T-ball and make friends. The camp focuses on teaching kids the fundamentals of throwing, catching, and batting skills.

General information:

- The camp meets twice per week, on Mondays and Wednesdays.
- There will be 4 teams, and each team will have a maximum of 13 players.
- Each participant will receive a camp T-shirt and a hat.
- Lunch will be provided along with snacks.

When: June 5th–July 12th, Monday/Wednesday, 10:00 a.m.–2:00 p.m.

Where: Central Square Park. In case of bad weather, the camp will be held in an indoor arena at Central Square.

Registration: Registration opens May 15th, in person at the Central Square Community Center or online at www.centralsquare.org. Due to limited spaces, register early!

Cost: $45 per child

Our camp needs parent volunteer coaches. Please contact the community center if you are able to volunteer. Training will be provided.

① 티볼 캠프에 필요한 자원봉사 참여를 유도하기 위해
② 티볼에 관심 있는 여름 캠프 참가자를 모집하기 위해
③ 여름 스포츠 캠프 홍보를 위한 온라인 사이트 안내를 위해
④ 티볼을 배울 수 있는 여름 캠프의 어른 회원 모집을 안내하기 위해
⑤ 여름 티볼 실내 캠핑 시즌 등록 안내와 자원봉사자 모집을 안내하기 위해

02 [10강 2번]

Future Scientists Program에 관한 다음 안내문의 내용과 일치하지 <u>않는</u> 것은?

Future Scientists Program

We are now inviting applicants for the 2023 Future Scientists Program!

The Future Scientists Program provides opportunities for those interested in science and research to participate as research assistants (RA) with our institute. Research assistant positions will last for three months.

Eligibility Requirements

- Current university or community college students, or recent graduates
- Those who are able to dedicate at least 5 hours per week for the duration of the program

Important Dates

- March 1: application period opens.
- April 15: application period closes.
- May 3: results of application process will be announced.
- June 1: program begins.
- August 31: program ends.

Application Requirements

- Complete the online application form.
- Send two letters of recommendation to fsp23_letters@institute.org.
- There is a $20 USD application fee.

*eligibility 자격, 적격(성)

① 프로그램의 지원 자격은 대학생 혹은 최근 졸업자이다.
② 6월부터 8월까지 프로그램 지원자에 대한 심사가 진행된다.
③ 온라인으로 추천서 2장과 함께 지원서를 작성한다.
④ 프로그램 진행 기간 동안 최소 일주일에 5시간을 근무해야 한다.
⑤ 연구 조교의 역할은 3개월간 이어지게 된다.

다음 안내문의 목적으로 가장 적절한 것은?

Jericho Vet Hospital Canine Therapeutic Massage Class

Therapeutic massage is very beneficial because it helps dogs release their physical and emotional stress. Come join our class to learn ten basic massage techniques that you can use on your dogs to help them relax.

Class Information

- The class is conducted by a certified canine massage therapist.
- Participants will observe a therapeutic massage session and learn about the ten techniques applied.
- Date & Time: Saturday, March 25, 9 a.m. – 11 a.m.
- Cost: $30 per person
- Only 10 spaces are available on a first-come-first-served basis.

To reserve your spot, email us at jerichovethospitalctmc@abd.com or give us a call at 999–123–5210.

*canine 개의

① 개 치료 마사지사 자격증 취득 과정을 안내하기 위해
② 개 치료 마사지 수업 참가의 중요성을 홍보하기 위해
③ 반려견을 편하게 해 주는 개 치료 마사지 수업을 홍보하기 위해
④ 개 치료 마사지 수업 장소로 선정된 동물 병원 10곳을 안내하기 위해
⑤ 개 치료 마사지 수업이 제대로 운영되는지를 관찰할 인원 모집을 안내하기 위해

2023 Farmers' Market Scavenger Hunt에 관한 다음 안내문의 내용과 일치하지 <u>않는</u> 것은?

2023 Farmers' Market Scavenger Hunt

Bring your kids to the 2023 Farmers' Market Scavenger Hunt for a fun day at the farmers' market!

Date and time: Saturday, June 3rd (9 a.m. – 12:30 p.m.)
Place: Hillsdale County Farmers' Market outdoor parking lot

Participants should be children ages 5 to 12.

General information:
- Arrive at the market, get instructions and a list of items to find from any vendor, and start looking.
- The first ten scavenger hunt finishers each receive a $5 coupon to anything at the market.
- All participants will be entered into a drawing for another chance to win a prize at 1:00 p.m.

For more information, email hcfm@freshhillsdale .com or call 375–288–0761.

*scavenger hunt 보물찾기 게임 **vendor 노점

① 농산물 시장에서 특정 연령을 대상으로 열리는 행사이다.
② 어떤 노점에서든 지침과 품목의 목록을 받을 수 있다.
③ 보물찾기를 끝내면 선착순 10명까지 쿠폰을 받을 수 있다.
④ 모든 참가자는 오후 1시에 최종 우승자로 뽑히는 기회를 얻는다.
⑤ 더 많은 정보를 위해 접근 가능한 경로는 두 가지 방법이 있다.

Central Square Summer Youth T-ball Camp에 관한 다음 안내문의 내용과 일치하는 것은?

Central Square Summer Youth T-ball Camp

Enroll your child in a fun summer camp to learn T-ball and make friends. The camp focuses on teaching kids the fundamentals of throwing, catching, and batting skills.

General information:
- The camp meets twice per week, on Mondays and Wednesdays.
- There will be 4 teams, and each team will have a maximum of 13 players.
- Each participant will receive a camp T-shirt and a hat.
- Lunch will be provided along with snacks.

When: June 5th–July 12th, Monday/Wednesday, 10:00 a.m.–2:00 p.m.

Where: Central Square Park. In case of bad weather, the camp will be held in an indoor arena at Central Square.

Registration: Registration opens May 15th, in person at the Central Square Community Center or online at www.centralsquare.org. Due to limited spaces, register early!

Cost: $45 per child

Our camp needs parent volunteer coaches. Please contact the community center if you are able to volunteer. Training will be provided.

① 캠프 참가자는 월요일과 수요일 중에 참가일을 선택할 수 있다.
② 아이를 등록시키면 최대 인원이 제한된 4개의 팀 중 한 곳에 소속된다.
③ 모든 참가자 및 학부모는 캠프 티셔츠와 모자를 제공받게 된다.
④ 5월 15일부터 온라인으로 주민 센터나 안내된 웹사이트에서 등록할 수 있다.
⑤ 코치로서 훈련 경험이 있는 부모들은 자원봉사에 지원할 수 있다.

다음 안내문의 목적으로 가장 적절한 것은?

Future Scientists Program

We are now inviting applicants for the 2023 Future Scientists Program!

The Future Scientists Program provides opportunities for those interested in science and research to participate as research assistants (RA) with our institute. Research assistant positions will last for three months.

Eligibility Requirements
- Current university or community college students, or recent graduates
- Those who are able to dedicate at least 5 hours per week for the duration of the program

Important Dates
- March 1: application period opens.
- April 15: application period closes.
- May 3: results of application process will be announced.
- June 1: program begins.
- August 31: program ends.

Application Requirements
- Complete the online application form.
- Send two letters of recommendation to fsp23_letters@institute.org.
- There is a $20 USD application fee.

*eligibility 자격, 적격(성)

① 2023년도 미래 과학자 프로그램에 참여할 대학생과 대학원생을 모집하기 위해
② 고등학생들에게 미래 과학자 프로그램 참여를 통한 대학 진학을 안내하기 위해
③ 2023년도 미래 과학자 프로그램 참여자들을 초대하는 행사의 홍보를 위해
④ 대학생 및 졸업자들에게 연구 조교로서 미래 과학자 프로그램에 참여할 것을 안내하기 위해
⑤ 2023년도 미래 과학자 프로그램을 위한 후원금을 모금하기 위해

Jericho Vet Hospital Canine Therapeutic Massage Class에 관한 다음 안내문의 내용과 일치하는 것은?

Jericho Vet Hospital Canine Therapeutic Massage Class

Therapeutic massage is very beneficial because it helps dogs release their physical and emotional stress. Come join our class to learn ten basic massage techniques that you can use on your dogs to help them relax.

Class Information

- The class is conducted by a certified canine massage therapist.
- Participants will observe a therapeutic massage session and learn about the ten techniques applied.
- Date & Time: Saturday, March 25, 9 a.m. – 11 a.m.
- Cost: $30 per person
- Only 10 spaces are available on a first-come-first-served basis.

To reserve your spot, email us at jerichovethospitalctmc@abd.com or give us a call at 999 – 123 – 5210.

*canine 개의

① 개 치료 마사지 수업은 매주 토요일에 2시간 동안 진행된다.
② 수업 참여자는 신체와 감정의 스트레스를 풀 수 있다.
③ 10개의 치료 마사지 수업을 듣게 된다.
④ 공인된 개 치료 마사지 전문가가 수업을 진행한다.
⑤ 선착순으로 10개의 자리만 남아 있으며 예약은 불가하다.

다음 안내문의 목적으로 가장 적절한 것은?

2023 Farmers' Market Scavenger Hunt

Bring your kids to the 2023 Farmers' Market Scavenger Hunt for a fun day at the farmers' market!

Date and time: Saturday, June 3rd (9 a.m. – 12:30 p.m.)
Place: Hillsdale County Farmers' Market outdoor parking lot

Participants should be children ages 5 to 12.

General information:

- Arrive at the market, get instructions and a list of items to find from any vendor, and start looking.
- The first ten scavenger hunt finishers each receive a $5 coupon to anything at the market.
- All participants will be entered into a drawing for another chance to win a prize at 1:00 p.m.

For more information, email hcfm@freshhillsdale.com or call 375 – 288 – 0761.

*scavenger hunt 보물찾기 게임   **vendor 노점

① 아이들을 위한 농장 체험을 홍보하기 위해
② Farmers' Market에서 발매하는 쿠폰을 홍보하기 위해
③ 시장에서 열리는 보물찾기 게임을 안내하기 위해
④ Farmers' Market 행사 참가자들에게 상품 추첨을 안내하기 위해
⑤ 보물찾기 게임, 그리기 대회 등 시장에서 열리는 다양한 행사를 알리기 위해

10강 1번

Central Square Summer Youth T-ball Camp

Enroll your child in a fun summer camp to learn T-ball and make friends. The camp focuses on teaching kids the fundamentals of throwing, catching, and batting skills.

General information:

- The camp meets twice per week, on Mondays and Wednesdays.
- There will be 4 teams, and each team will have a maximum of 13 players.
- Each participant will receive a camp T-shirt and a hat.
- Lunch will be provided along with snacks.

When: June 5th – July 12th, Monday / Wednesday, 10:00 a.m. – 2:00 p.m.

Where: Central Square Park. 날씨가 좋지 않은 경우, 캠프는 Central Square의 실내 경기장에서 개최됩니다.

Registration: Registration opens May 15th, in person at the Central Square Community Center or online at www.centralsquare.org. Due to limited spaces, register early!

Cost: $45 per child

Our camp needs parent ___(A)___ coaches. Please contact the community center if you are able to ___(B)___ . Training will be provided.

09 윗글의 밑줄 친 우리말 의미와 일치하도록 보기 의 단어를 순서대로 배열하여 조건 에 맞게 문장을 완성하시오.

> 보기 in / bad weather / in an indoor arena / of / the camp / case / hold

> 조건 · 부사구로 문장을 시작할 것
> · 필요시 어형을 바꿔 쓸 것

_____

at Central Square.

10 윗글의 빈칸 (A), (B)에 공통으로 들어갈 단어를 영영 뜻풀이를 참고하여 쓰시오.

> someone who is not paid for the work that they do; to do some work without getting paid

_____

Future Scientists Program

We are now inviting applicants for the 2023 Future Scientists Program!

미래 과학자 프로그램은 과학과 연구에 관심 있는 사람들이 우리 기관에서 연구 조교로 참여할 기회를 제공합니다. Research assistant positions will last for three months.

Eligibility Requirements
- Current university or community college students, or recent graduates
- Those who are able to dedicate at least 5 hours per week for the duration of the program

Important Dates
- March 1: application period opens.
- April 15: application period closes.
- May 3: results of application process will be announced.
- June 1: program begins.
- August 31: program ends.

Application Requirements
- Complete the online application form.
- Send two letters of recommendation to fsp23_letters@institute.org.
- There is a $20 USD application fee.

*eligibility 자격, 적격(성)

11 윗글의 밑줄 친 우리말 의미와 일치하도록 보기 의 단어를 활용하여 조건 에 맞게 문장을 완성하시오.

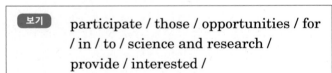

보기 participate / those / opportunities / for / in / to / science and research / provide / interested /

조건
· 〈보기〉의 단어를 모두 사용할 것
· 필요시 어형을 바꿔 쓸 것

The Future Scientists Program _____

_____

_____

as research assistants (RA) with our institute.

12 윗글을 읽고 다음 질문에 대한 답을 찾아 우리말로 쓰시오. (두 가지를 각각 25자 내외로 쓸 것)

Q: According to the passage, who can apply for Future Scientists Program?

A: (1) _____

_____

(2) _____

_____

Jericho Vet Hospital Canine Therapeutic Massage Class

Therapeutic massage is very beneficial because it helps dogs release their physical and emotional stress. Come join our class to learn ten basic massage techniques that you can use on your dogs to help them relax.

Class Information

- The class is conducted by a certified canine massage therapist.
- Participants will observe a(n) _____ massage session and learn about the ten techniques applied.
- Date & Time: Saturday, March 25, 9 a.m.–11 a.m.
- Cost: $30 per person
- 선착순으로 10명 자리만 가능합니다.

To reserve your spot, email us at jerichovethospitalctmc@abd.com or give us a call at 999–123–5210.

*canine 개의

13 윗글의 빈칸에 들어갈 단어를 영영 뜻풀이를 참고하여 본문에서 찾아 쓰시오.

> helping to treat or cure illness

_____

14 윗글의 밑줄 친 우리말 의미와 일치하도록 보기 의 단어를 활용하여 조건 에 맞게 문장을 완성하시오.

> 보기 be / 10 spaces / available / a / basis / first-come-first-served / on

> 조건 ·〈보기〉의 단어를 모두 사용할 것
> · 필요시 어형을 바꿔 쓸 것

Only _____

_____.

2023 Farmers' Market Scavenger Hunt

Bring your kids to the 2023 Farmers' Market Scavenger Hunt for a fun day at the farmers' market!

Date and time: Saturday, June 3rd (9 a.m.–12:30 p.m.)
Place: Hillsdale County Farmers' Market outdoor parking lot

Participants should be children ages 5 to 12.

General information:
- Arrive at the market, get instructions and a list of items to find from any vendor, and start looking.
- The first ten scavenger hunt finishers each receive a $5 coupon to anything at the market.
- All participants will be entered into a _____ for another chance to win a prize at 1:00 p.m.

For more information, email hcfm@freshhillsdale.com or call 375–288–0761.

*scavenger hunt 보물찾기 게임   **vendor 노점

15 윗글에서 다음 질문에 대한 답을 찾아 우리말로 쓰시오. (35자 내외)

Q: What can the first ten finishers do with the coupons they receive?

A: _____

_____

16 윗글의 빈칸에 들어갈 단어를 영영 뜻풀이를 참고하여 쓰시오. (단, 주어진 글자로 시작하여 동명사 형태로 쓸 것)

> an act of choosing something such as a winning ticket from a group without knowing which one you are choosing

d_____

❶ Sometimes it's important to disagree. ❷ All the great social reforms which took place in the eighteenth century, for instance, began with the dedicated campaigns of a handful of people who saw something wrong, and did not let it rest. ❸ Slavery was widely accepted in Europe in the eighteenth century, but as a result of consistent campaigning, the slave trade was made illegal near the beginning of the nineteenth century, and the owning of slaves became illegal a few years later. ❹ Social psychologists Moscovici and Nemeth showed that if just a few people stick to a particular view, which they are convinced is right, then over time they can have a great deal of influence on a larger group. ❺ The important thing, though, is that those people who are in the minority and trying to influence the majority should be seen to be genuine, consistent and resisting social pressure. ❻ If we see people acting like that, over time we become curious about why they are doing it and so are likely to think more seriously about what they are saying.

❶ 때로는 의견이 다른 것이 중요하다. ❷ 예를 들어, 18세기에 일어난 모든 위대한 사회 개혁은 잘못된 것을 보고 그것을 그대로 두지 않은 몇 안 되는 사람들의 헌신적인 운동으로 시작되었다. ❸ 노예제가 18세기에 유럽에서 널리 받아들여졌으나, 일관적인 운동의 결과로 노예 무역이 19세기 초 무렵에 불법화되었고, 노예 소유가 몇 년 후에 불법화되었다. ❹ 사회 심리학자 Moscovici와 Nemeth는 단지 소수의 사람이라도 자신이 옳다고 확신하는 특정한 관점을 고수하면, 시간이 지남에 따라 그들은 더 큰 집단에 많은 영향을 미칠 수 있다는 것을 보여 주었다. ❺ 그러나 중요한 것은 소수파에 속하면서 다수파에 영향을 미치려고 하고 있는 그런 사람들은 진실하고 일관적이며 사회적 압력에 저항하고 있다고 여겨져야 한다는 것이다. ❻ 사람들이 그렇게 행동하고 있는 것을 본다면, 시간이 지남에 따라 우리는 그들이 왜 그것을 하고 있는지에 대해 궁금해지고, 그래서 그들이 말하고 있는 것에 대해 아마도 더 진지하게 생각할 것이다.

Word List

□ **disagree** 의견이 다르다 □ **reform** 개혁 □ **take place** 일어나다, 발생하다 □ **dedicated** 헌신적인
□ **campaign** (조직적인) 운동, 캠페인; 운동[캠페인]을 벌이다 □ **a handful of** 소수의 □ **rest** (문제가 처리되지 않고) 그대로 있다
□ **slavery** 노예제 □ **consistent** 일관적인 □ **illegal** 불법적인 □ **own** 소유하다 □ **psychologist** 심리학자 □ **stick to** ~을 고수하다
□ **convince** 확신시키다 □ **a great deal of** 많은, 다량의 □ **influence** 영향; 영향을 미치다 □ **minority** 소수 집단 □ **majority** 다수집단
□ **genuine** 진실한, 진심 어린 □ **consistent** 일관된 □ **resist** 저항하다 □ **pressure** 압력

• Word Test

1	psychologist		12 압력	
2	resist		13 소수의	
3	stick to		14 노예제	
4	illegal		15 헌신적인	
5	take place		16 일관적인	
6	rest		17 소수 집단	
7	a great deal of		18 일관된	
8	disagree		19 확신시키다	
9	campaign		20 진실한, 진심 어린	
10	influence		21 개혁	
11	majority		22 소유하다	

Sometimes it's important to ❶ [agree/disagree]. All the great social reforms which took place in the eighteenth century, for instance, began with the dedicated campaigns of a handful of people who saw something ❷ [wrong/right], and did not let it rest. Slavery was widely accepted in Europe in the eighteenth century, but as a result of consistent campaigning, the slave trade was made illegal near the beginning of the nineteenth century, and the owning of slaves became illegal a few years later. Social psychologists Moscovici and Nemeth showed that if just a few people stick to a particular view, ❸ [what/which] they are convinced is right, then over time they can have a great deal of influence on a larger group. The important thing, ❹ [therefore/though], is that those people who are in the minority and trying to influence the majority should be seen to be genuine, consistent and resisting social pressure. If we see people acting like that, over time we become curious about why they are doing it and ❺ [so/that] are likely to think more seriously about what they are saying.

Sometimes it's important to disagree. All the great social reforms which took place in the eighteenth century, for instance, ❶ _____ (begin) with the dedicated campaigns of a handful of people who saw something wrong, and did not let it ❷ _____ (rest). Slavery was widely accepted in Europe in the eighteenth century, but as a result of consistent campaigning, the slave trade was made illegal near the beginning of the nineteenth century, and the owning of slaves became illegal a few years later. Social psychologists Moscovici and Nemeth showed that if just a few people stick to a particular view, which they ❸ _____ (convince) is right, then over time they can have a great deal of influence on a larger group. The important thing, though, is that those people who are in the minority and ❹ _____ (try) to influence the majority should be seen to be genuine, consistent and resisting social pressure. If we see people acting like that, over time we become curious about why they are doing it and so ❺ _____ (be) likely to think more seriously about what they are saying.

Sometimes it's important to disagree. All the great social reforms which took place in the eighteenth century, ❶ _____ _____ (예를 들어), began with the dedicated campaigns of ❷ _____ _____ _____ _____ (몇 안 되는 사람들) who saw something wrong, and did not let it rest. Slavery was widely accepted in Europe in the eighteenth century, but ❸ _____ _____ _____ _____ (~의 결과로) consistent campaigning, the slave trade was made illegal near the beginning of the nineteenth century, and the owning of slaves became illegal a few years later. Social psychologists Moscovici and Nemeth showed that if just a few people ❹ _____ _____ _____ _____ _____ (특정한 관점을 고수하다), which they are convinced is right, then over time they can have a great deal of influence on a larger group. The important thing, though, is that those ❺ _____ _____ _____ _____ _____ _____ (소수파에 속하는 사람들) and trying to influence the majority should be seen to be genuine, consistent and resisting social pressure. If we see people acting like that, over time we become curious about why they are doing it and so are likely to think more seriously about what they are saying.

❶ Attention is selective. ❷ We cannot focus on everything, and the knowledge we bring to a given situation allows us to direct our attention to the most important elements and to ignore the rest. ❸ The extent to which our schemas and expectations guide our attention was powerfully demonstrated by an experiment in which participants watched a videotape of two "teams" of three people, each passing a basketball back and forth. ❹ The members of one team wore white shirts, and the members of the other team wore black shirts. ❺ Each participant was asked to count the number of passes made by the members of one of the teams. ❻ Forty-five seconds into the action, a person wearing a gorilla costume strolled into the middle of the action. ❼ Although a large black gorilla might seem hard to miss, only half the participants noticed it! ❽ The participants' schemas about what is likely to happen in a game of catch directed their attention so intently to some parts of the videotape that they failed to see a rather dramatic stimulus they did not expect to see.

❶ 주의는 선택적이다. ❷ 우리는 모든 것에 다 집중할 수는 없으며, 어떤 특정한 상황에 끌어오는 지식 때문에 가장 중요한 요소로 주의를 돌리고 나머지는 무시할 수 있다. ❸ 우리의 스키마와 기대가 주의를 이끄는 정도는 참가자들이 3명으로 구성된 두 '팀'이 각자 농구공을 주고받으며 패스하는 비디오테이프를 보는 실험으로 매우 효과적으로 입증되었다. ❹ 한 팀의 구성원들은 흰색 셔츠를 입었고, 다른 팀 구성원들은 검은색 셔츠를 입었다. ❺ 각 참가자는 한 팀의 구성원들이 한 패스의 횟수를 세어 보라는 요청을 받았다. ❻ 활동이 시작되고 45초 후, 고릴라 의상을 입은 한 사람이 그 활동의 한가운데로 걸어 들어갔다. ❼ 커다란 검은 고릴라는 놓치기 어려워 보이겠지만, 참가자의 절반만이 그것을 알아챘다! ❽ 캐치볼 게임에서 일어날 가능성이 있는 일에 관한 스키마 때문에 참가자들은 비디오테이프의 일부분에 매우 열중하여 주의를 기울였으므로, 자신들이 볼 것으로 예상하지 못한 꽤 인상적인 자극물을 보지 못했다.

Word List

□ **attention** 주의(력)　□ **selective** 선택적인, 선별적인　□ **direct** 돌리다, 향하게 하다　□ **element** 요소　□ **ignore** 무시하다
□ **extent** 정도, 규모　□ **schema** 스키마, 도식(과거의 경험과 지식에 의해 형성된 개인의 인지 구조)　□ **demonstrate** 입증하다
□ **experiment** 실험　□ **back and forth** 주고받으며, 왔다 갔다, 앞뒤로　□ **costume** 의상, 복장　□ **stroll** 거닐다　□ **miss** 놓치다
□ **intently** 골똘히, 열중하여　□ **dramatic** 인상적인, 극적인　□ **stimulus** 자극, 자극물

• Word Test

1	stroll	9	돌리다, 향하게 하다
2	element	10	의상, 복장
3	extent	11	인상적인, 극적인
4	schema	12	입증하다
5	back and forth	13	주의(력)
6	selective	14	자극, 자극물
7	ignore	15	실험
8	intently	16	놓치다

Attention is selective. We cannot focus on everything, and the knowledge we bring to a given situation allows us to direct our attention to the most important elements and to ❶ approve / ignore the rest. The extent ❷ which / to which our schemas and expectations guide our attention was powerfully demonstrated by an experiment in which participants watched a videotape of two "teams" of three people, each passing a basketball back and forth. The members of one team wore white shirts, and the members of ❸ the other / another team wore black shirts. Each participant was asked to count the number of passes made by the members of one of the teams. Forty-five seconds into the action, a person wearing a gorilla costume strolled into the middle of the action. ❹ Although / Because a large black gorilla might seem hard to miss, only half the participants noticed it! The participants' schemas about what is likely to happen in a game of catch directed their attention so intently to some parts of the videotape ❺ which / that they failed to see a rather dramatic stimulus they did not expect to see.

Attention is selective. We cannot focus on everything, and the knowledge we bring to a given situation ❶ _____ (allow) us to direct our attention to the most important elements and to ignore the rest. The extent to which our schemas and expectations guide our attention was powerfully demonstrated by an experiment in which participants watched a videotape of two "teams" of three people, each ❷ _____ (pass) a basketball back and forth. The members of one team wore white shirts, and the members of the other team wore black shirts. Each participant ❸ _____ (ask) to count the number of passes made by the members of one of the teams. Forty-five seconds into the action, a person ❹ _____ (wear) a gorilla costume strolled into the middle of the action. Although a large black gorilla might seem hard to miss, only half the participants noticed it! The participants' schemas about what is likely to happen in a game of catch directed their attention so intently to some parts of the videotape that they ❺ _____ (fail) to see a rather dramatic stimulus they did not expect to see.

Attention is selective. We cannot focus on everything, and the knowledge we bring to a given situation allows us to direct our attention to ❶ _____ _____ _____ _____ (가장 중요한 요소들) and to ignore the rest. The extent to which our schemas and expectations guide our attention was powerfully demonstrated by an experiment in which participants watched a videotape of two "teams" of three people, each passing a basketball back and forth. The members of one team wore white shirts, and the members of the other team wore black shirts. Each participant was asked to ❷ _____ _____ _____ (횟수를 세다) of passes made by the members of one of the teams. Forty-five seconds into the action, a person wearing a gorilla costume strolled into the middle of the action. Although a large black gorilla might seem hard to miss, only ❸ _____ _____ _____ (참가자들의 절반) noticed it! The participants' schemas about ❹ _____ _____ _____ _____ _____ (일어날 가능성이 있는 일) in a game of catch directed their attention so intently to some parts of the videotape that they ❺ _____ _____ _____ (보지 못했다) a rather dramatic stimulus they did not expect to see.

❶ With the rise of modern science new habits of mind developed. ❷ The method of the sciences and the image of scientific narratives became unquestioned and reinforced the new habits of mind, becoming an accomplice to those that would best accommodate the new image. ❸ These habits of mind became a duplication in the classroom of what the sciences were supposed to be doing in the laboratory. ❹ They developed clear and distinct ideas imitating mathematical models that are hypothetical, abstract, ahistorical, and humanly disembodied. ❺ Descartes, Newton, Galileo, Locke, and Rousseau are the best examples. ❻ The mind was trained to repeat certain logical operations until a habit was developed of reading the world according to those skills. ❼ Even if the reading was supposed to be disembodied and therefore objective, the result was that the viewpoints and skills became embodied in those using them. ❽ For the older habits of mind, external cosmologies (now considered outdated) were substituted in all classrooms.

*accomplice 공범　**duplication 복제, 복제품　***cosmology 우주론

❶ 현대 과학의 부상과 함께 새로운 사고 습관이 생겨났다. ❷ 과학의 방법과 과학적 담론의 이미지는 의심의 여지가 없게 되었고 새로운 사고 습관을 강화하여, 새로운 이미지를 가장 잘 수용할 사람들의 공범자가 되었다. ❸ 이러한 사고 습관은 과학이 실험실에서 해야 할 일에 대한 교실 내의 복제품이 되었다. ❹ 그것들은 가상적이고, 추상적이며, 몰역사적이고, 인간적 견지에서 현실로부터 유리된 수학적 모델을 모방한 분명하고 뚜렷이 다른 아이디어를 개발했다. ❺ 데카르트, 뉴턴, 갈릴레오, 로크, 루소가 가장 좋은 예이다. ❻ 정신은 특정한 논리적 연산을 반복하도록 훈련되어, 마침내 그런 기술에 따라 세상을 해석하는 습관이 생겼다. ❼ 비록 그 해석은 현실로부터 유리되었고 따라서 객관적이라고 생각되었지만, 결과적으로 그 관점과 기술은 그것을 사용하는 사람들에게서 구현되었다. ❽ 구식 사고 습관이 모든 교실에서 (지금은 시대에 뒤떨어진 것으로 간주되는) 외부 우주론으로 대체되었다.

Word List

□ habit 습관　□ method 방법　□ narrative 서술, 이야기　□ unquestioned 의심의 여지가 없는, 의심할 수 없는　□ reinforce 강화하다
□ accommodate 수용하다　□ laboratory 실험실　□ distinct 뚜렷이 다른　□ imitate 모방하다, 흉내 내다
□ hypothetical 가상적인, 가설[가정]의　□ abstract 추상적인　□ ahistorical 몰역사적인, 역사와 무관한　□ humanly 인간적으로
□ disembodied 현실에서 유리된, 실체 없는　□ operation 연산　□ objective 객관적인　□ viewpoint 관점　□ external 외부의
□ outdated 시대에 뒤떨어진　□ substitute ~ for... ⋯ 대신에 ~을 쓰다, ~으로 ⋯을 대체하다

Word Test

1	operation	11	강화하다
2	hypothetical	12	뚜렷이 다른
3	unquestioned	13	추상적인
4	ahistorical	14	시대에 뒤떨어진
5	disembodied	15	관점
6	narrative	16	실험실
7	external	17	객관적인
8	substitute ~ for...	18	방법
9	imitate	19	인간적으로
10	accommodate	20	습관

With the rise of modern science new habits of mind developed. The method of the sciences and the image of scientific narratives became ❶ unquestioned/questionable and reinforced the new habits of mind, becoming an accomplice to those that would best accommodate the new image. These habits of mind became a duplication in the classroom of ❷ what/which the sciences were supposed to be doing in the laboratory. They developed clear and distinct ideas imitating mathematical models ❸ that/who are hypothetical, abstract, ahistorical, and humanly disembodied. Descartes, Newton, Galileo, Locke, and Rousseau are the best examples. The mind was trained to repeat certain logical operations ❹ until/since a habit was developed of reading the world according to those skills. Even if the reading was supposed to be disembodied and therefore objective, the result was that the viewpoints and skills became embodied in those using them. For the older habits of mind, external cosmologies (now considered ❺ updated/outdated) were substituted in all classrooms.

*accomplice 공범   **duplication 복제, 복제품   ***cosmology 우주론

With the rise of modern science new habits of mind developed. The method of the sciences and the image of scientific narratives became unquestioned and ❶ _____ (reinforce) the new habits of mind, ❷ _____ (become) an accomplice to those that would best accommodate the new image. These habits of mind became a duplication in the classroom of what the sciences were supposed to be doing in the laboratory. They developed clear and distinct ideas ❸ _____ (imitate) mathematical models that are hypothetical, abstract, ahistorical, and humanly disembodied. Descartes, Newton, Galileo, Locke, and Rousseau are the best examples. The mind was trained to repeat certain logical operations until a habit ❹ _____ (develop) of reading the world according to those skills. Even if the reading was supposed to be disembodied and therefore objective, the result was that the viewpoints and skills became embodied in those ❺ _____ (use) them. For the older habits of mind, external cosmologies (now considered outdated) were substituted in all classrooms.

*accomplice 공범   **duplication 복제, 복제품   ***cosmology 우주론

With ❶ _____ _____ _____ _____ _____ (현대 과학의 부상) new habits of mind developed. The method of the sciences and the image of scientific narratives became unquestioned and reinforced the new ❷ _____ _____ _____ (사고 습관들), becoming an accomplice to those that would best accommodate the new image. These habits of mind became a duplication in the classroom of what the sciences were supposed to be doing in the laboratory. They developed ❸ _____ _____ _____ _____ (분명하고 뚜렷이 다른 아이디어들) imitating mathematical models that are hypothetical, abstract, ahistorical, and humanly disembodied. Descartes, Newton, Galileo, Locke, and Rousseau are ❹ _____ _____ _____ (가장 좋은 사례들). The mind was trained to ❺ _____ _____ _____ _____ (특정한 논리적 연산들을 반복하다) until a habit was developed of reading the world according to those skills. Even if the reading was supposed to be disembodied and therefore objective, the result was that the viewpoints and skills became embodied in those using them. For the older habits of mind, external cosmologies (now considered outdated) were substituted in all classrooms.

*accomplice 공범   **duplication 복제, 복제품   ***cosmology 우주론

❶ Commodities do not go to market ail on their own. ❷ Someone has to take them there. ❸ Goods must be moved, prices agreed, and only after a long and complicated process will the commodity in question be there for the end-user to enjoy. ❹ This applies to films and videos as much as it does to any other commodity, and it applies even in that sector of the film and video business that likes to think of itself as remote from and even antagonistic to the regular processes of commodity exchange. ❺ But perhaps because of this aversion, the process by which commodities get to market — generally referred to in the film trade as distribution — is the least studied of all the aspects of cinema and other forms of moving image. ❻ A lot is written about film and video production, about the films and videos produced and about how they are perceived/received by the spectator, but very little about the intermediate stages between production and consumption. ❼ Sometimes it seems as if, in the world of cinema and the moving image, commodities do indeed mysteriously get to market all on their own.

*antagonistic 상반되는 **aversion 반감

❶ 상품은 자력으로 시장에 나오지 않는다. ❷ 누군가가 그것을 거기에 가지고 가야 한다. ❸ 상품은 이동되어야 하고, 가격은 합의되어야 하며, 길고 복잡한 과정을 거친 후에야 실수요자가 누릴 수 있도록 해당 상품이 거기에 있게 될 것이다. ❹ 이것은 다른 어떠한 상품에도 적용되는 것만큼 영화와 비디오에도 적용되며, 그것은 상품 거래의 일상적인 과정과는 아주 다르고 심지어 상반된다고 여기고 싶어 하는 영화와 비디오 사업 분야에도 적용된다. ❺ 그러나 아마도 이러한 반감 때문에, 상품이 시장에 도달하는 과정은, 일반적으로 영화 시장에서는 배급으로 일컬어지는데 영화와 다른 동영상 형태의 모든 측면 중에서 가장 적게 연구된다. ❻ 영화와 비디오 제작, 제작된 영화와 비디오, 그리고 영화와 비디오가 관객에게 어떻게 인식되고 받아들여지는지에 관해 쓴 글은 많지만, 제작과 소비 사이의 중간 단계에 관해서 쓴 글은 거의 없다. ❼ 때로는 영화와 동영상 분야에서는 마치 상품이 정말로 신비롭게도 자력으로 시장에 이르는 것처럼 보인다.

Word List
□ commodity 상품   □ (all) on one's own 자력으로, 자기 스스로   □ goods 상품, 제품   □ complicated 복잡한
□ in question 문제의, 논의가 되고 있는   □ apply 적용하다   □ sector 분야, 부문, 영역   □ remote 아주 다른, 관계가 없는
□ regular 일반적인   □ refer 언급하다   □ distribution 배급. 유통   □ aspect 양상, 측면   □ perceive 여기다   □ spectator 관객
□ intermediate 중간의   □ stage 단계   □ consumption 소비   □ mysteriously 신비롭게, 이상하게

• Word Test

1	(all) on one's own	10	적용하다
2	intermediate	11	배급. 유통
3	in question	12	단계
4	complicated	13	상품, 제품
5	refer	14	신비롭게, 이상하게
6	commodity	15	일반적인
7	remote	16	관객
8	aspect	17	소비
9	perceive	18	분야, 부문, 영역

Commodities do not go to market all on their own. Someone has to take them there. Goods must be moved, prices agreed, and only after a long and complicated process ❶ | will the commodity in question / the commodity in question will | be there for the end-user to enjoy. This applies to films and videos as much as it does to any other commodity, and it applies even in that sector of the film and video business that likes to think of ❷ | itself / themselves | as remote from and even antagonistic to the regular processes of commodity exchange. But perhaps because of this aversion, the process ❸ | which / by which | commodities get to market — generally referred to in the film trade as distribution — is ❹ | the least / the most | studied of all the aspects of cinema and other forms of moving image. A lot is written about film and video production, about the films and videos produced and about how they are perceived/received by the spectator, ❺ | and / but | very little about the intermediate stages between production and consumption. Sometimes it seems as if, in the world of cinema and the moving image, commodities do indeed mysteriously get to market all on their own.   *antagonistic 상반되는   **aversion 반감

Commodities do not go to market all on their own. Someone has to take them there. Goods must be moved, prices ❶ _____ (agree), and only after a long and complicated process will the commodity in question be there for the end-user ❷ _____ (enjoy). This applies to films and videos as much as it does to any other commodity, and it applies even in that sector of the film and video business that ❸ _____ (like) to think of itself as remote from and even antagonistic to the regular processes of commodity exchange. But perhaps because of this aversion, the process by which commodities get to market — generally referred to in the film trade as distribution — ❹ _____ (be) the least studied of all the aspects of cinema and other forms of moving image. A lot is written about film and video production, about the films and videos ❺ _____ (produce) and about how they are perceived/received by the spectator, but very little about the intermediate stages between production and consumption. Sometimes it seems as if, in the world of cinema and the moving image, commodities do indeed mysteriously get to market all on their own.   *antagonistic 상반되는   **aversion 반감

Commodities do not go to market ❶ _____ _____ _____ _____ (모두 자력으로). Someone has to take them there. Goods must be moved, prices agreed, and only after a long and complicated process will the commodity in question be there for the end-user to enjoy. This applies to films and videos as much as it does to any other commodity, and it applies even in that sector of the film and video business that likes to think of itself as remote from and even antagonistic to the regular processes of commodity exchange. But perhaps because of this aversion, the process by which commodities get to market — ❷ _____ _____ _____ (일반적으로 ~으로 일컬어지는) in the film trade as distribution — is ❸ _____ _____ _____ (가장 적게 연구되는) of all the aspects of cinema and other forms of moving image. A lot is written about film and video production, about the films and videos produced and about how they are perceived/received by the spectator, but very little about the ❹ _____ _____ _____ (~ 사이의 중간 단계들) production and consumption. Sometimes ❺ _____ _____ _____ (~인 것처럼 보이다), in the world of cinema and the moving image, commodities do indeed mysteriously get to market all on their own.   *antagonistic 상반되는   **aversion 반감

다음 글의 주제로 가장 적절한 것은?

Sometimes it's important to disagree. All the great social reforms which took place in the eighteenth century, for instance, began with the dedicated campaigns of a handful of people who saw something wrong, and did not let it rest. Slavery was widely accepted in Europe in the eighteenth century, but as a result of consistent campaigning, the slave trade was made illegal near the beginning of the nineteenth century, and the owning of slaves became illegal a few years later. Social psychologists Moscovici and Nemeth showed that if just a few people stick to a particular view, which they are convinced is right, then over time they can have a great deal of influence on a larger group. The important thing, though, is that those people who are in the minority and trying to influence the majority should be seen to be genuine, consistent and resisting social pressure. If we see people acting like that, over time we become curious about why they are doing it and so are likely to think more seriously about what they are saying.

① difficulties of campaigning for minority rights
② the power of minorities to cause social change
③ policies that brought slavery to an end in Europe
④ effects disobedience has on a minorty's social status
⑤ the impact of the overwhelming majority on legal issues

다음 빈칸에 들어갈 말로 가장 적절한 것은?

Attention is selective. We cannot focus on everything, and the knowledge we bring to a given situation allows us to direct our attention to the most important elements and to ignore the rest. The extent to which _____ was powerfully demonstrated by an experiment in which participants watched a videotape of two "teams" of three people, each passing a basketball back and forth. The members of one team wore white shirts, and the members of the other team wore black shirts. Each participant was asked to count the number of passes made by the members of one of the teams. Forty-five seconds into the action, a person wearing a gorilla costume strolled into the middle of the action. Although a large black gorilla might seem hard to miss, only half the participants noticed it! The participants' schemas about what is likely to happen in a game of catch directed their attention so intently to some parts of the videotape that they failed to see a rather dramatic stimulus they did not expect to see.

① our schemas and expectations guide our attention
② we ignore unexpected features that stray from the rules
③ we become attentive to what others ask during a game
④ our prior knowledge affects our actions as a group member
⑤ our expectations for our team encourage good sportsmanship

03 11강 3번

다음 글의 제목으로 가장 적절한 것은?

With the rise of modern science new habits of mind developed. The method of the sciences and the image of scientific narratives became unquestioned and reinforced the new habits of mind, becoming an accomplice to those that would best accommodate the new image. These habits of mind became a duplication in the classroom of what the sciences were supposed to be doing in the laboratory. They developed clear and distinct ideas imitating mathematical models that are hypothetical, abstract, ahistorical, and humanly disembodied. Descartes, Newton, Galileo, Locke, and Rousseau are the best examples. The mind was trained to repeat certain logical operations until a habit was developed of reading the world according to those skills. Even if the reading was supposed to be disembodied and therefore objective, the result was that the viewpoints and skills became embodied in those using them. For the older habits of mind, external cosmologies (now considered outdated) were substituted in all classrooms.

*accomplice 공범 **duplication 복제, 복제품 ***cosmology 우주론

① A Subjective Scientific Process Based on Objective Result
② Limitations of a Dehumanized Scientific Way of Thinking
③ Theoretical Challenges: Blind Spots in Laboratory Research
④ Alternative Ways of Thinking Emerging with Modern Science
⑤ New Scientific Methods Applied by the Mechanism of Thinking

04 11강 4번

밑줄 친 commodities do indeed mysteriously get to market all on their own이 다음 글에서 의미하는 바로 가장 적절한 것은?

Commodities do not go to market all on their own. Someone has to take them there. Goods must be moved, prices agreed, and only after a long and complicated process will the commodity in question be there for the end-user to enjoy. This applies to films and videos as much as it does to any other commodity, and it applies even in that sector of the film and video business that likes to think of itself as remote from and even antagonistic to the regular processes of commodity exchange. But perhaps because of this aversion, the process by which commodities get to market — generally referred to in the film trade as distribution — is the least studied of all the aspects of cinema and other forms of moving image. A lot is written about film and video production, about the films and videos produced and about how they are perceived/received by the spectator, but very little about the intermediate stages between production and consumption. Sometimes it seems as if, in the world of cinema and the moving image, commodities do indeed mysteriously get to market all on their own.

*antagonistic 상반되는 **aversion 반감

① A film's production process is less likely to be publicized.
② The market for movie distribution has been barely secured.
③ The notion of videos as commodities is not widely accepted.
④ The impact of end-users on movie screening prices is negligible.
⑤ Little is known about how a movie becomes available to an audience.

다음 빈칸에 들어갈 말로 가장 적절한 것은?

Sometimes it's important to disagree. All the great social reforms which took place in the eighteenth century, for instance, began with the dedicated campaigns of a handful of people who saw something wrong, and did not _____. Slavery was widely accepted in Europe in the eighteenth century, but as a result of consistent campaigning, the slave trade was made illegal near the beginning of the nineteenth century, and the owning of slaves became illegal a few years later. Social psychologists Moscovici and Nemeth showed that if just a few people stick to a particular view, which they are convinced is right, then over time they can have a great deal of influence on a larger group. The important thing, though, is that those people who are in the minority and trying to influence the majority should be seen to be genuine, consistent and resisting social pressure. If we see people acting like that, over time we become curious about why they are doing it and so are likely to think more seriously about what they are saying.

① stick to it
② let it rest
③ carry it out
④ bring it up
⑤ make it go further

다음 글의 제목으로 가장 적절한 것은?

Attention is selective. We cannot focus on everything, and the knowledge we bring to a given situation allows us to direct our attention to the most important elements and to ignore the rest. The extent to which our schemas and expectations guide our attention was powerfully demonstrated by an experiment in which participants watched a videotape of two "teams" of three people, each passing a basketball back and forth. The members of one team wore white shirts, and the members of the other team wore black shirts. Each participant was asked to count the number of passes made by the members of one of the teams. Forty-five seconds into the action, a person wearing a gorilla costume strolled into the middle of the action. Although a large black gorilla might seem hard to miss, only half the participants noticed it! The participants' schemas about what is likely to happen in a game of catch directed their attention so intently to some parts of the videotape that they failed to see a rather dramatic stimulus they did not expect to see.

① Interpreting Information While Ignoring Unfavorable Data
② Exaggeration in Our Memory: Favoring Our Schema
③ Psychological Principles of Designing Team Uniforms
④ Intense Pressure Impacting Our Expectations and Schema
⑤ The Effect Our Cognitive Framework Has on Our Attention

다음 빈칸에 들어갈 말로 가장 적절한 것은?

With the rise of modern science new habits of mind developed. The method of the sciences and the image of scientific narratives became unquestioned and reinforced the new habits of mind, becoming an accomplice to those that would best accommodate the new image. These habits of mind became a duplication in the classroom of what the sciences were supposed to be doing in the laboratory. They developed clear and distinct ideas imitating mathematical models that are hypothetical, abstract, ahistorical, and humanly disembodied. Descartes, Newton, Galileo, Locke, and Rousseau are the best examples. The mind was trained to repeat certain logical operations until a habit was developed of reading the world according to those skills. Even if the reading was supposed to be disembodied and therefore objective, the result was that the viewpoints and skills _____. For the older habits of mind, external cosmologies (now considered outdated) were substituted in all classrooms.

*accomplice 공범 **duplication 복제, 복제품 ***cosmology 우주론

① became embodied in those using them
② freed people from subjective interpretation
③ paved the way for their unbiased perspectives
④ supported scientific approaches to human issues
⑤ removed some obstacles to logical judgment in mankind

다음 빈칸에 들어갈 말로 가장 적절한 것은?

Commodities do not go to market all on their own. Someone has to take them there. Goods must be moved, prices agreed, and only after a long and complicated process will the commodity in question be there for the end-user to enjoy. This applies to films and videos as much as it does to any other commodity, and it applies even in that sector of the film and video business that likes to think of itself as remote from and even antagonistic to the regular processes of commodity exchange. But perhaps because of this aversion, the process by which commodities get to market — generally referred to in the film trade as distribution — is the least studied of all the aspectss of cinema and other forms of moving image. A lot is written about film and video production, about the films and videos produced and about how they are perceived/received by the spectator, but very little about _____. Sometimes it seems as if, in the world of cinema and the moving image, commodities do indeed mysteriously get to market all on their own.

*antagonistic 상반되는 **aversion 반감

① economic impacts of the film industry on society
② the stages of film development as cultural products
③ how ticket prices are dictated by a host of economic factors
④ the intermediate stages between production and consumption
⑤ the extent to which consumers influence the direction of film-making

Sometimes it's important to ① disagree. All the great social reforms which took place in the eighteenth century, for instance, began with the dedicated campaigns of a handful of people who saw something wrong, and did not let it rest. Slavery was widely accepted in Europe in the eighteenth century, but as a result of consistent campaigning, the slave trade was made illegal near the beginning of the nineteenth century, and the owning of slaves became illegal a few years later. Social psychologists Moscovici and Nemeth showed that if just a few people ② stick to a particular view, which they are convinced is right, then over time they can have a great deal of influence on a larger group. The important thing, though, is that those people who are in the minority and trying to influence the majority should be seen to be genuine, consistent and ③ accepting social pressure. If we see people acting like that, over time we become ④ curious about why they are doing it and so are likely to think more ⑤ indifferently about what they are saying.

09 윗글의 밑줄 친 ①~⑤ 중 문맥상 어색한 것을 2개 찾아 그 번호를 쓰고 고쳐 쓰시오.

(1) _____ → _____

(2) _____ → _____

10 윗글의 밑줄 친 did not let it rest가 문맥적으로 의미하는 바를 찾아 우리말로 쓰시오. (15자 내외)

_____

Attention is selective. We cannot focus on everything, and 어떤 주어진 상황으로 가져오는 지식은 우리로 하여금 우리의 주의를 가장 중요한 요소들에 돌리게 한다 and to ignore the rest. The extent to which our schemas and expectations guide our attention was powerfully demonstrated by an experiment in which participants watched a videotape of two "teams" of three people, each passing a basketball back and forth. The members of one team wore white shirts, and the members of the other team wore black shirts. Each participant was asked to count the number of passes made by the members of one of the teams. Forty-five seconds into the action, a person wearing a gorilla costume strolled into the middle of the action. Although a large black gorilla might seem hard to miss, only half the participants noticed it! The participants' _____ about what is likely to happen in a game of catch directed their attention so intently to some parts of the videotape that they failed to see a rather dramatic stimulus they did not expect to see.

고난도

11 윗글의 밑줄친 우리말 의미와 일치하도록 보기 의 단어를 순서대로 배열하여 문장을 완성하시오. (단, 필요시 어형을 바꾸거나 중복 사용할 것)

> 보기 important / we / attention / direct / to / the most / allow / elements

the knowledge we bring to a given situation

_____

_____

12 윗글의 빈칸에 들어갈 단어를 영영 뜻풀이를 참고하여 본문에서 찾아 알맞은 형태로 쓰시오.

> a plan that just shows the main parts of something

_____

With the rise of modern science new habits of mind developed. The method of the sciences and the image of scientific narratives became unquestioned and reinforced the new habits of mind, becoming an accomplice to those that would best accommodate the new image. These habits of mind became a duplication in the classroom of what the sciences were supposed to be doing in the laboratory. They developed clear and distinct ideas imitating mathematical models that are hypothetical, abstract, ahistorical, and humanly _____. Descartes, Newton, Galileo, Locke, and Rousseau are the best examples. The mind was trained to repeat certain logical operations until a habit was developed of reading the world according to those skills. Even if the reading was supposed to be disembodied and therefore objective, the result was that the viewpoints and skills became embodied in those using them. For the older habits of mind, external cosmologies (now considered outdated) were substituted in all classrooms.

*accomplice 공범 **duplication 복제, 복제품 ***cosmology 우주론

13 윗글의 빈칸에 들어갈 단어를 영영 뜻풀이를 참고하여 본문에서 찾아 쓰시오.

separated from the body; lacking in any firm relation to reality

_____

14 윗글의 밑줄 친 a habit이 가리키는 구체적인 내용을 우리말로 쓰시오. (30자 내외)

_____

Commodities do not go to market all on their own. Someone has to take them there. Goods must be moved, prices agreed, 그리고 길고 복잡한 과정을 거친 뒤에야 실수요자가 누릴 수 있도록 해당 상품이 거기에 있게 될 것이다. This applies to films and videos as much as it does to any other commodity, and it applies even in that sector of the film and video business that likes to think of itself as remote from and even antagonistic to the regular processes of commodity exchange. But perhaps because of this aversion, the process by which commodities get to market — generally referred to in the film trade as distribution — is the least studied of all the aspects of cinema and other forms of moving image. A lot is written about film and video production, about the films and videos produced and about how they are perceived/received by the spectator, but very little about the intermediate stages between production and consumption. Sometimes it seems as if, in the world of cinema and the moving image, commodities do indeed mysteriously get to market all on their own.

*antagonistic 상반되는 **aversion 반감

15 윗글을 읽고 다음 질문에 영어로 답하시오. (10단어 내외)

Q: What aspect of film is little written about?

A: _____

_____

16 윗글의 밑줄 친 우리말 의미와 일치하도록 보기 의 단어를 순서대로 배열하여 문장을 완성하시오.

보기 there / be / enjoy / the commodity / the end-user / in question / will / to / for

and only after a long and complicated process

_____

_____

❶ On April 12, 1955, the day that the US government announced that the new polio vaccine was safe and effective, its inventor, Jonas Salk, was asked on television who owned the vaccine. ❷ He famously replied, "Well, the people, I would say. There is no patent. Could you patent the sun?" ❸ The vaccine was common property; it belonged to the people who had donated money for the public interest. ❹ Salk was later pitied for his decision. ❺ He could have earned $7 billion if his vaccine had been patented. ❻ His attitude to patenting, however, is not unique. ❼ Even in the era of excessive property protection, there is a new interest in open sources and access, global goods, and the notion of the commons. ❽ Elon Musk, CEO of Tesla Motors, decided in June 2014 to release all of his patents. ❾ Technological leadership is not defined by patents. ❿ The future of sustainable transport will be better served by openly sharing information and knowledge. ⓫ "All our patents belong to you."

*polio 소아마비

❶ 1955년 4월 12일, 미국 정부가 새로운 소아마비 백신이 안전하고 효과적이라고 발표한 그 날, 그것의 발명자 Jonas Salk는 텔레비전에 출연하여 그 백신을 소유한 사람이 누구인지를 질문 받았다. ❷ 그는 유명한 대답을 했다. "음, 국민이라고 말씀드리고 싶습니다. 특허는 없습니다. 태양에 대해 특허를 얻을 수 있습니까?" ❸ 백신은 공동 재산이며, 그것은 공공의 이익을 위해 돈을 기부한 사람들의 것이라는 말이었다. ❹ Salk는 나중에 자신의 결정에 대해 동정을 받았다. ❺ 만약 그의 백신이 특허를 받았다면 그는 70억 달러를 벌 수 있었을 것이다. ❻ 그러나 특허에 대한 그의 태도는 유일한 것이 아니다. ❼ 과도한 재산 보호 시대에도 오픈 소스와 액세스, 지구 공공재, 공유 자원이라는 개념에 대한 새로운 관심이 있다. ❽ Tesla Motors의 최고 경영자 Elon Musk는 2014년 6월에 자신의 모든 특허를 풀기로 결정했다. ❾ 특허가 기술적 리더십의 특성을 나타내는 것은 아니다. ❿ 정보와 지식을 공개적으로 공유함으로써 지속 가능한 운송의 미래가 더 잘 제공될 것이다. ⓫ "우리의 모든 특허는 여러분의 것입니다."

Word List

□ **announce** 발표하다　□ **effective** 효과적인　□ **own** 소유하다　□ **patent** 특허; 특허를 얻다[획득하다]　□ **property** 재산
□ **belong to** ~에 속하다　□ **donate** 기부하다　□ **public interest** 공익　□ **pity** 동정하다, 애석하게 여기다　□ **attitude** 태도
□ **unique** 유일한, 유례가 없는　□ **era** 시대　□ **excessive** 과도한　□ **access** 접근, 접근권　□ **notion** 개념
□ **define** ~의 특성을 나타내다　□ **sustainable** 지속 가능한　□ **transport** 운송

• Word Test

1	own	10	운송
2	effective	11	태도
3	public interest	12	지속 가능한
4	define	13	과도한
5	unique	14	발표하다
6	notion	15	기부하다
7	patent	16	동정하다, 애석하게 여기다
8	belong to	17	시대
9	access	18	재산

On April 12, 1955, the day ❶ that / what the US government announced that the new polio vaccine was safe and effective, its inventor, Jonas Salk, was asked on television who owned the vaccine. He famously replied, "Well, the people, I would say. There is no patent. Could you patent the sun?" The vaccine was ❷ uncommon / common property; it belonged to the people who had donated money for the public interest. Salk was later pitied for his decision. He ❸ has earned / could have earned $7 billion if his vaccine had been patented. His attitude to patenting, ❹ however / thus, is not unique. Even in the era of excessive property protection, there is a new interest in open sources and access, global goods, and the notion of the commons. Elon Musk, CEO of Tesla Motors, decided in June 2014 to release all of his patents. Technological leadership is ❺ defined / not defined by patents. The future of sustainable transport will be better served by openly sharing information and knowledge. "All our patents belong to you."

*polio 소아마비

On April 12, 1955, the day that the US government announced that the new polio vaccine was safe and effective, its inventor, Jonas Salk, ❶ _____ (ask) on television who owned the vaccine. He famously replied, "Well, the people, I would say. There is no patent. Could you patent the sun?" The vaccine was common property; it belonged to the people who ❷ _____ (donate) money for the public interest. Salk was later pitied for his decision. He could have earned $7 billion if his vaccine had been patented. His attitude to patenting, however, is not unique. Even in the era of excessive property protection, there is a new interest in open sources and access, global goods, and the notion of the commons. Elon Musk, CEO of Tesla Motors, decided in June 2014 ❸ _____ (release) all of his patents. Technological leadership is not defined by patents. The future of sustainable transport will be better served by openly ❹ _____ (share) information and knowledge. "All our patents belong to you."

*polio 소아마비

On April 12, 1955, the day that the US government announced that the new polio vaccine was safe and effective, its inventor, Jonas Salk, was asked on television who owned the vaccine. He famously replied, "Well, the people, I would say. There is no patent. Could you patent the sun?" The vaccine was ❶ _____ _____ (공동 재산); it ❷ _____ _____ _____ _____ (사람들에게 속했다) who had donated money ❸ _____ _____ _____ _____ (공공의 이익을 위해). Salk was later pitied for his decision. He could have earned $7 billion if his vaccine had been patented. His attitude to patenting, however, is not unique. Even ❹ _____ _____ _____ _____ (~의 시대에) excessive property protection, there is a new interest in open sources and access, global goods, and the notion of the commons. Elon Musk, CEO of Tesla Motors, decided in June 2014 to release all of his patents. Technological leadership is not defined by patents. The future of sustainable transport ❺ _____ _____ _____ _____ (더 잘 제공될 것이다) by openly sharing information and knowledge. "All our patents belong to you."

*polio 소아마비

❶ By the early 1990s, the decline of the southwestern willow flycatcher was clear. ❷ In 1993, the U.S. Fish and Wildlife Service (FWS) formally proposed listing the flycatcher as a federal endangered species and designating critical habitat, an important step under the Endangered Species Act that prevents damage to specific areas. ❸ The task of writing the rule that listed the bird as endangered under the act fell to Rob Marshall. ❹ Marshall, a Yale-trained biologist with FWS in Arizona, was becoming disillusioned by the overall implementation of the Endangered Species Act. ❺ The FWS was highly politicized by powerful, moneyed interests that saw species listings and particularly habitat designations as a threat to business: ❻ if a species is listed but no critical habitat is designated, a now-common pattern, then restrictions on business are far fewer. ❼ This created an atmosphere in which it was extremely difficult for technical biological staff to maintain their integrity, says Marshall. ❽ For example, the process to list the flycatcher as endangered began in 1992, the proposed rule didn't come out until 1995, and it took until 1997 to produce the final ruling to list it. ❾ The FWS only completed the listing because the watchdog organization Center for Biological Diversity sued them.

*willow flycatcher 버드나무 딱새 **implementation 시행, 이행 ***integrity 변함없는 원칙 고수, 무결함

❶ 1990년대 초에 이르러 남서부의 버드나무 딱새의 감소가 뚜렷했다. ❷ 1993년, 미국 어류·야생동물 관리국(FWS)은 딱새를 연방 멸종 위기종으로 등재하고 보존 서식지를 지정할 것을 공식적으로 제안했는데, 이는 특정 지역의 피해를 예방하는, 멸종 위기종 법령에 따라 이루어진 중요한 조치였다. ❸ 그 법령에 따라 그 새를 멸종 위기종으로 등재하는 규칙을 작성하는 일이 Rob Marshall에게 돌아갔다. ❹ 애리조나주의 FWS 소속으로 예일(대학교)에서 교육받은 생물학자인 Marshall은 멸종 위기종 법령의 전반적인 시행에 환멸을 느껴가고 있었다. ❺ FWS는 종의 등재, 특히 서식지 지정을 사업에 대한 위협으로 보는 강력하고 돈 많은 이해관계자들에 의해 매우 정치화되어 있었다. ❻ 현재 흔한 패턴인데, 어떤 종이 등재되지만 보존 서식지가 지정되지 않으면, 사업에 대한 제한이 훨씬 더 적기 때문이다. ❼ 이것으로 인해 기술 생물학 직원들이 변함없는 원칙 고수를 유지하는 것이 극도로 어려운 분위기가 만들어졌다고 Marshall은 말한다. ❽ 예를 들어, 딱새를 멸종 위기종으로 등재하려는 과정은 1992년에 시작되었지만, 제안된 규칙은 1995년에서야 나왔으며, 그것을 등재하기 위한 최종 판결은 1997년이 되어서야 나왔다. ❾ FWS는 감시 단체 조직인 생물학적 다양성 센터가 그들을 고소했기 때문에 등재를 마쳤을 뿐이었다.

Word List

□ **decline** 감소 □ **formally** 공식적으로 □ **propose** 제안하다 □ **list** 목록에 포함시키다 □ **federal** 연방의
□ **endangered species** 멸종 위기종 □ **designate** 지정하다 □ **critical habitat** (멸종 위기종의) 보존 서식지 □ **specific** 특정한
□ **disillusioned** 환멸을 느낀 □ **overall** 전반적인 □ **politicize** 정치화하다 □ **interest** 이해관계(자), 이익 □ **species** (생물의) 종
□ **threat** 위협 □ **restriction** 제한 □ **atmosphere** 분위기 □ **maintain** 유지하다 □ **watchdog** 감시 단체 □ **sue** 고소하다

• Word Test

1 list _____
2 sue _____
3 threat _____
4 watchdog _____
5 critical habitat _____
6 interest _____
7 formally _____
8 disillusioned _____
9 overall _____
10 endangered species _____

11 특정한 _____
12 지정하다 _____
13 제한 _____
14 (생물의) 종 _____
15 제안하다 _____
16 분위기 _____
17 연방의 _____
18 감소 _____
19 정치화하다 _____
20 유지하다 _____

By the early 1990s, the decline of the southwestern willow flycatcher was clear. In 1993, the U.S. Fish and Wildlife Service (FWS) formally proposed listing the flycatcher as a federal endangered species and designating critical habitat, an important step under the Endangered Species Act ❶ [that / and] prevents damage to specific areas. The task of writing the rule ❷ [then / that] listed the bird as endangered under the act fell to Rob Marshall. Marshall, a Yale-trained biologist with FWS in Arizona, was becoming disillusioned by the overall implementation of the Endangered Species Act. The FWS was highly politicized by powerful, moneyed interests that saw species listings and particularly habitat designations ❸ [as / for] a threat to business: if a species is listed but no critical habitat is designated, a now-common pattern, then restrictions on business are far fewer. This created an atmosphere ❹ [that / in which] it was extremely difficult for technical biological staff to maintain their integrity, says Marshall. For example, the process to list the flycatcher as endangered began in 1992, the proposed rule didn't come out until 1995, and it took until 1997 to produce the final ruling to list it. The FWS only completed the listing because the watchdog organization Center for Biological Diversity sued ❺ [it / them].

*willow flycatcher 버드나무 딱새 **implementation 시행, 이행 ***integrity 변함없는 원칙 고수, 무결함

By the early 1990s, the decline of the southwestern willow flycatcher was clear. In 1993, the U.S. Fish and Wildlife Service (FWS) formally proposed listing the flycatcher as a federal endangered species and ❶ _____ (designate) critical habitat, an important step under the Endangered Species Act that prevents damage to specific areas. The task of writing the rule that listed the bird as endangered under the act fell to Rob Marshall. Marshall, a Yale-trained biologist with FWS in Arizona, was becoming disillusioned by the overall implementation of the Endangered Species Act. The FWS was highly politicized by powerful, moneyed interests that ❷ _____ (see) species listings and particularly habitat designations as a threat to business: if a species is listed but no critical habitat ❸ _____ (designate), a now-common pattern, then restrictions on business are far fewer. This created an atmosphere in which it was extremely difficult for technical biological staff ❹ _____ (maintain) their integrity, says Marshall. For example, the process ❺ _____ (list) the flycatcher as endangered began in 1992, the proposed rule didn't come out until 1995, and it took until 1997 to produce the final ruling to list it. The FWS only completed the listing because the watchdog organization Center for Biological Diversity sued them.

*willow flycatcher 버드나무 딱새 **implementation 시행, 이행 ***integrity 변함없는 원칙 고수, 무결함

By the early 1990s, the decline of the southwestern willow flycatcher was clear. In 1993, the U.S. Fish and Wildlife Service (FWS) formally proposed listing the flycatcher as a federal ❶ _____ _____ (멸종 위기종) and designating critical habitat, an important step under the Endangered Species Act that ❷ _____ _____ _____ _____ _____ (특정 지역들의 피해를 예방하다). The task of writing the rule that listed the bird as endangered ❸ _____ _____ _____ (법령 하에서) fell to Rob Marshall. Marshall, a Yale-trained biologist with FWS in Arizona, was becoming disillusioned by the overall implementation of the Endangered Species Act. The FWS was highly politicized by powerful, moneyed interests that saw species listings and particularly habitat designations as ❹ _____ _____ _____ _____ (사업에 대한 위협): if a species is listed but no critical habitat is designated, a now-common pattern, then restrictions on business are far fewer. This created an atmosphere in which it was extremely difficult for technical biological staff to maintain their integrity, says Marshall. For example, the process to list the flycatcher as endangered began in 1992, the proposed rule didn't come out until 1995, and it took until 1997 to produce ❺ _____ _____ _____ (최종 판결) to list it. The FWS only completed the listing because the watchdog organization Center for Biological Diversity sued them.

*willow flycatcher 버드나무 딱새   **implementation 시행, 이행   ***integrity 변함없는 원칙 고수, 무결함

❶ Translating theory into something that can be assessed in the physical environment means that phenomena are made measurable. ❷ It is often assumed that the phenomenon being measured is the same no matter how it is measured. ❸ Translations of theory into practice may differ, but these do not alter the nature of the phenomenon being measured. ❹ Without this assumption, measurement between different individuals made in different places or at different times could not be compared. ❺ The assumption does not, however, mean that this viewpoint is correct. ❻ Within quantum physics there is a view that the observer and the phenomenon cannot be separated. ❼ The observer and phenomenon make up a single system, a measurement system. ❽ In this context it is not possible to separate the measurement made from the measurement system within which it was made. ❾ The measurement and the phenomenon become combined in an unbreakable link in the measurement system. ❿ It is impossible to talk of a separate existence for the phenomenon and so also, therefore, to talk of an independent measurement of that phenomenon. ⓫ This means that within the supposedly objective, hard science of physics, it is accepted that reality and how it is measured form an inseparable whole.

❶ 이론을 물리적 환경에서 가늠할 수 있는 어떤 것으로 고쳐 말하는 것은 현상의 측정이 가능하게 된다는 것을 의미한다. ❷ 측정되고 있는 현상은 그것이 어떻게 측정이 되든지 간에 동일하다고 가정하는 경우가 많다. ❸ 이론을 실제로 고쳐 말한 것들이 다를 수도 있지만, 이것들이 측정되고 있는 현상의 본질을 바꾸지는 않는다. ❹ 이러한 가정이 없다면, 서로 다른 장소 혹은 서로 다른 시간에 이루어진 서로 다른 개인 간의 측정은 비교될 수 없다. ❺ 하지만 그 가정은 이 관점이 옳다는 것을 뜻하지는 않는다. ❻ 양자 물리학에서는 관찰자와 현상이 분리될 수 없다는 견해가 있다. ❼ 관찰자와 현상은 하나의 시스템, 즉 측정 시스템을 이룬다. ❽ 이러한 환경에서는 이루어진 측정과 그것이 이루어진 측정 시스템을 분리하는 것은 가능하지 않다. ❾ 측정과 현상은 측정 시스템 안에서 깨뜨릴 수 없는 고리로 결합된다. ❿ 현상이 별개로 존재한다는 것에 대해 말하는 것이 불가능하므로, 따라서 그 현상의 독립된 측정에 대해 말하는 것 역시 불가능하다. ⓫ 이는 이른바 객관적이라는, 물리학이라는 자연 과학에서 현실과 그것이 측정되는 방법이 불가분의 총체를 형성한다는 것이 용인된다는 것을 의미한다.

Word List

□ translate ~ into ... ~을 …으로 고쳐 말하다[옮기다] □ assess 가늠하다, 평가하다 □ phenomenon 현상(*pl.* phenomena)
□ measurable 측정 가능한 □ assume 가정하다, 추정하다 □ alter 바꾸다 □ nature 본질 □ assumption 가정
□ quantum physics 양자 물리학 □ separate 분리하다 □ make up ~을 이루다 □ context 맥락, 전후사정
□ unbreakable 깨뜨릴 수 없는 □ supposedly 이른바, 생각건대 □ hard science 자연 과학 □ inseparable 불가분의, 분리할 수 없는

• Word Test

1	hard science	9	본질
2	assume	10	불가분의, 분리할 수 없는
3	quantum physics	11	가정
4	make up	12	분리하다
5	alter	13	측정 가능한
6	translate ~ into ...	14	맥락, 전후사정
7	unbreakable	15	이른바, 생각건대
8	phenomenon	16	가늠하다, 평가하다

Translating theory into something that can be assessed in the physical environment means that phenomena are made ❶ measurable/measured . It is often assumed that the phenomenon being measured is the same no matter ❷ how / what it is measured. Translations of theory into practice may differ, but these do not alter the nature of the phenomenon being measured. ❸ With/Without this assumption, measurement between different individuals made in different places or at different times could not be compared. The assumption does not, however, mean that this viewpoint is correct. Within quantum physics there is a view that the observer and the phenomenon cannot be separated. The observer and phenomenon make up a single system, a measurement system. In this context it is not possible to separate the measurement made from the measurement system ❹ for which / within which it was made. The measurement and the phenomenon become combined in an unbreakable link in the measurement system. It is impossible to talk of a separate existence for the phenomenon and so also, ❺ however/therefore , to talk of an independent measurement of that phenomenon. This means that within the supposedly objective, hard science of physics, it is accepted that reality and how it is measured form an inseparable whole.

Translating theory into something that can be assessed in the physical environment ❶ _____ (mean) that phenomena are made measurable. It is often assumed that the phenomenon ❷ _____ (be) measured is the same no matter how it is measured. Translations of theory into practice may differ, but these do not alter the nature of the phenomenon being measured. Without this assumption, measurement between different individuals ❸ _____ (make) in different places or at different times could not be compared. The assumption does not, however, mean that this viewpoint is correct. Within quantum physics there is a view that the observer and the phenomenon cannot be separated. The observer and phenomenon make up a single system, a measurement system. In this context it is not possible to separate the measurement made from the measurement system within which it ❹ _____ (make). The measurement and the phenomenon become combined in an unbreakable link in the measurement system. It is impossible to talk of a separate existence for the phenomenon and so also, therefore, to talk of an independent measurement of that phenomenon. This means that within the supposedly objective, hard science of physics, it is accepted that reality and how it is measured ❺ _____ (form) an inseparable whole.

Translating theory into something that can be assessed in the physical environment means that phenomena are made measurable. It is often assumed that the phenomenon being measured is the same ❶ _____ _____ _____ _____ _____ _____ (그것이 어떻게 측정이 되든지 간에). Translations of theory into practice may differ, but these do not alter ❷ _____ _____ _____ _____ _____ (현상의 본질) being measured. Without this assumption, measurement between different individuals made in different places or at different times could not be compared. The assumption does not, however, mean that this viewpoint is correct. Within quantum physics ❸ _____ _____ _____ _____ (견해가 있다) that the observer and the phenomenon cannot be separated. The observer and phenomenon make up a single system, a measurement system. ❹ _____ _____ _____ (이러한 상황에서는) it is not possible to separate the measurement made from the measurement system within which it was made. The measurement and the phenomenon become combined in an unbreakable link in the measurement system. It is impossible to talk of a separate existence for the phenomenon and so also, therefore, to talk of an independent measurement of that phenomenon. This means that within the supposedly objective, hard science of physics, it is accepted that reality and how it is measured ❺ _____ _____ _____ _____ (불가분의 총체를 형성하다).

❶ Why are certain languages mistakenly thought to be primitive? ❷ There are several reasons. ❸ Some people consider other languages ugly or "primitive sounding" if those languages make use of sounds or sound combinations they find unclear because the sounds are greatly different from those of the languages they themselves speak. ❹ Such a view is based on the ethnocentric attitude that the characteristics of one's own language are obviously superior. ❺ But words that seem unpronounceable to speakers of one language — and are therefore considered obscure or even grotesque — are easily acquired by even the youngest native speakers of the language in which they occur. ❻ To a native speaker of English, the Czech word *scvrnkls* "you flicked off (something) with your finger" looks quite strange, and its pronunciation may sound odd and even impossible because there is no vowel among the eight consonants; for native speakers of Czech, of course, *scvrnkls* is just another word. ❼ Which speech sounds are used and how they are combined to form words and utterances vary from one language to the next, and speakers of no language can claim that their language has done the selecting and combining better than another.

*obscure 불분명한, 이해하기 어려운　**grotesque 괴상한　***flick (손가락 등으로) 튀기다

❶ 왜 특정한 언어는 원시적이라고 잘못 생각되는가? ❷ 몇 가지 이유가 있다. ❸ 어떤 사람들은 소리가 자신이 쓰는 언어의 소리와 매우 달라서 불분명하다고 생각하는 소리나 소리의 결합을 다른 언어가 사용한다면 그 언어를 흉하거나 '원시적으로 들리는'것으로 여긴다. ❹ 그러한 견해는 자기 언어의 특징이 명백히 우수하다는 자기 민족 중심적인 태도에 근거한다. ❺ 그러나 어느 한 언어의 사용자에게 발음하기 너무 힘들어 보이는 단어들, 그리고 그렇기 때문에 불분명하거나 심지어 괴상하다고 여겨지는 단어들은 그것들이 나타나는 언어의 가장 어린 현지인 화자조차 쉽게 습득한다. ❻ 영어 모국어 화자에게, "당신이 손가락으로 (무언가를) 튀겼다"라는 체코어 단어 'scvrnkls'는 상당히 이상하게 보이며, 8개의 자음 사이에 모음이 없기 때문에 발음이 이상하고 심지어 불가능하게 들릴 수 있지만, 체코어 모국어 화자에게는 물론 'scvrnkls'는 그저 또 하나의 (보통) 단어일 뿐이다. ❼ 어떤 말소리가 사용되고, 그것들이 어떻게 결합하여 단어와 발화를 구성하는지는 언어마다 다르며, 어떤 언어 사용자도 자신의 언어가 다른 언어보다 선택과 결합을 더 잘했다고 주장할 수 없다.

Word List

□ mistakenly 잘못되어, 실수로　□ primitive 원시적인　□ make use of ~을 이용하다　□ combination 조합, 결합
□ ethnocentric 자기 민족 중심적인　□ characteristics 특징　□ obviously 명백히, 확실히　□ superior 우월한
□ unpronounceable 발음하기 너무 힘든　□ acquire 습득하다　□ odd 이상한　□ vowel 모음　□ consonant 자음
□ utterance 발화　□ vary 다르다　□ claim 주장하다　□ select 선택하다　□ combine 결합하다

• Word Test

1	utterance	10	명백히, 확실히
2	select	11	이상한
3	unpronounceable	12	특징
4	combination	13	결합하다
5	make use of	14	잘못되어, 실수로
6	consonant	15	자기 민족 중심적인
7	primitive	16	모음
8	vary	17	우월한
9	acquire	18	주장하다

Why are certain languages mistakenly thought to be primitive? There are several reasons. Some people consider other languages ugly or "primitive sounding" if those languages make use of sounds or sound combinations they find unclear because the sounds are greatly different from those of the languages they themselves speak. Such a view is based on the ethnocentric attitude that the characteristics of one's own language are obviously ❶ inferior / superior. But words that seem unpronounceable to speakers of one language — and are therefore considered obscure or even grotesque — are ❷ hardly / easily acquired by even the youngest native speakers of the language ❸ in which / how they occur. To a native speaker of English, the Czech word *scvrnkls* "you flicked off (something) with your finger" looks quite strange, and its pronunciation may sound odd and even ❹ impossible / impossibility because there is no vowel among the eight consonants; for native speakers of Czech, of course, *scvrnkls* is just another word. Which speech sounds are used and how they are combined to form words and utterances vary from one language to the next, ❺ and / but speakers of no language can claim that their language has done the selecting and combining better than another.

*obscure 불분명한, 이해하기 어려운   **grotesque 괴상한   ***flick (손가락 등으로) 튀기다

Why are certain languages mistakenly ❶ _____ (think) to be primitive? There are several reasons. Some people consider other languages ugly or "primitive sounding" if those languages make use of sounds or sound combinations they find unclear because the sounds are greatly different from those of the languages they themselves speak. Such a view is based on the ethnocentric attitude that the characteristics of one's own language ❷ _____ (be) obviously superior. But words that seem unpronounceable to speakers of one language — and are therefore considered obscure or even grotesque — are easily acquired by even the youngest native speakers of the language in which they occur. To a native speaker of English, the Czech word *scvrnkls* "you flicked off (something) with your finger" ❸ _____ (look) quite strange, and its pronunciation may sound odd and even impossible because there is no vowel among the eight consonants; for native speakers of Czech, of course, *scvrnkls* is just another word. Which speech sounds ❹ _____ (use) and how they are combined to form words and utterances ❺ _____ (vary) from one language to the next, and speakers of no language can claim that their language has done the selecting and combining better than another.

*obscure 불분명한, 이해하기 어려운   **grotesque 괴상한   ***flick (손가락 등으로) 튀기다

• 유형 3 우리말에 맞게 빈칸에 알맞은 말을 쓰시오.

Why are certain languages mistakenly thought to be primitive? ❶ ________ ________ ________ ________ (몇 가지 이유들이 있다). Some people ❷ ________ ________ ________ ________ (다른 언어들을 흉하다고 여기다) or "primitive sounding" if those languages (소리들을 사용하다) make use of sounds or sound combinations they find unclear because the sounds are greatly different from those of the languages they themselves speak. ❸ ________ ________ ________ (그러한 견해) is based on the ethnocentric attitude that the characteristics of one's own language are obviously superior. But words that seem unpronounceable to speakers of one language — and are therefore considered obscure or even grotesque — are easily acquired by even the youngest native speakers of the language in which they occur. To ❹ ________ ________ ________ ________ ________ (영어 모국어 화자), the Czech word *scvrnkls* "you flicked off (something) with your finger" looks quite strange, and its pronunciation may sound odd and even impossible because there is no vowel among the eight consonants; for native speakers of Czech, of course, *scvrnkls* is just another word. Which speech sounds are used and how they are combined ❺ ________ ________ ________ ________ ________ (단어들과 발화들을 구성하기 위해) vary from one language to the next, and speakers of no language can claim that their language has done the selecting and combining better than another.

*obscure 불분명한, 이해하기 어려운 **grotesque 괴상한 ***flick (손가락 등으로) 튀기다

01 12강 1번

다음 글의 제목으로 가장 적절한 것은?

On April 12, 1955, the day that the US government announced that the new polio vaccine was safe and effective, its inventor, Jonas Salk, was asked on television who owned the vaccine. He famously replied, "Well, the people, I would say. There is no patent. Could you patent the sun?" The vaccine was common property; it belonged to the people who had donated money for the public interest. Salk was later pitied for his decision. He could have earned $7 billion if his vaccine had been patented. His attitude to patenting, however, is not unique. Even in the era of excessive property protection, there is a new interest in open sources and access, global goods, and the notion of the commons. Elon Musk, CEO of Tesla Motors, decided in June 2014 to release all of his patents. Technological leadership is not defined by patents. The future of sustainable transport will be better served by openly sharing information and knowledge. "All our patents belong to you."

*polio 소아마비

① Do What Is Right, Not What is Easy!
② Deprivation of Private Assets for the Public Good
③ The Influence of Intellectual Property on Our Lifespan
④ Sacrificing Individual Rights for Public Health
⑤ Placing Public Interest over Personal Interest

고난도

02 12강 2번

주어진 글 다음에 이어질 글의 순서로 가장 적절한 것은?

By the early 1990s, the decline of the southwestern willow flycatcher was clear. In 1993, the U.S. Fish and Wildlife Service (FWS) formally proposed listing the flycatcher as a federal endangered species and designating critical habitat, an important step under the Endangered Species Act that prevents damage to specific areas.

(A) For example, the process to list the flycatcher as endangered began in 1992, the proposed rule didn't come out until 1995, and it took until 1997 to produce the final ruling to list it. The FWS only completed the listing because the watchdog organization Center for Biological Diversity sued them.

(B) The task of writing the rule that listed the bird as endangered under the act fell to Rob Marshall. Marshall, a Yale-trained biologist with FWS in Arizona, was becoming disillusioned by the overall implementation of the Endangered Species Act.

(C) The FWS was highly politicized by powerful, moneyed interests that saw species listings and particularly habitat designations as a threat to business: if a species is listed but no critical habitat is designated, a now-common pattern, then restrictions on business are far fewer. This created an atmosphere in which it was extremely difficult for technical biological staff to maintain their integrity, says Marshall.

*willow flycatcher 버드나무 딱새 **implementation 시행, 이행
***integrity 변함없는 원칙 고수, 무결함

① (A) – (C) – (B)　　② (B) – (A) – (C)
③ (B) – (C) – (A)　　④ (C) – (A) – (B)
⑤ (C) – (B) – (A)

03 [12강] 3번

다음 빈칸에 들어갈 말로 가장 적절한 것은?

Translating theory into something that can be assessed in the physical environment means that phenomena are made measurable. It is often assumed that the phenomenon being measured is the same no matter how it is measured. Translations of theory into practice may differ, but these do not alter the nature of the phenomenon being measured. Without this assumption, measurement between different individuals made in different places or at different times could not be compared. The assumption does not, however, mean that this viewpoint is correct. Within quantum physics there is a view that the observer and the phenomenon cannot be separated. The observer and phenomenon make up a single system, a measurement system. In this context it is not possible to separate the measurement made from the measurement system within which it was made. The measurement and the phenomenon become combined in an unbreakable link in the measurement system. It is impossible to talk of a separate existence for the phenomenon and so also, therefore, to talk of an independent measurement of that phenomenon. This means that within the supposedly objective, hard science of physics, it is accepted that _____.

① physics assumptions are shared between practitioners
② reality and how it is measured form an inseparable whole
③ measured reality doesn't conform to theoretical knowledge
④ ties between measured values and phenomena are made to last
⑤ the measurements of a physical phenomenon are permanently invariant

04 [12강] 4번

다음 글에서 전체 흐름과 관계 없는 문장은?

Why are certain languages mistakenly thought to be primitive? There are several reasons. Some people consider other languages ugly or "primitive sounding" if those languages make use of sounds or sound combinations they find unclear because the sounds are greatly different from those of the languages they themselves speak. ① Such a view is based on the ethnocentric attitude that the characteristics of one's own language are obviously superior. ② But words that seem unpronounceable to speakers of one language — and are therefore considered obscure or even grotesque — are easily acquired by even the youngest native speakers of the language in which they occur. ③ By the same token, however, the language of a tribal society would have elaborate vocabularies for prominent aspects of the culture. ④ To a native speaker of English, the Czech word *scvrnkls* "you flicked off (something) with your finger" looks quite strange, and its pronunciation may sound odd and even impossible because there is no vowel among the eight consonants; for native speakers of Czech, of course, *scvrnkls* is just another word. ⑤ Which speech sounds are used and how they are combined to form words and utterances vary from one language to the next, and speakers of no language can claim that their language has done the selecting and combining better than another.

*obscure 불분명한, 이해하기 어려운 **grotesque 괴상한
***flick (손가락 등으로) 튀기다

주어진 글 다음에 이어질 글의 순서로 가장 적절한 것은?

On April 12, 1955, the day that the US government announced that the new polio vaccine was safe and effective, its inventor, Jonas Salk, was asked on television who owned the vaccine. He famously replied, "Well, the people, I would say. There is no patent. Could you patent the sun?"

(A) Elon Musk, CEO of Tesla Motors, decided in June 2014 to release all of his patents. Technological leadership is not defined by patents. The future of sustainable transport will be better served by openly sharing information and knowledge. "All our patents belong to you."

(B) His attitude to patenting, however, is not unique. Even in the era of excessive property protection, there is a new interest in open sources and access, global goods, and the notion of the commons.

(C) The vaccine was common property; it belonged to the people who had donated money for the public interest. Salk was later pitied for his decision. He could have earned $7 billion if his vaccine had been patented.

*polio 소아마비

① (A) – (C) – (B)
② (B) – (A) – (C)
③ (B) – (C) – (A)
④ (C) – (A) – (B)
⑤ (C) – (B) – (A)

글의 흐름으로 보아, 주어진 문장이 들어가기에 가장 적절한 곳은?

This created an atmosphere in which it was extremely difficult for technical biological staff to maintain their integrity, says Marshall.

By the early 1990s, the decline of the southwestern willow flycatcher was clear. (①) In 1993, the U.S. Fish and Wildlife Service (FWS) formally proposed listing the flycatcher as a federal endangered species and designating critical habitat, an important step under the Endangered Species Act that prevents damage to specific areas. (②) The task of writing the rule that listed the bird as endangered under the act fell to Rob Marshall. Marshall, a Yale-trained biologist with FWS in Arizona, was becoming disillusioned by the overall implementation of the Endangered Species Act. (③) The FWS was highly politicized by powerful, moneyed interests that saw species listings and particularly habitat designations as a threat to business: if a species is listed but no critical habitat is designated, a now-common pattern, then restrictions on business are far fewer. (④) For example, the process to list the flycatcher as endangered began in 1992, the proposed rule didn't come out until 1995, and it took until 1997 to produce the final ruling to list it. (⑤) The FWS only completed the listing because the watchdog organization Center for Biological Diversity sued them.

*willow flycatcher 버드나무 딱새   **implementation 시행, 이행
***integrity 변함없는 원칙 고수, 무결함

07 12강 3번

다음 글의 제목으로 가장 적절한 것은?

Translating theory into something that can be assessed in the physical environment means that phenomena are made measurable. It is often assumed that the phenomenon being measured is the same no matter how it is measured. Translations of theory into practice may differ, but these do not alter the nature of the phenomenon being measured. Without this assumption, measurement between different individuals made in different places or at different times could not be compared. The assumption does not, however, mean that this viewpoint is correct. Within quantum physics there is a view that the observer and the phenomenon cannot be separated. The observer and phenomenon make up a single system, a measurement system. In this context it is not possible to separate the measurement made from the measurement system within which it was made. The measurement and the phenomenon become combined in an unbreakable link in the measurement system. It is impossible to talk of a separate existence for the phenomenon and so also, therefore, to talk of an independent measurement of that phenomenon. This means that within the supposedly objective, hard science of physics, it is accepted that reality and how it is measured form an inseparable whole.

① Basic Assumptions of Modern Theories of Physics
② The Discrepancy between a Theory and Its Reality
③ Misguided Beliefs on the Measurability of Physical Realities
④ Independent or Bound?: Reality and Its Measurement
⑤ Contrasting Views on a Physically Impossible Phenomenon

08 12강 4번

다음 글의 요지로 가장 적절한 것은?

Why are certain languages mistakenly thought to be primitive? There are several reasons. Some people consider other languages ugly or "primitive sounding" if those languages make use of sounds or sound combinations they find unclear because the sounds are greatly different from those of the languages they themselves speak. Such a view is based on the ethnocentric attitude that the characteristics of one's own language are obviously superior. But words that seem unpronounceable to speakers of one language — and are therefore considered obscure or even grotesque — are easily acquired by even the youngest native speakers of the language in which they occur. To a native speaker of English, the Czech word *scvrnkls* "you flicked off (something) with your finger" looks quite strange, and its pronunciation may sound odd and even impossible because there is no vowel among the eight consonants; for native speakers of Czech, of course, *scvrnkls* is just another word. Which speech sounds are used and how they are combined to form words and utterances vary from one language to the next, and speakers of no language can claim that their language has done the selecting and combining better than another.

*obscure 불분명한, 이해하기 어려운 **grotesque 괴상한
***flick (손가락 등으로) 튀기다

① 발음 및 발화의 어려움으로 타 언어를 열등하다고 판단할 수 없다.
② 이상하게 들리는 발음은 화자의 발달 단계에 따른 자연스러운 현상이다.
③ 각 언어의 철자 조합과 그것이 만드는 발화 소리의 결합은 임의적이다.
④ 원시적 언어의 조음상 특징은 하나의 모음에 붙는 자음의 숫자와 관련이 있다.
⑤ 민족 중심적인 화자의 잘못된 태도는 사용하는 모국어 발음의 정교함에 근거한다.

12강 1번

On April 12, 1955, the day that the US government announced that the new polio vaccine was safe and effective, its inventor, Jonas Salk, was asked on television who owned the vaccine. He famously replied, "Well, the people, I would say. There is no patent. Could you patent the sun?" The vaccine was common property; it belonged to the people who had donated money for the public interest. Salk was later pitied for his decision. 그의 백신이 특허를 받았다면 그는 70억 달러를 벌 수 있었을 것이다. His attitude to patenting, however, is not unique. Even in the era of excessive property protection, there is a new interest in open sources and access, global goods, and the notion of the commons. Elon Musk, CEO of Tesla Motors, decided in June 2014 to release all of his patents. Technological leadership is not defined by patents. The future of _____ transport will be better served by openly sharing information and knowledge. "All our patents belong to you."

*polio 소아마비

09 윗글의 밑줄 친 우리말 의미와 일치하도록 **보기** 의 단어를 순서대로 배열하여 문장을 완성하시오.

> **보기** could / vaccine / patented / earned / $7 billion / if / his / been / have / had

He _____

_____.

10 윗글의 빈칸에 들어갈 단어를 영영 뜻풀이를 참고하여 쓰시오. (단, 주어진 글자로 시작할 것)

> capable of continuing for a long time at the same level

s_____

12강 2번

By the early 1990s, the decline of the southwestern willow flycatcher was clear. In 1993, the U.S. Fish and Wildlife Service (FWS) formally proposed listing the flycatcher as a federal endangered species and designating _____, an important step under the Endangered Species Act that prevents damage to specific areas. The task of writing the rule that listed the bird as endangered under the act fell to Rob Marshall. Marshall, a Yale-trained biologist with FWS in Arizona, was becoming disillusioned by the overall implementation of the Endangered Species Act. The FWS was highly politicized by powerful, moneyed interests that saw species listings and particularly habitat designations as a threat to business: if a species is listed but no critical habitat is designated, a now-common pattern, then restrictions on business are far fewer. <u>This</u> created an atmosphere in which it was extremely difficult for technical biological staff to maintain their integrity, says Marshall. For example, the process to list the flycatcher as endangered began in 1992, the proposed rule didn't come out until 1995, and it took until 1997 to produce the final ruling to list it. The FWS only completed the listing because the watchdog organization Center for Biological Diversity sued them.

*willow flycatcher 버드나무 딱새 **implementation 시행, 이행
***integrity 변함없는 원칙 고수, 무결함

11 윗글의 빈칸에 들어갈 단어를 영영 뜻풀이를 참고하여 본문에서 찾아 쓰시오. (단, 각각 주어진 글자로 시작할 것)

> the specific areas that are necessary for the survival or recovery of a listed wildlife species

c_____   h_____

12 윗글의 밑줄 친 This가 가리키는 것을 본문에서 찾아 우리말로 쓰시오. (25자 내외)

_____

_____

Translating theory into something that can be assessed in the physical environment means that phenomena are made measurable. It is often assumed that the phenomenon being measured is the same no matter how it is measured. Translations of theory into practice may differ, but these do not alter the nature of the phenomenon being measured. Without <u>this assumption</u>, measurement between different individuals made in different places or at different times could not be compared. The assumption does not, however, mean that this viewpoint is correct. Within quantum physics there is a view that the observer and the phenomenon cannot be separated. The observer and phenomenon make up a single system, a measurement system. In this context it is not possible to _____(A)_____ the measurement made from the measurement system within which it was made. The measurement and the phenomenon become combined in an unbreakable link in the measurement system. It is impossible to talk of a _____(B)_____ existence for the phenomenon and so also, therefore, to talk of an independent measurement of that phenomenon. This means that within the supposedly objective, hard science of physics, it is accepted that reality and how it is measured form an inseparable whole.

13 윗글의 밑줄 친 this assumption이 가리키는 것을 본문에서 찾아 우리말로 쓰시오. (30자 내외)

_____

_____

14 윗글의 빈칸 (A), (B)에 공통으로 들어갈 단어를 본문에서 찾아 쓰시오. (단, 주어진 글자로 시작할 것)

s_____

Why are certain languages mistakenly thought to be primitive? There are several reasons. Some people consider other languages ugly or "primitive sounding" if those languages make use of sounds or sound combinations they find unclear because the sounds are greatly different from (A) <u>that</u> of the languages they themselves speak. Such a view is based on the ethnocentric attitude that the characteristics of one's own language are obviously superior. But words that seem unpronounceable to speakers of one language — and are therefore considered obscure or even grotesque — (B) <u>is</u> easily acquired by even the youngest native speakers of the language in which they occur. To a native speaker of English, the Czech word *scvrnkls* "you flicked off (something) with your finger" looks quite strange, and its pronunciation may sound odd and even impossible because there is no vowel among the eight consonants; for native speakers of Czech, of course, *scvrnkls* is just another word. Which speech sounds are used and how they are combined to form words and utterances vary from one language to the next, and speakers of (C) <u>any</u> language can claim that their language has done the selecting and combining better than another.

*obscure 불분명한, 이해하기 어려운 **grotesque 괴상한
***flick (손가락 등으로) 튀기다

15 윗글의 밑줄 친 부분을 어법상 알맞은 형태로 고쳐 쓰시오.

(A) that → _____

(B) is   → _____

(C) any → _____

16 윗글의 내용을 한 문장으로 요약하려고 한다. 빈칸 (A)와 (B)에 들어갈 알맞은 말을 본문에서 찾아 쓰시오.

Attitudes that regard certain languages as primitive stem from a(n) _____(A)_____ belief that one's language is _____(B)_____ to another

(A) _____ (B) _____

❶ When we bemoan the lack of originality in the world, we blame it on the absence of creativity. ❷ If only people could generate more novel ideas, we'd all be better off. ❸ But in reality, the biggest barrier to originality is not idea generation — it's idea selection. ❹ In one analysis, when over two hundred people dreamed up more than a thousand ideas for new ventures and products, 87 percent were completely unique. ❺ Our companies, communities, and countries don't necessarily suffer from a shortage of novel ideas. ❻ They're constrained by a shortage of people who excel at choosing the right novel ideas. ❼ The Segway, a two-wheeled, self-balancing personal transporter, was a false positive: it was forecast as a hit but turned out to be a miss. ❽ *Seinfeld*, an American sitcom television series, was a false negative: it was expected to fail but ultimately flourished.

*bemoan 한탄하다

❶ 우리가 세상에서의 독창성의 부재를 한탄할 때, 우리는 그것을 창의성의 부재 탓으로 돌린다. ❷ 사람들이 더 많은 참신한 아이디어를 만들어 낼 수만 있다면, 우리 모두의 형편은 더 나을 것이다. ❸ 그러나 실제로는, 독창성의 가장 큰 장벽은 아이디어 생성이 아니고, 아이디어 선택이다. ❹ 어떤 분석에서, 200명이 넘는 사람들이 새로운 벤처 사업과 제품에 관해 1,000개가 넘는 아이디어를 생각해 냈을 때, 87퍼센트는 완전히 독특했다. ❺ 우리 회사, 지역 사회, 국가가 반드시 참신한 아이디어의 부족을 겪는 것은 아니다. ❻ 그것들은 알맞은 참신한 아이디어를 선택하는 데 탁월한 사람들의 부족으로 인해 제약을 받는다. ❼ 이륜 자가 균형 개인 운송기인 Segway는 긍정 오류였는데, 그것은 인기 제품으로 예측되었지만 실책으로 판명되었다. ❽ 미국의 시트콤 텔레비전 시리즈인 *Seinfeld*는 부정 오류였는데, 그것은 실패할 것이라고 예상되었지만 결국 매우 성공했다.

Word List

□ originality 독창성 □ blame 탓하다 □ absence 부재 □ novel 참신한, 새로운 □ better off (형편이) 더 나은 □ barrier 장벽 □ generation 생성 □ analysis 분석 □ dream up ~을 생각해 내다 □ venture 벤처 사업 □ unique 독특한 □ suffer from ~을 겪다 □ shortage 부족 □ constrain 제약하다 □ excel 뛰어나다 □ transporter 운송기 □ false positive 긍정 오류(거짓인 것이 참으로 잘못 판정되는 오류) □ forecast 예측하다 □ turn out ~으로 판명되다 □ false negative 부정 오류(참인 것이 거짓으로 잘못 판정되는 오류) □ ultimately 결국 □ flourish 매우 성공하다, 번성하다

• Word Test

1	excel		12	부족
2	turn out		13	독창성
3	constrain		14	장벽
4	dream up		15	예측하다
5	transporter		16	결국
6	better off		17	생성
7	suffer from		18	벤처 사업
8	blame		19	부재
9	false positive		20	독특한
10	analysis		21	매우 성공하다, 번성하다
11	false negative		22	참신한, 새로운

When we bemoan the lack of originality in the world, we blame it on the ❶ absence / presence of creativity. If only people could generate more novel ideas, we'd all be better off. ❷ But / And in reality, the biggest barrier to originality is not idea generation — it's idea selection. In one analysis, when over two hundred people dreamed up more than a thousand ideas for new ventures and products, 87 percent were completely ❸ common / unique . Our companies, communities, and countries don't necessarily suffer from a shortage of novel ideas. They're constrained by a(n) ❹ excess / shortage of people who excel at choosing the right novel ideas. The Segway, a two-wheeled, self-balancing personal transporter, was a false positive: it was forecast as a hit but turned out to be a miss. *Seinfeld*, an American sitcom television series, was a false negative: it was expected to fail but ultimately ❺ to flourish / flourished .

*bemoan 한탄하다

When we bemoan the lack of originality in the world, we blame it on the absence of creativity. If only people could generate more novel ideas, we'd all be better off. But in reality, the biggest barrier to originality is not idea generation — it's idea selection. In one analysis, when over two hundred people dreamed up more than a thousand ideas for new ventures and products, 87 percent ❶ _____ (be) completely unique. Our companies, communities, and countries don't necessarily ❷ _____ (suffer) from a shortage of novel ideas. They're constrained by a shortage of people who excel at ❸ _____ (choose) the right novel ideas. The Segway, a two-wheeled, self-balancing personal transporter, was a false positive: it was forecast as a hit but ❹ _____ (turn) out to be a miss. *Seinfeld*, an American sitcom television series, ❺ _____ (be) a false negative: it was expected to fail but ultimately flourished.

*bemoan 한탄하다

When we bemoan ❶ _____ _____ _____ _____ (독창성의 부재) in the world, we blame it on the absence of creativity. If only people could generate more novel ideas, we'd all be better off. But ❷ _____ _____ (실제로는), the biggest barrier to originality is not idea generation — it's idea selection. In one analysis, when over two hundred people dreamed up more than a thousand ideas for new ventures and products, 87 percent were completely unique. Our companies, communities, and countries don't necessarily suffer from a(n) ❸ _____ _____ _____ _____ (참신한 아이디어들의 부족). They're constrained by a shortage of people who excel at choosing the right novel ideas. The Segway, a two-wheeled, self-balancing personal transporter, was ❹ _____ _____ _____ (긍정 오류): it was forecast as a hit but ❺ _____ _____ _____ _____ _____ (실책으로 판명되었다). *Seinfeld*, an American sitcom television series, was a false negative: it was expected to fail but ultimately flourished.

*bemoan 한탄하다

❶ A striking experiment was performed accidentally by Japanese anthropologists attempting to relieve an overpopulation and hunger problem in a community of monkeys on an island in south Japan. ❷ The anthropologists threw grains of wheat on a sandy beach. ❸ Now it is very difficult to separate wheat grains one by one from sand grains; such an effort might even expend more energy than eating the collected wheat would provide. ❹ But one brilliant monkey, Imo, perhaps by accident or out of pique, threw handfuls of the mixture into the water. ❺ Wheat floats; sand sinks, a fact that Imo clearly noted. ❻ Through the sifting process she was able to eat well. ❼ While older monkeys, set in their ways, ignored her, the younger monkeys appeared to grasp the importance of her discovery, and imitated it. ❽ In the next generation, the practice was more widespread; today all monkeys on the island are competent at water sifting, an example of a cultural tradition among the monkeys.

*expend (에너지·시간 등을) 쓰다[들이다]   **out of pique 욱해서

❶ 하나의 주목할 만한 실험이 일본 남부의 한 섬에 있는 원숭이 군집에서 개체 수 과잉과 배고픔 문제를 덜어 주려던 일본인 인류학자들에 의해 우연히 행해졌다. ❷ 그 인류학자들은 밀알을 모래사장에 던졌다. ❸ 그런데 밀알을 모래알에서 하나씩 분리하는 것은 매우 어려운 일이어서, 그런 노력에는 오히려 모은 밀을 먹음으로써 얻는 것보다 더 많은 에너지가 쓰일지도 모른다. ❹ 그러나 아마도 우연인지 아니면 욱해서인지, 영리한 원숭이 Imo가 그 혼합물 몇 줌을 물속에 던졌다. ❺ 밀은 뜨지만, 모래는 가라앉는데, 바로 Imo가 분명히 주목한 사실이다. ❻ 거르는 과정을 통해 그 암컷은 잘 먹을 수 있었다. ❼ 나이가 더 많은 원숭이들은, 자기 방식이 몸에 배어, 그 암컷을 무시했지만, 더 어린 원숭이들은 그 원숭이가 발견한 것의 중요성을 이해하는 것 같았고, 그것을 모방했다. ❽ 다음 세대에, 그 수완은 더 널리 퍼졌고, 오늘날 그 섬의 모든 원숭이는 물로 걸러 내는 데 능숙한데, 이는 원숭이들의 문화적 전통의 한 예이다.

Word List

□ **striking** 주목할 만한, 놀라운 □ **accidentally** 우연히 □ **anthropologist** 인류학자 □ **relieve** 덜어 주다 □ **overpopulation** 개체 수[인구] 과잉 □ **community** (동물의) 군집, 집단 □ **grain** 낟알 □ **wheat** 밀 □ **brilliant** 영리한, 우수한 □ **by accident** 우연히 □ **mixture** 혼합물 □ **float** 뜨다 □ **sink** 가라앉다 □ **note** 주목하다 □ **sift** 거르다, 선별하다 □ **set in one's way** 자기 방식이 몸에 밴 □ **ignore** 무시하다 □ **grasp** 이해하다 □ **imitate** 모방하다 □ **practice** 수완, 숙련 □ **widespread** 널리 퍼진 □ **competent** 능숙한

• Word Test

1	grain	12	영리한, 우수한
2	note	13	능숙한
3	overpopulation	14	무시하다
4	by accident	15	덜어 주다
5	wheat	16	가라앉다
6	mixture	17	인류학자
7	practice	18	거르다, 선별하다
8	community	19	뜨다
9	set in one's way	20	널리 퍼진
10	accidentally	21	모방하다
11	grasp	22	주목할 만한, 놀라운

A striking experiment was performed accidentally by Japanese anthropologists attempting to ❶ cause / relieve an overpopulation and hunger problem in a community of monkeys on an island in south Japan. The anthropologists threw grains of wheat on a sandy beach. Now it is very ❷ easy / difficult to separate wheat grains one by one from sand grains; such an effort might even expend more energy than eating the collected wheat would provide. But one brilliant monkey, Imo, perhaps by accident or out of pique, threw handfuls of the mixture into the water. Wheat floats; sand sinks, a fact that Imo clearly noted. ❸ Through / Despite the sifting process she was able to eat well. ❹ While / Since older monkeys, set in their ways, ignored her, the younger monkeys appeared to grasp the importance of her discovery, and imitated it. In the next generation, the practice was more ❺ limited / widespread ; today all monkeys on the island are competent at water sifting, an example of a cultural tradition among the monkeys.

*expend (에너지·시간 등을) 쓰다[들이다]   **out of pique 욱해서

A striking experiment was performed accidentally by Japanese anthropologists attempting ❶ _____ (relieve) an overpopulation and hunger problem in a community of monkeys on an island in south Japan. The anthropologists threw grains of wheat on a sandy beach. Now it is very difficult ❷ _____ (separate) wheat grains one by one from sand grains; such an effort might even expend more energy than ❸ _____ (eat) the collected wheat would provide. But one brilliant monkey, Imo, perhaps by accident or out of pique, threw handfuls of the mixture into the water. Wheat floats; sand ❹ _____ (sink), a fact that Imo clearly noted. Through the sifting process she was able to eat well. While older monkeys, set in their ways, ignored her, the younger monkeys appeared to grasp the importance of her discovery, and ❺ _____ (imitate) it. In the next generation, the practice was more widespread; today all monkeys on the island are competent at water sifting, an example of a cultural tradition among the monkeys.

*expend (에너지·시간 등을) 쓰다[들이다]   **out of pique 욱해서

A striking experiment was performed accidentally by Japanese anthropologists attempting to relieve an overpopulation and hunger problem in ❶ _____ _____ _____ _____ (원숭이들 군집) on an island in south Japan. The anthropologists threw grains of wheat on a sandy beach. Now it is very difficult to separate wheat grains one by one from sand grains; ❷ _____ _____ _____ (그런 노력) might even expend more energy than eating the collected wheat would provide. But one brilliant monkey, Imo, perhaps ❸ _____ _____ (우연히) or out of pique, threw handfuls of the mixture into the water. Wheat floats; sand sinks, a fact that Imo clearly noted. Through the sifting process she was able to eat well. While older monkeys, set in their ways, ignored her, the younger monkeys appeared to ❹ _____ _____ _____ (중요성을 이해하다) of her discovery, and imitated it. In the next generation, the practice was more widespread; today all monkeys on the island are competent at water sifting, an example of ❺ _____ _____ _____ (문화적 전통) among the monkeys.

*expend (에너지·시간 등을) 쓰다[들이다]   **out of pique 욱해서

❶ The fact that a majority of the global population has at least some level of multilingual competence surely indicates that adding a second language is not a particularly remarkable feat. ❷ And yet, especially within powerful linguistic groups, it is common to find references to the difficulties involved or to the peculiar lack of language talents supposedly possessed. ❸ In the modern world, for example, English and American monolinguals often complain that they have no aptitude for foreign-language learning. ❹ This is usually accompanied by expressions of envy for those multilingual Europeans, and sometimes (more subtly) by a linguistic smugness reflecting a deeply held conviction that, after all, those clever "others" who don't already know English will have to accommodate in a world made increasingly safe for anglophones. ❺ All such attitudes, of course, reveal more about social dominance and convention than they do about aptitude.

*feat 재주 **smugness 우쭐거림 ***anglophone 영어 사용자

❶ 세계 인구의 대다수가 적어도 어느 정도 수준의 다중 언어 능력을 갖고 있다는 사실은 분명히 제2 언어를 추가하는 것이 특별히 주목할 만한 재주는 아니라는 것을 보여 준다. ❷ 하지만 특히 영향력 있는 언어 집단 내에서, 관련된 어려움이나 아마도 갖추고 있는 것으로 생각했던 언어 재능이 이상하게 결핍되어 있는 데 대해 언급하는 것을 흔히 볼 수 있다. ❸ 예를 들어, 현대 세계에서, 영국과 미국의 단일 언어 사용자는 자주 자신이 외국어 학습에 소질이 없다고 불평한다. ❹ 이것은 대개 복수의 언어가 가능한 유럽인에 대한 부러움의 표현과, 때로는 (더 미묘하게) 영어를 아직 알지 못하는 똑똑한 '다른 사람들'이 어쨌든 간에 결국 영어 사용자에게 갈수록 더 안전해지는 세상에 순응해야만 할 것이라는 깊이 박힌 확신을 나타내는 언어상의 우쭐거림을 수반한다. ❺ 물론, 이러한 모든 태도는 소질에 대한 것보다는 사회적 우위와 관습에 대한 것을 더 많이 드러낸다.

Word List

□ **majority** 대다수 □ **population** 인구 □ **multilingual** 여러 언어를 사용할 수 있는 □ **competence** 능력
□ **indicate** 보여 주다, 나타내다 □ **remarkable** 주목할 만한 □ **linguistic** 언어의 □ **reference** 언급, 논급 □ **involve** 관련시키다
□ **peculiar** 이상한, 특이한 □ **supposedly** 아마 □ **monolingual** 단일 언어 사용자 □ **complain** 불평하다, 투덜거리다
□ **aptitude** 소질, 적성 □ **accompany** 수반하다 □ **subtly** 미묘하게, 섬세하게 □ **reflect** 반영하다, 보여주다 □ **conviction** 확신, 신념
□ **accommodate** 순응하다, 적응하다 □ **increasingly** 갈수록 더, 점점 더 □ **dominance** 지배, 우세 □ **convention** 관습, 관례

● Word Test

1	indicate	12	이상한, 특이한
2	accommodate	13	언급, 논급
3	majority	14	능력
4	supposedly	15	인구
5	involve	16	불평하다, 투덜거리다
6	aptitude	17	관습, 관례
7	conviction	18	미묘하게, 섬세하게
8	monolingual	19	언어의
9	accompany	20	갈수록 더, 점점 더
10	multilingual	21	주목할 만한
11	dominance	22	반영하다, 보여주다

The fact that a ❶ majority / minority of the global population has at least some level of multilingual competence surely indicates that adding a second language is not a particularly remarkable feat. ❷ Then / And yet, especially within powerful linguistic groups, it is common to find references to the difficulties involved or to the peculiar lack of language talents supposedly possessed. In the modern world, for example, English and American ❸ multilinguals / monolinguals often complain that they have no aptitude for foreign-language learning. This is usually accompanied by expressions of envy for those ❹ monolingual / multilingual Europeans, and sometimes (more subtly) by a linguistic smugness reflecting a deeply held conviction that, after all, those clever "others" who don't already know English will have to accommodate in a world made increasingly safe for anglophones. All such attitudes, of course, reveal more about social dominance and convention ❺ than / because they do about aptitude.

*feat 재주 **smugness 우쭐거림 ***anglophone 영어 사용자

The fact that a majority of the global population has at least some level of multilingual competence surely ❶ _____ (indicate) that adding a second language is not a particularly remarkable feat. And yet, especially within powerful linguistic groups, it is common to find references to the difficulties ❷ _____ (involve) or to the peculiar lack of language talents supposedly possessed. In the modern world, for example, English and American monolinguals often complain that they have no aptitude for foreign-language learning. This is usually accompanied by expressions of envy for those multilingual Europeans, and sometimes (more subtly) by a linguistic smugness ❸ _____ (reflect) a deeply held conviction that, after all, those clever "others" who don't already know English will have to accommodate in a world ❹ _____ (make) increasingly safe for anglophones. All such attitudes, of course, reveal more about social dominance and convention than they do about aptitude.

*feat 재주 **smugness 우쭐거림 ***anglophone 영어 사용자

The fact that ❶ _____ _____ _____ (~의 대다수) the global population has at least some level of multilingual competence surely indicates that adding a second language is not a particularly remarkable feat. And yet, especially within powerful linguistic groups, it is common to find references to ❷ _____ _____ _____ (관련된 어려움들) or to the peculiar lack of language talents supposedly possessed. In the modern world, for example, English and American monolinguals often complain that they ❸ _____ _____ _____ _____ (~에 소질이 없다) foreign-language learning. This is usually accompanied by expressions of envy for those multilingual Europeans, and sometimes (more subtly) by a linguistic smugness reflecting ❹ _____ _____ _____ _____ (깊이 박힌 확신) that, after all, those clever "others" who don't already know English will have to accommodate in ❺ _____ _____ _____ _____ _____ (갈수록 더 안전해지는 세상) for anglophones. All such attitudes, of course, reveal more about social dominance and convention than they do about aptitude.

*feat 재주 **smugness 우쭐거림 ***anglophone 영어 사용자

❶ A gentleman came into my stress-management office and said, 'I'm mad at my boss. I don't like my job. I don't like the people that work with me. No one appreciates my work. I'm really angry.' ❷ When I began teaching him about how his own thinking creates his angry feelings he said, 'With all due respect, Dr. Carlson, I'm angry almost all the time, but I almost never think angry thoughts.' ❸ Do you see where he was being fooled? ❹ Until that moment, he believed that 'thinking' meant the same thing as 'pondering.' ❺ Even though he may not have dwelled on his misery for hours at a time, he was nevertheless continually thinking negatively, a moment here and a moment there. ❻ He spent nearly all of his time thinking about the little things that irritated and annoyed him. ❼ It was almost as if the unstated goal of his life was to analyse it and to give his opinions on how various things affected him. ❽ His negative thoughts were creating his negative feelings and emotions and he didn't even know he was thinking them. ❾ He was a victim of his own thinking.

*ponder 심사숙고하다

❶ 한 신사가 내 스트레스 관리 상담실에 들어와서 말했다. '전 제 상사에게 분노가 치밀어요. 전 제 직업이 마음에 들지 않아요. 전 저와 함께 일하는 사람들을 좋아하지 않아요. 아무도 제 일의 가치를 인정하지 않아요. 전 정말로 화가 나요.' ❷ 내가 그에게 그의 생각이 어떻게 그의 분노의 느낌을 만들어 내는지에 관해 알려 주기 시작했을 때, 그는 말했다. '송구스럽지만, Carlson 박사님, 저는 거의 내내 화가 나 있지만, 화가 났다는 생각을 거의 하지 않습니다.' ❸ 여러분은 그가 어디에서 속고 있었는지 아는가? ❹ 그 순간까지 그는 '생각하는 것'이 '심사숙고하는 것'과 같은 의미라고 믿었다. ❺ 비록 그는 한 번에 몇 시간씩 자신의 불행에 대해 곰곰이 생각해 보지는 않았을지 모르지만, 그럼에도 그는 여기서 잠깐, 저기서 잠깐, 계속해서 부정적인 생각을 하고 있었던 것이다. ❻ 그는 자신의 거의 모든 시간을 자신을 짜증나고 성가시게 하는 사소한 것들에 대해 생각하는 데 썼다. ❼ 마치 그의 삶에서 무언의 목표는 삶을 분석하고 다양한 것들이 어떻게 그에게 영향을 미치는지에 대해 자신의 의견을 제시하는 것인 듯했다. ❽ 그의 부정적인 생각은 그의 부정적인 느낌과 감정을 만들어 내고 있었는데, 그는 자신이 그것을 생각하고 있다는 것조차 알지 못했다. ❾ 그는 본인이 스스로 하는 생각의 희생자였다.

Word List

□ management 관리　□ appreciate ~의 가치를 인정하다　□ with all due respect 송구하지만　□ fool 속이다
□ dwell on ~에 대해 곰곰이 생각하다　□ misery 불행　□ nevertheless 그럼에도(불구하고)　□ continually 계속해서
□ negatively 부정적으로　□ irritate 짜증 나게 하다　□ annoy 성가시게 하다　□ unstated 무언의, 말로 표현되지 않은
□ analyse 분석하다　□ various 다양한　□ affect 영향을 미치다　□ victim 희생자, 피해자

• Word Test

1	unstated	_____	9	부정적으로	_____
2	nevertheless	_____	10	속이다	_____
3	irritate	_____	11	관리	_____
4	appreciate	_____	12	희생자, 피해자	_____
5	analyse	_____	13	성가시게 하다	_____
6	dwell on	_____	14	계속해서	_____
7	with all due respect	_____	15	다양한	_____
8	affect	_____	16	불행	_____

A gentleman came into my stress-management office and said, 'I'm mad at my boss. I don't like my job. I don't like the people ❶ [that / what] work with me. No one appreciates my work. I'm really angry.' When I began teaching him about how his own thinking creates his angry feelings he said, 'With all due respect, Dr. Carlson, I'm angry almost all the time, ❷ [but / so] I almost never think angry thoughts.' Do you see ❸ [when / where] he was being fooled? Until that moment, he believed that 'thinking' meant the same thing as 'pondering.'Even though he may not have dwelled on his misery for hours at a time, he was ❹ [eventually / nevertheless] continually thinking negatively, a moment here and a moment there. He spent nearly all of his time thinking about the little things that irritated and annoyed him. It was almost as if the unstated goal of his life was to analyse it and to give his opinions on how various things affected him. His negative thoughts were creating his negative feelings and emotions and he didn't even know he was thinking ❺ [it / them]. He was a victim of his own thinking.

*ponder 심사숙고하다

A gentleman came into my stress-management office and said, 'I'm mad at my boss. I don't like my job. I don't like the people that work with me. No one appreciates my work. I'm really angry.' When I began teaching him about how his own thinking ❶ _____ (create) his angry feelings he said, 'With all due respect, Dr. Carlson, I'm angry almost all the time, but I almost never think angry thoughts.' Do you see where he was ❷ _____ (be) fooled? Until that moment, he believed that 'thinking' meant the same thing as 'pondering.'Even though he may not have dwelled on his misery for hours at a time, he was nevertheless continually ❸ _____ (think) negatively, a moment here and a moment there. He spent nearly all of his time ❹ _____ (think) about the little things that irritated and annoyed him. It was almost as if the unstated goal of his life was ❺ _____ (analyse) it and to give his opinions on how various things affected him. His negative thoughts were creating his negative feelings and emotions and he didn't even know he was thinking them. He was a victim of his own thinking.

*ponder 심사숙고하다

A gentleman came into my stress-management office and said, 'I'm mad at my boss. I don't like my job. I don't like the ❶ _____ _____ _____ _____ _____ (나와 함께 일하는 사람들). No one appreciates my work. I'm really angry.' When I began teaching him about how his own thinking creates his angry feelings he said, 'With all due respect, Dr. Carlson, I'm angry ❷ _____ _____ _____ _____ (거의 내내), but I almost never think angry thoughts.' Do you see where he was being fooled? Until that moment, he believed that 'thinking' meant ❸ _____ _____ _____ _____ (~와 같은 것) 'pondering.'Even though he may not have ❹ _____ _____ _____ _____ (그의 불행에 대해 곰곰이 생각했다) for hours at a time, he was nevertheless continually thinking negatively, a moment here and a moment there. He spent nearly all of his time thinking about the little things that irritated and annoyed him. It was almost as if the unstated goal of his life was to analyse it and to give his opinions on how various things affected him. His negative thoughts were creating his negative feelings and emotions and he didn't even know he was thinking them. He was ❺ _____ _____ _____ (~의 희생자) his own thinking.

*ponder 심사숙고하다

❶ Caregivers for the old do much more than simply perform tasks. ❷ They provide intellectual engagement, social interaction, and emotional support, key factors in long-term health and longevity. ❸ As society has grown more urban and as family homes have become less multigenerational, greater numbers of the elderly now live alone. ❹ This shift brings with it diminished opportunities for social interaction. ❺ In the United States, a 2010 American Association of Retired Persons study found that over a third of respondents age forty-five and older were lonely as measured on the UCLA loneliness scale. ❻ Interactions with robots offer an opportunity to counteract, if not entirely remedy, the effects of such social isolation. ❼ Brain scan studies using fMRI have shown people have a measurable emotional response to robots similar to that measured when interacting with other people, at least in certain situations. ❽ While robots and technology can't entirely fill our need for social interaction, they may be able to provide some level of engagement.

❶ 고령자를 돌보는 사람들은 단순히 업무를 수행하는 것보다 훨씬 더 많은 일을 한다. ❷ 그들은 지적 관여, 사회적 상호 작용, 정서적 지원을 제공하는데, 그것들은 장기간의 건강과 장수의 핵심 요소이다. ❸ 사회가 더욱 도시화되고 가정이 덜 다세대화되면서, 더 많은 수의 고령자가 현재 혼자 살고 있다. ❹ 이러한 변화는 사회적 상호 작용을 위한 기회의 감소를 수반한다. ❺ 미국에서, 2010년 미국 은퇴자 협회의 한 연구는 UCLA 외로움 척도로 측정했을 때 45세 이상의 응답자 중 3분의 1 넘는 사람들이 외로움을 느낀다는 것을 알아냈다. ❻ 로봇과의 상호 작용은 그러한 사회적 고립의 영향을 완전히 치료하는 것까지는 아니더라도, 그에 대응할 기회를 제공한다. ❼ 기능적 자기 공명 영상법(fMRI)을 이용한 뇌 스캔 연구는 사람들이 최소한 특정한 상황에서는 다른 사람과 상호 작용을 할 때 측정된 감정 반응과 유사한 주목할 만한 감정 반응을 로봇에게 보인다는 것을 보여주었다. ❽ 로봇과 기술이 사회적 상호 작용에 대한 우리의 필요를 완전히 충족시켜 줄 수는 없지만, 그것들이 어느 정도의 관여는 제공할 수 있을 것이다.

Word List

□ caregiver 돌보는 사람 □ perform 수행하다 □ task 과제, 업무 □ engagement 관여, 참여 □ interaction 상호 작용
□ emotional 정서적 □ factor 요인, 요소 □ long-term 장기간의 □ longevity 장수 □ urban 도시화의, 도시의
□ multigenerational 다세대의 □ shift 변화 □ diminished 감소된 □ respondent 응답자 □ measure 측정하다
□ counteract 대응하다 □ remedy 치료하다 □ isolation 고립

• Word Test

1	multigenerational		10	장기간의	
2	engagement		11	감소된	
3	caregiver		12	고립	
4	factor		13	과제, 업무	
5	respondent		14	장수	
6	perform		15	대응하다	
7	interaction		16	도시화의, 도시의	
8	shift		17	측정하다	
9	remedy		18	정서적	

Caregivers for the old do much more than simply perform tasks. They provide intellectual engagement, social interaction, and emotional support, key factors in long-term health and longevity. As society has grown more urban and as family homes have become ❶ `less / more` multigenerational, greater numbers of the elderly now live alone. This shift brings with it diminished opportunities for social interaction. In the United States, a 2010 American Association of Retired Persons study found that over a third of respondents age forty-five and older were lonely as ❷ `measured / measuring` on the UCLA loneliness scale. Interactions with robots offer an opportunity to counteract, ❸ `if / if not` entirely remedy, the effects of such social isolation. Brain scan studies using fMRI have shown people have a measurable emotional response to robots similar to ❹ `that / those` measured when interacting with other people, at least in certain situations. While robots and technology can't entirely fill our need for social interaction, they may be able to provide some level of engagement.

Caregivers for the old ❶ _____ (do) much more than simply perform tasks. They provide intellectual engagement, social interaction, and emotional support, key factors in long-term health and longevity. As society ❷ _____ (grow) more urban and as family homes have become less multigenerational, greater numbers of the elderly now live alone. This shift brings with it diminished opportunities for social interaction. In the United States, a 2010 American Association of Retired Persons study found that over a third of respondents age forty-five and older were lonely as measured on the UCLA loneliness scale. Interactions with robots offer an opportunity ❸ _____ (counteract), if not entirely remedy, the effects of such social isolation. Brain scan studies ❹ _____ (use) fMRI have shown people have a measurable emotional response to robots similar to that measured when ❺ _____ (interact) with other people, at least in certain situations. While robots and technology can't entirely fill our need for social interaction, they may be able to provide some level of engagement.

Caregivers for the old do much more than simply perform tasks. They provide intellectual engagement, social interaction, and emotional support, key factors in long-term ❶ _____ _____ _____ (건강과 장수). As society has grown more urban and as family homes have become less multigenerational, greater numbers of the elderly now live alone. This shift brings with it diminished opportunities for social interaction. In the United States, a 2010 American Association of Retired Persons study found that over ❷ _____ _____ _____ _____ (응답자들의 3분의 1) age forty-five and older were lonely as measured on the UCLA loneliness scale. Interactions with robots ❸ _____ _____ _____ (기회를 제공하다) to counteract, if not entirely remedy, the effects of such social isolation. Brain scan studies using fMRI have shown people have a measurable emotional response to robots similar to that measured when interacting with other people, at least in certain situations. While robots and technology can't entirely ❹ _____ _____ _____ (우리의 필요를 충족시키다) for social interaction, they may be able to provide ❺ _____ _____ _____ _____ (어느 정도의 관여).

❶ How are films made and produced? ❷ A news item, an event, a novel or the biography of an important person might suggest suitable themes. ❸ The film director's first job is to write a short account of the subject and to present it for a producer. ❹ This simple, untechnical plan is called a *treatment*. ❺ Movie director Jean Renoir and his scriptwriter wrote several unused treatments for *La Grande Illusion*. ❻ One of them is easy to get hold of; it is quite different from the final film. ❼ If a producer and a group of actors are interested in the scheme, the director or the scriptwriter rewrites the text in order to give a full list of shots, described in their order, with stage directions and technical terms clearly marked; this is the scenario. ❽ There is a good scenario of *October (Ten Days That Shook the World)* written by Eisenstein himself but, once again, it is far removed from the three finished versions of the film we can see today. ❾ It is difficult to put into practice what was decided beforehand, and important alterations occur in the course of production.

❶ 영화는 어떻게 만들어지고 제작되는가? ❷ 뉴스거리, 사건, 소설 또는 중요한 인물의 전기가 적절한 주제를 제시할 수도 있다. ❸ 영화감독의 첫 번째 일은 주제에 대해 짧게 기술하여 그것을 제작자에게 제시하는 것이다. ❹ 이 간단하고 비전문적인 초안은 '트리트먼트'라고 불린다. ❺ 영화감독 Jean Renoir와 그의 대본작가는 *La Grande Illusion*을 위한 몇 개의 사용되지 않은 트리트먼트를 썼다. ❻ 그중 하나는 구하기 쉬운데, 그것은 최종 영화와는 상당히 다르다. ❼ 제작자 및 일단의 배우들이 그 기획에 관심이 있는 경우, 감독이나 대본 작가는 순서대로 기술되어 있고 무대 지시 및 전문 용어가 명확하게 표시된 숏의 목록 전체를 제공하기 위하여 원고를 다시 작성하는데, 이것이 시나리오이다. ❽ Eisenstein이 직접 쓴 *October (Ten Days That Shook the World)*의 좋은 시나리오가 있지만, 그것 역시 오늘날 우리가 볼 수 있는 그 영화의 세 가지 최종 버전과는 매우 다르다. ❾ 사전에 결정된 것을 실행에 옮기는 것은 어려우며, 제작 과정에서 중요한 변경이 생긴다.

Word List

□ biography 전기   □ suitable 적절한   □ theme 주제   □ account 기술, 설명   □ present 제시하다, 보여 주다
□ untechnical 비전문적인   □ scriptwriter 대본 작가   □ get hold of ~을 구하다[손에 넣다]   □ scheme 기획, 개요
□ shot 숏(영화에서 한 대의 카메라가 계속해서 잡는 장면)   □ direction 지시   □ term 용어   □ mark 표시하다
□ removed from ~과 다른[동떨어진]   □ put into practice ~을 실행에 옮기다   □ beforehand 사전에, 미리   □ alteration 변경, 수정
□ in the course of ~의 과정에서

• Word Test

1	put into practice		10	적절한	
2	scriptwriter		11	전기	
3	in the course of		12	비전문적인	
4	term		13	기획, 개요	
5	direction		14	기술, 설명	
6	shot		15	표시하다	
7	get hold of		16	변경, 수정	
8	present		17	주제	
9	removed from		18	사전에, 미리	

❶ How / Why are films made and produced? A news item, an event, a novel or the biography of an important person might suggest suitable themes. The film director's first job is to write a short account of the subject and to present it for a producer. This simple, untechnical plan is called a *treatment*. Movie director Jean Renoir and his scriptwriter wrote several unused treatments for *La Grande Illusion*. One of them is ❷ easy / difficult to get hold of; it is quite different from the final film. If a producer and a group of actors are ❸ disinterested / interested in the scheme, the director or the scriptwriter rewrites the text in order to give a full list of shots, described in their order, with stage directions and technical terms clearly marked; this is the scenario. There is a good scenario of *October (Ten Days That Shook the World)* written by Eisenstein himself ❹ and / but, once again, it is far removed from the three finished versions of the film we can see today. It is difficult to put into practice ❺ that / what was decided beforehand, and important alterations occur in the course of production.

How are films made and produced? A news item, an event, a novel or the biography of an important person might suggest suitable themes. The film director's first job is to write a short account of the subject and ❶ _____ (present) it for a producer. This simple, untechnical plan is called a *treatment*. Movie director Jean Renoir and his scriptwriter wrote several unused treatments for *La Grande Illusion*. One of them is easy to get hold of; it is quite different from the final film. If a producer and a group of actors are interested in the scheme, the director or the scriptwriter ❷ _____ (rewrite) the text in order to give a full list of shots, described in their order, with stage directions and technical terms clearly ❸ _____ (mark); this is the scenario. There is a good scenario of *October (Ten Days That Shook the World)* ❹ _____ (write) by Eisenstein himself but, once again, it is far removed from the three finished versions of the film we can see today. It is difficult ❺ _____ (put) into practice what was decided beforehand, and important alterations occur in the course of production.

How are films made and produced? A news item, an event, a novel or the biography of an important person might suggest suitable themes. The film director's first job is to write a short account of the subject and to present it for a producer. This simple, untechnical plan is called a *treatment*. Movie director Jean Renoir and his scriptwriter wrote several unused treatments for *La Grande Illusion*. One of them is ❶ _____ _____ _____ _____ _____ (구하기 쉬운); it is quite different from the final film. If a producer and a group of actors are interested in the scheme, the director or the scriptwriter rewrites the text in order to give ❷ _____ _____ _____ _____ (~의 목록 전체) shots, described in their order, with stage directions and technical terms clearly marked; this is the scenario. There is a good scenario of *October (Ten Days That Shook the World)* written by Eisenstein himself but, once again, it is far removed from the three finished ❸ _____ _____ _____ (영화의 버전들) we can see today. It is difficult to ❹ _____ _____ _____ (실행에 옮기다) what was decided beforehand, and important alterations occur in ❺ _____ _____ _____ _____ (제작 과정).

❶ Our present-day thinking is based on a succession of historically evolved mentalities; on mental edifices which previous generations have constructed, pulled down, renovated and extended. ❷ Past events are compressed in images and metaphors which determine our present thinking even if we are not always aware of them. ❸ Common sense is the thickly viscous form of the past, the reflex of history which, like the story about a puppet and a chess-playing machine, always triumphs. ❹ The puppet dressed in Turkish garb was sitting in front of a chessboard on a large table. ❺ A cunning arrangement of mirrors created the impression of being able to see underneath the table. ❻ In actual fact, there was a dwarf sitting underneath who was a chess master, and controlled the puppet. ❼ We can imagine the continuous effect of historical experience acting like an ugly, unloved and happily forgotten dwarf, moving the pieces in the chess game of our everyday life.

* edifice (사고의) 체계 ** viscous 끈적이는 *** garb 복장

❶ 우리의 현재 사고는 역사적으로 진화된 일련의 사고방식, 즉 이전 세대들이 구성하고, 허물고, 보수하고, 확장해 온 사고 체계에 기반을 두고 있다. ❷ 과거의 사건들은 우리가 항상 의식하고 있지는 않더라도 우리의 현재 사고를 결정하는 이미지와 은유 속에 압축된다. ❸ 상식은 걸쭉하게 끈적이는 형태의 과거, 즉 꼭두각시와 체스 경기 기계 장치에 관한 이야기처럼 항상 승리하는 역사의 반영이다. ❹ 튀르키예식 복장을 한 꼭두각시가 커다란 탁자 위에 놓인 체스판 앞에 앉아 있었다. ❺ 거울의 교묘한 배치는 탁자 안을 볼 수 있다는 인상을 만들어 냈다. ❻ 사실, 체스 달인이면서 그 꼭두각시를 조종하는 난쟁이가 그 안에 앉아 있었다. ❼ 우리는 역사적 경험의 지속적인 영향력이 추하고, 사랑받지 못하고, 다행히 잊힌 난쟁이처럼 행동하는 것, 즉 우리 일상생활의 체스 게임에서(체스) 말들을 움직이는 것을 상상할 수 있다.

Word List

□ **a succession of** 일련의　□ **evolve** 진화하다　□ **mentality** 사고방식　□ **previous** 이전의　□ **construct** 구성하다
□ **renovate** 보수하다　□ **extend** 확장하다　□ **compress** 압축하다　□ **metaphor** 은유, 비유　□ **common sense** 상식
□ **thickly** 걸쭉하게　□ **reflex** 반영, 반사　□ **puppet** 꼭두각시　□ **triumph** 승리하다　□ **chessboard** 체스판
□ **cunning** 교묘한, 교활한　□ **arrangement** 배치, 배열　□ **dwarf** 난쟁이　□ **continuous** 지속적인　□ **effect** 영향

• Word Test

1	continuous	11	사고방식
2	previous	12	영향
3	triumph	13	구성하다
4	renovate	14	상식
5	evolve	15	배치, 배열
6	thickly	16	반영, 반사
7	dwarf	17	교묘한, 교활한
8	compress	18	은유, 비유
9	a succession of	19	확장하다
10	chessboard	20	꼭두각시

Our present-day thinking is based on a succession of historically evolved mentalities; on mental edifices ❶ which / in which previous generations have constructed, pulled down, renovated and extended. ❷ Future / Past events are compressed in images and metaphors which determine our present thinking ❸ even so / even if we are not always aware of them. Common sense is the thickly viscous form of the past, the reflex of history ❹ in which / which, like the story about a puppet and a chess-playing machine, always triumphs. The puppet dressed in Turkish garb was sitting in front of a chessboard on a large table. A cunning arrangement of mirrors created the impression of being able to see underneath the table. In actual fact, there was a dwarf sitting underneath ❺ what / who was a chess master, and controlled the puppet. We can imagine the continuous effect of historical experience acting like an ugly, unloved and happily forgotten dwarf, moving the pieces in the chess game of our everyday life.

*edifice (사고의) 체계   **viscous 끈적이는   ***garb 복장

Our present-day thinking is based on a succession of historically evolved mentalities; on mental edifices which previous generations have constructed, pulled down, renovated and ❶ _____ (extend). Past events are compressed in images and metaphors which determine our present thinking even if we are not always aware of them. Common sense is the thickly viscous form of the past, the reflex of history which, like the story about a puppet and a chess-playing machine, always ❷ _____ (triumph). The puppet dressed in Turkish garb was sitting in front of a chessboard on a large table. A cunning arrangement of mirrors created the impression of ❸ _____ (be) able to see underneath the table. In actual fact, there was a dwarf sitting underneath who was a chess master, and ❹ _____ (control) the puppet. We can imagine the continuous effect of historical experience acting like an ugly, unloved and happily forgotten dwarf, ❺ _____ (move) the pieces in the chess game of our everyday life.

*edifice (사고의) 체계   **viscous 끈적이는   ***garb 복장

Our present-day thinking is based on ❶ _____ _____ _____ _____ _____
(역사적으로 진화된 일련의 사고방식들); on mental edifices which ❷ _____ _____ (이전 세대들) have constructed, pulled down, renovated and extended. Past events are compressed in images and metaphors which ❸ _____ _____ _____ _____ (우리의 현재 사고를 결정하다) even if we are not always aware of them. Common sense is the thickly viscous form of the past, the reflex of history which, like the story about a puppet and a chess-playing machine, always triumphs. The puppet dressed in Turkish garb was sitting in front of a chessboard on a large table. A(n) ❹ _____ _____ _____ _____ (거울들의 교묘한 배치) created the impression of being able to see underneath the table. In actual fact, there was a dwarf sitting underneath who was a chess master, and controlled the puppet. We can imagine the continuous effect of historical experience acting like an ugly, unloved and happily forgotten dwarf, moving the pieces in the chess game of ❺ _____ _____ _____
(우리의 일상생활).

*edifice (사고의) 체계   **viscous 끈적이는   ***garb 복장

❶ The word "entertainment" derives from the Latin *tenere*, which means "to hold or keep steady, busy, or amused." ❷ The notion of making money by keeping an audience steady, busy, or amused remains central to those in the business of entertainment. ❸ Media practitioners, then, define entertainment as material that grabs the audience's attention and leaves agreeable feelings, as opposed to challenging their views of themselves and the world. ❹ However, this doesn't mean that people who work in the entertainment business always stay away from informing or persuading. ❺ Many movies that are categorized under "entertainment" by their production firms have been written and produced with the intention of making a political point (think of *The Day After Tomorrow*, *Syriana*, or *Blood Diamond*) or an educational point (like *Schindler's List. Crash*, or *Letters from Iwo Jima*). ❻ When media practitioners label a product as "entertainment," though, they are signaling to their audiences that their primary concern should be with enjoyment, not with any other messages that may be included.

*practitioner (전문직) 종사자

❶ '엔터테인먼트'라는 단어는 라틴어 *tenere*에서 유래하는데, 그 말은 '안정되거나, 열중하거나, 즐거운 상태를 지속하거나 유지하는 것'을 의미한다. ❷ 관객을 안정되거나, 열중하거나, 즐거운 상태로 있게 함으로써 돈을 번다는 개념은 엔터테인먼트 사업에 종사하는 사람들에게 여전히 가장 중요하다. ❸ 그래서 미디어 종사자들은 엔터테인먼트를 청중이 자신과 세상에 대하여 가지는 견해에 이의를 제기하는 것이 아니라 그들의 관심을 붙들어 기분 좋은 감정을 남기는 재료로 정의한다. ❹ 하지만, 이것이 엔터테인먼트 업계에서 일하는 사람들이 항상 정보를 제공하거나 설득하는 것을 멀리한다는 것을 의미하지는 않는다. ❺ 제작사에 의해 '엔터테인먼트'로 분류되는 많은 영화가 정치적 논점(*The Day After Tomorrow*, *Syriana*, 또는 *Blood Diamond*를 생각해 보라)이나 교육적 논점(*Schindler's List. Crash*, 또는 *Letters from Iwo Jima*와 같이)을 만들려는 의도에서 쓰이고 제작되었다. ❻ 그러나 미디어 종사자들이 제작물을 '엔터테인먼트'라고 일컬을 때, 그들은 청중에게 자신들의 주 관심사가 아마도 즐거움에 있을 것이며, 포함될 수도 있는 어떤 다른 메시지에 있지는 않으리라는 신호를 보내고 있다.

Word List

□ **derive from** ~에서 유래하다 　□ **steady** 지속적인, 안정된 　□ **amused** 즐거운 　□ **notion** 개념 　□ **central** 가장 중요한, 중심적인
□ **define** 정의하다 　□ **grab** 붙들다, 붙잡다 　□ **agreeable** 기분 좋은 　□ **as opposed to** ~이 아니라, ~과 대조적으로
□ **challenge** 이의를 제기하다 　□ **categorize** 분류하다 　□ **production** 제작 　□ **intention** 의도 　□ **label** 일컫다, 부르다
□ **signal** 신호를 보내다 　□ **primary** 주된, 일차적인 　□ **concern** 관심사 　□ **include** 포함하다

• Word Test

1	label		10	관심사
2	grab		11	신호를 보내다
3	notion		12	지속적인, 안정된
4	as opposed to		13	분류하다
5	primary		14	포함하다
6	central		15	정의하다
7	intention		16	기분 좋은
8	challenge		17	제작
9	derive from		18	즐거운

The word "entertainment" derives from the Latin *tenere*, ❶ which / that means "to hold or keep steady, busy, or amused." The notion of making money by keeping an audience steady, busy, or amused remains central to those in the business of entertainment. Media practitioners, then, define entertainment as material that / what grabs the audience's attention and leaves agreeable feelings, as opposed to challenging their views of themselves and the world. ❷ Likewise / However , this doesn't mean that people who work in the entertainment business always stay away from informing or persuading. Many movies that are categorized under "entertainment" by their production firms have been written and produced ❸ with / without the intention of making a political point (think of *The Day After Tomorrow, Syriana*, or *Blood Diamond*) or an educational point (like *Schindler's List. Crash*, or *Letters from Iwo Jima*). When media practitioners label a product as "entertainment," ❹ though / therefore , they are signaling to their audiences that their primary concern should be with enjoyment, not with any other messages that may be included.

*practitioner (전문직) 종사자

The word "entertainment" derives from the Latin *tenere*, which ❶ _____ (mean) "to hold or keep steady, busy, or amused." The notion of making money by keeping an audience steady, busy, or amused ❷ _____ (remain) central to those in the business of entertainment. Media practitioners, then, define entertainment as material that ❸ _____ (grab) the audience's attention and leaves agreeable feelings, as opposed to challenging their views of themselves and the world. However, this doesn't mean that people who work in the entertainment business always stay away from informing or persuading. Many movies that ❹ _____ (categorize) under "entertainment" by their production firms have been written and produced with the intention of ❺ _____ (make) a political point (think of *The Day After Tomorrow, Syriana*, or *Blood Diamond*) or an educational point (like *Schindler's List. Crash*, or *Letters from Iwo Jima*). When media practitioners label a product as "entertainment," though, they are signaling to their audiences that their primary concern should be with enjoyment, not with any other messages that may be included.

*practitioner (전문직) 종사자

The word "entertainment" derives from the Latin *tenere*, which means "to hold or keep steady, busy, or amused." The notion of making money by keeping an audience steady, busy, or amused remains central to ❶ _____ _____ _____ _____ (업계에 있는 사람들) of entertainment. Media practitioners, then, define entertainment as material that ❷ _____ _____ _____ _____ (청중들의 관심을 붙들다) and leaves agreeable feelings, as opposed to challenging their views of themselves and the world. However, this doesn't mean that people who work in the entertainment business always ❸ _____ _____ _____ (~을 멀리하다) informing or persuading. Many movies that are categorized under "entertainment" by their production firms have been written and produced ❹ _____ _____ _____ _____ (~의 의도를 가지고) making a political point (think of *The Day After Tomorrow, Syriana*, or *Blood Diamond*) or an educational point (like *Schindler's List. Crash*, or *Letters from Iwo Jima*). When media practitioners label a product as "entertainment," though, they are signaling to their audiences that ❺ _____ _____ _____ (그들의 주된 관심사) should be with enjoyment, not with any other messages that may be included.

*practitioner (전문직) 종사자

❶ Ritual is a set of catalytic messages, effecting transformation of state from one season of the year or one stage of the life cycle to another. ❷ *State* refers either to a social and biological stage in life — adolescence or adulthood, for example — or to social status, such as graduate student or doctor of philosophy. ❸ Many vertebrate species — especially birds but fish and mammals, too — have ritual. ❹ In these animals ritual is triggered by certain messages or symbols in response to chemical messages from the genes. ❺ For example, among the three-spined stickleback fish, the male's zigzag courtship dance, whereby he entices a prospective mate to his nest, is triggered by the sight of her red belly, which is the signal that she is biologically ready to lay eggs. ❻ We assume, further, that the form of the zigzag dance itself is genetically programmed in the male's nervous system. ❼ In any case, the ritual effects his transformation into a parent that tends the eggs in his nest.

*catalytic 촉매(작용)의 **vertebrate 척추동물(의) ***entice 유인하다

❶ 의식은 촉매 작용을 하는 일단의 메시지인데, 한 해의 한 계절에서 다른 계절로, 혹은 생애 주기의 한 단계에서 다른 단계로 상태가 전환되는 결과를 초래한다. ❷ '상태'는 예를 들면, 청소년기나 성인기와 같은 삶의 사회적, 생물학적 단계나, 대학원생이나 박사와 같은 사회적 지위를 말한다. ❸ 많은 척추동물 종, 특히 조류, 그러나 어류와 포유류도 의식을 갖고 있다. ❹ 이들 동물에서 의식은 유전자에서 나오는 화학적 메시지에 반응하여 어떤 정해진 메시지나 상징에 의해 촉발된다. ❺ 예를 들면, 큰 가시고기 사이에서 장래의 짝을 자신의 둥지로 유인하는 수단인 수컷의 지그재그 구애춤은 암컷의 붉은 배를 보면 촉발되는데, 그것은 그 암컷이 생물학적으로 알을 낳을 준비가 되었다는 신호이다. ❻ 우리는 더 나아가 지그재그 춤의 형태 자체가 수컷의 신경계에 유전적으로 프로그램화되어 있다고 추정한다. ❼ 어쨌든, 그 의식은 수컷이 자신의 둥지에서 알을 보살피는 부모로 전환되는 결과를 초래한다.

Word List

□ ritual 의식, 제사　□ effect 결과로 ~을 초래하다[가져오다]　□ transformation 전환, 변환　□ state 상태　□ biological 생물학적
□ adolescence 청소년기　□ social status 사회적 지위　□ doctor of philosophy 박사, 박사 학위　□ species (생물의) 종
□ trigger 촉발하다, 일으키다　□ in response to ~에 대한 반응으로　□ three-spined stickleback 큰가시고기
□ courtship dance 구애 춤　□ whereby 그것으로 인하여　□ prospective 장래의, 미래의　□ belly 배　□ assume 추정하다, 가정하다
□ genetically programmed 유전적으로 프로그램화된

• Word Test

1	genetically programmed	_____	10	촉발하다, 일으키다	_____
2	three-spined stickleback	_____	11	사회적 지위	_____
3	doctor of philosophy	_____	12	그것으로 인하여	_____
4	adolescence	_____	13	배	_____
5	prospective	_____	14	생물학적	_____
6	courtship dance	_____	15	~에 대한 반응으로	_____
7	effect	_____	16	추정하다, 가정하다	_____
8	transformation	_____	17	상태	_____
9	species	_____	18	의식, 제사	_____

Ritual is a set of catalytic messages, ❶ effecting / affecting transformation of state from one season of the year or one stage of the life cycle to another. *State* refers either ❷ for / to a social and biological stage in life — adolescence or adulthood, for example — or to social status, such as graduate student or doctor of philosophy. Many vertebrate species — especially birds but fish and mammals, too — have ritual. In these animals ritual is triggered by certain messages or symbols in response to chemical messages from the genes. For example, among the three-spined stickleback fish, the male's zigzag courtship dance, ❸ whereas / whereby he entices a prospective mate to his nest, is triggered by the sight of her red belly, ❹ which / that is the signal that she is biologically ready to lay eggs. We assume, further, that the form of the zigzag dance ❺ itself / it is genetically programmed in the male's nervous system. In any case, the ritual effects his transformation into a parent that tends the eggs in his nest.

*catalytic 촉매(작용)의   **vertebrate 척추동물(의)   ***entice 유인하다

Ritual is a set of catalytic messages, ❶ _____ (effect) transformation of state from one season of the year or one stage of the life cycle to another. *State* refers either to a social and biological stage in life — adolescence or adulthood, for example — or to social status, such as graduate student or doctor of philosophy. Many vertebrate species — especially birds but fish and mammals, too — ❷ _____ (have) ritual. In these animals ritual is triggered by certain messages or symbols in response to chemical messages from the genes. For example, among the three-spined stickleback fish, the male's zigzag courtship dance, whereby he entices a prospective mate to his nest, ❸ _____ (trigger) by the sight of her red belly, which ❹ _____ (be) the signal that she is biologically ready to lay eggs. We assume, further, that the form of the zigzag dance itself is genetically programmed in the male's nervous system. In any case, the ritual effects his transformation into a parent that ❺ _____ (tend) the eggs in his nest.

*catalytic 촉매(작용)의   **vertebrate 척추동물(의)   ***entice 유인하다

Ritual is a set of catalytic messages, effecting ❶ _____ _____ _____ (상태의 전환) from one season of the year or one stage of ❷ _____ _____ _____ (생애 주기) to another. *State* refers either to a social and biological stage in life — adolescence or adulthood, for example — or to social status, such as graduate student or doctor of philosophy. Many vertebrate species — especially birds but fish and mammals, too — have ritual. In these animals ritual is triggered by certain messages or symbols ❸ _____ _____ _____ (~에 반응하여) chemical messages from the genes. For example, among the three-spined stickleback fish, the male's zigzag courtship dance, whereby he entices a prospective mate to his nest, is triggered ❹ _____ _____ _____ _____ (~의 광경에 의해) her red belly, which is the signal that she is biologically ready to lay eggs. We assume, further, that the form of the zigzag dance itself is genetically programmed in the male's nervous system. ❺ _____ _____ _____ (어쨌든), the ritual effects his transformation into a parent that tends the eggs in his nest.

*catalytic 촉매(작용)의   **vertebrate 척추동물(의)   ***entice 유인하다

❶ Post-traumatic stress syndrome became common knowledge but not the concept of post-traumatic growth, which is actually far more widespread. ❷ Most people who undergo trauma ultimately feel that the experience has made them stronger, wiser, more mature, more tolerant and understanding, or in some other way better people. ❸ The influential psychologist Martin Seligman has often lamented that so much attention is lavished on post-traumatic stress syndrome rather than post-traumatic growth because it causes people to mistakenly expect that bad events will have mainly negative effects. ❹ After being exposed to a terrifying event, at least 80 percent of people do not experience post-traumatic stress syndrome. ❺ Even though a single bad event is more powerful than a good event, over time people respond in so many constructive ways that they typically emerge more capable than ever of confronting life's challenges. ❻ Bad can make us stronger in the end.

*post-traumatic (정신적) 외상(外傷) 후의 **lament 한탄하다 ***lavish 낭비하다

❶ 정신적 외상(外傷) 후 스트레스 증후군은 상식이 되었지만, 정신적 외상 후 성장이라는 개념은 그렇지 않은데, 이것은 실제로 훨씬 더 널리 퍼져 있다. ❷ 정신적 외상을 겪는 대부분의 사람들은 궁극적으로 그 경험이 자신을 더 강하고, 더 현명하고, 더 성숙하고, 더 관용적이고 이해심 있고, 혹은 어떤 다른 면에서 더 나은 사람으로 만들었다고 생각한다. ❸ 영향력 있는 심리학자 Martin Seligman이 자주 한탄했던 것은, 정신적 외상 후 스트레스 증후군이 사람들에게 안 좋은 사건은 주로 부정적인 영향을 미칠 것이라고 잘못 예상하도록 하기 때문에, 정신적 외상 후 성장보다는 그것에 아주 많은 관심이 낭비된다는 것이었다. ❹ 끔찍한 사건을 접한 후에, 적어도 80퍼센트의 사람은 정신적 외상 후 스트레스 증후군을 경험하지 않는다. ❺ 비록 단 한 번의 안 좋은 사건이 좋은 사건보다 더 강력할지라도, 시간이 지나면서 사람들은 매우 많은 건설적인 방식으로 반응하여 보통 그 어느 때보다도 삶의 난제에 맞설 수 있는 더 많은 능력을 갖춘 상태로 일어선다. ❻ 안 좋은 것이 결국 우리를 더 강하게 만들 수 있다.

Word List

□ concept 개념 □ widespread 널리 퍼져 있는 □ undergo 겪다 □ trauma 정신적 외상, 트라우마 □ ultimately 궁극적으로 □ mature 성숙한 □ tolerant 관용적인 □ influential 영향력 있는, 유력한 □ psychologist 심리학자 □ be exposed to ~을 접하다, ~에 노출되다 □ terrifying 무서운 □ constructive 건설적인 □ typically 일반적으로, 보통은 □ emerge (곤경 등을 이기고) 일어서다, (곤경 등에서) 벗어나다 □ capable of ~을 할 수 있는 □ confront 맞서다, 대면[직면]하다

• **Word Test**

1	typically	9	관용적인
2	influential	10	정신적 외상, 트라우마
3	constructive	11	~을 접하다, ~에 노출되다
4	widespread	12	개념
5	ultimately	13	심리학자
6	undergo	14	맞서다, 대면[직면]하다
7	capable of	15	성숙한
8	emerge	16	무서운

Post-traumatic stress syndrome became common knowledge but not the concept of post-traumatic growth, ❶ which / that is actually far more widespread. Most people who undergo trauma ultimately feel that the experience has made ❷ it / them stronger, wiser, more mature, more tolerant and understanding, or in some other way better people. The influential psychologist Martin Seligman has often lamented that so much attention is lavished on post-traumatic stress syndrome ❸ as well as / rather than post-traumatic growth because it causes people to mistakenly expect that bad events will have mainly negative effects. After ❹ being exposed / be exposed to a terrifying event, at least 80 percent of people do not experience post-traumatic stress syndrome. Even though a single bad event is more powerful than a good event, over time people respond in so many constructive ways that they typically emerge more capable than ever of confronting life's challenges. Bad can make us ❺ stronger / weaker in the end.

*post-traumatic (정신적) 외상(外傷) 후의   **lament 한탄하다   ***lavish 낭비하다

Post-traumatic stress syndrome became common knowledge but not the concept of post-traumatic growth, which ❶ _____ (be) actually far more widespread. Most people who undergo trauma ultimately ❷ _____ (feel) that the experience has made them stronger, wiser, more mature, more tolerant and understanding, or in some other way better people. The influential psychologist Martin Seligman has often lamented that so much attention ❸ _____ (lavish) on post-traumatic stress syndrome rather than post-traumatic growth because it causes people to mistakenly ❹ _____ (expect) that bad events will have mainly negative effects. After being exposed to a terrifying event, at least 80 percent of people do not experience post-traumatic stress syndrome. Even though a single bad event is more powerful than a good event, over time people respond in so many constructive ways that they typically emerge more capable than ever of ❺ _____ (confront) life's challenges. Bad can make us stronger in the end.

*post-traumatic (정신적) 외상(外傷) 후의   **lament 한탄하다   ***lavish 낭비하다

Post-traumatic stress syndrome became common knowledge but not the concept of post-traumatic growth, which is actually ❶ _____ _____ _____ (훨씬 더 널리 퍼진). Most people who undergo trauma ultimately feel that the experience has made them stronger, wiser, more mature, more tolerant and understanding, or ❷ _____ _____ _____ _____ (어떤 다른 면에서) better people. The influential psychologist Martin Seligman has often lamented that so much attention is lavished on post-traumatic stress syndrome rather than post-traumatic growth because it causes people to mistakenly expect that bad events will ❸ _____ _____ _____ _____ (주로 부정적인 영향들을 가지다). After being exposed to a terrifying event, at least 80 percent of people do not experience post-traumatic stress syndrome. Even though a single bad event is more powerful than a good event, over time people respond in so ❹ _____ _____ _____ (많은 건설적인 방식들) that they typically emerge more capable than ever of confronting life's challenges. Bad can make us stronger ❺ _____ _____ _____ (결국).

*post-traumatic (정신적) 외상(外傷) 후의   **lament 한탄하다   ***lavish 낭비하다

❶ There is a common misconception that the reason we have hunger is because the earth is straining to feed an ever-growing population. ❷ This is not the case. ❸ The world uses only about a third of its arable land for crop production. ❹ And even that third we use inefficiently. ❺ China, for instance, has dramatically higher crop yields per acre than the United States, primarily because, even though the two countries are comparable in size, China has three times the population of the United States and only one-sixth the arable land, so its population has to grow crops more efficiently. ❻ Planet earth is in fact such a prodigious producer of food that in the United States, enough food is thrown away to keep all of the hungry people in the world fed.

*arable 경작할 수 있는　**prodigious 거대한

❶ 우리가 기아를 겪는 이유는 지구가 끊임없이 증가하는 인구를 먹여 살리기 위해 무리하고 있기 때문이라는 흔한 오해가 있다. ❷ 이것은 사실이 아니다. ❸ 세계는 농작물 생산을 위해 경작할 수 있는 땅의 약 3분의 1만을 사용하고 있다. ❹ 그리고 그 3분의 1마저도 우리는 비효율적으로 사용하고 있다. ❺ 예를 들어, 중국은 미국보다 에이커당 농작물 수확량이 훨씬 더 높은데, 주된 이유는 두 나라가 비슷한 크기임에도 불구하고, 중국은 미국의 3배 인구를 가지고 있고 경작지 면적은 6분의 1에 불과해, 그 주민들이 더 효율적으로 작물을 재배해야만 하기 때문이다. ❻ 사실 지구라는 행성은 매우 거대한 식량 생산자여서, 미국에서는 전 세계의 모든 굶주린 사람들을 먹여 살리기에 충분한 양의 음식이 버려진다.

Word List

☐ misconception 오해, 그릇된 생각　☐ hunger 기아, 굶주림　☐ strain 무리하다, 안간힘을 쓰다　☐ feed 먹이다　☐ population 인구
☐ case 경우, 문제　☐ crop 작물　☐ inefficiently 비효율적으로　☐ dramatically 극적으로, 매우　☐ yield 수확량　☐ primarily 주로
☐ comparable 비교할 만한, 비슷한

• Word Test

1　dramatically　_____
2　strain　_____
3　population　_____
4　hunger　_____
5　case　_____
6　primarily　_____

7　수확량　_____
8　비교할 만한, 비슷한　_____
9　먹이다　_____
10　작물　_____
11　오해, 그릇된 생각　_____
12　비효율적으로　_____

There is a common misconception ❶ that/which the reason we have hunger is because the earth is straining to feed an ever-growing population. This is not the case. The world uses only about a third of its arable land for crop production. And even that third we use ❷ inefficiently/efficiently. China, for instance, has dramatically higher crop yields per acre than the United States, primarily because, even though the two countries are ❸ compared/comparable in size, China has three times the population of the United States and only one-sixth the arable land, ❹ since/so its population has to grow crops more efficiently. Planet earth is in fact such a prodigious producer of food ❺ that/in which in the United States, enough food is thrown away to keep all of the hungry people in the world fed.

*arable 경작할 수 있는   **prodigious 거대한

There is a common misconception that the reason we have hunger ❶ _____ (be) because the earth is straining ❷ _____ (feed) an ever-growing population. This is not the case. The world uses only about a third of its arable land for crop production. And even that third we use inefficiently. China, for instance, ❸ _____ (have) dramatically higher crop yields per acre than the United States, primarily because, even though the two countries are comparable in size, China has three times the population of the United States and only one-sixth the arable land, so its population has ❹ _____ (grow) crops more efficiently. Planet earth is in fact such a prodigious producer of food that in the United States, enough food is thrown away ❺ _____ (keep) all of the hungry people in the world fed.

*arable 경작할 수 있는   **prodigious 거대한

There is ❶ _____ _____ _____ (흔한 오해) that the reason we have hunger is because the earth is straining to feed an ever-growing population. This is not the case. The world uses only about ❷ _____ _____ _____ (~의 3분의 1) its arable land for crop production. And even that third we use inefficiently. China, for instance, has ❸ _____ _____ _____ _____ (훨씬 더 높은 농작물 수확량) per acre than the United States, primarily because, even though the two countries are comparable in size, China has ❹ _____ _____ _____ _____ (3배의 인구) of the United States and only one-sixth the arable land, so its population has to grow crops more efficiently. Planet earth is in fact such a prodigious ❺ _____ _____ _____ (식량의 생산자) that in the United States, enough food is thrown away to keep all of the hungry people in the world fed.

*arable 경작할 수 있는   **prodigious 거대한

204

❶ There is a saying made famous by the Nobel memorial prize-winning economist Milton Friedman that 'There's no such thing as a free lunch' — that we can't magic wealth out of nothing (say, by printing money) or shift costs into the ether. ❷ Friedman's view was that if we legislate to reduce a burden on some citizens, or to increase the advantages they may enjoy, there will be repercussions somewhere down the line that will involve a cost for others and might even ultimately mean the measure is counterproductive. ❸ So even if a meal is priced at zero, someone, somewhere is paying for it. ❹ Modern economics may disparage the concept of free lunches, yet, today, one often gets a sense from key economists and policy-makers that a free lunch isn't that far away. ❺ Economics aims to show how we can generate growth by identifying more efficient ways of organising society, thereby making us richer and, hopefully, happier, with the least amount of sacrifice on our part. ❻ Such a utopia is achievable, economists believe, because they understand the mechanisms that drive everything from business investment and production decisions to consumer purchase choices, to individual attitudes to saving.

*ether 하늘, 창공 **repercussion 반향 ***disparage 폄하하다

❶ 노벨 기념 경제학상 수상자인 경제학자 Milton Friedman에 의해 유명해진 '공짜 점심 같은 것은 없다'라는 말이 있는데, 이는 우리가(예를 들어, 돈을 찍어 냄으로써) 무(無)에서 마법으로 부(富)를 만들어 내거나 비용을 하늘로 전가할 수 없다는 것이다. ❷ Friedman의 견해는 만약 우리가 일부 시민의 부담을 줄이거나 그들이 누릴 수도 있는 이익을 증가시키는 법률을 제정한다면, 다른 사람의 희생이 수반될 것이고 심지어 궁극적으로 그 조치가 역효과를 낳는 것을 의미할 수도 있는 반향이 미래에 어딘가에서 있으리라는 것이었다. ❸ 그래서 한 끼 식사의 가격이 0원이라도 누군가는 어딘가에서 그 식사비를 지불하고 있는 것이다. ❹ 현대 경제학이 공짜 점심이라는 개념을 폄하할 수도 있겠지만, 오늘날 사람들은 주요 경제학자와 정책 입안자로부터 공짜 점심이 그리 멀리 떨어져 있지 않다는 것을 자주 감지한다. ❺ 경제학은 사회를 조직하는 더 효율적인 방법을 찾아냄으로써 우리가 어떻게 성장을 가져올 수 있는지를 보여 주고, 그렇게 함으로써 우리의 가장 적은 희생으로 우리를 더 부유하게, 그리고 잘만 되면 더 행복하게 만들어 주는 것을 목표로 한다. ❻ 경제학자들은 자신들이 사업 투자와 생산 결정에서부터 소비자의 구매 선택, 저축에 대한 개인의 태도에 이르기까지의 모든 것을 구동하는 기제를 이해하고 있기 때문에 그런 유토피아가 달성 가능하다고 믿는다.

Word List

□ **memorial** 기념물, 기념의 □ **economist** 경제학자 □ **magic** 마법으로 만들다[나타나게 하다] □ **shift** 전가하다, 옮기다
□ **legislate** 법률을 제정하다 □ **burden** 부담, 짐 □ **down the line** 미래에, 나중에 □ **involve** 수반하다, 포함하다
□ **ultimately** 궁극적으로, 결국 □ **measure** 조치 □ **counterproductive** 역효과를 낳는 □ **get a sense** 감지하다, 감을 잡다
□ **generate** 발생시키다 □ **identify** 찾아내다, 확인하다 □ **organise** 조직하다 □ **thereby** 그렇게 함으로써, 그것에 의하여
□ **sacrifice** 희생 □ **mechanism** 기제, 방법 □ **drive** 구동하다, 추진하다 □ **attitude** 태도

• Word Test

1 counterproductive _____
2 organise _____
3 get a sense _____
4 down the line _____
5 identify _____
6 magic _____
7 shift _____
8 involve _____
9 thereby _____
10 drive _____

11 법률을 제정하다 _____
12 태도 _____
13 경제학자 _____
14 부담, 짐 _____
15 기제, 방법 _____
16 조치 _____
17 궁극적으로, 결국 _____
18 기념물, 기념의 _____
19 희생 _____
20 발생시키다 _____

There is a saying made famous by the Nobel memorial prize-winning economist Milton Friedman that 'There's no such thing as a free lunch' — ❶ | that / whether | we can't magic wealth out of nothing (say, by printing money) or shift costs into the ether. Friedman's view was that if we legislate to reduce a burden on some citizens, or to increase the advantages they may enjoy, there will be repercussions somewhere down the line that will ❷ | revolve / involve | a cost for others and might even ultimately mean the measure is ❸ | productive / counterproductive |. So even if a meal is priced at zero, someone, somewhere is paying for it. Modern economics may disparage the concept of free lunches, yet, today, ❹ | it / one | often gets a sense from key economists and policy-makers that a free lunch isn't that far away. Economics aims to show how we can generate growth by identifying more efficient ways of organising society, ❺ | thereby / while | making us richer and, hopefully, happier, with the least amount of sacrifice on our part. Such a utopia is achievable, economists believe, because they understand the mechanisms that drive everything from business investment and production decisions to consumer purchase choices, to individual attitudes to saving.

*ether 하늘, 창공 **repercussion 반향 ***disparage 폄하하다

There is a saying ❶ _____ (make) famous by the Nobel memorial prize-winning economist Milton Friedman that 'There's no such thing as a free lunch'— that we can't magic wealth out of nothing (say, by printing money) or shift costs into the ether. Friedman's view was that if we legislate to reduce a burden on some citizens, or ❷ _____ (increase) the advantages they may enjoy, there will be repercussions somewhere down the line that will involve a cost for others and might even ultimately mean the measure is counterproductive. So even if a meal ❸ _____ (price) at zero, someone, somewhere is paying for it. Modern economics may disparage the concept of free lunches, yet, today, one often gets a sense from key economists and policy-makers that a free lunch isn't that far away. Economics aims ❹ _____ (show) how we can generate growth by identifying more efficient ways of organising society, thereby ❺ _____ (make) us richer and, hopefully, happier, with the least amount of sacrifice on our part. Such a utopia is achievable, economists believe, because they understand the mechanisms that drive everything from business investment and production decisions to consumer purchase choices, to individual attitudes to saving.

*ether 하늘, 창공 **repercussion 반향 ***disparage 폄하하다

There is a saying made famous by the Nobel memorial prize-winning economist Milton Friedman that 'There's ❶ _____ _____ _____ _____ (~와 같은 것은 없다) a free lunch'— that we can't magic wealth out of nothing (say, by printing money) or shift costs into the ether. Friedman's view was that if we legislate to ❷ _____ _____ _____ (부담을 줄이다) on some citizens, or to increase the advantages they may enjoy, there will be repercussions somewhere down the line that will involve a cost for others and might even ultimately mean the measure is counterproductive. So even if a meal is priced at zero, someone, somewhere is paying for it. Modern economics may disparage ❸ _____ _____ _____ _____ _____ (공짜 점심들이라는 개념), yet, today, one often gets a sense from key economists and policy-makers that a free lunch isn't that far away. Economics aims to show how we can generate growth by identifying more efficient ways of organising society, thereby making us richer and, hopefully, happier, with ❹ _____ _____ _____ (가장 적은 분량) of sacrifice on our part. Such a utopia is achievable, economists believe, because they understand the mechanisms that drive everything from business investment and production decisions to consumer purchase choices, to individual attitudes to saving.

*ether 하늘, 창공   **repercussion 반향   ***disparage 폄하하다

01 13강 1번

다음 글에서 전체 흐름과 관계 <u>없는</u> 문장은?

When we bemoan the lack of originality in the world, we blame it on the absence of creativity. If only people could generate more novel ideas, we'd all be better off. But in reality, the biggest barrier to originality is not idea generation — it's idea selection. In one analysis, when over two hundred people dreamed up more than a thousand ideas for new ventures and products, 87 percent were completely unique. ① This disproves the idea that uniqueness and originality are more distinct than similar. ② Our companies, communities, and countries don't necessarily suffer from a shortage of novel ideas. ③ They're constrained by a shortage of people who excel at choosing the right novel ideas. ④ The Segway, a two-wheeled, self-balancing personal transporter, was a false positive: it was forecast as a hit but turned out to be a miss. ⑤ *Seinfeld*, an American sitcom television series, was a false negative: it was expected to fail but ultimately flourished.

*bemoan 한탄하다

02 13강 2번

cultural tradition에 관한 다음 글의 내용과 일치하지 <u>않는</u> 것은?

A striking experiment was performed accidentally by Japanese anthropologists attempting to relieve an overpopulation and hunger problem in a community of monkeys on an island in south Japan. The anthropologists threw grains of wheat on a sandy beach. Now it is very difficult to separate wheat grains one by one from sand grains; such an effort might even expend more energy than eating the collected wheat would provide. But one brilliant monkey, Imo, perhaps by accident or out of pique, threw handfuls of the mixture into the water. Wheat floats; sand sinks, a fact that Imo clearly noted. Through the sifting process she was able to eat well. While older monkeys, set in their ways, ignored her, the younger monkeys appeared to grasp the importance of her discovery, and imitated it. In the next generation, the practice was more widespread; today all monkeys on the island are competent at water sifting, an example of a cultural tradition among the monkeys.

*expend (에너지·시간 등을) 쓰다[들이다]   **out of pique 욱해서

① 실험으로서 의도한 것이 아닌 인류학자의 행동이 원숭이 집단에 관한 연구로 이어졌다.
② 모래알과 밀알을 분리할 때의 소모 에너지가 밀알 섭취로 얻는 것보다 더 클 수도 있다.
③ 밀알을 물에 띄우기 위해 원숭이 Imo는 모래와 밀알 혼합물을 물속에 던졌다.
④ 모든 원숭이가 Imo의 방식을 따라 밀알과 모래알을 구분한 것은 아니다.
⑤ 물로 걸러내는 이 지식이 세대를 거쳐 전파되어 원숭이들의 문화적 전통이 되었다.

03 13강 3번

밑줄 친 All such attitudes, of course, reveal more about social dominance and convention than they do about aptitude.가 다음 글에서 의미하는 바로 가장 적절한 것은?

The fact that a majority of the global population has at least some level of multilingual competence surely indicates that adding a second language is not a particularly remarkable feat. And yet, especially within powerful linguistic groups, it is common to find references to the difficulties involved or to the peculiar lack of language talents supposedly possessed. In the modern world, for example, English and American monolinguals often complain that they have no aptitude for foreign-language learning. This is usually accompanied by expressions of envy for those multilingual Europeans, and sometimes (more subtly) by a linguistic smugness reflecting a deeply held conviction that, after all, those clever "others" who don't already know English will have to accommodate in a world made increasingly safe for anglophones. All such attitudes, of course, reveal more about social dominance and convention than they do about aptitude.

*feat 재주 **smugness 우쭐거림 ***anglophone 영어 사용자

① English speakers are safer in more places than multilingual people.
② A person's ability is determined by how many languages he or she uses.
③ Those who are not good at language learning boast of their social status.
④ It is better to speak one important language than to speak multiple languages.
⑤ One's attitude toward language acquisition and its necessity reflects the position of their society.

04 13강 4번

글의 흐름으로 보아, 주어진 문장이 들어가기에 가장 적절한 곳은?

> It was almost as if the unstated goal of his life was to analyse it and to give his opinions on how various things affected him.

A gentleman came into my stress-management office and said, 'I'm mad at my boss. I don't like my job. I don't like the people that work with me. No one appreciates my work. I'm really angry.' When I began teaching him about how his own thinking creates his angry feelings he said, 'With all due respect, Dr. Carlson, I'm angry almost all the time, but I almost never think angry thoughts.' Do you see where he was being fooled? (①) Until that moment, he believed that 'thinking' meant the same thing as 'pondering.' (②) Even though he may not have dwelled on his misery for hours at a time, he was nevertheless continually thinking negatively, a moment here and a moment there. (③) He spent nearly all of his time thinking about the little things that irritated and annoyed him. (④) His negative thoughts were creating his negative feelings and emotions and he didn't even know he was thinking them. (⑤) He was a victim of his own thinking.

*ponder 심사숙고하다

다음 글의 내용을 한 문장으로 요약하고자 한다. 빈칸 (A), (B)에 들어갈 말로 가장 적절한 것은?

Caregivers for the old do much more than simply perform tasks. They provide intellectual engagement, social interaction, and emotional support, key factors in long-term health and longevity. As society has grown more urban and as family homes have become less multigenerational, greater numbers of the elderly now live alone. This shift brings with it diminished opportunities for social interaction. In the United States, a 2010 American Association of Retired Persons study found that over a third of respondents age forty-five and older were lonely as measured on the UCLA loneliness scale. Interactions with robots offer an opportunity to counteract, if not entirely remedy, the effects of such social isolation. Brain scan studies using fMRI have shown people have a measurable emotional response to robots similar to that measured when interacting with other people, at least in certain situations. While robots and technology can't entirely fill our need for social interaction, they may be able to provide some level of engagement.

Modern changes in society and families are making more elderly people socially _____(A)_____, but the development of robot technology is expected to have a(n) ____(B)____ role in solving the problem.

	(A)		(B)
①	troublesome	⋯⋯	important
②	isolated	⋯⋯	considerable
③	dependent	⋯⋯	imaginary
④	active	⋯⋯	leading
⑤	lonely	⋯⋯	insignificant

06 13강 6번

films에 관한 다음 글의 내용과 일치하지 <u>않는</u> 것은?

How are films made and produced? A news item, an event, a novel or the biography of an important person might suggest suitable themes. The film director's first job is to write a short account of the subject and to present it for a producer. This simple, untechnical plan is called a *treatment*. Movie director Jean Renoir and his scriptwriter wrote several unused treatments for *La Grande Illusion*. One of them is easy to get hold of; it is quite different from the final film. If a producer and a group of actors are interested in the scheme, the director or the scriptwriter rewrites the text in order to give a full list of shots, described in their order, with stage directions and technical terms clearly marked; this is the scenario. There is a good scenario of *October (Ten Days That Shook the World)* written by Eisenstein himself but, once again, it is far removed from the three finished versions of the film we can see today. It is difficult to put into practice what was decided beforehand, and important alterations occur in the course of production.

① 영화감독은 적절성을 따져 선정한 주제를 초안으로 만들어 제작자에게 보여 준다.
② '트리트먼트'라고 불리는 초안은 완성본 영화와는 매우 다르다.
③ 관계자들에 의해 선택되지 않은 대부분의 '트리트먼트'는 구하기 쉽다.
④ '트리트먼트'를 토대로 순서, 무대 지시, 전문 용어 등을 세밀하게 기술하여 시나리오를 다시 작성한다.
⑤ 최종적으로 작성된 시나리오는 제작 과정에서 내용이 변경될 가능성이 있다.

밑줄 친 a dwarf sitting underneath who was a chess master, and controlled the puppet가 다음 글에서 의미하는 바로 가장 적절한 것은?

Our present-day thinking is based on a succession of historically evolved mentalities; on mental edifices which previous generations have constructed, pulled down, renovated and extended. Past events are compressed in images and metaphors which determine our present thinking even if we are not always aware of them. Common sense is the thickly viscous form of the past, the reflex of history which, like the story about a puppet and a chess-playing machine, always triumphs. The puppet dressed in Turkish garb was sitting in front of a chessboard on a large table. A cunning arrangement of mirrors created the impression of being able to see underneath the table. In actual fact, there was a dwarf sitting underneath who was a chess master, and controlled the puppet. We can imagine the continuous effect of historical experience acting like an ugly, unloved and happily forgotten dwarf, moving the pieces in the chess game of our everyday life.

*edifice (사고의) 체계 **viscous 끈적이는 ***garb 복장

① a group who turns a blind eye to reality and tries to write a new history
② a person who works for his or her own gain by deceiving others
③ a historical system of thought that implicitly influences current thinking
④ a person who manipulates others to distort their perception of reality
⑤ a thing that is disappearing from people's memories every day

다음 글의 내용을 한 문장으로 요약하고자 한다. 빈칸 (A), (B)에 들어갈 말로 가장 적절한 것은?

The word "entertainment" derives from the Latin *tenere*, which means "to hold or keep steady, busy, or amused." The notion of making money by keeping an audience steady, busy, or amused remains central to those in the business of entertainment. Media practitioners, then, define entertainment as material that grabs the audience's attention and leaves agreeable feelings, as opposed to challenging their views of themselves and the world. However, this doesn't mean that people who work in the entertainment business always stay away from informing or persuading. Many movies that are categorized under "entertainment" by their production firms have been written and produced with the intention of making a political point (think of *The Day After Tomorrow, Syriana*, or *Blood Diamond*) or an educational point (like *Schindler's List. Crash*, or *Letters from Iwo Jima*). When media practitioners label a product as "entertainment," though, they are signaling to their audiences that their primary concern should be with enjoyment, not with any other messages that may be included.

*practitioner (전문직) 종사자

Since the essence of the entertainment industry is to make the audience _____(A)_____, even if an informative or persuasive work is made, its focus is ultimately on creating _____(B)_____.

	(A)		(B)
①	sincere	……	greed
②	happy	……	pleasure
③	political	……	intention
④	educational	……	joy
⑤	doubtful	……	heroism

09 **13강** 9번

글의 흐름으로 보아, 주어진 문장이 들어가기에 가장 적절한 곳은?

> In these animals ritual is triggered by certain messages or symbols in response to chemical messages from the genes.

Ritual is a set of catalytic messages, effecting transformation of state from one season of the year or one stage of the life cycle to another. (①) *State* refers either to a social and biological stage in life — adolescence or adulthood, for example — or to social status, such as graduate student or doctor of philosophy. (②) Many vertebrate species — especially birds but fish and mammals, too — have ritual. (③) For example, among the three-spined stickleback fish, the male's zigzag courtship dance, whereby he entices a prospective mate to his nest, is triggered by the sight of her red belly, which is the signal that she is biologically ready to lay eggs. (④) We assume, further, that the form of the zigzag dance itself is genetically programmed in the male's nervous system. (⑤) In any case, the ritual effects his transformation into a parent that tends the eggs in his nest.

*catalytic 촉매(작용)의   **vertebrate 척추동물(의)   ***entice 유인하다

10 **13강** 10번

다음 글의 밑줄 친 부분 중, 어법상 틀린 것은?

Post-traumatic stress syndrome became common knowledge but not the concept of post-traumatic growth, ① which is actually far more widespread. Most people who undergo trauma ultimately feel that the experience has made them stronger, wiser, more mature, more tolerant and understanding, or in some other way better people. The influential psychologist Martin Seligman has often lamented ② that so much attention is lavished on post-traumatic stress syndrome rather than post-traumatic growth because it causes people ③ to mistakenly expect that bad events will have mainly negative effects. After ④ being exposed to a terrifying event, at least 80 percent of people do not experience post-traumatic stress syndrome. Even though a single bad event is more powerful than a good event, over time people ⑤ responding in so many constructive ways that they typically emerge more capable than ever of confronting life's challenges. Bad can make us stronger in the end.

*post-traumatic (정신적) 외상(外傷) 후의   **lament 한탄하다
***lavish 낭비하다

11 **13강** 11번

다음 글의 주제로 가장 적절한 것은?

There is a common misconception that the reason we have hunger is because the earth is straining to feed an ever-growing population. This is not the case. The world uses only about a third of its arable land for crop production. And even that third we use inefficiently. China, for instance, has dramatically higher crop yields per acre than the United States, primarily because, even though the two countries are comparable in size, China has three times the population of the United States and only one-sixth the arable land, so its population has to grow crops more efficiently. Planet earth is in fact such a prodigious producer of food that in the United States, enough food is thrown away to keep all of the hungry people in the world fed.

*arable 경작할 수 있는   **prodigious 거대한

① the truth behind the hunger problem
② the benefits of efficient farming practices
③ the relationship between hunger and population
④ the actual food production capacity of Earth
⑤ debating the problem of hunger and abandoned food

12 13강 12번

밑줄 친 the concept of free lunches가 다음 글에서 의미하는 바로 가장 적절한 것은?

There is a saying made famous by the Nobel memorial prize-winning economist Milton Friedman that 'There's no such thing as a free lunch' — that we can't magic wealth out of nothing (say, by printing money) or shift costs into the ether. Friedman's view was that if we legislate to reduce a burden on some citizens, or to increase the advantages they may enjoy, there will be repercussions somewhere down the line that will involve a cost for others and might even ultimately mean the measure is counterproductive. So even if a meal is priced at zero, someone, somewhere is paying for it. Modern economics may disparage the concept of free lunches, yet, today, one often gets a sense from key economists and policy-makers that a free lunch isn't that far away. Economics aims to show how we can generate growth by identifying more efficient ways of organising society, thereby making us richer and, hopefully, happier, with the least amount of sacrifice on our part. Such a utopia is achievable, economists believe, because they understand the mechanisms that drive everything from business investment and production decisions to consumer purchase choices, to individual attitudes to saving.

*ether 하늘, 창공 **repercussion 반향 ***disparage 폄하하다

① a free meal given to someone lawfully
② enjoying the benefits of burdening others
③ providing something for free by minimizing social costs
④ organizing society more efficiently to bring about growth
⑤ data on the core policies of economists and policymakers

13 13강 1번

다음 글의 요지로 가장 적절한 것은?

When we bemoan the lack of originality in the world, we blame it on the absence of creativity. If only people could generate more novel ideas, we'd all be better off. But in reality, the biggest barrier to originality is not idea generation — it's idea selection. In one analysis, when over two hundred people dreamed up more than a thousand ideas for new ventures and products, 87 percent were completely unique. Our companies, communities, and countries don't necessarily suffer from a shortage of novel ideas. They're constrained by a shortage of people who excel at choosing the right novel ideas. The Segway, a two-wheeled, self-balancing personal transporter, was a false positive: it was forecast as a hit but turned out to be a miss. *Seinfeld*, an American sitcom television series, was a false negative: it was expected to fail but ultimately flourished.

*bemoan 한탄하다

① 창의적으로 생각하는 사람이 많아지면 세상을 바꿀 수 있다.
② 독창성과 창의성의 연관 관계는 독특하며 두 가지 오류를 발생시킨다.
③ 새로운 아이디어를 만들어 내는 것과 선택하는 것이 병행되어야 한다.
④ 수많은 창의적 생각을 제대로 선택하지 못하기 때문에 독창성이 부재한다.
⑤ 긍정 오류와 부정 오류는 새로운 독창적 아이디어에 대한 방해 요인이다.

14 13강 2번

다음 글의 밑줄 친 부분 중, 어법상 틀린 것은?

A striking experiment was performed accidentally by Japanese anthropologists ① attempting to relieve an overpopulation and hunger problem in a community of monkeys on an island in south Japan. The anthropologists threw grains of wheat on a sandy beach. Now it ② is very difficult to separate wheat grains one by one from sand grains; such an effort might even expend more energy than ③ eating the collected wheat would provide. But one brilliant monkey, Imo, perhaps by accident or out of pique, threw handfuls of the mixture into the water. Wheat floats; sand sinks, a fact ④ that Imo clearly noted. Through the sifting process she was able to eat well. While older monkeys, ⑤ setting in their ways, ignored her, the younger monkeys appeared to grasp the importance of her discovery, and imitated it. In the next generation, the practice was more widespread; today all monkeys on the island are competent at water sifting, an example of a cultural tradition among the monkeys.

* expend (에너지·시간 등을) 쓰다[들이다]   **out of pique 욱해서

15 13강 3번

다음 글의 제목으로 가장 적절한 것은?

The fact that a majority of the global population has at least some level of multilingual competence surely indicates that adding a second language is not a particularly remarkable feat. And yet, especially within powerful linguistic groups, it is common to find references to the difficulties involved or to the peculiar lack of language talents supposedly possessed. In the modern world, for example, English and American monolinguals often complain that they have no aptitude for foreign-language learning. This is usually accompanied by expressions of envy for those multilingual Europeans, and sometimes (more subtly) by a linguistic smugness reflecting a deeply held conviction that, after all, those clever "others" who don't already know English will have to accommodate in a world made increasingly safe for anglophones. All such attitudes, of course, reveal more about social dominance and convention than they do about aptitude.

*feat 재주   **smugness 우쭐거림   ***anglophone 영어 사용자

① What Really Hinders Multilingual Learning?
② The Problematic Worldview of Monolingual Learners
③ Regression to a Single Dominant Language and Social Safety
④ The Relationship between Language Learning and Aptitude
⑤ The Influence of Social Dominance and Conventions on Attitudes

16 13강 4번

다음 글의 주제로 가장 적절한 것은?

A gentleman came into my stress-management office and said, 'I'm mad at my boss. I don't like my job. I don't like the people that work with me. No one appreciates my work. I'm really angry.' When I began teaching him about how his own thinking creates his angry feelings he said, 'With all due respect, Dr. Carlson, I'm angry almost all the time, but I almost never think angry thoughts.' Do you see where he was being fooled? Until that moment, he believed that 'thinking' meant the same thing as 'pondering.' Even though he may not have dwelled on his misery for hours at a time, he was nevertheless continually thinking negatively, a moment here and a moment there. He spent nearly all of his time thinking about the little things that irritated and annoyed him. It was almost as if the unstated goal of his life was to analyse it and to give his opinions on how various things affected him. His negative thoughts were creating his negative feelings and emotions and he didn't even know he was thinking them. He was a victim of his own thinking.

*ponder 심사숙고하다

① the way negative thoughts make people angry
② the reason people need to consult a psychiatrist
③ the difference between thinking and contemplating
④ the effect of constantly thinking negatively on one's emotions
⑤ the importance of controlling one's anger for stress management

17 13강 5번

다음 글에서 전체 흐름과 관계 없는 문장은?

Caregivers for the old do much more than simply perform tasks. They provide intellectual engagement, social interaction, and emotional support, key factors in long-term health and longevity. As society has grown more urban and as family homes have become less multigenerational, greater numbers of the elderly now live alone. This shift brings with it diminished opportunities for social interaction. ① In the United States, a 2010 American Association of Retired Persons study found that over a third of respondents age forty-five and older were lonely as measured on the UCLA loneliness scale. ② A decrease in physical activity has led to increased depression, adding to the national toll of mental illness. ③ Interactions with robots offer an opportunity to counteract, if not entirely remedy, the effects of such social isolation. ④ Brain scan studies using fMRI have shown people have a measurable emotional response to robots similar to that measured when interacting with other people, at least in certain situations. ⑤ While robots and technology can't entirely fill our need for social interaction, they may be able to provide some level of engagement.

18 13강 6번

다음 글의 주제로 가장 적절한 것은?

How are films made and produced? A news item, an event, a novel or the biography of an important person might suggest suitable themes. The film director's first job is to write a short account of the subject and to present it for a producer. This simple, untechnical plan is called a *treatment*. Movie director Jean Renoir and his scriptwriter wrote several unused treatments for *La Grande Illusion*. One of them is easy to get hold of; it is quite different from the final film. If a producer and a group of actors are interested in the scheme, the director or the scriptwriter rewrites the text in order to give a full list of shots, described in their order, with stage directions and technical terms clearly marked; this is the scenario. There is a good scenario of *October (Ten Days That Shook the World)* written by Eisenstein himself but, once again, it is far removed from the three finished versions of the film we can see today. It is difficult to put into practice what was decided beforehand, and important alterations occur in the course of production.

① the reason scenarios have complex content
② early steps in the filmmaking process that are often later revised
③ the reason film directors should be involved in scenario creation
④ different perspectives of the producer and director of a movie
⑤ the process by which drafts and scenarios become different from the final film

19 13강 7번

다음 글의 요지로 가장 적절한 것은?

Our present-day thinking is based on a succession of historically evolved mentalities; on mental edifices which previous generations have constructed, pulled down, renovated and extended. Past events are compressed in images and metaphors which determine our present thinking even if we are not always aware of them. Common sense is the thickly viscous form of the past, the reflex of history which, like the story about a puppet and a chess-playing machine, always triumph. The puppet dressed in Turkish garb was sitting in front of a chessboard on a large table. A cunning arrangement of mirrors created the impression of being able to see underneath the table. In actual fact, there was a dwarf sitting underneath who was a chess master, and controlled the puppet. We can imagine the continuous effect of historical experience acting like an ugly, unloved and happily forgotten dwarf, moving the pieces in the chess game of our everyday life.

*edifice (사고의) 체계 **viscous 끈적이는 ***garb 복장

① 상식은 과거의 역사적 내용 중에서 기만적인 승리를 반영한 것이다.
② 현재 세대의 사고는 이전 세대의 정신적 사고 체계를 그대로 계승한 것이다.
③ 체스 경기에서 중요한 것은 이전 세대의 사고방식을 응용하는 것이다.
④ 역사적 경험이 현재 사고 체계에 지속적으로 영향을 끼치고 있다.
⑤ 과거의 여러 가지 사고 체계가 일상생활의 상상력에 영향을 미치게 된다.

20 13강 8번

다음 글의 제목으로 가장 적절한 것은?

The word "entertainment" derives from the Latin *tenere*, which means "to hold or keep steady, busy, or amused." The notion of making money by keeping an audience steady, busy, or amused remains central to those in the business of entertainment. Media practitioners, then, define entertainment as material that grabs the audience's attention and leaves agreeable feelings, as opposed to challenging their views of themselves and the world. However, this doesn't mean that people who work in the entertainment business always stay away from informing or persuading. Many movies that are categorized under "entertainment" by their production firms have been written and produced with the intention of making a political point (think of *The Day After Tomorrow, Syriana*, or *Blood Diamond*) or an educational point (like *Schindler's List. Crash*, or *Letters from Iwo Jima*). When media practitioners label a product as "entertainment," though, they are signaling to their audiences that their primary concern should be with enjoyment, not with any other messages that may be included.

*practitioner (전문직) 종사자

① Hidden Messages in Movies
② The Fate of the Film Industry
③ The Public's Goal: The Pursuit of Pleasure
④ The Nature of the Entertainment Business
⑤ Diversification of the Entertainment Industry

21 13강 9번

ritual에 관한 다음 글의 내용과 일치하지 <u>않는</u> 것은?

Ritual is a set of catalytic messages, effecting transformation of state from one season of the year or one stage of the life cycle to another. *State* refers either to a social and biological stage in life — adolescence or adulthood, for example — or to social status, such as graduate student or doctor of philosophy. Many vertebrate species — especially birds but fish and mammals, too — have ritual. In these animals ritual is triggered by certain messages or symbols in response to chemical messages from the genes. For example, among the three-spined stickleback fish, the male's zigzag courtship dance, whereby he entices a prospective mate to his nest, is triggered by the sight of her red belly, which is the signal that she is biologically ready to lay eggs. We assume, further, that the form of the zigzag dance itself is genetically programmed in the male's nervous system. In any case, the ritual effects his transformation into a parent that tends the eggs in his nest.

*catalytic 촉매(작용)의 **vertebrate 척추동물(의) ***entice: 유인하다

① 의식은 생애 주기에서 단계별 상태 전환의 결과를 가져온다.
② 삶의 단계적 상태는 사회 생물학적 혹은 사회적 지위를 나타낸다.
③ 거의 모든 동물들이 유전자에서 나오는 화학적 메시지에 반응하여 의식을 행한다.
④ 큰 가시고기에게는 암컷의 붉은 배가 구애 의식을 위한 유전적 상징이다.
⑤ 구애 의식을 통해 큰 가시고기의 수컷은 사회적 지위가 부모로 전환된다.

22 13강 10번

다음 글의 내용을 한 문장으로 요약하고자 한다. 빈칸 (A), (B)에 들어갈 말로 가장 적절한 것은?

Post-traumatic stress syndrome became common knowledge but not the concept of post-traumatic growth, which is actually far more widespread. Most people who undergo trauma ultimately feel that the experience has made them stronger, wiser, more mature, more tolerant and understanding, or in some other way better people. The influential psychologist Martin Seligman has often lamented that so much attention is lavished on post-traumatic stress syndrome rather than post-traumatic growth because it causes people to mistakenly expect that bad events will have mainly negative effects. After being exposed to a terrifying event, at least 80 percent of people do not experience post-traumatic stress syndrome. Even though a single bad event is more powerful than a good event, over time people respond in so many constructive ways that they typically emerge more capable than ever of confronting life's challenges. Bad can make us stronger in the end.

*post-traumatic (정신적) 외상(外傷) 후의 **lament 한탄하다
***lavish 낭비하다

↓

Despite the _____(A)_____ belief that trauma has largely negative effects, most people ultimately emerge from difficulty with a(n) _____(B)_____ spirit.

	(A)		(B)
①	dominant	……	energetic
②	powerful	……	generous
③	widespread	……	strengthened
④	rational	……	positive
⑤	constructive	……	revitalized

23 [13강 11번]

다음 글에서 전체 흐름과 관계 없는 문장은?

There is a common misconception that the reason we have hunger is because the earth is straining to feed an ever-growing population. ① This is not the case. ② The world uses only about a third of its arable land for crop production. And even that third we use inefficiently. ③ Most of the remaining two-thirds of the land is used for other purposes such as residential areas, which is increasing environmental pollution levels. ④ China, for instance, has dramatically higher crop yields per acre than the United States, primarily because, even though the two countries are comparable in size, China has three times the population of the United States and only one-sixth the arable land, so its population has to grow crops more efficiently. ⑤ Planet earth is in fact such a prodigious producer of food that in the United States, enough food is thrown away to keep all of the hungry people in the world fed.

*arable 경작할 수 있는 **prodigious 거대한

24 [13강 12번]

다음 글의 요지로 가장 적절한 것은?

There is a saying made famous by the Nobel memorial prize-winning economist Milton Friedman that 'There's no such thing as a free lunch' — that we can't magic wealth out of nothing (say, by printing money) or shift costs into the ether. Friedman's view was that if we legislate to reduce a burden on some citizens, or to increase the advantages they may enjoy, there will be repercussions somewhere down the line that will involve a cost for others and might even ultimately mean the measure is counterproductive. So even if a meal is priced at zero, someone, somewhere is paying for it. Modern economics may disparage the concept of free lunches, yet, today, one often gets a sense from key economists and policy-makers that a free lunch isn't that far away. Economics aims to show how we can generate growth by identifying more efficient ways of organising society, thereby making us richer and, hopefully, happier, with the least amount of sacrifice on our part. Such a utopia is achievable, economists believe, because they understand the mechanisms that drive everything from business investment and production decisions to consumer purchase choices, to individual attitudes to saving.

*ether 하늘, 창공   **repercussion 반향   ***disparage 폄하하다

① 경제학자들은 사회 조직을 더 효율적으로 운영하는 방법을 연구한다.
② 사회의 일부가 혜택을 받으면 나머지 부분은 손해를 감수해야 한다.
③ 경제학에 근거한 법률 제정을 통하여 무료 급식을 시행할 수 있다.
④ 사람들은 최근 공짜 점심과 같은 긍정적인 경제 신호를 인식하고 있다.
⑤ 오늘날의 경제학은 최소 비용으로 최대 효과를 내는 것을 목표로 하고 있다.

[13강 1번]

When we bemoan the lack of originality in the world, we blame it on the absence of creativity. If only people could generate more novel ideas, we'd all be better off. But in reality, the biggest barrier to originality is not idea generation — it's idea selection. In one analysis, when over two hundred people dreamed up more than a thousand ideas for new ventures and products, 87 percent were completely unique. Our companies, communities, and countries don't necessarily suffer from a shortage of novel ideas. They're constrained by a shortage of people who excel at choosing the right novel ideas. The Segway, a two-wheeled, self-balancing personal transporter, was a false positive: it was forecast as a hit but turned out to be a miss. *Seinfeld*, an American sitcom television series, was a false negative: it was expected to fail but ultimately flourished.

*bemoan 한탄하다

25 윗글을 읽고 다음 질문에 영어로 답하시오. (단, (1)은 7단어, (2)는 6단어로 쓸 것)

Q: What does the passage give as an example of the right choice of a novel idea and the wrong choice of a novel idea?

A: (1) 긍정 오류: _____

_____

(2) 부정 오류: _____

_____

26 윗글의 내용을 한 문장으로 요약하려고 한다. 빈칸 (A)와 (B)에 들어갈 알맞은 말을 보기 에서 찾아 쓰시오.

보기   sufficiency / insufficiency / attractive / unattractive

The reason for the lack of ingenuity in the world around us is not due to a(n) ___(A)___ of original ideas but due to a lack of people with the talent for selecting ___(B)___ original ideas.

(A) _____ (B) _____

13강 2번

A striking experiment was performed accidentally by Japanese anthropologists attempting to relieve an overpopulation and hunger problem in a community of monkeys on an island in south Japan. The anthropologists threw grains of wheat on a sandy beach. Now it is very difficult to separate wheat grains one by one from sand grains; 그런 노력에는 오히려 모은 밀을 먹음으로써 얻는 것보다 더 많은 에너지가 쓰일지도 모른다. But one brilliant monkey, Imo, perhaps by accident or out of pique, threw handfuls of the mixture into the water. Wheat floats; sand sinks, a fact that Imo clearly noted. Through the sifting process she was able to eat well. While older monkeys, set in their ways, ignored her, the younger monkeys appeared to grasp the importance of her discovery, and imitated it. In the next generation, the practice was more widespread; today all monkeys on the island are competent at water sifting, an example of a cultural tradition among the monkeys.

*expend (에너지·시간 등을) 쓰다[들이다]   **out of pique 욱해서

27 윗글의 밑줄 친 우리말 의미와 일치하도록 보기 의 단어를 순서대로 배열하여 영작하시오.

보기   wheat / expend / eating / collected / than / an / would provide / the / effort / more / might even / such / energy

_____

_____

고난도

28 윗글의 밑줄 친 부분을 가주어 it으로 시작하는 문장으로 바꿔 쓰시오.

→ _____

_____

The fact that a majority of the global population has at least some level of multilingual competence surely ① indicating that adding a second language is not a particularly remarkable feat. And yet, especially within powerful linguistic groups, it is common to find references to the difficulties ② involving or to the peculiar lack of language talents supposedly possessed. In the modern world, for example, English and American monolinguals often complain that they have no _____(A)_____ for foreign-language learning. This is usually ③ accompanied by expressions of envy for those multilingual Europeans, and sometimes (more subtly) by a linguistic smugness reflecting a deeply held conviction ④ that, after all, those clever "others" who don't already know English will have to accommodate in a world made increasingly ⑤ safely for anglophones. All such attitudes, of course, reveal more about social dominance and convention than they do about _____(B)_____.

*feat 재주 **smugness 우쭐거림 ***anglophone 영어 사용자

고난도

29 윗글의 밑줄 친 부분 중, 어법상 틀린 것을 3개 찾아 그 번호를 쓰고 고쳐 쓰시오.

(1) _____ → _____

(2) _____ → _____

(3) _____ → _____

30 윗글의 빈칸 (A), (B)에 공통으로 들어갈 단어를 영영 뜻풀이를 참고하여 쓰시오. (단, 주어진 글자로 시작할 것)

> natural ability that makes it easy for you to do something well

a_____

A gentleman came into my stress-management office and said, 'I'm mad at my boss. I don't like my job. I don't like the people that work with me. No one appreciates my work. I'm really angry.' When I began teaching him about how his own thinking creates his angry feelings he said, 'With all due respect, Dr. Carlson, I'm angry almost all the time, but I almost never think angry thoughts.' Do you see where he was being fooled? Until that moment, he believed that 'thinking' meant the same thing as 'pondering.' Even though he may not have dwelled on his misery for hours at a time, he was nevertheless continually thinking negatively, a moment here and a moment there. 그는 자신의 거의 모든 시간을 자신을 짜증 나고 성가시게 하는 사소한 것들에 대해 생각하는 데 썼다. It was almost as if the unstated goal of his life was to analyse it and to give his opinions on how various things affected him. His negative thoughts were creating his negative feelings and emotions and he didn't even know he was thinking them. He was a victim of his own thinking.

*ponder 심사숙고하다

31 윗글에서 다음 질문에 대한 답을 찾아 우리말로 쓰시오. (50자 내외)

Q: According to the passage, how was the gentleman a victim of his own thinking?

A: _____

_____

32 윗글의 밑줄 친 우리말 의미와 일치하도록 보기 의 단어를 순서대로 배열하여 문장을 완성하시오. (단, 필요시 어형을 바꿔 쓸 것)

> 보기 nearly / the little things / and / him / his time / irritate / all / thinking about / that / annoy / of

He spent _____

_____.

Caregivers for the old do much ① more than simply perform tasks. They provide intellectual engagement, social interaction, and emotional support, key factors in long-term health and longevity. As society has grown more urban and as family homes have become less multigenerational, greater numbers of the elderly now live alone. This shift brings with it ② diminished opportunities for social interaction. In the United States, a 2010 American Association of Retired Persons study found that over a third of respondents age forty-five and older were lonely as measured on the UCLA loneliness scale. Interactions with robots offer an opportunity to counteract, if not entirely remedy, the effects of such social ③ connection. Brain scan studies using fMRI have shown people have a measurable emotional response to robots ④ similar to that measured when interacting with other people, at least in certain situations. While robots and technology can't entirely ⑤ fill our need for social interaction, they may be able to provide some level of engagement.

33 윗글을 읽고 다음 질문에 영어로 답하시오. (10단어 내외)

Q: What has happened as society has gotten more urban and as family homes have become less multigenerational?

A: _____

_____

34 윗글의 밑줄 친 부분 중 문맥상 어색한 것을 1개 찾아 그 번호를 쓰고 고쳐 쓰시오.

_____ → _____

How are films made and produced? A news item, an event, a novel or the biography of an important person might suggest suitable themes. The film director's first job is to write a short account of the subject and to present it for a producer. This simple, untechnical plan is called a *treatment*. Movie director Jean Renoir and his scriptwriter wrote several unused treatments for *La Grande Illusion*. One of them is easy to get hold of; it is quite different from the final film. If a producer and a group of actors are interested in the scheme, the director or the scriptwriter rewrites the text in order to give a full list of shots, described in their order, with stage directions and technical terms clearly marked; this is the scenario. There is a good scenario of *October (Ten Days That Shook the World)* written by Eisenstein himself but, once again, it is far removed from the three finished versions of the film we can see today. It is difficult to put into practice what was decided beforehand, and important alterations occur in the course of production.

35 윗글의 밑줄 친 it이 가리키는 것을 본문에서 찾아 쓰시오. (5단어)

_____

🚩 고난도

36 윗글의 내용을 한 문장으로 요약하려고 한다. 보기 의 단어를 순서대로 배열하여 문장을 완성하시오.

보기 modifications / same / as / the / critical / film

We can hardly see _____ _____ _____ _____ presented in the first treatment or scenario since, in the process of making a film, _____ _____ of the treatment and the scenario are unavoidable.

Our present-day thinking is based on a succession of historically evolved mentalities; on mental edifices which previous generations have constructed, pulled down, renovated and extended. 과거의 사건들은 우리가 항상 의식하고 있지는 않더라도 우리의 현재 사고를 결정하는 이미지와 은유 속에 압축된다. Common sense is the thickly viscous form of the past, the reflex of history which, like the story about a puppet and a chess-playing machine, always triumphs. The puppet dressed in Turkish garb was sitting in front of a chessboard on a large table. A cunning arrangement of mirrors created the impression of being able to see underneath the table. In actual fact, there was a dwarf sitting underneath who was a chess master, and controlled the puppet. We can imagine the continuous effect of historical experience acting like an ugly, unloved and happily forgotten dwarf, moving the pieces in the chess game of our everyday life.

*edifice (사고의) 체계 **viscous 끈적이는 ***garb 복장

37 윗글의 밑줄 친 우리말 의미와 일치하도록 보기 의 단어를 순서대로 배열하여 문장을 완성하시오.

> 보기
>
> present / compressed / our / are / which / images / determine / past / thinking / metaphors / in / events / and

_____

_____ even if we are not always aware of them.

38 윗글의 내용을 한 문장으로 요약하려고 한다. 빈칸 (A)와 (B)에 들어갈 알맞은 말을 본문에서 찾아 쓰시오. (단, 필요시 어형을 바꿔 쓸 것)

> Like the dwarf which _____(A)_____ the puppet sitting at the chess table, the mentalities of the previous generations have a hidden (yet constant) _____(B)_____ on our present daily life and decision-making.

(A) _____ (B) _____

The word "entertainment" derives from the Latin _tenere_, which means "to hold or keep steady, busy, or amused." The notion of making money by keeping an audience steady, busy, or amused (A) remain central to those in the business of entertainment. Media practitioners, then, define entertainment as material that grabs the audience's attention and leaves agreeable feelings, as opposed to (B) challenge their views of themselves and the world. However, this doesn't mean that people who work in the entertainment business always stay away from informing or persuading. 제작사에 의해 '엔터테인먼트'로 분류되는 많은 영화가 정치적 논점(_The Day After Tomorrow, Syriana,_ 또는 _Blood Diamond_를 생각해 보라)이나 교육적 논점(_Schindler's List, Crash,_ 또는 _Letters from Iwo Jima_와 같이)을 만들려는 의도에서 쓰이고 제작되었다. When media practitioners label a product as "entertainment," though, they are signaling to their audiences (C) what their primary concern should be with enjoyment, not with any other messages that may be included.

*practitioner (전문직) 종사자

39 윗글의 밑줄 친 부분을 어법상 알맞은 형태로 고쳐 쓰시오.

(A) remain → _____

(B) challenge → _____

(C) what → _____

고난도

40 윗글의 밑줄 친 우리말 의미와 일치하도록 보기 의 단어를 활용하여 조건 에 맞게 문장을 완성하시오.

보기 make / produce / categorize under / of / the intention / with

조건
· 관계대명사 that을 활용할 것
· 현재완료 시제의 수동태를 활용할 것
· 필요시 어형을 바꿔 쓸 것

Many movies _____ _____ _____ _____ "entertainment" by their production firms _____ _____ _____ _____ _____ a political point(think of *The Day After Tomorrow, Syriana,* or *Blood Diamond*) or an educational point(like *Schindler's List, Crash,* or *Letters from Iwo Jima*).

13강 9번

Ritual is a set of catalytic messages, effecting ____(A)____ of state from one season of the year or one stage of the life cycle to another. *State* refers either to a social and biological stage in life — adolescence or adulthood, for example — or to social status, such as graduate student or doctor of philosophy. Many vertebrate species — especially birds but fish and mammals, too — have ritual. In these animals ritual is triggered by certain messages or symbols in response to chemical messages from the genes. For example, among the three-spined stickleback fish, the male's zigzag courtship dance, whereby he entices a prospective mate to his nest, is triggered by the sight of her red belly, which is the signal that she is biologically ready to lay eggs. We assume, further, that the form of the zigzag dance itself is genetically programmed in the male's nervous system. In any case, the ritual effects his ____(B)____ into a parent that tends the eggs in his nest.

*catalytic 촉매(작용)의 **vertebrate 척추동물(의) ***entice 유인하다

41 윗글을 읽고 다음 질문에 영어로 답하시오. (5단어)

Q: What is the ritual of the three-spined stickleback fish that enables the male fish to attract a mate to his nest?

A: The ritual of the male three-spined stickleback fish is _____ .

42 윗글의 빈칸 (A), (B)에 공통으로 들어갈 단어를 영영 뜻풀이를 참고하여 쓰시오. (단, 주어진 글자로 시작할 것)

a change into someone or something completely different, or the process by which this happens

t_____

Post-traumatic stress syndrome became common knowledge but not the concept of post-traumatic growth, which is actually ① <u>far</u> more widespread. Most people who undergo trauma ultimately feel that the experience has made them stronger, wiser, more mature, more ② <u>tolerant</u> and understanding, or in some other way better people. The influential psychologist Martin Seligman has often lamented that so much attention is lavished on post-traumatic stress syndrome rather than post-traumatic growth because it causes people ③ <u>mistakenly expect</u> that bad events will have mainly negative effects. After ④ <u>exposing</u> to a terrifying event, at least 80 percent of people do not experience post-traumatic stress syndrome. Even though a single bad event is more powerful than a good event, over time people respond in so many constructive ways ⑤ <u>which</u> they typically emerge more capable than ever of confronting life's challenges. Bad can make us stronger in the end.

*post-traumatic (정신적) 외상(外傷) 후의　　**lament 한탄하다
***lavish 낭비하다

고난도

43 윗글의 밑줄 친 부분 중, 어법상 틀린 것을 3개 찾아 그 번호를 쓰고 고쳐 쓰시오.

(1) _____ → _____

(2) _____ → _____

(3) _____ → _____

44 윗글의 내용을 한 문장으로 요약하려고 한다. 빈칸 (A)와 (B)에 들어갈 알맞은 말을 보기 에서 찾아 쓰시오.

> 보기　get over / suffer from / make use of / responsibilities / emergencies / adversities

> Generally, it is believed that most people ___(A)___ trauma after experiencing a terrible event, however, they actually end up becoming stronger against the ___(B)___ of life.

(A) _____　(B) _____

There is a common misconception that the reason we have hunger is because the earth is straining to feed an ever-growing population. This is not the case. The world uses only about a third of its arable land for crop production. And even that third we use inefficiently. China, for instance, has dramatically higher crop yields per acre than the United States, primarily because, even though the two countries are comparable in size, China has three times the population of the United States and only one-sixth the arable land, so its population has to grow crops more efficiently. Planet earth is in fact such a prodigious producer of food that in the United States, 전 세계의 모든 굶주린 사람들을 먹여 살리기에 충분한 양의 음식이 버려진다.

*arable 경작할 수 있는 **prodigious 거대한

45 윗글에서 다음 질문에 대한 답을 찾아 우리말로 쓰시오. (60자 내외)

Q: Although the size of China and the United States is almost the same, why does China have much higher crop yields than the United States?

A: _____

_____

46 윗글의 밑줄 친 우리말 의미와 일치하도록 보기 의 단어를 활용하여 조건 에 맞게 문장을 완성하시오.

보기　all of / keep / feed

조건
· to부정사를 활용할 것
· 필요시 어형을 바꿔 쓸 것
· 빈칸 부분에 총 11단어로 쓸 것

enough food is thrown away _____

There is a saying made famous by the Nobel memorial prize-winning economist Milton Friedman that 'There's no such thing as a free lunch' — that we can't magic wealth out of nothing (say, by printing money) or shift costs into the ether. Friedman's view was that if we legislate to reduce a burden on some citizens, or to increase the advantages they may enjoy, there will be repercussions somewhere down the line that will involve a cost for others and might even ultimately mean the measure is _____.
So even if a meal is priced at zero, someone, somewhere is paying for it. Modern economics may disparage the concept of free lunches, yet, today, one often gets a sense from key economists and policy-makers that a free lunch isn't that far away. Economics aims to show how we can generate growth by identifying more efficient ways of organising society, thereby making us richer and, hopefully, happier, with the least amount of sacrifice on our part. Such a utopia is achievable, economists believe, because they understand the mechanisms that drive everything from business investment and production decisions to consumer purchase choices, to individual attitudes to saving.

*ether 하늘, 창공　**repercussion 반향　***disparage 폄하하다

47 윗글의 빈칸에 들어갈 단어를 영영 뜻풀이를 참고하여 쓰시오. (단, 주어진 글자로 시작할 것)

having the opposite result to the one you intended

c_____

48 윗글의 밑줄 친 Such a utopia가 가리키는 것을 본문에서 찾아 우리말로 쓰시오. (35자 내외)

_____

_____

❶ Random sampling doesn't mean just choosing the people to participate in the study haphazardly — there's a difference between the meaning of the word 'random' in everyday use and its meaning in statistics and research methods. ❷ A random sample is a sample in which every member of the population has an equally likely chance of being selected for the study — and that isn't as easy as it sounds. ❸ Most sampling methods will unconsciously favour some people, and not others. ❹ Picking names at random out of a telephone directory means that people who are ex-directory or who don't use landlines are not going to be included. ❺ In a psychological study, that could introduce a bias, because those people may be different from others in some important way — for example, by being younger, or more suspicious of strangers.

*haphazardly 되는 대로

❶ 무작위 표본 추출은 연구에 참여할 사람을 그저 되는 대로 선택하는 것을 의미하지 않는데, 일상적으로 사용되는 '무작위적'이라는 단어의 의미와 통계학과 연구 방법에서의 그것의 의미 사이에는 차이가 있다. ❷ 무작위 표본은 모집단의 모든 구성원이 연구를 위해 선택될 가능성이 똑같이 있을 법한 표본인데, 그것은 들리는 것만큼 쉽지 않다. ❸ 대부분의 표본 추출 방법은 무심결에 일부 사람들은 편애하고 일부 다른 사람들은 편애하지 않기 마련이다. ❹ 무작위로 전화번호부에서 이름을 고르는 것은 전화번호부에 올라 있지 않거나 유선 전화를 사용하지 않는 사람들이 포함되지 않으리라는 것을 의미한다. ❺ 심리학 연구에서, 그것은 편향을 끌어들일 수도 있는데, 그런 사람들이 어떤 중요한 면에서, 가령 더 어리거나 낯선 사람들을 더 의심함으로써, 다른 사람들과 다를 수도 있기 때문이다.

Word List

□ random 무작위의, 무작위적인　□ sampling 표본 추출, 샘플링　□ statistics 통계학　□ method 방법　□ population 모집단
□ equally 동일하게　□ select 선정하다　□ unconsciously 무심결에, 무의식적으로　□ favour 편들다, 선호하다
□ at random 무작위로　□ telephone directory 전화번호부　□ ex-directory 전화번호부에 올라 있지 않은　□ landline 유선 전화
□ psychological 심리학의　□ bias 편향, 치우침　□ suspicious 의심하는

• Word Test

1	ex-directory		9	모집단	
2	method		10	선정하다	
3	at random		11	편향, 치우침	
4	unconsciously		12	유선 전화	
5	equally		13	심리학의	
6	statistics		14	편들다, 선호하다	
7	telephone directory		15	표본 추출, 샘플링	
8	suspicious		16	무작위의, 무작위적인	

Random sampling doesn't mean just choosing the people to participate in the study haphazardly — there's a ❶ difference/similarity between the meaning of the word 'random' in everyday use and its meaning in statistics and research methods. A random sample is a sample ❷ that/in which every member of the population has an equally likely chance of being selected for the study — and that isn't as easy as it sounds. Most sampling methods will ❸ consciously/unconsciously favour some people, and not others. Picking names at random out of a telephone directory means that people who are ex-directory or who don't use landlines are not going to be included. In a psychological study, that could introduce a bias, because those people may be ❹ different from/similar to others in some important way — for example, by being younger, or more suspicious of strangers.

*haphazardly 되는 대로

Random sampling doesn't mean just choosing the people ❶ _____ (participate) in the study haphazardly — there's a difference between the meaning of the word 'random' in everyday use and its meaning in statistics and research methods. A random sample is a sample in which every member of the population has an equally likely chance of ❷ _____ (select) for the study — and that isn't as easy as it ❸ _____ (sound). Most sampling methods will unconsciously favour some people, and not others. Picking names at random out of a telephone directory means that people who are ex-directory or who don't use landlines are not going to ❹ _____ (include). In a psychological study, that could introduce a bias, because those people may be different from others in some important way — for example, by ❺ _____ (be) younger, or more suspicious of strangers.

*haphazardly 되는 대로

Random sampling doesn't mean just choosing the people to ❶ _____ _____ _____ _____ (연구에 참여하다) haphazardly — there's a difference between the meaning of the word 'random' ❷ _____ _____ _____ (일상적으로 사용되는) and its meaning in statistics and research methods. A random sample is a sample in which every member of the population has ❸ _____ _____ _____ _____ (똑같이 있을 법한 가능성) of being selected for the study — and that isn't ❹ _____ _____ _____ _____ _____ (들리는 것만큼 쉬운). Most sampling methods will unconsciously favour some people, and not others. Picking names at random out of a telephone directory means that people who are ex-directory or who don't use landlines are not going to be included. In a psychological study, that could introduce a bias, because those people may be different from others 어떤 중요한 면에서 ❺ _____ _____ _____ _____ (어떤 중요한 면에서) — for example, by being younger, or more suspicious of strangers.

*haphazardly 되는 대로

❶ Spatial position can be indicative of social status. ❷ Historical analyses of hundreds of paintings indicate that when two people appear in the same picture the more dominant, powerful person is usually facing to the right. ❸ For example, relative to men, women are more often displayed showing the left cheek, consistent with gender roles that consider them as less agentic. ❹ In other words, traditionally weak and submissive characters have been assigned to their respective place by where they are situated in space. ❺ From the 15th century to the 20th century, however, this gender bias in paintings has become less pronounced, therefore paralleling increasingly modern views of women's role in society.

*agentic 주도적인 **submissive 복종하는

❶ 공간적 위치는 사회적 지위를 나타낼 수 있다. ❷ 수백 점의 그림에 대한 역사적 분석에 따르면, 두 사람이 같은 그림에 등장할 때, 더 우월하고 유력한 사람이 보통 오른쪽을 향하고 있다. ❸ 예를 들어, 남성과 비교하여, 여성은 왼쪽 뺨을 보이는 모습으로 더 자주 제시되는데, 이는 그들을 덜 주도적이라고 여기는 성 역할과 일치한다. ❹ 다시 말해, 전통적으로 약하고 복종적인 인물들은 그들이 공간상 놓이는 위치에 의해 각각의 지위가 정해졌다. ❺ 그러나 15세기부터 20세기까지 그림에서의 이런 성 편견은 덜 두드러지게 되었으며, 그리하여 사회에서 여성의 역할에 대한 점점 더 현대적 관점과 유사해졌다.

Word List

□ spatial 공간의, 공간적인 □ be indicative of ~을 나타내다, ~을 보여 주다 □ status 지위 □ analysis 분석(*pl.* analyses)
□ indicate 나타내다, 말하다 □ dominant 우월한, 지배적인 □ relative to ~과 비교하여 □ display 제시하다, 나타내다, 보여 주다
□ consistent 일치하는, 일관된 □ assign 정하다, 배정하다, 부여하다 □ respective 각각의, 각자의 □ situate 두다, 위치시키다
□ gender bias 성 편견 □ pronounced 두드러진, 뚜렷한 □ parallel 유사하다 □ increasingly 점점 더

• Word Test

1	display		9	지위	
2	parallel		10	우월한, 지배적인	
3	pronounced		11	일치하는, 일관된	
4	analysis		12	성 편견	
5	situate		13	점점 더	
6	be indicative of		14	각각의, 각자의	
7	relative to		15	공간의, 공간적인	
8	assign		16	나타내다, 말하다	

Spatial position can be indicative of social status. Historical analyses of hundreds of paintings indicate ❶ that / what when two people appear in the same picture the more dominant, powerful person is usually facing to the right. For example, relative to men, women are more often displayed showing the left cheek, ❷ inconsistent / consistent with gender roles that consider them as less agentic. In other words, traditionally weak and submissive characters have been assigned to their respective place ❸ by how / by where they are situated in space. From the 15th century to the 20th century, ❹ however / moreover , this gender bias in paintings has become less pronounced, therefore paralleling increasingly modern views of women's role in society.

*agentic 주도적인 **submissive 복종하는

Spatial position can be indicative of social status. Historical analyses of hundreds of paintings indicate that when two people ❶ _____ (appear) in the same picture the more dominant, powerful person is usually ❷ _____ (face) to the right. For example, relative to men, women are more often ❸ _____ (display) showing the left cheek, consistent with gender roles that consider them as less agentic. In other words, traditionally weak and submissive characters have been assigned to their respective place by where they ❹ _____ (situate) in space. From the 15th century to the 20th century, however, this gender bias in paintings has become less ❺ _____ (pronounce), therefore paralleling increasingly modern views of women's role in society.

*agentic 주도적인 **submissive 복종하는

Spatial position can be indicative of social status. Historical analyses of hundreds of paintings indicate that when two people appear in the same picture the more dominant, powerful person is usually ❶ _____ _____ _____ _____ (오른쪽을 향하는). For example, ❷ _____ _____ _____ (남성들과 비교하여), women are more often displayed showing the left cheek, consistent with gender roles that consider them as less agentic. ❸ _____ _____ _____ (다시 말해), traditionally weak and submissive characters have been assigned to their respective place by where they are situated in space. From the 15th century to the 20th century, however, this ❹ _____ _____ (성 편견) in paintings has become less pronounced, therefore paralleling increasingly modern views of ❺ _____ _____ _____ _____ (사회에서 여성들의 역할).

*agentic 주도적인 **submissive 복종하는

❶ Within travel destinations, it is not uncommon to see higher sticker prices in areas most frequented by tourists; prices are much lower elsewhere where locals shop. ❷ A few smart tourists soon learn to get away from these "tourist traps" to find better deals where there are not as many tourists. ❸ Most tourists will not, because it doesn't pay to spend their scarce vacation time attempting to find cheaper restaurants, souvenirs, and so on outside the tourist areas. ❹ If the time spent in searching and shopping for the best deals is included as part of the prices of the purchases, "prices" are actually lower in the tourist areas for most tourists. ❺ In sum, locational price differences are generally not considered price discrimination.

❶ 여행 목적지 내에, 관광객이 가장 자주 찾는 지역에서 더 높은 표시 가격을 보는 것은 드문 일이 아니며, 지역 사람들이 쇼핑하는 다른 곳에서는 가격이 훨씬 더 낮다. ❷ 소수의 현명한 관광객은 관광객이 그만큼 많지 않은 곳에서 더 좋은 거래를 찾기 위해 이러한 '관광객 함정'으로부터 벗어나는 것을 곧 배우게 된다. ❸ 대부분의 관광객은 그렇게 하지 않을 것인데, 이는 더 싼 식당, 기념품 등을 관광지 밖에서 애써 찾으려고 자신의 부족한 휴가 시간을 쓰는 것이 이득이 되지 않기 때문이다. ❹ 최상의 거래를 찾고 쇼핑하는 데 소비된 시간이 구매 가격의 일부로 포함된다면, 관광지에서의 '가격'은 대부분의 관광객들에게 사실상 더 낮다. ❺ 요컨대, 장소에 따른 가격 차이는 일반적으로 가격 차별로 여겨지지 않는다.

Word List

☐ destination 목적지, 행선지   ☐ sticker price 표시 가격   ☐ area 지역   ☐ frequent 자주 가다   ☐ local 지역 주민   ☐ trap 덫
☐ deal 거래   ☐ scarce 부족한, 적은   ☐ souvenir 기념품   ☐ include 포함시키다   ☐ actually 실제로   ☐ in sum 요컨대
☐ locational 장소에 따른, 위치 선정의   ☐ price discrimination 가격 차별(동등한 원가의 상품을 구매자에 따라 다른 값에 파는 일)

• **Word Test**

1 sticker price _____
2 area _____
3 locational _____
4 local _____
5 scarce _____
6 in sum _____
7 price discrimination _____

8 덫 _____
9 자주 가다 _____
10 실제로 _____
11 목적지, 행선지 _____
12 포함시키다 _____
13 거래 _____
14 기념품 _____

Within travel destinations, it is not uncommon to see higher sticker prices in areas most frequented by tourists; prices are much lower elsewhere ❶ when / where locals shop. ❷ A few / A little smart tourists soon learn to get away from these "tourist traps" to find better deals where there are not as many tourists. Most tourists will not, because it doesn't pay to spend their ❸ sufficient / scarce vacation time attempting to find cheaper restaurants, souvenirs, and so on outside the tourist areas. If the time spent in searching and shopping for the best deals is included as part of the prices of the purchases, "prices" are actually ❹ lower / higher in the tourist areas for most tourists. In sum, locational price differences are generally not considered price discrimination.

Within travel destinations, it is not uncommon to see higher sticker prices in areas most ❶ _____ (frequent) by tourists; prices are much lower elsewhere where locals shop. A few smart tourists soon learn to get away from these "tourist traps" ❷ _____ (find) better deals where there are not as many tourists. Most tourists will not, because it doesn't pay to spend their scarce vacation time ❸ _____ (attempt) to find cheaper restaurants, souvenirs, and so on outside the tourist areas. If the time ❹ _____ (spend) in searching and shopping for the best deals is included as part of the prices of the purchases, "prices" are actually lower in the tourist areas for most tourists. In sum, locational price differences are generally not considered price discrimination.

Within travel destinations, it is not uncommon to see higher sticker prices in ❶ _____ _____ _____ (가장 자주 찾게 되는 지역들) by tourists; prices are much lower elsewhere where locals shop. A few smart tourists soon learn to get away from these "tourist traps" to ❷ _____ _____ _____ (더 좋은 거래들을 찾다) where there are not as many tourists. Most tourists will not, because it doesn't pay to spend their scarce vacation time attempting to find cheaper restaurants, souvenirs, and so on outside the tourist areas. If the time spent in searching and shopping for the best deals is included ❸ _____ _____ _____ (~의 일부로) the prices of the purchases, "prices" are actually lower in the tourist areas for most tourists. ❹ _____ _____ (요컨대), locational price differences are generally not considered ❺ _____ _____ (가격 차별).

❶ The desire for esteem can be used effectively by society to influence how people act. ❷ Systems of prestige are found in all cultures, and in general prestige is used to recognize and reward people who do what is most useful to the culture. ❸ People will labor for years, even decades, in the hope of securing the esteem of their fellows and the accompanying right to think well of themselves. ❹ By linking prestige and esteem to particular activities or accomplishments, a culture can direct many people to devote their energies in those directions. ❺ It is no accident that in small societies struggling for survival, prestige comes with bringing in large amounts of protein (hunting) or defeating the most dangerous enemies (fighting). ❻ By the same token, the prestige of motherhood probably rises and falls with the society's need to increase population, and the prestige of entertainers rises and falls with how much time and money the population can devote to leisure activities.

❶ 존경에 대한 욕구는 사람들이 행동하는 방식에 영향을 미치도록 사회에 의해 효과적으로 사용될 수 있다. ❷ 명망의 체계는 모든 문화에서 발견되며, 일반적으로 명망은 그 문화에 가장 유용한 일을 하는 사람들을 인정하고 보상하기 위해 사용된다. ❸ 사람들은 동료의 존경과 자신을 호의적으로 생각하는 그에 수반하는 권리를 확보하려는 희망으로 수년, 심지어 수십 년 동안 노력할 것이다. ❹ 명망과 존경을 특정한 활동이나 성취와 연결시킴으로써, 각 문화는 많은 사람이 자신의 에너지를 그 방향으로 쏟게 할 수 있다. ❺ 생존을 위해 애쓰는 작은 사회에서 명망이 많은 양의 단백질을 들여오거나(사냥) 또는 가장 위험한 적을 물리치는 것(전투)에 따라오는 것은 우연한 일이 아니다. ❻ 같은 이유로, 어머니가 된다는 것의 명망은 아마도 인구를 늘려야 하는 사회의 필요성에 따라 오르락내리락할 것이고, 연예인이라는 명망은 사람들이 여가 활동에 얼마나 많은 시간과 돈을 쏟을 수 있는지에 따라 오르락내리락한다.

Word List

□ esteem 존경 □ effectively 효과적으로 □ influence 영향을 미치다 □ prestige 명망, 명성 □ in general 일반적으로 □ reward 보상하다 □ labor 노력하다 □ decade 10년 □ secure 확보하다 □ fellow 동료 □ accompanying 수반하는 □ link 연결하다 □ accomplishment 성취 □ direct 지시하다, 지휘하다 □ devote 쏟다, 바치다 □ struggle 애쓰다, 발버둥치다 □ protein 단백질 □ by the same token 같은 이유로 □ population 인구, 주민 □ entertainer 연예인

• Word Test

1 accompanying _____

2 prestige _____

3 by the same token _____

4 direct _____

5 devote _____

6 labor _____

7 secure _____

8 accomplishment _____

9 influence _____

10 population _____

11 애쓰다, 발버둥치다 _____

12 존경 _____

13 연예인 _____

14 효과적으로 _____

15 보상하다 _____

16 단백질 _____

17 일반적으로 _____

18 연결하다 _____

19 동료 _____

20 10년 _____

The desire for esteem can be used effectively by society to influence ❶ which / how people act. Systems of prestige are found in all cultures, and in general prestige is used to recognize and reward people who do ❷ which / what is most useful to the culture. People will labor for years, even decades, in the hope of securing the esteem of their fellows and the accompanying right to think well of themselves. By ❸ unlinking / linking prestige and esteem to particular activities or accomplishments, a culture can direct many people to devote their energies in those directions. ❹ It / This is no accident that in small societies struggling for survival, prestige comes with bringing in large amounts of protein (hunting) or defeating the most dangerous enemies (fighting). By the same token, the prestige of motherhood probably rises and falls with the society's need to ❺ increase / decrease population, and the prestige of entertainers rises and falls with how much time and money the population can devote to leisure activities.

The desire for esteem can be used effectively by society ❶ _____ (influence) how people act. Systems of prestige ❷ _____ (find) in all cultures, and in general prestige is used to recognize and reward people who do what is most useful to the culture. People will labor for years, even decades, in the hope of ❸ _____ (secure) the esteem of their fellows and the accompanying right to think well of themselves. By linking prestige and esteem to particular activities or accomplishments, a culture can direct many people ❹ _____ (devote) their energies in those directions. It is no accident that in small societies struggling for survival, prestige comes with bringing in large amounts of protein (hunting) or ❺ _____ (defeat) the most dangerous enemies (fighting). By the same token, the prestige of motherhood probably rises and falls with the society's need to increase population, and the prestige of entertainers rises and falls with how much time and money the population can devote to leisure activities.

The ❶ _____ _____ _____ (존경에 대한 욕구) can be used effectively by society to influence how people act. Systems of prestige are found in all cultures, and ❷ _____ _____ (일반적으로) prestige is used to recognize and reward people who do what is most useful to the culture. People will labor for years, even decades, ❸ _____ _____ _____ _____ (~하려는 희망으로) securing the esteem of their fellows and the accompanying right to think well of themselves. By linking prestige and esteem to particular activities or accomplishments, a culture can direct many people to devote their energies in those directions. It is no accident that in small societies struggling for survival, prestige comes with bringing in large amounts of protein (hunting) or defeating the most dangerous enemies (fighting). ❹ _____ _____ _____ _____ (같은 이유로), the prestige of motherhood probably rises and falls with the society's need to increase population, and the prestige of entertainers rises and falls with how much time and money the population can devote to leisure activities.

다음 빈칸에 들어갈 말로 가장 적절한 것은?

Random sampling doesn't mean just choosing the people to participate in the study haphazardly — there's a difference between the meaning of the word 'random' in everyday use and its meaning in statistics and research methods. A random sample is a sample in which every member of the population _____ for the study — and that isn't as easy as it sounds. Most sampling methods will unconsciously favour some people, and not others. Picking names at random out of a telephone directory means that people who are ex-directory or who don't use landlines are not going to be included. In a psychological study, that could introduce a bias, because those people may be different from others in some important way — for example, by being younger, or more suspicious of strangers.

*haphazardly 되는 대로

① has an equally likely chance of being selected
② collectively takes responsibility for unjust acts
③ is notified of what kind of personal information will be used
④ has no contact with people outside of the experiment
⑤ is selected without prejudice against their ethnic background

(A), (B), (C)의 각 네모 안에서 어법에 맞는 표현으로 가장 적절한 것은?

Spatial position can be indicative of social status. Historical analyses of hundreds of paintings indicate that when two people appear in the same picture the more dominant, powerful person is usually facing to the right. For example, (A) relative/relatively to men, women are more often displayed showing the left cheek, consistent with gender roles that consider them as less agentic. In other words, traditionally weak and submissive characters have been assigned to their respective place by (B) where/whom they are situated in space. From the 15th century to the 20th century, however, this gender bias in paintings has become less pronounced, therefore (C) paralleled/paralleling increasingly modern views of women's role in society.

*agentic 주도적인 **submissive 복종하는

	(A)	(B)	(C)
①	relative	where	paralleled
②	relative	where	paralleling
③	relative	whom	paralleled
④	relatively	whom	paralleling
⑤	relatively	where	paralleled

03 14강 3번

다음 빈칸에 들어갈 말로 가장 적절한 것은?

Within travel destinations, it is not uncommon to see higher sticker prices in areas most frequented by tourists; prices are much lower elsewhere where locals shop. A few smart tourists soon learn to get away from these "tourist traps" to find better deals where there are not as many tourists. Most tourists will not, because it doesn't pay to spend their scarce vacation time attempting to find cheaper restaurants, souvenirs, and so on outside the tourist areas. If the time spent in searching and shopping for the best deals is included as part of the prices of the purchases, "prices" are actually lower in the tourist areas for most tourists. In sum, locational price differences _____.

① are generally not considered price discrimination
② are not reflected in the quality of travel packages
③ encourage travelers to spend more in local areas
④ bring travel agents to the outer regions of tourist attractions
⑤ prohibit tourists from getting significant price discounts

04 14강 4번

다음 빈칸에 들어갈 말로 가장 적절한 것은?

The desire for esteem can be used effectively by society to influence how people act. Systems of prestige are found in all cultures, and in general prestige is used to recognize and reward people who do what is most useful to the culture. People will labor for years, even decades, in the hope of securing the esteem of their fellows and the accompanying right to think well of themselves. By linking prestige and esteem to particular activities or accomplishments, a culture can _____. It is no accident that in small societies struggling for survival, prestige comes with bringing in large amounts of protein (hunting) or defeating the most dangerous enemies (fighting). By the same token, the prestige of motherhood probably rises and falls with the society's need to increase population, and the prestige of entertainers rises and falls with how much time and money the population can devote to leisure activities.

① order people to accomplish tasks for a particular authority
② direct many people to devote their energies in those directions
③ keep people from indulging in basic human physiological needs
④ redirect people's energies to dull them in an immediate crisis
⑤ ease survival competition among its active participants

다음 글의 제목으로 가장 적절한 것은?

Random sampling doesn't mean just choosing the people to participate in the study haphazardly — there's a difference between the meaning of the word 'random' in everyday use and its meaning in statistics and research methods. A random sample is a sample in which every member of the population has an equally likely chance of being selected for the study — and that isn't as easy as it sounds. Most sampling methods will unconsciously favour some people, and not others. Picking names at random out of a telephone directory means that people who are ex-directory or who don't use landlines are not going to be included. In a psychological study, that could introduce a bias, because those people may be different from others in some important way — for example, by being younger, or more suspicious of strangers.

*haphazardly 되는 대로

① Prejudice in Everyday Conversation
② Randomized Trials in Marketing Research
③ How to Reduce Errors in Sampling Methods
④ Not Arbitrary but Impartial Random Sampling
⑤ The Importance of Not Treating People as Numbers

다음 빈칸에 들어갈 말로 가장 적절한 것은?

Spatial position can _____. Historical analyses of hundreds of paintings indicate that when two people appear in the same picture the more dominant, powerful person is usually facing to the right. For example, relative to men, women are more often displayed showing the left cheek, consistent with gender roles that consider them as less agentic. In other words, traditionally weak and submissive characters have been assigned to their respective place by where they are situated in space. From the 15th century to the 20th century, however, this gender bias in paintings has become less pronounced, therefore paralleling increasingly modern views of women's role in society.

*agentic 주도적인 **submissive 복종하는

① be indicative of social status
② determine where actions unfold
③ suggest the hierarchy of social needs
④ reflect characteristics of social movements
⑤ be illustrative of gender neutrality in languages

07 14강 3번

다음 글의 제목으로 가장 적절한 것은?

Within travel destinations, it is not uncommon to see higher sticker prices in areas most frequented by tourists; prices are much lower elsewhere where locals shop. A few smart tourists soon learn to get away from these "tourist traps" to find better deals where there are not as many tourists. Most tourists will not, because it doesn't pay to spend their scarce vacation time attempting to find cheaper restaurants, souvenirs, and so on outside the tourist areas. If the time spent in searching and shopping for the best deals is included as part of the prices of the purchases, "prices" are actually lower in the tourist areas for most tourists. In sum, locational price differences are generally not considered price discrimination.

① How to Avoid High Prices during Your Trip
② A Secret among Residents: Local-Only Pricing
③ Reasons for High Prices in Travel Destinations
④ The High But Low Prices of Travel Destinations
⑤ Affordable Prices for Tourists during Off-Season

08 14강 4번

다음 글의 요지로 가장 적절한 것은?

The desire for esteem can be used effectively by society to influence how people act. Systems of prestige are found in all cultures, and in general prestige is used to recognize and reward people who do what is most useful to the culture. People will labor for years, even decades, in the hope of securing the esteem of their fellows and the accompanying right to think well of themselves. By linking prestige and esteem to particular activities or accomplishments, a culture can direct many people to devote their energies in those directions. It is no accident that in small societies struggling for survival, prestige comes with bringing in large amounts of protein (hunting) or defeating the most dangerous enemies (fighting). By the same token, the prestige of motherhood probably rises and falls with the society's need to increase population, and the prestige of entertainers rises and falls with how much time and money the population can devote to leisure activities.

① 각 문화가 가지는 고유한 명망의 체계는 시간이 지남에 따라 변화한다.
② 사람은 자신이 인정받고 보상받는 기준으로 동료로부터의 존경을 꼽는다.
③ 생존에 대한 사회적 요구가 충족된 사회에서는 명망에 대한 욕구가 발현된다.
④ 인구가 급격히 감소하고 있는 문화는 모성애에 대한 존경의 상실이 선행한다.
⑤ 존경과 명망을 이용하여 사람들이 사회에 유용한 일을 하도록 유도할 수 있다.

Random sampling doesn't mean just choosing the people (A) participate in the study haphazardly — there's a difference between the meaning of the word 'random' in everyday use and its meaning in statistics and research methods. A random sample is a sample in which every member of the population has an equally likely chance of being selected for the study — and that isn't as easy as it sounds. Most sampling methods will (B) unconscious favour some people, and not others. (C) Pick names at random out of a telephone directory means that people who are ex-directory or who don't use landlines are not going to be included. In a psychological study, that could introduce a bias, because those people may be different from others in some important way — for example, by being younger, or more suspicious of strangers.

*haphazardly 되는 대로

09 윗글의 밑줄 친 부분을 어법상 알맞은 형태로 고쳐 쓰시오.

(A) participate → _____

(B) unconscious → _____

(C) Pick → _____

10 윗글의 밑줄 친 that이 가리키는 것을 본문에서 찾아 우리말로 쓰시오. (35자 내외)

_____

_____

Spatial position can be indicative of social status. Historical analyses of hundreds of paintings indicate that when two people appear in the same picture the more dominant, powerful person is usually facing to the right. For example, relative to men, women are more often displayed showing the left cheek, _____ with gender roles that consider them as less agentic. In other words, 전통적으로 약하고 복종적인 인물들은 그들이 공간상 놓이는 위치에 의해 각각의 지위가 정해졌다. From the 15th century to the 20th century, however, this gender bias in paintings has become less pronounced, therefore paralleling increasingly modern views of women's role in society.

*agentic 주도적인 **submissive 복종하는

11 윗글의 빈칸에 들어갈 단어를 영영 뜻풀이를 참고하여 쓰시오. (단, 주어진 글자로 시작할 것)

> containing statements or ideas that are similar or that have the same aim

c_____

12 윗글의 밑줄 친 우리말 의미와 일치하도록 보기 의 단어를 순서대로 배열하여 문장을 완성하시오.

> 보기 to / situated / they / where / been / by / respective / their / place / have / are / assigned

traditionally weak and submissive characters

_____

_____ in space

Within travel destinations, it is not uncommon to see higher sticker prices in areas most frequented by tourists; ① prices are much lower elsewhere where locals shop. A few smart tourists soon learn to get away from these "tourist traps" to find better deals where there are not as many tourists. Most tourists will not, ② because it doesn't pay to spend their sufficient vacation time attempting to find cheaper restaurants, souvenirs, and so on outside the tourist areas. 최상의 거래를 찾고 쇼핑하는 데 소비된 시간이 구매 가격의 일부로 포함된다면, "prices" are actually lower in the tourist areas for most tourists. In sum, ③ locational price differences are generally not considered price discrimination.

13 윗글의 밑줄 친 부분 중 문맥상 어색한 것을 1개 찾아 그 번호를 쓰고 고쳐 쓰시오. (어색한 부분의 번호, 어색한 부분, 알맞게 고친 정답을 차례대로 쓸 것)

_____, _____ → _____

14 윗글의 밑줄 친 우리말 의미와 일치하도록 보기 의 단어를 활용하여 조건 에 맞게 문장을 완성하시오.

보기 shop for / spend in / the best deals / search / include

조건 · 조건의 부사절로 쓸 것
· 분사구를 활용할 것
· 필요시 어형을 바꿔 쓰고, 총 14단어로 쓸 것

_____

_____

as part of the prices of the purchases

The desire for esteem ① can be used effectively by society to influence how people act. Systems of prestige are found in all cultures, and in general prestige is used to recognize and ② rewarding people who do what is most useful to the culture. People will labor for years, even decades, in the hope of ③ securing the esteem of their fellows and the accompanying right to think well of themselves. By linking prestige and esteem to particular activities or accomplishments, a culture can direct many people to devote their energies in those directions. It is no accident that in small societies ④ struggled for survival, prestige comes with bringing in large amounts of protein (hunting) or defeating the most dangerous enemies (fighting). By the same token, the prestige of motherhood probably rises and falls with the society's need to increase population, and the prestige of entertainers rises and falls with how much time and money ⑤ can the population devote to leisure activities.

15 윗글의 밑줄 친 부분 중, 어법상 틀린 것을 3개 찾아 그 번호를 쓰고 고쳐 쓰시오.

(1) _____ → _____

(2) _____ → _____

(3) _____ → _____

16 윗글의 내용을 한 문장으로 요약하려고 한다. 빈칸 (A)와 (B)에 들어갈 알맞은 말을 본문에서 찾아 쓰시오.

A society drives people to accomplish what it considers to be ___(A)___ by using people's ___(B)___ for prestige and esteem.

(A) _____ (B) _____

❶ What do we want to hear when asking the question why John slammed the door? ❷ Probably not that John put more than average energy into his act, giving the door more speed (which resulted in a heavy collision of the door with the doorpost, a loud noise and the lamp rocking back and forth). ❸ We normally are not interested in a report of the chain of causes and effects leading up to the slamming. ❹ Neither do we expect to hear a report about micro-processes in John's body causing his movements. ❺ The why-question asks for reasons — 'He felt offended', for instance. ❻ Even when we think in a materialistic frame of mind that the state of being offended can be traced in John's brain, we usually will not be interested in an answer in neurological terms. ❼ So, normally, in our day-to-day why-questions about people's actions we expect to hear about their reasons.

❶ John이 왜 문을 쾅 닫았느냐는 질문을 할 때, 우리는 무엇을 듣고 싶어 하는가? ❷ 아마도 John이 자기 행위에 보통 수준이 넘는 힘을 주어서 문의 속도를 더 높였다(그것이 결과적으로 문이 문설주에 심하게 충돌하게 하고, 큰 소리가 나게 하고, 등이 이리저리 흔들리게 했다)는 것은 아닐 것이다. ❸ 대개 우리는 그 쾅 닫힘까지 이르는 일련의 원인과 결과에 대한 보고에는 관심이 없다. ❹ 또한 우리는 John의 움직임을 유발한 그의 몸속의 미세한 과정에 대한 보고를 듣는 것도 기대하지 않는다. ❺ 그 왜라는 질문은 가령 '그가 화가 났다'처럼 이유를 요구한다. ❻ 심지어 우리가 유물론적인 사고방식으로 화가 난 상태의 원인을 John의 뇌에서 밝혀낼 수 있다고 생각할 때도, 대개 우리는 신경학 용어로 된 대답에는 관심을 두지 않을 것이다. ❼ 그러므로 대개 우리는 사람들의 행동에 대한 우리의 일상의 왜라는 질문에서 그들의 이유에 대해 듣기를 기대한다.

Word List

□ **slam** (문 따위를) 쾅 닫다　□ **result in** (결과적으로) ~하게 하다　□ **collision** 충돌, 부딪힘　□ **doorpost** 문설주, 문기둥
□ **rock** 흔들리다　□ **back and forth** 앞뒤로, 왔다갔다 하는　□ **normally** 대개　□ **cause and effect** 원인과 결과
□ **lead up to** ~까지 이르다　□ **offended** 화가 난　□ **materialistic** 유물론의, 물질주의의　□ **frame of mind** (특정한 때의) 사고방식[기분]
□ **state** 상태　□ **trace** (원인을) 밝혀내다, 추적하다　□ **neurological** 신경학의, 신경의　□ **term** 용어

• Word Test

1	neurological		9	충돌, 부딪힘
2	back and forth		10	상태
3	doorpost		11	사고방식[기분]
4	result in		12	화가 난
5	slam		13	흔들리다
6	lead up to		14	(원인을) 밝혀내다, 추적하다
7	normally		15	원인과 결과
8	materialistic		16	용어

What do we want to hear when asking the question why John slammed the door? Probably not that John put more than average energy into his act, giving the door more speed (which resulted in a heavy ❶ collision / collapse of the door with the doorpost, a loud noise and the lamp rocking back and forth). We normally are not interested in a report of the chain of causes and effects leading up ❷ to / for the slamming. ❸ Neither / Whether do we expect to hear a report about micro-processes in John's body causing his movements. The why-question asks for reasons — 'He felt offended', for instance. Even when we think in a materialistic frame of mind ❹ which / that the state of being offended can be traced in John's brain, we usually will not be interested in an answer in neurological terms. So, ❺ normally / relatively , in our day-to-day why-questions about people's actions we expect to hear about their reasons.

What do we want to hear when ❶ _____ (ask) the question why John slammed the door? Probably not that John put more than average energy into his act, ❷ _____ (give) the door more speed (which resulted in a heavy collision of the door with the doorpost, a loud noise and the lamp rocking back and forth). We normally are not interested in a report of the chain of causes and effects ❸ _____ (lead) up to the slamming. Neither do we expect to hear a report about micro-processes in John's body ❹ _____ (cause) his movements. The why-question asks for reasons — 'He felt offended', for instance. Even when we think in a materialistic frame of mind that the state of ❺ _____ (offend) can trace in John's brain, we usually will not be interested in an answer in neurological terms. So, normally, in our day-to-day why-questions about people's actions we expect to hear about their reasons.

What do we want to hear when asking the question why John slammed the door? Probably not that John put more than average energy into his act, giving the door more speed (which ❶ _____ _____ (결과적으로 ~하게 했다) a heavy collision of the door with the doorpost, a loud noise and the lamp rocking back and forth). We normally are not interested in a report of ❷ _____ _____ _____ _____ _____ _____ (일련의 원인들과 결과들) leading up to the slamming. Neither do we expect to hear a report about micro-processes in John's body causing his movements. The why-question asks for reasons — 'He felt offended', for instance. Even when we think in a materialistic frame of mind that ❸ _____ _____ _____ _____ _____ (화가 난 상태) can be traced in John's brain, we usually will not be interested in an answer ❹ _____ _____ _____ (신경학 용어들로 된). So, normally, in our day-to-day why-questions about people's actions we expect to hear about their reasons.

❶ We can presume that the components of love proposed by Sternberg can be found in all cultures. ❷ Intimacy, passion, and commitment are most likely cultural universals. ❸ Evidence of this comes from many sources, including cultural anthropology, psychological research, and love poetry from across the world. ❹ What does appear to vary across cultures, however, is the emphasis placed on the different components of love and on different types of relationships. ❺ In collectivist cultures like those found in Asia and Africa, relationships with family may take priority over relationships with lovers and friends. ❻ In individualistic cultures, like those of Northern Europe and North America, friendships and romantic relationships compete with family for priority (and often win). ❼ Likewise, the concept of duty (similar to Sternberg's concept of commitment) is absolutely central to Chinese Confucianism. ❽ In contrast, judging by the mountains of romance novels, love songs, and beauty products found in North America, it is the passionate side of love that is prized in this culture.

❶ 우리는 Sternberg가 제안한 사랑의 구성 요소가 모든 문화에서 발견될 수 있다고 추정할 수 있다. ❷ 친밀감, 열정, 헌신은 문화적으로 보편적 특성일 가능성이 매우 크다. ❸ 이것의 증거는 문화 인류학, 심리학적 연구, 그리고 전 세계의 사랑의 시를 포함한 많은 출처에서 나온다. ❹ 그러나 정말 문화에 따라 다르게 보이는 것은 사랑의 서로 다른 구성 요소를 어떻게 강조하고 서로 다른 관계 유형을 어떻게 강조하는지이다. ❺ 아시아와 아프리카에서 보이는 것과 같은 집단주의 문화에서는, 가족과의 관계가 연인이나 친구와의 관계보다 우선할 수 있다. ❻ 북유럽과 북미의 문화와 같은 개인주의 문화에서는, 우정과 연인 관계가 우선순위를 두고 가족과 경쟁한다(그리고 흔히 이긴다). ❼ 마찬가지로, (Sternberg의 헌신 개념과 유사한) 의무라는 개념은 중국 유교에 절대적으로 중요하다. ❽ 이와 대조적으로, 북미에서 보이는 산더미처럼 많은 로맨스 소설, 사랑의 노래, 미용 제품으로 판단해 보면, 이 문화에서 소중히 여겨지는 것은 바로 사랑의 열정적인 면이다.

Word List

□ **presume** 추정하다　□ **component** 구성요소　□ **propose** 제안하다　□ **intimacy** 친밀감　□ **passion** 열정　□ **commitment** 헌신
□ **universal** 보편적 특성　□ **evidence** 증거　□ **anthropology** 인류학　□ **emphasis** 강조, 중점　□ **collectivist culture** 집단주의 문화
□ **priority** 우선순위　□ **individualistic** 개인주의적인　□ **concept** 개념　□ **Confucianism** 유교　□ **in contrast** 대조적으로
□ **passionate** 열정적인　□ **prize** 소중히 여기다

• Word Test

1	Confucianism		10	증거	
2	intimacy		11	헌신	
3	passionate		12	구성요소	
4	individualistic		13	우선순위	
5	collectivist culture		14	제안하다	
6	presume		15	강조, 중점	
7	anthropology		16	개념	
8	prize		17	대조적으로	
9	universal		18	열정	

We can presume that the components of love proposed by Sternberg can be found in all cultures. Intimacy, passion, and commitment are most likely cultural universals. Evidence of ❶ these / this comes from many sources, including cultural anthropology, psychological research, and love poetry from across the world. What does appear to vary across cultures, ❷ however/therefore, is the emphasis placed on the different components of love and on different types of relationships. In collectivist cultures like those found in Asia and Africa, relationships with family may take priority over relationships with lovers and friends. In individualistic cultures, like ❸ that / those of Northern Europe and North America, friendships and romantic relationships compete with family for priority (and often win). Likewise, the concept of duty (similar to Sternberg's concept of commitment) is absolutely central to Chinese Confucianism. In contrast, judging by the mountains of romance novels, love songs, and beauty products found in North America, it is the passionate side of love that is ❹ prized / released in this culture.

We can presume that the components of love proposed by Sternberg can be found in all cultures. Intimacy, passion, and commitment ❶ _____ (be) most likely cultural universals. Evidence of this comes from many sources, ❷ _____ (include) cultural anthropology, psychological research, and love poetry from across the world. What does appear to vary across cultures, however, is the emphasis placed on the different components of love and on different types of relationships. In collectivist cultures like those ❸ _____ (find) in Asia and Africa, relationships with family may take priority over relationships with lovers and friends. In individualistic cultures, like those of Northern Europe and North America, friendships and romantic relationships compete with family for priority (and often win). Likewise, the concept of duty (similar to Sternberg's concept of commitment) is absolutely central to Chinese Confucianism. In contrast, ❹ _____ (judge) by the mountains of romance novels, love songs, and beauty products found in North America, it is the passionate side of love that ❺ _____ (be) prized in this culture.

We can presume that the components of love proposed by Sternberg can be found in all cultures. Intimacy, passion, and commitment are most likely cultural universals. Evidence of this comes from many sources, including cultural anthropology, psychological research, and love poetry from across the world. What does appear to ❶ _____ _____ _____ (문화들에 따라 다르다), however, is the emphasis placed on the different components of love and on different types of relationships. In collectivist cultures like those found in Asia and Africa, relationships with family may ❷ _____ _____ _____ (~보다 우선하다) relationships with lovers and friends. In individualistic cultures, like those of Northern Europe and North America, friendships and romantic relationships ❸ _____ _____ (~와 경쟁하다) family for priority (and often win). Likewise, the concept of duty (similar to Sternberg's concept of commitment) is absolutely central to Chinese Confucianism. In contrast, judging by ❹ _____ _____ _____ (~의 산더미) romance novels, love songs, and beauty products found in North America, it is the passionate side of love that is prized in this culture.

❶ It could be argued that the 'processual' nature of personhood means that one becomes a person as one 'goes along' in society. ❷ Indeed, the African philosopher Ifeanyi Menkiti takes this position. ❸ He maintains that children are not fully human. ❹ Following Kwame Gyekye, a Ghanaian philosopher, however, I would argue that the fact that personhood must be earned is not a denial of personhood to children. ❺ It is an affirmation of the view that *personhood is an ongoing process* attained through interactions with others and one's community. ❻ It requires one to affirm ideals and standards thought to be constitutive of the life of a community. ❼ These are standards such as generosity, benevolence and respect. ❽ A number of sayings in some African societies refer to people who have failed to meet standards expected of a fully human person. ❾ These are sayings such as *ga e se motho* (Tswana) or *a ku si muntu* (Nguni), literally meaning 'he or she is not a person'. ❿ Because one can fall short of these standards at any stage in the life cycle, personhood could be regarded as a *becoming*. ⓫ It is an unpredictable, open-ended process during which personhood may be achieved, lost, and regained, depending on a person's circumstances.

*affirmation 지지, 확인   **benevolence 자비심

❶ 사람다움의 '과정적' 본질은 우리가 사회에서 '살아가'면서 한 사람이 된다는 것을 의미한다고 주장할 수 있다. ❷ 사실, 아프리카의 철학자 Ifeanyi Menkiti는 이 입장을 취한다. ❸ 그는 아이들은 완전한 사람이 아니라고 주장한다. ❹ 그러나 나는 가나의 철학자 Kwame Gyekye를 따라, 사람다움이 획득되어야 한다는 사실이 아이들에게 사람다움이 있는 것을 부인하는 것은 아니라고 주장하고 싶다. ❺ 그것은 '사람다움이' 다른 사람 및 공동체와의 상호 작용을 통해 얻어지는 '진행 중인 과정이라는' 견해에 대한 지지이다. ❻ 그 때문에 우리는 공동체의 삶을 구성하는 것으로 여겨지는 이상과 규범을 지지해야 한다. ❼ 이것은 관용, 자비심, 존경과 같은 규범이다. ❽ 일부 아프리카 사회의 여러 속담은 온전한 인격체의 인간에게 기대되는 규범을 충족하지 못한 사람들을 언급한다. ❾ 이것들은 *ga e se motho*(츠와나족)나 *a ku si muntu*(응구니족)와 같은 속담인데, 말 그대로 '그는 사람이 아니다'라는 뜻이다. ❿ 사람은 생애 주기의 어느 단계에서도 이 규범에 미치지 못할 수 있으므로, 사람다움은 '되어 가는 일'로 여겨질 수도 있을 것이다. ⓫ 그것은 개인의 환경에 따라 사람다움이 성취되며, 상실되고, 다시 회복될 수 있는, 예측할 수 없고 정해진 결말이 없는 과정이다.

Word List

□ **processual** 과정의, 절차의   □ **personhood** 개인적 특질   □ **indeed** 사실, 정말로   □ **philosopher** 철학자   □ **maintain** 주장하다
□ **denial** (존재의) 부인   □ **ongoing** 진행 중인   □ **attain** 얻다, 이루다   □ **interaction** 상호 작용   □ **ideal** 이상
□ **be constitutive of** ~을 구성하다   □ **generosity** 관용   □ **literally** 말 그대로   □ **fall short of** ~에 미치지 못하다, 미흡하다
□ **regain** 회복하다, 되찾다   □ **circumstances** 환경

• Word Test

1 literally _____
2 interaction _____
3 be constitutive of _____
4 circumstances _____
5 attain _____
6 processual _____
7 indeed _____
8 fall short of _____

9 개인적 특질 _____
10 이상 _____
11 관용 _____
12 (존재의) 부인 _____
13 철학자 _____
14 주장하다 _____
15 진행 중인 _____
16 회복하다, 되찾다 _____

It could be argued that the 'processual' nature of personhood means that one becomes a person as one 'goes along' in society. ❶ Indeed / Rather , the African philosopher Ifeanyi Menkiti takes this position. He maintains that children are not fully human. Following Kwame Gyekye, a Ghanaian philosopher, however, I would argue that the fact that personhood must ❷ earn / be earned is not a denial of personhood to children. It is an affirmation of the view ❸ that / what *personhood is an ongoing process* attained through interactions with others and one's community. It requires one to affirm ideals and standards thought to be constitutive of the life of a community. These are standards such as generosity, benevolence and respect. ❹ A number of / The number of sayings in some African societies refer to people who have failed to meet standards expected of a fully human person. These are sayings such as *ga e se motho* (Tswana) or *a ku si muntu* (Nguni), literally meaning 'he or she is not a person'. Because one can fall short of these standards at any stage in the life cycle, personhood could be regarded as a *becoming*. It is an unpredictable, open-ended process ❺ for / during which personhood may be achieved, lost, and regained, depending on a person's circumstances.

*affirmation 지지, 확인   **benevolence 자비심

It could be argued that the 'processual' nature of personhood means that one becomes a person as one 'goes along' in society. Indeed, the African philosopher Ifeanyi Menkiti takes this position. He maintains that children are not fully human. Following Kwame Gyekye, a Ghanaian philosopher, however, I would argue that the fact that personhood must be earned ❶ _____ (be) not a denial of personhood to children. It is an affirmation of the view that *personhood is an ongoing process* ❷ _____ (attain) through interactions with others and one's community. It requires one to affirm ideals and standards ❸ _____ (think) to be constitutive of the life of a community. These are standards such as generosity, benevolence and respect. A number of sayings in some African societies refer to people who ❹ _____ (fail) to meet standards expected of a fully human person. These are sayings such as *ga e se motho* (Tswana) or *a ku si muntu* (Nguni), literally meaning 'he or she is not a person'. Because one can fall short of these standards at any stage in the life cycle, personhood could be regarded as a *becoming*. It is an unpredictable, open-ended process during which personhood may ❺ _____ (achieve), lost, and regained, depending on a person's circumstances.

*affirmation 지지, 확인   **benevolence 자비심

It could be argued that the 'processual' nature of personhood means that one becomes a person as one 'goes along' in society. Indeed, the African philosopher Ifeanyi Menkiti ❶ _____ _____ _____ (이 입장을 취한다). He maintains that children are not fully human. Following Kwame Gyekye, a Ghanaian philosopher, however, I would argue that the fact that personhood must be earned is not a denial of personhood to children. It is an affirmation of the view that *personhood is an ongoing process* attained through interactions with others and one's community. It requires one to affirm ideals and standards thought to be constitutive of the life of a community. These are standards such as generosity, benevolence and respect. A number of sayings in some African societies ❷ _____ _____ (~을 언급하다) people who have failed to meet standards expected of ❸ _____ _____ _____ _____ (온전한 인격체). These are sayings such as *ga e se motho* (Tswana) or *a ku si muntu* (Nguni), literally meaning 'he or she is not a person'. Because one can ❹ _____ _____ _____ (~에 미치지 못하다) these standards at any stage in the life cycle, personhood could be regarded as a *becoming*. It is an unpredictable, open-ended process during which personhood may be achieved, lost, and regained, depending on a person's circumstances.

*affirmation 지지, 확인 **benevolence 자비심

❶Some countries grow cash crops. ❷These are crops that are in high demand and can be grown in large quantities in specific areas of the world. ❸For example, sugar needs a hot, damp climate; coffee needs a hot climate, rainfall, and higher mountain elevations. ❹Tea needs to grow on hillsides in rainy areas. ❺Bananas grow well in tropical environments. ❻Because there is a worldwide demand for specific items such as these, the farmers in tropical countries grow as much of these commodities as they can. ❼These cash crops are sold all around the world and bring in a lot of money, but there are risks to specializing in just one commodity for trade. ❽If these farmers grow too much of a particular cash crop, that creates more supply than demand, which drops the price of the commodity. ❾If the climate is bad, and the cash crop does not grow well one year, that hurts the country selling it because that crop may be the only one the country provides in large enough quantities to make a living from.

*cash crop 환금 작물(시장에 내다 팔기 위하여 재배하는 농작물)

❶ 몇몇 나라들은 환금 작물을 재배한다. ❷ 이것들은 수요가 많고 세계의 특정 지역에서 대량으로 재배될 수 있는 작물이다. ❸ 예를 들어, 설탕은 덥고 습한 기후를 필요로 하고, 커피는 더운 기후, 강우, 더 높은 고도의 산지를 필요로 한다. ❹ 차는 강우가 많은 지역의 비탈에서 자라야 한다. ❺ 바나나는 열대 환경에서 잘 자란다. ❻ 이것들과 같은 특정 품목에 대한 전 세계적인 수요가 있기 때문에, 열대 국가의 농부들은 가능한 한 이 상품들을 많이 재배한다. ❼ 이 환금 작물들은 전 세계적으로 팔리고 많은 돈을 벌어들이지만, 무역을 위해 단 하나의 상품만을 전문으로 하는 것에는 위험이 있다. ❽ 만약 이 농부들이 특정 환금 작물을 너무 많이 재배하면, 그것은 수요보다 더 많은 공급을 만들어 내고, 그 때문에 그 상품의 가격이 떨어진다. ❾ 만약 기후가 나빠서, 한 해에 환금 작물이 잘 자라지 않으면, 그것은 그 환금 작물을 파는 나라에 해를 끼치는데, 그 작물은 그 나라가 생계를 유지하게 할 수 있을 만큼 충분히 많이 제공하는 유일한 작물일 수도 있기 때문이다.

Word List

□ **in high demand** 수요가 많은　□ **quantity** 양　□ **specific** 특정한　□ **damp** 습한　□ **rainfall** 강우　□ **elevation** 고도
□ **hillside** (작은 산이나 언덕의) 비탈　□ **tropical** 열대의　□ **demand** 수요　□ **commodity** 상품　□ **risk** 위험
□ **specialize in** ~을 전문으로 하다　□ **supply** 공급　□ **make a living** 생계를 유지하다

• Word Test

1	elevation	_____	8	특정한	_____
2	quantity	_____	9	상품	_____
3	risk	_____	10	공급	_____
4	damp	_____	11	수요가 많은	_____
5	make a living	_____	12	강우	_____
6	demand	_____	13	~을 전문으로 하다	_____
7	hillside	_____	14	열대의	_____

Some countries grow cash crops. These are crops that are in high demand and can be grown in large quantities in specific areas of the world. ❶ For example / In addition , sugar needs a hot, damp climate; coffee needs a hot climate, rainfall, and higher mountain elevations. Tea needs to grow on hillsides in rainy areas. Bananas grow well in tropical environments. Because there is a worldwide demand for specific items such as ❷ this / these , the farmers in tropical countries grow as much of these commodities as they can. These cash crops are sold all around the world and bring in a lot of money, but there are risks to ❸ specialize / specializing in just one commodity for trade. If these farmers grow too much of a particular cash crop, that creates more supply than demand, ❹ what / which drops the price of the commodity. If the climate is bad, and the cash crop does not grow well one year, that hurts the country selling it ❺ because / although that crop may be the only one the country provides in large enough quantities to make a living from.

*cash crop 환금 작물(시장에 내다 팔기 위하여 재배하는 농작물)

Some countries grow cash crops. These are crops that are in high demand and can ❶ _____ (grow) in large quantities in specific areas of the world. For example, sugar needs a hot, damp climate; coffee needs a hot climate, rainfall, and higher mountain elevations. Tea needs to grow on hillsides in rainy areas. Bananas grow well in tropical environments. Because there is a worldwide demand for specific items such as these, the farmers in tropical countries grow as much of these commodities as they can. These cash crops ❷ _____ (sell) all around the world and bring in a lot of money, but there are risks to specializing in just one commodity for trade. If these farmers grow too much of a particular cash crop, that ❸ _____ (create) more supply than demand, which drops the price of the commodity. If the climate is bad, and the cash crop does not grow well one year, that hurts the country ❹ _____ (sell) it because that crop may be the only one the country provides in large enough quantities to make a living from.

*cash crop 환금 작물(시장에 내다 팔기 위하여 재배하는 농작물)

Some countries grow cash crops. These are crops that are in high demand and can be grown ❶ _____ _____ _____ (대량으로) in specific areas of the world. For example, sugar needs a hot, damp climate; coffee needs a hot climate, rainfall, and ❷ _____ _____ _____ (더 높은 고도들의 산지). Tea needs to grow on hillsides in rainy areas. Bananas grow well in tropical environments. Because there is a worldwide demand for specific items such as these, the farmers in tropical countries grow as much of these commodities as they can. These cash crops are sold all around the world and ❸ _____ _____ _____ _____ _____ _____ (많은 돈을 벌어들이다), but there are risks to specializing in just one commodity for trade. If these farmers grow too much of a particular cash crop, that creates more supply than demand, which drops the price of the commodity. If the climate is bad, and the cash crop does not grow well one year, that hurts the country selling it because that crop may be the only one the country provides in large enough quantities to ❹ _____ _____ _____ _____ (~로 생계를 유지하다).

*cash crop 환금 작물(시장에 내다 팔기 위하여 재배하는 농작물)

❶ Some might have had the impression that early scientists like Newton and Galileo belonged to a small sect that conjured science out of the blue as a result of mystical investigation. ❷ This wasn't so. ❸ Their work did not take place in a cultural vacuum: ❹ it was the product of many ancient traditions. ❺ One of these was Greek philosophy, which encouraged the belief that the world could be explained by logic, reasoning, and mathematics. ❻ Another was agriculture, from which people learned about order and chaos by observing the cycles and rhythms of nature, interrupted periodically by sudden and unpredictable disasters. ❼ And then there were religions which encouraged belief in a created world order. ❽ The founding assumption of science is that the physical universe is neither random nor absurd; ❾ it is not just a meaningless jumble of objects and phenomena randomly placed side by side. ❿ Rather, there is a coherent *scheme of things*. ⓫ This is often expressed by the simple saying that there is order in nature. ⓬ But scientists have gone beyond this vague notion to formulate a system of well-defined *laws*.

*sect 종파 **conjure (마법으로) 불러내다 ***jumble 뒤범벅

❶ 어떤 이는 아마도 뉴턴과 갈릴레오와 같은 초기 과학자들이 신비로운 연구의 결과로 느닷없이 마법으로 과학을 불러낸 작은 종파에 속했다는 인상을 가졌을지도 모른다. ❷ 이것은 그렇지 않았다. ❸ 그들의 작업은 문화적 공백에서 일어나지 않았다. ❹ 그것은 고대의 많은 전통의 산물이었던 것이다. ❺ 이것들 가운데 하나가 그리스 철학이었는데, 그것은 논리, 추론, 수학으로 세상이 설명될 수 있다는 믿음을 부추겼다. ❻ 다른 하나는 농업이었는데, 이로부터 사람들은 갑작스럽고, 예측할 수 없는 재난에 의해 주기적으로 방해를 받는 자연의 순환과 리듬을 관찰함으로써 질서와 혼돈에 대해 배웠다. ❼ 그리고 다음으로 창조된 세계 질서에 대한 믿음을 부추긴 종교가 있었다. ❽ 과학의 기초적인 가정은 물리적인 우주가 제멋대로이지도 않고 터무니없지도 않다는 것이다. ❾ 그것은 우주가 단지 무작위로 나란히 놓인 사물과 현상의 무의미한 뒤범벅은 아니라는 것이다. ❿ 오히려, 일관성 있는 '사물의 체계'가 있다. ⓫ 이것은 흔히 자연에는 질서가 있다는 간단한 경구로 표현된다. ⓬ 하지만 과학자는 이 막연한 개념을 넘어서 잘 정의된 '법칙' 체계를 정립해 왔다.

Word List

□ impression 인상 □ out of the blue 느닷없이 □ investigation 연구 □ vacuum 공백 □ philosophy 철학 □ logic 논리 □ agriculture 농업 □ chaos 혼돈 □ interrupt 방해하다, 중단시키다 □ periodically 주기적으로 □ unpredictable 예측할 수 없는 □ disaster 재난 □ founding 기초적인 □ assumption 가정 □ random 제멋대로의 □ absurd 터무니없는, 황당한 □ phenomenon 현상 (*pl.* phenomena) □ randomly 무작위로 □ coherent 일관성 있는 □ scheme of things 사물의 체계 □ saying 경구, 격언 □ order 질서 □ vague 막연한 □ formulate 정립하다

• Word Test

1 philosophy _____
2 phenomenon _____
3 coherent _____
4 out of the blue _____
5 unpredictable _____
6 formulate _____
7 assumption _____
8 scheme of things _____
9 vacuum _____
10 interrupt _____
11 absurd _____
12 investigation _____

13 인상 _____
14 혼돈 _____
15 무작위로 _____
16 기초적인 _____
17 막연한 _____
18 주기적으로 _____
19 재난 _____
20 논리 _____
21 농업 _____
22 제멋대로의 _____
23 경구, 격언 _____
24 질서 _____

네모 안에서 옳은 어법·어휘를 고르시오.

Some might have had the impression that early scientists like Newton and Galileo belonged to a small sect that conjured science out of the blue as a result of mystical ❶ evaluation/investigation. This wasn't so. Their work did not take place in a cultural vacuum: it was the product of many ❷ ancient/modern traditions. One of these was Greek philosophy, which encouraged the belief that the world could be explained by logic, reasoning, and mathematics. Another was agriculture, from ❸ whom/which people learned about order and chaos by observing the cycles and rhythms of nature, interrupted periodically by sudden and ❹ predictable/unpredictable disasters. And then there were religions which encouraged belief in a created world order. The founding assumption of science is that the physical universe is neither random nor absurd; it is not just a ❺ worthwhile/meaningless jumble of objects and phenomena randomly placed side by side. Rather, there is a coherent *scheme of things*. This is often expressed by the simple saying that there is order in nature. But scientists have gone beyond this vague notion to formulate a system of well-defined *laws*.

*sect 종파   **conjure (마법으로) 불러내다   ***jumble 뒤범벅

• 유형 2 괄호 안의 동사를 알맞은 형태로 쓰시오.

Some might ❶ _____(have) the impression that early scientists like Newton and Galileo belonged to a small sect that conjured science out of the blue as a result of mystical investigation. This wasn't so. Their work did not take place in a cultural vacuum: it was the product of many ancient traditions. One of these was Greek philosophy, which encouraged the belief that the world could ❷ _____(explain) by logic, reasoning, and mathematics. Another was agriculture, from which people learned about order and chaos by observing the cycles and rhythms of nature, ❸ _____(interrupt) periodically by sudden and unpredictable disasters. And then there were religions which encouraged belief in a created world order. The founding assumption of science is that the physical universe is neither random nor absurd; it is not just a meaningless jumble of objects and phenomena randomly ❹ _____(place) side by side. Rather, there is a coherent *scheme of things*. This is often expressed by the simple saying that there is order in nature. But scientists ❺ _____(go) beyond this vague notion to formulate a system of well-defined *laws*.

*sect 종파   **conjure (마법으로) 불러내다   ***jumble 뒤범벅

• 유형 3 우리말에 맞게 빈칸에 알맞은 말을 쓰시오.

Some might have had the impression that early scientists like Newton and Galileo belonged to a small sect that conjured science ❶ _____ _____ _____ _____ (느닷없이) as a result of mystical investigation. This wasn't so. Their work did not take place ❷ _____ _____ _____ _____ (문화적 공백에서): it was the product of many ancient traditions. One of these was Greek philosophy, which encouraged the belief that the world could be explained by logic, reasoning, and mathematics. Another was agriculture, from which people learned about order and chaos by observing the cycles and rhythms of nature, interrupted periodically by sudden and unpredictable disasters. And then there were religions which encouraged belief in a created world order. The founding assumption of science is that the physical universe is neither random nor absurd; it is not just a meaningless jumble of objects and phenomena randomly placed ❸ _____ _____ _____ (나란히). Rather, there is a coherent *scheme of things*. This is often expressed by the simple saying that there is order in nature. But scientists have gone ❹ _____ _____ _____ _____ (이 막연한 개념을 넘어서) to formulate a system of well-defined *laws*.

*sect 종파   **conjure (마법으로) 불러내다   ***jumble 뒤범벅

❶ In English, many spelling errors could be avoided if we systematically transcribed each sound with a fixed letter. ❷ For instance, if we were to avoid writing the sound *f* with both the letter "f" and with "ph," life would be much simpler. ❸ There is little doubt that we could easily get rid of this and many other useless redundancies whose acquisition eats up many years of childhood. ❹ In fact, this is the timid direction that American spelling reform took when it simplified the irregular British spellings of "behaviour" or "analyse" into "behavior" and "analyze." ❺ Many more steps could have been taken along the same lines. ❻ As expert readers, we cease to be aware of the absurdity of our spelling. ❼ Even a letter as simple as "x" is unnecessary, as it stands for two phonemes *ks* that already have their own spelling. ❽ In Türkiye, one takes a "taksi." ❾ That country, which in the space of one year adopted the Roman alphabet, drastically simplified its spelling, and taught three million people how to read, sets a beautiful example of the feasibility of spelling reform.

*redundancy 군더더기 **phoneme 음소 ***feasibility 실현 가능성

❶ 영어에서 우리가 각각의 음을 고정된 글자로 체계적으로 표기한다면 많은 철자 오류를 피할 수 있을 것이다. ❷ 예를 들어, 만약 우리가 'f'음을 글자 'f'와 'ph'로 둘 다 쓰는 것을 피한다면, 생활이 훨씬 더 수월해질 것이다. ❸ 우리가 이것과 습득하는 데 수년의 유년 시절을 잡아먹는 여타 많은 불필요한 군더더기를 쉽게 없앨 수 있다는 것에는 거의 의심의 여지가 없다. ❹ 사실, 이것은 미국의 철자 개혁이 'behaviour'나 'analyse'의 불규칙한 영국 철자를 'behavior'와 'analyze'로 단순화했을 때 취했던 소심한 방향이다. ❺ 더욱 많은 조치가 같은 방식으로 취해질 수도 있었을 것이다. ❻ 숙련된 독자로서 우리는 우리 철자의 불합리성을 의식하지 않게 된다. ❼ 'X'와 같이 간단한 글자조차 이미 자체의 철자가 있는 두 개의 음소 'ks'를 나타내기 때문에 불필요하다. ❽ 튀르키예에서는 'taksi'를 탄다. ❾ 그 나라는 일년의 기간 내에 로마자를 채택하여 철자를 대폭 단순화하고 삼백만 명의 사람들에게 읽는 법을 가르쳤는데, 철자 개혁의 실현 가능성을 보여 주는 훌륭한 본보기가 된다.

Word List

□ avoid 피하다　□ systematically 체계적으로　□ transcribe (말소리를 기호로) 표기하다　□ fixed 고정된　□ get rid of ~을 없애다
□ acquisition 습득　□ timid 소심한, 소극적인　□ reform 개혁; 개혁하다　□ simplify 단순화하다　□ irregular 불규칙한
□ cease to *do* ~이 아니게 되다　□ absurdity 불합리성, 부조리　□ stand for ~을 나타내다[상징하다]　□ in the space of ~의 기간 내에
□ adopt 채택하다　□ drastically 대폭(적으로), 과감하게　□ set an example of ~의 본보기가 되다

• Word Test

1	timid	9	체계적으로
2	set an example of	10	대폭(적으로), 과감하게
3	in the space of	11	~을 없애다
4	acquisition	12	고정된
5	transcribe	13	불규칙한
6	stand for	14	채택하다
7	reform	15	단순화하다
8	cease to *do*	16	불합리성, 부조리

In English, many spelling errors could be avoided if we systematically transcribed each sound with a ❶ fixed / variable letter. For instance, if we were to avoid writing the sound *f* with both the letter "f" and with "ph," life would be much simpler. There is ❷ few / little doubt that we could easily get rid of this and many other useless redundancies ❸ which / whose acquisition eats up many years of childhood. In fact, this is the timid direction that American spelling reform took when it simplified the ❹ regular / irregular British spellings of "behaviour" or "analyse" into "behavior" and "analyze." Many more steps could have been taken along the same lines. As expert readers, we cease to be aware of the ❺ integrity / absurdity of our spelling. Even a letter as simple as "x" is unnecessary, as it stands for two phonemes *ks* that already have their own spelling. In Tiirkiye, one takes a "taksi." That country, which in the space of one year adopted the Roman alphabet, drastically simplified its spelling, and taught three million people how to read, sets a beautiful example of the feasibility of spelling reform.

*redundancy 군더더기   **phoneme 음소   ***feasibility 실현 가능성

In English, many spelling errors could ❶ _____ (avoid) if we systematically transcribed each sound with a fixed letter. For instance, if we were to avoid ❷ _____ (write) the sound *f* with both the letter "f" and with "ph," life would be much simpler. There is little doubt that we could easily get rid of this and many other useless redundancies whose acquisition eats up many years of childhood. In fact, this is the timid direction that American spelling reform took when it simplified the irregular British spellings of "behaviour" or "analyse" into "behavior" and "analyze." Many more steps could ❸ _____ (take) along the same lines. As expert readers, we cease to be aware of the absurdity of our spelling. Even a letter as simple as "x" is unnecessary, as it stands for two phonemes *ks* that already ❹ _____ (have) their own spelling. In Tiirkiye, one takes a "taksi." That country, which in the space of one year adopted the Roman alphabet, drastically simplified its spelling, and taught three million people how to read, ❺ _____ (set) a beautiful example of the feasibility of spelling reform.

*redundancy 군더더기   **phoneme 음소   ***feasibility 실현 가능성

In English, many spelling errors could be avoided if we systematically transcribed each sound with a fixed letter. For instance, if we were to avoid writing the sound *f* with both the letter "f" and with "ph," life would be much simpler. There is little doubt that we could ❶ _____ _____ _____ _____ (~을 쉽게 없애다) this and many other useless redundancies whose acquisition ❷ _____ _____ (~을 잡아먹다) many years of childhood. In fact, this is the timid direction that American spelling reform took when it simplified the irregular British spellings of "behaviour" or "analyse" into "behavior" and "analyze." Many more steps could have been taken ❸ _____ _____ _____ _____ (같은 방식으로). As expert readers, we cease to be aware of the absurdity of our spelling. Even a letter as simple as "x" is unnecessary, as it stands for two phonemes *ks* that already have their own spelling. In Tiirkiye, one takes a "taksi." That country, which ❹ _____ _____ _____ _____ _____ (일 년의 기간 내에) adopted the Roman alphabet, drastically simplified its spelling, and taught three million people how to read, sets a beautiful example of the feasibility of spelling reform.

*redundancy 군더더기   **phoneme 음소   ***feasibility 실현 가능성

01 15강 1번

다음 글의 제목으로 가장 적절한 것은?

What do we want to hear when asking the question why John slammed the door? Probably not that John put more than average energy into his act, giving the door more speed (which resulted in a heavy collision of the door with the doorpost, a loud noise and the lamp rocking back and forth). We normally are not interested in a report of the chain of causes and effects leading up to the slamming. Neither do we expect to hear a report about micro-processes in John's body causing his movements. The why-question asks for reasons — 'He felt offended', for instance. Even when we think in a materialistic frame of mind that the state of being offended can be traced in John's brain, we usually will not be interested in an answer in neurological terms. So, normally, in our day-to-day why-questions about people's actions we expect to hear about their reasons.

① The True Aim of the Question Why
② Wonder: The Main Cause of Behavior
③ How to Know the Exact Intent of a Question
④ The Need to Always Ask Why in Everyday Life
⑤ The Importance of Identifying Cause and Effect

02 15강 2번

다음 글의 밑줄 친 부분 중, 문맥상 낱말의 쓰임이 적절하지 <u>않은</u> 것은?

We can presume that the components of love proposed by Sternberg can be found in all cultures. Intimacy, passion, and commitment are most likely cultural ① <u>universals</u>. Evidence of this comes from many sources, including cultural anthropology, psychological research, and love poetry from across the world. What does appear to ② <u>vary</u> across cultures, however, is the emphasis placed on the different components of love and on different types of relationships. In collectivist cultures like those found in Asia and Africa, relationships with family may take ③ <u>priority</u> over relationships with lovers and friends. In individualistic cultures, like those of Northern Europe and North America, friendships and romantic relationships compete with family for priority (and often ④ <u>win</u>). Likewise, the concept of duty (similar to Sternberg's concept of commitment) is absolutely central to Chinese Confucianism. In contrast, judging by the mountains of romance novels, love songs, and beauty products found in North America, it is the passionate side of love that is ⑤ <u>undervalued</u> in this culture.

03 15강 3번

다음 글에서 필자가 주장하는 바로 가장 적절한 것은?

It could be argued that the 'processual' nature of personhood means that one becomes a person as one 'goes along' in society. Indeed, the African philosopher Ifeanyi Menkiti takes this position. He maintains that children are not fully human. Following Kwame Gyekye, a Ghanaian philosopher, however, I would argue that the fact that personhood must be earned is not a denial of personhood to children. It is an affirmation of the view that *personhood is an ongoing process* attained through interactions with others and one's community. It requires one to affirm ideals and standards thought to be constitutive of the life of a community. These are standards such as generosity, benevolence and respect. A number of sayings in some African societies refer to people who have failed to meet standards expected of a fully human person. These are sayings such as *ga e se motho* (Tswana) or *a ku si muntu* (Nguni), literally meaning 'he or she is not a person'. Because one can fall short of these standards at any stage in the life cycle, personhood could be regarded as a *becoming*. It is an unpredictable, open-ended process during which personhood may be achieved, lost, and regained, depending on a person's circumstances.

*affirmation 지지, 확인 **benevolence 자비심

① 아이들을 완전한 존재로 바라보는 관점은 한계가 있다.
② 사람은 공동체의 이상에 도달되어야만 인정받을 수 있다.
③ 사람이 공동체 규범에서 벗어나서 사는 것은 힘든 일이다.
④ 사람다움이란 이상과 규범을 통해 성취되어가는 과정이다.
⑤ 사회의 일원으로 인정받는 생애주기는 공동체마다 다르다.

04 15강 4번

다음 글의 내용과 일치하지 <u>않는</u> 것은?

Some countries grow cash crops. These are crops that are in high demand and can be grown in large quantities in specific areas of the world. For example, sugar needs a hot, damp climate; coffee needs a hot climate, rainfall, and higher mountain elevations. Tea needs to grow on hillsides in rainy areas. Bananas grow well in tropical environments. Because there is a worldwide demand for specific items such as these, the farmers in tropical countries grow as much of these commodities as they can. These cash crops are sold all around the world and bring in a lot of money, but there are risks to specializing in just one commodity for trade. If these farmers grow too much of a particular cash crop, that creates more supply than demand, which drops the price of the commodity. If the climate is bad, and the cash crop does not grow well one year, that hurts the country selling it because that crop may be the only one the country provides in large enough quantities to make a living from.

*cash crop 환금 작물(시장에 내다 팔기 위하여 재배하는 농작물)

① 환금 작물은 많은 수요를 충족하기 위해 특정 지역에서 대량으로 재배된다.
② 환금 작물의 재배를 위해서 각 작물에 맞는 기후와 지형이 필요하다.
③ 특정 지역의 환금 작물 수요를 충족하기 위해 주로 열대지역에서 재배한다.
④ 특정 작물이 과도하게 재배되는 경우 가격의 하락을 초래하기도 한다.
⑤ 기후 탓으로 재배가 어려워진 환금 작물은 국가 경제에도 영향을 끼친다.

05 15강 5번

밑줄 친 in a cultural vacuum이 다음 글에서 의미하는 바로 가장 적절한 것은?

Some might have had the impression that early scientists like Newton and Galileo belonged to a small sect that conjured science out of the blue as a result of mystical investigation. This wasn't so. Their work did not take place <u>in a cultural vacuum</u>:

it was the product of many ancient traditions. One of these was Greek philosophy, which encouraged the belief that the world could be explained by logic, reasoning, and mathematics. Another was agriculture, from which people learned about order and chaos by observing the cycles and rhythms of nature, interrupted periodically by sudden and unpredictable disasters. And then there were religions which encouraged belief in a created world order. The founding assumption of science is that the physical universe is neither random nor absurd; it is not just a meaningless jumble of objects and phenomena randomly placed side by side. Rather, there is a coherent *scheme of things*. This is often expressed by the simple saying that there is order in nature. But scientists have gone beyond this vague notion to formulate a system of well-defined *laws*.

*sect 종파 **conjure (마법으로) 불러내다 ***jumble: 뒤범벅

① without outside influence
② as a result of hard work
③ without cultural prejudice
④ by sudden discovery
⑤ with accumulated knowledge

06 15강 6번

다음 글의 밑줄 친 부분 중, 문맥상 낱말의 쓰임이 적절하지 <u>않은</u> 것은?

In English, many spelling errors could be avoided if we systematically transcribed each sound with a fixed letter. For instance, if we were to ① <u>avoid</u> writing the sound *f* with both the letter "f" and with "ph," life would be much simpler. There is little doubt that we could easily get rid of this and many other ② <u>useless</u> redundancies whose acquisition eats up many years of childhood. In fact, this is the ③ <u>timid</u> direction that American spelling reform took when it simplified the irregular British spellings of "behaviour" or "analyse" into

"behavior" and "analyze." Many more steps could have been taken along the same lines. As expert readers, we cease to be aware of the absurdity of our spelling. Even a letter as simple as "x" is ④ <u>necessary</u>, as it stands for two phonemes *ks* that already have their own spelling. In Tiirkiye, one takes a "taksi." That country, which in the space of one year adopted the Roman alphabet, drastically ⑤ <u>simplified</u> its spelling, and taught three million people how to read, sets a beautiful example of the feasibility of spelling reform.

*redundancy 군더더기 **phoneme 음소 ***feasibility 실현 가능성

07 15강 1번

다음 빈칸에 들어갈 말로 가장 적절한 것은?

What do we want to hear when asking the question why John slammed the door? Probably not that John put more than average energy into his act, giving the door more speed (which resulted in a heavy collision of the door with the doorpost, a loud noise and the lamp rocking back and forth). We normally are not interested in a report of the chain of causes and effects leading up to the slamming. Neither do we expect to hear a report about micro-processes in John's body causing his movements. The why-question asks for reasons — 'He felt offended', for instance. Even when we think in a materialistic frame of mind that the state of being offended can be traced in John's brain, we usually will not be interested in an answer in neurological terms. So, normally, in our day-to-day why-questions about people's actions we expect to _____.

① win the favor of others
② hear about their reasons
③ reveal a causal relationship
④ show our interest in others
⑤ find out the neurological reasonings

08 15강 2번

글의 흐름으로 보아, 주어진 문장이 들어가기에 가장 적절한 곳은?

> What does appear to vary across cultures, however, is the emphasis placed on the different components of love and on different types of relationships.

We can presume that the components of love proposed by Sternberg can be found in all cultures. Intimacy, passion, and commitment are most likely cultural universals. (①) Evidence of this comes from many sources, including cultural anthropology, psychological research, and love poetry from across the world. (②) In collectivist cultures like those found in Asia and Africa, relationships with family may take priority over relationships with lovers and friends. (③) In individualistic cultures, like those of Northern Europe and North America, friendships and romantic relationships compete with family for priority (and often win). (④) Likewise, the concept of duty (similar to Sternberg's concept of commitment) is absolutely central to Chinese Confucianism. (⑤) In contrast, judging by the mountains of romance novels, love songs, and beauty products found in North America, it is the passionate side of love that is prized in this culture.

09 15강 3번

다음 빈칸에 들어갈 말로 가장 적절한 것은?

It could be argued that the 'processual' nature of personhood means that one becomes a person as one 'goes along' in society. Indeed, the African philosopher Ifeanyi Menkiti takes this position. He maintains that children are not fully human. Following Kwame Gyekye, a Ghanaian philosopher, however, I would argue that the fact that personhood must be earned is not a denial of personhood to children. It is an affirmation of the view that *personhood is* _____ attained through interactions with others and one's community. It requires one to affirm ideals and standards thought to be constitutive of the life of a community. These are standards such as generosity, benevolence and respect. A number of sayings in some African societies refer to people who have failed to meet standards expected of a fully human person. These are sayings such as *ga e se motho* (Tswana) or *a ku si muntu* (Nguni), literally meaning 'he or she is not a person'. Because one can fall short of these standards at any stage in the life cycle, personhood could be regarded as a *becoming*. It is an unpredictable, open-ended process during which personhood may be achieved, lost, and regained, depending on a person's circumstances.

*affirmation 지지, 확인 **benevolence 자비심

① an ongoing process
② an unattainable goal
③ a voluntary acquisition
④ a dependent performance
⑤ an unavoidable procedure

10 15강 4번

다음 글의 밑줄 친 부분 중, 어법상 틀린 것은?

Some countries grow cash crops. These are crops that are in high demand and can ① grow in large quantities in specific areas of the world. For example, sugar needs a hot, damp climate; coffee needs a hot climate, rainfall, and higher mountain elevations. Tea needs to grow on hillsides in rainy areas. Bananas grow well in tropical environments. Because there is a worldwide demand for specific items such as ② these, the farmers in tropical countries grow as much of these commodities as they can. These cash crops are sold all around the world and ③ bring in a lot of money, but there are risks to specializing in just one commodity for trade. If these farmers grow too much of a particular cash crop, that creates more supply than demand, ④ which drops the price of the commodity. If the climate is bad, and the cash crop does not grow well one year, that hurts the country selling it because that crop may be the only one the country provides in large ⑤ enough quantities to make a living from.

*cash crop 환금 작물(시장에 내다 팔기 위하여 재배하는 농작물)

11 15강 5번

다음 글의 밑줄 친 부분 중, 문맥상 낱말의 쓰임이 적절하지 않은 것은?

Some might have had the impression that early scientists like Newton and Galileo belonged to a small sect that conjured science out of the blue as a result of mystical investigation. This wasn't so. Their work did not take place in a cultural vacuum: it was the product of many ancient traditions. One of these was Greek philosophy, which ① encouraged the belief that the world could be explained by logic, reasoning, and mathematics. Another was agriculture, from which people learned about order and chaos by observing the cycles and rhythms of nature, ② interrupted periodically by sudden and unpredictable disasters. And then there were religions which encouraged belief in a created world order. The founding assumption of science is that the physical universe is neither random nor absurd; it is not just a ③ meaningless jumble of objects and phenomena randomly placed side by side. Rather, there is a ④ incoherent *scheme of things*. This is often expressed by the simple saying that there is order in nature. But scientists have gone beyond this ⑤ vague notion to formulate a system of well-defined *laws*.

*sect 종파   **conjure (마법으로) 불러내다   ***jumble 뒤범벅

12 15강 6번

다음 글의 주제로 가장 적절한 것은?

In English, many spelling errors could be avoided if we systematically transcribed each sound with a fixed letter. For instance, if we were to avoid writing the sound *f* with both the letter "f" and with "ph," life would be much simpler. There is little doubt that we could easily get rid of this and many other useless redundancies whose acquisition eats up many years of childhood. In fact, this is the timid direction that American spelling reform took when it simplified the irregular British spellings of "behaviour" or "analyse" into "behavior" and "analyze." Many more steps could have been taken along the same lines. As expert readers, we cease to be aware of the absurdity of our spelling. Even a letter as simple as "x" is unnecessary, as it stands for two phonemes *ks* that already have their own spelling. In Tiirkiye, one takes a "taksi." That country, which in the space of one year adopted the Roman alphabet, drastically simplified its spelling, and taught three million people how to read, sets a beautiful example of the feasibility of spelling reform.

*redundancy 군더더기   **phoneme 음소   ***feasibility 실현 가능성

① the reason Americans make spelling errors
② a suggestion for reducing English spelling mistakes
③ the difficulties of matching spelling with pronunciation
④ the effects of teaching methods that reduce errors
⑤ the importance of teaching spelling to children

What do we want to hear when asking the question why John slammed the door? Probably not ① that John put more than average energy into his act, ② gives the door more speed (which resulted in a heavy collision of the door with the doorpost, a loud noise and the lamp rocking back and forth). We normally are not interested in a report of the chain of causes and effects ③ leading up to the slamming. 또한 우리는 John의 움직임을 유발한 그의 몸속의 미세한 과정에 대한 보고를 듣는 것도 기대하지 않는다. The why-question asks for reasons — 'He felt offended', for instance. Even when we think in a materialistic frame of mind ④ that the state of ⑤ offending can be traced in John's brain, we usually will not be interested in an answer in neurological terms. So, normally, in our day-to-day why-questions about people's actions we expect to hear about their reasons.

고난도

13 윗글의 밑줄 친 부분 중, 어법상 틀린 것을 2개 찾아 그 번호를 쓰고 고쳐 쓰시오.

(1) _____ → _____

(2) _____ → _____

14 윗글의 밑줄 친 우리말 의미와 일치하도록 보기 의 단어를 활용하여 조건 에 맞게 문장을 완성하시오.

보기   hear a report / cause / expect / his movements

조건   · neither로 시작하는 강조 문장으로 쓸 것
     · 필요 시 단어를 추가할 것

_____ _____ _____

_____ _____ _____

about micro-processes in John's body _____

_____ .

We can presume that the components of love proposed by Sternberg can be found in all cultures. Intimacy, passion, and commitment are most likely cultural universals. Evidence of this comes from many sources, including cultural anthropology, psychological research, and love poetry from across the world. What does appear to vary across cultures, however, is the emphasis placed on the different components of love and on different types of relationships. In collectivist cultures like those found in Asia and Africa, relationships with family may take priority over relationships with lovers and friends. In individualistic cultures, like those of Northern Europe and North America, friendships and romantic relationships compete with family for priority (and often win). Likewise, the concept of duty (similar to Sternberg's concept of commitment) is absolutely central to Chinese Confucianism. In contrast, judging by the mountains of romance novels, love songs, and beauty products found in North America, 이 문화에서 소중히 여겨지는 것은 바로 사랑의 열정적인 면이다.

15 윗글의 밑줄 친 우리말 의미와 일치하도록 보기 의 단어를 순서대로 배열하여 문장을 완성하시오.

보기   in / is / of love / it / that / prized / this culture / is / the passionate side

_____

_____

16 윗글의 내용을 한 문장으로 요약하려고 한다. 빈칸 (A)와 (B)에 들어갈 알맞은 말을 보기 에서 찾아 쓰시오.

보기   individualistic   passionate
      collectivistic   psychological

The emphasis placed on the different components of love and on different types of relationships varies across cultures; in ____(A)____ cultures, people often place more importance on familial relationships, whereas friendship and love often take priority in ____(B)____ cultures.

(A) _____ (B) _____

15강 3번

It could be argued that the 'processual' nature of personhood (A) <u>meaning</u> that one becomes a person as one 'goes along' in society. Indeed, the African philosopher Ifeanyi Menkiti takes this position. He maintains that children are not fully human. Following Kwame Gyekye, a Ghanaian philosopher, however, 나는 사람다움이 획득되어야 한다는 사실이 아이들에게 사람다움이 있는 것을 부인하는 것은 아니라고 주장하고 싶다. It is an affirmation of the view (B) <u>what</u> *personhood is an ongoing process* attained through interactions with others and one's community. It requires one to affirm ideals and standards thought to be constitutive of the life of a community. These are standards such as generosity, benevolence and respect. A number of sayings in some African societies refer to people who have failed to meet standards (C) <u>expect</u> of a fully human person. These are sayings such as *ga e se motho* (Tswana) or *a ku si muntu* (Nguni), literally meaning 'he or she is not a person'. Because one can fall short of these standards at any stage in the life cycle, personhood could be regarded as a *becoming*. It is an unpredictable, open-ended process during which personhood may be achieved, lost, and regained, depending on a person's circumstances.

*affirmation 지지. 확인 **benevolence 자비심

17 윗글의 밑줄 친 부분을 어법상 알맞은 형태로 고쳐 쓰시오.

(A) meaning → _____

(B) what → _____

(C) expect → _____

고난도

18 윗글의 밑줄 친 우리말과 일치하도록 보기 의 단어를 활용하여 조건 에 맞게 문장을 완성하시오.

보기   fact / I / argue / earn / that / the / personhood / must / would / that

조건   · 〈보기〉의 단어를 반드시 모두 사용할 것
     · 필요 시 어형을 바꿔 쓸 것

_____ is not a denial of personhood to children

Some countries grow cash crops. These are crops that are in ① high demand and can be grown in large quantities in ② specific areas of the world. For example, sugar needs a hot, damp climate; coffee needs a hot climate, rainfall, and higher mountain elevations. Tea needs to grow on hillsides in rainy areas. Bananas grow well in tropical environments. Because there is a worldwide demand for specific items such as these, the farmers in tropical countries grow as much of these commodities as they can. These cash crops are sold all around the world and bring in a lot of money, but there are ③ risks to specializing in just one commodity for trade. If these farmers grow too much of a particular cash crop, that creates more supply than demand, which ④ rises the price of the commodity. If the climate is bad, and the cash crop does not grow well one year, that hurts the country selling it because that crop may be the only one the country provides in large enough ⑤ quantities to make a living from.

*cash crop 환금 작물(시장에 내다 팔기 위하여 재배하는 농작물)

19 윗글의 밑줄 친 부분 중 문맥상 어색한 것을 1개 찾아 그 번호를 쓰고 고쳐 쓰시오.

_____ → _____

20 윗글에서 다음 질문에 대한 답을 찾아 우리말로 쓰시오. (20자 내외)

Q: Why do the farmers in tropical countries grow specific commodities such as sugar, coffee, tea, and bananas?

A: _____

_____

Some might have had the impression that early scientists like Newton and Galileo belonged to a small sect ① that conjured science out of the blue as a result of mystical investigation. This wasn't so. Their work did not take place in a cultural vacuum: it was the product of many ancient traditions. One of (A) these was Greek philosophy, ② which encouraged the belief that the world could be explained by logic, reasoning, and mathematics. Another was agriculture, ③ which people learned about order and chaos by observing the cycles and rhythms of nature, ④ interrupts periodically by sudden and unpredictable disasters. And then there were religions which encouraged belief in a created world order. The founding assumption of science is that the physical universe is neither random ⑤ nor absurd; (B) it is not just a meaningless jumble of objects and phenomena randomly placed side by side. Rather, there is a coherent *scheme of things*. This is often expressed by the simple saying that there is order in nature. But scientists have gone beyond this vague notion to formulate a system of well-defined *laws*.

*sect 종파 **conjure (마법으로) 불러내다 ***jumble 뒤범벅

*penetrate 뚫고

21 윗글의 밑줄 친 부분 중, 어법상 틀린 것을 2개 찾아 그 번호를 쓰고 고쳐 쓰시오.

(1) _____ → _____

(2) _____ → _____

22 윗글의 밑줄 친 (A), (B)가 각각 가리키는 것을 본문에서 찾아 쓰시오. (단, (A)는 6단어, (B)는 3단어로 쓸 것)

(A) _____

(B) _____

In English, many spelling errors could be avoided if we systematically transcribed each sound with a fixed letter. For instance, if we were to avoid writing the sound *f* with both the letter "f" and with "ph," life would be much simpler. 우리가 이것과 습득하는 데 수년의 유년 시절을 잡아먹는 여타 많은 불필요한 군더더기를 쉽게 없앨 수 있다는 것에는 거의 의심의 여지가 없다. In fact, this is the timid direction that American spelling reform took when it simplified the _____ British spellings of "behaviour" or "analyse" into "behavior" and "analyze." Many more steps could have been taken along the same lines. As expert readers, we cease to be aware of the absurdity of our spelling. Even a letter as simple as "x" is unnecessary, as it stands for two phonemes *ks* that already have their own spelling. In Tiirkiye, one takes a "taksi." That country, which in the space of one year adopted the Roman alphabet, drastically simplified its spelling, and taught three million people how to read, sets a beautiful example of the feasibility of spelling reform.

*redundancy 군더더기   **phoneme 음소   ***feasibility 실현 가능성

고난도

23 윗글의 밑줄 친 우리말 의미와 일치하도록 보기 의 단어를 활용하여 문장을 완성하시오. (단, 필요 시 어형을 바꿔 쓸 것)

보기   who / childhood / eats up / many other
/ redundancies / acquisition /
many years of / useless

There is little doubt that we could easily get rid of

this and _____

_____

_____

24 윗글의 빈칸에 들어갈 단어를 영영 뜻풀이를 참고하여 쓰시오. (단, 주어진 글자로 시작할 것)

not normal or usual; not following the usual rule or general practice

i_____

261

❶ When we are in groups, we tend to feel that we, personally, aren't as responsible as we would be if we were acting on our own. ❷ So the decisions that the group makes can easily become extreme. ❸ Occasionally, groups reach riskier decisions — they decide to take actions which are more challenging or unsafe than they should be. ❹ Sometimes, though, they make choices that are too cautious. ❺ It's known as group polarization: a tendency towards extremes. ❻ A lot depends on how the discussions in the group develop. ❼ If one person is advocating a risky strategy early on, others may begin to think of even more challenging examples, and that leads the discussion towards reaching a riskier decision. ❽ But if someone advocates more cautious approaches at an early stage, this too can influence the direction of the discussion, resulting in a more cautious decision than the group members might have made individually.

❶ 우리는 집단 속에 있을 때, 혼자서 행동하고 있는 경우에 책임이 있을 만큼 개인적으로 책임이 있지는 않다고 생각하는 경향이 있다. ❷ 그래서 집단이 내리는 결정은 쉽게 극단적이 될 수 있다. ❸ 이따금 집단은 더 위험한 결정에 도달하는데, 즉 그것(집단)은 응당 그러해야 하는 것보다 더 도전적이거나 안전하지 않은 행동을 취하기로 결정한다. ❹ 하지만, 때로 그것(집단)은 너무 신중한 선택을 한다. ❺ 그것은 집단 양극화라고 알려져 있는데, 극단적인 행위로 향하는 경향이다. ❻ 많은 것이 집단 내의 논의가 어떻게 전개 되느냐에 좌우된다. ❼ 어느 한 사람이 초기에 위험한 전략을 옹호하고 있다면, 다른 사람들은 훨씬 더 도전적인 예를 생각하기 시작할 수도 있고, 그것은 논의를 더 위험한 결정에 도달하는 방향으로 이끈다. ❽ 그러나 누군가가 초기 단계에서 더 신중한 접근법을 옹호한다면, 이것도 또한 논의의 방향에 영향을 미칠 수 있으며, 결국 집단 구성원이 개별적으로 내렸을지도 모르는 것보다 더 신중한 결정에 이르게 한다.

Word List

□ **tend to** *do* ~하는 경향이 있다　□ **responsible** 책임이 있는, 책임을 져야 할　□ **on one's own** 혼자서, 단독으로
□ **extreme** 극단적인; 극단적인 행위[수단/조체]　□ **occasionally** 이따금　□ **risky** 위험한　□ **challenging** 도전적인　□ **cautious** 신중한
□ **polarization** 양극화　□ **tendency** 경향　□ **advocate** 옹호하다, 지지하다　□ **strategy** 전략
□ **result in** 결국 ~에 이르게 하다, ~을 야기[초래]하다　□ **individually** 개별적으로

• Word Test

1　polarization　_____

2　result in　_____

3　cautious　_____

4　challenging　_____

5　individually　_____

6　tend to *do*　_____

7　extreme　_____

8　위험한　_____

9　옹호하다, 지지하다　_____

10　책임이 있는, 책임을 져야 할　_____

11　이따금　_____

12　경향　_____

13　혼자서, 단독으로　_____

14　전략　_____

네모 안에서 옳은 어법·어휘를 고르시오.

When we are in groups, we tend to feel that we, personally, aren't as responsible as we would be if we were acting on our own. So the decisions that the group makes can easily become ❶ extreme / moderate . Occasionally, groups reach riskier decisions — they decide to take actions which are more challenging or unsafe than they should be. Sometimes, ❷ though / so , they make choices that are too cautious. It's known as group polarization: a tendency ❸ forward / towards extremes. A lot depends on how the discussions in the group develop. If one person is advocating a risky strategy early on, others may begin to think of even more challenging examples, and ❹ that / what leads the discussion towards reaching a riskier decision. But if someone advocates more cautious approaches at an early stage, this too can influence the direction of the discussion, resulting in a more cautious decision than the group members might have made ❺ collectively / individually .

● 유형 2 괄호 안의 동사를 알맞은 형태로 쓰시오.

When we are in groups, we tend to feel that we, personally, aren't as responsible as we would be if we were acting on our own. So the decisions that the group ❶ _____ (make) can easily become extreme. Occasionally, groups reach riskier decisions — they decide to take actions which are more challenging or unsafe than they should be. Sometimes, though, they make choices that ❷ _____ (be) too cautious. It's known as group polarization: a tendency towards extremes. A lot ❸ _____ (depend) on how the discussions in the group develop. If one person is advocating a risky strategy early on, others may begin to think of even more challenging examples, and that ❹ _____ (lead) the discussion towards reaching a riskier decision. But if someone advocates more cautious approaches at an early stage, this too can influence the direction of the discussion, resulting in a more cautious decision than the group members might ❺ _____ (make) individually.

● 유형 3 우리말에 맞게 빈칸에 알맞은 말을 쓰시오.

When we are in groups, we ❶ _____ _____ (~하는 경향이 있다) feel that we, personally, aren't as responsible as we would be if we were acting on our own. So the decisions that the group makes can easily become extreme. Occasionally, groups reach riskier decisions — they ❷ _____ _____ _____ _____ (행동들을 취하기로 결정하다) which are more challenging or unsafe than they should be. Sometimes, though, they make choices that are too cautious. It's known as group polarization: a tendency towards extremes. A lot depends on how the discussions in the group develop. If one person is advocating a risky strategy ❸ _____ _____ (초기에), others may begin to think of even more challenging examples, and that leads the discussion towards reaching a riskier decision. But if someone advocates more cautious approaches ❹ _____ _____ _____ _____ (초기 단계에서), this too can influence the direction of the discussion, resulting in a more cautious decision than the group members might have made individually.

❶ Advertising in the United States is a relatively large and stable marketplace with a dollar volume of activity closely tied to the overall health of the economy. ❷ The same is true of other mature industrialized nations, especially those of Western Europe. ❸ One significant difference, however, is the way commercial media evolved. ❹ In the United States, radio and television systems began as commercial ventures; in many other countries media were largely or completely government supported for years. ❺ Different models of commercial support are still evolving and the precise configurations vary by country. ❻ This evolution does not mean, however, that governments are uninvolved in steering the development of media. ❼ As Joseph Straubhaar observes, television systems are often "stubbornly national," which means advertisers must tailor "global" media plans to the regulatory policies and cultural expectations of individual countries.

*configuration 형태, 구조   **stubbornly 완강하게, 고집스럽게

❶ 미국에서 광고는 활동의 달러 총액이 경제의 전반적인 건전성과 밀접하게 관련이 있는 비교적 크고 안정적인 시장이다. ❷ 다른 성숙한 산업 국가, 특히 서유럽 국가들에도 마찬가지이다. ❸ 그러나 한 가지 중요한 차이점은 상업 매체가 발전한 방식이다. ❹ 미국에서 라디오와 텔레비전 방송 시스템은 상업적인 사업으로 시작되었는데, 많은 다른 국가에서는 매체가 오랫동안 주로 또는 전적으로 정부 지원형이었다. ❺ 상업적 지원의 여러 가지 모형이 여전히 발전 중이며 정확한 형태는 국가마다 다르다. ❻ 그러나 이러한 발전이 정부가 매체의 전개 방향을 잡아 가는 데 관여하지 않는다는 것을 의미하는 것은 아니다. ❼ Joseph Straubhaar가 평하는 것처럼, 텔레비전 방송 시스템은 흔히 '완강하게 국가적'인데, 이것은 광고주가 '세계적인' 매체 계획을 개별 국가의 규제 정책과 문화 기대에 맞춰야 한다는 것을 의미한다.

Word List

□ **relatively** 비교적, 상대적으로   □ **stable** 안정적인   □ **marketplace** 시장   □ **overall** 전반적인   □ **mature** 성숙한, 발달한
□ **industrialized** 산업화된   □ **significant** 중요한, 상당한   □ **commercial** 상업의   □ **evolve** 발전하다, 진화하다
□ **venture** 모험적 사업   □ **precise** 정확한, 정밀한   □ **steer** (일정한 방향으로) 향하게 하다, 이끌다   □ **tailor** 맞추다, 적응시키다
□ **regulatory** 규제의

• Word Test

1	steer		8	비교적, 상대적으로
2	evolve		9	모험적 사업
3	industrialized		10	상업의
4	tailor		11	안정적인
5	mature		12	규제의
6	marketplace		13	정확한, 정밀한
7	overall		14	중요한, 상당한

Advertising in the United States is a relatively large and stable marketplace with a dollar volume of activity closely ❶ tied / tying to the overall health of the economy. The same is true of other mature industrialized nations, especially ❷ these / those of Western Europe. One significant difference, however, is the way commercial media evolved. In the United States, radio and television systems began as commercial ventures; in many other countries media were largely or completely government supported for years. Different models of commercial support are still evolving and the ❸ inexact / precise configurations vary by country. This evolution does not mean, however, that governments are ❹ involved / uninvolved in steering the development of media. As Joseph Straubhaar observes, television systems are often "stubbornly national," which means advertisers must tailor "global" media plans to the regulatory policies and cultural ❺ exceptions / expectations of individual countries.

*configuration 형태, 구조   **stubbornly 완강하게, 고집스럽게

Advertising in the United States ❶ _____ (be) a relatively large and stable marketplace with a dollar volume of activity closely tied to the overall health of the economy. The same is true of other mature industrialized nations, especially those of Western Europe. One significant difference, however, is the way commercial media ❷ _____ (evolve). In the United States, radio and television systems began as commercial ventures; in many other countries media ❸ _____ (be) largely or completely government supported for years. Different models of commercial support ❹ _____ (be) still evolving and the precise configurations vary by country. This evolution does not mean, however, that governments are uninvolved in steering the development of media. As Joseph Straubhaar observes, television systems are often "stubbornly national," which ❺ _____ (mean) advertisers must tailor "global" media plans to the regulatory policies and cultural expectations of individual countries.

*configuration 형태, 구조   **stubbornly 완강하게, 고집스럽게

Advertising in the United States is a relatively large and stable marketplace with a dollar volume of activity ❶ _____ _____ _____ (~와 밀접하게 관련이 있는) the overall health of the economy. ❷ _____ _____ _____ _____ _____ (~에도 마찬가지이다) other mature industrialized nations, especially those of Western Europe. One significant difference, however, is the way commercial media evolved. In the United States, radio and television systems began as commercial ventures; in many other countries media were largely or completely ❸ _____ _____ (정부 지원형) for years. Different models of commercial support are still evolving and the precise configurations vary by country. This evolution does not mean, however, that governments are uninvolved ❹ _____ _____ _____ _____ (전개 방향을 잡아 가는 데) of media. As Joseph Straubhaar observes, television systems are often "stubbornly national," which means advertisers must tailor "global" media plans to the regulatory policies and cultural expectations of individual countries.

*configuration 형태, 구조   **stubbornly 완강하게, 고집스럽게

❶ Some people think that facts are the same as *events*, which they regard as the "objective," "hard core" elements of this universe. ❷ The main reason for thinking this is that events seem the best candidates to offer us a rock-solid foundation for our facts. ❸ True, events do happen or do not happen; you can neglect them but not deny them. ❹ So by replacing facts with events, we might think we have found the strong objective foundation that we strive for. ❺ However, facts and events are concepts very different from each other. ❻ Unlike facts, events are dated, tied to space and time, whereas facts are detached from space and time. ❼ It is even considered a fact that certain events did not occur; ❽ it is a fact, for instance, that Darwin did not have a copy of Mendel's 1866 article in his collection. ❾ Apparently, a fact is not the same as an event; the best we can say is that a fact is a description of an event, but not the event itself.

❶ 어떤 사람들은 사실이 '사건'과 같다고 생각하는데, 그들은 사건을 이 우주의 '객관적이고' '핵심적인' 요소로 간주한다. ❷ 이렇게 생각하는 주된 이유는 사건이 우리에게 우리가 가진 사실에 대한 확고부동한 토대를 제공하는 가장 좋은 후보처럼 보이기 때문이다. ❸ 사건은 실제로 일어나거나 혹은 일어나지 않는 것이 사실이므로, 여러분은 그것을 무시할 수는 있지만 그것을 부인할 수는 없다. ❹ 그래서 사실을 사건으로 대체함으로써, 우리는 우리가 얻으려고 노력하는 강력한 객관적인 토대를 찾았다고 생각할 수도 있다. ❺ 그러나 사실과 사건은 서로 매우 다른 개념이다. ❻ 사실과 달리, 사건은 날짜가 있어 시공간에 묶여 있는 반면에, 사실은 시공간에서 분리되어 있다. ❼ 심지어 특정한 사건이 일어나지 않았다는 것조차 사실로 여겨지는데, ❽ 예를 들어, Darwin이 장서에 Mendel의 1866년 논문 한 편을 가지고 있지 않았던 것은 사실이다. ❾ 분명히, 사실은 사건과 같지 않은데, 우리가 말할 수 있는 최선의 것은 사실은 사건에 관한 기술이지만, 사건 그 자체는 아니라는 것이다.

Word List

□ regard ~ as ... ~을 …으로 간주하다   □ objective 객관적인, 실증적인   □ hard core 핵심적인   □ element 요소, 요인
□ candidate 후보(자)   □ rock-solid 확고부동한, 굳건한   □ foundation 토대, 기초   □ neglect 무시하다   □ replace 대체하다
□ strive for ~을 얻으려고 노력하다   □ be detached from ~에서 분리되다   □ article 논문, 기사   □ apparently 분명히, 명백히
□ description 기술, 서술

Word Test

1	be detached from		8	기술, 서술
2	strive for		9	대체하다
3	article		10	토대, 기초
4	regard ~ as ...		11	요소, 요인
5	hard core		12	객관적인, 실증적인
6	rock-solid		13	분명히, 명백히
7	candidate		14	무시하다

Some people think that facts are the same as *events*, which they regard as the "objective," "hard core" elements of this universe. The main reason for thinking this is ❶ that / which events seem the best candidates to offer us a rock-solid foundation for our facts. True, events do happen or do not happen; you can neglect them ❷ and / but not deny them. So by replacing facts with events, we might think we have found the strong ❸ objective / subjective foundation that we strive for. However, facts and events are concepts very different from each other. Unlike facts, events are dated, tied to space and time, ❹ likewise / whereas facts are detached from space and time. It is even considered a fact that certain events did not occur; it is a fact, for instance, that Darwin did not have a copy of Mendel's 1866 article in his collection. ❺ Apparently / Relatively , a fact is not the same as an event; the best we can say is that a fact is a description of an event, but not the event itself.

Some people think that facts are the same as *events*, which they regard as the "objective," "hard core" elements of this universe. The main reason for thinking this ❶ _____ (be) that events seem the best candidates to offer us a rock-solid foundation for our facts. True, events do happen or do not happen; you can neglect them but not ❷ _____ (deny) them. So by replacing facts with events, we might think we ❸ _____ (find) the strong objective foundation that we strive for. However, facts and events are concepts very different from each other. Unlike facts, events are dated, tied to space and time, whereas facts are detached from space and time. It is even ❹ _____ (consider) a fact that certain events did not occur; it is a fact, for instance, that Darwin did not have a copy of Mendel's 1866 article in his collection. Apparently, a fact is not the same as an event; the best we can say is that a fact is a description of an event, but not the event itself.

Some people think that facts are the same as *events*, which they regard as the "objective," "hard core" elements of this universe. The main reason for thinking this is that events seem the best candidates to offer us a rock-solid foundation for our facts. True, events do happen or do not happen; you can neglect them but not deny them. So ❶ _____ _____ _____ _____ _____ (사실들을 사건들로 대체함으로써), we might think we have found the strong objective foundation that we ❷ _____ _____ (~을 얻으려고 노력하다). However, facts and events are concepts very different from each other. Unlike facts, events are dated, tied to space and time, whereas facts ❸ _____ _____ _____ (~에서 분리되어 있다) space and time. It is even considered a fact that certain events did not occur; it is a fact, for instance, that Darwin did not have a copy of Mendel's 1866 article in his collection. Apparently, a fact is not the same as an event; ❹ _____ _____ _____ _____ _____ (우리가 말할 수 있는 최선의 것) is that a fact is a description of an event, but not the event itself.

❶ The extent to which decision making is shared with subordinates or concentrated at the top of the hierarchy differs across organizations. ❷ Thus, organizations can vary from strongly centralized decision-making practices to highly participatory decision-making practices. ❸ In participatory decision making, subordinates have much more input into how decisions are made. ❹ Research shows that greater participation in decision making improves employees' satisfaction with the decisions, but does not necessarily translate into better group performance. ❺ Therefore, research has investigated when participatory decision making is most useful, and when it is less important. ❻ When the workers are highly educated, intelligent, and have considerable expertise in their areas, participatory decision making is more effective. ❼ Additionally, when the task at hand is highly complex and knowledge about local conditions is important to the decision, participatory decision making is important. ❽ Finally, in times of crisis, when the decisions have very strong impact, participatory decision making is useful.

*subordinate 하급자　**hierarchy 위계, 계층

❶ 의사 결정이 하급자와 공유되거나 위계의 정상부에 집중되는 정도는 조직마다 다르다. ❷ 따라서 조직은 강력한 중앙 집권형 의사 결정 관행에서 고도의 참여형 의사 결정 관행에 이르기까지 다양할 수 있다. ❸ 참여형 의사 결정에서, 하급자는 어떻게 결정이 내려지는가에 관해 훨씬 더 많은 의견을 낸다. ❹ 연구에 따르면, 의사 결정에 더 많이 참여하는 것은 그 결정에 대한 직원들의 만족도를 향상하지만, 반드시 더 나은 집단 성과로 이어지는 것은 아니다. ❺ 그러므로 연구는 참여형 의사 결정이 가장 유용한 때와 그것이 덜 중요한 때를 조사했다. ❻ 근로자가 고학력이고, 지적이며, 자신의 분야에서 상당한 전문 지식을 가지고 있을 때, 참여형 의사 결정이 더 효과적이다. ❼ 게다가, 당면한 과제가 매우 복잡하고 현지 상황에 관한 지식이 의사 결정에 중요할 때, 참여형 의사 결정이 중요하다. ❽ 마지막으로, 결정이 매우 강력한 영향을 미치는 위기 시기에, 참여형 의사 결정이 유용하다.

Word List

□ extent 정도, 범위　□ concentrate 집중시키다　□ organization 조직　□ thus 따라서　□ centralized 중앙 집권화된
□ practice 관행　□ participatory 참여의　□ input 의견, 조언　□ necessarily 반드시, 필연적으로
□ translate into ~으로 이어지다, (결과가) ~이 되다　□ performance 성과　□ investigate 조사하다　□ considerable 상당한
□ expertise 전문 지식, 전문 기술　□ at hand 당면한　□ impact 영향

• Word Test

1	considerable	_____	9	조직	_____
2	concentrate	_____	10	영향	_____
3	centralized	_____	11	따라서	_____
4	translate into	_____	12	조사하다	_____
5	input	_____	13	참여의	_____
6	practice	_____	14	반드시, 필연적으로	_____
7	at hand	_____	15	정도, 범위	_____
8	expertise	_____	16	성과	_____

The extent to which decision making is shared with subordinates or concentrated at the top of the hierarchy differs across organizations. Thus, organizations can vary from strongly ❶ centralized/centralizing decision-making practices to highly participatory decision-making practices. In participatory decision making, subordinates have much ❷ more / less input into how decisions are made. Research shows that greater participation in decision making improves employees' ❸ satisfaction/dissatisfaction with the decisions, but does not necessarily translate into better group performance. ❹ However/Therefore , research has investigated when participatory decision making is most useful, and when it is less important. When the workers are highly educated, intelligent, and have considerable expertise in their areas, participatory decision making is more ❺ effective/evitable . Additionally, when the task at hand is highly complex and knowledge about local conditions is important to the decision, participatory decision making is important. Finally, in times of crisis, when the decisions have very strong impact, participatory decision making is useful.

*subordinate 하급자 **hierarchy 위계, 계층

The extent to which decision making ❶ _____ (share) with subordinates or concentrated at the top of the hierarchy differs across organizations. Thus, organizations can vary from strongly centralized decision-making practices to highly participatory decision-making practices. In participatory decision making, subordinates have much more input into how decisions ❷ _____ (make). Research shows that greater participation in decision making ❸ _____ (improve) employees' satisfaction with the decisions, but does not necessarily translate into better group performance. Therefore, research ❹ _____ (investigate) when participatory decision making is most useful, and when it is less important. When the workers are highly educated, intelligent, and have considerable expertise in their areas, participatory decision making is more effective. Additionally, when the task at hand is highly complex and knowledge about local conditions ❺ _____ (be) important to the decision, participatory decision making is important. Finally, in times of crisis, when the decisions have very strong impact, participatory decision making is useful.

*subordinate 하급자 **hierarchy 위계, 계층

The extent to which decision making is shared with subordinates or concentrated at the top of the hierarchy ❶ _____ _____ _____ (조직들마다 다르다). Thus, organizations can vary from strongly centralized decision-making practices to highly participatory decision-making practices. In participatory decision making, subordinates have much more input into how decisions are made. Research shows that greater participation in decision making improves employees' satisfaction with the decisions, but does not ❷ _____ _____ _____ (반드시 ~로 이어지다) better group performance. Therefore, research has investigated when participatory decision making is most useful, and when it is less important. When the workers are highly educated, intelligent, and have considerable expertise in their areas, participatory decision making is more effective. Additionally, when ❸ _____ _____ _____ (당면한 과제) is highly complex and knowledge about local conditions is important to the decision, participatory decision making is important. Finally, ❹ _____ _____ _____ _____ (위기 시기에), when the decisions have very strong impact, participatory decision making is useful.

*subordinate 하급자 **hierarchy 위계, 계층

❶ Insects attract collectors' attention because they are extremely diverse and often bear spectacular colors. ❷ To biologists, however, bright coloration has been a constantly renewed puzzle because it makes an insect a highly visible prey to prospective predators. ❸ Charles Darwin understood that bright colors or exaggerated forms could evolve via sexual selection, the process by which individuals compete for access to mates and fertilization opportunities. ❹ However, he felt sexual selection could not account for the striking color pattern of nonreproductive larvae in, for example, *Pseudosphinx* hawk moth caterpillars. ❺ In a reply to Darwin about this puzzle, Alfred R. Wallace proposed that bright colors could advertise the distastefulness of the caterpillars to experienced predators. ❻ Indeed, prey that are not edible to predators are predicted to gain by exhibiting very recognizable colors; experienced predators can then correctly identify and subsequently avoid attacking such prey. ❼ E. B. Poulton later developed this idea, expanded it to other warning signals (i.e., sounds or smells), and coined the term aposematism to describe this phenomenon (from the Greek "away" and "sign").

*larva 유충, 애벌레 (*pl.* larvae)
**Pseudosphinx hawk moth Pseudosphinx 속(屬) 박각시나방　***caterpillar 애벌레

❶ 곤충은 매우 다양하고 흔히 화려한 색깔을 띠기 때문에 수집가의 관심을 끈다. ❷ 그러나 생물학자에게 강렬한 천연색은 끊임없이 다시 등장하는 난제가 되어 왔는데, 그것 때문에 곤충은 (자신의) 포식자가 될 가능성이 있는 동물의 눈에 아주 잘 뜨이는 먹이가 되기 때문이다. ❸ Charles Darwin은 강렬한 색이나 과장된 형태가 성 선택, 즉 개체들이 짝에 접근하여 수정할 기회를 얻으려고 경쟁하는 과정을 통해 진화할 수 있다고 여겼다. ❹ 그러나 그는 성 선택이 가령 'Pseudosphinx' 속(屬) 박각시나방 애벌레에 속하는 비생식 유충의 눈에 뜨이는 색깔 패턴을 설명할 수 없다고 생각했다. ❺ 이 난제에 대해 Darwin에게 보낸 답장에서 Alfred R. Wallace는 강렬한 색깔이 경험 많은 포식자에게 애벌레의 맛이 고약하다는 것을 짐짓 드러낼 수 있다는 의견을 제시했다. ❻ 정말로, 포식자가 먹을 수 없는 먹이는 매우 잘 알아볼 수 있는 색깔을 보임으로써 이득을 얻을 것으로 예측되는데, 그러면 경험 많은 포식자는 그런 먹이를 정확히 식별한 후에 공격하지 않을 수 있다. ❼ E. B. Poulton은 나중에 이 생각을 발전시켜 그것을 다른 경고 신호(즉, 소리나 냄새)로 확장했고, 이 현상을 기술하기 위해(그리스어 '떨어져'와 '신호'라는 말로부터) aposematism(경계색)이라는 용어를 만들어 냈다.

Word List

□ **attract** (주목 등을) 끌다　□ **diverse** 다양한　□ **bear** (눈에 보이게) 띠다[지니다]　□ **spectacular** 화려한
□ **coloration** (생물의) 천연색, 채색　□ **renewed** 다시 등장하는, (관심·강도가) 새로워진　□ **prey** 먹이
□ **prospective** (~이 될) 가능성이 있는, 장래의　□ **predator** 포식자　□ **exaggerated** 과장된　□ **fertilization** 수정, 수태, 비옥화
□ **account for** ~을 설명하다　□ **striking** 눈에 뜨이는, 두드러지는　□ **nonreproductive** 비생식의　□ **advertise** 짐짓 드러내다, 광고하다
□ **distastefulness** 맛이 고약함　□ **edible** 먹을 수 있는　□ **identify** 식별하다　□ **subsequently** 그 후, 뒤에　□ **expand** 확장하다
□ **coin** (새로운 말을) 만들어 내다　□ **term** 용어

1	coloration	12	짐짓 드러내다, 광고하다
2	attract	13	화려한
3	subsequently	14	먹이
4	prospective	15	다시 등장하는, 새로워진
5	diverse	16	과장된
6	bear	17	용어
7	fertilization	18	먹을 수 있는
8	account for	19	확장하다
9	coin	20	포식자
10	distastefulness	21	식별하다
11	nonreproductive	22	눈에 뜨이는, 두드러지는

• 유형 **1** 네모 안에서 옳은 어법·어휘를 고르시오.

Insects attract collectors' attention because they are extremely diverse and often bear spectacular colors. To biologists, however, bright coloration has been a ❶ constant/constantly renewed puzzle because it makes an insect a highly visible prey to prospective predators. Charles Darwin understood that bright colors or exaggerated forms could evolve via sexual selection, the process ❷ by/for which individuals compete for access to mates and fertilization opportunities. However, he felt sexual selection could not account for the striking color pattern of nonreproductive larvae in, ❸ for example/in other words, Pseudosphinx hawk moth caterpillars. In a reply to Darwin about this puzzle, Alfred R. Wallace proposed that bright colors could advertise the distastefulness of the caterpillars to ❹ experienced/inexperienced predators. Indeed, prey that are not edible to predators are predicted to gain by exhibiting very recognizable colors; experienced predators can then correctly identify and ❺ subsequently/substantially avoid attacking such prey. E. B. Poulton later developed this idea, expanded it to other warning signals (i.e., sounds or smells), and coined the term aposematism to describe this phenomenon (from the Greek "away" and "sign").

*larva 유충, 애벌레 (*pl.* larvae)   **Pseudosphinx hawk moth Pseudosphinx 속(屬) 박각시나방   ***caterpillar 애벌레

Insects attract collectors' attention because they are extremely diverse and often bear spectacular colors. To biologists, however, bright coloration ❶ _____ (be) a constantly renewed puzzle because it makes an insect a highly visible prey to prospective predators. Charles Darwin understood that bright colors or exaggerated forms could evolve via sexual selection, the process by which individuals compete for access to mates and fertilization opportunities. However, he felt sexual selection could not account for the striking color pattern of nonreproductive larvae in, for example, *Pseudosphinx* hawk moth caterpillars. In a reply to Darwin about this puzzle, Alfred R. Wallace proposed that bright colors could advertise the distastefulness of the caterpillars to experienced predators. Indeed, prey that ❷ _____ (be) not edible to predators are predicted to gain by exhibiting very recognizable colors; experienced predators can then correctly identify and subsequently avoid ❸ _____ (attack) such prey. E. B. Poulton later developed this idea, ❹ _____ (expand) it to other warning signals (i.e., sounds or smells), and ❺ _____ (coin) the term aposematism to describe this phenomenon (from the Greek "away" and "sign").

*larva 유충, 애벌레 (*pl.* larvae) **Pseudosphinx hawk moth Pseudosphinx 속(屬) 박각시나방 ***caterpillar 애벌레

Insects attract collectors' attention because they are extremely diverse and often bear spectacular colors. To biologists, however, bright coloration has been a constantly renewed puzzle because it makes an insect a highly visible prey to prospective predators. Charles Darwin understood that bright colors or exaggerated forms could ❶ _____ _____ (~을 통해 진화하다) sexual selection, the process by which individuals compete for access to mates and fertilization opportunities. However, he felt sexual selection could not ❷ _____ _____ (~을 설명하다) the striking color pattern of nonreproductive larvae in, for example, *Pseudosphinx* hawk moth caterpillars. ❸ _____ _____ _____ _____ (~에게 보낸 답장에서) Darwin about this puzzle, Alfred R. Wallace proposed that bright colors could advertise the distastefulness of the caterpillars to experienced predators. Indeed, prey that are not edible to predators ❹ _____ _____ _____ _____ (이득을 얻을 것으로 예측되다) by exhibiting very recognizable colors; experienced predators can then correctly identify and subsequently avoid attacking such prey. E. B. Poulton later developed this idea, expanded it to other warning signals (i.e., sounds or smells), and coined the term aposematism to describe this phenomenon (from the Greek "away" and "sign").

*larva 유충, 애벌레 (*pl.* larvae) **Pseudosphinx hawk moth Pseudosphinx 속(屬) 박각시나방 ***caterpillar 애벌레

❶ In ancient and medieval times considerable respect was accorded to language by those working in the scientific field. ❷ According to the ancient metaphysical *Weltanschauung*, it was believed that the structure of reality and of thought were so closely allied that they were interchangeable. ❸ A *logical* statement — not only a matter of thinking but also of linguistics — was automatically a *true* statement of reality. ❹ Since such a statement happened to be true, it did not need to be subjected to experimental testing. ❺ However, in modern times it was realized for the first time that trust in the accord between reality and thinking was based on a grossly exaggerated notion of the scope of human reason. ❻ In order to discover whether a logical statement (i.e. the logical language) was really true (i.e. agreed with reality), the statement should be tested against empirical reality in an experiment. ❼ The emphasis on the physical experiment is characteristic of modern science. ❽ Later again it was realized that even this approach overrated the importance of thinking: ❾ from the outset research should be directed by experiments, although that experimental action — like any action — required the support of logical thought.

*Weltanschauung 세계관   **empirical 경험적인

❶ 고대와 중세 시대에는 과학 분야에 종사하는 사람들에 의해 언어가 상당한 존중을 받았다. ❷ 고대의 형이상학적 '세계관'에 따르면, 현실의 구조와 사고의 구조가 매우 밀접하게 연관되어 있어 그것들은 상호 대체가 가능하다고 여겨졌다. ❸ '논리적' 진술은, 사고의 문제일 뿐만 아니라 언어학의 문제이기도 하여, 자동적으로 현실에 대한 '사실적' 진술이었다. ❹ 그러한 진술이 마침 사실이었기 때문에, 그것은 실험에 의한 검증을 받을 필요가 없었다. ❺ 하지만 현대에는 현실과 사고 사이의 일치에 대한 믿음이 인간 이성의 범위에 대한 크게 과장된 개념에 기초하고 있다는 것이 처음으로 인식되었다. ❻ 논리적 진술(즉, 논리적 언어)이 정말 사실인지(즉, 현실과 일치하는지) 알아내기 위해, 그 진술은 실험에서 경험적 현실과 비교하여 검증되어야 했다. ❼ 물리적 실험을 강조하는 것이 현대 과학의 특징이다. ❽ 이후 다시 이 접근법조차 사고의 중요성을 과대평가했다는 것이 인식되었다. ❾ 즉, 그 실험 행동은 어떤 행동과 마찬가지로 논리적 사고의 뒷받침이 필요했지만, 연구는 처음부터 실험이 이끌어야 했다.

Word List	
□ medieval 중세의 □ considerable 상당한 □ accord 일치, 조화; 주다 □ metaphysical 형이상학적인 □ allied 연관된, 동맹한	
□ interchangeable 교체할 수 있는 □ logical 논리적인 □ statement 진술, 말 □ linguistics 언어학	
□ be subjected to ~을 받다 □ grossly 크게, 심하게 □ exaggerated 과장된 □ notion 개념 □ scope 범위 □ reason 이성	
□ emphasis 강조 □ overrate 과대평가하다 □ outset 처음, 시작	

• Word Test

1	metaphysical		10	중세의	
2	grossly		11	언어학	
3	allied		12	범위	
4	outset		13	논리적인	
5	accord		14	상당한	
6	be subjected to		15	진술, 말	
7	overrate		16	과장된	
8	notion		17	이성	
9	interchangeable		18	강조	

In ancient and medieval times considerable respect was accorded to language by those working in the scientific field. According to the ancient metaphysical *Weltanschauung*, it was believed that the structure of reality and of thought were ❶ [so / very] closely allied that they were interchangeable. A *logical* statement — not only a matter of thinking ❷ [and / but] also of linguistics — was automatically a *true* statement of reality. Since such a statement happened to be true, it did not need to be subjected to experimental testing. However, in modern times it was realized for the first time that trust in the accord between reality and thinking was based on a grossly exaggerated notion of the scope of human reason. In order to discover ❸ [whether / even if] a logical statement (i.e. the logical language) was really true (i.e. agreed with reality), the statement should be tested against empirical reality in an experiment. The emphasis on the physical experiment is ❹ [characteristic/characterization] of modern science. Later again it was realized that even this approach ❺ [overrated/underrated] the importance of thinking: from the outset research should be directed by experiments, although that experimental action — like any action — required the support of logical thought.

*Weltanschauung 세계관   **empirical 경험적인

In ancient and medieval times considerable respect ❶ _____ (accord) to language by those working in the scientific field. According to the ancient metaphysical *Weltanschauung*, it ❷ _____ (believe) that the structure of reality and of thought were so closely allied that they were interchangeable. A *logical* statement — not only a matter of thinking but also of linguistics — ❸ _____ (be) automatically a *true* statement of reality. Since such a statement happened to be true, it did not need to be subjected to experimental testing. However, in modern times it ❹ _____ (realize) for the first time that trust in the accord between reality and thinking was based on a grossly exaggerated notion of the scope of human reason. In order to discover whether a logical statement (i.e. the logical language) was really true (i.e. agreed with reality), the statement should be tested against empirical reality in an experiment. The emphasis on the physical experiment is characteristic of modern science. Later again it was realized that even this approach overrated the importance of thinking: from the outset research should ❺ _____ (direct) by experiments, although that experimental action — like any action — required the support of logical thought.

*Weltanschauung 세계관   **empirical 경험적인

In ancient and medieval times considerable respect was accorded to language by those working in the scientific field. According to the ancient metaphysical *Weltanschauung*, it was believed that the structure of reality and of thought were so closely allied that they were interchangeable. A *logical* statement — not only a matter of thinking but also of linguistics — was automatically a *true* statement of reality. Since such a statement ❶ _____ _____ _____ _____ (마침 사실이었다), it did not ❷ _____ _____ _____ _____ _____ (~을 받을 필요가 있다) experimental testing. However, in modern times it was realized for the first time that ❸ _____ _____ _____ _____ (일치에 대한 믿음) between reality and thinking was based on a grossly exaggerated notion of the scope of human reason. In order to discover whether a logical statement (i.e. the logical language) was really true (i.e. agreed with reality), the statement should be tested against empirical reality in an experiment. The emphasis on the physical experiment is characteristic of modern science. Later again it was realized that even this approach overrated the importance of thinking: ❹ _____ _____ _____ (처음부터) research should be directed by experiments, although that experimental action — like any action — required the support of logical thought.

*Weltanschauung 세계관 **empirical 경험적인

다음 글의 제목으로 가장 적절한 것은?

When we are in groups, we tend to feel that we, personally, aren't as responsible as we would be if we were acting on our own. So the decisions that the group makes can easily become extreme. Occasionally, groups reach riskier decisions — they decide to take actions which are more challenging or unsafe than they should be. Sometimes, though, they make choices that are too cautious. It's known as group polarization: a tendency towards extremes. A lot depends on how the discussions in the group develop. If one person is advocating a risky strategy early on, others may begin to think of even more challenging examples, and that leads the discussion towards reaching a riskier decision. But if someone advocates more cautious approaches at an early stage, this too can influence the direction of the discussion, resulting in a more cautious decision than the group members might have made individually.

① Methods for Effective Decision-Making
② Group Decisions *vs.* Individual Decisions
③ The Secret to Gathering Group Opinions
④ Are Moderate Opinions Essential to a Group?
⑤ Group Decisions: Able to Go to Both Ends

다음 글에서 전체 흐름과 관계 <u>없는</u> 문장은?

Advertising in the United States is a relatively large and stable marketplace with a dollar volume of activity closely tied to the overall health of the economy. The same is true of other mature industrialized nations, especially those of Western Europe. One significant difference, however, is the way commercial media evolved. ① In the United States, radio and television systems began as commercial ventures; in many other countries media were largely or completely government supported for years. ② Different models of commercial support are still evolving and the precise configurations vary by country. ③ This evolution does not mean, however, that governments are uninvolved in steering the development of media. ④ Since the way media evolves is very diverse, various national support measures are being sought, leading to competition in media. ⑤ As Joseph Straubhaar observes, television systems are often "stubbornly national," which means advertisers must tailor "global" media plans to the regulatory policies and cultural expectations of individual countries.

*configuration 형태, 구조 **stubbornly 완강하게, 고집스럽게

다음 글의 제목으로 가장 적절한 것은?

Some people think that facts are the same as *events*, which they regard as the "objective," "hard core" elements of this universe. The main reason for thinking this is that events seem the best candidates to offer us a rock-solid foundation for our facts. True, events do happen or do not happen; you can neglect them but not deny them. So by replacing facts with events, we might think we have found the strong objective foundation that we strive for. However, facts and events are concepts very different from each other. Unlike facts, events are dated, tied to space and time, whereas facts are detached from space and time. It is even considered a fact that certain events did not occur; it is a fact, for instance, that Darwin did not have a copy of Mendel's 1866 article in his collection. Apparently, a fact is not the same as an event; the best we can say is that a fact is a description of an event, but not the event itself.

① Why We Miss the Facts in Events
② Are Facts and Events Really the Same?
③ The Importance of Fact-Based Thinking
④ Incidents Containing Both Fact and Fiction
⑤ How to Distinguish Whether It Is True or Not

04 16강 4번

주어진 글 다음에 이어질 글의 순서로 가장 적절한 것은?

The extent to which decision making is shared with subordinates or concentrated at the top of the hierarchy differs across organizations. Thus, organizations can vary from strongly centralized decision-making practices to highly participatory decision-making practices.

(A) Therefore, research has investigated when participatory decision making is most useful, and when it is less important. When the workers are highly educated, intelligent, and have considerable expertise in their areas, participatory decision making is more effective.

(B) In participatory decision making, subordinates have much more input into how decisions are made. Research shows that greater participation in decision making improves employees' satisfaction with the decisions, but does not necessarily translate into better group performance.

(C) Additionally, when the task at hand is highly complex and knowledge about local conditions is important to the decision, participatory decision making is important. Finally, in times of crisis, when the decisions have very strong impact, participatory decision making is useful.

*subordinate 하급자 **hierarchy 위계, 계층

① (A) – (C) – (B)
② (B) – (A) – (C)
③ (B) – (C) – (A)
④ (C) – (A) – (B)
⑤ (C) – (B) – (A)

05 16강 5번

다음 글의 밑줄 친 부분 중, 문맥상 낱말의 쓰임이 적절하지 <u>않은</u> 것은?

Insects attract collectors' attention because they are extremely diverse and often bear pectacular colors. To biologists, however, bright coloration has been a constantly renewed puzzle because it makes an insect a highly ① visible prey to prospective predators. Charles Darwin understood that bright colors or exaggerated forms could evolve via sexual selection, the process by which individuals compete for ② access to mates and fertilization opportunities. However, he felt sexual selection could not account for the striking color pattern of ③ nonreproductive larvae in, for example, *Pseudosphinx* hawk moth caterpillars. In a reply to Darwin about this puzzle, Alfred R. Wallace proposed that bright colors could advertise the ④ tastefulness of the caterpillars to experienced predators. Indeed, prey that are not edible to predators are predicted to ⑤ gain by exhibiting very recognizable colors; experienced predators can then correctly identify and subsequently avoid attacking such prey. E. B. Poulton later developed this idea, expanded it to other warning signals (i.e., sounds or smells), and coined the term aposematism to describe this phenomenon (from the Greek "away" and "sign").

*larva 유충, 애벌레 (*pl.* larvae)
**Pseudosphinx hawk moth: Pseudosphinx 속(屬) 박각시나방
***caterpillar 애벌레

06 16강 6번

다음 글의 밑줄 친 부분 중, 문맥상 낱말의 쓰임이 적절하지 <u>않은</u> 것은?

In ancient and medieval times considerable respect was accorded to language by those working in the scientific field. According to the ancient metaphysical *Weltanschauung*, it was believed that the structure of reality and of thought were so closely allied that they were ① interchangeable. A *logical* statement — not only a matter of thinking but also of linguistics — was automatically a ② *true* statement of reality. Since such a statement happened to be true, it did not need to be ③ subjected to experimental testing. However, in modern times it was realized for the first time that trust in the accord between reality and thinking was based on a grossly ④ exaggerated notion of the scope of human reason. In order to discover whether a logical statement (i.e. the logical language) was really true (i.e. agreed with reality), the statement should be tested against empirical reality in an experiment. The emphasis on the physical experiment is characteristic of modern science. Later again it was realized that even this approach ⑤ underrated the importance of thinking: from the outset research should be directed by experiments, although that experimental action — like any action — required the support of logical thought.

*Weltanschauung 세계관 **empirical 경험적인

07 16강 1번

주어진 글 다음에 이어질 글의 순서로 가장 적절한 것은?

When we are in groups, we tend to feel that we, personally, aren't as responsible as we would be if we were acting on our own. So the decisions that the group makes can easily become extreme. Occasionally, groups reach riskier decisions — they decide to take actions which are more challenging or unsafe than they should be.

(A) If one person is advocating a risky strategy early on, others may begin to think of even more challenging examples, and that leads the discussion towards reaching a riskier decision.

(B) But if someone advocates more cautious approaches at an early stage, this too can influence the direction of the discussion, resulting in a more cautious decision than the group members might have made individually.

(C) Sometimes, though, they make choices that are too cautious. It's known as group polarization: a tendency towards extremes. A lot depends on how the discussions in the group develop.

① (A) – (C) – (B)　　② (B) – (A) – (C)
③ (B) – (C) – (A)　　④ (C) – (A) – (B)
⑤ (C) – (B) – (A)

다음 빈칸에 들어갈 말로 가장 적절한 것은?

Advertising in the United States is a relatively large and stable marketplace with a dollar volume of activity closely tied to the overall health of the economy. The same is true of other mature industrialized nations, especially those of Western Europe. One significant difference, however, is the way _____. In the United States, radio and television systems began as commercial ventures; in many other countries media were largely or completely government supported for years. Different models of commercial support are still evolving and the precise configurations vary by country. This evolution does not mean, however, that governments are uninvolved in steering the development of media. As Joseph Straubhaar observes, television systems are often "stubbornly national," which means advertisers must tailor "global" media plans to the regulatory policies and cultural expectations of individual countries.

*configuration 형태, 구조   **stubbornly 완강하게, 고집스럽게

① commercial media evolved
② broadcasting systems affect society
③ countries support their own industries
④ media help industrial development
⑤ consumers perceive advertisements

다음 글의 밑줄 친 부분 중, 어법상 틀린 것은?

Some people think that facts are the same as *events*, ① which they regard as the "objective," "hard core" elements of this universe. The main reason for thinking this is that events seem the best candidates to offer us a rock-solid foundation for our facts. True, events do happen or do not happen; you can neglect them but not deny them. So by replacing facts with events, we might think we have found the strong objective foundation that we strive for. However, facts and events are concepts very ② different from each other. Unlike facts, events are dated, tied to space and time, whereas facts ③ are detached from space and time. It even ④ considered a fact that certain events did not occur; it is a fact, for instance, that Darwin did not have a copy of Mendel's 1866 article in his collection. Apparently, a fact is not the same as an event; the best we can say is ⑤ that a fact is a description of an event, but not the event itself.

10 16강 4번

다음 글의 주제로 가장 적절한 것은?

The extent to which decision making is shared with subordinates or concentrated at the top of the hierarchy differs across organizations. Thus, organizations can vary from strongly centralized decision-making practices to highly participatory decision-making practices. In participatory decision making, subordinates have much more input into how decisions are made. Research shows that greater participation in decision making improves employees' satisfaction with the decisions, but does not necessarily translate into better group performance. Therefore, research has investigated when participatory decision making is most useful, and when it is less important. When the workers are highly educated, intelligent, and have considerable expertise in their areas, participatory decision making is more effective. Additionally, when the task at hand is highly complex and knowledge about local conditions is important to the decision, participatory decision making is important. Finally, in times of crisis, when the decisions have very strong impact, participatory decision making is useful.

*subordinate 하급자 **hierarchy 위계, 계층

① the problems that occur when decision-making is overly centralized
② a decision-making method driven by workers' inclinations
③ the features and effective uses of participatory decision-making
④ the effects of decision-making methods on corporate profitability
⑤ ways to increase employees' satisfaction with an organization

11 16강 5번

다음 글의 제목으로 가장 적절한 것은?

Insects attract collectors' attention because they are extremely diverse and often bear spectacular colors. To biologists, however, bright coloration has been a constantly renewed puzzle because it makes an insect a highly visible prey to prospective predators. Charles Darwin understood that bright colors or exaggerated forms could evolve via sexual selection, the process by which individuals compete for access to mates and fertilization opportunities. However, he felt sexual selection could not account for the striking color pattern of nonreproductive larvae in, for example, *Pseudosphinx* hawk moth caterpillars. In a reply to Darwin about this puzzle, Alfred R. Wallace proposed that bright colors could advertise the distastefulness of the caterpillars to experienced predators. Indeed, prey that are not edible to predators are predicted to gain by exhibiting very recognizable colors; experienced predators can then correctly identify and subsequently avoid attacking such prey. E. B. Poulton later developed this idea, expanded it to other warning signals (i.e., sounds or smells), and coined the term aposematism to describe this phenomenon (from the Greek "away" and "sign").

*larva 유충, 애벌레 (*pl.* larvae)
**Pseudosphinx hawk moth: Pseudosphinx 속(屬) 박각시나방
***caterpillar 애벌레

① Protective Color: A Strong Protective Feature
② Two Scientists' Hard Work on a Difficult Puzzle
③ The Secret Behind an Insect's Bright Coloration
④ An Amazing Ability of Predators: Prey Identification
⑤ Fighting against Fate: A Fierce Escape from Predators

12 16강 6번

주어진 글 다음에 이어질 글의 순서로 가장 적절한 것은?

In ancient and medieval times considerable respect was accorded to language by those working in the scientific field. According to the ancient metaphysical *Weltanschauung*, it was believed that the structure of reality and of thought were so closely allied that they were interchangeable. A *logical* statement — not only a matter of thinking but also of linguistics — was automatically a *true* statement of reality.

(A) In order to discover whether a logical statement (i.e. the logical language) was really true (i.e. agreed with reality), the statement should be tested against empirical reality in an experiment. The emphasis on the physical experiment is characteristic of modern science.

(B) Since such a statement happened to be true, it did not need to be subjected to experimental testing. However, in modern times it was realized for the first time that trust in the accord between reality and thinking was based on a grossly exaggerated notion of the scope of human reason.

(C) Later again it was realized that even this approach overrated the importance of thinking: from the outset research should be directed by experiments, although that experimental action — like any action — required the support of logical thought.

*Weltanschauung 세계관 **empirical 경험적인

① (A) – (C) – (B)
② (B) – (A) – (C)
③ (B) – (C) – (A)
④ (C) – (A) – (B)
⑤ (C) – (B) – (A)]

16강 1번

When we are in groups, we tend to feel that we, personally, aren't as responsible as we would be if we were acting on our own. So the decisions that the group makes can easily become extreme. Occasionally, groups reach riskier decisions — they decide to take actions which are more challenging or unsafe than they should be. Sometimes, though, they make choices that are too cautious. It's known as group polarization: a tendency towards extremes. A lot depends on how the discussions in the group develop. If one person is advocating a risky strategy early on, others may begin to think of even more challenging examples, and that leads the discussion towards reaching a riskier decision. But if someone advocates more cautious approaches at an early stage, this too can influence the direction of the discussion, resulting in a more cautious decision than the group members might have made individually.

13

윗글에서 다음 질문에 대한 답을 찾아 우리말로 쓰시오. (50자 내외)

Q: Why does the writer think that the decisions a group make can easily become extreme?

A: _____

_____

14

윗글의 내용을 한 문장으로 요약하려고 한다. 빈칸 (A)와 (B)에 들어갈 알맞은 말을 보기 에서 찾아 쓰시오.

보기 individuals   groups   advocates approaches

Due to feelings of shared responsibility, decisions made by _____(A)_____ easily tend to the extremes compared to those made by _____(B)_____, and therefore they tend to be either too risky or prudent.

(A) _____ (B) _____

Advertising in the United States is a relatively large and stable marketplace with a dollar volume of activity closely (A) <u>ties</u> to the overall health of the economy. The same is true of other mature industrialized nations, especially (B) <u>that</u> of Western Europe. One significant difference, however, is the way commercial media evolved. In the United States, radio and television systems began as commercial ventures; in many other countries media (C) <u>was</u> largely or completely government supported for years. Different models of commercial support are still evolving and the precise configurations vary by country. This evolution does not mean, however, that governments are uninvolved in steering the development of media. As Joseph Straubhaar observes, television systems are often "stubbornly _____," which means advertisers must tailor "global" media plans to the regulatory policies and cultural expectations of individual countries.

*configuration 형태, 구조   **stubbornly 완강하게, 고집스럽게

15 윗글의 밑줄 친 부분을 어법상 알맞은 형태로 고쳐 쓰시오.

(A) ties → _____

(B) that → _____

(C) was → _____

16 윗글의 빈칸에 들어갈 단어를 영영 뜻풀이를 참고하여 쓰시오. (단, 주어진 글자로 시작할 것)

relating to or belonging to a nation or country

n_____

Some people think that facts are the same as *events*, which they regard as the "objective," "hard core" elements of this universe. The main reason for thinking this is that events seem the best candidates to offer us a rock-solid foundation for our facts. True, events do happen or do not happen; you can neglect them but not deny them. So by replacing facts with events, we might think we have found the strong objective foundation that we strive for. However, facts and events are concepts very different from each other. Unlike facts, events are dated, tied to space and time, whereas facts are detached from space and time. <u>심지어 특정한 사건이 일어나지 않았다는 것조차 사실로 여겨진다</u>; it is a fact, for instance, that Darwin did not have a copy of Mendel's 1866 article in his collection. Apparently, a fact is not the same as an event; the best we can say is that a fact is a description of an event, but not the event itself.

17 윗글의 밑줄 친 우리말 의미와 일치하도록 보기 의 단어를 활용하여 조건 에 맞게 문장을 완성하시오.

보기   is / not / a fact / did / that / occur / it / consider / certain events / even

조건   · 〈가주어–진주어〉 구문을 활용할 것
· 필요 시 어형을 바꿀 것

_____

_____

18 윗글을 읽고 다음 질문에 영어로 답하시오. (20단어 내외)

Q: According to the passage, why are facts and events different concepts from each other?

A: _____

_____

_____

The extent ① <u>to which</u> decision making is shared with subordinates or concentrated at the top of the hierarchy differs across organizations. Thus, organizations can vary from ② <u>strong</u> centralized decision-making practices to highly participatory decision-making practices. In participatory decision making, subordinates have ③ <u>much</u> more input into how decisions are made. Research shows that greater participation in decision making improves employees' satisfaction with the decisions, but ④ <u>do</u> not necessarily translate into better group performance. 그러므로 연구는 참여형 의사결정이 가장 유용한 때와 그것이 덜 중요한 때를 조사했다. When the workers are highly educated, intelligent, and have considerable expertise in their areas, participatory decision making is more effective. Additionally, when the task at hand is highly complex and knowledge about local conditions ⑤ <u>is</u> important to the decision, participatory decision making is important. Finally, in times of crisis, when the decisions have very strong impact, participatory decision making is useful.

*subordinate 하급자   **hierarchy 위계, 계층

고난도

19 윗글의 밑줄 친 부분 중, 어법상 <u>틀린</u> 것을 2개 찾아 그 번호를 쓰고 고쳐 쓰시오.

(1) ＿＿＿＿＿＿ → ＿＿＿＿＿＿

(2) ＿＿＿＿＿＿ → ＿＿＿＿＿＿

20 윗글의 밑줄 친 우리말과 일치하도록 [보기]의 단어를 활용하여 [조건]에 맞게 문장을 완성하시오.

[보기] most / is / when / it / participatory decision making / less important / useful / has investigated

[조건] · <보기>의 단어를 반드시 모두 사용할 것
· 필요 시 단어를 중복 사용하고 어형을 바꿔 쓸 것

Therefore, research ＿＿＿＿＿＿＿＿＿＿＿＿

＿＿＿＿＿＿＿＿ and ＿＿＿＿＿＿＿＿

＿＿＿＿＿＿＿＿＿＿＿＿＿＿＿＿.

Insects attract collectors' attention because they are extremely diverse and often bear pectacular colors. To biologists, however, bright coloration has been a constantly renewed puzzle because it makes an insect a highly visible prey to prospective predators. Charles Darwin understood that bright colors or exaggerated forms could evolve via sexual selection, the process by which individuals compete for access to mates and fertilization opportunities. However, he felt sexual selection could not account for the striking color pattern of nonreproductive larvae in, for example, *Pseudosphinx* hawk moth caterpillars. In a reply to Darwin about this puzzle, Alfred R. Wallace proposed that bright colors could advertise the distastefulness of the caterpillars to experienced predators. Indeed, prey that are not _____ to predators are predicted to gain by exhibiting very recognizable colors; experienced predators can then correctly identify and subsequently avoid attacking such prey. E. B. Poulton later developed this idea, expanded it to other warning signals (i.e., sounds or smells), and coined the term aposematism to describe this phenomenon (from the Greek "away" and "sign").

*larva 유충, 애벌레 (*pl.* larvae)
**Pseudosphinx hawk moth: Pseudosphinx 속(屬) 박각시나방
***caterpillar 애벌레

21 윗글의 밑줄 친 this puzzle이 문맥적으로 의미하는 바를 찾아 우리말로 쓰시오. (40자 내외)

_____

_____

22 윗글의 빈칸에 들어갈 단어를 영영 뜻풀이를 참고하여 쓰시오. (단, 주어진 글자로 시작할 것)

suitable for use as food or safe to eat

e_____

In ancient and medieval times considerable respect was accorded to language by those working in the scientific field. According to the ancient metaphysical *Weltanschauung*, 현실의 구조와 사고의 구조가 매우 밀접하게 연관되어 있어 그것들은 상호 대체가 가능하다고 여겨졌다. A *logical* statement — not only a matter of thinking but also of linguistics — was automatically a *true* statement of reality. Since such a statement happened to be true, it did not need to be subjected to experimental testing. However, in modern times it was realized for the first time that trust in the accord between reality and thinking was based on a grossly exaggerated notion of the scope of human reason. In order to discover whether a logical statement (i.e. the logical language) was really true (i.e. agreed with reality), the statement should be tested against empirical reality in an experiment. The emphasis on the physical experiment is characteristic of modern science. Later again it was realized that even this approach overrated the importance of thinking: from the outset research should be directed by experiments, although that experimental action — like any action — required the support of logical thought.

*Weltanschauung 세계관 **empirical 경험적인

23 윗글의 밑줄 친 우리말 의미와 일치하도록 보기 의 단어를 활용하여 조건 에 맞게 문장을 완성하시오.

보기 so / of reality / of thought / closely allied / that / believed

조건
· ⟨가주어-진주어⟩, ⟨so ~ that ...⟩ 구문을 활용할 것
· 필요 시 단어를 추가할 것

_____ _____ _____ _____

the structure _____ _____ and

_____ _____ were _____

_____ _____ _____ they were

interchangeable

24 윗글의 내용을 한 문장으로 요약하려고 한다. 빈칸 (A) 와 (B)에 들어갈 알맞은 말을 본문에서 찾아 쓰시오. (단, 각각 3단어로 쓸 것)

In ancient and medieval times, ___(A)___ was considered ___(B)___ of reality in itself and did not require experimental testing, whereas in modern science the necessity of verifying it against reality in physical experiments was realized.

(A) _____

(B) _____

❶ There are several theories about why older people experience "long-term" time compression so much more acutely than young people. ❷ It has been observed, for example, that for a twenty-year-old, ten years is half a lifetime, but for a fifty-year-old, the same span represents just 20 percent of one's life. ❸ As we age, a decade becomes an ever-smaller proportion of our life experience. ❹ Others have emphasized the fact that, in a ten-year span, younger people encounter more "turning points" than older people. ❺ In just ten years, a younger person is likely to graduate from college, woo and win a mate, start a family, and buy a house. ❻ Older people, in contrast, can easily pass a decade doing the same job and living in the same house with the same spouse. ❼ The absence of frequent life-changing events may partly explain why older people feel that the later decades seem to pass so quickly.

*compression 압축 **woo 구애하다

❶ 고령자들이 왜 젊은 사람들보다 훨씬 더 강렬하게 '장기' 시간 압축을 경험하는지에 관한 몇 가지 이론이 있다. ❷ 예를 들어, 20세에게는 10년이 반평생이지만, 50세에게는 같은 기간이 자기 인생의 단지 20퍼센트에 해당한다고들 말해 왔다. ❸ 우리가 나이가 들면서, 10년이 우리의 인생 경험에서 차지하는 부분은 늘 더 작아진다. ❹ 다른 사람들은 10년의 기간 동안에, 더 젊은 사람들이 고령자들보다 더 많은 '전환점'에 맞닥뜨린다는 사실을 강조해왔다. ❺ 단 10년 동안에 더 젊은 사람은 아마도 대학을 졸업하고, 구애해서 배우자를 얻고, 가정을 이루고, 집을 살 것이다. ❻ 그에 반해서, 고령자들은 똑같은 일을 하고 똑같은 배우자와 똑같은 집에서 살면서 쉽게 10년을 보낼 수 있다. ❼ 인생을 바꿀 만한 빈번한 사건의 부재가 왜 고령자들이 만년의 수십 년이 매우 빨리 지나가는 것 같다고 느끼는지를 얼마간 설명할 수도 있다.

Word List	
□ theory 이론 □ acutely 강렬하게 □ observe 말하다, 관찰하다 □ span 기간 □ represent 해당하다, 나타내다 □ proportion 부분, 비율 □ emphasize 강조하다 □ encounter 맞닥뜨리다, 만나다 □ turning point 전환점, 전기 □ mate 짝 □ in contrast 대조적으로 □ spouse 배우자 □ absence 부재 □ frequent 빈번한	

• Word Test

1	encounter		8	이론	
2	span		9	전환점, 전기	
3	represent		10	강조하다	
4	mate		11	말하다, 관찰하다	
5	in contrast		12	빈번한	
6	acutely		13	배우자	
7	absence		14	부분, 비율	

There are several theories about why older people experience "long-term" time compression so much more ❶ acute / acutely than young people. It has been observed, for example, that for a twenty-year-old, ten years is half a lifetime, but for a fifty-year-old, the same span represents just 20 percent of one's life. As we age, a decade becomes an ever-smaller proportion of our life experience. Others have emphasized the fact that, in a ten-year span, younger people encounter more "turning points" than older people. In just ten years, a younger person is likely to graduate from college, woo and win a mate, start a family, and buy a house. Older people, ❷ in contrast / in other words , can easily pass a decade doing the same job and living in the same house with the same spouse. The ❸ absence / presence of frequent life-changing events may ❹ partly / relatively explain why older people feel that the ❺ later / earlier decades seem to pass so quickly.

*compression 압축 **woo 구애하다

There are several theories about why older people experience "long-term" time compression so much more acutely than young people. It ❶ _____ (observe), for example, that for a twenty-year-old, ten years is half a lifetime, but for a fifty-year-old, the same span represents just 20 percent of one's life. As we age, a decade ❷ _____ (become) an ever-smaller proportion of our life experience. Others ❸ _____ (emphasize) the fact that, in a ten-year span, younger people encounter more "turning points" than older people. In just ten years, a younger person is likely to graduate from college, woo and win a mate, start a family, and buy a house. Older people, in contrast, can easily pass a decade ❹ _____ (do) the same job and living in the same house with the same spouse. The absence of frequent life-changing events may partly explain why older people feel that the later decades seem to pass so quickly.

*compression 압축 **woo 구애하다

There are several theories about why older people experience "long-term" time compression so much more acutely than young people. It has been observed, for example, that for a twenty-year-old, ten years is ❶ _____ _____ _____ (반평생), but for a fifty-year-old, the same span represents just 20 percent of one's life. ❷ _____ _____ _____ (우리가 나이가 들면서), a decade becomes an ever-smaller proportion of our life experience. Others have emphasized the fact that, in a ten-year span, younger people encounter more "turning points" than older people. In just ten years, a younger person is likely to ❸ _____ _____ (~을 졸업하다) college, woo and win a mate, start a family, and buy a house. Older people, in contrast, can easily pass a decade doing the same job and living in the same house with the same spouse. The absence of ❹ _____ _____ _____ (인생을 바꿀 만한 빈번한 사건들) may partly explain why older people feel that the later decades seem to pass so quickly.

*compression 압축 **woo 구애하다

❶ Social mobility is upward or downward movement in social position over time in a society. ❷ That movement can be specific to individuals who change social positions or to categories of people, such as racial or ethnic groups. ❸ Social mobility between generations is referred to as intergenerational mobility. ❹ The self-made myth suggests that social position in the United States is largely up to the individual, implying that mobility is quite common and easy to achieve for those who apply themselves. ❺ However, what people believe and what is fact are often not the same. ❻ A recent experimental study found that Americans substantially and consistently overestimate the amount of income mobility and educational access in society. ❼ The higher one's social class, the more likely they are to overestimate social mobility. ❽ In other words, wealthy Americans tend to subscribe to the belief that pulling oneself out of poverty is easier than it actually is and that one's wealth is a result of hard work and initiative, rather than luck or birth.

❶ 사회 이동은 사회 내에서 시간의 흐름에 따른 사회적 지위의 상승 또는 하강 이동이다. ❷ 그 이동은 사회적 지위가 바뀌는 개인 또는 인종이나 민족 집단과 같은 부류의 사람들에 특유한 것일 수 있다. ❸ 세대 사이에서의 사회 이동은 세대 간 이동이라고 불린다. ❹ 자수성가에 관한 근거 없는 믿음은 미국에서는 사회적 지위가 주로 개인에 달려 있음을 시사하는데, 이는 열심히 노력하는 사람들에게 이동은 아주 흔하고 성취하기 쉬운 것임을 의미한다. ❺ 그러나 사람들이 믿는 것과 사실인 것은 흔히 같지 않다. ❻ 최근의 한 실험 연구는 미국인들이 사회에서의 소득 이동의 양과 교육 접근성을 상당히 그리고 일관되게 실제보다 더 높게 어림한다는 것을 발견했다. ❼ 사람들의 사회 계층이 더 높을수록 그들이 사회 이동을 실제보다 더 높게 어림할 가능성이 더 크다. ❽ 다시 말해, 부유한 미국인들은 자신이 가난에서 벗어나는 것이 실제로 그런 것보다 더 쉬우며, 사람들의 부는 운이나 출생보다는 근면과 진취성의 결과라는 믿음에 동의하는 경향이 있다.

Word List

□ social mobility 사회 이동　□ specific 특정한　□ ethnic 민족의, 인종의　□ be referred to as ~으로 불리다
□ intergenerational 세대 간의　□ mobility 이동성　□ self-made 자수성가의　□ myth 신화　□ largely 주로, 대체로
□ be up to ~에 달려 있다　□ imply 의미하다　□ apply oneself 열심히 노력하다, 전념하다　□ substantially 상당히
□ consistently 일관되게　□ overestimate 실제보다 더 높게 어림하다, 과대평가하다　□ subscribe to ~에 동의하다　□ poverty 가난
□ initiative 진취성, 주도권

• Word Test

1	overestimate	10	진취성, 주도권
2	social mobility	11	의미하다
3	myth	12	민족의, 인종의
4	substantially	13	세대 간의
5	mobility	14	~에 달려 있다
6	self-made	15	일관되게
7	subscribe to	16	특정한
8	be referred to as	17	주로, 대체로
9	apply oneself	18	가난

Social mobility is upward or downward movement in social position over time in a society. That movement can be specific to individuals who change social positions or to categories of people, such as racial or ethnic groups. Social mobility between generations is referred ❶ [by / to] as intergenerational mobility. The self-made myth suggests that social position in the United States is largely up to the individual, implying that mobility is quite common and easy to achieve for those who apply ❷ [himself / themselves]. However, what people believe and what is fact are often not the same. A recent experimental study found that Americans substantially and consistently overestimate the amount of income mobility and educational access in society. The higher one's social class, the ❸ [more / most] likely they are to overestimate social mobility. In other words, wealthy Americans tend to ❹ [subscribe / prescribe] to the belief that pulling oneself out of poverty is easier than it actually is and that one's wealth is a result of hard work and ❺ [initiative / initiation], rather than luck or birth.

Social mobility is upward or downward movement in social position over time in a society. That movement can be specific to individuals who change social positions or to categories of people, such as racial or ethnic groups. Social mobility between generations ❶ _____ (be) referred to as intergenerational mobility. The self-made myth ❷ _____ (suggest) that social position in the United States is largely up to the individual, ❸ _____ (imply) that mobility is quite common and easy to achieve for those who apply themselves. However, what people believe and what is fact ❹ _____ (be) often not the same. A recent experimental study found that Americans substantially and consistently overestimate the amount of income mobility and educational access in society. The higher one's social class, the more likely they are ❺ _____ (overestimate) social mobility. In other words, wealthy Americans tend to subscribe to the belief that pulling oneself out of poverty is easier than it actually is and that one's wealth is a result of hard work and initiative, rather than luck or birth.

Social mobility is upward or downward movement in social position ❶ _____ _____ (시간의 흐름에 따른) in a society. That movement can be specific to individuals who change social positions or to categories of people, such as racial or ethnic groups. Social mobility between generations is referred to as intergenerational mobility. The self-made myth suggests that social position in the United States ❷ _____ _____ _____ _____ (주로 ~에 달려 있다) the individual, implying that mobility is quite common and easy to achieve for those who apply themselves. However, ❸ _____ _____ _____ (사람들이 믿는 것) and what is fact are often not the same. A recent experimental study found that Americans substantially and consistently overestimate the amount of income mobility and educational access in society. The higher one's social class, the more likely they are to overestimate social mobility. In other words, wealthy Americans tend to subscribe to the belief that ❹ _____ _____ _____ _____ _____ (자신이 가난에서 벗어나는 것) is easier than it actually is and that one's wealth is a result of hard work and initiative, rather than luck or birth.

❶ In Ancient Greece, many private individuals believed in the powers of magic, such as farmers who were always dependent on the weather. ❷ Even though the use of magic was widespread in Ancient Greece, there remained an official caution over its use. ❸ We know that the Greek authorities believed that magic was an activity capable of results, but they grew concerned about those who practiced harmful magic. ❹ So it was established that those who practiced harmful magic could be punished by civic action. ❺ This may be the reason why magic in the classical world was held in low esteem and condemned by speakers and writers. ❻ Likewise, we find certain intellectuals realizing that the power of magic could be abused. ❼ For example, Plato believed that those who sold spells and curse tablets should be punished. ❽ Epicurean and Stoic philosophers also believed that magic should be eliminated. ❾ This mistrust of magic, along with religion and a separation of humans from the divine world, created a need to develop new methods of understanding the world. ❿ It is thus understandable that the Ancient Greeks created the foundations for philosophy.

*civic 시민의   **curse tablet 저주 서판

❶ 고대 그리스에서는 항상 날씨에 의존하는 농부와 같은 많은 사사로운 개개인들이 마법의 힘을 믿었다. ❷ 고대 그리스에서 마법의 사용이 널리 퍼져 있었음에도 불구하고 그것의 사용에 대한 공식적인 경고가 존속하였다. ❸ 우리는 그리스 당국이 마법이 성과를 낼 수 있는 활동이라고 믿었지만 해로운 마법을 행하는 사람들에 대해 점차 걱정하게 되었음을 알고 있다. ❹ 그래서 해로운 마법을 행하는 사람들은 시민 행동에 의해 처벌될 수도 있다고 정해졌다. ❺ 이것이 바로 고대 그리스·로마 사회에서 마법이 웅변가들과 작가들에게 낮게 평가되고 비난받은 이유일 것이다. ❻ 마찬가지로, 우리는 특정 지식인들이 마법의 힘이 남용될 수 있다고 인식하고 있었음을 안다. ❼ 예를 들어, 플라톤은 주문(呪文)과 저주 서판을 파는 사람들은 처벌을 받아야 한다고 믿었다. ❽ 에피쿠로스학파와 스토아학파 철학자들도 마법은 없어져야 한다고 믿었다. ❾ 이러한 마법에 대한 불신은 종교와 신적인 세계로부터 인간을 분리하는 것과 함께 세상을 이해하는 새로운 방법을 개발할 필요를 만들어 냈다. ❿ 따라서 고대 그리스인들이 철학의 기초를 만든 것은 이해할만하다.

Word List

□ **dependent on** ~에게 의존하고 있는   □ **widespread** 광범위한, 널리 퍼진   □ **caution** 경고, 주의   □ **authorities** 당국, 관계자
□ **practice** 실행하다   □ **establish** (제도·법률 따위를) 정하다, 마련하다   □ **classical** 고대 그리스 로마의, 고전적인
□ **hold in low esteem** ~을 낮게 평가하다, ~을 경시하다   □ **condemn** 비난하다, 규탄하다   □ **likewise** 마찬가지로
□ **intellectual** 지식인   □ **abuse** 남용하다   □ **spell** 주문(呪文), 마법   □ **eliminate** 없애다   □ **mistrust** 불신   □ **separation** 분리
□ **divine** 신성한, 신의   □ **foundation** 기반, 기초

• Word Test

1	eliminate	10	경고, 주의
2	divine	11	분리
3	hold in low esteem	12	당국, 관계자
4	classical	13	~에게 의존하고 있는
5	widespread	14	기반, 기초
6	practice	15	남용하다
7	establish	16	불신
8	likewise	17	지식인
9	spell	18	비난하다, 규탄하다

In Ancient Greece, many private individuals believed in the powers of magic, such as farmers who were always ❶ dependent/independent on the weather. Even though the use of magic was widespread in Ancient Greece, there remained an official caution over ❷ its/their use. We know that the Greek authorities believed that magic was an activity capable of results, but they grew concerned about those who practiced ❸ harmful/innocent magic. So it was established that those who practiced harmful magic could be punished by civic action. This may be the reason why magic in the classical world was held in low esteem and condemned by speakers and writers. ❹ Likewise/Otherwise, we find certain intellectuals realizing that the power of magic could be abused. For example, Plato believed that those who sold spells and curse tablets should be punished. Epicurean and Stoic philosophers also believed that magic should be eliminated. This mistrust of magic, along with religion and a separation of humans from the divine world, created a need to develop new methods of understanding the world. It is thus understandable ❺ that/which the Ancient Greeks created the foundations for philosophy.

*civic 시민의 **curse tablet 저주 서판

In Ancient Greece, many private individuals believed in the powers of magic, such as farmers who were always dependent on the weather. Even though the use of magic was widespread in Ancient Greece, there remained an official caution over its use. We know that the Greek authorities believed that magic was an activity capable of results, but they grew concerned about those who practiced harmful magic. So it ❶ _____ (establish) that those who practiced harmful magic could ❷ _____ (punish) by civic action. This may be the reason why magic in the classical world was held in low esteem and condemned by speakers and writers. Likewise, we find certain intellectuals ❸ _____ (realize) that the power of magic could ❹ _____ (abuse). For example, Plato believed that those who sold spells and curse tablets should be punished. Epicurean and Stoic philosophers also believed that magic should ❺ _____ (eliminate). This mistrust of magic, along with religion and a separation of humans from the divine world, created a need to develop new methods of understanding the world. It is thus understandable that the Ancient Greeks created the foundations for philosophy.

*civic 시민의 **curse tablet 저주 서판

In Ancient Greece, many private individuals believed in the powers of magic, such as farmers who were always dependent on the weather. Even though the use of magic was widespread in Ancient Greece, there remained an official caution over its use. We know that the Greek authorities believed that magic was an activity capable of results, but they ❶ _____ _____ _____ (~에 대해 점차 걱정하게 되었다) those who practiced harmful magic. So it was established that those who practiced harmful magic could be punished by civic action. This may be the reason why magic in the classical world ❷ _____ _____ _____ _____ _____ (낮게 평가되다) and condemned by speakers and writers. Likewise, we find certain intellectuals realizing that the power of magic could be abused. For example, Plato believed that those who sold spells and curse tablets should be punished. Epicurean and Stoic philosophers also believed that magic should be eliminated. This mistrust of magic, ❸ _____ _____ (~와 함께) religion and a separation of humans from the divine world, created a need to develop new methods of understanding the world. It is thus understandable that the Ancient Greeks created ❹ _____ _____ _____ _____ (철학의 기초들).

*civic 시민의 **curse tablet 저주 서판

❶ The development psychologist Jerome Kagan measured changes in children's temperament between the ages of 4 months and 7 years. ❷ He classified several healthy 4-month-old infants as high reactors (easily excited or fearful) or low reactors (relaxed and unafraid), depending upon their responses to an unfamiliar stimulus. ❸ Kagan waved colorful mobiles in front of a baby, played a tape saying, "Hello baby, how are you doing today?" and popped a balloon behind the baby's head. ❹ High reactors moved around violently and cried, while low reactors rested or even laughed during the tests. ❺ By the time these infants were 4 years old, some of the high reactors were quite shy, subdued, and quiet, while others had moved toward the center of Kagan's "shy-bold" continuum. ❻ By the age of 7, only 15 percent of the initially low reactors were enthusiastic, fearless, and highly sociable kids, and the rest had moved closer to the center. ❼ None of the high reactors became fearless, and none of the low reactors became fearful; ❽ in other words, environment only moderately affected the final outcome.

*temperament 기질 **subdued 차분해진

❶ 발달 심리학자 Jerome Kagan은 생후 4개월에서 7세 사이 아동들의 기질 변화를 측정했다. ❷ 그는 몇 명의 생후 4개월 된 건강한 유아들을 낯선 자극에 대한 반응에 따라 (쉽게 흥분하거나 두려워하는)고반응자 혹은 (느긋하고 두려워하지 않는)저반응자로 분류했다. ❸ Kagan은 아기 앞에서 알록달록한 모빌을 흔들고, "안녕 아기야, 오늘 어떻게 지내고 있니?"라는 내용의 테이프를 틀고, 아기 머리 뒤에서 풍선을 터뜨렸다. ❹ 고반응자는 격렬하게 움직이며 울었지만, 저반응자는 실험 중에 가만히 있거나 심지어 웃기도 했다. ❺ 이 유아들이 4살이 되었을 때, 고반응자들 중 일부는 상당히 수줍고, 차분하고, 조용했으며, 한편 또 다른 일부는 Kagan의 '수줍음과 대담함' 연속선의 중심 쪽으로 이동했다. ❻ 7살이 되었을 때, 초기 저반응자들 중 15퍼센트만이 열정적이고, 두려움이 없으며, 매우 사교적인 아이들이었고, 나머지는 중앙으로 더 가까이 이동했다. ❼ 고반응자들 중 아무도 겁이 없게 되지 않았고, 저반응자들 중 아무도 두려움을 갖게 되지 않았다. ❽ 다시 말해서, 환경은 최종 결과에 그저 어느 정도만 영향을 미쳤다.

Word List

□ psychologist 심리학자　□ measure 측정하다　□ classify 분류하다　□ reactor 반응자　□ relaxed 느긋한　□ unfamiliar 낯선　□ stimulus 자극 (*pl.* stimuli)　□ wave 흔들다　□ pop 터뜨리다　□ violently 격렬하게　□ continuum 연속선　□ initially 초기에　□ enthusiastic 열정적인　□ sociable 사교적인　□ moderately 적당히　□ outcome 결과

• Word Test

1	relaxed	_____	9	터뜨리다	_____
2	moderately	_____	10	결과	_____
3	stimulus	_____	11	흔들다	_____
4	reactor	_____	12	사교적인	_____
5	enthusiastic	_____	13	심리학자	_____
6	measure	_____	14	초기에	_____
7	classify	_____	15	격렬하게	_____
8	continuum	_____	16	낯선	_____

The development psychologist Jerome Kagan measured changes in children's temperament between the ages of 4 months and 7 years. He classified several healthy 4-month-old infants as high reactors (easily excited or fearful) or low reactors (relaxed and unafraid), depending upon their responses to an unfamiliar ❶ stimuli/stimulus . Kagan waved colorful mobiles in front of a baby, played a tape saying, "Hello baby, how are you doing today?" and popped a balloon behind the baby's head. High reactors moved around violently and cried, ❷ as/while low reactors rested or even laughed during the tests. By the time these infants were 4 years old, some of the high reactors were quite shy, subdued, and quiet, while others had moved toward the center of Kagan's "shy-bold" continuum. By the age of 7, only 15 percent of the ❸ initial/initially low reactors were enthusiastic, fearless, and ❹ high/highly sociable kids, and the rest had moved closer to the center. None of the high reactors became fearless, and none of the low reactors became fearful; in other words, environment only ❺ drastically/moderately affected the final outcome. *temperament 기질 **subdued 차분해진

The development psychologist Jerome Kagan measured changes in children's temperament between the ages of 4 months and 7 years. He ❶ _____ (classify) several healthy 4-month-old infants as high reactors (easily excited or fearful) or low reactors (relaxed and unafraid), depending upon their responses to an unfamiliar stimulus. Kagan waved colorful mobiles in front of a baby, played a tape ❷ _____ (say), "Hello baby, how are you doing today?" and ❸ _____ (pop) a balloon behind the baby's head. High reactors moved around violently and cried, while low reactors rested or even laughed during the tests. By the time these infants ❹ _____ (be) 4 years old, some of the high reactors were quite shy, subdued, and quiet, while others ❺ _____ (move) toward the center of Kagan's "shy-bold" continuum. By the age of 7, only 15 percent of the initially low reactors were enthusiastic, fearless, and highly sociable kids, and the rest had moved closer to the center. None of the high reactors became fearless, and none of the low reactors became fearful; in other words, environment only moderately affected the final outcome. *temperament 기질 **subdued 차분해진

The development psychologist Jerome Kagan measured changes in children's temperament between the ages of 4 months and 7 years. He classified several healthy 4-month-old infants as high reactors (easily excited or fearful) or low reactors (relaxed and unafraid), ❶ _____ _____ (~에 따라) their responses to an unfamiliar stimulus. Kagan waved colorful mobiles in front of a baby, played a tape saying, "Hello baby, how are you doing today?" and popped a balloon behind the baby's head. High reactors ❷ _____ _____ _____ (격렬하게 움직였다) and cried, while low reactors rested or even laughed during the tests. By the time these infants were 4 years old, some of the high reactors were quite shy, subdued, and quiet, while others had moved toward the center of Kagan's "shy-bold" continuum. ❸ _____ _____ _____ _____ _____ (7살이 되었을 때), only 15 percent of the initially low reactors were enthusiastic, fearless, and highly sociable kids, and the rest had moved closer to the center. None of the high reactors became fearless, and none of the low reactors became fearful; ❹ _____ _____ _____ (다시 말해서), environment only moderately affected the final outcome.

*temperament 기질 **subdued 차분해진

01 [17강 1번]

글의 흐름으로 보아, 주어진 문장이 들어가기에 가장 적절한 곳은?

> Others have emphasized the fact that, in a ten-year span, younger people encounter more "turning points" than older people.

There are several theories about why older people experience "long-term" time compression so much more acutely than young people. (①) It has been observed, for example, that for a twenty-year-old, ten years is half a lifetime, but for a fifty-year-old, the same span represents just 20 percent of one's life. (②) As we age, a decade becomes an ever-smaller proportion of our life experience. (③) In just ten years, a younger person is likely to graduate from college, woo and win a mate, start a family, and buy a house. (④) Older people, in contrast, can easily pass a decade doing the same job and living in the same house with the same spouse. (⑤) The absence of frequent life-changing events may partly explain why older people feel that the later decades seem to pass so quickly.

*compression 압축   **woo 구애하다

02 [17강 2번]

다음 빈칸에 들어갈 말로 가장 적절한 것은?

Social mobility is upward or downward movement in social position over time in a society. That movement can be specific to individuals who change social positions or to categories of people, such as racial or ethnic groups. Social mobility between generations is referred to as intergenerational mobility. The self-made myth suggests that social position in the United States is _____, implying that mobility is quite common and easy to achieve for those who apply themselves. However, what people believe and what is fact are often not the same. A recent experimental study found that Americans substantially and consistently overestimate the amount of income mobility and educational access in society. The higher one's social class, the more likely they are to overestimate social mobility. In other words, wealthy Americans tend to subscribe to the belief that pulling oneself out of poverty is easier than it actually is and that one's wealth is a result of hard work and initiative, rather than luck or birth.

① largely up to the individual
② preceded by personal happiness
③ too difficult to achieve personally
④ something everyone wants to occupy
⑤ what people want to aim for in their lives

주어진 글 다음에 이어질 글의 순서로 가장 적절한 것은?

In Ancient Greece, many private individuals believed in the powers of magic, such as farmers who were always dependent on the weather. Even though the use of magic was widespread in Ancient Greece, there remained an official caution over its use. We know that the Greek authorities believed that magic was an activity capable of results, but they grew concerned about those who practiced harmful magic.

(A) This mistrust of magic, along with religion and a separation of humans from the divine world, created a need to develop new methods of understanding the world. It is thus understandable that the Ancient Greeks created the foundations for philosophy.

(B) So it was established that those who practiced harmful magic could be punished by civic action. This may be the reason why magic in the classical world was held in low esteem and condemned by speakers and writers.

(C) Likewise, we find certain intellectuals realizing that the power of magic could be abused. For example, Plato believed that those who sold spells and curse tablets should be punished. Epicurean and Stoic philosophers also believed that magic should be eliminated.

*civic 시민의 **curse tablet 저주 서판

① (A) – (C) – (B)   ② (B) – (A) – (C)
③ (B) – (C) – (A)   ④ (C) – (A) – (B)
⑤ (C) – (B) – (A)

다음 글의 제목으로 가장 적절한 것은?

The development psychologist Jerome Kagan measured changes in children's temperament between the ages of 4 months and 7 years. He classified several healthy 4-month-old infants as high reactors (easily excited or fearful) or low reactors (relaxed and unafraid), depending upon their responses to an unfamiliar stimulus. Kagan waved colorful mobiles in front of a baby, played a tape saying, "Hello baby, how are you doing today?" and popped a balloon behind the baby's head. High reactors moved around violently and cried, while low reactors rested or even laughed during the tests. By the time these infants were 4 years old, some of the high reactors were quite shy, subdued, and quiet, while others had moved toward the center of Kagan's "shy-bold" continuum. By the age of 7, only 15 percent of the initially low reactors were enthusiastic, fearless, and highly sociable kids, and the rest had moved closer to the center. None of the high reactors became fearless, and none of the low reactors became fearful; in other words, environment only moderately affected the final outcome.

*temperament 기질 **subdued 차분해진

① Ever Persistent: A Psychologist's Research
② Early Education: Able to Change Temperament?
③ Temperamental Characteristics of Each Age Group
④ Environment: Helpful to Changes in Temperament?
⑤ The Classification of Temperament: Are Two Classes Enough?

다음 글의 밑줄 친 부분 중, 어법상 틀린 것은?

There are several theories about why older people experience "long-term" time compression so much more ① <u>acutely</u> than young people. It ② <u>has observed</u>, for example, that for a twenty-year-old, ten years is half a lifetime, but for a fifty-year-old, the same span represents just 20 percent of one's life. As we age, a decade becomes an ever-smaller proportion of our life experience. ③ <u>Others</u> have emphasized the fact that, in a ten-year span, younger people encounter more "turning points" than older people. In just ten years, a younger person is likely to graduate from college, woo and win a mate, start a family, and buy a house. Older people, in contrast, can easily pass a decade doing the same job and ④ <u>living</u> in the same house with the same spouse. The absence of frequent life-changing events may partly explain ⑤ <u>why</u> older people feel that the later decades seem to pass so quickly.

*compression 압축 **woo 구애하다

주어진 글 다음에 이어질 글의 순서로 가장 적절한 것은?

Social mobility is upward or downward movement in social position over time in a society. That movement can be specific to individuals who change social positions or to categories of people, such as racial or ethnic groups. Social mobility between generations is referred to as intergenerational mobility.

(A) In other words, wealthy Americans tend to subscribe to the belief that pulling oneself out of poverty is easier than it actually is and that one's wealth is a result of hard work and initiative, rather than luck or birth.

(B) A recent experimental study found that Americans substantially and consistently overestimate the amount of income mobility and educational access in society. The higher one's social class, the more likely they are to overestimate social mobility.

(C) The self-made myth suggests that social position in the United States is largely up to the individual, implying that mobility is quite common and easy to achieve for those who apply themselves. However, what people believe and what is fact are often not the same.

① (A) – (C) – (B)　　② (B) – (A) – (C)
③ (B) – (C) – (A)　　④ (C) – (A) – (B)
⑤ (C) – (B) – (A)

다음 빈칸에 들어갈 말로 가장 적절한 것은?

In Ancient Greece, many private individuals believed in the powers of magic, such as farmers who were always dependent on the weather. Even though the use of magic was widespread in Ancient Greece, there remained an official caution over its use. We know that the Greek authorities believed that magic was an activity capable of results, but they grew concerned about those who practiced harmful magic. So it was established that those who practiced harmful magic could be punished by civic action. This may be the reason why magic in the classical world was held in low esteem and condemned by speakers and writers. Likewise, we find certain intellectuals realizing that the power of magic could be abused. For example, Plato believed that those who sold spells and curse tablets should be punished. Epicurean and Stoic philosophers also believed that magic should be eliminated. _____, along with religion and a separation of humans from the divine world, created a need to develop new methods of understanding the world. It is thus understandable that the Ancient Greeks created the foundations for philosophy.

*civic 시민의 **curse tablet 저주 서판

① The abuse of magic
② This mistrust of magic
③ This achievement of magic
④ The over-reliance on magic
⑤ Criticism of the intellectuals of the time

Kagan에 관한 다음 글의 내용과 일치하지 <u>않는</u> 것은?

The development psychologist Jerome Kagan measured changes in children's temperament between the ages of 4 months and 7 years. He classified several healthy 4-month-old infants as high reactors (easily excited or fearful) or low reactors (relaxed and unafraid), depending upon their responses to an unfamiliar stimulus. Kagan waved colorful mobiles in front of a baby, played a tape saying, "Hello baby, how are you doing today?" and popped a balloon behind the baby's head. High reactors moved around violently and cried, while low reactors rested or even laughed during the tests. By the time these infants were 4 years old, some of the high reactors were quite shy, subdued, and quiet, while others had moved toward the center of Kagan's "shy-bold" continuum. By the age of 7, only 15 percent of the initially low reactors were enthusiastic, fearless, and highly sociable kids, and the rest had moved closer to the center. None of the high reactors became fearless, and none of the low reactors became fearful; in other words, environment only moderately affected the final outcome.

*temperament 기질 **subdued 차분해진

① 아동들의 기질 변화를 조사하기 위해 몇차례에 걸쳐 관찰하였다.
② 피실험자를 낯선 자극에 대한 반응에 따라 분류하였다.
③ 4세 아이들을 관찰했을 때 유아기 때와 큰 차이가 없었다.
④ 7세가 된 초기 저반응 아이들의 15%만이 열정적임을 관찰하였다.
⑤ 고반응을 보였던 유아들이 7세가 되어 겁이 없어진 것을 발견했다.

There are several theories about why older people experience "long-term" time compression so much more ① <u>acutely</u> than young people. It has been observed, for example, that for a twenty-year-old, ten years ② <u>are</u> half a lifetime, but for a fifty-year-old, the same span represents just 20 percent of one's life. As we age, a decade becomes an ever-smaller proportion of our life experience. Others have emphasized the fact ③ <u>that</u>, in a ten-year span, younger people encounter more "turning points" than older people. In just ten years, a younger person is likely ④ <u>to graduate</u> from college, woo and win a mate, start a family, and buy a house. Older people, in contrast, can easily pass a decade doing the same job and ⑤ <u>live</u> in the same house with the same spouse. The absence of frequent life-changing events may partly explain why older people feel that the later decades seem to pass so quickly.

*compression 압축 **woo 구애하다

고난도

09 윗글의 밑줄 친 부분 중, 어법상 틀린 것을 2개 찾아 그 번호를 쓰고 고쳐 쓰시오.

(1) _____ → _____

(2) _____ → _____

10 윗글에서 다음 질문에 대한 답을 찾아 영어로 답하시오. (6단어)

Q: According to the passage, what might make older people feel that the later decades seem to pass so quickly?

A: _____

Social mobility is upward or downward movement in social position over time in a society. That movement can be specific to individuals who change social positions or to categories of people, such as racial or ethnic groups. Social mobility between generations (A) <u>refer to</u> as intergenerational mobility. The self-made myth suggests that social position in the United States is largely up to the individual, (B) <u>implies</u> that mobility is quite common and easy to achieve for those who apply themselves. However, what people believe and (C) <u>which</u> is fact are often not the same. A recent experimental study found that Americans substantially and consistently overestimate the amount of income mobility and educational access in society. The higher one's social class, the more likely they are to overestimate social mobility. In other words, wealthy Americans tend to subscribe to the belief that pulling oneself out of poverty is easier than <u>it</u> actually is and that one's wealth is a result of hard work and initiative, rather than luck or birth.

고난도

11 윗글의 밑줄 친 부분을 어법상 알맞은 형태로 고쳐 쓰시오.

(A) refer to → _____

(B) implies → _____

(C) which → _____

12 윗글의 밑줄 친 it이 가리키는 것을 본문에서 찾아 쓰시오. (5단어)

_____

In Ancient Greece, many private individuals believed in the powers of magic, such as farmers who were always dependent on the weather. Even though the use of magic was widespread in Ancient Greece, there remained an official caution over its use. 우리는 그리스 당국이 마법이 성과를 낼 수 있는 활동이라고 믿었지만 해로운 마법을 행하는 사람들에 대해 점차 걱정하게 되었음을 알고 있다. So it was established that those who practiced harmful magic could be punished by civic action. This may be the reason why magic in the classical world was held in low esteem and _____ by speakers and writers. Likewise, we find certain intellectuals realizing that the power of magic could be abused. For example, Plato believed that those who sold spells and curse tablets should be punished. Epicurean and Stoic philosophers also believed that magic should be eliminated. This mistrust of magic, along with religion and a separation of humans from the divine world, created a need to develop new methods of understanding the world. It is thus understandable that the Ancient Greeks created the foundations for philosophy.

*civic 시민의 **curse tablet 저주 서판

고난도

13 윗글의 밑줄 친 우리말 의미와 일치하도록 보기 의 단어를 순서대로 배열하여 문장을 완성하시오.

> 보기 results / grew / an activity / they / magic / concerned about / was / who / practiced / harmful magic / those / capable of

We know that the Greek authorities believed that

_____,

but _____.

14 윗글의 빈칸에 들어갈 단어를 영영 뜻풀이를 참고하여 쓰시오. (단, 주어진 글자로 시작하여 알맞은 형태로 쓸 것)

> to express strong and define disapproval of someone or something

c_____

The development psychologist Jerome Kagan measured changes in children's temperament between the ages of 4 months and 7 years. He classified several healthy 4-month-old infants as high reactors (easily excited or fearful) or low reactors (relaxed and unafraid), 낯선 자극에 대한 그들의 반응에 따라. Kagan waved colorful mobiles in front of a baby, played a tape saying, "Hello baby, how are you doing today?" and popped a balloon behind the baby's head. High reactors moved around violently and cried, while low reactors rested or even laughed during the tests. By the time these infants were 4 years old, some of the high reactors were quite shy, subdued, and quiet, while others had moved toward the center of Kagan's "shy-bold" continuum. By the age of 7, only 15 percent of the initially low reactors were enthusiastic, fearless, and highly sociable kids, and the rest had moved closer to the center. None of the high reactors became ____(A)____, and none of the low reactors became ____(B)____; in other words, environment only moderately affected the final outcome.

*temperament 기질 **subdued 차분해진

고난도

15 윗글의 빈칸 (A)와 (B)에 들어갈 말을 본문에서 찾아 쓰시오. (각각 1단어로 쓸 것)

(A) _____ (B) _____

16 윗글의 밑줄 친 우리말과 일치하도록 보기 의 단어를 순서대로 배열하여 문장을 완성하시오.

> 보기 unfamiliar / upon / their / to / responses / stimulus / depending / an

_____

❶ We do know that the ability to question, whether verbally or through other means, is one of the things that separates us from lower primates. ❷ Paul Harris, an education professor at Harvard University who has studied questioning in children, observes, "Unlike other primates, we humans are designed so that the young look to the old for cultural information." ❸ He sees this as an important "evolutionary divide" — that from an early age, even before speech, humans will use some form of questioning to try to gain information. ❹ A child may pick up a kiwi fruit and indicate, through a look or gesture directed at a nearby adult, a desire to know more. ❺ Chimpanzees don't do this; they may "ask" for a treat through signaling, but it's a simple request for food, as opposed to an information-seeking question.

❻ So then, one of the primary drivers of questioning is an awareness of what we don't know — which is a form of higher awareness that separates not only man from monkey but also the smart and curious person from the dullard who doesn't know or care. ❼ Good questioners tend to be aware of, and quite comfortable with, their own ignorance ❽ (Richard Saul Wurman, the founder of the TED Conferences, has been known to brag, "I know more about my ignorance than you know about yours"). ❾ But they constantly examine that vast ignorance using the question flashlight — or, if you prefer, they attack it with the question spade.

*primate 영장류   **brag 호언장담하다   ***spade 삽

❶ 말로든 아니면 다른 수단을 통해서든 질문을 하는 능력이 우리와 하등 영장류를 구분 짓는 것들 중 하나라는 것을 우리는 정말이지 알고 있다. ❷ 아이들에게 질문하는 것을 연구해 온 Paul Harris 하버드 대학교 교육학 교수는 "우리 인간은 다른 영장류와 달리 어린 사람은 연장자가 문화적 정보를 주리라고 기대하도록 설계되어 있다."라고 말한다. ❸ 그는 이것을 중요한 '진화의 경계선'으로 보는데, 즉 어린 나이부터 심지어 말을 하기 전에도 인간은 정보를 얻고자 어떤 형태의 질문을 (으레) 사용할 거라는 것이다. ❹ 어린이는 키위를 집어서 가까이 있는 어른을 향한 시선이나 몸짓을 통해 더 많은 것을 알고 싶다는 욕구를 나타낼 수도 있다. ❺ 침팬지들은 이것을 하지 않는데, 즉 그들은 신호 보내기를 통해 맛있는 것을 '요구할' 수 있지만, 그것은 정보를 찾는 질문이 아니라, 음식을 달라는 단순한 요청이다. ❻ 그렇다면 질문하기의 주요한 동인(動因) 중 하나는 우리가 모르는 것에 대한 인식이라는 것인데, 그것은 인간과 원숭이뿐만 아니라 똑똑하고 호기심 많은 사람과 모르거나 신경 쓰지 않는 둔한 사람을 구분 짓는 더 수준 높은 인식의 한 형태이다. ❼ 훌륭한 질문자들은 자신들의 무지를 인식하고 그것에 대해 꽤 편안하게 느끼는 경향이 있다 ❽ (TED 콘퍼런스의 창시자인 Richard Saul Wurman은 "여러분이 여러분 자신의 무지에 대해 아는 것보다 제가 저의 무지에 대해 더 많이 알고 있습니다"라고 호언장담한다고 알려졌다). ❾ 그러나 그들은 질문이라는 손전등을 사용하여 그 방대한 무지를 끊임없이 조사하는데, 여러분이 이 말이 더 좋다면, 질문이라는 삽으로 그것을 공격하는 것이다.

Word List

□ verbally 말로   □ means 수단   □ separate 구분 짓다   □ observe 말하다, 관찰하다   □ look to ~ for... ~이 …을 주리라고 기대하다
□ evolutionary 진화론적인   □ divide 경계선, 분수령   □ speech 말, 발화   □ gain 얻다   □ signal 신호하다
□ as opposed to ~이 아니라   □ primary 주요한   □ driver 동인(動因)   □ awareness 인식   □ dullard 둔한 사람
□ ignorance 무지   □ founder 창시자   □ vast 방대한

• Word Test

1	gain		10	수단
2	driver		11	진화론적인
3	observe		12	주요한
4	as opposed to		13	구분 짓다
5	look to ~ for...		14	말, 발화
6	dullard		15	방대한
7	founder		16	무지
8	divide		17	신호하다
9	verbally		18	인식

We do know that the ability to question, whether verbally or through other means, is one of the things that separates us ❶ to / from lower primates. Paul Harris, an education professor at Harvard University who has studied questioning in children, observes, "❷ Like / Unlike other primates, we humans are designed so that the young look to the old for cultural information." He sees this as an important "evolutionary divide" — that from an early age, even before speech, humans will use some form of questioning to try to gain information. A child may pick up a kiwi fruit and ❸ ensure / indicate , through a look or gesture directed at a nearby adult, a desire to know more. Chimpanzees don't do this; they may "ask" for a treat through signaling, but it's a simple request for food, as opposed to an information-seeking question.

So then, one of the primary drivers of questioning is an awareness of what we don't know — which is a form of higher awareness that separates not only man from monkey but also the smart and curious person from the dullard ❹ which / who doesn't know or care. Good questioners tend to be aware of, and quite ❺ embarrassed/comfortable with, their own ignorance (Richard Saul Wurman, the founder of the TED Conferences, has been known to brag, "I know more about my ignorance than you know about yours"). But they constantly examine that vast ignorance using the question flashlight — or, if you prefer, they attack it with the question spade.

*primate 영장류 **brag 호언장담하다 ***spade 삽

We do know that the ability to question, whether verbally or through other means, ❶ _____ (be) one of the things that separates us from lower primates. Paul Harris, an education professor at Harvard University who has studied questioning in children, observes, "Unlike other primates, we humans ❷ _____ (design) so that the young look to the old for cultural information." He sees this as an important "evolutionary divide" — that from an early age, even before speech, humans will use some form of questioning to try to gain information. A child may pick up a kiwi fruit and indicate, through a look or gesture ❸ _____ (direct) at a nearby adult, a desire to know more. Chimpanzees don't do this; they may "ask" for a treat through signaling, but it's a simple request for food, as opposed to an information-seeking question.

So then, one of the primary drivers of questioning ❹ _____ (be) an awareness of what we don't know — which is a form of higher awareness that separates not only man from monkey but also the smart and curious person from the dullard who doesn't know or care. Good questioners tend to be aware of, and quite comfortable with, their own ignorance (Richard Saul Wurman, the founder of the TED Conferences, ❺ _____ (know) to brag, "I know more about my ignorance than you know about yours"). But they constantly examine that vast ignorance ❻ _____ (use) the question flashlight — or, if you prefer, they attack it with the question spade.

*primate 영장류 **brag 호언장담하다 ***spade 삽

We do know that ❶ _____ _____ _____ _____ (질문을 하는 능력), whether verbally or through other means, is one of the things that separates us from lower primates. Paul Harris, an education professor at Harvard University who has studied questioning in children, observes, "Unlike other primates, we humans are designed ❷ _____ _____ (~하도록) the young look to the old for cultural information." He sees this as an important "evolutionary divide" — that from an early age, even before speech, humans will use some form of questioning to try to gain information. A child may pick up a kiwi fruit and indicate, through a look or gesture directed at a nearby adult, a desire to know more. Chimpanzees don't do this; they may "ask" for a treat through signaling, but it's a simple request for food, ❸ _____ _____ _____ (~이 아닌 반대로) an information-seeking question.

So then, one of the primary drivers of questioning is an awareness of what we don't know — which is a form of higher awareness that separates not only man from monkey but also the smart and curious person from the dullard who doesn't know or care. Good questioners ❹ _____ _____ _____ _____ (~을 인식하려는 경향이 있다), and quite comfortable with, their own ignorance (Richard Saul Wurman, the founder of the TED Conferences, has been known to brag, "I know more about my ignorance than you know about yours"). But they constantly examine that vast ignorance using the question flashlight — or, if you prefer, they attack it with the question spade.

*primate 영장류 **brag 호언장담하다 ***spade 삽

❶ You attract whatever you spend time pondering, including whatever you love and whatever you fear. ❷ Your soul will rise to achieve your highest hope and will also fall to the depths of your basest appetite and your life will be a direct reflection of all your desires. ❸ This holds true for both your conscious and unconscious thoughts, which may seem a bit confusing at first. ❹ For example, you may want prosperity and believe that you're working toward bringing more of it into your life. ❺ Your savings account, however, remains empty. ❻ This is because unconsciously you're thinking, *I'm afraid of poverty, and I don't think I'll ever be rich*. ❼ Even though you've made an effort to increase your wealth, your pessimistic thinking with respect to money is so ingrained that it actually cancels out your positive steps. ❽ Yet with continued effort and vigilance against negative self-talk, you can turn around and create a prosperous life.

❾ The outer world of your circumstances is shaped by the inner world of your thoughts. ❿ Every seed of thought that you sow or allow to fall into your mind and take root eventually blossoms into action. ⓫ And once again, good thoughts bear sweet fruit, while bad ones bear rotten fruit. ⓬ A person doesn't end up homeless or in jail by the tyranny of fate or by chance, but as the direct result of cynical thinking and corrupt desires. ⓭ Similarly, a model citizen doesn't suddenly commit a crime due to a chance occurrence, but because he or she secretly fostered the criminal thought for a long time.

*pessimistic 비관적인, 회의적인 **vigilance 경계, 조심 ***tyranny 횡포, 폭정

❶ 여러분은 여러분이 사랑하는 모든 것과 두려워하는 모든 것을 포함해서 여러분이 숙고하며 시간을 보내는 것은 무엇이든 끌어모은다. ❷ 여러분의 정신은 고조되어 최상의 희망을 성취할 것이고, 또한 가장 기본적인 욕구의 나락으로 떨어져, 여러분의 삶은 모든 욕망의 직접적인 반영이 될 것이다. ❸ 이것은 여러분의 의식적 사고와 무의식적인 사고 둘 다에 딱 들어맞는데, 이것은 처음에는 약간 혼란스러워 보일 수도 있다. ❹ 예를 들면, 여러분은 부를 원하고 그것을 더 많이 여러분의 삶에 가져오도록 노력하고 있다고 믿을지도 모른다. ❺ 그러나 여러분의 예금 계좌는 계속 비어있다. ❻ 이것은 '나는 가난이 두렵고 나는 결코 부자가 될 것으로 생각하지 않는다.'라고 여러분이 무의식적으로 생각하고 있기 때문이다. ❼ 비록 여러분이 부를 늘리기 위해 노력을 해 왔더라도, 돈에 관한 여러분의 비관적인 생각이 매우 뿌리 깊어 그것은 실제로 여러분의 긍정적인 조치를 상쇄한다. ❽ 그러나 지속적으로 노력하고 부정적인 자기 대화를 경계한다면, 여러분은 더 나아져서 유복한 삶을 이룰 수 있다.

❾ 여러분 환경의 외부 세계는 여러분 사고의 내부 세계에 의해 형성된다. ❿ 여러분이 뿌리거나 여러분의 마음에 떨어져 뿌리를 내리게 하는 모든 생각의 씨앗은 결국에는 개화하여 행동이 될 것이다. ⓫ 다시 한번 말하지만, 좋은 생각은 달콤한 열매를 맺지만, 나쁜 생각은 썩은 열매를 맺는다. ⓬ 사람은 운명의 횡포나 우연에 의해 결국 노숙자가 되거나 교도소에 가는 것이 아니라 부정적인 생각과 타락한 욕망의 직접적인 결과로 그렇게 되는 것이다. ⓭ 마찬가지로, 모범 시민이 갑자기 우연한 사건으로 범죄를 저지르는 것이 아니라 오랫동안 은밀하게 범죄에 관한 생각을 품었기 때문에 그런 것이다.

Word List

□ attract 끌어모으다 □ ponder 숙고하다, 곰곰이 생각하다 □ base 기본의 □ appetite 욕구, 식욕 □ reflection 반영, 반사
□ unconscious 무의식적인 □ confusing 혼란스러운 □ prosperity 부, (금전적) 성공 □ savings account 예금 계좌, 적금 계좌
□ with respect to ~에 관하여 □ ingrain 깊이 배게 하다 □ cancel out ~을 상쇄하다 □ sow (씨를) 뿌리다
□ eventually 결국, 언젠가는 □ blossom 개화하다, 꽃 피다 □ rotten 썩은 □ cynical 부정적인, 냉소적인 □ corrupt 타락한, 부패한
□ commit a crime 범죄를 저지르다 □ occurrence 발생

1	sow	11	부, (금전적) 성공
2	ingrain	12	혼란스러운
3	base	13	~에 관하여
4	savings account	14	타락한, 부패한
5	cynical	15	발생
6	commit a crime	16	썩은
7	reflection	17	무의식적인
8	eventually	18	개화하다, 꽃 피다
9	ponder	19	끌어모으다
10	cancel out	20	욕구, 식욕

• 유형 1 네모 안에서 옳은 어법·어휘를 고르시오.

You attract ❶ whatever/whenever you spend time pondering, including whatever you love and whatever you fear. Your soul will rise to achieve your highest hope and will also fall to the depths of your basest appetite and your life will be a direct ❷ meditation/reflection of all your desires. This holds true for both your conscious and unconscious thoughts, ❸ that/which may seem a bit confusing at first. For example, you may want prosperity and believe that you're working toward bringing more of it into your life. Your savings account, however, remains empty. This is because unconsciously you're thinking, *I'm afraid of poverty, and I don't think I'll ever be rich*. Even though you've made an effort to increase your wealth, your pessimistic thinking with respect to money is so ❹ ingrained/transient that it actually cancels out your positive steps. Yet with continued effort and vigilance against negative self-talk, you can turn around and create a prosperous life.

The outer world of your circumstances is shaped by the inner world of your thoughts. Every ❺ seed / seeds of thought that you sow or allow to fall into your mind and take root eventually blossoms into action. And once again, good thoughts bear sweet fruit, ❻ since/while bad ones bear rotten fruit. A person doesn't end up homeless or in jail by the tyranny of fate or by chance, but as the direct result of cynical thinking and corrupt desires. Similarly, a model citizen doesn't suddenly ❼ commit/prevent a crime due to a chance occurrence, but because he or she secretly fostered the criminal thought for a long time.

*pessimistic 비관적인, 회의적인   **vigilance 경계, 조심   ***tyranny 횡포, 폭정

You attract whatever you spend time ❶ _____ (ponder), including whatever you love and whatever you fear. Your soul will rise to achieve your highest hope and will also fall to the depths of your basest appetite and your life will be a direct reflection of all your desires. This holds true for both your conscious and unconscious thoughts, which may seem a bit confusing at first. For example, you may want prosperity and believe that you're working toward bringing more of it into your life. Your savings account, however, ❷ _____ (remain) empty. This is because unconsciously you're thinking, *I'm afraid of poverty, and I don't think I'll ever be rich*. Even though you've made an effort to increase your wealth, your pessimistic thinking with respect to money is so ingrained that it actually ❸ _____ (cancel) out your positive steps. Yet with continued effort and vigilance against negative self-talk, you can turn around and create a prosperous life.

The outer world of your circumstances ❹ _____ (shape) by the inner world of your thoughts. Every seed of thought that you sow or allow ❺ _____ (fall) into your mind and take root eventually blossoms into action. And once again, good thoughts bear sweet fruit, while bad ones bear rotten fruit. A person doesn't end up homeless or in jail by the tyranny of fate or by chance, but as the direct result of cynical thinking and corrupt desires. Similarly, a model citizen doesn't suddenly commit a crime due to a chance occurrence, but because he or she secretly fostered the criminal thought for a long time.

*pessimistic 비관적인, 회의적인   **vigilance 경계, 조심   ***tyranny 횡포, 폭정

You attract whatever you spend time pondering, including whatever you love and whatever you fear. Your soul will rise to achieve your highest hope and will also fall to the depths of your basest appetite and your life will be a direct reflection of all your desires. ❶ _____ _____ _____ _____ (이것은 ~에 딱 들어맞는다) both your conscious and unconscious thoughts, which may ❷ _____ _____ _____ _____ (약간 혼란스러워 보인다) at first. For example, you may want prosperity and believe that you're working toward bringing more of it into your life. Your savings account, however, remains empty. This is because unconsciously you're thinking, *I'm afraid of poverty, and I don't think I'll ever be rich*. Even though you've made an effort to increase your wealth, your pessimistic thinking ❸ _____ _____ _____ _____ (돈에 관한) is so ingrained that it actually cancels out your positive steps. Yet with continued effort and vigilance against negative self-talk, you can turn around and create a prosperous life.

The outer world of your circumstances is shaped by the inner world of your thoughts. Every seed of thought that you sow or allow to fall into your mind and take root eventually blossoms into action. And once again, good thoughts bear sweet fruit, while bad ones bear rotten fruit. A person doesn't end up homeless or in jail by the tyranny of fate or by chance, but ❹ _____ _____ _____ _____ _____ (~의 직접적인 결과로) cynical thinking and corrupt desires. Similarly, a model citizen doesn't suddenly commit a crime ❺ _____ _____ _____ _____ _____ (우연한 사건으로 인해), but because he or she secretly fostered the criminal thought for a long time.

*pessimistic 비관적인, 회의적인   **vigilance 경계, 조심   ***tyranny 횡포, 폭정

❶ Humans are motivated, at least in part, by empathy and concern for the welfare of others. ❷ We donate blood for strangers, contribute to charity, and punish violators of social norms. ❸ Chimpanzees are, together with bonobos, our closest relatives, and they similarly engage in cooperative hunting, comfort victims of aggression, and perform other collective activities. ❹ Would they show concern for the welfare of unrelated, familiar chimps if the benefits were at no cost to themselves?

❺ Researcher Joan Silk and her collaborators conducted an experiment with chimps that had lived together for fifteen years or more. ❻ Eighteen chimps were studied, from two different populations with different life histories and exposures to experiments. ❼ Pairs of chimps faced each other in opposing enclosures or sat side by side, and could see and hear each other. ❽ One chimp, the actor, was given the choice to pull one of two handles: if the actor pulled the "nice" handle, both the actor and the other chimp got food, and exactly the same portion. ❾ If the actor pulled the "nasty" handle, only the actor received food, and the other chimp got nothing. ❿ In a control test, only the actor was present. ⓫ Which handle did the chimps pull?

⓬ When no other chimp was present, the actors chose both options about equally frequently. ⓭ The chimps didn't care, and why should they? ⓮ Yet even when a second chimp arrived, the chimps didn't choose the "nice" option more often. ⓯ Although they could clearly see the other one displaying desperate begging gestures, or happily eating the food when it was dispensed, the chimps showed no sign of empathy. ⓰ It should be noted that they showed no spitefulness either. ⓱ What mattered to the actors more than the other chimp was whether the handle for the nice option was placed on their right or left side. ⓲ They had a much stronger preference for the right side than for the happiness of their partner. ⓳ Chimps simply did not seem to care about the welfare of unrelated group members.

*enclosure 울타리 안, 담장 안　**dispense 제공하다, 나눠 주다　***spitefulness 악의

❶ 인간은 최소한 어느 정도는 타인의 행복에 대한 공감과 관심에 의해 동기 부여를 받는다. ❷ 우리는 낯선 사람을 위해 헌혈을 하고, 자선 단체에 기부하며, 사회 규범을 위반하는 사람을 처벌한다. ❸ 침팬지는 보노보를 포함하여 우리의 가장 가까운 친척이며, 그것들은 비슷하게 협력적인 사냥을 하고, 공격의 희생자를 위로하며, 그 밖의 다른 집단 활동을 한다. ❹ 그들은 그 이익(다른 침팬지가 받는 이익)이 자기 자신에게 아무런 손실이 되지 않는다면 친족이 아닌 친숙한 침팬지들의 행복에 관심을 보일까?

❺ 연구자 Joan Silk와 그녀의 공동 연구자들은 15년 또는 그 이상 함께 살아온 침팬지들을 대상으로 실험을 수행했다. ❻ 18마리의 침팬지들이 연구되었는데, 그것들은 서로 다른 생활사를 갖고 있고 서로 다른 실험을 체험한 서로 다른 두 개체군에서 왔다. ❼ 여러 쌍의 침팬지들이 마주 보는 (반대편) 울타리 안에서 서로를 대면하거나 나란히 앉아 서로를 보고 들을 수 있었다. ❽ 행위자인 한 침팬지에게 두 손잡이 중 하나를 당길 수 있는 선택권이 주어졌는데, 그 행위자가 '착한(nice)' 손잡이를 당기면, 행위자와 다른 한 침팬지가 모두 먹이를 얻었고, 정확히 똑같은 몫이었다. ❾ 행위자가 '못된(nasty)' 손잡이를 당기면, 행위자만 음식을 받았고, 다른 한 침팬지는 아무것도 얻지 못했다. ❿ 대조 검사에서는 행위자만 있었다. ⓫ 침팬지들은 어떤 손잡이를 당겼을까?

⓬ 다른 침팬지가 없을 때, 행위자들은 거의 같은 빈도로 두 가지 선택권을 모두 택했다. ⓭ 침팬지들은 신경 쓰지 않았는데, 그것들이 왜 그러겠는가? ⓮ 그러나 다른 침팬지가 도착했을 때조차도, 침팬지들은 '착한' 선택권을 더 자주 택하지는 않았다. ⓯ 다른 침팬지가 절박하게 구걸하는 몸짓을 보이거나, 또는 음식이 제공될 때 행복하게 그것을 먹는 것을 분명히 볼 수 있었음에도 불구하고, 침팬지들은 전혀 공감하는 기색을 보이지 않았다. ⓰ 그것들이 또한 악의도 보이지 않았다는 것이 주목되어야 한다. ⓱ 행위자에게 다른 침팬지보다 더 중요했던 것은 착한 선택권을 위한 손잡이가 그것들의 오른쪽에 놓였는가 아니면 왼쪽에 놓였는가 하는 것이었다. ⓲ 그것들은 파트너의 행복보다는 오른쪽에 대한 훨씬 더 강한 선호를 가지고 있었다. ⓳ 침팬지들은 친족이 아닌 집단 구성원의 행복에 전혀 신경 쓰는 것처럼 보이지 않았다.

	□ **motivate** 동기를 부여하다 □ **in part** 부분적으로 □ **empathy** 공감 □ **welfare** 행복, 안녕 □ **contribute** 기여하다
Word List	□ **charity** 자선(단체) □ **violator** 위반하는 사람 □ **norm** 규범 □ **relative** 친척, (공통의 계통을 갖는) 동물[식물]
	□ **cooperative** 협력적인 □ **aggression** 공격 □ **unrelated** 친족이 아닌 □ **collaborator** 공동 연구자, 협력자
	□ **exposure** 체험[경험]하기 □ **opposing** 마주보는 □ **portion** 몫, 부분 □ **nasty** 못된, 고약한 □ **desperate** 절박한, 필사적인
	□ **beg** 애원하다, 구걸하다 □ **preference** 선호(도)

• Word Test

1	desperate		11	부분적으로	
2	portion		12	마주보는	
3	contribute		13	선호(도)	
4	unrelated		14	공동 연구자, 협력자	
5	cooperative		15	자선(단체)	
6	empathy		16	애원하다, 구걸하다	
7	violator		17	체험[경험]하기	
8	relative		18	행복, 안녕	
9	motivate		19	규범	
10	nasty		20	공격	

• 유형 1 네모 안에서 옳은 어법·어휘를 고르시오.

Humans are motivated, at least in part, by empathy and concern for the welfare of ❶ other / others . We donate blood for strangers, contribute to charity, and punish violators of social norms. Chimpanzees are, together with bonobos, our closest relatives, and they similarly engage in cooperative hunting, comfort victims of aggression, and perform other collective activities. Would they show concern for the welfare of unrelated, familiar chimps if the benefits were at no cost to themselves?

Researcher Joan Silk and her collaborators conducted an experiment with chimps that had lived together for fifteen years or more. Eighteen chimps ❷ studied / were studied , from two different populations with different life histories and exposures to experiments. Pairs of chimps faced each other in opposing enclosures or sat side by side, and could see and hear each other. One chimp, the actor, was given the choice to pull one of two handles: if the actor pulled the "nice" handle, both the actor and ❸ the other / another chimp got food, and exactly the same portion. If the actor pulled the "nasty" handle, only the actor received food, and the other chimp got nothing. In a control test, only the actor was present. Which handle did the chimps pull?

When no other chimp was present, the actors chose both options about equally frequently. The chimps didn't care, and why should they? Yet even when a second chimp arrived, the chimps didn't choose the "nice" option more often. ❹ Unless / Although they could clearly see the other one displaying desperate begging gestures, or happily eating the food when it was dispensed, the chimps showed no sign of empathy. It should be noted that they showed no spitefulness ❺ too / either . What mattered to the actors more than the other chimp was whether the handle for the nice option was placed on their right or left side. They had a much stronger preference for the right side than for the happiness of their partner. Chimps simply did not seem to care about the welfare of ❻ related / unrelated group members.

*enclosure 울타리 안, 담장 안 **dispense 제공하다, 나눠 주다 ***spitefulness 악의

Humans are motivated, at least in part, by empathy and concern for the welfare of others. We donate blood for strangers, contribute to charity, and punish violators of social norms. Chimpanzees are, together with bonobos, our closest relatives, and they similarly engage in cooperative hunting, ❶ _____ (comfort) victims of aggression, and perform other collective activities. Would they show concern for the welfare of unrelated, familiar chimps if the benefits were at no cost to themselves? Researcher Joan Silk and her collaborators conducted an experiment with chimps that ❷ _____ (live) together for fifteen years or more. Eighteen chimps were studied, from two different populations with different life histories and exposures to experiments. Pairs of chimps faced each other in opposing enclosures or sat side by side, and could see and hear each other. One chimp, the actor, ❸ _____ (give) the choice to pull one of two handles: if the actor pulled the "nice" handle, both the actor and the other chimp got food, and exactly the same portion. If the actor pulled the "nasty" handle, only the actor received food, and the other chimp got nothing. In a control test, only the actor was present. Which handle did the chimps pull?

When no other chimp was present, the actors chose both options about equally frequently. The chimps didn't care, and why should they? Yet even when a second chimp arrived, the chimps didn't choose the "nice" option more often. Although they could clearly see the other one displaying desperate begging gestures, or happily eating the food when it ❹ _____ (dispense), the chimps showed no sign of empathy. It should ❺ _____ (note) that they showed no spitefulness either. What mattered to the actors more than the other chimp ❻ _____ (be) whether the handle for the nice option was placed on their right or left side. They had a much stronger preference for the right side than for the happiness of their partner. Chimps simply did not seem to care about the welfare of unrelated group members.

*enclosure 울타리 안, 담장 안   **dispense 제공하다, 나눠 주다   ***spitefulness 악의

Humans are motivated, ❶ _____ _____ _____ _____ (최소한 어느 부분 정도는), by empathy and concern for the welfare of others. We donate blood for strangers, contribute to charity, and punish violators of social norms. Chimpanzees are, together with bonobos, our closest relatives, and they similarly engage in cooperative hunting, comfort victims of aggression, and perform other collective activities. Would they show concern for the welfare of unrelated, familiar chimps if the benefits were ❷ _____ _____ _____ _____ (~에게 아무런 손실이 아닌) themselves?

Researcher Joan Silk and her collaborators conducted an experiment with chimps that had lived together for fifteen years or more. Eighteen chimps were studied, from two different populations with different life histories and exposures to experiments. Pairs of chimps faced each other ❸ _____ _____ _____ (마주보는 울타리들 안에서) or sat side by side, and could see and hear each other. One chimp, the actor, was given the choice to pull one of two handles: if the actor pulled the "nice" handle, both the actor and the other chimp got food, and ❹ _____ _____ _____ _____ (정확히 똑같은 몫). If the actor pulled the "nasty" handle, only the actor received food, and the other chimp got nothing. In a control test, only the actor was present. Which handle did the chimps pull?

When no other chimp was present, the actors chose both options ❺ _____ _____ _____ (거의 같은 빈도로). The chimps didn't care, and why should they? Yet even when a second chimp arrived, the chimps didn't choose the "nice" option more often. Although they could clearly see the other one displaying desperate begging gestures, or happily eating the food when it was dispensed, the chimps showed no sign of empathy. It should be noted that they showed no spitefulness either. What mattered to the actors more than the other chimp was whether the handle for the nice option was placed on their right or left side. They had a much stronger preference for the right side than for the happiness of their partner. Chimps simply did not seem to care about the welfare of unrelated group members.

*enclosure 울타리 안, 담장 안   **dispense 제공하다, 나눠 주다   ***spitefulness 악의

❶ The main message from studies of change blindness is that people can miss obvious changes in what they see and hear. ❷ Despite this possibility, most people believe they will always notice large changes, that important events automatically draw their attention. ❸ This erroneous belief persists because people often do not find out about the things they fail to perceive. ❹ In addition, the phenomenon of change blindness is so counterintuitive that few people believe how much they do not see. ❺ *Change blindness blindness* is people's unawareness that they often do not notice apparently obvious changes in their environments.

❻ Imagine you are driving up a hill. ❼ At the top of the hill, there is an intersection. ❽ When you reach the top, you see another car heading straight into your lane, and in a flash you swerve to avoid a collision. ❾ The other car hits yours, but your last-minute swerve convinces eyewitnesses that you caused the accident by driving wildly. ❿ Change blindness blindness could be a factor in their reports: Perhaps out of a desire to help, the eyewitnesses believe they saw the whole accident, but they may have missed the critical moments because they were attending to their own activities.

⓫ Being aware of change blindness blindness is a critical thinking skill. ⓬ Thinking that we always notice large changes in our visual field may lead us to perceive things incorrectly, such as in erroneously believing something did or did not happen. ⓭ Recognizing the limitations of attention may help prevent us from misleading ourselves about our perceptions. ⓮ Knowledge about change blindness should make us more humble about what we really see and what we remember.

*counterintuitive 직관에 반하는 **swerve 방향을 바꾸다; 방향 전환 ***collision 충돌

❶ 변화맹에 관한 연구의 주된 메시지는 사람들이 자신이 보고 듣는 것에서의 분명한 변화를 놓칠 수 있다는 것이다. ❷ 이러한 가능성에도 불구하고, 대부분의 사람은 자신이 항상 큰 변화를 알아차릴 것이라고, 즉 중요한 사건은 자동으로 자신의 주의를 끈다고 믿는다. ❸ 이 잘못된 믿음은 사람들이 흔히 자신이 인지하지 못하는 것들에 대해 알아차리지 못하기 때문에 지속된다. ❹ 게다가, 변화맹 현상은 매우 직관에 반해서 자신이 얼마나 많이 보지 못하는지를 믿는 사람은 거의 없다. ❺ '변화맹을 보지 못하는 것'은 사람들이 자신의 환경에서 겉보기에 분명한 변화를 흔히 알아차리지 못한다는 것을 그들이 인식하지 못하는 것이다.

❻ 여러분이 차를 몰아 언덕을 올라가고 있다고 상상해 보라. ❼ 그 언덕 꼭대기에는 교차로가 있다. ❽ 꼭대기에 다다를 때, 여러분은 다른 차 하나가 여러분의 차선으로 곧장 진입하는 것을 보게 되고, 순간적으로 충돌을 피하고자 여러분은 방향을 바꾼다. ❾ 그 다른 차가 여러분의 차를 들이받지만, 여러분의 마지막 순간의 방향 전환은 여러분이 난폭하게 운전해서 사고를 냈다는 것을 목격자들에게 확신시킨다. ❿ 변화맹을 보지 못하는 것이 그들이 보고하는 내용의 한 요소가 될 수 있었는데, 어쩌면 돕고 싶은 마음에서, 그 목격자들은 자신들이 사고의 모든 것을 봤다고 믿지만, 그들은 자기 자신의 활동에 주의를 기울이고 있었기 때문에 결정적인 순간을 놓쳤을 수도 있다. ⓫ 변화맹을 보지 못하는 것을 인식하는 것은 중요한 사고 기술이다. ⓬ 우리가 항상 우리의 시계에서 큰 변화를 알아차린다고 생각하는 것은 우리가 어떤 일이 일어났거나 일어나지 않았다고 잘못 믿는 경우처럼, 사물을 잘못 인식하게 할 수도 있다. ⓭ 주의의 한계를 인식하는 것은 우리가 우리의 인식에 관해 우리 자신을 오도하지 못하게 하는 데 도움이 될 수도 있다. ⓮ 변화맹에 관해 알게 되면 우리는 우리가 실제로 보는 것과 우리가 기억하는 것에 관해 더 겸손하게 될 것이다.

Word List

□ change blindness 변화맹 □ obvious 분명한 □ automatically 자동으로 □ erroneous 잘못된 □ persist 지속되다
□ phenomenon 현상 □ unawareness 인식하지 못함 □ apparently 겉보기에는, 외관상으로 □ intersection 교차로
□ in a flash 순간적으로, 순식간에 □ convince 확신시키다 □ eyewitness 목격자 □ critical 결정적인, 중요한
□ attend to ~에 주의를 기울이다 □ incorrectly 잘못되게, 틀리게 □ limitation 한계 □ mislead 오도하다 □ humble 겸손한, 소박한

1	attend to	10	자동으로
2	apparently	11	겸손한, 소박한
3	erroneous	12	한계
4	in a flash	13	확신시키다
5	persist	14	변화맹
6	incorrectly	15	결정적인, 중요한
7	unawareness	16	분명한
8	eyewitness	17	교차로
9	mislead	18	현상

• 유형 1 네모 안에서 옳은 어법·어휘를 고르시오.

The main message from studies of change blindness is that people can miss obvious changes in what they see and hear. ❶ Despite / Due to this possibility, most people believe they will always notice large changes, that important events automatically draw their attention. This ❷ apparent / erroneous belief persists because people often do not find out about the things they fail to perceive. In addition, the phenomenon of change blindness is so counterintuitive ❸ that / which few people believe how much they do not see. *Change blindness blindness* is people's ❹ awareness / unawareness that they often do not notice apparently obvious changes in their environments.

Imagine you are driving up a hill. At the top of the hill, there is an intersection. When you reach the top, you see another car heading straight into your lane, and in a flash you swerve to avoid a collision. The other car hits yours, but your last-minute swerve convinces eyewitnesses ❺ that / which you caused the accident by driving wildly. Change blindness blindness could be a factor in their reports: Perhaps out of a desire to help, the eyewitnesses believe they saw the whole accident, but they may have missed the critical moments because they were attending to their own activities.

Being aware of change blindness blindness is a critical thinking skill. Thinking that we always notice large changes in our visual field may lead us to perceive things ❻ incorrect / incorrectly, such as in erroneously believing something did or did not happen. Recognizing the limitations of attention may help prevent us from misleading ourselves about our perceptions. Knowledge about change blindness should make us more ❼ humble / arrogant about what we really see and what we remember.

*counterintuitive 직관에 반하는   **swerve 방향을 바꾸다; 방향 전환   ***collision 충돌

The main message from studies of change blindness is that people can miss obvious changes in what they see and hear. Despite this possibility, most people believe they will always notice large changes, that important events automatically draw their attention. This erroneous belief persists because people often do not find out about the things they fail ❶ _____ (perceive). In addition, the phenomenon of change blindness is so counterintuitive that few people believe how much they do not see. *Change blindness blindness* is people's unawareness that they often do not notice apparently obvious changes in their environments.

Imagine you are driving up a hill. At the top of the hill, there is an intersection. When you reach the top, you see another car ❷ _____ (head) straight into your lane, and in a flash you swerve to avoid a collision. The other car hits yours, but your last-minute swerve convinces eyewitnesses that you caused the accident by driving wildly. Change blindness blindness could be a factor in their reports: Perhaps out of a desire to help, the eyewitnesses believe they saw the whole accident, but they may ❸ _____ (miss) the critical moments because they were attending to their own activities. Being aware of change blindness blindness is a critical thinking skill. Thinking that we always notice large changes in our visual field may lead us to perceive things incorrectly, such as in erroneously ❹ _____ (believe) something did or did not happen. Recognizing the limitations of attention may help prevent us from ❺ _____ (mislead) ourselves about our perceptions. Knowledge about change blindness should make us more humble about what we really see and what we remember.

*counterintuitive 직관에 반하는   **swerve 방향을 바꾸다; 방향 전환   ***collision 충돌

The main message from studies of change blindness is that people can miss obvious changes in what they see and hear. Despite this possibility, most people believe they will always notice large changes, that important events automatically ❶ _____ _____ _____ (그들의 주의를 끈다). This erroneous belief persists because people often do not find out about the things they fail to perceive. In addition, the phenomenon of change blindness is so counterintuitive that ❷ _____ _____ _____ (믿는 사람은 거의 없다) how much they do not see. *Change blindness blindness* is people's unawareness that they often do not notice apparently obvious changes in their environments.

Imagine you are driving up a hill. At the top of the hill, there is an intersection. When you reach the top, you see another car heading straight into your lane, and in a flash you swerve to avoid a collision. The other car hits yours, but your last-minute swerve convinces eyewitnesses that you caused the accident by driving wildly. Change blindness blindness could be a factor in their reports: ❸ _____ _____ _____ _____ _____ _____ _____ (어쩌면 돕고 싶은 마음에서), the eyewitnesses believe they saw the whole accident, but they may have missed the critical moments because ❹ _____ _____ _____ _____ (그들은 ~에 주의를 기울이고 있었다) their own activities.

Being aware of change blindness blindness is a critical thinking skill. Thinking that we always notice large changes in our visual field may lead us to perceive things incorrectly, such as in erroneously believing something did or did not happen. Recognizing ❺ _____ _____ _____ _____ (주의의 한계들) may help prevent us from misleading ourselves about our perceptions. Knowledge about change blindness should make us more humble about what we really see and what we remember.

*counterintuitive 직관에 반하는   **swerve 방향을 바꾸다; 방향 전환   ***collision 충돌

[01~02] 다음 글을 읽고, 물음에 답하시오.

We do know that the ability to question, whether verbally or through other means, is one of the things that separates us from lower primates. Paul Harris, an education professor at Harvard University who has studied questioning in children, observes, "Unlike other primates, we humans are designed so that the young look to the old for cultural information." He sees this as an important "evolutionary divide" — that from an early age, even before speech, humans will use some form of questioning to try to (a) gain information. A child may pick up a kiwi fruit and indicate, through a look or gesture directed at a nearby adult, a desire to (b) know more. Chimpanzees don't do this; they may "ask" for a treat through signaling, but it's a simple (c) request for food, as opposed to an information-seeking question.

So then, one of the primary drivers of questioning is an awareness of what we don't know — which is a form of higher awareness that separates not only man from monkey but also the smart and curious person from the dullard who doesn't know or care. Good questioners tend to be (d) unaware of, and quite comfortable with, their own ignorance (Richard Saul Wurman, the founder of the TED Conferences, has been known to brag, "I know more about my ignorance than you know about yours"). But they constantly examine that vast (e) ignorance using the question flashlight — or, if you prefer, they attack it with the question spade.

*primate 영장류 **brag 호언장담하다 ***spade 삽

01

윗글의 제목으로 가장 적절한 것은?

① Educational Effects of Questioning in Class
② Questioning: The Key to Exploring the Realm of Ignorance
③ Level of One's Questions: A Measure of Intellectual Ability
④ Evolutionary Boundaries: Humans and Lower Primates
⑤ An Awareness of Ignorance: The Essence of Meta-Learning

02

밑줄 친 (a)~(e) 중에서 문맥상 낱말의 쓰임이 적절하지 <u>않은</u> 것은?

① (a) ② (b) ③ (c)
④ (d) ⑤ (e)

[03~04] 다음 글을 읽고, 물음에 답하시오.

You attract whatever you spend time (a) pondering, including whatever you love and whatever you fear. Your soul will rise to achieve your highest hope and will also fall to the depths of your basest appetite and your life will be a direct reflection of all your desires. This holds true for both your conscious and unconscious thoughts, which may seem a bit confusing at first. For example, you may want prosperity and believe that you're working toward bringing more of it into your life. Your savings account, however, remains empty. This is because unconsciously you're thinking, *I'm* (b) *afraid of poverty, and I don't think I'll ever be rich*. Even though you've made an effort to increase your wealth, your (c) optimistic thinking with respect to money is so ingrained that it actually cancels out your positive steps. Yet with continued effort and vigilance against (d) negative self-talk, you can turn around and create a prosperous life. The outer world of your circumstances is shaped by the inner world of your thoughts. Every seed of thought that you sow or allow to fall into your mind and take root eventually blossoms into action. And once again, good thoughts bear sweet fruit, while bad ones bear rotten fruit. A person doesn't end up homeless or in jail by the tyranny of fate or by chance, but as the direct result of cynical thinking and corrupt desires. Similarly, a model citizen doesn't (e) suddenly commit a crime due to a chance occurrence, but because he or she secretly fostered the criminal thought for a long time.

*pessimistic 비관적인, 회의적인
**vigilance 경계, 조심 ***tyranny 횡포, 폭정

03

윗글의 제목으로 가장 적절한 것은?

① Reality: A Reflection of the Mind
② Repeated Actions Become Habits
③ Essential for Achievement: Pondering
④ The Unexpected Results of Involuntary Actions
⑤ The Secret to Building Wealth: Don't Be Afraid of Poverty

04

밑줄 친 (a)~(e) 중에서 문맥상 낱말의 쓰임이 적절하지 <u>않은</u> 것은?

① (a)　　　　② (b)　　　　③ (c)
④ (d)　　　　⑤ (e)

18강 5-6번

[05~06] 다음 글을 읽고, 물음에 답하시오.

Humans are motivated, at least in part, by empathy and concern for the welfare of others. We donate blood for strangers, contribute to charity, and punish violators of social norms. Chimpanzees are, together with bonobos, our closest relatives, and they similarly engage in cooperative hunting, comfort victims of aggression, and perform other collective activities. Would they show concern for the welfare of unrelated, familiar chimps if the (a) benefits were at no cost to themselves? Researcher Joan Silk and her collaborators conducted an experiment with chimps that had lived together for fifteen years or more. Eighteen chimps were studied, from two different populations with different life histories and exposures to experiments. Pairs of chimps faced each other in opposing enclosures or sat side by side, and could see and hear each other. One chimp, the actor, was given the choice to pull one of two handles: if the actor pulled the "nice" handle, both the actor and the other chimp got food, and exactly the same portion. If the actor pulled the "nasty" handle, only the actor received food, and the other chimp got nothing. In a control test, only the actor was present. Which handle did the chimps pull? When no other chimp was present, the actors chose both options about (b) equally frequently. The chimps didn't care, and why should they? Yet even when a second chimp arrived, the chimps didn't choose the (c) "nasty" option more often. Although they could clearly see the other one displaying desperate begging gestures, or happily eating the food when it was dispensed, the chimps showed no sign of (d) empathy. It should be noted that they showed no spitefulness either. What mattered to the actors more than the other chimp was whether the handle for the nice option was placed on their right or left side. They had a much stronger preference for the (e) right side than for the happiness of their partner. Chimps simply did not seem to care about the welfare of unrelated group members.

*enclosure 울타리 안, 담장 안
**dispense 제공하다. 나눠 주다   ***spitefulness 악의

05

윗글의 제목으로 가장 적절한 것은?

① Effects and Limitations of Controlled Experiments
② Deep and Genuine Empathy Displayed by Chimpanzees
③ A Biological Similarity Between Humans and Chimpanzees
④ Are Chimpanzees Close to Humans in Terms of Empathy?
⑤ Impressions of Empathic Behaviors Performed by Chimpanzees

06

밑줄 친 (a)~(e) 중에서 문맥상 낱말의 쓰임이 적절하지 <u>않은</u> 것은?

① (a)　　　　② (b)　　　　③ (c)
④ (d)　　　　⑤ (e)

[07~08] 다음 글을 읽고, 물음에 답하시오.

The main message from studies of change blindness is that people can miss obvious changes in what they see and hear. Despite this possibility, most people believe they will always notice large changes, that important events automatically draw their attention. This (a) erroneous belief persists because people often do not find out about the things they fail to perceive. In addition, the phenomenon of change blindness is so counterintuitive that few people believe how much they do not see. Change blindness blindness is people's unawareness that they often do not (b) notice apparently obvious changes in their environments.

Imagine you are driving up a hill. At the top of the hill, there is an intersection. When you reach the top, you see another car heading straight into your lane, and in a flash you swerve to avoid a collision. The other car hits yours, but your last-minute swerve convinces eyewitnesses that you caused the accident by driving wildly. Change blindness blindness could be a factor in their reports: Perhaps out of a desire to help, the eyewitnesses believe they saw the whole accident, but they may have (c) missed the critical moments because they were attending to their own activities.

Being aware of change blindness blindness is a critical thinking skill. Thinking that we always notice large changes in our visual field may lead us to perceive things (d) correctly, such as in erroneously believing something did or did not happen. Recognizing the limitations of attention may help prevent us from (e) misleading ourselves about our perceptions. Knowledge about change blindness should make us more humble about what we really see and what we remember.

*counterintuitive 직관에 반하는
**swerve 방향을 바꾸다; 방향 전환   ***collision 충돌

07

윗글의 제목으로 가장 적절한 것은?

① Controversy over the Statements of Eyewitnesses
② The Limits of Human Senses during Emergencies
③ The Difficulty of Admitting the Possibility of Making Mistakes
④ Traits for Focusing on Attention-Grabbing Events
⑤ Acknowledging Change Blindness Blindness

08

밑줄 친 (a)~(e) 중에서 문맥상 낱말의 쓰임이 적절하지 않은 것은?

① (a)   ② (b)   ③ (c)
④ (d)   ⑤ (e)

• 내신 만점 서술형

We do know that the ability to question, whether verbally or through other means, is one of the things that ① separate us from lower primates. Paul Harris, an education professor at Harvard University who has studied questioning in children, observes, "Unlike other primates, we humans are designed ② so that the young look to the old for cultural information." He sees this as an important "evolutionary divide" — that from an early age, even before speech, humans will use some form of questioning to try to gain information. A child may pick up a kiwi fruit and indicate, through a look or gesture ③ directed at a nearby adult, a desire to know more. Chimpanzees don't do this; they may "ask" for a treat through signaling, but it's a simple request for food, as opposed to an information-seeking question. So then, one of the primary drivers of questioning is an awareness of ④ which we don't know — which is a form of higher awareness that separates not only man from monkey but also the smart and curious person from the dullard who doesn't know or care. Good questioners tend to be aware of, and quite comfortable with, their own ignorance (Richard Saul Wurman, the founder of the TED Conferences, has been known to brag, "I know more about my ignorance than you know about yours"). But they constantly examine that vast ignorance ⑤ using the question flashlight — or, if you prefer, they attack it with the question spade.

*primate 영장류 **brag 호언장담하다 ***spade 삽

09 윗글의 밑줄 친 부분 중, 어법상 틀린 것을 2개 찾아 그 번호를 쓰고 고쳐 쓰시오.

(1) _____ → _____

(2) _____ → _____

10 윗글의 밑줄 친 this가 가리키는 것을 본문에서 찾아 우리말로 쓰시오. (40자 내외)

_____

_____

18강 3-4번

You attract whatever you spend time pondering, including whatever you love and whatever you fear. Your soul will rise to achieve your highest hope and will also fall to the depths of your basest appetite and your life will be a direct reflection of all your desires. 이것은 여러분의 의식적 사고와 무의식적인 사고 둘 다에 딱 들어맞는데, 이것은 처음에는 약간 혼란스러워 보일 수도 있다. For example, you may want prosperity and believe that you're working toward bringing more of it into your life. Your savings account, however, remains empty. This is because _____

you're thinking, *I'm afraid of poverty, and I don't think I'll ever be rich*. Even though you've made an effort to increase your wealth, your pessimistic thinking with respect to money is so ingrained that it actually cancels out your positive steps. Yet with continued effort and vigilance against negative self-talk, you can turn around and create a prosperous life.

The outer world of your circumstances is shaped by the inner world of your thoughts. Every seed of thought that you sow or allow to fall into your mind and take root eventually blossoms into action. And once again, good thoughts bear sweet fruit, while bad ones bear rotten fruit. A person doesn't end up homeless or in jail by the tyranny of fate or by chance, but as the direct result of cynical thinking and corrupt desires. Similarly, a model citizen doesn't suddenly commit a crime due to a chance occurrence, but because he or she secretly fostered the criminal thought for a long time.

*pessimistic 비관적인, 회의적인
**vigilance 경계, 조심 ***tyranny 횡포, 폭정

11 윗글의 밑줄 친 우리말 의미와 일치하도록 보기 의 단어를 활용하여 조건 에 맞게 문장을 완성하시오.

보기   for / your / which / true / may seem / conscious / hold / both / and / unconscious / thoughts

조건   · 〈both A and B〉 구문으로 쓸 것
       · 필요 시 어형을 바꿔 쓸 것

This _____

_____

a bit confusing at first.

12 윗글의 빈칸에 들어갈 단어를 본문에서 찾아 알맞은 형태로 쓰시오. (단, 주어진 글자로 시작할 것)

u_____

Humans are motivated, at least in part, by empathy and concern for the welfare of others. We donate blood for strangers, contribute to charity, and punish violators of social norms. Chimpanzees are, together with bonobos, our closest relatives, and they similarly engage in cooperative hunting, comfort victims of aggression, and perform other collective activities. Would they show concern for the welfare of unrelated, familiar chimps if the benefits (A) are at no cost to themselves? Researcher Joan Silk and her collaborators conducted an experiment with chimps that had lived together for fifteen years or more. Eighteen chimps were studied, from two different populations with different life histories and exposures to experiments. Pairs of chimps faced each other in opposing enclosures or sat side by side, and could see and hear each other. One chimp, the actor, was given the choice to pull one of two handles: if the actor pulled the "nice" handle, both the actor and the other chimp got food, and exactly the same portion. If the actor pulled the "nasty" handle, only the actor received food, and the other chimp got nothing. In a control test, only the actor was present. Which handle did the chimps pull?

When no other chimp was present, the actors chose both options about equally frequently. The chimps didn't care, and why should they? Yet even when a second chimp arrived, the chimps didn't choose the "nice" option more often. Although they could clearly see the other one displaying desperate begging gestures, or happily (B) eat the food when it was dispensed, the chimps showed no sign of empathy. It should be noted that they showed no spitefulness either. What mattered to the actors more than the other chimp was (C) what the handle for the nice option was placed on their right or left side. They had a much stronger preference for the right side than for the happiness of their partner. Chimps simply did not seem to care about the welfare of unrelated group members.

*enclosure 울타리 안, 담장 안
**dispense 제공하다. 나눠 주다   ***spitefulness 악의

13 윗글의 밑줄 친 부분을 어법상 알맞은 형태로 고쳐 쓰시오.

(A) are   → _____

(B) eat   → _____

(C) what → _____

14 윗글의 내용을 한 문장으로 요약하려고 한다. 빈칸 (A)와 (B)에 들어갈 알맞은 말을 보기 에서 찾아 쓰시오.

> 보기   welfare / empathy / preferences / contribution

Whereas humans are motivated by ____(A)____ for the happiness of others, an experiment has shown that chimpanzees, humans' close relatives, do not care about the happiness of other chimpanzees and just make choices based on their own ____(B)____.

(A) _____   (B) _____

The main message from studies of change blindness is that people can miss obvious changes in what they see and hear. Despite this possibility, most people believe they will always notice large changes, that important events automatically draw their attention. This erroneous belief persists because people often do not find out about the things they fail to perceive. In addition, the phenomenon of change blindness is so counterintuitive that few people believe how much they do not see. *Change blindness blindness* is people's unawareness that they often do not notice apparently obvious changes in their environments.

Imagine you are driving up a hill. At the top of the hill, there is an intersection. When you reach the top, you see another car heading straight into your lane, and in a flash you swerve to avoid a collision. The other car hits yours, but your last-minute swerve convinces eyewitnesses that you caused the accident by driving wildly. Change blindness blindness could be a factor in their reports: Perhaps out of a desire to help, the eyewitnesses believe they saw the whole accident, but they may have missed the critical moments because they were attending to their own activities.

Being aware of change blindness blindness is a critical thinking skill. Thinking that we always notice large changes in our visual field may lead us to perceive things incorrectly, such as in erroneously believing something did or did not happen. Recognizing the limitations of attention may help prevent us from misleading ourselves about our perceptions. Knowledge about change blindness should make us more humble about what we really see and what we remember.

*counterintuitive 직관에 반하는
**swerve 방향을 바꾸다; 방향 전환   ***collision 충돌

15 윗글의 밑줄 친 **This erroneous belief**가 가리키는 것을 본문에서 찾아 우리말로 쓰시오. (45자 내외)

_____

_____

16 윗글의 내용을 한 문장으로 요약하려고 한다. 보기 에서 알맞은 말을 골라 문장을 완성하시오.

> 보기   incorrect perceptions /
> change blindness / humble attitude

Recognizing the fact that we don't see _____ is an important thinking skill because it can lead to a(n) _____ about what we really see and remember, and therefore prevent us from having _____ of events.

❶ Although my family weren't really all that excited about having animals in the house, they'd been persuaded to take on a two-year-old dog called Sally, a Bull Terrier-Boxer cross. ❷ She was very attractive, being smooth-haired, mostly black with a white chest and reddish-brown eyebrows and rings around her legs, and a thin reddish-brown line around her white chest, dividing it from the rest of her black coat. ❸ Mum had been assured she was well-behaved and non-aggressive, but she didn't suspect just how thoroughly I was going to test that guarantee out!

❹ On the day of her arrival, Sally was given a big bone and let into the garden with it, where she soon settled down and started chewing contentedly. ❺ A few minutes later Mum was distracted by the arrival of a neighbour, and when she came back into the kitchen and looked out of the window, she saw, to her horror, her two-year-old (me) tottering across the grass to the dog and bending down to grab the bone from her jaws.

❻ Not having time to do anything more than yell out of the window, which might have triggered a bad reaction from the dog, my mother could only watch in fear at what might happen next. ❼ Apparently, after I'd casually reached down and grabbed the bone, I walked off with it, with poor Sally following along behind me. ❽ That moment was the start of a lifelong friendship. ❾ Because Sally was two and I was two when she came to the family, we grew up together. ❿ She was my constant escort and guardian.

⓫ I remember my Uncle Phil, who was a very kindly soul, waving an arm around my head once as he tried to swat a fly away from me. ⓬ Thinking he was going to hit me, Sally leapt between us and grabbed and held his arm. ⓭ She didn't bite him — she never bit — but she held him tight all the same. ⓮ From quite a young age I was completely safe to wander around the countryside, so long as I had my guardian with me. ⓯ She was my playmate and my best friend for 12 years, and we went everywhere together.

*totter 아장아장 걷다　**swat (파리 등을 잡기 위해) 찰싹 때리다

❶ 우리 가족은 집에서 동물을 기르는 것에 대해 사실 그렇게 신나지는 않았지만, 불테리어와 복서가 섞인 잡종인 Sally라고 불리는 2살 된 개를 맡도록 설득되었다. ❷ 그것은 털이 부드럽고 전반적으로 까만색이면서, 하얀색의 가슴과 적갈색 눈썹과 다리 주위에 고리 모양의 털을 갖고 있었고, 하얀색 가슴 주변의 가는 적갈색 선이 그것의 하얀색 가슴을 나머지 까만색 털과 구분 짓고 있어서 매우 매력적인 모습이었다. ❸ 엄마는 그것이 말을 잘 듣고 공격적이지 않다고 확신했지만, 내가 그 확신을 정말 철저하게 시험해 보리라는 것을 짐작도 하지 못했다!

❹ 그것이 도착한 날, Sally는 큰 뼈를 받아 그것을 가지고 정원으로 가게 되었는데, 그곳에서 그것은 곧 편안히 앉아 만족스럽게 (뼈를) 씹기 시작했다. ❺ 몇 분 후 엄마가 이웃의 방문에 정신이 딴 데 가 있었는데, 그녀가 부엌으로 돌아와 창밖을 내다보았을 때, 경악스럽게도 자신의 두 살배기 아기(내)가 잔디밭을 가로질러 개에게로 아장아장 걸어가 그것의 입에서 뼈를 움켜쥐기 위해 허리를 숙이는 것을 보았다.

❻ 창밖으로 소리를 지르는 것 말고는 다른 어떤 것도 할 겨를이 없었지만, 그것이 그 개에게서 나쁜 반응을 촉발할지도 몰라, 엄마는 다음에 일어날지도 모를 일을 두려워하며 그저 지켜볼 수밖에 없었다. ❼ 보아하니, 나는 태연하게 손을 뻗어 뼈를 움켜쥔 후, 그것을 가지고 걸어가 버렸고, 불쌍한 Sally는 내 뒤를 따라왔던 것 같다. ❽ 그 순간이 평생의 우정이 시작하는 순간이었다. ❾ Sally가 두 살이었고 그것이 집에 왔을 때 나도 두 살이었기 때문에, 우리는 함께 자랐다. ❿ 그것은 나의 변함 없는 호위대원이자 보호자였다.

⓫ 매우 다정한 분이셨던 Phil 삼촌이 파리를 찰싹 때려 나에게서 쫓아내려고 하면서 내 머리 주위로 팔을 한 번 휘둘렀던 것을 나는 기억한다. ⓬ 그가 나를 때릴 것으로 생각한 Sally는 우리 사이에 뛰어들어 그의 팔을 붙들고 늘어졌다. ⓭ 그것은 절대 물지 않기에 그를 물지는 않았지만, 그것은 여전히 삼촌을 단단히 잡고 있었다. ⓮ 꽤 어린 나이부터 나는 시골 주변을 돌아다녀도 내 보호자가 있는 한 안전했다. ⓯ 그것은 12년 동안 나의 놀이 친구이자 가장 친한 친구였고, 우리는 어디든 함께 다녔다.

Word List

□ take on 떠맡다　□ cross 잡종, (두 가지 다른 것, 동식물의) 혼합, 이종 교배　□ attractive 매력적인　□ divide 나누다, 구분 짓다　□ assure ~에게 확신시키다　□ well-behaved 얌전한, 품행이 바른　□ non-aggressive 공격적이지 않은　□ thoroughly 철저히, 대단히　□ guarantee 보증, 굳은 약속　□ chew 씹다　□ contentedly 만족스럽게　□ distracted 주의가 산만한　□ horror 공포　□ trigger 촉발하다　□ apparently 보아하니, 언뜻 보기에　□ escort 호위대(원)　□ all the same 여전히　□ wander 돌아다니다, 거닐다

1	apparently	10	공포
2	distracted	11	철저히, 대단히
3	all the same	12	얌전한, 품행이 바른
4	trigger	13	~에게 확신시키다
5	take on	14	돌아다니다, 거닐다
6	cross	15	매력적인
7	divide	16	씹다
8	guarantee	17	만족스럽게
9	non-aggressive	18	호위대(원)

• 유형 1 네모 안에서 옳은 어법·어휘를 고르시오.

Although my family weren't really all that excited about having animals in the house, they'd been persuaded to take on a two-year-old dog called Sally, a Bull Terrier-Boxer cross. She was very attractive, being smooth-haired, mostly black with a white chest and reddish-brown eyebrows and rings around her legs, and a thin reddish-brown line around her white chest, dividing it from the rest of her black coat. Mum had been assured she was well-behaved and non-aggressive, but she didn't suspect just how ❶ | thorough / thoroughly | I was going to test that guarantee out!

On the day of her arrival, Sally was given a big bone and let into the garden with it, ❷ | which / where | she soon settled down and started chewing contentedly. A few minutes later Mum was distracted by the arrival of a neighbour, and when she came back into the kitchen and looked out of the window, she saw, to her horror, her two-year-old (me) tottering across the grass to the dog and bending down to grab the bone from her jaws.

Not having time to do anything more than ❸ | yell / yelling | out of the window, which might have triggered a bad reaction from the dog, my mother could only watch in fear at what might happen next. ❹ | Apparently / Particularly |, after I'd casually reached down and grabbed the bone, I walked off with it, with poor Sally following along behind me. That moment was the start of a lifelong friendship. Because Sally was two and I was two when she came to the family, we grew up together. She was my constant escort and guardian.

I remember my Uncle Phil, who was a very kindly soul, ❺ | waves / waving | an arm around my head once as he tried to swat a fly away from me. Thinking he was going to hit me, Sally leapt between us and grabbed and held his arm. She didn't bite him — she never bit — but she held him tight all the same. From quite a young age I was completely safe to wander around the countryside, so long as I had my guardian with me. She was my playmate and my best friend for 12 years, and we went everywhere together.

*totter 아장아장 걷다 **swat (파리 등을 잡기 위해) 찰싹 때리다

Although my family weren't really all that excited about having animals in the house, they'd been persuaded to take on a two-year-old dog called Sally, a Bull Terrier-Boxer cross. She was very attractive, ❶ _____ (be) smooth-haired, mostly black with a white chest and reddish-brown eyebrows and rings around her legs, and a thin reddish-brown line around her white chest, ❷ _____ (divide) it from the rest of her black coat. Mum had been assured she was well-behaved and non-aggressive, but she didn't suspect just how thoroughly I was going to test that guarantee out!

On the day of her arrival, Sally ❸ _____ (give) a big bone and let into the garden with it, where she soon settled down and started chewing contentedly. A few minutes later Mum was distracted by the arrival of a neighbour, and when she came back into the kitchen and looked out of the window, she saw, to her horror, her two-year-old (me) tottering across the grass to the dog and ❹ _____ (bend) down to grab the bone from her jaws.

Not having time to do anything more than yell out of the window, which might have triggered a bad reaction from the dog, my mother could only watch in fear at what might happen next. Apparently, after I'd casually reached down and grabbed the bone, I walked off with it, with poor Sally ❺ _____ (follow) along behind me. That moment was the start of a lifelong friendship. Because Sally was two and I was two when she came to the family, we grew up together. She was my constant escort and guardian.

I remember my Uncle Phil, who was a very kindly soul, waving an arm around my head once as he tried to swat a fly away from me. ❻ _____ (think) he was going to hit me, Sally leapt between us and grabbed and held his arm. She didn't bite him — she never bit — but she held him tight all the same. From quite a young age I was completely safe to wander around the countryside, so long as I had my guardian with me. She was my playmate and my best friend for 12 years, and we went everywhere together.

*totter 아장아장 걷다   **swat (파리 등을 잡기 위해) 찰싹 때리다

Although my family weren't really all that excited about having animals in the house, they'd been persuaded to take on a two-year-old dog called Sally, a Bull Terrier-Boxer cross. She was very attractive, being smooth-haired, mostly black with a white chest and reddish-brown eyebrows and rings around her legs, and a thin reddish-brown line around her white chest, dividing it from the rest of her black coat. Mum had been assured she was ❶ _____ _____ _____ (말을 잘 듣고 공격적이지 않은), but she didn't suspect just how thoroughly I was going to test that guarantee out!

On the day of her arrival, Sally was given a big bone and let into the garden with it, where she soon ❷ _____ _____ (편안히 앉았다) and started chewing contentedly. A few minutes later Mum was distracted by the arrival of a neighbour, and when she came back into the kitchen and looked out of the window, she saw, to her horror, her two-year-old (me) tottering across the grass to the dog and bending down to grab the bone from her jaws.

❸ _____ _____ _____ _____ _____ _____ (다른 어떤 것도 할 겨를이 없었지만) more than yell out of the window, which might have triggered a bad reaction from the dog, my mother could only watch in fear at ❹ _____ _____ _____ _____ (다음에 일어날지도 모를 일). Apparently, after I'd casually reached down and grabbed the bone, I walked off with it, with poor Sally following along behind me. That moment was the start of a lifelong friendship. Because Sally was two and I was two when she came to the family, we grew up together. She was my constant escort and guardian.

I remember my Uncle Phil, who was a very kindly soul, waving an arm around my head once as he tried to swat a fly away from me. Thinking he was going to hit me, Sally leapt between us and grabbed and held his arm. She didn't bite him — she never bit — but she held him tight ❺ _____ _____ _____ (여전히). From quite a young age I was completely safe to wander around the countryside, ❻ _____ _____ _____ (~하는 한) I had my guardian with me. She was my playmate and my best friend for 12 years, and we went everywhere together.

*totter 아장아장 걷다   **swat (파리 등을 잡기 위해) 찰싹 때리다

❶ Mr. Johnson's three sons worked together in a local trading company. ❷ One Monday, Mr. Johnson went down to the company to speak to his sons' manager. ❸ The manager came out of his office and introduced himself. ❹ "Please come into my office," he said, and he motioned for Mr. Johnson to go first. ❺ As they walked into the office, the manager invited him to take a seat in the chair in front of the desk. ❻ Mr. Johnson sat down, but he seemed to be somewhat displeased.

❼ The manager asked him what he could help him with. ❽ "Well, all three of my boys got hired here the same day. All of them have been here the same amount of time, work the same number of hours and even have the same position," Mr. Johnson began. ❾ "That's a problem for you?" asked the manager. ❿ "No, it's not that," Mr. Johnson continued to explain. ⓫ "What I don't understand is, if they all have the same position and do the same amount of work, why do they all make different amounts of money?"

⓬ The manager listened to him quietly and fully understood his concerns. ⓭ He wanted to explain everything to Mr. Johnson, but then decided that it would be easier to show him why there was a significant difference in the salaries. ⓮ He called down to the warehouse and asked for the first son. ⓯ When he answered, the manager asked him about the shipment that was supposed to have arrived that morning. ⓰ The first son said he knew nothing about any shipment. ⓱ Then the manager called down for the second son, and also asked him about the shipment.

⓲ This son at least knew of the shipment, but he couldn't confirm whether it had arrived or not. ⓳ But he was going to find out and later inform the manager. ⓴ Then, the manager called down for the third son. ㉑ When the manager asked him about the shipment, he seemed to know all about it. ㉒ "Yes, sir, it arrived this morning. I did inventory on it and found that it's a crate short. But don't worry sir. I already sent a fax to the company's office and they are replacing the crate in the next shipment." ㉓ The manager turned to Mr. Johnson and said, "Now do you see why they make different amounts of money?"

*crate (물품 운송용 대형 나무) 상자

❶ Johnson씨의 세 아들이 지역의 어느 무역 회사에서 함께 일했다. ❷ 어느 월요일에 Johnson 씨는 아들들의 부장과 이야기를 나누기 위해 그 회사로 갔다. ❸ 부장이 자기 사무실에서 나와 자신을 소개했다. ❹ 그는 "제 사무실로 들어오시죠."라고 말하며, Johnson 씨에게 먼저 들어가라고 몸짓을 했다. ❺ 그들이 사무실로 들어가자, 부장은 그에게 책상 앞 의자에 앉으라고 권했다. ❻ Johnson 씨는 자리에 앉았지만, 다소 불만스러운 듯 보였다.

❼ 부장은 그에게 자신이 무엇을 도와줄지 물었다. ❽ "음, 제 아이들 셋이 모두 같은 날 이곳에 고용되었습니다. 그들은 모두 여기에서 근무한 기간이 같고, 근무 시간이 같고, 심지어 직위도 같습니다."라고 Johnson 씨가 말을 시작했다. ❾ "그게 아버님께 문제가 되는지요?"라고 부장이 물었다. ❿ "아니요, 그런 게 아닙니다." Johnson 씨가 계속해서 설명했다. ⓫ "제가 이해하지 못하는 것이 하나 있는데요, 그 아이들이 모두 직위가 같고 근무량이 같다면, 왜 그 아이들이 모두 서로 다른 액수의 봉급을 받을까요?"

⓬ 부장은 그의 말을 조용히 들었고 충분히 그의 염려를 이해했다. ⓭ 그는 Johnson 씨에게 모든 것을 설명해 주고 싶었지만, 왜 봉급에 상당한 차이가 있는지 그에게 보여 주는 것이 더 쉬우리라고 판단했다. ⓮ 그는 창고로 전화를 걸어 첫째 아들을 찾았다. ⓯ 그가 응답하자, 부장은 그에게 그 날 아침에 도착하기로 되어 있었던 화물에 관해 물었다. ⓰ 첫째 아들은 어떤 화물에 대해서도 전혀 모른다고 말했다. ⓱ 그다음에 부장은 전화로 둘째 아들을 찾아서, 역시 그에게도 그 화물에 관해 물었다.

⓲ 이 아들은 적어도 그 화물에 대해 알고 있기는 했지만, 그는 그것이 도착했는지 도착하지 않았는지 확인해 줄 수 없었다. ⓳ 하지만 그는 알아보고 나서 나중에 부장에게 알려 주겠다고 했다. ⓴ 그다음에, 부장은 전화로 셋째 아들을 찾았다. ㉑ 부장이 그에게 그 화물에 관해 물었을 때, 그는 그것에 대해 모두 알고 있는 것 같았다. ㉒ "네, 부장님, 그것은 오늘 아침에 도착했습니다. 제가 그것의 물품 목록을 만들어 보니 한 상자가 부족하다는 것을 알게 되었습니다. 하지만 걱정하지 마십시오. 제가 이미 그 회사 사무실로 팩스를 보냈으며, 그들은 다음 탁송분에 그 한 상자를 돌려줄 예정입니다." ㉓ 부장은 Johnson 씨를 향해 몸을 돌려 "이제 아버님께서는 그들이 왜 서로 다른 액수의 봉급을 받는지 아시겠습니까?"라고 말했다.

Word List

□ trading company 무역 회사   □ motion (손짓으로) 신호하다   □ displeased 불만스러운, 불쾌한   □ amount 양, 분량
□ concern 염려, 관심사   □ significant 상당한   □ warehouse 창고   □ shipment (탁송된) 화물   □ be supposed to ~하기로 되어 있다
□ confirm 확인하다   □ inform 알려 주다   □ inventory 물품 목록, 재고(품)   □ short 부족한   □ replace 돌려주다, 갚다

1	trading company		8	양, 분량
2	motion		9	상당한
3	shipment		10	알려 주다
4	short		11	확인하다
5	be supposed to		12	돌려주다, 갚다
6	concern		13	불만스러운, 불쾌한
7	inventory		14	창고

• 유형 1 네모 안에서 옳은 어법·어휘를 고르시오.

Mr. Johnson's three sons worked together in a local trading company. One Monday, Mr. Johnson went down to the company to speak to his sons' manager. The manager came out of his office and introduced himself. "Please come into my office," he said, and he ❶ forced / motioned for Mr. Johnson to go first. As they walked into the office, the manager invited him to take a seat in the chair in front of the desk. Mr. Johnson sat down, but he seemed to be somewhat displeased.

The manager asked him ❷ when / what he could help him with. "Well, all three of my boys got hired here the same day. All of them have been here the same amount of time, work the same number of hours and even have the same position," Mr. Johnson began. "That's a problem for you?" asked the manager. "No, it's not that," Mr. Johnson continued to explain. "What I don't understand is, if they all have the same position and do the same amount of work, why do they all make different amounts of money?"

The manager listened to him quietly and fully understood his concerns. He wanted to explain everything to Mr. Johnson, but then decided that it would be easier to show him why there was a ❸ significant / insignificant difference in the salaries. He called down to the warehouse and asked for the first son. When he answered, the manager asked him about the shipment that was supposed to have arrived that morning. The first son said he knew ❹ something / nothing about any shipment. Then the manager called down for the second son, and also asked him about the shipment.

This son at least knew of the shipment, but he couldn't confirm ❺ whether / whenever it had arrived or not. But he was going to find out and later inform the manager. Then, the manager called down for the third son. When the manager asked him about the shipment, he seemed to know all about it. "Yes, sir, it arrived this morning. I did inventory on it and found that it's a crate short. But don't worry sir. I already sent a fax to the company's office and they are ❻ replacing / representing the crate in the next shipment." The manager turned to Mr. Johnson and said, "Now do you see why they make different amounts of money?"

*crate (물품 운송용 대형 나무) 상자

Mr. Johnson's three sons worked together in a local trading company. One Monday, Mr. Johnson went down to the company to speak to his sons' manager. The manager came out of his office and introduced himself. "Please come into my office," he said, and he motioned for Mr. Johnson ❶ _____ (go) first. As they walked into the office, the manager invited him to take a seat in the chair in front of the desk. Mr. Johnson sat down, but he seemed to be somewhat displeased.

The manager asked him what he could help him with. "Well, all three of my boys got hired here the same day. All of them ❷ _____ (be) here the same amount of time, work the same number of hours and even have the same position," Mr. Johnson began. "That's a problem for you?" asked the manager. "No, it's not that," Mr. Johnson continued to explain. "What I don't understand is, if they all have the same position and do the same amount of work, why do they all make different amounts of money?"

The manager listened to him quietly and fully understood his concerns. He wanted to explain everything to Mr. Johnson, but then decided that it would be easier to show him why there was a significant difference in the salaries. He called down to the warehouse and asked for the first son. When he answered, the manager asked him about the shipment that was supposed to ❸ _____ (arrive) that morning. The first son said he ❹ _____ (know) nothing about any shipment. Then the manager called down for the second son, and also asked him about the shipment.

This son at least knew of the shipment, but he couldn't confirm whether it ❺ _____ (arrive) or not. But he was going to find out and later inform the manager. Then, the manager called down for the third son. When the manager asked him about the shipment, he seemed ❻ _____ (know) all about it. "Yes, sir, it arrived this morning. I did inventory on it and found that it's a crate short. But don't worry sir. I already sent a fax to the company's office and they are replacing the crate in the next shipment." The manager turned to Mr. Johnson and said, "Now do you see why they make different amounts of money?"

*crate (물품 운송용 대형 나무) 상자

Mr. Johnson's three sons worked together in a local trading company. One Monday, Mr. Johnson went down to the company to speak to his sons' manager. The manager came out of his office and introduced himself. "Please come into my office," he said, and he motioned for Mr. Johnson to go first. As they walked into the office, the manager invited him to take a seat in the chair in front of the desk. Mr. Johnson sat down, but he ❶ _____ _____ _____ _____ _____ (다소 불만스러운 듯 보였다).
The manager asked him what he could help him with. "Well, all three of my boys got hired here the same day. All of them have been here the same amount of time, work the same number of hours and even have the same position," Mr. Johnson began. "That's a problem for you?" asked the manager. "No, it's not that," Mr. Johnson continued to explain. "What I don't understand is, if they all have the same position and do the same amount of work, why do they all ❷ _____ _____ _____ _____ _____ (다른 액수의 돈을 받다)?"
The manager listened to him quietly and fully understood his concerns. He wanted to explain everything to Mr. Johnson, but then decided that it would be easier to show him why there was a significant difference in the salaries. He called down to the warehouse and asked for the first son. When he answered, the manager asked him about the shipment that ❸ _____ _____ _____ (~하기로 되어 있었다) have arrived that morning. The first son said he knew nothing about any shipment. Then the manager called down for the second son, and also asked him about the shipment. This son ❹ _____ _____ _____ _____ (적어도 ~에 대해 알고 있었다) the shipment, but he couldn't confirm whether it had arrived or not. But he was going to find out and later inform the manager. Then, the manager called down for the third son. When the manager asked him about the shipment, he seemed to know all about it. "Yes, sir, it arrived this morning. I ❺ _____ _____ _____ _____ (그것의 물품 목록을 만들었다) and found that it's a crate short. But don't worry sir. I already sent a fax to the company's office and they are replacing the crate in the next shipment." The manager turned to Mr. Johnson and said, "Now do you see why they make different amounts of money?"

*crate (물품 운송용 대형 나무) 상자

❶ Dhira was a shoeshine boy. ❷ He lost his father when he was very young and now lived with his mother and sister. ❸ He was a hard-working boy. ❹ After school, he would sit near a cinema hall and polish shoes for a living. ❺ One day it was very hot. ❻ Dhira sat under a tree counting his day's earnings when he overheard a passerby. ❼ "A thief has just escaped from the jewellery shop." ❽ Dhira stopped counting. ❾ He quickly put his money back in his pocket and asked the passerby, "When? Where?" "Just now. He stole a gold necklace and managed to run away. They say he has a beard."

❿ So saying the passerby went on his way. ⓫ Dhira was about to go towards the jewellery shop to find out more details when a customer accosted him. ⓬ "Boy, polish my shoes nicely. There's no hurry," he said looking at his wristwatch. ⓭ The customer was wearing a blue suit and a red tie. ⓮ He looked like a rich man. ⓯ Dhira sat down immediately to polish his shoes, though his mind was still on the theft. ⓰ Through the corner of his eye, Dhira saw two policemen approaching.

⓱ He was eager to ask them about the theft, but the customer seemed to have lost his temper. ⓲ "You, silly boy! You're not doing your job well," he cried glancing quickly at the policemen. ⓳ So Dhira concentrated his attention on polishing the shoe. ⓴ He said, "The other shoe, sir." ㉑ The man said, "Hurry up, there are only two minutes for the show to begin." ㉒ 'Funny!' Dhira said to himself. ㉓ 'A moment ago he was in no hurry, but now he is in a great hurry.' ㉔ As Dhira was about to shine it with a cloth, he found something sticking out of it at the back.

㉕ 'What can it be?' Dhira wondered. ㉖ He bent his head to take a closer look. ㉗ 'My goodness!' ㉘ "That'll do, boy. It's time," the man said taking his foot off the stand. ㉙ Dhira quickly tied the ends of the laces of the two shoes and got up without taking the coin the man held out. ㉚ He rushed to the policemen. ㉛ The man fell flat on his face when he tried to walk. ㉜ While he was struggling to get up, Dhira was back with the two policemen. ㉝ They caught hold of him. ㉞ Yes, he was the jewel thief! ㉟ The gold necklace was found in his shoe and his 'beard' in his pocket. ㊱ He was taken to the police station. ㊲ Dhira was rewarded by the police and by the jeweller. ㊳ His school, too, honoured him with a medal for his bravery.

*accost 다가와 말을 걸다

❶ Dhira는 구두닦이 소년이었다. ❷ 그는 아주 어렸을 때 아버지를 여의었고, 이제는 어머니와 누나와 함께 살고 있었다. ❸ 그는 열심히 일하는 소년이었다. ❹ 방과 후 그는 영화관 근처에 앉아 생계를 위해 구두를 닦곤 했다. ❺ 어느 날, 날이 무척 더웠다. ❻ Dhira가 나무 아래에 앉아 자신의 하루 수입을 세고 있었을 때, 한 행인의 말을 우연히 들었다. ❼ "도둑이 방금 보석상에서 도망쳤대." ❽ Dhira는 세는 것을 멈추었다. ❾ 그는 재빨리 자신의 돈을 호주머니에 다시 넣고 그 행인에게 물었다. "언제요? 어디서요?" "방금 전에. 그 사람이 금목걸이를 훔쳐 용케 달아났다네. 사람들 말로는 그 사람은 턱수염이 있대."

❿ 그렇게 말하고는 그 행인은 자신이 가던 길을 갔다. ⓫ Dhira가 더 자세한 정보를 알아보기 위해 보석상을 향해 막 가려는데 한 손님이 그에게 다가와 말을 걸었다. ⓬ "얘야, 내 구두 좀 잘 닦아다오. 서두를 필요는 없단다."라고 그가 자신의 손목시계를 보며 말했다. ⓭ 그 손님은 파란색 정장에 빨간색 넥타이를 착용하고 있었다. ⓮ 그는 부자처럼 보였다. ⓯ 자신의 마음은 여전히 그 절도 사건에 가 있었지만, Dhira는 그의 구두를 닦기 위해 곧 자리에 앉았다. ⓰ 곁눈질로, Dhira는 두 명의 경찰관이 다가오는 것을 보았다.

⓱ 그는 그들에게 그 절도 사건에 대해 간절히 묻고 싶었지만, 손님은 화가 난 듯이 보였다. ⓲ "너, 이 바보 녀석아! 네 일을 제대로 못 하고 있잖아."라고 그가 빠르게 경찰관들을 힐끗 보며 소리쳤다. ⓳ 그래서 Dhira는 구두를 닦는 것에 주의를 집중했다. ⓴ "다른 쪽 구두요, 손님." 하고 그가 말했다. ㉑ "서둘러, 쇼 시작이 2분밖에 안 남았어."라고 그 남자가 말했다. ㉒ '수상한데!'라고 Dhira는 속으로 생각했다. ㉓ '조금 전까지만 해도 그는 전혀 서두르지 않았는데, 지금은 몹시 서두르네.' ㉔ Dhira가 막 천으로 광을 내려다가, 그는 구두 뒤쪽에 무언가 삐져나와 있는 것을 발견했다.

㉕ '저게 뭘까?' 하고 Dhira는 궁금해했다. ㉖ 그는 더 자세히 보기 위해 고개를 숙였다. ㉗ '맙소사!' ㉘ "그만해라, 얘야. 시간 됐다."라고 남자가 말하며 받침대에서 발을 떼었다. ㉙ Dhira는 남자가 내민 동전을 받지 않고 재빨리 두 신발 끈의 끝을 묶고 일어났다. ㉚ 그는 경찰관들에게 달려갔다. ㉛ 그 남자는 걸어가려다 앞으로 넘어졌다. ㉜ 그가 일어나려고 버둥거리는 동안, Dhira는 두 명의 경찰관과 함께 돌아왔다. ㉝ 그들은 그를 붙잡았다. ㉞ 그렇다, 그는 보석 도둑이었다! ㉟ 그 금목걸이는 그의 구두 속에서 발견되었고, 그의 '턱수염'은 그의 호주머니 속에서 발견되었다. ㊱ 그는 경찰서로 연행되었다. ㊲ Dhira는 경찰과 보석상으로부터 포상을 받았다. ㊳ 그의 학교 역시 그의 용기에 대해 그에게 메달을 수여했다.

Word List

☐ shoeshine 구두닦이   ☐ polish 닦다, 광을 내다   ☐ count 세다   ☐ overhear 우연히 듣다   ☐ passerby 행인, 지나가는 사람
☐ jewellery 보석(류)   ☐ beard 턱수염   ☐ accost 말을 걸다   ☐ theft 절도 사건   ☐ be eager to *do* 간절히 ~하고 싶어 하다
☐ lose one's temper 화를 내다, 성질을 내다   ☐ glance 힐끗 보다   ☐ stick out of ~에서 삐져나오다   ☐ that'll do 그만해, 그것으로 됐어
☐ hold out ~을 내밀다   ☐ fall flat on one's face 앞으로 넘어지다   ☐ struggle 버둥거리다, 애쓰다   ☐ catch hold of ~을 (붙)잡다
☐ honour ~ with ... ~에게 ···을 수여하다   ☐ bravery 용기

• Word Test

1	stick out of	___	11	화를 내다, 성질을 내다	___
2	overhear	___	12	턱수염	___
3	accost	___	13	용기	___
4	be eager to *do*	___	14	행인, 지나가는 사람	___
5	hold out	___	15	버둥거리다, 애쓰다	___
6	that'll do	___	16	닦다, 광을 내다	___
7	shoeshine	___	17	~을 (붙)잡다	___
8	jewellery	___	18	힐끗 보다	___
9	fall flat on one's face	___	19	세다	___
10	honour ~ with ...	___	20	절도 사건	___

• 유형 1 네모 안에서 옳은 어법·어휘를 고르시오.

Dhira was a shoeshine boy. He lost his father when he was very young and now lived with his mother and sister. He was a hard-working boy. After school, he would sit near a cinema hall and polish shoes for a living. One day it was very hot. Dhira sat under a tree counting his day's earnings when he ❶ overheard / observed a passerby. "A thief has just escaped from the jewellery shop." Dhira stopped counting. He quickly put his money back in his pocket and asked the passerby, "When? Where?" "Just now. He stole a gold necklace and managed to run away. They say he has a beard."

So saying the passerby went on his way. Dhira was about to go towards the jewellery shop to find out more details when a customer accosted him. "Boy, polish my shoes nicely. There's no hurry," he said looking at his wristwatch. The customer was wearing a blue suit and a red tie. He looked like a rich man. Dhira sat down immediately to polish his shoes, ❷ when / though his mind was still on the theft. Through the corner of his eye, Dhira saw two policemen approaching.

He was eager to ask them about the theft, but the customer seemed to have lost his ❸ temper / threat. "You, silly boy! You're not doing your job well," he cried glancing quickly at the policemen. So Dhira concentrated his attention on polishing the shoe. He said, "❹ The other / Another shoe, sir." The man said, "Hurry up, there are only two minutes for the show to begin." 'Funny!' Dhira said to himself. 'A moment ago he was in no hurry, but now he is in a great hurry.' As Dhira was about to shine it with a cloth, he found something ❺ stuck / sticking out of it at the back.

'What can it be?' Dhira wondered. He bent his head to take a closer look. 'My goodness!' "That'll do, boy. It's time," the man said taking his foot off the stand.

Dhira quickly tied the ends of the laces of the two shoes and got up without taking the coin the man held out. He rushed to the policemen. The man fell flat on his face when he tried to walk. While he was struggling to get up, Dhira was back with the two policemen. They caught hold of him. Yes, he was the jewel thief! The gold necklace was found in his shoe and his 'beard' in his pocket. He was taken to the police station. Dhira was rewarded by the police and by the jeweller. His school, too, honoured him with a medal for his ❻ bravery / generosity.

*accost 다가와 말을 걸다

Dhira was a shoeshine boy. He lost his father when he was very young and now lived with his mother and sister. He was a hard-working boy. After school, he would sit near a cinema hall and polish shoes for a living. One day it was very hot. Dhira sat under a tree ❶ _____ (count) his day's earnings when he overheard a passerby. "A thief has just escaped from the jewellery shop." Dhira stopped counting. He quickly put his money back in his pocket and asked the passerby, "When? Where?" "Just now. He stole a gold necklace and managed to run away. They say he has a beard."

So ❷ _____ (say) the passerby went on his way. Dhira was about to go towards the jewellery shop to find out more details when a customer accosted him. "Boy, polish my shoes nicely. There's no hurry," he said ❸ _____ (look) at his wristwatch. The customer was wearing a blue suit and a red tie. He looked like a rich man. Dhira sat down immediately to polish his shoes, though his mind was still on the theft. Through the corner of his eye, Dhira saw two policemen approaching.

He was eager to ask them about the theft, but the customer seemed to ❹ _____ (lose) his temper. "You, silly boy! You're not doing your job well," he cried glancing quickly at the policemen. So Dhira concentrated his attention on polishing the shoe. He said, "The other shoe, sir." The man said, "Hurry up, there are only two minutes for the show to begin." 'Funny!' Dhira said to himself. 'A moment ago he was in no hurry, but now he is in a great hurry.' As Dhira was about to shine it with a cloth, he found something sticking out of it at the back.

'What can it be?' Dhira wondered. He bent his head to take a closer look. 'My goodness!' "That'll do, boy. It's time," the man said taking his foot off the stand.

Dhira quickly tied the ends of the laces of the two shoes and got up without taking the coin the man held out. He rushed to the policemen. The man fell flat on his face when he tried to walk. While he was struggling to get up, Dhira was back with the two policemen. They caught hold of him. Yes, he was the jewel thief! The gold necklace ❺ _____ (find) in his shoe and his 'beard' in his pocket. He ❻ _____ (take) to the police station. Dhira was rewarded by the police and by the jeweller. His school, too, honoured him with a medal for his bravery.

*accost 다가와 말을 걸다

Dhira was a shoeshine boy. He lost his father when he was very young and now lived with his mother and sister. He was a hard-working boy. After school, he would sit near a cinema hall and polish shoes ❶ _____ _____ _____ (생계를 위해). One day it was very hot. Dhira sat under a tree counting his day's earnings when he overheard a passerby. "A thief ❷ _____ _____ _____ _____ (방금 ~에서 도망쳤다) the jewellery shop." Dhira stopped counting. He quickly put his money back in his pocket and asked the passerby, "When? Where?" "Just now. He stole a gold necklace and ❸ _____ _____ _____ _____ (용케 달아났다). They say he has a beard."

So saying the passerby went on his way. Dhira was about to go towards the jewellery shop to find out more details when a customer accosted him. "Boy, polish my shoes nicely. There's no hurry," he said looking at his wristwatch. The customer was wearing a blue suit and a red tie. He looked like a rich man. Dhira sat down immediately to polish his shoes, though his mind was still on the theft. ❹ _____ _____ _____ _____ _____ _____ (곁눈질을 통해), Dhira saw two policemen approaching.

He was eager to ask them about the theft, but the customer seemed to have lost his temper. "You, silly boy! You're not doing your job well," he cried glancing quickly at the policemen. So Dhira ❺ _____ _____ _____ _____ (~에 그의 주의를 집중했다) polishing the shoe. He said, "The other shoe, sir."
The man said, "Hurry up, there are only two minutes for the show to begin." 'Funny!' Dhira said to himself. 'A moment ago he was in no hurry, but now he is in a great hurry.' As Dhira was about to shine it with a cloth, he found something sticking out of it at the back.
'What can it be?' Dhira wondered. He bent his head to take a closer look. 'My goodness!' "That'll do, boy. It's time," the man said taking his foot off the stand.
Dhira quickly tied the ends of the laces of the two shoes and got up without taking the coin the man held out. He rushed to the policemen. The man fell flat on his face when he tried to walk. While he was struggling to get up, Dhira was back with the two policemen. ❻ _____ _____ _____ _____ _____ (그들은 그를 붙잡았다). Yes, he was the jewel thief! The gold necklace was found in his shoe and his 'beard' in his pocket. He was taken to the police station. Dhira was rewarded by the police and by the jeweller. His school, too, honoured him with a medal for his bravery.

*accost 다가와 말을 걸다

❶ While working for the state parks management department in Michigan, Rob was told from his boss that the state had been very concerned recently with the large number of boating accidents that occur on state lakes and wished to reduce this number. ❷ The boss asked him to help determine some ways to reduce the number of boating accidents in the state. ❸ Rob was excited about this assignment. ❹ This was a chance for him to impress his boss by solving a serious problem.

❺ Rob started the project by looking at a lot of data. ❻ He wanted to see what events were associated with boating accidents and he used his knowledge of statistics to calculate correlations. ❼ Other governmental agencies and departments were generous in sharing data with Rob, and he found many interesting correlations. ❽ The most fascinating thing, though, was that there was a very high correlation, in the state of Michigan, between ice-cream consumption and boating accidents.

❾ Rob was quite excited about finding this correlation. ❿ First, it was a strong correlation. ⓫ Second, it seemed like an event the state might be able to do something about. ⓬ There were other strong correlations with boating accidents, such as the correlation between boating accidents and temperature, but most of these were things the state had no control over. ⓭ Rob realized the state might have some control over ice-cream consumption. ⓮ Just one short week after receiving the assignment, he marched into his boss's office with a plan to reduce boating accidents in the state.

⓯ Rob proposed to his boss that there be no ice-cream sales at all state beaches and all state parks that include a lake. ⓰ To make doubly sure that there would be no ice-cream consumption on state lakes, he proposed banning ice-cream sales in all stores within two miles of any Michigan lake. ⓱ The potential impact of this proposal was large, since no person in Michigan is ever more than six miles from an inland lake. ⓲ Rob knew the Michigan dairy industry would not be happy with the proposal and his boss would likely reject it, but he presented it to him anyway. ... ⓳ Rob still has his job with the parks management department, but his ice-cream proposal did not go over well. ⓴ The boss laughed at him and dismissed him from his office.

❶ 미시간주 주립 공원 관리부에서 일하면서, Rob은 자기 상사로부터 주 정부가 최근 주 호수에서 발생하는 많은 수의 뱃놀이 사고에 대해 매우 우려해 왔고, 이 수를 줄이기를 바라고 있다는 말을 들었다. ❷ 상사는 그에게 주에서의 뱃놀이 사고 수를 줄이기 위한 몇 가지 방법을 결정하는 데 도움을 달라고 요청했다. ❸ Rob은 이 임무에 신이 났다. ❹ 이것은 그가 심각한 문제를 해결함으로써 그의 상사에게 깊은 인상을 줄 기회였다.

❺ Rob은 많은 자료를 살펴보는 것으로 그 과제를 시작했다. ❻ 그는 어떤 사건들이 뱃놀이 사고와 연관이 있는지를 알고 싶었고, 상관관계를 계산하기 위해 자신의 통계학 지식을 사용했다. ❼ 다른 정부 기관들과 부서들은 Rob과의 자료 공유에 관대했고, 그는 많은 흥미로운 상관관계를 발견했다. ❽ 하지만 가장 흥미로운 것은 미시간주에서 아이스크림 소비와 뱃놀이 사고 사이에 매우 높은 상관관계가 있다는 것이었다.

❾ Rob은 이 상관관계를 찾은 것에 매우 흥분했다. ❿ 첫째, 그것은 강력한 상관관계였다. ⓫ 둘째, 그것은 주 정부가 (그것에 대해) 뭔가를 할 수도 있을 것 같은 일처럼 보였다. ⓬ 뱃놀이 사고와 기온 사이의 상관관계처럼, 뱃놀이 사고와 강력한 상관관계를 가지는 다른 것들이 있었지만, 이것들 대부분은 주 정부가 통제할 수 없는 것들이었다. ⓭ Rob은 주 정부가 아이스크림 소비를 어느 정도 통제할 수도 있을 거라고 이해했다. ⓮ 그 임무를 받은 지 불과 일주일 만에, 그는 주의 뱃놀이 사고를 줄이기 위한 계획을 갖고 상사의 사무실로 당당하게 걸어 들어갔다.

⓯ Rob은 상사에게 주의 모든 해변과, 호수를 포함하고 있는 모든 주립 공원에서 아이스크림 판매를 하지 말 것을 제안했다. ⓰ 주 호수에서 아이스크림 소비가 없도록 이중으로 확실히 하기 위해, 그는 어떤 미시간주의 호수라도 그 호수의 2마일 내에 있는 모든 상점에서 아이스크림 판매를 금지할 것을 제안했다. ⓱ 이 제안의 잠재적 영향은 컸는데, 왜냐하면 미시간에서는 어떤 사람도 내륙 호수로부터 6마일이 넘는 거리에 있지 않기 때문이다. ⓲ Rob은 미시간 낙농업계가 그 제안을 좋아하지 않으리라는 것과 자기 상사가 그것을 아마도 거부하리라는 것을 알았지만, 어쨌든 그는 그것을 그에게 제시했다. … ⓳ Rob은 여전히 공원 관리부에서 자기 일을 하고 있지만, 그의 아이스크림 제안은 잘 받아들여지지 않았다. ⓴ 그 상사는 그를 비웃고는 자기 사무실에서 그를 내보냈다.

Word List

□ management 관리 □ occur 발생하다 □ determine 결정하다 □ assignment 임무, 과제 □ impress 깊은 인상을 주다
□ associated with ~과 연관된 □ statistics 통계학 □ calculate 계산하다 □ correlation 상관관계 □ agency 기관
□ generous 너그러운, 후한 □ consumption 소비 □ temperature 기온, 온도 □ march 당당하게 걷다 □ doubly 이중으로
□ ban 금지하다 □ potential 잠재적인 □ inland 내륙의 □ dairy 낙농의 □ present 제시하다 □ go over 받아들여지다
□ dismiss 내보내다, 물러가게 하다

• Word Test

1	doubly	12	기온, 온도
2	correlation	13	관리
3	associated with	14	통계학
4	march	15	금지하다
5	potential	16	기관
6	assignment	17	너그러운, 후한
7	determine	18	계산하다
8	dairy	19	깊은 인상을 주다
9	inland	20	내보내다, 물러가게 하다
10	go over	21	소비
11	occur	22	제시하다

• 유형 1 네모 안에서 옳은 어법·어휘를 고르시오.

While working for the state parks management department in Michigan, Rob was told from his boss ❶ [that / who] the state had been very concerned recently with the large number of boating accidents that occur on state lakes and wished to reduce this number. The boss asked him to help ❷ [determine / facilitate] some ways to reduce the number of boating accidents in the state. Rob was excited about this assignment. This was a chance for him to impress his boss by solving a serious problem. Rob started the project by looking at a lot of data. He wanted to see ❸ [what / that] events were associated with boating accidents and he used his knowledge of statistics to calculate correlations. Other governmental agencies and departments were generous in sharing data with Rob, and he found many interesting correlations. The most fascinating thing, ❹ [though / however], was that there was a very high correlation, in the state of Michigan, between ice-cream consumption and boating accidents. Rob was quite excited about finding this correlation. First, it was a strong correlation. Second, it seemed like an event the state might be able to do something about. There were other strong correlations with boating accidents, such as the correlation between boating accidents and temperature, but most of these were things the state had ❺ [no / some] control over. Rob realized the state might have some control over ice-cream consumption. Just one short week after receiving the assignment, he marched into his boss's office with a plan to reduce boating accidents in the state.

Rob proposed to his boss that there be no ice-cream sales at all state beaches and all state parks that include a lake. To make doubly sure that there would be no ice-cream consumption on state lakes, he proposed ❻ [banning / permitting] ice-cream sales in all stores within two miles of any Michigan lake. The potential impact of this proposal was large, since no person in Michigan is ever more than six miles from an inland lake. Rob knew the Michigan dairy industry would not be happy with the proposal and his boss would likely reject it, but he presented it to him anyway. ... Rob still has his job with the parks management department, but his ice-cream proposal did not go over well. The boss laughed at him and ❼ [accused / dismissed] him from his office.

While ❶ _____ (work) for the state parks management department in Michigan, Rob ❷ _____ (tell) from his boss that the state had been very concerned recently with the large number of boating accidents that occur on state lakes and wished to reduce this number. The boss asked him to help determine some ways to reduce the number of boating accidents in the state. Rob was excited about this assignment. This was a chance for him ❸ _____ (impress) his boss by solving a serious problem.

Rob started the project by looking at a lot of data. He wanted to see what events were associated with boating accidents and he used his knowledge of statistics to calculate correlations. Other governmental agencies and departments were generous in sharing data with Rob, and he found many interesting correlations. The most fascinating thing, though, was that there was a very high correlation, in the state of Michigan, between ice-cream consumption and boating accidents.

Rob was quite excited about finding this correlation. First, it was a strong correlation. Second, it seemed like an event the state might be able to do something about. There were other strong correlations with boating accidents, such as the correlation between boating accidents and temperature, but most of these were things the state had no control over. Rob realized the state might have some control over ice-cream consumption. Just one short week after ❹ _____ (receive) the assignment, he marched into his boss's office with a plan to reduce boating accidents in the state.

Rob proposed to his boss that there ❺ _____ (be) no ice-cream sales at all state beaches and all state parks that include a lake. To make doubly sure that there would be no ice-cream consumption on state lakes, he proposed banning ice-cream sales in all stores within two miles of any Michigan lake. The potential impact of this proposal was large, since no person in Michigan ❻ _____ (be) ever more than six miles from an inland lake. Rob knew the Michigan dairy industry would not be happy with the proposal and his boss would likely reject it, but he presented it to him anyway. ... Rob still has his job with the parks management department, but his ice-cream proposal did not go over well. The boss laughed at him and dismissed him from his office.

While working for the state parks management department in Michigan, Rob was told from his boss that the state had been very concerned recently with ❶ _____ _____ _____ _____ (많은 수의) boating accidents that occur on state lakes and wished to reduce this number. The boss asked him to help determine some ways to reduce the number of boating accidents in the state. Rob was excited about this assignment. This was a chance for him to impress his boss by solving a serious problem.

Rob started the project by looking at a lot of data. He wanted to see what events were ❷ _____ _____ (~와 연관이 있는) boating accidents and he used his knowledge of statistics to calculate correlations. Other governmental agencies and departments were ❸ _____ _____ _____ _____ (자료 공유에 관대한) with Rob, and he found many interesting correlations. The most fascinating thing, though, was that there was a very high correlation, in the state of Michigan, between ice-cream consumption and boating accidents.

Rob was quite excited about finding this correlation. First, it was a strong correlation. Second, it seemed like an event the state might be able to do something about. There were other strong correlations with boating accidents, such as the correlation between boating accidents and temperature, but most of these were things the state had no control over. Rob realized the state might have some control over ice-cream consumption. ❹ _____ _____ _____ _____ (불과 일주일 만에) after receiving the assignment, he marched into his boss's office with a plan to reduce boating accidents in the state.

Rob proposed to his boss that there be no ice-cream sales at all state beaches and all state parks that include a lake. ❺ _____ _____ _____ _____ (이중으로 확실히 하기 위해) that there would be no ice-cream consumption on state lakes, he proposed banning ice-cream sales in all stores within two miles of any Michigan lake. The potential impact of this proposal was large, since no person in Michigan is ever more than six miles from an inland lake. Rob knew the Michigan dairy industry would not be happy with the proposal and his boss would likely reject it, but he presented it to him anyway. ... Rob still has his job with the parks management department, but his ice-cream proposal ❻ _____ _____ _____ _____ _____ (잘 받아들여지지 않았다). The boss laughed at him and dismissed him from his office.

(A)

Although my family weren't really all that excited about having animals in the house, they'd been persuaded to take on a two-year-old dog called Sally, a Bull Terrier-Boxer cross. She was very attractive, being smooth-haired, mostly black with a white chest and reddish-brown eyebrows and rings around her legs, and a thin reddish-brown line around her white chest, dividing it from the rest of (a) her black coat. Mum had been assured she was well-behaved and non-aggressive, but she didn't suspect just how thoroughly I was going to test that guarantee out!

(B)

Not having time to do anything more than yell out of the window, which might have triggered a bad reaction from the dog, my mother could only watch in fear at what might happen next. Apparently, after I'd casually reached down and grabbed the bone, I walked off with it, with poor Sally following along behind me. That moment was the start of a lifelong friendship. Because Sally was two and I was two when she came to the family, we grew up together. (b) She was my constant escort and guardian.

(C)

I remember my Uncle Phil, who was a very kindly soul, waving an arm around my head once as he tried to swat a fly away from me. Thinking he was going to hit me, Sally leapt between us and grabbed and held his arm. She didn't bite him — she never bit — but (c) she held him tight all the same. From quite a young age I was completely safe to wander around the countryside, so long as I had my guardian with me. She was my playmate and my best friend for 12 years, and we went everywhere together.

(D)

On the day of her arrival, Sally was given a big bone and let into the garden with it, where (d) she soon settled down and started chewing contentedly. A few minutes later Mum was distracted by the arrival of a neighbour, and when she came back into the kitchen and looked out of the window, she saw, to (e) her horror, her two-year-old (me) tottering across the grass to the dog and bending down to grab the bone from her jaws.

*totter 아장아장 걷다   **swat (파리 등을 잡기 위해) 찰싹 때리다

01

주어진 글 (A)에 이어질 내용을 순서에 맞게 배열한 것으로 가장 적절한 것은?

① (B) – (D) – (C) ② (C) – (B) – (D)
③ (C) – (D) – (B) ④ (D) – (B) – (C)
⑤ (D) – (C) – (B)

02

밑줄 친 (a)~(e) 중에서 가리키는 대상이 나머지 넷과 다른 것은?

① (a)   ② (b)   ③ (c)
④ (d)   ⑤ (e)

03

윗글에 관한 내용으로 적절하지 않은 것은?

① Sally는 가슴 주변에 가는 적갈색 선이 있었다.
② 엄마는 창밖으로 소리를 지르지 않고 바라만 보았다.
③ Sally가 가족에게 왔을 때 'I'와 같은 나이였다.
④ Sally는 Phil 삼촌이 'I'를 때릴 것이라 생각했다.
⑤ Sally가 집에 온 다음 날 삼촌이 집을 방문했다.

(A)

Mr. Johnson's three sons worked together in a local trading company. One Monday, Mr. Johnson went down to the company to speak to his sons' manager. The manager came out of his office and introduced himself. "Please come into (a) my office," he said, and he motioned for Mr. Johnson to go first. As they walked into the office, the manager invited him to take a seat in the chair in front of the desk. Mr. Johnson sat down, but he seemed to be somewhat displeased.

(B)

This son at least knew of the shipment, but he couldn't confirm whether it had arrived or not. But he was going to find out and later inform the manager. Then, the manager called down for the third son. When the manager asked him about the shipment, he seemed to know all about it. "Yes, sir, it arrived this morning. I did inventory on it and found that it's a crate short. But don't worry (b) sir. I already sent a fax to the company's office and they are replacing the crate in the next shipment." The manager turned to Mr. Johnson and said, "Now do you see why they make different amounts of money?"

(C)

The manager listened to him quietly and fully understood his concerns. (c) He wanted to explain everything to Mr. Johnson, but then decided that it would be easier to show him why there was a significant difference in the salaries. (d) He called down to the warehouse and asked for the first son. When he answered, the manager asked him about the shipment that was supposed to have arrived that morning. The first son said he knew nothing about any shipment. Then the manager called down for the second son, and also asked him about the shipment.

(D)

The manager asked him what he could help him with. "Well, all three of my boys got hired here the same day. All of them have been here the same amount of time, work the same number of hours and even have the same position," Mr. Johnson began. "That's a problem for (e) you?" asked the manager. "No, it's not that," Mr. Johnson continued to explain. "What I don't understand is, if they all have the same position and do the same amount of work, why do they all make different amounts of money?"

*crate (물품 운송용 대형 나무) 상자

04

주어진 글 (A)에 이어질 내용을 순서에 맞게 배열한 것으로 가장 적절한 것은?

① (B) – (D) – (C) ② (C) – (B) – (D)
③ (C) – (D) – (B) ④ (D) – (B) – (C)
⑤ (D) – (C) – (B)

05

밑줄 친 (a)~(e) 중에서 가리키는 대상이 나머지 넷과 다른 것은?

① (a) ② (b) ③ (c)
④ (d) ⑤ (e)

06

윗글에 관한 내용으로 적절하지 않은 것은?

① 부장은 Johnson씨에게 책상 앞 의자에 앉도록 청했다.
② 셋째 아들은 상대 회사 사무실로 팩스를 보내두었다.
③ 부장은 첫째 아들에게 아침에 오기로 한 화물에 대해 물었다.
④ Johnson씨의 세 아들은 입사일과 직급이 모두 같다.
⑤ Johnson씨는 세 아들이 맡은 업무량의 차이를 궁금해했다.

(A)

Dhira was a shoeshine boy. He lost his father when he was very young and now lived with his mother and sister. He was a hard-working boy. After school, he would sit near a cinema hall and polish shoes for a living. One day it was very hot. Dhira sat under a tree counting his day's earnings when he overheard a passerby. "A thief has just escaped from the jewellery shop." Dhira stopped counting. He quickly put his money back in (a) his pocket and asked the passerby, "When? Where?" "Just now. He stole a gold necklace and managed to run away. They say he has a beard."

(B)

'What can it be?' Dhira wondered. He bent his head to take a closer look. 'My goodness!' "That'll do, boy. It's time," the man said taking his foot off the stand. Dhira quickly tied the ends of the laces of the two shoes and got up without taking the coin the man held out. He rushed to the policemen. The man fell flat on his face when he tried to walk. While he was struggling to get up, Dhira was back with the two policemen. They caught hold of (b) him. Yes, he was the jewel thief! The gold necklace was found in his shoe and his 'beard' in his pocket. He was taken to the police station. Dhira was rewarded by the police and by the jeweller. His school, too, honoured him with a medal for his bravery.

(C)

So saying the passerby went on his way. Dhira was about to go towards the jewellery shop to find out more details when a customer accosted him. "Boy, polish my shoes nicely. There's no hurry," he said looking at his wristwatch. The customer was wearing a blue suit and a red tie. He looked like a rich man. Dhira sat down immediately to polish his shoes, though his mind was still on the theft. Through the corner of (c) his eye, Dhira saw two policemen approaching.

(D)

He was eager to ask them about the theft, but the customer seemed to have lost his temper. "You, silly boy! (d) You're not doing your job well," he cried glancing quickly at the policemen. So Dhira concentrated his attention on polishing the shoe. He said, "The other shoe, sir." The man said, "Hurry up, there are only two minutes for the show to begin." 'Funny!' Dhira said to himself. 'A moment ago he was in no hurry, but now he is in a great hurry.' As Dhira was about to shine it with a cloth, (e) he found something sticking out of it at the back.

07

주어진 글 (A)에 이어질 내용을 순서에 맞게 배열한 것으로 가장 적절한 것은?

① (B) – (D) – (C)   ② (C) – (B) – (D)
③ (C) – (D) – (B)   ④ (D) – (B) – (C)
⑤ (D) – (C) – (B)

08

밑줄 친 (a)~(e) 중에서 가리키는 대상이 나머지 넷과 다른 것은?

① (a)   ② (b)   ③ (c)
④ (d)   ⑤ (e)

09

Dhira에 대한 내용으로 적절하지 않은 것은?

① 하루 수입을 세면서 행인의 말을 들었다.
② 손님에게 동전을 받지 않고 일어섰다.
③ 자신의 용기에 대해 메달을 수여 받았다.
④ 손님에게 서두를 필요가 없다는 말을 들었다.
⑤ 손님에게 절도 사건에 대해 물어보고 싶었다.

(A)

While working for the state parks management department in Michigan, Rob was told from his boss that the state had been very concerned recently with the large number of boating accidents that occur on state lakes and wished to reduce this number. The boss asked (a) <u>him</u> to help determine some ways to reduce the number of boating accidents in the state. Rob was excited about this assignment. This was a chance for him to impress his boss by solving a serious problem.

(B)

Rob started the project by looking at a lot of data. He wanted to see what events were associated with boating accidents and he used (b) <u>his</u> knowledge of statistics to calculate correlations. Other governmental agencies and departments were generous in sharing data with Rob, and he found many interesting correlations. The most fascinating thing, though, was that there was a very high correlation, in the state of Michigan, between ice-cream consumption and boating accidents.

(C)

Rob proposed to his boss that there be no ice-cream sales at all state beaches and all state parks that include a lake. To make doubly sure that there would be no ice-cream consumption on state lakes, he proposed banning ice-cream sales in all stores within two miles of any Michigan lake. The potential impact of this proposal was large, since no person in Michigan is ever more than six miles from an inland lake. Rob knew the Michigan dairy industry would not be happy with the proposal and his boss would likely reject it, but (c) <u>he</u> presented it to him anyway. ... Rob still has his job with the parks management department, but his ice-cream proposal did not go over well. The boss laughed at him and dismissed him from (d) <u>his</u> office.

(D)

Rob was quite excited about finding this correlation. First, it was a strong correlation. Second, it seemed like an event the state might be able to do something about. There were other strong correlations with boating accidents, such as the correlation between boating accidents and temperature, but most of these were things the state had no control over. Rob realized the state might have some control over ice-cream consumption. Just one short week after receiving the assignment, he marched into (e) <u>his</u> boss's office with a plan to reduce boating accidents in the state.

10

주어진 글 (A)에 이어질 내용을 순서에 맞게 배열한 것으로 가장 적절한 것은?

① (B) – (D) – (C) ② (C) – (B) – (D)
③ (C) – (D) – (B) ④ (D) – (B) – (C)
⑤ (D) – (C) – (B)

11

밑줄 친 (a)~(e) 중에서 가리키는 대상이 나머지 넷과 <u>다른</u> 것은?

① (a) ② (b) ③ (c)
④ (d) ⑤ (e)

12

윗글에 관한 내용으로 적절하지 <u>않은</u> 것은?

① 상사는 주 정부가 보트 사고 수를 줄이기 원한다는 내용을 Rob에게 말했다.
② Rob은 다른 정부 기관과 부서들이 공유한 자료들을 통해 여러 상관관계를 밝혀냈다.
③ 사람들이 호수에서 6마일 이상 떨어져 살아서 Rob의 제안은 잠재적 영향이 컸다.
④ 보트 사고와 기온 사이의 상관관계는 주 정부가 통제할 수 없는 종류의 것이었다.
⑤ Rob은 주 정부가 아이스크림 소비를 통제할 수 있을 것이라 생각했다.

Although my family weren't really all that excited about having animals in the house, they'd been ① persuaded to take on a two-year-old dog called Sally, a Bull Terrier-Boxer cross. She was very attractive, being smooth-haired, mostly black with a white chest and reddish-brown eyebrows and rings around her legs, and a thin reddish-brown line around her white chest, dividing it from the rest of her black coat. Mum had been assured she was well-behaved and non-aggressive, but she didn't ② suspect just how thoroughly I was going to test that guarantee out!

On the day of her arrival, Sally was given a big bone and let into the garden with it, where she soon settled down and started chewing contentedly. A few minutes later Mum was distracted by the arrival of a neighbour, and when she came back into the kitchen and looked out of the window, she saw, to her ③ delight, her two-year-old (me) tottering across the grass to the dog and bending down to grab the bone from her jaws.

Not having time to do anything more than yell out of the window, which might have triggered a bad reaction from the dog, my mother could only watch in fear at what might happen next. Apparently, after I'd casually reached down and grabbed the bone, I walked off with it, with poor Sally following along behind me. That moment was the start of a lifelong friendship. Because Sally was two and I was two when she came to the family, we grew up together. She was my ④ occasional escort and guardian.

I remember my Uncle Phil, who was a very kindly soul, waving an arm around my head once as he tried to swat a fly away from me. Thinking he was going to hit me, Sally leapt between us and grabbed and held his arm. She didn't bite him — she never bit — but she held him tight all the same. From quite a young age I was completely ⑤ safe to wander around the countryside, so long as I had my guardian with me. She was my playmate and my best friend for 12 years, and we went everywhere together.

*totter 아장아장 걷다   **swat (파리 등을 잡기 위해) 찰싹 때리다

13 윗글의 밑줄 친 부분 중 문맥상 어색한 것을 2개 찾아 그 번호를 쓰고 고쳐 쓰시오.

(1) _____ → _____
(2) _____ → _____

14 윗글의 밑줄 친 부분을 접속사 Although로 시작하는 문장으로 바꿔 쓰시오.

Although _____

_____

Mr. Johnson's three sons worked together in a local trading company. One Monday, Mr. Johnson went down to the company to speak to his sons' manager. The manager came out of his office and introduced himself. "Please come into my office," he said, and he motioned for Mr. Johnson to go first. As they walked into the office, the manager invited him to take a seat in the chair in front of the desk. Mr. Johnson sat down, but he seemed to be somewhat displeased.

The manager asked him what he could help him with. "Well, all three of my boys got hired here the same day. All of them have been here the same amount of time, work the same number of hours and even have the same position," Mr. Johnson began. "That's a problem for you?" asked the manager. "No, it's not that," Mr. Johnson continued to explain. "What I don't understand is, if they all have the same position and do the same amount of work, why do they all make different amounts of money?"

The manager listened to him quietly and fully understood his concerns. He wanted to explain everything to Mr. Johnson, but 왜 봉급에 상당한 차이가 있는지 그에게 보여 주는 것이 더 쉬우리라고 판단했다. He called down to the warehouse and asked for the first son. When he answered, the manager asked him about the shipment that was supposed to have arrived that morning. The first son said he knew nothing about any shipment. Then the manager called down for the second son, and also asked him about the shipment.

This son at least knew of the shipment, but he couldn't confirm whether it had arrived or not. But he was going to find out and later inform the manager. Then, the manager called down for the third son. When the manager asked him about the shipment, he seemed to know all about it. "Yes, sir, it arrived this morning. I did inventory on it and found that it's a crate short. But don't worry sir. I already sent a fax to the company's office and they are replacing the crate in the next shipment." The

manager turned to Mr. Johnson and said, "Now do you see why they make different amounts of money?"

*crate (물품 운송용 대형 나무) 상자

15 윗글의 밑줄 친 우리말의 의미에 맞게 [보기]의 단어를 활용하여 [조건]에 맞게 문장을 완성하시오.

[보기] easier / significant / would / why
in the salaries / there / was

[조건]
· 〈가주어 – 진주어 to부정사구〉 구문을 쓸 것
· 의문사절을 쓸 것
· 총 16단어로 쓸 것

then decided that _____

_____

16 윗글의 내용을 한 문장으로 요약하려고 한다. [보기]의 단어를 순서대로 배열하여 문장을 완성하시오.

[보기] attitudes / differently / work /
gets / towards / paid

Even though all of Mr. Johnson's three sons have worked in a trading company for the same period, have the same position, and do the same hours, the reason each of them _____ _____ _____ is that they have different _____ _____ _____.

Dhira was a shoeshine boy. He lost his father when he was very young and now lived with his mother and sister. He was a hard-working boy. After school, he would sit near a cinema hall and polish shoes for a living. One day it was very hot. Dhira sat under a tree counting his day's earnings when he overheard a passerby. "A thief has just escaped from the jewellery shop." Dhira stopped counting. He quickly put his money back in his pocket and asked the passerby, "When? Where?" "Just now. He stole a gold necklace and managed (A) run away. They say he has a beard."

So saying the passerby went on his way. Dhira was about to go towards the jewellery shop to find out more details when a customer accosted him. "Boy, polish my shoes nicely. There's no hurry," he said looking at his wristwatch. The customer was wearing a blue suit and a red tie. He looked like a rich man. Dhira sat down immediately to polish his shoes, though his mind was still on the theft. Through the corner of his eye, Dhira saw two policemen (B) approached.

He was eager to ask them about the theft, but the customer seemed to have lost his temper. "You, silly boy! You're not doing your job well," he cried glancing quickly at the policemen. So Dhira concentrated his attention on polishing the shoe. He said, "The other shoe, sir." The man said, "Hurry up, there are only two minutes for the show to begin." 'Funny!' Dhira said to himself. 'A moment ago he was in no hurry, but now he is in a great hurry.' Dhira가 막 천으로 광을 내려다가, 그는 구두 뒤쪽에 무언가 삐져나와 있는 것을 발견했다.

'What can it be?' Dhira wondered. He bent his head to take a closer look. 'My goodness!' "That'll do, boy. It's time," the man said taking his foot off the stand.

Dhira quickly tied the ends of the laces of the two shoes and got up without taking the coin the man held out. He rushed to the policemen. The man fell flat on his face when he tried to walk. While he was struggling to get up, Dhira was back with the two policemen. They caught hold of him. Yes, he was the jewel thief! The gold necklace was found in his shoe and his 'beard' in his pocket. He was taken to the police station. Dhira (C) rewarded by the police and by the jeweller. His school, too, honoured him with a medal for his bravery.

*accost 다가와 말을 걸다

17 윗글의 밑줄 친 부분을 어법상 알맞은 형태로 고쳐 쓰시오.

(A) run   → _____

(B) approached → _____

(C) rewarded   → _____

18 윗글의 밑줄 친 우리말 의미와 일치하도록 보기 의 단어를 활용하여 문장을 완성하시오. (단, 필요시 어형을 바꿔 쓸 것)

> 보기   a cloth / out of it / be about to / sticking / find / at the back / shine / something / it / he / with

As Dhira _____

_____

While working for the state parks management department in Michigan, Rob was told from his boss that ① the state had been very concerned recently with the large number of boating accidents that occur on state lakes and wished to reduce this number. The boss asked him to help determine some ways to reduce the number of boating accidents in the state. Rob was excited about (A) this assignment. ② This was a chance him to impress his boss by solving a serious problem.

Rob started the project by looking at a lot of data. He wanted to see what events were associated with boating accidents and he used his knowledge of statistics to calculate correlations. Other governmental agencies and departments were generous in sharing data with Rob, and he found many interesting correlations. ③ The most fascinating thing, though, was what there was a very high correlation, in the state of Michigan, between ice-cream consumption and boating accidents.

Rob was quite excited about finding this correlation. First, it was a strong correlation. Second, ④ it seemed like an event the state might be able to do something about. There were other strong correlations with boating accidents, such as the correlation between boating accidents and temperature, but most of these were things the state had no control over. Rob realized the state might have some control over ice-cream consumption. Just one short week after receiving the assignment, he marched into his boss's office with a plan to reduce boating accidents in the state.

⑤ Rob proposed to his boss that there are no ice-cream sales at all state beaches and all state parks that include a lake. To make doubly sure that there would be no ice-cream consumption on state lakes, he proposed banning ice-cream sales in all stores within two miles of any Michigan lake. The potential impact of this proposal was large,

since no person in Michigan is ever more than six miles from an inland lake. Rob knew the Michigan dairy industry would not be happy with (B) the proposal and his boss would likely reject it, but he presented it to him anyway. ... Rob still has his job with the parks management department, but his ice-cream proposal did not go over well. The boss laughed at him and dismissed him from his office.

19 윗글의 밑줄 친 ①~⑤ 중 어법상 틀린 것을 3개 찾아 그 번호를 쓰고 고쳐 쓰시오. (틀린 부분의 번호, 틀린 부분, 알맞게 고친 정답을 차례대로 쓸 것)

(1) _____ , _____

→ _____

(2) _____ , _____

→ _____

(3) _____ , _____

→ _____

20 윗글의 밑줄 친 (A), (B)가 각각 가리키는 것을 본문에서 찾아 우리말로 쓰시오. ((A), (B) 각각 40자 내외)

(A) _____

_____

(B) _____

_____

지은이

NE능률 영어교육연구소

NE능률 영어교육연구소는 혁신적이며 효율적인 영어 교재를 개발하고
영어 학습의 질을 한 단계 높이고자 노력하는 NE능률의 연구 조직입니다.

능률 EBS 수능특강 변형 문제 〈영어(상)〉

펴 낸 이	주민홍
펴 낸 곳	서울특별시 마포구 월드컵북로 396(상암동) 누리꿈스퀘어 비즈니스타워 10층
	㈜NE능률 (우편번호 03925)
펴 낸 날	2023년 3월 5일 초판 제1쇄 발행
전　　화	02 2014 7114
팩　　스	02 3142 0356
홈 페 이 지	www.neungyule.com
등 록 번 호	제1-68호
I S B N	979-11-253-4162-8 53740
정　　가	19,000원

NE 능률

고객센터

교재 내용 문의 : contact.nebooks.co.kr (별도의 가입 절차 없이 작성 가능)
제품 구매, 교환, 불량, 반품 문의 : 02-2014-7114
☎ 전화문의는 본사 업무시간 중에만 가능합니다.

www.nebooks.co.kr NE 능률

내신과 수능을 한 번에, 문법과 구문을 동시에!

빠른 독해를 위한 바른 선택

빠른 독해 × 바른 독해

수능 유형과
소재 분석을 통한
실전 대비서
종합실전편

빠바 시리즈
360
만부 돌파!

NE Waffle
MP3 듣기

부록 휴대용 어휘 암기장
독해 지문 MP3 파일 제공
www.nebooks.co.kr

NE능률 영어교육연구소
신유승 허인혜 박서경 양은빈

전국 **온오프 서점** 판매중

체계적으로 완성하는
수능 독해 기본서 빠바

기초세우기

구문독해

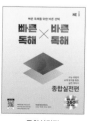
유형독해

종합실전편

최신 수능 경향 반영
· Email, 안내문 등 실용문 추가 [기초세우기, 구문독해]
· 수능 기출 문장 중심으로 구성 된 '구문훈련' [구문독해]
· 수능 중요도 상승에 따라 빈칸 추론 유닛 확대 [유형독해]
· 최신 수능 유형과 소재 분석 [종합실전편]

실전 대비 기능 강화
· 배운 구문과 문법 사항 재정리가 쉬워지는 Review Test [기초세우기]
· 수능 독해 Mini Test를 통한 실력 다지기 [구문독해, 유형독해]
· Mini Test에 장문과 고난도 지문 추가, '필수구문'의 문항화 [구문독해]
· 모의고사 3회분 수록 [종합실전편]

서술형 주관식 문제 재정비로 내신 대비 강화
· 최근 내신 출제 경향을 분석 반영한 주관식 문제 반영

NE능률 교재 MAP

아래 교재 MAP을 참고하여 본인의 현재 혹은 목표 수준에 따라 교재를 선택하세요.
NE능률 교재들과 함께 영어실력을 쑥쑥~ 올려보세요!
MP3 등 교재 부가 학습 서비스 및 자세한 교재 정보는 www.nebooks.co.kr 에서 확인하세요.

수능

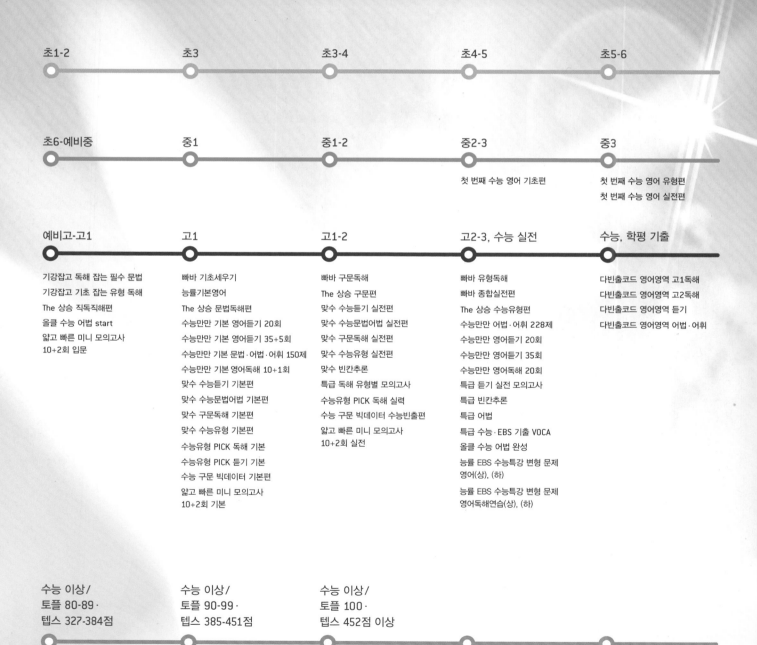

초1-2	초3	초3-4	초4-5	초5-6

초6-예비중	중1	중1-2	중2-3	중3
			첫 번째 수능 영어 기초편	첫 번째 수능 영어 유형편
				첫 번째 수능 영어 실전편

예비고-고1	고1	고1-2	고2-3, 수능 실전	수능, 학평 기출
기강잡고 독해 잡는 필수 문법	빠바 기초세우기	빠바 구문독해	빠바 유형독해	다빈출코드 영어영역 고1독해
기강잡고 기초 잡는 유형 독해	능률기본영어	The 상승 구문편	빠바 종합실전편	다빈출코드 영어영역 고2독해
The 상승 직독직해편	The 상승 문법독해편	맞수 수능듣기 실전편	The 상승 수능유형편	다빈출코드 영어영역 듣기
올클 수능 어법 start	수능만만 기본 영어듣기 20회	맞수 수능문법어법 실전편	수능만만 어법·어휘 228제	다빈출코드 영어영역 어법·어휘
얇고 빠른 미니 모의고사	수능만만 기본 영어듣기 35+5회	맞수 구문독해 실전편	수능만만 영어듣기 20회	
10+2회 입문	수능만만 기본 문법·어법·어휘 150제	맞수 수능유형 실전편	수능만만 영어듣기 35회	
	수능만만 기본 영어독해 10+1회	맞수 빈칸추론	수능만만 영어독해 20회	
	맞수 수능듣기 기본편	특급 독해 유형별 모의고사	특급 듣기 실전 모의고사	
	맞수 수능문법어법 기본편	수능유형 PICK 독해 실력	특급 빈칸추론	
	맞수 구문독해 기본편	수능 구문 빅데이터 수능빈출편	특급 어법	
	맞수 수능유형 기본편	얇고 빠른 미니 모의고사	특급 수능·EBS 기출 VOCA	
	수능유형 PICK 독해 기본	10+2회 실전	올클 수능 어법 완성	
	수능유형 PICK 듣기 기본		능률 EBS 수능특강 변형 문제 영어(상), (하)	
	수능 구문 빅데이터 기본편		능률 EBS 수능특강 변형 문제 영어독해연습(상), (하)	
	얇고 빠른 미니 모의고사 10+2회 기본			

수능 이상/ 토플 80-89· 텝스 327-384점	수능 이상/ 토플 90-99· 텝스 385-451점	수능 이상/ 토플 100· 텝스 452점 이상		

·2024학년도 수능 및 내신 대비·

능률 EBS 수능특강

변형 문제
영어(상)

612제

정답 및 해설

·2024학년도 수능 및 내신 대비·

능률
EBS 수능특강

변형 문제
영어(상)

612제

정답 및 해설

한눈에 보는 정답

1강
p.4
01 ④ 02 ④ 03 ③ 04 ① 05 ③ 06 ② 07 ③ 08 ② 09 ⑤ → covered 10 your vocal group 11 due to unprecedented levels of demand / we're unable to fulfil your order 12 refund 13 (1) ① → discussing (2) ③ → convinced (3) ⑤ → that 14 편지 수신인은 분석적인 주제에 대한 자신의 편집 방식을 보여 주기를 주저했다. 15 as much as I would like to speak at the conference 16 expert

2강
p.7
01 ② 02 ① 03 ③ 04 ① 05 ④ 06 ③ 07 ③ 08 ④ 09 the phone 10 (A) whatever (B) boring (C) order 11 we were asked to write a whole composition about some birds in Gaelic 12 ① → easily 13 that used to be a manor / used for events 14 Rosemary는 사람들이 점점 길어지는 낮을 즐기는 모습을 볼 수 있다. 15 (1) ① → was rejected (2) ③ → handed (3) ⑤ → attracting 16 accepted

3강
p.10
01 ② 02 ① 03 ③ 04 ⑤ 05 ⑤ 06 ③ 07 ① 08 ③ 09 there was little genetic pressure to stop people from becoming obese 10 사람들로 하여금 더 적은 열량을 섭취하게 하는 유전 돌연변이 11 (1) ① → suggested (2) ② → were (3) ④ → being expelled 12 profession 13 putting aside what one knows about the world that contradicts the story 14 예상치 못한 결과를 말하는 이야기는 독자들이 잘 알려진 사실을 확인하는 데 더 느려지게 만든다는 것 15 광고는 회사의 연간 지출에서 고정적인 요소일 수 있다는 것 16 causal

4강
p.13
01 ② 02 ④ 03 ② 04 ② 05 ③ 06 ④ 07 ② 08 ⑤ 09 The elements are personal freedom, meaningful work, and social tolerance. 10 (A) material (B) increase 11 (A) inbuilt (B) predator 12 (A) prioritizing (B) unlikely 13 오직 이 순간만을 위해 살아왔더라도 그럴 만한 가치가 있었을 거야. 14 Experiencing beauty can make life meaningful. 15 I've seen this innocent question spawn brilliant research projects 16 Innocent / research / inspiration / rational

5강
p.15
01 ② 02 ⑤ 03 ④ 04 ④ 05 ① 06 ④ 07 ④ 08 ④ 09 가능한 한 가장 낮은 가격에 주택을 구매하고자 하는 것 10 공공요금 납입금이 더 적게 든다. 11 The teacher should not be expected to flatter the prejudices either of the mob or of officials. 12 controversy 13 (A) resembling (B) to fill (C) necessarily 14 discipline yourself to differentiate between what is urgent and important and what is simply urgent 15 therefore convinced ourselves that our scientific endeavours were merely of interest to other scientists 16 (A) communicating (B) non-scientists

6강
p.18
01 ② 02 ② 03 ⑤ 04 ② 05 ② 06 ⑤ 07 ② 08 ③ 09 (도덕적) 의무에 대한 존경은 보편적이기 때문이다. 10 approve 11 (1) ② → to be strengthened (2) ⑤ → what 12 what suggestions their candidates made / have supported them unconditionally 13 ③ → useful 14 is it likely that you will experience emotions and behavioral reactions that are dysfunctional and self-defeating 15 갑작스러운 변화로 중단되는 상대적 안정의 긴 기간 다음에 더 큰 안정이 따르고 다시 더 많은 변화가 따르는 것 16 (A) steady (B) abrupt

7강
p.20
01 ④ 02 ④ 03 ③ 04 ⑤ 05 ③ 06 ② 07 ④ 08 ④ 09 exercise 10 Physical movement has been shown to have a positive effect on creative thinking. 11 unless there were such a thing as the universe to explain 12 ④ → systematically 13 change 14 직장에서의 보건과 안전, 피고용인의 권리, 고용주(로서)의 의무와 같은 문제들 15 (1) ① → that (2) ③ → is 16 advertisers will pay literally billions of dollars to broadcasters that can deliver mass audiences for sports

8강
p.23
01 ② 02 ④ 03 ③ 04 ③ 05 the most linguistically diverse country in the world 06 (1) ② → higher (2) ⑤ → increase 07 reversed 08 maintained its status as the African country with the highest GDP

9강
p.24
01 ④ 02 ④ 03 ③ 04 ⑤ 05 ③ 06 ② 07 ④ 08 ③ 09 몸이 앞으로 나아가도록 뒷지느러미발을 옆으로 둥글게 (회전하며) 움직일 수 있기 때문이다. 10 (A) measuring → measures (B) referred → refers to (C) to which → to when[to the time (when)] 11 (A) which → where (B) knew → known (C) married with → married[was married with] 12 Dissatisfied by what he saw in British schools for deaf people 13 (A) pursued (B) cover 14 made little impression 15 π(파이)값의 숫자를 가능한 한 많이 암기해서 암송하는 대회와 각종 파이를 먹는 것 16 passed a resolution recognising 14 March as National Pi Day

10강
p.27
01 ② 02 ② 03 ③ 04 ④ 05 ② 06 ④ 07 ④ 08 ③ 09 In case of bad weather, the camp will be held in an indoor arena 10 volunteer 11 provides opportunities for those interested in science and research to participate 12 (1) 현재 대학이나 지역 전문 대학의 학생, 또는 최근 대학 졸업자 (2) 프로그램 기간에 적어도 1주일에 5시간을 근무할 수 있는 사람 13 therapeutic 14 10 spaces are available on a first-come-first-served basis 15 자신들이 시장에서 구입하는 어떤 물건이든지 쿠폰을 사용해서 5달러 할인을 받을 수 있다. 16 drawing

11강
p.30
01 ② 02 ① 03 ④ 04 ⑤ 05 ② 06 ⑤ 07 ① 08 ④ 09 (1) ③ → resisting (2) ⑤ → seriously 10 잘못된 것을 보고 그대로 두지 않았다. 11 allows us to direct our attention to the most important elements 12 schemas 13 disembodied 14 특정한 논리적 연산을 통해 습득된 기술에 따라 세상을 해석하는 습관 15 (Little is written) About the intermediate stages between production and consumption. 16 will the commodity in question be there for the end-user to enjoy

2

1강

1번 ——————————————— p.6

• Word Test

1 숙박　2 완전히, 전적으로　3 경의를 표하다, 영예를 주다
4 뛰어난　5 공연하다　6 음역, 범위　7 특별히 출연시키다
8 불과 ~ 만에　9 상; 상을 주다　10 선곡, 발췌곡　11 state
12 celebrate　13 accept　14 cover
15 invitation　16 vocal　17 progressive
18 finalize　19 appreciate　20 accomplishment

유형 1

❶ accomplished　❷ yours　❸ performing
❹ covered　❺ could

유형 2

❶ holds　❷ has become　❸ be honored
❹ know

유형 3

❶ new and progressive artistic groups
❷ In a matter of one year
❸ your travel and lodging expenses
❹ as early as possible

2번 ——————————————— p.8

• Word Test

1 최신 정보　2 구매, 구매품　3 이행하다, 충족하다
4 알리다　5 매우, 극도로　6 방식, 종류　7 처리하다
8 추가의, 그 이상의　9 기념일, 기념행사　10 최근의
11 ~하게 되어 유감이다　12 provide　13 inconvenience
14 appreciate　15 loyal　16 original
17 support　18 apologize　19 payment
20 refund　21 demand　22 business day

유형 1

❶ interest　❷ with　❸ due to
❹ fulfil　❺ to write

유형 2

❶ have shown　❷ to provide
❸ are processing　❹ appreciate

유형 3

❶ in an extremely short space of time
❷ within 2-7 business days
❸ feel free to write
❹ for this inconvenience

3번 ——————————————— p.10

• Word Test

1 생각하다, 숙고하다　2 상당한　3 분석적인
4 전문적인, 기술적인　5 편집자　6 솔직히
7 오랫동안, 상세히　8 견해　9 editorial

---

10 background　11 candidate　12 appropriate
13 conclusion　14 demonstrate
15 hesitancy　16 convince

유형 1

❶ hesitancy　❷ Since　❸ substantial
❹ that　❺ regret

유형 2

❶ discussing　❷ have reviewed
❸ to demonstrate　❹ have interviewed　❺ are

유형 3

❶ reflected at length
❷ several other candidates
❸ during a necessary period
❹ make this decision

4번 ——————————————— p.12

• Word Test

1 ~라는 것을 알다　2 회의　3 곧 있을, 다가오는
4 영광스러운, 특권을 가진　5 ~의 분야에서　6 영광스러운
7 협회　8 경력　9 훌륭한, 명망 있는
10 대체[대신]할 사람, 대리인　11 expert
12 engagement　13 sincerely　14 notice
15 gathering　16 regional　17 organization
18 human resources　19 regrettably
20 advanced

유형 1

❶ privileged　❷ fully　❸ gathering
❹ because　❺ if

유형 2

❶ have invited　❷ considering
❸ been working　❹ has done
❺ to invite

유형 3

❶ out of the country　❷ to take my place
❸ throughout her career　❹ advanced notice

—————————————————— p.14

01 ④　02 ④　03 ③　04 ①　05 ③　06 ②
07 ③　08 ②　09 ⑤ → covered
10 your vocal group　11 due to unprecedented
levels of demand / we're unable to fulfil your
order　12 refund
13 (1) ① → discussing (2) ③ → convinced (3) ⑤ → that
14 편지 수신인은 분석적인 주제에 대한 자신의 편집 방식을 보여
주기를 주저했다.
15 as much as I would like to speak at the conference
16 expert

01 ④

동사구 will be covered를 수식하는 자리에 부사가 들어가야 하므로 entire를 entirely로 고쳐야 한다.

오답노트

① '기량이 뛰어난'이란 의미로 artist를 꾸미는 분사가 필요하므로 과거분사인 accomplished는 적절하다.
② your group을 대신하므로 소유대명사 yours는 적절하다.
③ '~함으로써'에 해당하는 문장을 완성하기 위해 전치사 by의 목적어가 필요하므로 performing은 적절하다.
⑤ know의 목적어 역할을 하는 명사절을 이끄는 '~인지'라는 뜻의 접속사 if는 적절하다.

02 ④

문제해설

이 글은 50주년 기념상품이 전례 없는 수준의 수요로 인해, 주문을 이행할 수 없는 상황이 되어 이를 알리고 환불과 관련된 세부 사항을 안내하는 내용의 편지글이므로, 빈칸에 들어갈 말로 적절한 것은 ④ '귀하의 최근 주문에 대한 최신 정보를 제공하기 위해서'이다.

오답노트

① 오배송에 대해 사과하려고
② 배송 지연을 알리려고
③ 환불 요청을 거절하기로 한 결정을 설명하려고
⑤ 사이즈, 스타일, 색상 교환 요청법을 설명하려고

03 ③

문제해설

지원자의 견해와 배경을 고려해 볼 때 편집자직에 적합하지 않다고 판단되어 채용할 수 없다는 내용이므로 '이 결정'이 의미하는 바로 가장 적절한 것은 ③ '귀하가 이 직책에 적합하지 않다고 귀하에게 알리는 것'이다.

오답노트

① 귀하의 작업 샘플을 다른 편집자에게 보내는 것
② 분석 능력과 전문 지식에 대한 자격을 요구하는 것
④ 최종 결정을 내리기 전 몇몇 다른 지원자를 면접하는 것
⑤ 지원자들에게 분석적인 주제에 대한 편집 방식 연수를 제공하는 것

04 ①

문제해설

인사관리협회의 지역 회의에 초청 연사로 저를 청해 주셔서 진심으로 명예롭고 영광스럽고, 이 모임에 상원 의원 몇 분을 초대했다는 점을 고려하면, 이 행사가 훌륭한 행사가 될 것임을 알고 있다고 말하는 주어진 글에 이어, 유감스럽게도, 회의 날 가족 행사로 인해 외국에 나가 있을 것이기 때문에 초대를 거절할 수밖에 없다고 밝히는 (A)가 오고, 이어 Julia Spencer 씨를 추천하며 그녀의 경력을 소개하는 (C)가 이어지고, 대체 연사로 그녀를 초대하기로 결정하시면 그녀에게 사전 고지할 수 있도록 제게 알려 달라고 말하며 행사의 성공적인 개최를 기원하는 내용인 (B)가 오는 것이 자연스럽다.

05 ③

문제해설

We will be honored if you help us celebrate this year's accomplishments in modern art by performing two selections for us on the evening of October 6.에서 글쓴이는 수신인에게 10월 6일 저녁 축하 공연에서 두 곡을 공연할 것을 요청했으므로, ③은 글의 내용과 일치하지 않는다.

06 ②

문제해설

We regret to inform you that ~ we're unable to fulfil your order for the FC Rainbow City 50 Year Anniversary Shirt 2XL.에서 기념 셔츠 2XL에 대한 주문을 이행할 수 없다고만 언급되고 다른 사이즈에 대한 내용은 없으므로, ②는 글의 내용과 일치하지 않는다.

07 ③

문제해설

지원자의 견해와 배경을 고려해 볼 때 편집자직에 적합하지 않다고 판단되어 채용할 수 없다는 내용의 글이므로, '또한, 어떤 자격증은 산업에서 직업을 얻는 필수 조건으로 작용할 수 있어 자격증을 따는 것이 직업 전망을 향상시킬 수 있다.'라는 ③은 글의 전체 흐름과 관계가 없다.

08 ②

문제해설

(A) '이 모임에 상원 의원 몇 분을 초대했다는 점을 고려하면, 이 행사가 명망 있는 행사가 될 것을 알고 있다'라는 의미이므로 prestigious(명망 있는)가 적절하다. pretentious는 '가식적인, 허세 부리는'이라는 뜻이다.
(B) 회의에서 연설하고 싶지만, 가족 행사로 인해 그날 외국에 나가 있을 것이라 유감이라는 의미이므로 문장 시작에 Regrettably(유감스럽게도)가 적절하다. Respectably는 '점잖게'라는 뜻이다.
(C) Julia Spencer 씨를 대체 연사로 초대하기로 결정하면, 그녀에게 사전 고지하도록 알려 달라는 의미이므로, alternate(대체자)가 적절하다. administrate는 '통치자, 집정자'라는 뜻이다.

09 ⑤ → covered

문제해설

초청을 수락한다면 이동 경비와 숙박비는 주최 측에서 부담한다고 하는 것이 자연스러우므로 charged(부과되다)는 '경비를 대다, 비용을 치르다'라는 의미의 cover를 사용하여 어법에 맞도록 covered로 바꿔 써야 한다.

10 your vocal group

문제해설

yours는 이어지는 문장에 나오는 your vocal group을 가리킨다.

11 due to unprecedented levels of demand / we're
unable to fulfil your order

문제해설

'전례 없는 수준의 수요로 인해'는 〈due to+명사구〉를 사용하여 due
to unprecedented levels of demand로, '~할 수 없다'는 〈be
unable to + 동사원형〉 형태로 나타낸다.

12 refund

문제해설

'특히나 무언가에 너무 많은 돈을 지불했거나 그 무언가를 원하지 않는다
고 판단했기 때문에 다시 얻게 되는 본인의 것인 돈'이라는 의미의 단어는
refund(환불금)이다.

13 (1) ① → discussing (2) ③ → convinced
(3) ⑤ → that

문제해설

① Thank you for sending ~ and discussing으로 병렬되는 구조
이므로 discuss를 discussing으로 고쳐야 한다.
③ 주어 I가 '확신하게 되는' 수동적 의미이므로 convincing을
convinced로 고쳐야 한다.
⑤ My conclusion is that ~ and that ~ 형태로 두 개의 that절이
and로 병렬되므로 what을 that으로 고쳐야 한다.

오답노트

② Since we talked를 통해 과거의 어느 시점 이후로 현재까지 이어져
온 시제임을 알 수 있으므로 현재완료시제의 have interviewed는 적
절하다.
④ 주어가 analytical skills and technical knowledge로 복수이
므로 동사 are는 적절하다.

14 편지 수신인은 분석적인 주제에 대한 자신의 편집 방식을 보
여 주기를 주저했다.

문제해설

필자와 편지 수신인 사이의 지난 대화에서 수신인이 하기를 주저했던 것은
I have reviewed your work ~ to demonstrate your editorial
approach to analytical topics.에 나타나 있다.

15 as much as I would like to speak at the conference

문제해설

'~이지만'이라는 양보의 의미는 as much as(~이지만)를 사용하고, 이
어서 '연설하고 싶다'는 I would like to speak로 쓰며, '회의에서'는 at
the conference로 써서 완성한다.

16 expert

문제해설

'특별한 기술을 가지고 있거나 특별한 주제에 대해 많이 알고 있는 사람'이
라는 의미의 단어는 expert(전문가)이다.

2강

1번 ————————————————————— p.19

• Word Test

1 떨쳐버리다, 흔들다   2 밀려들다   3 배송하다, 배달하다
4 번쩍이는   5 오두막   6 ~으로 초대하다   7 진동하다
8 (소식·정보를) 알아내다   9 머뭇거리는, 망설이는
10 exceptional   11 piece   12 art gallery
13 end table   14 slightly   15 recognize
16 occasionally   17 impact   18 relief

유형 **1**

❶ that   ❷ whatever   ❸ recognize
❹ hesitant   ❺ whether

유형 **2**

❶ picked   ❷ shook   ❸ had
❹ be shipped

유형 **3**

❶ couldn't shake the feeling   ❷ have an impact on
❸ felt relief flood   ❹ catch up on local news

2번 ————————————————————— p.21

• Word Test

1 참을성 있게   2 걸작, 명작   3 전반적으로
4 ~을 감동시키다   5 짧은 글, 작문   6 자기 연민
7 곧 오려고 하는, 다가오는   8 붉은   9 make a good job
10 notice   11 horrible   12 whole   13 spread
14 hesitation   15 tense   16 descend

유형 **1**

❶ composition   ❷ it   ❸ Without
❹ anything   ❺ better

유형 **2**

❶ were asked   ❷ read   ❸ was getting
❹ to pass   ❺ spread

유형 **3**

❶ patiently waiting for the praise
❷ more and more ruddy   ❸ blown away by
❹ started slowly to descend

3번 ————————————————————— p.23

• Word Test

1 한창, 최고점   2 접의자   3 줄무늬를 넣다
4 (군것질을 하여) 손가락이 끈끈한   5 저택, 장원(莊園)
6 방해, 소란   7 고리 모양으로 이동하다[움직이다]
8 붉은 벽돌을 쓴   9 뜨다   10 lengthen   11 wrap
12 calming   13 rectangle   14 track   15 petal
16 split   17 food stand   18 edge

유형 1

❶ that ❷ while ❸ its
❹ disturbance ❺ that

유형 2

❶ used ❷ selling ❸ is
❹ enjoying ❺ wraps

유형 3

❶ Spring is in bloom
❷ Two sets of train tracks
❸ on the edge of ❹ place to spend the day

4번 _____ p.25

• Word Test

1 불합격시키다, 거부하다 2 (전화기를) 들다
3 전화를 걸다, 다이얼을 돌리다 4 숨이 가쁜 5 소리 지르다
6 조수, 보조원 7 행정실, (사업체의) 본부
8 (주의·흥미 등을) 끌다 9 (심장이) 두근거리다 10 career
11 chance 12 admission 13 hand 14 expect
15 thrill 16 editor 17 overwhelmed
18 anxiety

유형 1

❶ However ❷ who ❸ hearing
❹ overwhelmed ❺ attention

유형 2

❶ were accepted ❷ had worked ❸ was
❹ handed ❺ attracting

유형 3

❶ my own chances of getting accepted
❷ I was short of breath ❸ more than anything
❹ A thrill ran through me

---

p.27

01 ② 02 ① 03 ③ 04 ① 05 ④ 06 ③
07 ③ 08 ④ 09 the phone
10 (A) whatever (B) boring (C) order
11 we were asked to write a whole composition about
some birds in Gaelic 12 ① → easily
13 that used to be a manor / used for events
14 Rosemary는 사람들이 점점 길어지는 낮을 즐기는 모습을 볼 수
있다. 15 (1) ① → was rejected (2) ③ → handed
(3) ⑤ → attracting 16 accepted

01 ②

문제해설

늦은 밤에 전화벨이 울려 깜짝 놀라 일어나 앉은 Sam은 수화기(탁자 위
에서 진동하고 있는 그 번쩍이는 금속 조각)를 집어 들고 나면 자신의 인
생이 바뀔 것 같은 느낌이 들었다고 말하는 주어진 글에 이어, 자신이 막
알게 될 것이 무엇이든지 간에 자신의 남은 인생에 영향을 미칠 것 같다

는 느낌을 받으며 떨리는 손으로 모르는 번호로부터 걸려온 전화를 받게
되는 (B)가 오고, 수화기 너머로 "오랜만이야! Joe가 오두막으로 초대
했던 지난 파티가 너무 지루하지는 않았겠지?"라고 응답한 친구 John
Havisham의 목소리가 들렸다는 (A)가 이어지고, 그 순간, 전화를 한 주
인공이 가끔 전화해서 지역 소식을 알아내는, 친구 John이라는 걸 알고
안도의 물결이 밀려드는 것을 느꼈다는 (C)가 오는 것이 자연스럽다.

02 ①

문제해설

나의 게일어 작문을 본 수녀님이, 안색이 점점 더 붉어지시더니 "네가 통과
할 거라고 생각하니?"라고 말씀하시며, "나는 전에 이런 걸 본 적이 없다."
라고 혹평하셨고, 그 순간 나는 그녀가 게일어로 된 나의 명작에 감동한 것
이 전혀 아니라는 것을 깨달았다는 내용이므로 '그녀는 게일어로 된 나의
명작에 감동한 것이 전혀 아니다'가 의미하는 바로 가장 적절한 것은 ① '나
의 게일어 명작은 그녀를 감동시키는 데 실패했다'이다.

오답노트

② 그녀는 나의 게일어 작문에 완전히 감동했다
③ 그녀는 일생 동안 한 번도 다른 게일어 명작을 본 적이 없었다.
④ 그녀는 나의 게일어 명작이 (바람 등에) 날아가지 않도록 보호하려고 노
력해 왔다
⑤ 그녀는 내 작품보다 더 나은 게일어 작문을 본적이 없었다.

03 ③

문제해설

지각동사 see의 목적격 보어 자리에는 원형부정사 혹은 현재분사가 필요
하므로, to enjoy를 enjoy나 enjoying으로 고쳐야 한다.

오답노트

① with 이하는 a small hill을 수식하는 전치사구이며, that절은 an
old house를 수식하는 관계절인데, 이때 〈used to + 동사원형〉은 '(과
거에) ~ 가 있었다(현재는 없음)'라는 의미로, used to be a manor는
적절하다.
② that절은 the miniature one을 수식하는 관계절이므로 주격 관계
대명사 that은 적절하다.
④ 주어는 a low redbrick building이므로 동사 자리에 본동사의 3인
칭 단수 현재형인 wraps는 적절하다.
⑤ 선행사 ropes를 수식하는 관계대명사절의 동사로 선행사의 수에 일치
시킨 복수형 동사 split은 적절하다.

04 ①

문제해설

the editor of our newspaper, who had worked his whole
high-school career for a Tufts admission, was rejected에
서 우리 신문사의 편집장, 즉 우리 (고등학교) 신문 편집장은, Tufts 대학
교 입학을 위해 고등학교 생활 내내 노력했는데도, 불합격했다고 했으므
로, ①은 글의 내용과 일치하지 않는다.

05 ④

문제해설

(A) 늦은 밤에 전화벨이 울려 깜짝 놀라 일어나 앉은 Sam이 수화기(탁자
위에서 진동하고 있는 그 번쩍이는 금속 조각)를 집어 들고 나면 자신의 인

생이 바뀔 것 같은 느낌이 들었다라는 의미이므로 picked up(수화기를 들다)가 적절하다. hang up은 '전화를 끊다'라는 뜻이다.
(B) 떨리는 손으로 모르는 번호로부터 걸려온 전화를 받게 되어 "Sam입니다."라며 걸걸하고 머뭇거리는 목소리로 전화를 받는다는 의미이므로 hesitant(머뭇거리는)가 적절하다. confident는 '자신감 있는'이라는 뜻이다.
(C) 긴장하면서 모르는 번호에서 온 전화를 받았지만, 이내 전화를 건 사람이 친구 John이라는 걸 알고 안도의 물결이 밀려드는 것을 느꼈다는 의미이므로, relief(안도)가 적절하다. grief는 '큰 슬픔, 비탄'이라는 뜻이다.

06 ③

문제해설

영어 작문에 자신이 있었던 나는 게일어로도 작문을 쉽게 할 수 있을 것으로 생각하고, 자신이 전반적으로 잘했다고 생각했으나, Cecilia 수녀가 글을 읽고 혹평을 한 상황에 처했으므로, 이런 상황에서는 자기 연민감이 서서히 들기 시작하는 것이 적합하므로, 빈칸에 들어갈 말로 적절한 것은 ③ '끔찍한 자기 연민감'이다.

오답노트

① 엄청난 안도감
② 분명한 질투의 감정
④ 강한 소속감
⑤ 증대되는 자신감

07 ③

문제해설

Two sets of train tracks loop around the park: the real one and the miniature one that is only for the summer and very small children.에서 두 개의 기차선로가 공원을 따라 고리 모양으로 나 있는데, 하나는 실제 선로이고, 다른 하나는 여름철과 아주 어린 아이들만을 위한 축소 모형 선로라고 했으므로, ③은 글의 내용과 일치하지 않는다.

08 ④

문제해설

재학 중인 고등학교에서 학생 두 명이 Tufts 대학교에 합격했지만, 신문 편집장은 Tufts 대학교 입학을 위해 고등학교 생활 내내 노력했는데도 불합격했다는 주어진 글에 이어, 그 소식을 듣고, 자신의 합격 가능성에 대한 불안감에 휩싸여 아침 내내 Tufts 대학교 생각만 하다가 10시 30분경에 집으로 전화하라는 쪽지를 받았다는 (C)가 오고, 가슴이 두근거리고 두 손이 떨리는 가운데, 인생에서 입학 허가를 무엇보다 바라는 마음으로 집으로 전화를 걸었다는 내용의 (A)가 이어진 뒤, 엄마가 합격 소식을 알려주자 기뻐하며 소리를 질렀다고 한 (B)가 오는 것이 자연스럽다.

09 the phone

문제해설

the flashing piece of metal은 앞 문장의 the phone을 가리킨다.

10 (A) whatever (B) boring (C) order

문제해설

(A) '그가 알게 될 것이 무엇이든지 간에'의 의미로 주어 역할을 하는 명사절이 필요하므로 however를 whatever로 고쳐야 한다.
(B) the last party가 주어로 능동의 의미가 되어야 하므로 bored를 현재분사 boring으로 고쳐야 한다.
(C) call to 뒤의 catch up on ~, ask ~, and order ~ 형태로 세 개의 동사구가 연결되는 병렬구조가 적절하므로 ordering을 order로 고쳐야 한다.

11 we were asked to write a whole composition about some birds in Gaelic

문제해설

'우리는 ~하라는 요구를 받았다'는 주어 we와 5형식 동사 ask의 수동태인 were asked to ~로 나타낸다. '어떤 새들에 관해 완전히 갖추어진 짧은 글을 쓰라(는)'는 asked to 뒤에 동사구인 write a whole composition about some birds로 나타낸다.

12 ① → easily

문제해설

앞 문장에서 게일어로도 그다지 어렵지 않으리라는 것을 알고 있었다고 했으므로 단어들이 아주 쉽게 떠올랐다는 내용이 자연스럽다. 따라서 laboriously(힘들게)를 easily(쉽게)와 같은 말로 바꿔 써야 한다.

13 that used to be a manor / used for events

문제해설

an old house를 꾸며주는 that절 안에 필요한 내용을 모두 넣어 영작한다. '한때는 저택이었다'는 that 뒤에 used to be a manor로 쓰고, '지금은 행사용으로 사용되고 있다'는 is now 뒤에 used for events로 써서 완성한다.

14 Rosemary는 사람들이 점점 길어지는 낮을 즐기는 모습을 볼 수 있다.

문제해설

이제 막 해가 지기 시작하고 있을 때 Rosemary가 새들의 노래에 귀를 기울이면서 볼 수 있는 것은 The sun is just starting to set ~ can see people enjoying the lengthening days.에 나타나 있다.

15 (1) ① → was rejected (2) ③ → handed
    (3) ⑤ → attracting

문제해설

① the editor of our newspaper가 주어이고 대학에서 떨어졌다(거부되었다)라는 수동의 의미를 나타내야 하므로 rejected는 was rejected로 고쳐야 한다.
③ an assistant came ~ and handed로 병렬되는 구조이므로 hands는 과거형 handed로 고쳐야 한다.
⑤ 목적어가 이어나오는 분사로 주어와 능동의 관계이므로 attracted는 attracting으로 고쳐야 한다.

오답노트

② all I could think about은 단수 취급하므로 was는 적절하다.
④ right를 수식하는 형용사적 용법의 to부정사 to expect는 적절하다.

16 accepted

문제해설

'누군가가 조직에 들어가는 것을 허락하다'라는 의미의 단어는 accept(받아들이다, 수락하다)이며, '합격되다', '합격될'이라는 수동의 의미를 나타내야 하므로 과거분사 accepted라고 써야 한다.

3강

1번 ———————————————————— p.33

• Word Test

1 개인, 사람 2 비만 3 (일부로) 포함하다 4 포유류의
5 번식하다 6 반면에 7 ~을 따라잡다 8 모으다, 수집하다
9 유전적인 10 (어떤 일에 소요되는) 기간 11 ~을 전달하다
12 pressure 13 current 14 obese
15 approximately 16 considerable 17 consume
18 evolutionary 19 scarce 20 abundant
21 degree 22 population

유형 1

❶ little ❷ much ❸ where
❹ abundant ❺ whatever

유형 2

❶ was ❷ to consume ❸ be passed
❹ required ❺ were incorporated

유형 3

❶ stop people from becoming obese
❷ on the other hand ❸ whenever we want it
❹ catch up with

2번 ———————————————————— p.35

• Word Test

1 결점이 없는, 완전한 2 협력자, 동맹국 3 떠돌다, 헤매다
4 신화, 근거 없는 믿음 5 쫓아내다, 추방하다 6 전제 조건
7 직업 8 말하다 9 실질적인 10 정말로 11 genius
12 conclusion 13 widow 14 coal
15 respectable 16 reformer 17 reliable
18 literary 19 psychologist 20 colleague

유형 1

❶ preconditions ❷ that ❸ who
❹ reliable ❺ while

유형 2

❶ suggested ❷ is ❸ dreamed
❹ was forced ❺ turns

유형 3

❶ is far from being faultless
❷ hid his clarinet from him
❸ after being expelled from home
❹ upon closer examination

3번 ———————————————————— p.38

• Word Test

1 ~을 정신없이 빠져들게 만들다 2 특징 3 ~을 제쳐 두다
4 ~과 모순되다, 반박하다 5 발견하다 6 거부하다, 거절하다
7 ~한 결과를 낳다 8 예증하다, 설명하다

9 다른 세상에 있는 것처럼 느끼게 하다　　10 ~에 동그라미를 치다
11 거짓말을 하는　　12 elect　　13 falsehood
14 nomination　　15 suspension　　16 outcome
17 clue　　18 disbelief　　19 narrative　　20 involved
21 emotionally　　22 make sense

유형 1
❶ transport　　❷ what　　❸ contradicts
❹ in which　　❺ fewer

유형 2
❶ experiencing　　❷ requires　　❸ suggests
❹ was elected　　❺ illustrated

유형 3
❶ as if being swept away　　❷ putting aside
❸ less likely to　　❹ make sense

4번　　　　　　　　　　　　　　　p.41

• Word Test
1 잘 보여 주다　　2 ~을 활용하다　　3 고정적인 요소
4 (특정한 활동을) 수행하다　　5 개념, 생각
6 시대에 뒤떨어진, 구식의　　7 주창, 계획, 진취성　　8 원인이 되는
9 부족　　10 이사회　　11 iceberg　　12 merely
13 performance　　14 method　　15 survey
16 based on　　17 reaction　　18 budget　　19 apply
20 annual

유형 1
❶ what　　❷ initiatives　　❸ whom
❹ fixture　　❺ increasingly

유형 2
❶ be heard　　❷ are　　❸ communicated
❹ remains　　❺ is

유형 3
❶ 20 years out of date　　❷ what they see and read
❸ the methods being used
❹ proven causal relationship

---

p.44
01 ②　　02 ①　　03 ③　　04 ⑤　　05 ③　　06 ③
07 ①　　08 ③　　09 there was little genetic
pressure to stop people from becoming obese
10 사람들로 하여금 더 적은 열량을 섭취하게 하는 유전 돌연변이
11 (1) ① → suggested　(2) ② → were　(3) ④ → being
expelled　　12 profession　　13 putting aside what
one knows about the world that contradicts the story
14 예상치 못한 결과를 말하는 이야기는 독자들이 잘 알려진 사실을
확인하는 데 더 느려지게 만든다는 것　　15 광고는 회사의 연간
지출에서 고정적인 요소일 수 있다는 것　　16 causal

01 ②

문제해설
an environment를 수식하는 관계사절에서 관계사 뒤에는 주어와 동사가 있는 완벽한 문장이 이어지고, 의미상으로도 '음식이 더 부족하고, 그것을 사냥하거나 채집하는 데 상당한 에너지 소비가 요구되는 환경에서'라는 의미의 관계부사절이 와야 하므로 which를 where 또는 in which로 고쳐야 한다.

오답노트
① 〈stop+목적어+from -ing〉 동명사 구문으로 동명사 becoming은 적절하다.
③ on the other hand는 삽입구이며, Mutations를 선행사로 하는 that절이 이어 나오고 있다. 따라서 주어는 Mutations이므로 동사는 복수 과거형 were가 적절하다.
④ only in ~ evolutionary time이 It's와 that 사이에 놓여 그 의미가 강조되고 있으므로, 강조구문의 that은 적절하다.
⑤ 한 문장 내에서 Evolution의 반복을 피하기 위해 대명사로 대체했으므로, 단수 대명사 it은 적절하다.

02 ①

문제해설
이 글은 성공한 음악가의 뒤에는 가족의 성원이 있었을 것이라는 믿음과 달리, 위대한 음악가의 부모는 악기를 감추거나, 음악가가 된 것을 간신히 받아들이거나, 음악가가 된 자식을 집에서 쫓아내기도 했다는 내용의 글이므로, (글을 통해 근거 없는 믿음으로 판명된) 빈칸에 들어갈 말로 가장 적절한 것은 ① '초보 음악가에게 부모가 주는 보편적 성원'이다.

오답노트
② 아이의 성공에 있어 전제 조건에 대한 강한 강조
③ 아이의 음악적 경력을 위한 무관심한 부모의 중요성
④ 음악 천재와 그 가족에 대한 재정적 지원의 중요성
⑤ 고난에도 불구하고 꿈을 추구하는 것이 언젠가는 보상받을 것이라는 믿음

03 ③

문제해설
(A) 이야기를 읽는 동안은 감정적으로 몰입되며 마치 참여자로서 정신없이 빠져드는 듯한 기분을 느낄 수 있다는 뜻이므로, involved(몰입된)가 적절하다. detached는 '거리를 두는, 무심한'이라는 뜻이다.
(B) 독자는 이야기에 몰입하며, 알고 있는 이야기와 모순되는 바를 제쳐둔다고 했으므로, 예상과 다른 결과가 있는 이야기는 잘 알려진 사실을 확인하는 데에 더 느려지게(slower) 만든다는 것이 적절하다. quicker는 '더 빠른'이라는 뜻이다.
(C) '피노키오 동그라미 치기(이야기를 읽다가 거짓(단서)을 발견할 때마다 동그라미를 치는 방식)' 연구에서, 이야기에 빠져든 독자일수록 거짓을 더 적게(fewer) 발견했다는 것이 적절하다. more를 사용하면 '더 많이' 발견한 게 된다.

04 ⑤

문제해설
주어진 문장은 세계 5대 브랜드 중 4개는 광고를 한 번도 한 적이 없으며,

이는 최고속 성장 10대 브랜드 중 7개도 마찬가지라는 내용으로, 설문 조사의 결과를 나타낸다. 따라서 가장 최근의 Brandchannel 설문 조사가 이 점을 보여 준다는 내용의 문장 뒤인 ⑤에 들어가는 것이 가장 적절하다.

05 ③

문제해설

대부분의 진화 기간에, 인간은 먹을 것이 부족한 환경이었기 때문에 비만을 막을 수 있는 돌연변이는 전달될 가능성이 적었고, 지난 세기부터 비만을 통제해야 할 정도로 먹을 것이 풍부해졌지만, 비만을 억제하는 유전적 압력을 당장 만들어 내기에는 진화 기간이 길다는 흐름이 자연스러우므로 ③의 short(짧은)는 long(긴)과 같은 말로 고쳐야 한다.

06 ③

문제해설

Robert Schumann's mother, the widow of a publisher and literary translator, reconciled herself only with difficulty to her son's choice of music as a profession.에서 출판업자이자 문학 번역가의 미망인이었던 Robert Schumann의 어머니가 자기 아들이 직업으로 음악을 선택한 것을 간신히 감수했다고 했으므로, ③은 글의 내용과 일치하지 않는다.

07 ①

문제해설

이야기를 경험하는 동안 독자들은 불신을 유예한다는 내용의 글로, '이야기를 즐기는 것은 이야기를 (A) 반박하는 세상에 대한 지식을 제쳐두는 것을 수반할 수도 있으며 이런 불신의 유예는 이야기에 나타난 (B) 결함(참이 아닌 잘못된 정보)을 인지하는 것을 더욱 어렵게 만들 수 있다.'와 같이 요약하는 것이 적절하다.

오답노트

② 설명하다 …… 교훈
③ 확실히 하다 …… 실현 가능성
④ 거부하다 …… 진실
⑤ 뒷받침하다 …… 거짓

08 ③

문제해설

많은 회사가 마케팅 활동에 많은 예산을 들이지만, 회사의 이사회는 이에 대해 점점 더 의문을 제기하고 있고, 최근 조사에서도 세계의 큰 브랜드나 빠르게 성장하고 있는 대다수의 브랜드들이 광고를 한 적이 없다는 내용의 글이므로, 글의 요지로 가장 적절한 것은 ③이다.

09 there was little genetic pressure to stop people from becoming obese

문제해설

'유전적 압력이 거의 없었다'를 앞에 두어 there was little genetic pressure로 쓰고, '사람들이 비만이 되는 것을 막을 수 있는'은 〈stop+목적어+from+v-ing〉 형태를 사용하되 이 부분이 pressure를 꾸며주도록 to부정사를 사용하여 to stop people from becoming obese로 쓰도록 한다.

10 사람들로 하여금 더 적은 열량을 섭취하게 하는 유전 돌연변이

문제해설

that mutation은 문장 앞부분의 Genetic mutations that drove people to consume fewer calories를 가리킨다.

11 (1) ① → suggested (2) ② → were
(3) ④ → being expelled

문제해설

① family support에 대해 부가적인 정보를 제시하는 분사구의 분사로 수동의 의미를 나타내므로 suggests를 과거분사 suggested로 고쳐야 한다.
② 가능성이 희박한 일을 상상하는 가정법 과거 문장이므로 동사 is를 were로 고쳐야 한다.
④ 〈after+v-ing〉 형태에서 -ing의 의미상 주어가 '쫓겨나게 됨'이라는 수동의 의미가 되어야 하므로 expelling을 being expelled로 고쳐야 한다.

오답노트

③ 동사가 필요한 자리이고 과거형이 와야 하므로 hid는 적절하다.
⑤ 주어가 복수이고 수동태의 동사가 필요한 자리이므로 were given은 적절하다.

12 profession

문제해설

'특히 높은 사회적 지위를 지닌 것으로, 해야 할 특별한 기술과 자격을 필요로 하는 직업'이라는 의미의 단어는 profession(직업)이다.

13 putting aside what one knows about the world that contradicts the story

문제해설

'알고 있는 바를 제쳐 두는 것'은 putting aside what one knows로 쓰고 '이야기와 모순되는 세상에 대해'는 about the world that contradicts the story로 쓴다. 동사 involve의 목적어로 동명사형인 putting aside가 먼저 오고 know와 contradict는 주어의 수와 일치시켜 단수 동사로 쓴다.

14 예상치 못한 결과를 말하는 이야기는 독자들이 잘 알려진 사실을 확인하는 데 더 느려지게 만든다는 것

문제해설

This suspension of disbelief가 의미하는 바는 앞의 A story that suggests an unexpected outcome ~ to verify well-known facts에 나타나 있다.

15 광고는 회사의 연간 지출에서 고정적인 요소일 수 있다는 것

문제해설

밑줄 친 this가 가리키는 내용은 바로 앞 문장의 Advertising may be a fixture in a company's annual send에 나타나 있다.

16 causal

'하나가 다른 것을 유발하는 두 사건 사이에 어떤 관계나 연결이 있는'이라는 의미의 단어는 causal(인과 관계의)이다.

4강

1번 ————————————————— p.50

• Word Test

1 소비 사회   2 대다수의   3 부상하다, 나타나다
4 풍요, 풍부   5 3배가 되다   6 주거, 주거지
7 복지, 행복, 안녕   8 비할 데 없는   9 1인당 소득
10 감지하다, 인지하다   11 genuine   12 factor
13 range   14 assumption   15 tolerance
16 income   17 generation   18 prosperity
19 material   20 unprecedented

유형 1

❶ has   ❷ material   ❸ abundance
❹ However   ❺ little

유형 2

❶ have lived   ❷ has produced   ❸ have moved
❹ have had   ❺ reaches

유형 3

❶ until the last few generations
❷ in a number of developed nations
❸ on a very low income   ❹ as a global average

2번 ————————————————— p.52

• Word Test

1 과대평가하다   2 몇 분의 1초 만에, 순식간에
3 타고나는, 천성의   4 이득, 이익   5 ~배로   6 끌림, 매력
7 지나치게 중시하다   8 특전[특권]을 주다   9 내재된
10 기제   11 감지하다, 발견하다   12 tendency
13 predator   14 permit   15 lottery   16 survival
17 evaluate   18 priority   19 urban
20 acknowledge   21 constantly   22 struggle

유형 1

❶ constantly   ❷ quicker   ❸ been seen
❹ why   ❺ unlikely

유형 2

❶ requiring   ❷ is   ❸ are set
❹ means   ❺ being caught

유형 3

❶ evaluated as good or bad ❷ give priority to
❸ in a fraction of a second ❹ Treats are privileged

3번 ————————————————— p.54

• Word Test

1 충족하다   2 (악곡의) 마디   3 (시간·수고 따위를 들일 만한)
그럴 만한 가치가 있는   4 행위자, 동인   5 ~에 국한하다
6 ~하는 한은, ~하는 정도까지는   7 전념, 헌신   8 울려 퍼지다
9 언명하다, (분명히) 말하다   10 phrase
11 symphony   12 existence   13 demand

14 specific　　15 spine　　16 loving　　17 responsibly
18 shiver

유형 1
❶ responsibly　　❷ dedication　　❸ confine
❹ so　　❺ whether

유형 2
❶ experiencing　　❷ listening　　❸ declared
❹ have lived

유형 3
❶ through our actions　　❷ fulfill the demands
❸ resound in your ears
❹ It would have been worth it

4번
p.56

• Word Test
1 ~하기로 되어 있다　　2 대처 방안　　3 결정적 실험　　4 경우
5 훌륭한, 화려한　　6 실행, 집행　　7 적용
8 가설 (pl. hypotheses)　　9 우선, 첫째로　　10 insight
11 formulate　　12 argue for　　13 deal with
14 innocent　　15 odd　　16 entirely　　17 inspiration
18 rational

유형 1
❶ entirely　　❷ generalization　　❸ whose
❹ inspiration　　❺ insights

유형 2
❶ argued　　❷ been made　　❸ are
❹ to deal　　❺ be done

유형 3
❶ is supposed to　　❷ in the first place
❸ on quite a few occasions　　❹ in terms of

p.58

01 ②　　02 ④　　03 ②　　04 ②　　05 ③　　06 ④
07 ②　　08 ⑤　　09 The elements are personal freedom, meaningful work, and social tolerance.
10 (A) material　(B) increase
11 (A) inbuilt　(B) predator
12 (A) prioritizing　(B) unlikely
13 오직 이 순간만을 위해 살아왔더라도 그럴 만한 가치가 있었을 거야.
14 Experiencing beauty can make life meaningful.
15 I've seen this innocent question spawn brilliant research projects
16 Innocent / research / inspiration / rational

01 ②

문제해설

(A) 돈으로 행복을 얻는다는 언급에 대한 부연 설명으로 수입의 증가가 물

질적 복지와 행복의 '향상, 증가'를 가져왔다는 내용으로 increases(향상, 증가)가 문맥상 적절하다. decrease는 '쇠퇴, 감소'라는 뜻이다.
(B) 선진국의 경우를 보면 소득과 행복의 양이 무조건 비례할 것이라는 예상과 다르게 소득의 증가가 행복으로 이어지는 경우는 소득이 '낮은' 경우에 한정된다는 내용이 문맥상 자연스러우므로 low(낮은, 적은)가 적절하다. high는 '높은, 많은'의 뜻이다.
(C) 1인당 소득이 일정 수준 이상이 되면 추가 소득이 행복의 증대를 가져오지 않아 수입이 두 배, 세 배로 늘어도 '체감되는' 행복으로 이어지지 않는다는 내용으로 perceived(체감되는, 인식되는)가 적절하다. material은 '물질적'이라는 뜻이다.

02 ④

문제해설

주어진 문장의 That is why ~에서 that은 ④ 앞에서 언급한 '우리의 뇌는 포식자가 목격되었다는 것을 인지하기 전에 이미 포식자를 감지할 수 있다'는 것을 지칭하고 있으며 이로 인해 우리는 우리가 행동하고 있다는 것을 알기도 전에 행동할 수 있다는 내용으로 이어진다. 따라서 ④에 주어진 문장이 들어가는 것이 가장 적절하다.

03 ②

문제해설

빈칸 앞에서는 우리는 행동을 통해서 뿐 아니라 아름다움, 선함, 위대함을 추구함으로서도 인생을 의미있게 만들 수 있다고 언급했고, 빈칸 뒤에서는 콘서트홀에서 교향곡을 감상하면서 느끼는 전율의 순간에 삶의 가치를 느낄 수 있음을 기술하고 있으므로 빈칸에 들어갈 말로 가장 적절한 것은 ② '아름다움을 경험하는 것'이다.

오답노트

① 타인을 사랑하는 것
③ 개인의 목표를 성취하는 것
④ 대의를 추구하는 것
⑤ 명곡을 연주하는 것

04 ②

문제해설

(A) 주어 a generalization(일반화)은 '지지를 얻게 되는 것이다'라는 수동의 의미로 과거분사인 argued가 적절하다.
(B) 선행사 a colleague가 사람이고, 이어지는 명사구 favourite question과 소유 관계이므로 소유격 관계대명사 whose가 적절하다.
(C) 문장의 주어가 Most of the books로 복수이며 동사구 are concerned with와 병렬 연결된 동사로 fail이 적절하다.

05 ③

문제해설

이 글은 최저 생계에 가깝게 살 경우에는 소득의 증가가 물질적 복지의 향상으로 행복의 증대로 이어지나 일정 소득 수준 이상에서는 수입의 증가가 행복의 체감으로 이어지지 않는다는 내용으로 '자녀가 있는 저소득층, 한부모 가정이 빈곤 관련 문제에 더 취약하다.'라고 서술하는 ③은 글의 전체 흐름과 관계가 없다.

06 ④

문제해설

(A) 생존 투쟁으로 나쁜 소식에 우선순위를 부여하는 기재를 가지고 있다는 내용이 전개되고 있으므로 손실에 대한 혐오가 이득에 대한 끌림보다 '더 크다'는 내용으로 greater(더 큰, 더 강력한)가 문맥상 적절하다. smaller는 '더 적은, 더 약한'의 뜻이다.
(B) 우리의 뇌는 포식자가 목격되었다는 것을 인지하는 것보다 '더 빨리' 포식자를 감지할 수 있기에 우리는 우리가 행동하고 있다는 것을 알기도 전에 행동할 수 있다는 내용으로 이어지는 것이 자연스러우므로 quicker(더 빠른)가 적절하다. slower는 '더 느린'의 뜻이다.
(C) 기회보다는 위협에 특전을 준다는 것을 재진술하는 문장에서 테러리스트 공격과 같이 일어나지 않을 법한 사건을 '지나치게 중시하고 있다'는 내용이 자연스러우므로 overweight(지나치게 중시하다, 과대평가하다)가 적절하다. underestimate는 '과소평가하다'의 뜻이다.

07 ②

문제해설

우리는 행동을 통해서 뿐 아니라 아름다움, 선함, 위대함을 추구함으로서도 인생을 의미있게 만들 수 있다고 언급하는 주어진 글 다음에, 아름다움을 경험하는 것이 어떻게 삶을 의미있게 만드는지 예를 들어 설명해보겠다는 (B)가 온 다음, 구체적 상황으로 콘서트홀에서 교향곡을 듣고 있는 상황을 제시하며 이 순간에 누군가 당신에게 삶이 의미있는지 물어보는 상황을 상상해 보라고 말하는 (A)가 온 뒤, 이 순간만으로도 삶의 가치를 느낄 수 있다는 말에 당신이 동의할 것이라는 (C)가 오는 것이 자연스럽다.

08 ⑤

문제해설

빈칸은 연구 방법과 실험 설계에 관한 대부분의 책이 어떠한지를 나타내는 내용에 해당된다. 빈칸 뒤에 역접의 접속사 yet에 이어 '창의적인 부분이 없다면 어떤 진정한 연구도 이루어지지 않을 것'이라는 내용이 있으므로, 빈칸에 들어갈 말로 가장 적절한 것은 (대부분의 책이) ⑤ '합리적인 부분과 관련이 있으며 창의적인 부분은 다루지 않는(다)'이다.

오답노트

① 연구 윤리의 의미와 중요성의 이유를 생략하는
② 연구자들에게 창의성의 중요성에 대해 알려주는
③ 합리적 요소와 창의적인 요소의 균형에 대해 다루고 있는
④ 새로운 연구 방법에 대한 영감을 주는 관점을 제시하는

09 The elements are personal freedom, meaningful work, and social tolerance.

문제해설

소득이 일정 범위에 이르렀을 때 행복을 더 증진시키는 요소들은 other factors such as personal freedom, meaningful work, and social tolerance add much more에 나타나 있다.

10 (A) material (B) increase

문제해설

소득이 일정 범위에 이르면 추가 소득이 행복을 체감할 정도로는 증대시키지 않는다는 내용의 글로, '대부분의 사람들이 최저 생계에 가깝게 살았을 때 (A) 물질적 복지가 더 많은 행복을 가져왔지만, 1인당 국민 소득이 연간 13,000달러에 도달함에 따라 그것은 체감되는 행복의 (B) 증대로 이어지지는 않는다.'와 같이 요약하는 것이 적절하다.

11 (A) inbuilt (B) predator

문제해설

(A) '어떤 것의 자연적인 부분이나 기본적인 부분으로 존재하는'이라는 의미의 단어는 inbuilt(내재된, 고유의)이다.
(B) '다른 동물을 죽여서 먹는 동물'이라는 의미의 단어는 predator(포식자, 포식 동물)이다.

12 (A) prioritizing (B) unlikely

문제해설

우리는 나쁜 소식이나 가능성이 별로 없는 일을 더 중시한다는 내용의 글로, '우리에게는 좋은 기회보다는 나쁜 소식과 (B) 일어날 것 같지 않은 상황에 (A) 우선 순위를 부여하여 생존할 수 있는 타고난 기제가 있다.'와 같이 요약하는 것이 적절하다.

13 오직 이 순간만을 위해 살아왔더라도 그럴 만한 가치가 있었을 거야.

문제해설

one answer에 해당하는 말은 이어지는 "It would have been worth it to have lived for this moment alone!"에 나타나 있다.

14 Experiencing beauty can make life meaningful.

문제해설

이 글은 아름다움을 경험하는 것이 삶을 의미있게 만들 수 있다고 하면서 그 예를 제시하고 있으므로, 요지는 본문의 experiencing beauty can make life meaningful에 나타나 있다.

15 I've seen this innocent question spawn brilliant research projects

문제해설

'나는 ~을 보아 왔다'는 현재완료형으로 표현하여 'I've seen ~'으로 쓰고(조건의 단어수에 따라), '이러한 순수한 질문'인 this innocent question을 목적어로, '훌륭한 연구 프로젝트를 탄생시키다'인 spawn brilliant research projects를 목적격 보어로 하여 문장을 완성한다.

16 Innocent / research / inspiration / rational

문제해설

'이것은 왜 그렇지?'라는 순수한 질문이 많은 훌륭한 연구 프로젝트를 탄생시키는 것을 보아 왔으며, 연구는 영감과 합리적 사고의 혼합으로 창의적인 부분이 없다면 진정한 연구 성과를 내지 못할 것이라는 내용의 글로, '순수한 질문은 훌륭한 연구 프로젝트를 탄생시킬 수 있으며, 연구는 창의적인 부분뿐만 아니라 합리적인 부분 역시 필요하다는 점에서 연구는 영감과 합리적 사고의 혼합임을 보여준다.'와 같이 요약하는 것이 적절하다.

5강

1번 p.64

• Word Test

1 주택 건설업자 2 공공요금 3 신경을 쓰는, 관심을 가진
4 지출 5 에너지 효율성이 높은 6 빈틈없이
7 ~한 결과를 낳다 8 consumer 9 attempt
10 maintain 11 aware 12 term 13 issue
14 insurance

유형 1
❶ while ❷ However ❸ Besides
❹ higher ❺ smaller

유형 2
❶ ignoring ❷ are purchased ❸ costs
❹ has

유형 3
❶ as little as possible ❷ in the short term
❸ in the case of ❹ in the total price of

2번 p.66

• Word Test

1 ~을 시비곡직에 따라 판단하다 2 입증 가능한 3 액면 그대로
4 ~에 가담하다 5 ~에 있다 6 ~에게 공평하게 대하다
7 군중 8 기꺼이 하는 마음 9 ~ 하지 않도록 경계하다
10 주입하다 11 노력하다; 노력 12 민족주의
13 impartial 14 resentment 15 virtue
16 prejudice 17 statement 18 strife 19 flatter
20 controversy 21 civil war 22 official
23 party 24 obvious

유형 1
❶ obvious ❷ strife ❸ to
❹ unless ❺ dishonest

유형 2
❶ to stand ❷ leading ❸ be expected
❹ are ❺ be shown

유형 3
❶ in other forms ❷ instill into
❸ at their face value ❹ consist in

3번 p.68

• Word Test

1 일, 과제 2 실행 목표 3 ~이 없을 경우[때]
4 (자선 단체·조직 등을 위한) 기금 모금 행사 5 약속
6 필연적으로, 어쩔 수 없이 7 ~와 관련이 없다 8 할당하다
9 훈련시키다 10 serious 11 urgent 12 volunteer
13 critical goal 14 apply 15 spirit
16 resemble 17 colleague 18 differentiate

유형 1
❶ management ❷ unimportant ❸ necessarily
❹ yourself ❺ allocate

유형 2
❶ resembling ❷ applies ❸ bringing
❹ to differentiate

유형 3
❶ have nothing to do with ❷ In the absence of
❸ fill up with ❹ in the spirit of helpfulness

4번 p.70

• Word Test

1 관여, 참여 2 대량의, 대중의 3 출현, 도래
4 ~은 … 덕분이다 5 (어쩔 수 없이) ~해야만 하다
6 미치다, 뻗다 7 근시안적인, 근시의 8 무지한 9 영향, 함축
10 노력, 시도 11 습득하다, 얻다 12 existence
13 safely 14 strategy 15 aspect 16 transport
17 effective 18 merely 19 expertise
20 convince 21 argue 22 theoretical

유형 1
❶ incorrect ❷ ignorant ❸ theoretical
❹ that ❺ scientist

유형 2
❶ are ❷ were ❸ compelled
❹ have done ❺ mastering

유형 3
❶ nearly all aspects of ❷ merely of interest to
❸ as many people as possible
❹ effective public engagement

p.72

O1 ② O2 ⑤ O3 ④ O4 ④ O5 ① O6 ④
O7 ④ O8 ④ O9 가능한 한 가장 낮은 가격에 주택을 구매하고자 하는 것 10 공공요금 납입금이 더 적게 든다.
11 The teacher should not be expected to flatter the prejudices either of the mob or of officials.
12 controversy
13 (A) resembling (B) to fill (C) necessarily
14 discipline yourself to differentiate between what is urgent and important and what is simply urgent 15 therefore convinced ourselves that our scientific endeavours were merely of interest to other scientists
16 (A) communicating (B) non-scientists

O1 ②

문제해설

주어진 문장은 새 주택의 경우, 현명한 소비자에게 이것은 가장 중요한 문

15

제는 아니라는 내용으로, 문장 앞에 **however**가 있으므로, 이와 상반된 내용의 문장이 앞에 제시되어 있어야 한다. ② 앞에 구매자들이 낮은 가격에 주택을 구매하려고 한다는 상반된 내용이 있으므로 이 문장 뒤인 ②에 주어진 문장이 들어가는 것이 가장 적절하다.

02 ⑤

문제해설

교사는 정치적 중립의 입장에서 공정성을 유지해야 하며 논쟁을 넘어 공정한 조사의 영역으로 들어가도록 노력해야 한다는 내용의 글로, '교사는 정치적 편견에 영향을 받지 말아야 하며 젊은이들로 하여금 특정 사람, 집단, 관점에 (A) 치우치게 하지 말아야 하고, 또한 공정치 못한 분노의 두려움 없이 과학적인 (B) 조사를 수행할 수 있어야 한다.'와 같이 요약하는 것이 적절하다.

오답노트

① 공정한 …… 판단 　　② 공정한 …… 조사
③ 논쟁하는 …… 판단 　　④ 치우친 …… 처벌

03 ④

문제해설

이번 주에 직면한 긴급한 일의 목록을 만들어 중대 목표와 실행 목표 목록과 비교해 보고 이것이 일치하는지 살펴보라는 주어진 글 다음에, 긴급한 일이 중대 목표와 실행 목표와 무관하다는 것을 발견할 것이며 시간 관리를 하지 않으면 긴급하지만 중요하지 않은 일을 하다가 시간이 간다고 언급하는 (C)가 온 다음, 타인을 도와주는 경우에도 똑같이 적용된다는 (A)가 온 뒤, 시간을 효과적으로 관리하기 위해서는 긴급하면서고 중요한 일과 긴급하기만 한 일을 구별하도록 훈련해야 한다는 (B)가 오는 것이 자연스럽다.

04 ④

문제해설

이 글은 과학이 이뤄낸 결과와 영향을 많은 사람이 알도록 과학자는 전략적으로 대중과 소통하기 위해 노력해야 한다는 내용으로, '효과적인 대중적 관여'가 의미하는 바로 가장 적절한 것은 ④ '보다 적극적이고 개방적인 방식으로 과학이 이루어낸 성과를 대중에게 전파하는 것'이다.

오답노트

① 현대 인간의 삶을 향상시킬 수 있도록 대중들과 소통하는 것
② 과학 연구의 모든 성과물을 이용자들에게 친근한 방식으로 재정리하는 것
③ 과학자들이 긴밀하게 협업할 수 있도록 의사소통 전략을 개선하는 것
⑤ 통신기술 개발을 통해 과학의 성취를 대중에게 보여주는 것

05 ①

문제해설

while이 이끄는 부사절에서 주어가 생략된 이후에 동사를 분사화한 구문으로 의미상의 주어인 **people**이 '무시하면서'라는 능동의 의미를 나타내므로 현재분사 **ignoring**으로 고쳐야 한다.

오답노트

② **that** 이후에 완전한 문장이 와서 명사절을 이끌고 문장 전체적으로 **be aware that** 구문을 이루는 **that**은 적절하다.

③ '집은 융자를 통해 구매되는 것'이라는 수동의 의미를 나타내야 하므로 **purchased**는 적절하다.
④ **Besides** 뒤에 명사구가 바로 이어져 전치사로 쓰일 수 있으므로 어법상 적절하다.
⑤ '집을 짓기 위해', '집을 짓는데'라는 의미의 목적을 나타내는 부사적 용법의 to부정사 **to build**는 적절하다.

06 ④

문제해설

이 글은 교사는 정치적 중립의 입장에서 공정성을 유지해야 하며 논쟁을 넘어 공정한 조사의 영역으로 들어가도록 노력해야 한다는 내용으로, 빈칸이 있는 문장은 교사는 학생들이 특정 사람, 집단, 관점에 치우치지 않는 탐구 습관을 들이도록 지도해야 한다는 내용이 자연스러우므로 빈칸에 들어갈 말로 가장 적절한 것은 ④ '공평한, 치우치지 않는'이다.

오답노트

① 공식적인 　　　　② 치우친
③ 자세한 　　　　　⑤ 예비의

07 ④

문제해설

시간 관리를 하지 않으면 긴급하지만 중요하지 않은 활동으로 시간을 보내기 쉬우므로 효과적인 시간 관리를 위해서는 긴급하면서도 중요한 일과 단지 긴급하기만 한 일을 구별해야 한다는 것이 문맥상 자연스러우므로 ④의 **unimportant**(중요하지 않은)를 **important**(중요한) 등으로 고쳐야 한다.

08 ④

문제해설

이 글은 과학이 이뤄낸 결과와 영향을 많은 사람이 알도록 과학자가 전략적으로 대중과 소통하기 위해 노력해야 한다는 내용으로, '과학은 타당성에 의문을 제기하거나 재고해 보도록 할 수는 있을지라도, 세상의 보편적인 진리나 객관적인 설명을 제공하지 않는다.'라는 내용의 ④는 글의 전체 흐름과 관계가 없다.

09 가능한 한 가장 낮은 가격에 주택을 구매하고자 하는 것

문제해설

밑줄 친 **this**가 가리키는 내용은 바로 앞 문장의 **most homebuyers are trying to buy a home for the lowest price possible**에 나타나 있다.

10 공공요금 납입금이 더 적게 든다.

문제해설

에너지 효율성이 더 높은 주택의 이점은 **a more energy-efficient home also will result in smaller utility payments**에 나타나 있다.

11 The teacher should not be expected to flatter the prejudices either of the mob or of officials.

문제해설

'~하도록 요구되어서는 안 된다'는 〈shoud not be + 과거분사〉 구문을

사용하여 should not be expected to로 나타내고, '군중이나 관리들의 편견'은 the prejudices of와 〈either A or B〉 구문을 결합하여 either of the mob or of officials로 나타낸다.

12 controversy

문제해설

'특히나, 많은 사람들이 강한 감정을 갖고 있는 공공 정책이나 도덕적 문제에 대한 의견 충돌'이라는 의미의 단어는 controversy(논쟁, 논란)이다.

13 (A) resembling (B) to fill (C) necessarily

문제해설

(A) 앞의 anything을 수식하는 분사로, '비슷하게 일치하는' 어떤 것이라는 능동의 의미가 적절하므로 현재분사 resembling으로 고쳐야 한다.
(B) 〈가주어 it ~ 진주어 to부정사구〉 구문으로, 밑줄 부분은 to부정사 자리이므로 filling을 to fill로 고쳐야 한다.
(C) 동사의 성격을 지닌 동명사 bringing은 부사의 수식을 받아야 하므로 necessary를 necessarily로 고쳐야 한다.

14 discipline yourself to differentiate between what is urgent and important and what is simply urgent

문제해설

'~와 …를 구별하도록'은 부사적 용법의 to부정사 to differentiate와 〈between ~ and …〉를 사용하여 나타내고, '~한 것'은 관계대명사 what을 사용하여 what is ~로 나타낸다.

15 therefore convinced ourselves that our scientific endeavours were merely of interest to other scientists

문제해설

'그러므로 ~라고 확신하다'는 주어인 우리가 우리자신에게 확신한다는 것이고, 주절이 가정법 과거시제를 나타내므로, therefore convinced ourselves that ~이라고 나타낸다. that 이하는 명사절로 주어인 scientific endeavours와 동사 were를 쓰고, '~에게 관심사일 뿐인'은 merely of interest to ~로 나타낸다.

16 (A) communicating (B) non-scientists

문제해설

현대 인간 생활의 모든 면이 거의 과학 덕분에 존재하는 상황에서, 과학적 노력과 업적이 단지 다른 과학자들의 관심사일 뿐이란 내용은 틀렸으며, 이런 과학적 결과들이 더 많은 비과학자들에게 미치도록, 과학자들은 대중과 소통하는 능력을 키워야 한다는 내용의 글로, '사람들이 과학 덕분에 현대 삶을 살아갈 수 있다는 믿음 속에서, 많은 과학자들은 과학적 결과들을 과학자들 외에 많은 (B) 비과학자들에게 전파하기 위해 효과적으로 대중과 (A) 소통하는 방법을 완전히 익혀야 한다.'와 같이 요약하는 것이 적절하다.

1번
p.78

● Word Test

1 ~을 못마땅하게 여기다 **2** 묶음, (한) 벌 **3** 희생하다
4 불충한 **5** 보편적인 **6** 배신하다
7 (부정어 뒤에서) 전혀, 도무지 **8** 항의하다
9 나오다, 모습을 드러내다 **10** 약속 **11** demand
12 moral **13** fair **14** chew **15** treatment
16 tribe **17** reinforce **18** preference
19 admiration **20** violate

유형 1

❶ universal ❷ somewhere ❸ violate
❹ them ❺ where

유형 2

❶ to admire ❷ sacrifices ❸ is
❹ disapprove ❺ are praised

유형 3

❶ demand fair treatment
❷ the admiration for duty
❸ disloyal to ❹ emerge from
❺ violate social commitments

2번
p.80

● Word Test

1 엮어서 만들다 **2** 후보 **3** 최저임금 **4** 열성적인, 헌신적인
5 의료 서비스, 보건 **6** 국경 **7** 대통령직
8 제안 (사항), 추천 **9** 가상의, 소위 [이른바] ~이라고 하는
10 강조하다 **11** switch **12** presidential election
13 statement **14** strengthen **15** voter
16 identification **17** tightly **18** justify
19 expand **20** local

유형 1

❶ compiled ❷ committed ❸ those
❹ justifying ❺ question

유형 2

❶ were told ❷ controlled
❸ underscoring ❹ were

유형 3

❶ As for ❷ In every case
❸ as if it did not matter
❹ once they had made up their minds

3번
p.82

● Word Test

1 괴로움을 주는, 고통스러운 **2** 비이성적인 **3** 슬퍼하다
4 자멸적인, 문제를 오히려 키우는 **5** 속상하게 하는
6 ~을 띠다, ~을 얻다 **7** 포함하다, 결합하다
8 인식하다, 감지하다 **9** function **10** distort
11 accurately **12** as a result of **13** unrealistically
14 further **15** extreme **16** tragic

유형 1

❶ negative   ❷ to be   ❸ distressing
❹ incorporate   ❺ that

유형 2

❶ are   ❷ has died   ❸ to work
❹ is gone

유형 3

❶ further from the truth
❷ serve a useful function
❸ move on with your life   ❹ look forward to

4번 ————————————————————— p.84

• Word Test

1 눈에 띄지 않는   2 특화하다   3 특징을 나타내다   4 소진화
5 가설   6 주기적인   7 적자생존   8 유전자 접합
9 계통, 혈통   10 중단시키다   11 대진화
12 phenomenon   13 natural selection
14 succession   15 gradual   16 continuous
17 wipe out   18 species   19 stability
20 challenge   21 evolution   22 diversify

유형 1

❶ fittest   ❷ that   ❸ it out
❹ gradual   ❺ succession

유형 2

❶ is characterized   ❷ are   ❸ occurs
❹ creating   ❺ wipe

유형 3

❶ is being challenged
❷ as the most likely phenomenon
❸ hundreds of thousands of years
❹ even wipe it out

---

p.86

01 ②   02 ②   03 ⑤   04 ②   05 ②   06 ⑤
07 ②   08 ③   09 (도덕적) 의무에 대한 존경은 보편적이기
때문이다.   10 approve   11 (1) ② → to be strengthened
(2) ⑤ → what   12 what suggestions their candidates
made / have supported them unconditionally
13 ③ → useful   14 is it likely that you will
experience emotions and behavioral reactions that
are dysfunctional and self-defeating   15 갑작스러운
변화로 중단되는 상대적 안정의 긴 기간 다음에 더 큰 안정이 따르고
다시 더 많은 변화가 따르는 것   16 (A) steady (B) abrupt

01 ②

문제해설

이 글은 도덕의식은 보편적으로 타고나는 것이므로 가르칠 필요가 없다는
내용으로 '전투에서 도망치는 사람들을 칭찬하는 사회는 없다.'는 말이 의
미하는 바로 가장 적절한 것은 ② '도덕의식은 후천적으로 배우는 것이라
기 보다는 이미 내재되어 있는 것이다.'이다.

오답노트

① 도덕의식은 저절로 생기는 것이 아니므로 끊임없는 교육이 필요하다.
③ 도덕적 감정은 의무를 수행함으로써 강화될 수 있다.
④ 목숨이 위협받는 상황에서는 누구도 부도덕하다는 비난을 받지 않는다.
⑤ 배신은 인간의 선척적인 특질이 아니라 환경으로부터 학습된 것이다.

02 ②

문제해설

글 초반의 one of our local comedians compiled a list of
all the recommendations ~ switched them, and asked
committed Democratic and Republican supporters about
them에서 각 정당의 대통령 후보의 제안 사항을 맞바꾸고 그것에 대해
지지자들에게 물었다고 했으므로, ②는 글의 내용과 일치하지 않는다.

03 ⑤

문제해설

선행사 emotions and behavioral reactions가 있고 뒤에 불완전
한 절이 이어지고 있으므로 what을 관계대명사 that 혹은 which로 고
쳐야 한다.

오답노트

① that절 내의 주어가 of negative thinking의 수식을 받는 all
forms이므로 복수동사 are는 적절하다.
② believe가 이끄는 5형식 문장에서 목적격 보어로 to be ~가 오는 것
은 적절하다.
③ 동사 are perceiving을 수식하는 부사 accurately는 적절하다.
④ 주절의 주어인 crying, grieving, and sadness 뒤에 동사
구 will allow ~가 이어지는 구문에서 등위접속사 and가 allow와
incorporate을 병렬 연결한 것이므로 적절하다.

04 ②

문제해설

진화론이 도전을 받고 있다고 하면서 기존 진화론 입장인 다윈의 진화론
에 대해 언급하고 있는 주어진 글 다음에 새로운 진화론을 주장하는 학자
와 그들의 이론을 소개하는 내용인 (B)가 온 다음, 이러한 주장이 나오게
된 가설인 종의 다양성과 새로운 계통에 대해 말하고 있는 (A)가 오는 것
이 자연스럽다. 이후 (A)에서 설명한 안정과 급격한 변화를 대진화로 볼 수
있다고 설명하는 (C)가 이어지는 것이 자연스럽다.

05 ②

문제해설

이 글은 도덕의식은 보편적으로 타고나는 것이므로 도덕적 의무를 가르칠
필요가 없다는 내용으로, 빈칸이 포함된 문장에서 선척적으로 가지고 있
는 '도덕적' 감정이 사회적 약속을 어기는 사람들을 못마땅하게 여기게 한
다는 내용이 이어지는 것이 자연스러우므로 빈칸에 들어갈 말로 가장 적절
한 것은 ② '도덕적인'이다.

오답노트

① 죄책(감)의   ③ 극단적인

④ 억누르는   ⑤ 모순된

06 ⑤

문제해설

주어진 문장은 그 대신에 지지자들이 자기 후보의 입장을 정당화하기 시작했다는 내용으로, 지지자들이 제안 사항의 목록의 진실성을 의심하지 않았다는 내용의 문장 뒤인 ⑤에 들어가는 것이 가장 적절하다.

07 ②

문제해설

모든 형태의 부정적인 생각이 불필요하거나 비이성적인 것은 아니며 너무 지나치지만 않는다면 부정적인 생각이 인생의 어려움을 극복하고 앞으로 나아갈 수 있도록 도움을 줄 수 있다는 내용의 글로, '부정적인 생각은 사람들에게 (A) 유해한 영향을 끼칠 것이라는 통념과는 달리, 지나치게 (B) 파괴적이지 않으면 사람들의 성장에 도움이 될 수 있다.'와 같이 요약하는 것이 적절하다.

오답노트

① 유해한 ······ 부유하게 만드는   ③ 파괴적인 ······ 부유하게 만드는
④ 유익한 ······ 파괴적인   ⑤ 유익한 ······ 안심시키는

08 ③

문제해설

진화는 안정과 급격한 변화가 계속 번갈아 일어나는 것이라는 진화론의 새로운 관점에 대해 설명하고 있으므로 '이것은 공립학교에서 진화론의 장단점을 다루는 논쟁의 이슈로 이끌어져 왔다.'는 내용의 ③은 글의 전체 흐름과 관계가 없다.

09 (도덕적) 의무에 대한 존경은 보편적이기 때문이다.

문제해설

사람들이 집단을 위해 희생하는 사람을 존경하도록 가르침 받을 필요가 없는 이유는 the admiration for duty is universal에 나타나 있다.

10 approve

문제해설

'좋거나 적절하다고 여기는 누군가 또는 어떤 것에 대해 긍정적인 감정을 가지다'라는 의미의 단어는 approve(인정하다, 괜찮다고 생각하다)이다.

11 (1) ② → to be strengthened (2) ⑤ → what

문제해설

② to부정사의 의미상 주어인 the American military가 '강화되어야' 한다는 것이므로 to부정사의 수동태인 〈to be + 과거분사〉가 적절하다. 따라서 to strengthen을 to be strengthened로 고쳐야 한다.
⑤ 가주어 it과 진주어로 의문사절이 쓰인 구문으로 '사실이 무엇인지'라는 의미의 진주어인 의문사절을 나타내기 위해 that을 what으로 고쳐야 한다.

오답노트

① 명사구 all the recommendations를 수식하는 분사구의 분사로 의미상 '민주당과 공화당의 대통령 후보 두 명 모두에 의해 만들어 지고 있

던'이라는 진행의 의미가 알맞으므로 현재분사 being은 적절하다. 수동의 의미가 있으므로, being을 생략해도 된다.
③ supporters를 가리키는 복수 대명사 those는 적절하다.
④ the need to 뒤의 expand, create와 and로 병렬 연결된 구조이므로 increase는 적절하다.

12 what suggestions their candidates made / have supported them unconditionally

문제해설

각 당의 대통령 후보들을 지지하는 사람들은 그들을 맹목적으로 지지한다는 내용의 글로, '각 당의 지지자들은, 그들의 후보들이 어떤 제안을 했는지에 상관없이, 자신들이 그들을 선택했던 그 순간 이후로 그들을 무조건 지지해 오고 있다.'와 같이 요약하는 것이 적절하다.

13 ③ → useful

문제해설

뒤의 예시에서 친한 친구가 죽어 극도로 슬프다면 충분히 슬퍼함으로써 어려운 상황을 이겨낼 수 있을 것이라는 내용이 제시되어 있으므로, '만약 여러분이 상황을 정확하게 인식하고 있다면, 괴로운 감정은 유용한 기능을 제공할 것이다'라는 내용이 문맥상 자연스럽다. 따라서 ③ useless(쓸모없는)를 useful(유용한) 등으로 고쳐야 한다.

14 is it likely that you will experience emotions and behavioral reactions that are dysfunctional and self-defeating

문제해설

'~할 가능성이 있다'는 〈it is likely that ~〉 구문을 사용해서 나타내는데, 앞에 부사절이 only when으로 시작하고 있으므로, 주절의 주어와 동사를 도치하여 is it likely that으로 쓴다. '역기능적이고 자멸적인 감정과 행동 반응'은 선행사인 emotions and behavioral reactions 뒤에 관계대명사 that이 이끄는 절을 써서 나타낸다.

15 갑작스러운 변화로 중단되는 상대적 안정의 긴 기간 다음에 더 큰 안정이 따르고 다시 더 많은 변화가 따르는 것

문제해설

밑줄 친 this가 가리키는 내용은 바로 앞 문장의 evolution is characterized by long periods of relative stability ~ by more changes에 나타나 있다.

16 (A) steady (B) abrupt

문제해설

진화를 자연 선택의 점진적인 과정으로 설명한 Darwin과 달리, Gould와 같은 진화론자들은 진화를 주기적이고 갑작스러운 큰 변화로 생각했다는 내용의 글로, 'Darwin의 진화론은 (A) 꾸준한 자연 선택의 과정인 소진화로 여겨질 수 있는 반면, Gould의 진화론은 주기적이고 (B) 갑작스러운 큰 변화인 대진화로 여겨질 수 있다.'와 같이 요약하는 것이 적절하다.

7강

1번 ———————————— p.92

• Word Test

1 인지의　2 영향　3 야외에서　4 빠져나가다
5 (수업) 시간　6 실험, 실험실　7 solution　8 claim
9 observation　10 philosopher　11 literally
12 stuck

유형 1

❶ literally　❷ Physical　❸ does
❹ that　❺ those

유형 2

❶ developing　❷ has been shown　❸ were
❹ is held　❺ moving

유형 3

❶ get unstuck　❷ have a positive effect on
❸ taking part in　❹ four times a week

2번 ———————————— p.94

• Word Test

1 더구나[하물며] ~은 아닌　2 ~이라고 할 정도로　3 매우 중요한
4 흥미로운　5 체계적인, 조직화된　6 균일성　7 구성
8 쓰레기 더미, 더러운 것　9 은하　10 분포시키다
11 알아내다, 해결하다　12 coherent　13 cosmos
14 unity　15 attain　16 unrelated　17 chaos
18 emerge　19 totality　20 astronomer
21 systematically　22 scale

유형 1

❶ unless　❷ Instead of　❸ as
❹ crucial　❺ its

유형 2

❶ to explain　❷ resemble
❸ are distributed　❹ evolve　❺ to attain

유형 3

❶ such a thing as
❷ On the largest scale of size
❸ in much the same way　❹ rather than

3번 ———————————— p.96

• Word Test

1 끊임없는, 지속적인　2 ~을 활용하다　3 잘 아는
4 운영되다, 운영하다　5 최신 정보를 계속 알다[유지하다]
6 통제하다, 지배하다　7 ~에[의] 영향을 받다　8 영향을 미치다
9 framework　10 legal　11 regulation　12 ease
13 accountant　14 stable　15 slightly
16 burden

유형 1

❶ which　❷ Nevertheless　❸ informed
❹ which　❺ direct

유형 2

❶ requires　❷ is　❸ be eased
❹ employs　❺ sells

유형 3

❶ is subject to　❷ by making use of
❸ keep up to date　❹ be aware of

4번 ———————————— p.98

• Word Test

1 상당한　2 차지하다　3 ~하는 것도 당연한 일이다
4 말[문자] 그대로, 그야말로　5 숫자, 자릿수　6 운동선수
7 수입　8 종사자, 개업자, 개업 의사　9 measure
10 by contrast　11 in relation to　12 absolute
13 spectator　14 overall　15 broadcaster
16 source

유형 1

❶ that　❷ despite　❸ the
❹ while　❺ that

유형 2

❶ is　❷ is　❸ paid
❹ watching　❺ creates

유형 3

❶ In absolute terms　❷ make up
❸ In relation to　❹ at the current stage

———————————————————— p.101

01 ④　02 ④　03 ③　04 ⑤　05 ③　06 ②
07 ④　08 ④　09 exercise
10 Physical movement has been shown to have a positive effect on creative thinking.
11 unless there were such a thing as the universe to explain　12 ④ → systematically　13 change
14 직장에서의 보건과 안전, 피고용인의 권리, 고용주(로서)의 의무와 같은 문제들　15 (1) ① → that (2) ③ → is
16 advertisers will pay literally billions of dollars to broadcasters that can deliver mass audiences for sports

01 ④

문제해설

아이디어를 떠올려야 할 때 막힌다면 빈칸의 내용을 함으로써 벗어나라는 내용으로, 이 글은 신체적 움직임이 창의적 사고에 긍정적인 영향을 끼친다는 내용의 글이므로, 빈칸에 들어갈 말로 가장 적절한 것은 ④ '말 그대로 책상에서 벗어남으로써'이다.

① 물리적으로 가구를 이동함으로써
② 실제로 운동하는 것에 대해 생각함으로써
③ 정신적으로 삶의 목표를 재조정함으로써
⑤ 자연 산책에 대해 긍정적으로 명상함으로써

④ 우주는 항상 시간의 지배를 받는다
⑤ 우주에서 어떤 것도 절대 똑같지 않다

02 ④

문제해설

(A) 뒷부분이 완전한 절을 이루고 있으며 동명사 finding의 목적절이 되어야 하므로 명사절 접속사 that이 적절하다.
(B) 주어인 Stars and galaxies billions of light-years away가 '(널리) 분포되어 있다'라는 수동의 의미를 나타내므로 분사 distributed가 적절하다.
(C) '답을 찾기 위해서'라는 의미의 목적을 나타내므로 to부정사의 부사적 용법인 To find가 적절하다.

03 ③

문제해설

주어진 문장은 사업가가 법률의 변화를 계속 인지하고 있어야 한다고 언급하고 있다. 그러므로 사업 운영을 위한 고용과 관련된 직장에서의 보건과 안전, 피고용인의 권리 등 전반적인 최신 정보를 인지하고 있어야 한다는 예를 보여주는 문장 앞인 ③에 주어진 문장이 들어가는 것이 가장 적절하다.

04 ⑤

문제해설

스포츠를 관람하는 많은 사람이 스포츠 산업에 상당한 수입을 창출한다는 것이 문맥상 자연스러우므로, ⑤의 insignificant(사소한)를 significant(상당한) 등으로 고쳐야 한다.

05 ③

문제해설

신체적 움직임이 창의적 사고에 긍정적인 영향을 끼친다는 내용의 글로, '신체적 움직임과 창의력 사이의 관계에 대한 연구들에서 신체적 움직임은 창의적으로 막힌 사람에게 (A) 동기를 부여해 주는 기폭제라는 것을 알아냈으며, 또한 신체적으로 활동적인 사람들이 오랜 기간 앉아 있던 사람들보다 새로운 사고를 (B) 더 많이 할 수 있다는 것을 보여 주었다.'와 같이 요약하는 것이 적절하다.

오답노트

① 방해하다 …… 더 많이   ② 발전시키다 …… 덜
④ 신장시키다 …… 덜   ⑤ 억누르다 …… 더 많이

06 ②

문제해설

이 글은 체계적이고 질서 정연한 우주의 존재에 관한 내용의 글이므로, 빈칸에 들어갈 말로 가장 적절한 것은 ② '혼돈보다는 질서가 있다'이다.

오답노트

① 우주론은 생명체를 탄생시켰다
③ 혼돈은 인간의 존재에서 질서를 찾는다

07 ④

문제해설

④ to keep의 의미상의 주어인 the businessman과 목적어가 동일한 대상이므로 him을 재귀대명사 himself로 고쳐야 한다.

오답노트

① 선행사가 사물이고, 전치사 within뒤에 전치사의 목적어로 (대)명사가 나와야 하므로 관계대명사인 which를 쓰는 것은 적절하다.
② 주어인 the framework of law가 단수이므로 단수동사 is는 적절하다.
③ 동사 may be eased를 수식하는 부사 slightly는 적절하다.
⑤ 조건의 부사절에서는 현재가 미래를 대신하므로 현재시제인 employs를 사용한 것은 적절하다.

08 ④

문제해설

주어진 문장의 that demand는 ④의 바로 앞 문장에서 언급한 운동선수 서비스에 관한 수요를 가리키고 ④ 다음 문장에서 언급되는 운동선수 서비스에 관한 큰 수요의 원천으로 스포츠 경기를 시청하기 위해서 큰 금액을 지불하는 팬들 그리고 스포츠 경기를 시청하는 대규모 팬들을 보유하고 있는 방송사에게 큰 금액을 지불하려는 광고주가 있다는 구체적 상황이 묘사되고 있으므로 주어진 문장은 ④에 들어가는 것이 가장 적절하다.

09 exercise

문제해설

빈칸 (A)에는 산책이라는 내용과 유사한 활동이, (B)에서는 뒤따르는 산책이나 자전거 타기를 예로 들 수 있는 활동이, 빈칸 (C)에서는 앉아서 지내는 생활과 대조되는 의미인 몸을 움직이는 활동이 적절하므로, 빈칸 (A), (B), (C)에 공통으로 들어갈 단어는 exercise이다.

10 Physical movement has been shown to have a positive effect on creative thinking.

문제해설

'신체적 움직임이 ~한 것으로 밝혀졌다'는 Physical movement has been shown to로 '~에 긍정적인 영향을 미치다'는 have a positive effect on으로 나타낸다. '창의적인 사고'는 creative thinking으로 나타낸다.

11 unless there were such a thing as the universe to explain

문제해설

'~이 있지 않다면'은 unless there were ~로 나타내고 '설명해야 할 우주'는 to부정사의 형용사적 용법을 이용하여 the universe to explain으로 나타낸다. '~와 같은 것'은 such a thing as ~로 쓴다.

12 ④ → systematically

문제해설

우주는 일관적인 통일성을 보이고, 모든 물리적 법칙이 우주에서 적용되는 등 혼돈이 아닌 질서 있는 체계가 있다고 언급하고 있으므로, 문맥상 ④ unsystematically(비체계적으로)를 systematically(체계적으로)와 같은 말로 바꿔 써야 한다.

13 change

문제해설

이 글은 사업가는 끊임없이 변화하는 법적 환경을 인지하고 있어야 한다는 내용으로, 빈칸 (A)에는 앞 문장의 기업 환경이 안정적인 환경과 대조되는 의미로 변화가, (B)에는 사업 운영에 영향을 주는 일반적인 법적 변화를 알고 있어야 한다는 내용이, 빈칸 (C)에서는 상품을 판매한다면 소비자 보호법의 변화에 대해 알고 있어야 한다는 내용이, 빈칸 (D)에는 주제를 재진술한 것으로 사업은 법적 규제를 받고 법은 항상 변화한다는 내용이 적절하므로, 빈칸 (A)~(D)에 공통으로 들어갈 말은 change이다.

14 직장에서의 보건과 안전, 피고용인의 권리, 고용주(로서)의 의무와 같은 문제들

문제해설

사업가가 사람을 고용하는 경우 어떤 문제에 대해 최신 정보가 필요한 지는 If he employs others ~ his duties as an employer.에 나타나 있다.

15 (1) ① → that (2) ③ → is

문제해설

① demand를 받는 대명사이므로 수일치를 하여 that으로 고쳐야 한다.
③ 주어가 the demand로 단수 명사이므로 단수 동사 is로 고쳐야 한다.

오답노트

② 뒤에 명사구가 있으므로 '~임에도 불구하고'라는 의미의 전치사 despite은 적절하다.
④ '입장하기 위해'라는 의미의 목적을 나타내는 부사적 용법의 to부정사 to attend는 적절하다.
⑤ 일반 동사를 강조하는 do가 enjoy 앞에 쓰인 것으로 적절하다.

16 advertisers will pay literally billions of dollars to broadcasters that can deliver mass audiences for sports

문제해설

'광고주는 말 그대로 ~을 지불할 것이다'는 advertisers will pay literally로 나타내고, '수십억 달러'는 billions of dollars로, '스포츠에 대규모의 시청자를 넘겨 줄 수 있는 방송사'는 선행사인 broadcasters 뒤에 that이 이끄는 관계절을 사용해서 나타낸다.

8강

1번 ———————————————————— p.107

• Word Test

1 ~의 면에서. ~과 관련하여 2 전국적으로 3 언어적으로
4 ~당 5 1위를 차지하다 6 list 7 diverse
8 inhabitant 9 immediately 10 language

유형 1
❶ linguistically ❷ followed ❸ where
❹ inhabitants

유형 2
❶ including ❷ spoken ❸ followed
❹ tops

유형 3
❶ per one million inhabitants
❷ throughout the country
❸ less than ❹ In terms of

2번 ———————————————————— p.109

• Word Test

1 (특히 미국이나 캐나다에 사는)히스패닉[라틴 아메리카](계)의
2 등록률 3 민족의 4 인종 5 나타내다 6 racial
7 compared to 8 table 9 ethnicity
10 decrease

유형 1
❶ ethnic ❷ both ❸ compared
❹ decrease

유형 2
❶ listed ❷ were ❸ was
❹ showed

유형 3
❶ listed in the table ❷ marked a decrease
❸ For Hispanics ❹ Among all the groups

3번 ———————————————————— p.111

• Word Test

1 직업의 2 조금씩 움직이다 3 근로자 4 진전, 증가
5 차지하다, 구성하다 6 역전시키다 7 engineering
8 physical science 9 double 10 significant
11 respectively 12 share

유형 1
❶ which ❷ lower ❸ significant
❹ that

유형 2
❶ comprised ❷ was reversed ❸ have made
❹ was ❺ inching

유형 3

❶ about three-quarters
❷ by one percentage point
❸ significant gains
❹ up to

4번
p.113

• Word Test

1 각각   2 (등급·등위·순위를) 차지하다   3 국내 총생산
4 ~에서 중도하차하다   5 목록   6 reach   7 status
8 despite   9 enter   10 maintain

유형 1

❶ maintained   ❷ while   ❸ reaching
❹ did

유형 2

❶ maintained   ❷ reaching   ❸ dropped
❹ having

유형 3

❶ maintained its status   ❷ fell to third
❸ dropped out of   ❹ did so

p.115

01 ②   02 ④   03 ③   04 ③   05 the most
linguistically diverse country in the world
06 (1) ② → higher (2) ⑤ → increase   07 reversed
08 maintained its status as the African country
with the highest GDP

01 ②

문제해설

현재 사용되는 언어의 수에서 인도네시아가 712개로 목록에서 2위를 차지하고, 인도가 아닌 나이지리아가 522개의 언어를 사용하여 인도네시아 뒤를 잇고 있으므로, 도표의 내용과 일치하지 않는 것은 ②이다.

02 ④

문제해설

히스패닉의 경우, 대학 등록률이 2010년보다 2018년에 4퍼센트포인트 더 높았으므로, 도표의 내용과 일치하지 않는 것은 더 낮았다고 나타내고 있는 ④이다.

03 ③

문제해설

여성은 생명 과학과 자연 과학 직업에서 상당한 진전을 보였는데, 1990년과 2019년 사이에 각각 14퍼센트포인트와 18퍼센트포인트의 증가를 나타냈으므로, 도표의 내용과 일치하지 않는 것은 ③이다.

04 ③

문제해설

모로코는 1990년, 2005년, 2020년에 상위 아프리카 8개국 중 5위를 차지했는데, 2020년 모로코의 GDP는 1,128억 달러에 달했으므로, 도표의 내용과 일치하지 않는 것은 ③이다.

05 the most linguistically diverse country in the world

문제해설

'세계에서'는 in the world로, '언어적으로 가장 다양한 나라'는 the most linguistically diverse country로 나타낸다.

06 (1) ② → higher (2) ⑤ → increase

문제해설

② 2010년의 대학 등록률은 백인과 흑인 둘 다 2000년대 보다 높았으므로 higher로 고쳐야 한다.
⑤ 표의 모든 집단 중, 아메리칸 인디언 / 알래스카 원주민이 2000년부터 2010년까지, 가장 높은 증가를 보였으므로 increase로 고쳐야 한다.

07 reversed

문제해설

'사건들, 과정 또는 상황의 순서나 전개를 원래의 반대로 바꾸다'라는 의미의 단어는 reverse(뒤바꾸다)이다. '역전되다'라는 수동의 의미를 나타내야 하므로 과거분사형인 reversed로 써야 한다.

08 maintained its status as the African country with the highest GDP

문제해설

'GDP가 가장 높은 아프리카 국가'는 high를 최상급으로 변형하여 the African country with the highest GDP로, '~로서 지위를 유지했다'는 maintain을 과거 동사로 변형하여 maintained its status as로 나타낸다.

1번 — p.119

• Word Test

1 따라서, 그러므로 2 둥글게 움직이다, 회전시키다 3 참물범
4 포효 5 나아가게 하다 6 ~과 관련이 있다 7 기동성 있는
8 뒷지느러미발 9 하기야 그래서 10 물개, 바다표범
11 (큰 짐승의) 수컷 12 manner 13 sea lion
14 sideways 15 ashore 16 enormous
17 visible 18 expend 19 massive 20 decorate
21 elegant 22 external

유형 1
❶ forward ❷ much ❸ which
❹ expend ❺ neither

유형 2
❶ being ❷ weighs ❸ is decorated
❹ make ❺ sleeps

유형 3
❶ clearly visible external ears
❷ much more mobile on land
❸ This massive animal
❹ refers to his roar ❺ a full-time job

2번 — p.121

• Word Test

1 ~으로 근무하다, ~의 역할을 하다 2 이웃
3 함께 가다, 동반하다 4 기관 5 청각 장애가 있는
6 establish 7 dissatisfied 8 principal
9 funding 10 attend

유형 1
❶ where ❷ what
❸ accompanied ❹ as

유형 2
❶ meeting ❷ to teach ❸ training
❹ known

유형 3
❶ the youngest in his class ❷ became interested in
❸ With funding from ❹ he received training
❺ served as the institution's principal

3번 — p.123

• Word Test

1 인상, 감명 2 조성하다, 만들다 3 분쟁, 갈등
4 저널리즘, 언론계 5 출산 6 시골의, 지방의
7 도시에서 자란 8 상인 9 취재하다 10 eventually
11 pursue 12 dialect 13 countryside
14 thinker 15 character 16 correspondent
17 so-called 18 tension

유형 1
❶ on ❷ where ❸ who
❹ rural

유형 2
❶ were ❷ following ❸ to cover
❹ set ❺ setting

유형 3
❶ instead of painting
❷ made little impression
❸ died in childbirth
❹ have success as a novelist
❺ a dramatic tension

4번 — p.125

• Word Test

1 결의안 2 매스컴[언론]의 관심[주목], 명성 3 의미가 있는, 중요한
4 섭취, 소비 5 물리학자 6 ~과 일치하다
7 (0부터 9까지의) 아라비아 숫자 8 다양한 9 inevitable
10 recognise 11 annually 12 memorise
13 attract 14 involve 15 worldwide
16 celebrate

유형 1
❶ has been ❷ that ❸ inevitable
❹ corresponded

유형 2
❶ was chosen ❷ corresponding
❸ recognising ❹ increasing
❺ to memorise

유형 3
❶ celebrated annually
❷ the first three digits ❸ passed a resolution
❹ in a vast variety of ways ❺ as possible

p.127

01 ④ 02 ④ 03 ③ 04 ③ 05 ③ 06 ②
07 ④ 08 ③ 09 몸이 앞으로 나아가도록 뒷지느러미발을
옆으로 둥글게 (회전하며) 움직일 수 있기 때문이다.
10 (A) measuring → measures (B) referred → refers
to (C) to which → to when[to the time (when)]
11 (A) which → where (B) knew → known
(C) married with → married[was married with]
12 Dissatisfied by what he saw in British schools for
deaf people 13 (A) pursued (B) cover
14 made little impression 15 π(파이)값의 숫자를 가능한
한 많이 암기해서 암송하는 대회와 각종 파이를 먹는 것
16 passed a resolution recognising 14 March as
National Pi Day

01 ④

문제해설

④ 동사 weigh의 주어는 복수 형태인 females이므로 weighs를 복수 동사 weigh로 고쳐야 한다.

오답노트

① 형용사 visible을 수식하는 것으로 부사 clearly를 쓰는 것은 적절하다.
② being이 이끄는 분사구문의 주어는 주절의 주어인 they와 같은 대상이며, 주어의 시제와 같으므로 현재분사 being으로 쓰는 것은 적절하다.
③ 관계대명사 which가 가리키는 것은 앞에 나온 주어 the name 'sea lion'이므로 계속적 용법의 주격 관계대명사 which를 쓰는 것은 적절하다.
⑤ 'A와 B 어느 쪽도 아닌'이라는 의미의 ⟨neither A nor B⟩ 구문이므로 동사 sleeps를 쓰는 것은 적절하다.

02 ④

문제해설

주어진 문장의 There는 ④ 앞 문장에 언급된 장소인 파리에 있는 청각 장애인들을 위한 학교를 가리키고, 그곳에서 Gallaudet에게 청각 장애인을 위한 교육을 해 준 Laurent Clerc와 Hartford로 함께 돌아왔다는 내용이 ④ 다음에 이어지고 있으므로, 주어진 문장이 들어가기에 가장 적절한 곳은 ④이다.

03 ③

문제해설

William Black이 저널리즘을 업으로 삼으면서 쓴 초기의 소설이 큰 인기를 얻지 못하자 저널리스트로서 일하면서 결국에는 소설가로서도 성공을 거두기 시작했다는 내용의 글이므로, 글의 제목으로 가장 적절한 것은 ③ 'William Black: 소설가이자 기자'이다.

오답노트

① 화가로서 Black의 성공적인 경력
② 작가들의 다양한 진로
④ Black이 저널리즘을 추구하기 위해 예술을 떠난 이유
⑤ 시골이 Black의 인생에 어떻게 영향을 미쳤는가?

04 ③

문제해설

(A) 종속절의 주어가 명사구 the American pattern of writing dates이므로 단수 동사 is가 적절하다.
(B) 명사 a resolution을 수식하는 분사구가 이어져야 하는데, 통과된 결의안이 3월 14일을 파이의 날로 '인정하는' 능동의 의미이므로 recognising이 적절하다.
(C) 문장의 동사가 involves이므로 '암기해서 외우는 대회'라는 의미의 명사 competitions를 수식하는 to memorize가 적절하다.

05 ③

문제해설

(A) 바다사자는 몸을 앞으로 움직이기 위해 뒷지느러미발을 회전하며 빠

르게 움직인다는 내용이 언급되었으므로 mobile(움직임이 자유로운)이 적절하다. immobile은 '움직이지 못하는'이라는 뜻이다.
(B) 앞 문장에 바다사자는 어른 남방바다사자보다 훨씬 더 크다는 내용이 언급되었으므로 massive(거대한)가 적절하다. modest는 '(크기가) 보통'이라는 뜻이다.
(C) 바다사자는 12월부터 3월까지 하렘을 지키기 위해 먹지도 오래 자지도 않는다는 내용이 언급되었으므로 full-time(전시간 근무의)이 적절하다. part-time은 '시간제의'라는 뜻이다.

06 ②

문제해설

Gallaudet가 청각 장애 아동을 가르치는 법을 배우기 위해 공부를 시작했으며 추후 미국 최초의 청각 장애인 학교까지 설립했다는 내용의 글이므로, 글의 제목으로 가장 적절한 것은 ② '청각 장애 교육에 있어서의 Gallaudet의 남다른 노력'이다.

오답노트

① 청각 장애 문화의 가치관 이해하기
③ 청각 장애인을 위한 학교 지원의 어려움
④ 미국의 청각 장애인의 권리 개척하기
⑤ EU에서 장애인을 위한 학교 설립

07 ④

문제해설

저널리즘을 업으로 삼으면서 쓴 소설이 큰 인기를 얻지 못했던 초창기와 달리, 런던으로 이주한 후에 저널리즘 일을 하면서 소설가로서도 성공을 거두기 시작했다는 것이 문맥상 자연스러우므로, ④의 hardship(어려움)을 success(성공)와 같은 말로 바꿔 써야 한다.

08 ③

문제해설

미국에서 파이의 날이 3월 14일로 지정된 이유가 수학 기호 π값인 3.14가 미국에서 사용하는 날짜 형식으로 풀어 보면 3월 14일과 동일하기 때문이라는 내용의 글이므로, 글의 제목으로 가장 적절한 것은 ③ '파이의 날의 날짜의 의미'이다.

오답노트

① Larry Shaw: 수학의 아이콘
② 수학자들이 파이의 날을 기념하는 방법
④ 파이의 날에 즐길 수 있는 최고의 명소들
⑤ 파이의 날에 파이를 먹는 전통

09 몸이 앞으로 나아가도록 뒷지느러미발을 옆으로 둥글게 (회전하며) 움직일 수 있기 때문이다.

문제해설

남방바다사자가 참물범보다 육지에서 더 빨리 움직일 수 있는 이유는 두 번째 문장 being able to ~ bodies forward에 나타나 있다.

10
(A) measuring → measures
(B) referred → refers to
(C) to which → to when[to the time (when)]

문제해설

(A) 등위접속사 and에 의해 동사 weighs와 병렬 연결되었으므로 measuring을 measures로 고쳐야 한다.
(B) 전치사 to와 함께 쓰여 '~에 관련되다'라는 의미가 되어야 하고, 주격 관계대명사 which 뒤의 동사 자리이며 현재 시제이므로 referred를 refers to로 고쳐야 한다.
(C) 'A에서 B까지'라는 의미의 〈from A to B〉 구문이고 '~하는 때'라는 의미의 부사절 접속사가 필요하므로 to when 또는 to the time (when)으로 고쳐야 한다.

11
(A) which → where (B) knew → known
(C) married with → married[was married with]

문제해설

(A) 뒤에 완전한 문장이 이어지고 선행사가 장소이므로 장소를 나타내는 관계부사 where로 고쳐야 한다.
(B) '~로 알려진'이라는 의미를 가진 분사구문으로 과거분사 형태인 known으로 고쳐야 한다.
(C) marry가 타동사이고 결혼 대상이 목적어로 제시되어 있으므로 전치사 with 없이 쓰이거나, be married with 형태로 고쳐야 한다.

12
Dissatisfied by what he saw in British schools for deaf people

문제해설

'영국의 청각 장애인 학교들에서'는 in British schools for deaf people이며, '본 것에 만족하지 못해서'는 dissatisfy를 분사구문으로 변형하되, 주어 Gallaudet와 수동의 관계이므로 과거분사구로 써서 Dissatisfied by what he saw로 나타낸다.

13
(A) pursued (B) cover

문제해설

(A) Black이 글쓰기를 추구한 구체적인 사례가 설명되어 있으므로 그림 대신 저널리즘을 '추구했다'가 문맥상 적합하다. 따라서 무언가를 '이루기 위해 노력하다'의 의미인 pursue가 적절한데 과거 시제이므로 pursued로 쓴다.
(B) 해외 특파원으로 유럽에 갔다는 내용 뒤에 오스트리아와 프러시아 사이의 분쟁이 '취재' 목적으로 자연스럽게 연결되므로, 'TV, 라디오, 또는 신문에 어떤 사건에 대해 보도하거나 서술하다'라는 의미의 cover(취재하다)가 적절하다.

14
made little impression

문제해설

make impression은 '인상을 주다'라는 의미이므로 '별다른 인상을 주지 못했다'는 부정의 의미를 나타내는 수량형용사 little을 사용하여 made little impression으로 나타낸다.

15
π(파이)값의 숫자를 가능한 한 많이 암기해서 암송하는 대회와 각종 파이를 먹는 것

문제해설

파이의 날을 기념하는 방식으로 언급한 두 가지는 and involves the inevitable ~ digits of π as possible에 나타나 있다.

16
passed a resolution recognising 14 March as National Pi Day

문제해설

'결의안을 통과시켰다'는 동사 pass를 과거형으로 써서 passed a resolution으로 나타내고, '전국 파이의 날로 인정하는'은 recognise를 분사로 바꿔 recognising 14 March as National Pi Day로 나타낸다.

10강

1번 ──────────────── p.132

• Word Test

1 실내의 2 (주로 복수로) 기초, 기본 3 ~의 경우에
4 두 번 5 ~당 6 직접 7 재미있는 8 ~과 함께
9 경기장 10 contact 11 registration 12 provide
13 focus on 14 limited 15 enroll 16 general
17 maximum 18 due to

유형 1

❶ on ❷ maximum ❸ Due
❹ if

유형 2

❶ to learn ❷ teaching ❸ be provided
❹ are

유형 3

❶ make friends ❷ twice per(a) week
❸ In case of bad weather ❹ in person

2번 ──────────────── p.135

• Word Test

1 기간 2 지역 전문 대학 3 요건
4 (시간·노력을) 쓰다, 바치다 5 추천서 6 참여하다
7 ~의 기간 중에 8 완료하다 9 연구 조교 10 applicant
11 fee 12 application 13 process 14 graduate
15 last 16 institute 17 current 18 recent

유형 1

❶ for ❷ recent ❸ who
❹ recommendation

유형 2

❶ interested ❷ will last ❸ to dedicate
❹ be announced

유형 3

❶ those interested in ❷ recent graduates
❸ the duration of the program ❹ application fee

3번 ──────────────── p.139

• Word Test

1 치료의 2 긴장을 풀다 3 (특정 활동을) 하다
4 이용 가능한 5 동물병원 6 풀어 주다, 방출하다
7 관찰하다, 보다 8 beneficial 9 certified 10 spot
11 emotional 12 apply 13 reserve
14 on a first-come-first-served basis

유형 1

❶ beneficial ❷ that ❸ available
❹ To reserve

유형 2

❶ to help ❷ is conducted ❸ applied

유형 3

❶ Come join ❷ The class is conducted
❸ per person
❹ on a first-come-first-served basis

4번 ──────────────── p.142

• Word Test

1 주차장 2 상품을 받다 3 물품, 품목
4 (보통 복수로) 지침 5 outdoor 6 drawing
7 participant 8 list

유형 1

❶ to ❷ instructions ❸ anything
❹ another

유형 2

❶ to find ❷ receive ❸ be entered

유형 3

❶ Bring your kids ❷ list of items
❸ coupon to anything
❹ drawing for another chance

────────────── p.145

01 ② 02 ② 03 ③ 04 ④ 05 ② 06 ④
07 ④ 08 ③ 09 In case of bad weather, the camp will be held in an indoor arena
10 volunteer 11 provides opportunities for those interested in science and research to participate
12 (1) 현재 대학이나 지역 전문 대학의 학생, 또는 최근 대학 졸업자 (2) 프로그램 기간에 적어도 1주일에 5시간을 근무할 수 있는 사람
13 therapeutic 14 10 spaces are available on a first-come-first-served basis 15 자신들이 시장에서 구입하는 어떤 물건이든지 쿠폰을 사용해서 5달러 할인을 받을 수 있다. 16 drawing

01 ②

문제해설

티볼을 배우는 데 관심이 있는 여름 캠프 참가자를 모집하는 내용이므로, 안내문의 목적으로 가장 적절한 것은 ②이다.

02 ②

문제해설

6월 1일 ~ 8월 31일까지는 미래 과학자 프로그램 자체가 진행되는 기간 (June 1: program begins. ~ August 31: program ends.)이므로, ②는 글의 내용과 일치하지 않는다.

03 ③

문제해설

개 치료 마사지 수업을 통해 반려견을 편안하게 해 주고 스트레스를 줄여 줄 수 있다고 안내하는 내용이므로, 글의 목적으로 가장 적절한 것은 ③이다.

04 ④

문제해설

모든 참가자는 1시에 (보물찾기 외에) 상품을 탈 수 있는 또 한 번의 기회를 얻게 된다(another chance to win a prize)고 했으므로, ④는 글의 내용과 일치하지 않는다.

05 ②

문제해설

4팀이 있을 것(There will be 4 teams)이고 각 팀에는 최대 13명의 선수가 있을 것이다(each team will have a maximum of 13 players)라고 했으므로, ②는 글의 내용과 일치한다.

오답노트

① meets twice per week, on Mondays and Wednesday라고 했으므로 오답이다.
③ 학부모는 참가자가 아니어서 티셔츠와 모자를 지급받지 못하므로 오답이다.
④ in person은 '직접' 대면하는 상황을 나타내는 말이므로 오답이다.
⑤ Training will be provided.는 자원봉사 코치를 신청한 부모들에게 '훈련이 제공된다'라는 뜻이므로 오답이다.

06 ④

문제해설

2023년 미래 과학자 프로그램에 연구 조교로서 참여할 것을 독려하면서 관련 일정과 지원에 필요한 여러 가지를 안내하는 내용이므로, 안내문의 목적으로 가장 적절한 것은 ④이다.

07 ④

문제해설

수업은 자격증이 있는 개 마사지 치료사에 의해 진행된다(conducted by a certified canine massage therapist)고 했으므로, 안내문의 내용과 일치하는 것은 ④이다.

오답노트

① 3월 25일 오전 9시부터 11시까지 두 시간 동안 진행되므로 오답이다.
② 반려견의 신체와 감정의 스트레스를 풀어 주는 것을 돕는 것이므로 오답이다.
③ 수업을 참관하면서 10가지 기본적인 마사지 기술을 배우게 되는 것이므로 오답이다.
⑤ 자리(spot) 예약을 하기 위한 연락처를 마지막 문단에서 안내하고 있으므로 오답이다.

08 ③

문제해설

Farmers' Market이라는 농산물 시장에서 열리는 보물찾기 행사를 홍

보하는 안내문이므로, 글의 목적으로 가장 적절한 것은 ③이다.

09 In case of bad weather, the camp will be held in an indoor arena

문제해설

'날씨가 좋지 않은 경우'는 '~할 경우'라는 의미의 in case of를 활용하여 In case of bad weather로 쓰고, '실내 경기장에서 개최된다'는 '~에서 개최되다'라는 수동의 의미이므로 동사 hold를 be held로 바꿔 문장을 완성한다.

10 volunteer

문제해설

'자신이 하는 일에 대해 보수를 받지 않는 사람; 돈을 받지 않고 일을 하다'를 의미하는 단어는 volunteer(자원봉사자; 자원봉사하다)이다.

11 provides opportunities for those interested in science and research to participate

문제해설

'…에게 ~하는 기회를 제공하다'는 〈provide+목적어+to-v〉 구문을 활용하여 provides opportunities to participate로 나타낸다. '과학과 연구에 관심 있는 사람들'은 전치사 for와 '~하는 사람들'이라는 의미의 those who를 활용해서 for those who are interested in science and research인데 〈관계대명사+be동사〉가 생략된 형태이고 제시되어 있지 않으므로 who are를 생략하고 쓴다.

12 (1) 현재 대학이나 지역 전문 대학의 학생, 또는 최근 대학 졸업자
(2) 프로그램 기간에 적어도 1주일에 5시간을 근무할 수 있는 사람

문제해설

미래 과학자 프로그램에 지원할 수 있는 사람은 Eligibility Requirements에 나타나 있다.

13 therapeutic

문제해설

'병을 치료하거나 치유하는 것을 돕는'을 의미하는 단어는 therapeutic(치료상의, 치료법의)이다.

14 10 spaces are available on a first-come-first-served basis

문제해설

'10명 자리만 가능하다'는 Only가 문두에 제시되어 있으므로 10 spaces are available로 나타내고, '선착순으로'는 on a first-come-first-served basis로 써서 문장을 완성한다.

15 자신들이 시장에서 구입하는 어떤 물건이든지 쿠폰을 사용해서 5달러 할인을 받을 수 있다.

문제해설

자신들이 시장에서 구입하는 어떤 물건이든지 쿠폰을 사용해서 5달러 할인을 받을 수 있다.

16 drawing

문제해설

'자신도 어떤 것을 뽑고 있는지를 알지 못한 채 여럿 가운데서 당첨 복권 같은 것을 뽑는 일'을 의미하는 단어는 draw인데 동명사 형태로 쓰라고 했으므로 정답은 drawing(제비뽑기, 추첨)이다.

11강

1번
p.152

● Word Test

1 심리학자　2 저항하다　3 ~을 고수하다　4 불법적인
5 일어나다, 발생하다　6 (문제가 처리되지 않고) 그대로 있다
7 많은, 다량의　8 의견이 다르다　9 (조직적인)운동, 캠페인; 운동[캠페인]을 벌이다　10 영향; 영향을 미치다　11 다수집단
12 pressure　13 a handful of　14 slavery
15 dedicated　16 consistent　17 minority
18 consistent　19 convince　20 genuine
21 reform　22 own

유형 1

❶ disagree　❷ wrong　❸ which
❹ though　❺ so

유형 2

❶ began　❷ rest　❸ are convinced
❹ trying　❺ are

유형 3

❶ for instance　❷ a handful of people
❸ as a result of　❹ stick to a particular view
❺ people who are in the minority

2번
p.154

● Word Test

1 거닐다　2 요소　3 정도, 규모　4 스키마, 도식(과거의 경험과 지식에 의해 형성된 개인의 인지 구조)　5 주고받으며, 왔다 갔다, 앞뒤로　6 선택적인, 선별적인　7 무시하다　8 골똘히, 열중하여　9 direct　10 costume　11 dramatic
12 demonstrate　13 attention　14 stimulus
15 experiment　16 miss

유형 1

❶ ignore　❷ to which　❸ the other
❹ Although　❺ that

유형 2

❶ allows　❷ passing　❸ was asked
❹ wearing　❺ failed

유형 3

❶ the most important elements
❷ count the number
❸ half the participants
❹ what is likely to happen
❺ failed to see

3번
p.156

● Word Test

1 연산　2 가상적인, 가설[가정]의　3 의심의 여지가 없는, 의심할 수 없는　4 몰역사적인, 역사와 무관한　5 현실에서 유리된, 실체

없는　　**6** 서술, 이야기　　**7** 외부의　　**8** …대신에 ~을 쓰다, ~으로 …을 대체하다　　**9** 모방하다, 흉내 내다　　**10** 수용하다
11 reinforce　　**12** distinct　　**13** abstract
14 outdated　　**15** viewpoint　　**16** laboratory
17 objective　　**18** method　　**19** humanly　　**20** habit

유형 1
1 unquestioned　　**2** what　　**3** that
4 until　　**5** outdated

유형 2
1 reinforced　　**2** becoming　　**3** imitating
4 was developed　　**5** using

유형 3
1 the rise of modern science
2 habits of mind　　**3** clear and distinct ideas
4 the best examples
5 repeat certain logical operations

4번　　　　　　　　　　　　　　　　　　p.158

• Word Test
1 자력으로, 자기 스스로　　**2** 중간의　　**3** 문제의, 논의가 되고 있는
4 복잡한　　**5** 언급하다　　**6** 상품　　**7** 아주 다른, 관계가 없는
8 양상, 측면　　**9** 여기다　　**10** apply　　**11** distribution
12 stage　　**13** goods　　**14** mysteriously　　**15** regular
16 spectator　　**17** consumption　　**18** sector

유형 1
1 will the commodity in question　　**2** itself
3 by which　　**4** the least　　**5** but

유형 2
1 agreed　　**2** to enjoy　　**3** likes
4 is　　**5** produced

유형 3
1 all on their own　　**2** generally referred to
3 the least studied
4 intermediate stages between
5 it seems as if

p.160
1 ②　　**2** ①　　**3** ④　　**4** ⑤　　**5** ②　　**6** ⑤
7 ①　　**8** ④　　**9** (1) ③ → resisting
(2) ⑤ → seriously　　**10** 잘못된 것을 보고 그대로 두지 않았다.
11 allows us to direct our attention to the most important elements　　**12** schemas　　**13** disembodied
14 특정한 논리적 연산을 통해 습득된 기술에 따라 세상을 해석하는 습관　　**15** (Little is written) About the intermediate stages between production and consumption.
16 will the commodity in question be there for the end-user to enjoy

---

01 ②

문제해설
위대한 사회 개혁은 잘못된 것을 보고 지속적으로 자신의 관점을 고수하는 소수에 의해서 실현된다는 내용이며, 이러한 요지를 18세기 노예제가 불법화된 과정을 예를 들어 서술하고 있으므로, 글의 주제로 가장 적절한 것은 ② '사회 변화를 일으키는 소수의 힘'이다.

오답노트
① 소수의 권리를 위한 캠페인의 어려움
③ 유럽에서 노예제를 종결한 정책들
④ 불복종이 소수의 사회적 지위에 미치는 영향
⑤ 법적 사안에 대한 압도적인 다수의 영향

02 ①

문제해설
주의 집중은 선택적이기 때문에 주어진 상황에 대한 우리 지식이 인도하는 가장 중요한 요소 이외의 것은 무시한다는 내용의 글이다. 빈칸 다음에 실험 참가자들이 농구공을 주고받는 영상에서 과업 수행 중에 눈에 띄는 고릴라 옷을 입은 사람을 인식하지 못했다는 결과를 언급하고, 이에 대한 시사점으로 주어진 상황에서 작동하는 스키마와 기대 때문에 눈에 띄는 자극을 인지하지 못했다고 했으므로, 빈칸에 들어갈 말로 가장 적절한 것은 ① '우리의 스키마와 기대가 우리의 주의를 이끈다'이다.

오답노트
② 우리는 규칙에서 벗어난 예상치 못한 요소를 무시한다
③ 우리는 게임 중에 다른 사람이 요청한 것에 주의를 기울이게 된다
④ 우리의 사전 지식이 집단의 일원으로서 우리 행동에 영향을 준다
⑤ 우리의 팀에 대한 우리의 기대가 좋은 스포츠맨십을 장려한다

03 ④

문제해설
현대 과학의 부상과 함께 생겨난 새로운 사고 습관 및 이러한 사고 습관의 특징과 대표하는 사상가 등에 대한 내용의 글이므로, 글의 제목으로 가장 적절한 것은 ④ '현대 과학과 함께 등장하는 대안적 사고방식'이다.

오답노트
① 객관적 결과에 기초한 주관적인 과학적 과정
② 비인간적인 과학적 사고방식의 한계
③ 이론적 과제: 실험실 연구의 사각지대
⑤ 사고 메커니즘이 적용된 새로운 과학적 방법들

04 ⑤

문제해설
상품이 시장에 나오기까지의 과정을 거친 후에야 수요자가 누릴 수 있고, 이 과정이 영화와 비디오에도 적용되어 영화 배급으로 일컬어지는데, 이러한 제작과 소비 사이의 중간 단계에 대해 알려진 바가 거의 없다는 내용의 글이다. 그러므로 영화와 영상 분야에서 '마치 상품(영화)이 신비롭게 저절로 시장에 이르는 것처럼 보인다'가 의미하는 바로 가장 적절한 것은 ⑤ '관객들이 어떻게 영화를 볼 수 있게 되는지에 대해서는 거의 알려져 있지 않다.'이다.

① 영화의 제작 과정은 공개될 가능성이 적다.
② 영화 배급 시장은 거의 확보되지 않았다.
③ 비디오가 상품이라는 개념은 널리 받아들여지지 않는다.
④ 영화 상영 가격에 대한 최종 사용자의 영향은 미비하다.

05 ②

문제해설

위대한 사회 개혁은 잘못된 것을 보고 지속적으로 자신의 관점을 고수하는 소수에 의해서 실현된다는 내용의 글이다. 빈칸을 포함한 문장은 이러한 요지를 18세기 노예제 불법화 과정을 예를 들어 서술하는 내용으로, 소수의 사람들이 무엇인가 잘못되었음을 보고 어떻게 하지 않았는지를 묻고 있는데, 빈칸 뒤에 이어지는 내용이 지속적인 운동(캠페인)으로 노예제 불법화가 성립되었다고 설명하고 있고, 사회 심리학자들의 연구에서도 소수의 사람들이 자신들이 옳다고 확신하는 특정 관점을 고수한다는 내용이 이어진다. 따라서 부정어 not 뒤의 빈칸에 들어갈 말로 가장 적절한 것은 ② '그것을 그대로 두다'이다.

오답노트

① 그것을 고수하다
③ 그것을 실행하다
④ 문제를 제기하다(말을 꺼내다)
⑤ 그것을 퍼뜨리다

06 ⑤

문제해설

우리는 모든 것에 다 집중하지 못하고 선택적 집중을 한다는 내용으로, 우리의 스키마와 기대가 주의를 이끄는 정도를 실험 상황을 예시로 들며 설명하고 있다. 실험 참가자들이 관찰한 영상에 등장한 고릴라 옷을 입은 사람의 등장을 알아차리지 못한 이유는 예상하는 것과 스키마에서 벗어났기 때문이라고 설명하고 있으므로, 글의 제목으로 가장 적절한 것은 ⑤ '우리의 인지 구조가 주의력에 미치는 영향'이다.

오답노트

① 비호의적인 데이터를 무시하는 동안의 정보 해석하기
② 우리 기억의 과장: 우리의 스키마에 맞추기
③ 팀 단체복을 디자인하는 심리학적 원리들
④ 우리의 기대와 스키마에 영향을 미치는 강한 압박

07 ①

문제해설

현대 과학의 부상과 함께 새로운 사고 습관이 생겨났다는 내용의 글로, 빈칸 앞에서 비록 과학의 부상과 함께 생겨난 사고 방식이 현실과 유리되었고 객관적이라고 생각되었지만 결과적으로는 그러한 앞의 내용과 상반되거나 다른 내용이 빈칸에 들어가야 한다. 따라서 빈칸에 들어갈 말로 가장 적절한 것은 ① '그것들을 사용하는 사람들에게서 구현되었다'이다.

오답노트

② 사람들을 주관적인 해석으로부터 해방시켰다
③ 그들의 편견 없는 관점을 위한 길을 닦았다
④ 인간의 문제에 대한 과학적 접근법을 지지했다
⑤ 인류의 논리적 판단을 방해하는 몇몇 장애물을 제거했다

08 ④

문제해설

영화와 영상의 배급의 과정에 대해서는 알려진 바가 거의 없다는 내용의 글로, 빈칸 앞에 but과 부정 형용사 little이 있기 때문에 영화와 영상이 관객에게 어떻게 인식되고 수용되는지에 대한 글은 많다는 앞의 내용과 대조적인 내용이 들어가야 한다. 빈칸 다음 문장에서 영화 배급은 중간 단계 없이 저절로 이루어지는 것 같다고 하고 있으므로, 빈칸에 들어갈 말로 가장 적절한 것은 ④ '제작과 소비의 중간 단계'이다.

오답노트

① 영화 산업이 사회에 미치는 경제적 영향
② 문화 상품으로서 영화 발전의 단계
③ 표 가격이 어떻게 많은 경제적 요인에 의해 결정되는지
⑤ 소비자들이 영화 제작 방향에 영향을 미치는 정도

09 (1) ③ → resisting (2) ⑤ → seriously

문제해설

③ 소수파에 속하는 사람들은 다수파의 사회적 압력에 저항할 것이므로, accepting(기꺼이 받아들이는)을 resisting(저항하는)과 같은 말로 바꿔 써야 한다.
⑤ 소수의 사람들이 진실하고 일관되게 행동하고 있다면 대중들도 점차 소수가 말하는 것에 대해 더 관심을 더 갖게 될 것이므로, indifferently(무관심하게)를 seriously(진지하게)와 같은 말로 바꿔 써야 한다.

10 잘못된 것을 보고 그대로 두지 않았다.

문제해설

did not let it rest는 '그것을 그대로 두지 않았다'는 뜻으로, 대명사 it은 앞에 나오는 something wrong을 가리킨다.

11 allows us to direct our attention to the most important elements

문제해설

'…로 하여금 주의를 ~로 돌리게 해 주다'는 ⟨allow+목적어+to-v⟩ 구문을 활용해서 쓴다. 주어가 the knowledge we bring to a given situation이므로 단수 동사 allows를 쓰고, 목적어 us와 to direct our attention 순서로 쓴다. 이어서 '가장 중요한 요소들에'는 전치사 to 다음에 대상 the most important elements를 써서 문장을 완성한다.

12 schemas

문제해설

'어떤 것의 중요한 부분만 보여 주는 계획[생각]'이라는 의미의 단어는 schemas이다.

13 disembodied

문제해설

'몸에서 분리된; 현실과의 확고한 관계가 결여된'이라는 의미로 본문에서 찾을 수 있는 단어는 disembodied이다.

14 특정한 논리적 연산을 통해 습득된 기술에 따라 세상을 해석하는 습관

문제해설

a habit이 있는 절의 주어부는 a habit of reading the world according to those skills이며, those skills의 내용은 The mind was trained to repeat certain logical operations에 나타나 있다.

15 (Little is written) About the intermediate stages between production and consumption.

문제해설

영화의 어떤 측면에 대해 쓰인 글이 거의 없는지는 but very little about the intermediate stages between production and consumption에 나타나 있다.

16 will the commodity in question be there for the end-user to enjoy

문제해설

부사구 only after a long and complicated process가 문장 앞으로 나와 도치된 형태이므로 〈조동사+주어+동사원형〉 어순으로 쓴다. '해당 상품'은 the commodity in question으로 쓰고, '실수요자가 누릴 수 있도록'은 의미상 주어 〈for+목적격〉과 to부정사를 이용하여 for the end-user to enjoy로 써서 문장을 완성한다.

1번 ——————————————— p.166

• Word Test

1 소유하다   2 효과적인   3 공익   4 ~의 특성을 나타내다
5 유일한, 유례가 없는   6 개념   7 특허; 특허를 얻다[획득하다]
8 ~에 속하다   9 접근, 접근권   10 transport
11 attitude   12 sustainable   13 excessive
14 announce   15 donate   16 pity   17 era
18 property

유형 1

❶ that   ❷ common
❸ could have earned   ❹ however
❺ not defined

유형 2

❶ was asked   ❷ had donated   ❸ to release
❹ sharing

유형 3

❶ common property   ❷ belonged to the people
❸ for the public interest ❹ in the era of
❺ will be better served

2번 ——————————————— p.168

• Word Test

1 목록에 포함시키다   2 고소하다   3 위협   4 감시 단체
5 (멸종 위기종의) 보존 서식지   6 이해관계(자), 이익
7 공식적으로   8 환멸을 느낀   9 전반적인   10 멸종 위기종
11 specific   12 designate   13 restriction
14 species   15 propose   16 atmosphere
17 federal   18 decline   19 politicize
20 maintain

유형 1

❶ that   ❷ that   ❸ as
❹ in which   ❺ them

유형 2

❶ designating   ❷ saw
❸ is designated ❹ to maintain   ❺ to list

유형 3

❶ endangered species
❷ prevents damage to specific areas
❸ under the act   ❹ a threat to business
❺ the final ruling

3번 ——————————————— p.171

• Word Test

1 자연 과학   2 가정하다, 추정하다   3 양자 물리학
4 ~을 이루다   5 바꾸다   6 ~을 …으로 고쳐 말하다[옮기다]
7 깨뜨릴 수 없는   8 현상   9 nature   10 inseparable

11 assumption　12 separate　13 measurable
14 context　15 supposedly　16 assess

4번 　　　　　　　　　　　　　　　　p.174

유형 1
❶ measurable　❷ how　❸ Without
❹ within which　❺ therefore

유형 2
❶ means　❷ being　❸ made
❹ was made　❺ form

유형 3
❶ no matter how it is measured
❷ the nature of the phenomenon
❸ there is a view　❹ In this context
❺ form an inseparable whole

4번

p.174

• Word Test

1 발화　2 선택하다　3 발음하기 너무 힘든　4 조합, 결합
5 ~을 이용하다　6 자음　7 원시적인　8 다르다
9 습득하다　10 obviously　11 odd
12 characteristics　13 combine　14 mistakenly
15 ethnocentric　16 vowel　17 superior　18 claim

유형 1
❶ superior　❷ easily　❸ in which
❹ impossible　❺ and

유형 2
❶ thought　❷ are　❸ looks
❹ are used　❺ vary

유형 3
❶ There are several reasons
❷ consider other languages ugly
❸ Such a view　❹ a native speaker of English
❺ to form words and utterances

p.177

01 ⑤　02 ③　03 ②　04 ③　05 ⑤　06 ④
07 ④　08 ①　9 could have earned $7 billion if
his vaccine had been patented
10 sustainable　11 critical habitat
12 보존 서식지가 지정되지 않으면 사업에 대한 제한이 훨씬 적은 것
13 측정되고 있는 현상은 그것이 어떻게 측정이 되든지 간에 동일하다는
가정　14 separate　15 (A) those　(B) are　(C) no
16 (A) ethnocentric　(B) superior

01 ⑤

문제해설

Jonas Salk와 Elon Musk가 자신들이 소유한 특허권을 포기하고 공
공의 이익에 기여했다는 내용의 글로, 두 사례는 개인의 특허 소유권을 자

발적으로 포기함으로써 오히려 다수의 이익을 도모했다는 역설적인 시사
점을 가지고 있으므로, 글의 제목으로 가장 적절한 것은 ⑤ '개인의 이익보
다 공공의 이익을 우선시하는 것'이다.

오답노트

① 쉬운 일이 아니라 옳은 일을 하라!
② 공공의 이익을 위한 사적 자산 탈취
③ 지적 재산이 우리의 수명에 미치는 영향
④ 공중 보건을 위한 개인 권리 희생

02 ③

문제해설

1990년 초 남서부의 버드나무 딱새의 감소로 미국 어류·야생동물 관리
국(FWS)이 이를 멸종 위기종으로 등재하고 서식지를 지정할 것을 제안
하였고, 이는 해당 법령에 따라 이뤄진 조치라는 주어진 글 다음에, 그 법
령에 따른 과업이 Marshall에게 주어졌으나 시행에 환멸을 가지게 되었
다는 내용의 (B)가 이어지고, FWS의 서식지 지원 사업이 재력 있는 이해
관계자들에 의해 정치화되어 있고 서식지 지정에 어려움이 있다는 내용인
(C) 다음에, 그 예시에 해당하는 (A)가 마지막에 오는 것이 글의 순서로 가
장 적절하다.

03 ②

문제해설

측정되고 있는 현상은 어디서 어떻게 측정이 되든 동일하다는 가정을 언급
하고, 그러한 관점이 옳지 않을 수 있다는 상반된 입장을 양자 물리학의 견
해를 들어 설명하는 글이다. 측정과 현상에 있어 후자의 의견이 서술된 글
의 후반부에 빈칸이 위치하고, 빈칸이 있는 문장 앞에서 현상과 측정이 별
개로 존재하지 않고 해당 현상의 독립된 측정이 불가능하다고 말하고 있
으므로, 빈칸에 들어갈 말로 가장 적절한 것은 ② '현실과 그것이 측정되는
방법은 불가분의 총체를 형성한다'이다.

오답노트

① 물리학적 가정은 실천하는 사람들 간에 공유된다
③ 측정된 현실은 그것의 이론적 지식과 일치하지 않는다
④ 측정된 값과 현상 사이의 관계는 지속된다
⑤ 물리적 현상의 측정은 영구적으로 변하지 않는다

04 ③

문제해설

특정 언어가 원시적이라고 생각하는 것은 잘못된 견해이며, 이는 자신의
언어가 우수하다는 자민족 중심의 태도에 근거한다는 내용의 글이다. 이에
대한 근거로 발음이 어려워 괴상하다고 여겨지는 단어를 어린 화자조차 쉽
게 습득한다며 반론하고 있고, 언어는 언어일 뿐 우월성을 주장할 수 없다
고 서술하고 있으므로, '그러나 같은 이유로 부족 사회의 언어는 문화의 두
드러진 측면을 위한 정교한 어휘를 가질 것이다'라는 내용의 ③은 글의 전
체 흐름과 관계가 없다.

05 ⑤

문제해설

소아마비 백신을 발명한 Jonas Salk가 백신의 특허 소유에 대한 질문에
답하는 주어진 글 다음에, 그의 대답의 의미가 공공을 위해 백신을 기부하
는 것이라는 내용인 (C)가 이어지고, 특허에 대한 Salk와 같은 태도를 취

한 추가적인 사례가 있음을 설명하는 (B)가 온다. 마지막으로 공공의 이익을 위해 개인이 특허권을 포기한 추가 사례로 Elon Musk의 일화를 소개한 (A)가 오는 것이 자연스럽다.

06 ④

문제해설

주어진 문장의 This는 강력하고 돈 많은 이해 관계자들에 의해 서식지 지정 사업이 매우 정치화되어 있고, 어떤 종을 등재만 하고 보존 서식지를 지정하지 않는 패턴을 의미하며, 주어진 문장에서 Marshall이 언급한 어려움에 대한 예시가 ④ 다음 문장에서 이어지고 있으므로, 주어진 문장이 들어가기에 가장 적절한 곳은 ④이다.

07 ④

문제해설

이론의 해석과 관련하여 측정되고 있는 현상은 어디서 어떻게 측정이 되든 동일하다는 가정을 언급하고, 그러한 관점이 옳지 않을 수 있다는 상반된 입장을 양자 물리학의 견해를 빌려 서술하는 내용의 글이므로, 글의 제목으로 가장 적절한 것은 ④ '독립적인가 아니면 결속되어 있는가?: 현실과 그 측정'이다.

오답노트

① 현대 물리 이론의 기본적 가정
② 이론과 그 현실의 불일치
③ 물리적 현실의 측정 가능성에 대한 잘못된 믿음
⑤ 물리적으로 불가능한 현상에 대한 대조적인 견해

08 ①

문제해설

특정 언어가 원시적이라고 잘못 인식하는 이유 중 하나로 모국어와 다른 소리를 들어 말하고 있고, 발음상 힘들어 보이는 단어를 어린 화자조차 쉽게 습득하고 있으며, 발화 및 발음상의 차이로 언어 간 우월을 주장할 수 없다고 서술하고 있으므로, 글의 요지로 가장 적절한 것은 ①이다.

09 could have earned $7 billion if his vaccine had been patented

문제해설

과거 사실의 반대되는 일을 가정하는 가정법 과거완료를 활용해서 주절의 동사는 〈조동사+have+p.p.〉 형태로 쓰고, 조건절은 주어 his vaccine이 '특허를 받았다면'이라는 수동의 의미이므로 수동태로 써서 〈if+주어+had been p.p.〉 형태로 나타낸다.

10 sustainable

문제해설

'동일한 수준으로 오랫동안 계속될 수 있는'을 의미하는 단어는 sustainable(지속 가능한)이다.

11 critical habitat

문제해설

'등재된 야생 생물 종의 생존이나 회복을 위해 필요한 특정 지역'에 해당하는 말은 critical habitat(보존 서식지)이다.

12 보존 서식지가 지정되지 않으면 사업에 대한 제한이 훨씬 적은 것

문제해설

밑줄 친 This가 가리키는 내용은 앞 문장 if a species is listed ~ designated에 나타나 있다.

13 측정되고 있는 현상은 그것이 어떻게 측정이 되든지 간에 동일하다는 가정

문제해설

밑줄 친 this assumption이 가리키는 것은 두 번째 문장의 the phenomenon being measured is the same no matter how it is measured에 나타나 있다.

14 separate

문제해설

측정과 현상은 측정 시스템 안에서 분리할 수 없이 결합되어 있다는 내용이 이어지고 있으므로, 빈칸에 공통으로 들어갈 단어는 separate(분리하다; 별개의)이다.

15 (A) those (B) are (C) no

문제해설

(A) 앞의 the sounds를 받는 대명사가 필요한 자리이므로 that을 those로 고쳐야 한다.
(B) 문장의 주어가 words로 복수이므로 is를 are로 고쳐야 한다.
(C) 문맥상 어떤 언어 사용자도 자신의 언어가 다른 언어보다 더 우수하다고 주장할 수 없다는 부정의 내용이 되어야 하므로 any를 no로 고쳐야 한다.

16 (A) ethnocentric (B) superior

문제해설

특정한 언어가 다른 언어보다 더 우수하다고 주장할 수 없다는 내용의 글이므로, '특정한 언어들을 원시적이라고 여기는 태도는 자신의 언어가 다른 언어보다 (B) 우수하다는 (A) 자기 민족 중심적인 믿음에서 기인한다.'와 같이 요약하는 것이 가장 적절하다.

13강

1번

• Word Test

1 뛰어나다   2 ~으로 판명되다   3 제약하다   4 ~을 생각해 내다
5 운송기   6 (형편이) 더 나은   7 ~을 겪다   8 탓하다
9 긍정 오류(거짓인 것이 참으로 잘못 판정되는 오류)   10 분석
11 부정 오류(참인 것이 거짓으로 잘못 판정되는 오류)
12 shortage   13 originality   14 barrier
15 forecast   16 ultimately   17 generation
18 venture   19 absence   20 unique   21 flourish
22 novel

유형 1

❶ absence   ❷ But   ❸ unique
❹ shortage   ❺ flourished

유형 2

❶ were   ❷ suffer   ❸ choosing
❹ turned   ❺ was

유형 3

❶ the lack of originality   ❷ in reality
❸ shortage of novel ideas   ❹ a false positive
❺ turned out to be a miss

2번

• Word Test

1 낟알   2 주목하다   3 개체 수[인구] 과잉   4 우연히
5 밀   6 혼합물   7 수완, 숙련   8 (동물의) 군집, 집단
9 자기 방식이 몸에 밴   10 우연히   11 이해하다
12 brilliant   13 competent   14 ignore
15 relieve   16 sink   17 anthropologist   18 sift
19 float   20 widespread   21 imitate
22 striking

유형 1

❶ relieve   ❷ difficult   ❸ Through
❹ While   ❺ widespread

유형 2

❶ to relieve   ❷ to separate   ❸ eating
❹ sinks   ❺ imitated

유형 3

❶ a community of monkeys   ❷ such an effort
❸ by accident   ❹ grasp the importance
❺ a cultural tradition

3번

• Word Test

1 보여 주다, 나타내다   2 순응하다, 적응하다   3 대다수
4 아마   5 관련시키다   6 소질, 적성   7 확신, 신념
8 단일 언어 사용자   9 수반하다   10 여러 언어를 사용할 수 있는
11 지배, 우세   12 peculiar   13 reference
14 competence   15 population   16 complain
17 convention   18 subtly   19 linguistic
20 increasingly   21 remarkable   22 reflect

유형 1

❶ majority   ❷ And yet
❸ monolinguals   ❹ multilingual   ❺ than

유형 2

❶ indicates   ❷ involved   ❸ reflecting
❹ made

유형 3

❶ a majority of   ❷ the difficulties involved
❸ have no aptitude for
❹ a deeply held conviction
❺ a world made increasingly safe

4번

• Word Test

1 무언의, 말로 표현되지 않은   2 그럼에도(불구하고)
3 짜증 나게 하다   4 ~의 가치를 인정하다   5 분석하다
6 ~에 대해 곰곰이 생각하다   7 송구하지만   8 영향을 미치다
9 negatively   10 fool   11 management
12 victim   13 annoy   14 continually   15 various
16 misery

유형 1

❶ that   ❷ but   ❸ where
❹ nevertheless   ❺ them

유형 2

❶ creates   ❷ being   ❸ thinking
❹ thinking   ❺ to analyse

유형 3

❶ people that work with me
❷ almost all the time   ❸ the same thing as
❹ dwelled on his misery   ❺ a victim of

5번

• Word Test

1 다세대의   2 관여, 참여   3 돌보는 사람   4 요인, 요소
5 응답자   6 수행하다   7 상호 작용   8 변화
9 치료하다   10 long-term   11 diminished
12 isolation   13 task   14 longevity
15 counteract   16 urban   17 measure
18 emotional

유형 1

❶ less   ❷ measured   ❸ if not
❹ that

유형 2

① do   **②** has grown
③ to counteract   **④** using   **⑤** interacting

유형 3

① health and longevity   **②** a third of respondents
③ offer an opportunity   **④** fill our need
⑤ some level of engagement

6번   p.193

• Word Test

1 ~을 실행에 옮기다   2 대본 작가   3 ~의 과정에서   4 용어
5 지시   6 숏(영화에서 한 대의 카메라가 계속해서 잡는 장면)
7 ~을 구하다[손에 넣다]   8 제시하다, 보여 주다
9 ~과 다른[동떨어진]   10 suitable   11 biography
12 untechnical   13 scheme   14 account
15 mark   16 alteration   17 theme
18 beforehand

유형 1

① How   **②** easy   **③** interested
④ but   **⑤** what

유형 2

① to present   **②** rewrites   **③** marked
④ written   **⑤** to put

유형 3

① easy to get hold of   **②** a full list of
③ versions of the film   **④** put into practice
⑤ the course of production

7번   p.195

• Word Test

1 지속적인   2 이전의   3 승리하다   4 보수하다
5 진화하다   6 걸쭉하게   7 난쟁이   8 압축하다
9 일련의   10 체스판   11 mentality   12 effect
13 construct   14 common sense   15 arrangement
16 reflex   17 cunning   18 metaphor   19 extend
20 puppet

유형 1

① which   **②** Past   **③** even if
④ which   **⑤** who

유형 2

① extended   **②** triumphs   **③** being
④ controlled   **⑤** moving

유형 3

① a succession of historically evolved mentalities
② previous generations
③ determine our present thinking
④ cunning arrangement of mirrors
⑤ our everyday life

8번   p.197

• Word Test

1 일컫다, 부르다   2 붙들다, 붙잡다   3 개념
4 ~이 아니라, ~과 대조적으로   5 주된, 일차적인
6 가장 중요한, 중심적인   7 의도   8 이의를 제기하다
9 ~에서 유래하다   10 concern   11 signal
12 steady   13 categorize   14 include   15 define
16 agreeable   17 production   18 amused

유형 1

① which   **②** However   **③** with
④ though

유형 2

① means   **②** remains   **③** grabs
④ are categorized   **⑤** making

유형 3

① those in the business
② grabs the audience's attention
③ stay away from   **④** with the intention of
⑤ their primary concern

9번   p.199

• Word Test

1 유전적으로 프로그램화된   2 큰가시고기   3 박사, 박사 학위
4 청소년기   5 장래의, 미래의   6 구애 춤
7 결과로 ~을 초래하다[가져오다]   8 전환, 변환   9 (생물의) 종
10 trigger   11 social status   12 whereby
13 belly   14 biological   15 in response to
16 assume   17 state   18 ritual

유형 1

① effecting   **②** to   **③** whereby
④ which   **⑤** itself

유형 2

① effecting   **②** have   **③** is triggered
④ is   **⑤** tends

유형 3

① transformation of state   **②** the life cycle
③ in response to   **④** by the sight of
⑤ In any case

10번   p.201

• Word Test

1 일반적으로, 보통은   2 영향력 있는, 유력한   3 건설적인
4 널리 퍼져 있는   5 궁극적으로   6 겪다   7 ~을 할 수 있는
8 (곤경 등을 이기고) 일어서다, (곤경 등에서) 벗어나다.
9 tolerant   10 trauma   11 be exposed to
12 concept   13 psychologist   14 confront
15 mature   16 terrifying

유형 1

1. which
2. them
3. rather than
4. being exposed
5. stronger

유형 2

1. is
2. feel
3. is lavished
4. expect
5. confronting

유형 3

1. far more widespread
2. in some other way
3. have mainly negative effects
4. many constructive ways
5. in the end

11번

p.203

• Word Test

1 극적으로, 매우　2 무리하다, 안간힘을 쓰다　3 인구
4 기아, 굶주림　5 경우, 문제　6 주로　7 yield
8 comparable　9 feed　10 crop
11 misconception　12 inefficiently

유형 1

1. that
2. inefficiently
3. comparable
4. so
5. that

유형 2

1. is
2. to feed
3. has
4. to grow
5. to keep

유형 3

1. a common misconception
2. a third of
3. dramatically higher crop yields
4. three times the population
5. producer of food

12번

p.205

• Word Test

1 역효과를 낳는　2 조직하다　3 감지하다, 감을 잡다
4 미래에, 나중에　5 찾아내다, 확인하다
6 마법으로 만들다[나타나게 하다]　7 전가하다, 옮기다
8 수반하다, 포함하다　9 그렇게 함으로써, 그것에 의하여
10 구동하다, 추진하다　11 legislate　12 attitude
13 economist　14 burden　15 mechanism
16 measure　17 ultimately　18 memorial
19 sacrifice　20 generate

유형 1

1. that
2. involve
3. counterproductive
4. one
5. thereby

유형 2

1. made
2. to increase
3. is priced
4. to show
5. making

유형 3

1. no such thing as
2. reduce a burden
3. the concept of free lunches
4. the least amount

p.208

01 ①　02 ③　03 ⑤　04 ④　05 ②　06 ③
07 ③　08 ②　09 ③　10 ⑤　11 ①　12 ③
13 ④　14 ⑤　15 ①　16 ④　17 ②　18 ②
19 ④　20 ④　21 ③　22 ③　23 ③　24 ⑤
25 (1) the Segway, a two-wheeled, self-balancing personal transporter　(2) *Seinfeld*, an American sitcom television series　26 (A) insufficiency (B) attractive　27 such an effort might even expend more energy than eating the collected wheat would provide　28 it appeared that the younger monkeys grasped the importance of her discovery
29 (1) ① → indicates　(2) ② → involved　(3) ⑤ → safe
30 aptitude　31 그의 부정적인 생각이 부정적인 느낌과 감정을 만들어 내고 있었는데, 자신이 그것을 생각하고 있다는 것조차 알지 못했기 때문이다.　32 nearly all of his time thinking about the little things that irritated and annoyed him　33 Greater numbers of the elderly now live alone.　34 ③ → isolation　35 a good scenario of *October*　36 the same film as, critical modifications　37 Past events are compressed in images and metaphors which determine our present thinking　38 (A) controlled (B) effect
39 (A) remains (B) challenging (C) that
40 that are categorized under, have been written and produced with the intention of making
41 the male's zigzag courtship dance
42 transformation　43 (1) ③ → to mistakenly expect　(2) ④ → being exposed　(3) ⑤ → that
44 (A) suffer from (B) adversities
45 중국은 미국의 3배 인구를 가지고 있고 경작지 면적은 6분의 1에 불과해서 그 주민들이 더 효율적으로 작물을 재배해야 하기 때문이다.
46 to keep all of the hungry people in the world fed　47 counterproductive　48 우리의 가장 적은 희생으로 우리가 더 부유하게, 그리고 잘만 되면 더 행복하게 만들어 주는 것

01 ①

문제해설

창의성이 부족하여 독창성이 없는 것이 아니라, 많은 창의적인 생각이 존재하지만 그에 대한 선택을 잘못하기 때문이라는 내용의 글이므로, '이것은 독특함과 독창성이 유사하기보다는 구별되는 것이라는 개념을 반증한다.'라는 내용의 ①은 글의 전체 흐름과 관계가 없다.

02 ③

문제해설

perhaps by accident or out of pique에서 원숭이 Imo가 아마도 알 수 없는 이유로 모래와 밀 혼합물을 물속에 던졌다고 했으므로, ③은 글의 내용과 일치하지 않는다.

03 ⑤

문제해설

영향력 있는 언어 집단, 즉 영어만 쓰는 사용자는 다중 언어를 구사하는 집단을 부러워하기도 하지만, 이는 결국 영어를 사용하는 사회가 우세한 지위를 가지고 있다는 사실에 기댄 우쭐함에 기인한다는 내용의 글이다. 따라서 '이러한 모든 태도는 소질에 대한 것보다는 사회적 우위와 관습에 대한 것을 더 많이 드러낸다.'가 의미하는 바로 가장 적절한 것은 ⑤ '언어 습득과 그 필요성에 관한 태도는 자신이 속한 사회의 지위를 반영한다.'이다.

오답노트

① 영어를 사용하는 사람이 다중 언어 사용자보다 더 많은 곳에서 더 안전하다.
② 한 사람의 능력은 자신이 사용하는 언어에 의해 결정된다.
③ 언어 학습에 소질이 없는 사람은 본인의 지위를 자랑한다.
④ 다중 언어를 구사하는 것보다 한 개의 중요한 언어를 구사하는 것이 낫다.

04 ④

문제해설

주어진 문장은 그것은 마치 삶의 목표가 자신에게 영향을 끼치는 것들을 분석하여 의견을 제시하는 것인 듯했다는 내용으로, ④ 앞부분에서 단순하게 생각과 숙고의 차이와 부정적인 생각을 지속하고, 거의 모든 시간을 자신을 괴롭히고 짜증 나게 하는 작은 것들에 대해서 생각한다는 내용이므로, 주어진 문장이 들어가기에 가장 적절한 곳은 ④이다.

05 ②

문제해설

사회와 가정이 도시화 및 핵가족화되면서 혼자 사는 고령자들이 증가하여 사회적 상호 작용의 기회가 많이 줄었으나 로봇이 특정 상황에서만 적용됨에도 불구하고 우리의 필요성을 어느 정도 충족시켜 줄 수 있을 것이라는 가능성을 제시하는 내용이므로, '사회와 가정의 현대적 변화는 더 많은 고령자가 사회적으로 (A) 고립되도록 만들고 있지만, 로봇 기술의 발전이 문제 해결에 (B) 상당한 역할을 할 것으로 기대되고 있다.'와 같이 요약하는 것이 가장 적절하다.

오답노트

	(A)	(B)
①	골칫거리인	중요한
③	의존적인	가상의
④	활동적인	주도적인
⑤	외로운	중요하지 않은

06 ③

문제해설

영화 제작의 처음부터 끝까지의 과정에 대한 글로, 어떤 주제가 정해지면 그것에 따른 여러 개의 간단하고 비전문적인 초안인 '트리트먼트'가 작성되고 그중 하나가 구체적으로 시나리오화된다는 내용의 글이다. 이 '트리트먼트' 중 하나를 구하기 쉽다고 한 것은 *La Grande Illusion*에 국한되며 대부분의 경우에 해당되는 것이 아니므로, ③은 글의 내용과 일치하지 않는다.

07 ③

문제해설

과거로부터 이어져 온 사고 체계가 은연중에 우리의 현재 사고를 결정하는 데 많은 영향을 끼치고 있다는 내용의 글이므로, '체스 달인이면서 그 꼭두각시를 조종하는 난쟁이가 그 안에 앉아 있었다'가 의미하는 것은 ③ '현재의 사고에 은연중에 영향을 끼치는 역사적인 사고 체계'가 가장 적절하다.

오답노트

① 현실을 외면하고 새로운 역사를 쓰려고 하는 집단
② 타인을 기만함으로써 자신의 이득을 위해 일하는 사람
④ 타인을 조종하여 그들의 현실 인식을 왜곡시키는 사람
⑤ 매일 사람들의 기억 속에서 사라져 가는 것

08 ②

문제해설

엔터테인먼트라는 어휘의 본질적인 의미와 그 사업에 종사하는 사람들에게 그것이 가장 중요하게 여겨지는 가치가 '청중의 즐거움'에 있기 때문에, 즐거움과 다른 내용을 다룬다고 할지라도 결국 주된 관심사는 즐거움을 주려는 의도에 있다는 내용이므로, '엔터테인먼트 산업의 본질은 관객을 (A) 행복하게 만들어 주는 것에 있으므로 유익한 정보를 주거나 설득력 있는 작품이 만들어진다고 해도, 그것의 초점은 결국 (B) 즐거움을 만들어 내는 것이다.'와 같이 요약하는 것이 가장 적절하다.

오답노트

	(A)	(B)
①	진실된	탐욕
③	정치적인	의도
④	교육적인	기쁨
⑤	의심 많은	영웅적 행위

09 ③

문제해설

주어진 문장은 이들 동물에서 의식은 유전자에서 나오는 화학적 메시지에 반응하여 어떤 정해진 메시지나 상징에 의해 촉발된다는 내용이며, ③ 앞에서 이러한 의식에 대해 언급되고 있고 ③ 다음 문장에서 반응의 예시를 들고 있으므로, 주어진 문장이 들어가기에 가장 적절한 곳은 ③이다.

10 ⑤

문제해설

⑤ 부사절 Even though 다음에 주절의 주어인 people의 동사가 필요하므로, responding을 repond로 고쳐야 한다.

오답노트

① 관계대명사의 계속적 용법으로 the concept of post-traumatic growth를 선행사로 하는 which는 적절하다.
② 동사 has oftne lamented의 목적절을 이끄는 명사절 접속사 that은 적절하다.

③ 5형식 동사 causes의 목적격 보어인 to부정사구 to mistakenly expect는 적절하다.
④ 내용상 끔찍한 사건에 '노출이 되는' 수동의 의미이므로 전치사 after의 목적어로 수동형 동명사 being exposed는 적절하다.

11 ①

문제해설

인류가 겪고 있는 기아 문제가 실제로는 인구 증가, 경작할 땅의 부족 혹은 불충분한 식량 생산량 때문이 아닌 비효율적인 농사법과 낭비되는 음식물 때문이라고 주장하는 내용의 글이므로, 글의 주제로 가장 적절한 것은 ① '기아 문제 이면의 진실'이다.

오답노트

② 효율적인 농사법의 이점
③ 기아와 인구의 상관관계
④ 지구의 실제 식량 생산 능력
⑤ 기아 및 버려지는 음식 문제에 대한 논의

12 ③

문제해설

무료 점심을 소재로 누군가 공짜로 점심을 먹는다는 것은 다른 누군가에게 비용이 전가되는 역효과가 일어날 수 있다는 경제학 이론에 대해 설명하는 글이므로, '공짜 점심의 개념'이 의미하는 것으로 가장 적절한 것은 ③ '사회적 비용의 최소화를 통해 어떤 것을 무료로 제공하는 것'이다.

오답노트

① 합법적으로 누군가에게 주어지는 무료 식사
② 타인에게 부담을 주면서 혜택을 누리는 것
④ 사회를 좀 더 효율적으로 조직하여 성장을 가져오는 것
⑤ 경제학자들과 정책 입안자들의 핵심적인 정책을 담은 자료

13 ④

문제해설

독창성의 부재가 창의성의 부족 탓이 아니며, 분석 결과가 보여 주듯이 참신한 생각은 부족하지 않지만 수많은 창의적 생각을 제대로 선별하지 못하는 오류가 결국 독창성의 부재로 이어진다는 내용의 글이므로, 글의 요지로 가장 적절한 것은 ④이다.

14 ⑤

문제해설

⑤ while 부사절에서 삽입구인 setting in their ways는 내용상 '그들의 방식에 정착되어'라는 수동의 의미이므로, 현재분사 setting을 과거분사 set으로 고쳐야 한다.

오답노트

① '~을 시도하면서'라는 의미로 명사 anthropologists를 수식하는 분사구문이므로 attempting은 적절하다.
② now는 '현재'를 가리키는 말이 아니라, 밀알이 모래에 던져진 그 상황을 뜻하여 '자, 이제' 혹은 '그런데' 정도의 의미로 쓰여 과거의 상황이지만 사실적 진리를 언급하므로 is는 적절하다.
③ than에 의해 연결된 비교 대상이 명사구 such an effort이므로 동

명사 eating은 적절하다.
④ 선행사가 the fact인 목적격 관계대명사 that은 적절하다.

15 ①

문제해설

지배적 단일 언어 사용자가 제2외국어를 습득하려 할 때 흔히 본인의 소질이 없음을 탓하지만, 실제 그 본질에는 지배적 언어에 대한 우월감이 있으며 이것은 사회적 우위와 관습이 배경에 있다는 내용의 글이므로, 글의 제목으로 가장 적절한 것은 ① '정말로 무엇이 다중 언어 학습을 방해하는가?'이다.

오답노트

② 단일 언어 학습자가 가지는 문제적 세계관
③ 지배적 단일 언어로의 회귀와 사회 안전성
④ 언어 학습과 소질 사이의 관계
⑤ 사회적 지배성과 관습이 태도에 끼치는 영향

16 ④

문제해설

불행의 원인에 대해 심사숙고하지 않고 자신을 짜증 나고 성가시게 만드는 사소한 것들만 생각하면서 그 사실조차 인지하지 못하는 부정적인 생각의 희생자에 관한 글이므로, 글의 주제로 가장 적절한 것은 ④ '끊임없이 부정적으로 생각하는 것이 감정에 미치는 영향'이다.

오답노트

① 부정적인 생각이 사람들을 화나게 만드는 방식
② 정신과 의사와의 상담이 필요한 이유
③ 생각하는 것과 심사숙고하는 것의 차이
⑤ 스트레스 관리를 위한 분노 조절의 중요성

17 ②

문제해설

사회의 도시화와 가정이 덜 다세대화되면서 고령자들의 외로움 지수가 상승하고 사회적 상호 작용의 기회가 점점 감소하는 상황 개선에 로봇이 일조할 수 있다는 내용의 글이다. 따라서 '신체적 활동의 감소는 우울증으로 이어져 정신 질환 치료의 국가적 비용을 가중한다.'는 내용의 ②는 글의 전체 흐름과 관계가 없다.

18 ②

문제해설

영화 제작 시 어떤 주제를 선정하여 몇 가지 초안을 만든 후, 그중 하나가 선정되어 시나리오 작업을 거치게 되는데, 이때 좋은 시나리오조차도 다시 제작 과정에서 변경되는 일이 많다는 내용이므로, ② '종종 나중에 변경이 되는 영화 제작 과정의 초기 단계'가 글의 주제로 가장 적절하다.

오답노트

① 시나리오들이 복잡한 내용을 가지는 이유
③ 영화감독이 시나리오 창작에 포함되어야 하는 이유
④ 영화의 제작자와 감독의 다른 시각
⑤ 초안과 시나리오가 최종 영화와 달라지게 되는 과정

19 ④

문제해설

현재 이전의 세대들이 건설해 온 사고 체계에 기반해서 현재 세대가 사고 결정을 내리고 있으며, 마치 체스 게임에서 난쟁이 체스 달인이 꼭두각시를 통해 경기 내용에 영향을 끼치듯이 과거 세대의 사고 체계가 현재 사고를 움직인다는 내용의 글이므로, ④가 글의 요지로 가장 적절하다.

20 ④

문제해설

'엔터테인먼트'라는 어휘의 본질적인 의미가 즐거움에 있으며, 그 사업에 종사하는 사람들에게 가장 중요한 가치 또한 청중의 즐거움이라는 내용의 글이므로, 글의 제목으로 가장 적절한 것은 ④ '엔터테인먼트 사업의 본질'이다.

오답노트

① 영화 속에 감춰진 메시지
② 영화 산업의 숙명
③ 대중의 목표: 즐거움 추구
⑤ 엔터테인먼트 산업의 다각화

21 ③

문제해설

의식은 유전적으로 촉발되어 행해지게 되는 일종의 메시지로서, 의식을 통하여 한 개체가 사회적 혹은 생물학적 단계로 전환하게 된다는 내용이며, 거의 모든 동물이 아닌 많은 척추동물 종들이 이러한 의식을 행한다고 했으므로, ③은 글의 내용과 일치하지 않는다.

22 ③

문제해설

대부분의 사람은 어려움을 긍정적인 생각으로 극복하고 그 속에서 오히려 더 성장한다는 내용이므로, '정신적 외상이 대체로 부정적인 영향을 가지고 있다는 (A) 널리 퍼진 믿음에도 불구하고, 대부분의 사람은 (B) 강화된 기상(정신)으로 결국은 난관에서 벗어난다.'와 같이 요약하는 것이 가장 적절하다.

오답노트

(A)		(B)
① 지배적인	……	활동적인
② 강력한	……	관대한
④ 이성적인	……	긍정적인
⑤ 건설적인	……	생기가 회복된

23 ③

전 세계 기아 문제가 비효율적인 농사법, 불균형적인 음식 낭비 등에 있다고 주장하는 내용의 글이므로, '나머지 3분의 2를 차지하는 땅 대부분은 주거 지역과 같은 다른 용도로 사용되며, 이는 환경 오염 수치를 증가시키고 있다.'라는 내용의 ③은 전체 글의 흐름과 관계가 없다.

24 ⑤

사회의 일부가 다른 사람들의 부담이나 이익을 위해 희생당하는 불균형을 유발하기 때문에 소위 '공짜 점심'과 같은 무료에 가까운 재화나 서비스의 이용은 불가능하다는 과거 경제학에 반해, 현대의 경제학은 더 효율적인 방식을 활용하여 가장 적은 희생(최소 비용)으로 사회를 더 부유하고 행복하게 만들 것을 목표로 하고 있다고 했으므로, 글의 요지로 가장 적절한 것은 ⑤이다.

25 (1) the Segway, a two-wheeled, self-balancing personal transporter
(2) *Seinfeld*, an American sitcom television series

문제해설

참신한 아이디어 선택의 긍정 오류와 부정 오류의 예는 글의 후반부인 The Segway, a two-wheeled, self-balancing personal transporter, ~ ultimately flourished.에 나타나 있다.

26 (A) insufficiency (B) attractive

문제해설

세상에 독창성이 부재하는 이유는 참신한 아이디어의 부족이 아니라 참신한 아이디어를 선택하는 데 탁월한 사람들의 부족 때문이라는 내용의 글이므로, '우리 주변의 세계에서 독창성이 부재하는 이유는 기발한 생각의 (A) 부족 때문이 아니라 (B) 마음을 끄는 기발한 생각을 선택하는 재능을 가진 사람들이 부족하기 때문이다.'와 같이 요약하는 것이 가장 적절하다.

27 such an effort might even expend more energy than eating the collected wheat would provide

문제해설

'그런 노력'은 〈such a(n)+(형용사)+명사〉의 어순으로 쓰고, '~보다 더 많은 에너지가 쓰일지도 모른다'는 might even expend more energy than으로 쓴다. than 뒤에 '모은 밀을 먹음으로써 얻는 것'에 해당하는 표현을 이어 쓴다.

28 it appeared that the younger monkeys grasped the importance of her discovery

문제해설

〈appear to-v〉 구문을 〈it appears that+주어+동사 ~〉로 바꿔 쓰면, 시제가 과거이므로 it appeared that 뒤에 주어인 the younger monkeys를 쓰고, to grasp을 과거 동사인 grasped로 쓴다.

29 (1) ① → indicates (2) ② → involved
(3) ⑤ → safe

문제해설

① The fact that ~ competence가 주어인 문장의 본동사 자리이므로 분사 indicating을 시제와 수에 맞게 현재형 indicates로 고쳐야 한다.
② 앞의 the difficulties를 수식하는 분사로, '관련된' 어려움이라는 수동의 의미가 적절하므로 현재분사 involving을 과거분사 involved로 고쳐야 한다.
⑤ made로 시작하는 분사구가 a world를 수식하는 구조로, '안전해지는' 세상이라는 의미를 나타낸다. 밑줄 친 부분은 a world를 보충 설명하는 보어 자리이므로 부사 safely를 형용사 safe로 고쳐야 한다.

③ '~을 수반하다'라는 의미의 〈be accompanied by〉 구문이므로 accompanied는 적절하다.
④ a deeply held conviction과 동격인 절을 이끄는 명사절 접속사 that은 적절하다.

30 aptitude

문제해설

'무언가를 잘 하게 하는 것을 쉽게 만들어 주는 타고난 능력'이라는 의미의 단어는 aptitude(소질, 적성)이다.

31 그의 부정적인 생각이 부정적인 느낌과 감정을 만들어 내고 있었는데, 자신이 그것을 생각하고 있다는 것조차 알지 못했기 때문이다.

문제해설

그 신사가 어떻게 본인이 스스로 하는 생각의 희생자가 되었는지는 His negative thoughts were creating his negative feelings ~ didn't even know he was thinking them.에 나타나 있다.

32 nearly all of his time thinking about the little things that irritated and annoyed him

문제해설

'~하는 데 시간·돈을 쓰다'는 〈spend+시간·돈+v-ing〉 구문을 사용해서 나타내고, '자신을 짜증 나고 성가시게 하는 사소한 것들'은 선행사 the little things뒤에 관계대명사 that이 이끄는 절을 써서 나타낸다.

33 Greater numbers of the elderly now live alone.

문제해설

사회가 더욱 도시화되고 가정이 덜 다세대화되면서 어떤 일이 발생했는지는 greater numbers of the elderly now live alone에 나타나 있다.

34 ③ → isolation

문제해설

많은 수의 고령자가 혼자 살게 되어 사회적 상호 작용의 기회가 감소하는 상황에서, 로봇과의 상호 작용은 사회적 고립의 영향을 완전히 치료하는 것까지는 아니더라도 그에 대응할 기회를 제공한다는 내용이 문맥상 자연스럽다. 따라서 ③의 connection(연결, 관련성)을 isolation(고립)과 같은 말로 바꿔야 한다.

35 a good scenario of *October*

문제해설

밑줄 친 it이 가리키는 내용은 바로 앞의 There is a good scenario of *October* (*Ten Days That Shook the World*) written by Eisenstein himself에 나타나 있다.

36 the same film as, critical modifications

문제해설

수차례의 변경을 통해 영화가 제작된다는 내용의 글로, '영화 제작 과정에서 트리트먼트와 시나리오의 중요한 수정은 피할 수 없기 때문에 우리는 첫 번째 트리트먼트 또는 시나리오에 제시된 것과 똑같은 영화를 거의 볼 수 없다.'와 같이 요약하는 것이 적절하다.

37 Past events are compressed in images and metaphors which determine our present thinking

문제해설

'~ 속에 압축된다'는 be compressed in으로 나타내고, '우리의 현재 사고를 결정하는 이미지와 은유'는 선행사 images and metaphors 뒤에 〈관계대명사+동사+목적어〉의 어순으로 써서 문장을 완성한다.

38 (A) controlled (B) effect

문제해설

체스를 두는 꼭두각시를 조종하는 난쟁이처럼, 과거 세대의 사고 체계가 현재의 사고와 결정에 영향을 준다는 내용의 글로, '체스 탁자에 앉아 있는 꼭두각시를 (A) 조종하는 난쟁이처럼, 이전 세대들의 사고방식은 우리의 현재 매일의 생활과 의사 결정에 숨은 (그렇지만 끊임없는) (B) 영향을 미친다.'와 같이 요약하는 것이 적절하다.

39 (A) remains (B) challenging (C) that

문제해설

(A) The notion이 주어인 문장의 본동사 자리이므로 단수 동사 remains로 고쳐야 한다.
(B) as opposed to는 '~와 대조적으로'라는 의미로 전치사 to 뒤에는 동명사가 와야 한다. 따라서 challenge를 challenging으로 고쳐야 한다.
(C) signaling의 목적어로 쓰인 명사절을 이끄는 접속사 자리로 뒤에 완벽한 문장이 이어지고 있으므로 what을 명사절 접속사 that으로 고쳐야 한다.

40 that are categorized under, have been written and produced with the intention of making

문제해설

'~으로 분류되는'은 관계대명사 that 뒤에 수동태 are categorized under로 나타낸다. '~을 만들려는 의도에서 쓰이고 제작되었다'는 현재완료 시제의 수동태 〈have been+p.p.〉와 〈with the intention of+v-ing〉로 나타낸다.

41 the male's zigzag courtship dance

문제해설

수컷 짝을 자신의 둥지로 유인하는 것을 가능하게 하는 큰가시고기의 의식이 무엇인지는 among the three-spined stickleback fish, the male's zigzag courtship dance, ~ to his nest에 나타나 있다.

42 transformation

문제해설

'완전히 다른 어떤 사람이나 무언가로의 변화 또는 이것이 발생되는 과정'
이라는 의미의 단어는 transformation(변환, 전환)이다.

43 (1) ③ → to mistakenly expect
(2) ④ → being exposed (3) ⑤ → that

문제해설

③ 동사 cause는 목적격 보어로 to부정사를 취하므로 expect를 to
expect로 고쳐야 하는데, 이처럼 부사가 있는 경우 부사는 to와 동사원
형 사이에 들어가야 하므로 to mistakenly expect로 고쳐야 한다.
④ 끔찍한 사건에 (사람들이) '노출된'이라는 수동의 의미를 나타내야 하므
로 exposing을 동명사 수동태 being exposed로 고쳐야 한다.
⑤ '매우 …해서 ~하다'라는 의미의 〈so ~ that …〉 구문으로 which를
that으로 고쳐야 한다.

오답노트

① 비교급을 강조하여 '훨씬'이라는 의미를 나타내는 far는 적절하다.
② 동사 made의 목적격 보어 자리로 형용사 tolerant는 적절하다.

44 (A) suffer from (B) adversities

문제해설

정신적 외상을 겪은 대부분의 사람이 끔찍한 사건으로부터 부정적인 영향
을 받을 것으로 예상하지만, 이들은 오히려 더 강한 사람으로 성장하게 된
다는 내용의 글로, '일반적으로, 대부분의 사람이 끔찍한 사건을 겪은 후에
정신적 외상으로 (A) 고통을 받는다고 여겨지지만, 사실상 그들은 삶에서
의 (B) 역경들에 대항해서 결국에는 더 강해지게 된다.'와 같이 요약하는
것이 가장 적절하다.

45 중국은 미국의 3배 인구를 가지고 있고 경작지 면적은 6분
의 1에 불과해서 그 주민들이 더 효율적으로 작물을 재배해
야 하기 때문이다.

문제해설

중국과 미국의 크기가 거의 같을지라도 중국이 미국보다 훨씬 더 높은 농
작물 수확량을 거두는 이유는 even though the two countries are
comparable in size, ~ has to grow crops more efficiently에
나타나 있다.

46 to keep all of the hungry people in the world fed

문제해설

'~을 먹여 살리기에'는 enough food를 수식하는 형용사적 용법의 to
부정사를 활용해서 〈to keep+목적어+목적격 보어〉로 나타낸다. 목적어
all of the hungry people in the world가 '먹여지는'이라는 수동의
의미이므로 feed의 과거분사 fed를 쓰는 것에 유의한다.

47 counterproductive

문제해설

'자신이 의도한 것과 반대되는 결과를 갖게 되는'이라는 의미의 단어는
counterproductive(역효과를 낳는)이다.

48 우리의 가장 적은 희생으로 우리가 더 부유하게, 그리고 잘
만 되면 더 행복하게 만들어 주는 것

문제해설

밑줄 친 Such a utopia가 가리키는 내용은 앞 문장의 Economics
aims to show ~ thereby making us richer and, hopefully,
happier, with the least amount of sacrifice on our part.에
나타나 있다.

14강

1번 ——————————————— p.226

• Word Test

1 전화번호부에 올라 있지 않은 2 방법 3 무작위로
4 무심결에, 무의식적으로 5 동일하게 6 통계학
7 전화번호부 8 의심하는 9 population 10 select
11 bias 12 landline 13 psychological
14 favour 15 sampling 16 random

유형 1

❶ difference ❷ in which
❸ unconsciously ❹ different from

유형 2

❶ to participate ❷ being selected ❸ sounds
❹ be included ❺ being

유형 3

❶ participate in the study ❷ in everyday use
❸ an equally likely chance ❹ as easy as it sounds
❺ in some important way

2번 ——————————————— p.228

• Word Test

1 제시하다, 나타내다, 보여 주다 2 유사하다 3 두드러진, 뚜렷한
4 분석(pl. analyses) 5 두다, 위치시키다 6 ~을 나타내다,
~을 보여 주다 7 ~과 비교하여 8 정하다, 배정하다, 부여하다
9 status 10 dominant 11 consistent
12 gender bias 13 increasingly 14 respective
15 spatial 16 indicate

유형 1

❶ that ❷ consistent ❸ by where
❹ however

유형 2

❶ appear ❷ facing ❸ displayed
❹ are situated ❺ pronounced

유형 3

❶ facing to the right ❷ relative to men
❸ In other words ❹ gender bias
❺ women's role in society

3번 ——————————————— p.230

• Word Test

1 표시 가격 2 지역 3 장소에 따른, 위치 선정의 4 지역 주민
5 부족한, 적은 6 요컨대 7 가격 차별(동등한 원가의 상품을
구매자에 따라 다른 값에 파는 일) 8 trap 9 frequent
10 actually 11 destination 12 include 13 deal
14 souvenir

유형 1

❶ where ❷ A few ❸ scarce
❹ lower

유형 2

❶ frequented ❷ to find ❸ attempting
❹ spent

유형 3

❶ areas most frequented ❷ find better deals
❸ as part of ❹ In sum
❺ price discrimination

4번 ——————————————— p.232

• Word Test

1 수반하는 2 명망, 명성 3 같은 이유로 4 지시하다, 지휘하다
5 쏟다, 바치다 6 노력하다 7 확보하다 8 성취
9 영향을 미치다 10 인구, 주민 11 struggle
12 esteem 13 entertainer 14 effectively
15 reward 16 protein 17 in general 18 link
19 fellow 20 decade

유형 1

❶ how ❷ what ❸ linking
❹ It ❺ increase

유형 2

❶ to influence ❷ are found ❸ securing
❹ to devote ❺ defeating

유형 3

❶ desire for esteem ❷ in general
❸ in the hope of ❹ By the same token

—————————————————— p.234

01 ① 02 ② 03 ① 04 ② 05 ④ 06 ①
07 ④ 08 ⑤ 09 (A) to participate
(B) unconsciously (C) Picking[To pick]
10 무작위 표본에서 모집단의 모든 구성원이 연구를 위해 선택될
가능성이 똑같이 있을 법한 것 11 consistent
12 have been assigned to their respective place by
where they are situated 13 ② sufficient → scarce
14 If the time spent in searching and shopping for
the best deals is included 15 (1) ② → (to) reward
(2) ④ → struggling (3) ⑤ → the population can
devote 16 (A) useful (B) desire

01 ①

문제해설

연구에 있어 무작위 표본 추출에 대해 설명하는 내용으로, 빈칸 앞에서 '무
작위'라는 말의 의미가 일상에서와 연구 방법에서 차이가 있음을 밝히고

있고, 빈칸 뒤에서는 연구 방법에서 무작위가 쉽지 않은 이유에 대해 설명하고 있으므로, 빈칸에 들어갈 말로 가장 적절한 것은 ① '선택될 가능성이 똑같이 있을 법하다'이다.

오답노트

② 부당한 행동에 대해 공동으로 책임을 진다
③ 어떤 종류의 개인 정보가 사용될 것인지 통보를 받는다
④ 실험 이외의 사람들과 접촉하지 않는다
⑤ 그들의 민족적 배경에 대한 편견 없이 선발된다

02 ②

문제해설

(A) being이 생략된 독립 분사구문으로, 보어로 쓰인 형용사 relative가 적절하다.
(B) 전치사 by 뒤의 장소를 나타내는 간접의문문이므로, 의문사 where가 적절하다.
(C) 분사구문 자리로 의미상 주어는 주절의 내용이므로, 〈관계대명사(which)+be동사〉가 생략된 형태이다. 앞 부분의 절의 내용이 주어와 능동의 관계가 되어야 하므로 현재분사 paralleling이 적절하다.

03 ①

문제해설

관광객이 자주 찾는 지역은 다른 곳보다 가격이 높지만, 더 저렴한 식당이나 기념품을 찾는 데 소비되는 시간이 가격에 포함된다고 가정하면 관광지의 가격이 대부분 관광객들에게 더 낮다고 언급하고 있으므로, 마지막 요약 문장은 장소에 따른 가격 차이가 사실상 없다는 내용이 되어야 한다. 따라서 빈칸에 들어갈 말로 가장 적절한 것은 ① '일반적으로 가격 차별로 여겨지지 않는다'이다.

오답노트

② 여행 패키지의 품질에 반영되지 않는다
③ 여행자들에게 지방에서 더 많은 돈을 쓰도록 장려한다
④ 여행사 직원을 관광지의 외부 지역으로 데리고 간다
⑤ 관광객들이 대폭적으로 가격 할인을 받는 것을 금지한다

04 ②

문제해설

빈칸 앞에서 존경에 대한 욕구는 행동 방식에 영향을 미치게 하고 명망은 문화에 기여한 사람들을 인정하고 보상하기 위해 사용된다고 했으며, 빈칸이 있는 문장에서는 명망과 존경을 특정 활동 및 성취와 연결시킴으로써 문화가 할 수 있는 바를 묻고 있다. 빈칸 뒤에서는 문화적 요구 상황에 명망을 사용하여 사람들의 에너지를 쏟게 만드는 예시가 이어지므로, 빈칸에 들어갈 말로 가장 적절한 것은 ② '많은 사람이 자신의 에너지를 그 방면으로 쏟게 하다'이다.

오답노트

① 사람들에게 특정한 권한을 위해 임무를 수행하도록 명령하다
③ 사람들이 기본적인 인간의 생리적 욕구에 탐닉하는 것을 막다
④ 당면한 위기에 사람들을 둔감하게 만들기 위해 사람들의 에너지의 방향을 바꾸다
⑤ 그것의 적극적인 참가자들 간의 생존 경쟁을 완화하다

05 ④

문제해설

연구에 있어 무작위 표본 추출에 대해 설명하는 내용으로, 빈칸 앞에서 '무작위'라는 말의 의미가 일상에서와 달리 모든 사람이 연구를 위해 선택될 가능성이 똑같이 있으며, 이러한 의미는 무의식적으로 작용하는 편애와 편견들에 의해서 실현하기 어렵다고 설명하고 있으므로, 글의 제목으로 가장 적절한 것은 ④ '임의적이 아닌 동등한 무작위 표본 추출'이다.

오답노트

① 일상 대화에서의 편견
② 마케팅 연구의 무작위 시험
③ 표본 추출에서 오류를 줄이는 방법
⑤ 사람들을 수치로 다루지 않는 것의 중요성

06 ①

문제해설

빈칸을 포함한 첫 번째 문장에 이어서 수백 점의 그림을 분석한 바에 따르면 오른쪽에 위치한 사람이 더 우월하고 유력한 사람이고, 덜 주도적으로 여겨진 여성이 왼쪽 뺨을 보인다고 설명하고 있다. 또한 공간상 위치에 의해 그림에서 각각 지위가 정해졌다는 내용이 이어지고 있으므로, 빈칸에 들어갈 말로 가장 적절한 것은 ① '사회적 지위를 나타내다'이다.

오답노트

② 행동이 전개되는 장소를 결정하다
③ 사회적 욕구의 계층을 제시하다
④ 사회 운동의 특징을 반영하다
⑤ 언어의 성 중립성을 잘 보여 주다

07 ④

문제해설

관광객이 자주 찾는 지역은 다른 곳보다 가격이 높지만, 더 저렴한 가격을 찾는 데 소비되는 시간이 가격에 포함된다고 가정하면 관광지의 가격이 대부분 관광객들에게 더 낮아서 지역별 가격 차이가 가격 차별은 아니라는 내용이므로, 글의 제목으로 가장 적절한 것은 ④ '비싸지만 저렴한 여행지 가격'이다.

오답노트

① 여행하는 동안 비싼 가격을 피하는 방법
② 거주자들 사이의 비밀: 지역 전용 가격
③ 여행지의 가격이 비싼 이유
⑤ 비수기 관광객을 위한 저렴한 가격

08 ⑤

문제해설

존경에 대한 욕구는 사람들의 행동 방식에 영향을 미치도록 사회에 의해 사용될 수 있으며, 명망은 문화에 유용한 일을 한 사람들을 인정하고 보상하기 위해 사용된다는 내용의 글이므로, 글의 요지로 가장 적절한 것은 ⑤이다.

09 (A) to participate (B) unconsciously
  (C) Picking[To pick]

문제해설

(A) '참여할'이라는 의미로 the people을 수식하는 형용사적 용법의 to부정사 to participate로 고쳐야 한다.
(B) 동사 favour를 수식하는 자리이므로 형용사 unconscious를 부사 unconsciously로 고쳐야 한다.
(C) 본동사 means가 뒤에 있으므로 means 앞에는 주어 자리에 맞는 동명사나 to부정사가 적절하다. 따라서 Pick을 Picking 또는 To pick으로 고쳐야 한다.

10 무작위 표본에서 모집단의 모든 구성원이 연구를 위해 선택될 가능성이 똑같이 있을 법한 것

문제해설

밑줄 친 that이 가리키는 내용은 바로 앞 문장의 in which every member of the population has an equally likely chance ~ the study에 나타나 있다.

11 consistent

문제해설

'유사하거나 같은 목적을 갖고 있는 진술 또는 아이디어를 포함하는'이라는 의미의 단어는 consistent(일치하는)이다.

12 have been assigned to their respective place by where they are situated

문제해설

'각각의 지위가 정해졌다'는 '(사람을) 배치하다'라는 의미의 동사 assign을 활용해서 현재완료 수동태 have been assigned를 쓰고 이어서 to their respective place를 쓴다. '그들이 공간상 놓이는 위치에 의해'는 전치사 by 다음에 관계부사절을 이끄는 where를 쓰고, 그들이 '놓이는' 수동의 의미이므로 수동태 are situated로 써서 문장을 완성한다.

13 ② sufficient → scarce

문제해설

대부분의 관광객들은 관광객이 많지 않은 곳에서 더 좋은 거래를 찾으러 다니지는 않을 것인데, 그 이유는 더 싼 기념품 등을 관광지 밖에서 애써 찾기 위해 자신의 부족한 휴가 시간을 쓰는 것이 이득이 되지 않기 때문이라는 내용이 문맥상 자연스럽다. 따라서 ②의 sufficient(풍부한)를 scarce(부족한)와 같은 말로 바꿔야 한다.

14 If the time spent in searching and shopping for the best deals is included

문제해설

조건의 접속사 If 뒤에 주어인 '~하는 데 소비된 시간'은 the time과 이를 수동의 의미로 수식하는 과거분사구 〈spent in+v-ing〉로 나타낸다. '~의 일부로 포함된다'는 현재시제 수동태 is included로 나타낸다.

15 (1) ② → (to) reward (2) ④ → struggling
  (3) ⑤ → the population can devote

문제해설

② is used 뒤의 to부정사 to recognize와 and로 병렬 연결된 형태이므로 rewarding을 (to) reward로 고쳐야 한다.
④ small societies를 '생존을 위해 애쓰는'이라는 능동의 의미로 수식하는 것이 적절하므로 struggled를 현재분사 struggling으로 고쳐야 한다.
⑤ 의문사절은 〈의문사+주어+동사〉의 어순으로 써야 하므로 how much time and money 뒤에 주어 the population과 동사구 can devote를 써야 한다.

오답노트

① 주어 The desire for esteem이 '사용될 수 있다'는 수동의 의미를 나타내므로 수동태인 can be used는 적절하다.
③ 전치사구 in the hope of 뒤의 동명사 securing은 적절하다.

16 (A) useful (B) desire

문제해설

사람들은 존경과 명망을 얻기 위한 욕구로 자신이 소속된 사회나 문화에서 유용하다고 여겨지는 일을 한다는 내용의 글이므로, '사회는 명망과 존경에 대한 사람들의 (B) 욕구를 이용해서 사람들로 하여금 그것(사회)이 (A) 유용하다고 여기는 것들을 이루게 한다.'와 같이 요약하는 것이 적절하다.

15강

1번 ——————————————— p.240

• Word Test

1 신경학의, 신경의　2 앞뒤로, 왔다갔다 하는　3 문설주, 문기둥
4 (결과적으로) ~하게 하다　5 (문 따위를) 쾅 닫다
6 ~까지 이르다　7 대개　8 유물론의, 물질주의의
9 collision　10 state　11 frame of mind
12 offended　13 rock　14 trace
15 cause and effect　16 term

유형 1

❶ collision　❷ to　❸ Neither
❹ that　❺ normally

유형 2

❶ asking　❷ giving　❸ leading
❹ causing　❺ being offended

유형 3

❶ resulted in
❷ the chain of causes and effects
❸ the state of being offended
❹ in neurological terms

2번 ——————————————— p.242

• Word Test

1 유교　2 친밀감　3 열정적인　4 개인주의적인
5 집단주의 문화　6 추정하다　7 인류학　8 소중히 여기다
9 보편적 특성　10 evidence　11 commitment
12 component　13 priority　14 propose
15 emphasis　16 concept　17 in contrast
18 passion

유형 1

❶ this　❷ however
❸ those　❹ prized

유형 2

❶ are　❷ including　❸ found
❹ judging　❺ is

유형 3

❶ vary across cultures　❷ take priority over
❸ compete with　❹ the mountains of

3번 ——————————————— p.244

• Word Test

1 말 그대로　2 상호 작용　3 ~을 구성하다　4 환경
5 얻다, 이루다　6 과정의, 절차의　7 사실, 정말로
8 ~에 미치지 못하다, 미흡하다　9 personhood　10 ideal
11 generosity　12 denial　13 philosopher
14 maintain　15 ongoing　16 regain

유형 1

❶ Indeed　❷ be earned　❸ that
❹ A number of　❺ during

유형 2

❶ is　❷ attained　❸ thought
❹ have failed　❺ be achieved

유형 3

❶ takes this position　❷ refer to
❸ a fully human person　❹ fall short of

4번 ——————————————— p.247

• Word Test

1 고도　2 양　3 위험　4 습한　5 생계를 유지하다
6 수요　7 (작은 산이나 언덕의) 비탈　8 specific
9 commodity　10 supply　11 in high demand
12 rainfall　13 specialize in　14 tropical

유형 1

❶ For example　❷ these　❸ specializing
❹ which　❺ because

유형 2

❶ be grown　❷ are sold　❸ creates
❹ selling

유형 3

❶ in large quantities
❷ higher mountain elevations
❸ bring in a lot of money　❹ make a living from

5번 ——————————————— p.249

• Word Test

1 철학　2 현상　3 일관성 있는　4 느닷없이
5 예측할 수 없는　6 정립하다　7 가정　8 사물의 체계
9 공백　10 방해하다, 중단시키다　11 터무니없는, 황당한
12 연구　13 impression　14 chaos　15 randomly
16 founding　17 vague　18 periodically
19 disaster　20 logic　21 agriculture
22 random　23 saying　24 order

유형 1

❶ investigation　❷ ancient　❸ which
❹ unpredictable　❺ meaningless

유형 2

❶ have had　❷ be explained　❸ interrupted
❹ placed　❺ have gone

유형 3

❶ out of the blue　❷ in a cultural vacuum
❸ side by side　❹ beyond this vague notion

6번 _____ p.251

● Word Test

1 소심한, 소극적인   2 ~의 본보기가 되다   3 ~의 기간 내에
4 습득   5 (말소리를 기호로) 표기하다   6 ~을 나타내다[상징하다]
7 개혁; 개혁하다   8 ~이 아니게 되다   9 systematically
10 drastically   11 get rid of   12 fixed
13 irregular   14 adopt   15 simplify
16 absurdity

유형 1

❶ fixed   ❷ little   ❸ whose
❹ irregular   ❺ absurdity

유형 2

❶ be avoided   ❷ writing
❸ have been taken   ❹ have   ❺ sets

유형 3

❶ easily get rid of   ❷ eats up
❸ along the same lines   ❹ in the space of one year

_____ p.253

01 ①   02 ⑤   03 ④   04 ③   05 ①   06 ④
07 ②   08 ②   09 ①   10 ①   11 ④   12 ②
13 ② → giving   ⑤ → being offended
14 Neither do we expect to hear a report, causing his movements   15 it is the passionate side of love that is prized in this culture
16 (A) collectivistic   (B) individualistic
17 (A) means   (B) that   (C) expected
18 I would argue that the fact that personhood must be earned   19 ④ → drops
20 특정 품목에 대한 전 세계적인 수요가 있기 때문에
21 (1) ③ → from which[where]   (2) ④ → interrupted
22 (A) the product of many ancient traditions
(B) the physical universe   23 many other useless redundancies whose acquisition eats up many years of childhood   24 irregular

01 ①

문제해설

우리가 다른 사람들의 행동에 대해 왜라는 질문을 할 때, 우리가 결국 듣고 싶어 하는 것은 그들의 행동에 대한 이유라고 설명하고 있다. 예를 들어 John이 왜 문을 쾅 닫았냐는 질문을 할 때는 그가 화가 나서 그랬다와 같은 이유를 요구하고 기대한다는 것이다. 따라서 글의 제목으로 가장 적절한 것은 ① '이유를 묻는 진정한 목적'이다.

오답노트

② 놀라움: 행동의 주요 원인
③ 질문의 의도를 정확히 아는 방법
④ 일상생활에서 항상 이유를 물어야 할 필요성
⑤ 원인과 결과를 정확히 밝혀내는 것의 중요성

02 ⑤

문제해설

Sternberg가 제안한 사랑의 구성 요소가 문화적으로 보편적인 특성이 있는 반면에 문화 간의 차이에 따라 구성 요소가 강조되는 정도와 다른 구성 요소와의 관계가 상이하다는 예시를 나열하고 있는 글이다. 특히 헌신의 개념은 중국 유교 문화에서는 절대적이며 이와 대조적으로 북미 문화권에서는 사랑의 열정이 강조되고 있다는 문맥이 자연스러우므로 ⑤의 undervalued (과소평가된)을 prized (소중히 여겨지는)으로 바꿔야 한다.

03 ④

문제해설

'사람다움'이라는 과정은 공동체 안에서 다른 사람들과의 상호작용을 통해 소속되어있는 공동체에서 요구하는 이상과 규범을 충족해 가며 각자가 진행되어 가는 과정이라고 말하고 있으므로, 필자의 주장으로 가장 적절한 것은 ④이다.

04 ③

문제해설

Because there is a worldwide demand for specific items such as these, the farmers in tropical countries grow as much of these commodities as they can.에서 전 세계적인 수요가 있기 때문에 열대 국가의 농부들이 가능한 한 이 상품들을 많이 재배한다고 했으므로, 특정 지역의 수요를 충족하기 위해 열대지역에서 재배한다고 언급한 ③은 글의 내용과 일치하지 않는다.

05 ①

문제해설

뉴턴이나 갈릴레오 같은 초기 과학자들이 느닷없이 마법과 같이 과학을 불러낸 것이 아니라 고대의 많은 전통들의 산물들이었다는 내용으로, '문화적 공백에서'라는 말이 의미하는 바로 가장 적절한 것은 ③ '외부의 영향 없이'이다.

오답노트

② 고된 노력의 결과로
③ 문화적 편견 없이
④ 갑작스러운 발견으로
⑤ 축적된 지식으로

06 ④

문제해설

영어에서 각각의 음과 철자가 체계적으로 연결된다면 많은 철자 오류를 피할 수 있다는 내용으로 예를 들어 두 개의 음소 ks가 철자 그대로 사용된다면 x가 ks 발음을 내는 데 사용될 필요가 없다는 게 문맥상 자연스럽다. 따라서 ④의 necessary(필요한)는 unnecessary(불필요한)와 같은 말로 바꿔야 한다.

07 ②

문제해설

우리가 'John이 왜 문을 쾅 닫았나'라는 질문을 할 때, 정작 우리가 무엇

을 듣고 싶어하는지에 대한 질문을 첫 문장에 제시하고, 글의 중반에서 그 질문에 '그가 화가 났다'라는 이유를 요구하는 것이라고 답하고 있다. 본문에 나열된 다른 내용, 즉 그 행동에 대한 구체적인 분석이나 일련의 원인과 결과에 대한 보고 또는 그 원인을 신경학적 용어로 분석하는 것 등에는 관심이 없다는 내용을 설명하고 있으므로, 빈칸에 들어갈 말로 가장 적절한 것은 ② '그들의 이유에 대해 듣다'이다.

오답노트

① 다른 사람들의 환심을 얻다
③ 인과관계를 밝히다
④ 다른 사람들에 대한 관심을 보여주다
⑤ 신경학적인 논거를 발견하다

08 ②

문제해설

Sternberg가 제안한 사랑의 구성 요소가 모든 문화권에서 발견되는 보편적인 특성이지만, 각 구성 요소가 어떻게 강조되는지에 따라 문화마다 각 요소에 대한 강조가 다르다는 내용으로 이에 대한 예시를 들어 설명하고 있는 글이다. 따라서 however를 동반해서 문화권마다 다를 수 있다는 내용의 주어진 문장은 각 예시들 앞에 나오는 것이 자연스러우므로 가장 적절한 곳은 ②이다.

09 ①

문제해설

'사람다움'은 다른 사람들과의 상호작용을 통해 공동체에서 요구되는 이상과 규범을 충족해 가는 과정이고, 그 과정은 사람마다 각자의 생애주기와 환경에 따라 'a becoming (되어가는 일)'이라고 글의 후반부에 반복되고 있으므로 빈칸에 들어갈 말로 가장 적절한 것은 ① '진행 중인 과정'이다.

오답노트

② 달성할 수 없는 목표
③ 자발적인 습득
④ 의존적인 행동
⑤ 피할 수 없는 과정

10 ①

문제해설

동사 grow는 crops를 선행사로 하는 관계사절 that절 안에서 are in high demand와 병렬구조를 이루고, grow의 행위 주체인 crops와 수동의 의미이기 때문에 ① grow를 be grown으로 고쳐야 한다.

오답노트

② these는 specific items의 구체적인 설명을 위해 사용된 such as 뒤에 나온 대명사로서 앞 문장들에서 예시로 나열된 설탕, 커피, 차, 바나나를 지칭하고 있으므로 복수형 대명사 these는 적절하다.
③ These cash crops를 주어로 are sold all around the world와 병렬구조를 이루고 의미상 능동이므로 bring은 적절하다.
④ 앞 절에 언급된 내용인 수요보다 더 많은 공급을 만들어낸다는 부분을 가리키는 which는 적절하다.
⑤ quantities를 수식하고 있으므로 형용사 enough의 쓰임은 적절하다.

11 ④

문제해설

초기 과학자들이 신비로운 연구의 결과로 그들의 작업을 만들어낸 것이 아니라, 고대의 많은 전통 산물, 즉 그리스 철학이나 농업, 종교 등에 기반을 두고 있다는 내용이다. 그중에서 종교가 이야기하는 창조된 세계 질서에 대한 내용에서 우주는 무작위로 놓여진 무의미한 뒤범벅이 아니고 일관성 있는 사물의 체계이며 이것을 두고 자연에는 질서가 있다는 간단한 경구를 설명하는 문맥이므로 ④의 incoherent(일관성이 없는)는 coherent(일관성 있는)와 같은 말로 바꿔야 한다.

12 ②

문제해설

영어에서 체계적인 방식으로 각각의 음이 고정된 글자로 표기된다면 많은 철자 오류를 줄일 수 있으므로 이에 대한 철자 개혁의 필요성을 주장하는 내용의 글이므로, 글의 주제로 가장 적절한 것은 ② '영어 철자 오류를 줄이기 위한 제언'이다.

오답노트

① 미국인들이 철자 오류를 범하는 이유
③ 철자와 발음을 연결하는 어려움
④ 오류를 줄이는 교수 방법의 효과
⑤ 아이들 대상 철자 교육의 중요성

13 ② → giving ⑤ → being offended

문제해설

② 주어인 John의 동작을 설명하는 분사구문이므로, 현재분사 giving으로 고쳐야 한다.
⑤ '화가 난 상태'라는 수동의 의미이고 전치사 뒤에는 명사나 동명사를 써야 하므로 being offended로 고쳐야 한다.

오답노트

① Probably 앞에 It is가 생략된 형태로 문장의 주격 보어 역할을 하는 명사절을 이끄는 that은 적절하다.
③ 주어인 a report of the chain of causes and effects와 능동 관계이므로 분사구문에서 현재분사 leading을 쓰는 것은 적절하다.
④ a materialistic frame of mind와 동격을 이루는 명사절을 이끄는 접속사 that은 적절하다.

14 Neither do we expect to hear a report, causing his movements

문제해설

부정문인 앞 문장에 이어 '~도 또한 그러하다'라는 의미의 neither로 문장이 시작되므로 〈조동사+주어+동사〉의 형태로 문장을 완성하고, 목적어로 to부정사를 가지는 expect 다음에 to hear a report를 쓴다. 'John의[그의] 움직임을 유발한'은 능동의 의미이므로 현재분사 causing을 사용하여 causing his movements로 쓴다.

15 it is the passionate side of love that is prized in this culture

문제해설

〈it is ~ that ...〉 강조 구문을 사용하되, 문맥상 이 문화에서 소중히 여겨지는 '무엇'이 강조 대상이 되어야 하므로 the passionate side of love를 it is와 that 사이에 위치시키고 주어인 the passionate side of love가 '소중히 여겨지는' 것이므로 동사는 수동태가 되도록 is prized로 쓴다.

16 (A) collectivistic (B) individualistic

문제해설

사랑의 구성 요소와 관계 유형이 문화에 따라 다르다는 내용이므로, '사랑의 서로 다른 구성 요소 및 서로 다른 관계 유형에 대해 이루어지는 강조는 문화에 따라 달라지는데, (A) 집단주의 문화에서는 가족과의 관계를 종종 더 중요하게 생각하는 반면, (B) 개인주의 문화에서는 우정과 연인 관계가 종종 우선순위를 갖는다.'와 같이 요약하는 것이 가장 적절하다.

17 (A) means (B) that (C) expected

문제해설

(A) 주어 the 'processual' nature of personhood 뒤에 나오는 동사 자리이고, 변함 없는 사실에 대해 말하는 것이므로 현재분사 meaning을 현재형 동사 means로 고쳐야 한다.
(B) that personhood is an ongoing process ~와 the view는 동격 관계이므로 명사절의 접속사 that으로 고쳐야 한다.
(C) standards를 수식하는 분사구이고 온전한 인격체의 인간에게 '기대되는'이라는 수동의 의미가 되어야 하므로 현재분사 expecting을 과거분사 expected로 고쳐야 한다.

18 I would argue that the fact that personhood must be earned

문제해설

'나는 주장하고 싶다'는 I would argue 다음에 argue의 목적어 역할을 하는 접속사 that을 쓰고, '~이라는 사실'은 the fact와 동격의 명사절을 이끄는 접속사 that을 사용해서 문장을 만든다. '획득되어야' 한다는 수동의 의미이므로 earn을 be earned로 바꿔서 쓴다.

19 ④ → drops

문제해설

농부들이 특정 환금 작물을 너무 많이 재배할 경우, 그것이 수요보다 더 많은 공급을 만들어 내고 이는 상품 가격이 하락하는 결과를 가져오게 되므로, ④ rises(오르다)를 drops(떨어지다)와 같은 말로 바꿔 써야 한다.

20 특정 품목에 대한 전 세계적인 수요가 있기 때문에

문제해설

열대 국가의 농부들이 설탕, 커피, 차, 바나나와 같은 특정한 상품들을 재배하는 이유는 Because there is a worldwide demand for specific items such as these에 나타나 있다.

21 (1) ③ → from which[where]
　　(2) ④ → interrupted

문제해설

③ 뒤에 완전한 절이 이어지고 있고, 선행사 agriculture가 관계대명사

절에서 전치사 from의 목적어 역할을 해야 하므로 관계대명사 which를 〈전치사+관계대명사〉의 형태인 from which 또는 관계부사 where로 고쳐야 한다. learn from은 '~에서 배우다'라는 의미이다.
④ the cycles and rhythms of nature를 부가적으로 설명하는 분사구이고, '방해를 받는'이라는 수동의 의미이므로 interrupts를 과거분사 interrupted로 고쳐야 한다.

오답노트

① a small sect를 수식하는 관계대명사 that은 적절하다.
② Greek philosophy를 부연 설명하는 계속적 용법의 관계대명사 which는 적절하다.
⑤ 'A도 B도 둘 다 아닌'의 의미인 〈neither A nor B〉 구문이므로 nor는 적절하다.

22 (A) the product of many ancient traditions
　　(B) the physical universe

문제해설

(A)는 앞에서 언급된 'the product of many ancient traditions(고대의 많은 전통의 산물)', (B)는 'the physical universe(물리적인 우주)'를 가리킨다.

23 many other useless redundancies whose acquisition eats up many years of childhood

문제해설

many other useless redundancies를 먼저 쓴 후, '습득하는 데 수년의 유년 시절을'은 '그것의 습득'이라는 의미가 되도록 소유격 관계대명사 whose를 사용해서 whose acquisition으로 연결하고, '수년의 유년 시절'은 many years of를 사용하여 many years of childhood로 나타낸다.

24 irregular

문제해설

'평범한 또는 보통의; 통상의 규칙 또는 일반적인 관행을 따르지 않는'이라는 의미의 단어는 irregular(불규칙한)이다.

16강

1번 ——————————————————— p.262

• Word Test
1 양극화　2 결국 ~에 이르게 하다, ~을 야기[초래]하다
3 신중한　4 도전적인　5 개별적으로　6 ~하는 경향이 있다
7 극단적인; 극단적인 행위[수단/조처]　8 risky　9 advocate
10 responsible　11 occasionally　12 tendency
13 on one's own　14 strategy

유형 1
❶ extreme　❷ though　❸ towards
❹ that　❺ individually

유형 2
❶ makes　❷ are　❸ depends
❹ leads　❺ have made

유형 3
❶ tend to　❷ decide to take actions
❸ early on　❹ at an early stage

2번 ——————————————————— p.264

• Word Test
1 (일정한 방향으로) 향하게 하다, 이끌다　2 발전하다, 진화하다
3 산업화된　4 맞추다, 적응시키다　5 성숙한, 발달한
6 시장　7 전반적인　8 relatively　9 venture
10 commercial　11 stable　12 regulatory
13 precise　14 significant

유형 1
❶ tied　❷ those　❸ precise
❹ uninvolved　❺ expectations

유형 2
❶ is　❷ evolved　❸ were
❹ are　❺ means

유형 3
❶ closely tied to　❷ The same is true of
❸ government supported
❹ in steering the development

3번 ——————————————————— p.266

• Word Test
1 ~에서 분리되다　2 ~을 얻으려고 노력하다　3 논문, 기사
4 ~을 …으로 간주하다　5 핵심적인　6 확고부동한, 굳건한
7 후보(자)　8 description　9 replace
10 foundation　11 element　12 objective
13 apparently　14 neglect

유형 1
❶ that　❷ but　❸ objective
❹ whereas　❺ Apparently

유형 2
❶ is　❷ deny　❸ have found
❹ considered

유형 3
❶ by replacing facts with events
❷ strive for　❸ are detached from
❹ the best we can say

4번 ——————————————————— p.268

• Word Test
1 상당한　2 집중시키다　3 중앙 집권화된
4 ~으로 이어지다, (결과가) ~이 되다　5 의견, 조언　6 관행
7 당면한　8 전문 지식, 전문 기술　9 organization
10 impact　11 thus　12 investigate
13 participatory　14 necessarily　15 extent
16 performance

유형 1
❶ centralized　❷ more　❸ satisfaction
❹ Therefore　❺ effective

유형 2
❶ is shared　❷ are made　❸ improves
❹ has investigated　❺ is

유형 3
❶ differs across organizations
❷ necessarily translate into
❸ the task at hand　❹ in times of crisis

5번 ——————————————————— p.270

• Word Test
1 (생물의) 천연색, 채색　2 (주목 등을) 끌다　3 그 후, 뒤에
4 (~이 될) 가능성이 있는, 장래의　5 다양한
6 (눈에 보이게) 띠다[지니다]　7 수정, 수태, 비옥화
8 ~을 설명하다　9 (새로운 말을) 만들어 내다　10 맛이 고약함
11 비생식의　12 advertise　13 spectacular　14 prey
15 renewed　16 exaggerated　17 term
18 edible　19 expand　20 predator　21 identify
22 striking

유형 1
❶ constantly　❷ by　❸ for example
❹ experienced　❺ subsequently

유형 2
❶ has been　❷ are　❸ attacking
❹ expanded　❺ coined

유형 3

1 evolve via　2 account for　3 In a reply to　4 are predicted to gain

6번

p.273

• Word Test

1 형이상학적인　2 크게, 심하게　3 연관된, 동맹한
4 처음, 시작　5 일치, 조화; 주다　6 ~을 받다　7 과대평가하다
8 개념　9 교체할 수 있는　10 medieval　11 linguistics
12 scope　13 logical　14 considerable
15 statement　16 exaggerated　17 reason
18 emphasis

유형 1

1 so　2 but　3 whether
4 characteristic　5 overrated

유형 2

1 was accorded　2 was believed　3 was
4 was realized　5 be directed

유형 3

1 happened to be true　2 need to be subjected to
3 trust in the accord　4 from the outset

p.276

01 ⑤　02 ④　03 ②　04 ②　05 ④　06 ⑤
07 ④　08 ①　09 ④　10 ③　11 ③　12 ②

13 우리는 집단 속에 있을 때, 혼자서 행동하고 있는 경우에 책임을 져야 할 만큼의 개인적으로 책임이 있지는 않다고 생각하는 경향이 있기 때문이다.　14 (A) groups　(B) individuals

15 (A) tied　(B) those　(C) were　16 national

17 It is even considered a fact that certain events did not occur　18 Unlike facts, events are dated, tied to space and time, whereas facts are detached from space and time.　19 (1) ② → strongly　(2) ④ → does

20 has investigated when participatory decision making is most useful, when it is less important

21 성 선택이 박각시나방 애벌레에 속하는 비생식 유충의 눈에 뜨이는 색깔 패턴을 설명할 수 없다는 것　22 edible

23 it was believed that, of reality, of thought, so closely allied that

24 (A) a logical statement　(B) a true statement

01 ⑤

문제해설

집단이 내리는 결정이 때로는 도전적이고 안전하지 않은 방향으로, 때로는 너무 신중한 방향으로 쉽게 극단적이 될 수 있다는 내용이다. 따라서 글의 제목으로 가장 적절한 것은 ⑤ '집단의 의사결정: 양 끝으로 갈 수 있는'이다.

오답노트

① 효과적인 의사결정의 방법들

② 집단의 결정 대 개인의 결정
③ 집단의 의사를 모으는 비결
④ 중도적 의견이 집단에 필수적인가?

02 ④

문제해설

상업 매체가 발전하는 방식을 다룬 글로서, 많은 국가에서 정부 지원형으로 매체가 발전해 가고 있으며, 그에 따라 정부가 매체의 전개 방향을 잡아가는 데 관여를 피할 수 없다는 내용과 함께 텔레비전 방송 시스템이 완강하게 국가적이라는 Joseph Straubhaar의 평가를 인용하는 맥락이다. 따라서 '미디어가 진화하는 방식이 매우 다양하기 때문에 다양한 국가적 지원 방안이 모색되고 있으며, 미디어 경쟁으로 이어진다'는 ④가 글의 전체 흐름과 관계가 없다.

03 ②

문제해설

사람들이 사실이 사건과 같다고들 생각하는데 그렇게 생각하는 이유를 설명하고 두 개념이 서로 분명히 다른 개념임을 설명하는 글이므로 글의 제목으로 가장 적절한 것은 ② '사실과 사건은 정말로 같은 것인가?'이다.

오답노트

① 우리가 사건에서 사실을 놓치는 이유
③ 사실에 기반한 사고의 중요성
④ 사실과 허구를 모두 포함하고 있는 사건들
⑤ 사실 여부를 구별하는 방법

04 ②

문제해설

조직의 의사 결정 방식이 강력한 중앙 집권형에서 고도의 참여형 의사 결정 관행까지 다양하다는 내용으로 참여형 의사 결정이 직원의 만족도를 올리기는 하지만 더 나은 성과로 이어지지 않는 경우도 있다는 (B)가 먼저 나오고, 따라서 어떨 때 가장 유용하고 어떨 때 덜 중요한지 연구 결과를 소개하면서 참여형 의사 결정이 효과적인 첫 번째 사례를 소개하고 있는 (A)가 나온 다음에 추가적으로(Additionally) 참여형 의사 결정이 효과적인 사례를 덧붙이고 있는 (C)가 이어지는 것이 자연스러우므로 글의 순서로는 ②가 가장 적절하다.

05 ④

문제해설

포식자가 먹을 수 없는 먹이가 매우 잘 알아볼 수 있는 색깔을 보임으로써 이득을 얻을 것이라는 예측을 제시한 Alfred R. Wallace의 의견이므로 맛이 고약함이 문맥상 자연스럽다. 따라서 ④의 tastefulness(좋은 맛을 가짐)는 distastefulness(맛이 고약함)와 같은 말로 바꿔야 한다.

06 ⑤

문제해설

시대별로 논리적 진술의 검증 필요성이 어떻게 변화되었는지를 다룬 글로써, 현대에 들어와서는 논리적 진술이 정말 사실인지 알아내기 위해서는 실험을 통해 검증되어야 한다는 입장이었다. 그런데 처음부터 실험이 이끌었어야 할 검증 절차에서 실험 행동 자체가 논리적 사고를 뒷받침으로 삼았다는 것은 이 접근법조차도 사고의 중요성을 과대평가했다는 문맥이므로 ⑤의 underrated(과소평가된)을 overrated(과대평가된) 정도로 바꿔야 한다.

07 ④

문제해설

집단은 개인보다 더 쉽게 극단적인 결정을 내릴 수 있으며 더 도전적이고 위험한 결정을 내릴 수 있다는 내용의 주어진 글 다음에는, though가 이끄는 문장을 통해 집단이 너무 신중한 결정을 내릴 수도 있다는 대조되는 내용으로 시작하여 이러한 집단 양극화는 집단 내에서 논의가 어떻게 진행되느냐에 좌우된다는 (C)가 이어지고, 양극단의 사례 중에서 위험한 전략을 옹호하여 더 위험한 결정에 도달하는 내용인 (A)가 문맥상 먼저 나오고, 이와 반대되는 신중한 접근법을 옹호하면 더 신중한 결정에 이르게 된다는 (B)가 오는 것이 자연스럽다.

08 ①

문제해설

미국이 다른 서유럽 국가들과 마찬가지로, 광고 등의 상업 매체가 경제 전반에 밀접하게 관련이 있는 점은 동일하지만, 중요한 차이점은 이것에 관한 방식이라는 게 빈칸의 내용이다. 뒤에 이어지는 내용을 보면 미국의 경우 상업적인 사업으로 발전해 온 반면 많은 다른 국가들은 전적으로 정부 지원형이었다는 내용으로 보아 빈칸에 들어갈 말로 가장 적절한 것은 ① '상업 매체가 발전한'이다.

오답노트

② 방송 시스템이 사회에 영향을 끼치는
③ 국가들이 자국의 산업을 지원하는
④ 미디어가 산업 발전에 도움을 주는
⑤ 소비자들이 광고를 인식하는

09 ④

문제해설

④ It은 형식상의 가주어이고 that certain events did not occur가 내용상의 주어로서 that절이 a fact(사실)로 여겨진다는 의미이므로 ④ considered를 is considered로 고쳐서 It is even considered의 형태가 되어야 한다.

오답노트

① 앞 절의 events를 선행사로 하는 목적격 관계대명사로 which는 적절하다.
② different from each other가 형용사구로 앞에 위치한 concepts를 수식하고 있으므로 형용사 different가 적절하다.
③ facts are detached from space and time에서 facts가 시공간에서 분리되어있다는 의미로 수동형 are detached는 적절하다.
⑤ 우리가 말할 수 있는 최선의 것(the best we can say)이라는 주어의 보어절로 쓰이는 명사절이 필요하므로 접속사 that은 적절하다.

10 ③

문제해설

조직의 의사 결정 방식은 중앙 집권형부터 참여형까지 다양한데 특히 참여형 의사 결정 방식이 어떨 때 유용하고 중요하게 적용되는지를 사례를 들어 설명하는 글이므로, 글의 주제로 가장 적절한 것은 ③ '참여형 의사 결정 방식의 특징과 효과적 사용'이다.

오답노트

① 의사 결정이 지나치게 중앙 집중적일 때 발생하는 문제점
② 근로자의 성향에 따른 의사 결정 방식
④ 의사 결정 방식이 기업 이윤에 끼치는 영향
⑤ 근로자의 조직에 대한 만족도를 올리기 위한 방법

11 ③

문제해설

곤충의 강렬한 천연색이 눈에 띄어 포식자의 먹이가 되기 쉽다고 생각되었는데 오히려 그것이 포식자의 공격을 피하게 하는 경계색이 될 수 있다는 새로운 연구를 소개한 글이기 때문에, 글의 제목으로 가장 적절한 것은 ③ '곤충의 강렬한 천연색 뒤에 숨겨진 비밀'이다.

오답노트

① 보호색: 강한 보호적 특성
② 어려운 난제에 관한 두 과학자의 노고
④ 포식자의 놀라운 능력: 먹이 식별법
⑤ 운명과의 싸움: 포식자로부터의 치열한 탈출

12 ②

문제해설

논리적 진술이 곧 현실에 대한 사실적 진술이었다는 주어진 문장의 마지막 내용 다음에는, 그렇기 때문에 논리적 진술이 실험에 의해 검증받을 필요가 없다고 이야기하는 (B)가 이어지고, (B)의 뒷부분에 현대에 들어와서 인식이 바뀌어 인간이 이성에 대한 의존이 지나치게 과장되었다고 이야기하고 있다. 그래서 (A)에서 논리적 진술이 정말 사실인지 알아내기 위해서는 실험을 통해 검증되어야 한다는 입장이 이어졌고, 나중에 이 입장조차도 사고의 중요성을 과대평가했다는 문맥이 (C)에서 이어지므로 적절한 글의 순서로는 ②가 가장 적절하다.

13 우리는 집단 속에 있을 때, 혼자서 행동하고 있는 경우에 책임을 져야 할 만큼의 개인적으로 책임이 있지는 않다고 생각하는 경향이 있기 때문이다.

문제해설

집단이 내리는 결정이 쉽게 극단적이 될 수 있는 이유는 앞 문장 When we are in groups, we tend to ~ if we were acting on our own.에 나타나 있다.

14 (A) groups (B) individuals

문제해설

집단이 내리는 결정은 쉽게 극단적이 되는 경향이 있다는 집단 양극화에 관한 내용의 글이므로, '공동의 책임감 때문에 (A) 집단에 의한 결정이 (B) 개인에 의한 결정에 비해 쉽게 극단적 경향이 있고, 그것들(그 결정들)이 지나치게 위험하거나 신중하게 되는 경향이 있다.'와 같이 요약하는 것이 가장 적절하다.

15 (A) tied (B) those (C) were

문제해설

(A) 〈with+목적어+분사〉 구문으로, 주어인 a dollar volume of activity를 '관련된'이라는 수동의 의미로 꾸며줘야 하므로 ties를 과거분사 tied로 고쳐야 한다.
(B) 앞에 언급된 other mature industrialized nations를 대신하는 대명사이므로 that을 those로 고쳐야 한다.

(C) media는 medium((대중) 매체)의 복수형이므로 단수 동사 was를 복수 동사 were로 고쳐야 한다.

16 national

문제해설

'나라와 연관이 있거나 속하는'이라는 의미의 단어는 national(국가의)이다.

17 It is even considered a fact that certain events did not occur

문제해설

가주어 it과 that 진주어를 활용한다. 가주어 It 다음에 '~으로 여겨지다'는 수동태로 써야 하므로 consider를 is considered로 바꿔 쓰고 이어서 보어인 a fact 다음에 진주어 that절을 넣어 문장을 완성한다.

18 Unlike facts, events are dated, tied to space and time, whereas facts are detached from space and time.

문제해설

사실과 사건이 서로 다른 개념인 이유는 Unlike facts, events are dated, ~ detached from space and time.에서 사건(events)은 날짜가 있어 시공간에 묶이는 반면, 사실(facts)은 시공간과 분리되어 있기 때문이라는 것에서 알 수 있다.

19 (1) ② → strongly (2) ④ → does

문제해설

② centralized가 뒤에 나온 명사구 decision-making practices를 수식하는 형용사이므로 strong은 이를 강조하는 부사 strongly로 고쳐야 한다.
④ shows의 목적어 역할을 하는 that 명사절 안에서 등위접속사 but에 의해 동사 improves와 병렬 연결되어 있으므로 do를 does로 고쳐야 한다.

오답노트

① 선행사 The extent가 관계대명사절에서 전치사 to의 목적어 역할을 해야 하므로 to which는 적절하다.
③ 이어지는 more input이 비교급이므로 비교급을 강조하는 부사 much는 적절하다.
⑤ 주어가 knowledge이므로 단수 동사 is는 적절하다.

20 has investigated when participatory decision making is most useful, when it is less important

문제해설

동사 has investigated 다음에 '~한 때'라는 의미의 부사절 접속사 when을 활용하여 '참여형 의사 결정이 가장 유용한 때'와 '그것이 덜 중요한 때'를 각각 when participatory decision making is most useful과 when it is less important로 써서 나타낸다.

21 성 선택이 박각시나방 애벌레에 속하는 비생식 유충의 눈에 뜨이는 색깔 패턴을 설명할 수 없다는 것

문제해설

밑줄 친 this puzzle은 앞 문장에 제시된 sexual selection could not account for the striking color pattern ~ Pseudosphinx hawk moth caterpillars를 가리킨다.

22 edible

문제해설

'음식으로 사용하기에 적절하거나 먹기에 안전한'이라는 의미의 단어는 edible(먹을 수 있는, 먹어도 되는)이다.

23 it was believed that, of reality, of thought, so closely allied that

문제해설

'~이라고 여겨졌다'는 〈가주어-진주어〉 구문으로 쓰라는 조건이 있으므로 문장 맨 앞에 가주어 it, 동사 was believed 뒤에 진주어를 이끄는 접속사 that을 쓴다. '매우 밀접하게 연관되어 있어'는 〈so ~ that ...〉 구문을 활용해서 so closely allied that으로 나타낸다.

24 (A) a logical statement (B) a true statement

문제해설

고대와 중세 시대에는 논리적 진술 자체가 현실에 대한 사실적 진술이라고 생각했기 때문에 실험에 의해 검증을 받을 필요가 없었지만, 현대에는 그것이 사실인지 알아내기 위해 검증하는 물리적 실험의 필요성을 깨닫게 되었다는 내용의 글이므로, (A)에는 a logical statement(논리적 진술), (B)에는 a true statement(사실적 진술)가 가장 적절하다.

17강

1번 ——————————————— p.286

● Word Test

1 맞닥뜨리다, 만나다　2 기간　3 해당하다, 나타내다　4 짝
5 대조적으로　6 강렬하게　7 부재　8 theory
9 turning point　10 emphasize　11 observe
12 frequent　13 spouse　14 proportion

유형 1

❶ acutely　❷ in contrast　❸ absence
❹ partly　❺ later

유형 2

❶ has been observed　❷ becomes
❸ have emphasized　❹ doing

유형 3

❶ half a lifetime　❷ As we age
❸ graduate from　❹ frequent life-changing events

2번 ——————————————— p.288

● Word Test

1 실제보다 더 높게 어림하다, 과대평가하다　2 사회 이동　3 신화
4 상당히　5 이동성　6 자수성가의　7 ~에 동의하다
8 ~으로 불리다　9 열심히 노력하다, 전념하다　10 initiative
11 imply　12 ethnic　13 intergenerational
14 be up to　15 consistently　16 specific
17 largely　18 poverty

유형 1

❶ to　❷ themselves　❸ more
❹ subscribe　❺ initiative

유형 2

❶ is　❷ suggests　❸ implying
❹ are　❺ to overestimate

유형 3

❶ over time　❷ is largely up to
❸ what people believe
❹ pulling oneself out of poverty

3번 ——————————————— p.290

● Word Test

1 없애다　2 신성한, 신의　3 ~을 낮게 평가하다, ~을 경시하다
4 고대 그리스 로마의, 고전적인　5 광범위한, 널리 퍼진
6 실행하다　7 (제도·법률 따위를) 정하다, 마련하다
8 마찬가지로　9 주문(呪文), 마법　10 caution
11 separation　12 authorities　13 dependent on
14 foundation　15 abuse　16 mistrust
17 intellectual　18 condemn

유형 1

❶ dependent　❷ its　❸ harmful
❹ Likewise　❺ that

유형 2

❶ was established　❷ be punished　❸ realizing
❹ be abused　❺ be eliminated

유형 3

❶ grew concerned about
❷ was held in low esteem
❸ along with　❹ the foundations for philosophy

4번 ——————————————— p.293

● Word Test

1 느긋한　2 적당히　3 자극　4 반응자　5 열정적인
6 측정하다　7 분류하다　8 연속선　9 pop
10 outcome　11 wave　12 sociable
13 psychologist　14 initially　15 violently
16 unfamiliar

유형 1

❶ stimulus　❷ while　❸ initially
❹ highly　❺ moderately

유형 2

❶ classified　❷ saying　❸ popped
❹ were　❺ had moved

유형 3

❶ depending upon　❷ moved around violently
❸ By the age of 7　❹ in other words

——————————————— p.295

01 ③　02 ①　03 ③　04 ④　05 ②　06 ⑤
07 ②　08 ⑤　09 ② → is ⑤ → living
10 the absence of frequent life-changing events
11 (A) is referred to　(B) implying　(C) what
12 pulling oneself out of poverty　13 magic was
an activity capable of results, they grew concerned
about those who practiced harmful magic
14 condemned　15 (A) fearless　(B) fearful
16 depending upon their responses to an unfamiliar
stimulus

01 ③

문제해설

주어진 문장은 다른 사람들은 같은 10년의 기간 동안에, 더 젊은 사람들이
고령자들보다 더 많은 전환점에 맞닥뜨린다는 사실을 강조해 왔다는 내용
이다. 그러므로 나이가 들면서 10년이 우리의 인생에서 차지하는 부분이
더 작아지기 때문이라는 첫 이론이 제시된 다음에, 주어진 문장에서 언급
한 전환점에 대한 예가 제시되는 내용의 사이인 ③에 오는 것이 가장 적절
하다.

02 ①

문제해설

미국에서는 개인의 노력에 따라 사회적 이동이 아주 흔하고 성취하기 쉬운 일이라는 내용의 글로써 미국에서는 부 또한 운이나 출생보다는 각 개인의 근면과 진취성의 결과라는 믿음을 더 높게 어림한다는 내용이므로 빈칸에 들어갈 말로 가장 적절한 것은 ① '주로 개인에게 달려있는'이다.

오답노트

② 개인의 행복이 우선하는
③ 개인적으로 달성하기 너무 어려운
④ 모든 사람이 성취하고자 하는 어떤 것
⑤ 사람들이 자신의 인생에서 목표로 삼는 것

03 ③

문제해설

고대 그리스 당국이 해로운 마법을 행하는 사람들에 대해 점차 걱정하게 되었다는 내용의 주어진 글 다음에는, 그 결과 해로운 마법을 행하는 사람들이 시민 행동에 의해 처벌될 수 있도록 정해졌으며 이것이 바로 마법이 낮게 평가되고 비난받은 이유일 것이라는 (B)가 오고, 특정 지식인들도 마법이 남용될 수 있다고 인식했음을 언급하면서 예시로 플라톤 등을 언급하는 (C)가 이어지며, 이를 배경으로 철학의 기초가 만들어졌다는 (A)의 내용으로 마무리하는 것이 자연스러우므로, 글의 순서로는 ③이 가장 적절하다.

04 ④

문제해설

자극에 대한 반응에 따라 분류한 유아들이 나이가 들면서 기질의 변화가 생기는지에 대해 연구한 내용으로 나이대별의 관찰을 통해 환경에 의해 크게 영향을 받지 않는다는 내용이므로 글의 제목으로 가장 적절한 것은 ④ '환경: 기질의 변화에 도움이 되는가?'이다.

오답노트

① 끊임없이 지속되는: 한 심리학자의 연구
② 조기 교육: 기질을 변화시킬 수 있는가?
③ 각 나이대의 기질적 특징
⑤ 기질의 분류: 두 가지로 충분한가?

05 ②

문제해설

② 주어 It이 형식상 주어이고 that절이 내용상 주어로서 관찰되어 온 것이므로 observe는 수동형이 적절하다. 따라서 has observed를 has been observed로 고쳐야 한다.

오답노트

① 고령자들이 젊은 사람들보다 훨씬 더 강렬하게 장기 시간 압축을 경험한다는 맥락으로 동사 experience를 수식하므로 부사 acutely는 적절하다.
③ 몇 가지 이론을 소개하는 맥락에서 다른 연구를 소개하는 문장의 주어로써 다른 사람들을 지칭하는 대명사 Others는 적절하다.
④ 고령자들이 쉽게 10년을 보낼 수 있다는 주절을 부연 설명하는 분사구문 doing과 병렬구조를 이루므로 living은 적절하다.
⑤ 의문사 why가 이끄는 명사절이 동사 explain의 목적어로 쓰인 것이므로 why는 적절하다.

06 ⑤

문제해설

주어진 글에서 사회 이동과 세대 간 이동에 대해 소개한 다음에는, 특히 자수성가에 대한 근거 없는 믿음이 미국에서는 사회적 지위가 주로 개인에 달려있음을 시사한다는 (C)가 이어지고 이에 대한 최근의 한 실험 결과를 소개하는 (B)가 이어진 뒤에 마지막으로 In other words를 활용해 실험 결과를 다시 재진술하는 (A)가 나오는 것이 자연스러우므로 적절한 글의 순서로는 ⑤가 가장 적절하다.

07 ②

문제해설

고대 그리스에서 널리 퍼져 있던 마법에 대한 믿음과 관행이 해로운 마법을 행하는 사람들로 인해 금지되고 당대 지식인들의 비난과 낮은 평가가 결국 고대 그리스인들이 철학의 기초를 마련했다는 내용이므로 빈칸에 들어갈 말로 가장 적절한 것은 ② '마법에 대한 불신'이다.

오답노트

① 마법의 남용
③ 마법의 이러한 성취
④ 마법에 대한 지나친 의존
⑤ 당대 지식인들의 비판 의식

08 ⑤

문제해설

None of the high reactors became fearless, ~에서 고반응자들 중 아무도 겁이 없게 되지 않았다는 말은 결국 여전히 겁이 있었다는 내용이므로, ⑤ 고반응을 보였던 유아들이 7세가 되어 겁이 없어진 것을 발견했다는 설명은 글의 내용과 일치하지 않는다.

09 ② → is ⑤ → living

문제해설

② ten years가 '10년이라는 기간'의 의미로 개념상 하나의 수치를 나타내므로 복수 동사 are로 고쳐야 한다.
⑤ '~하면서'라는 동시상황을 나타내는 분사구문으로, 등위접속사 and에 의해 doing과 병렬로 연결되었으므로 live를 living으로 고쳐야 한다.

오답노트

① '강렬하게' 경험한다는 의미이며 동사 experience를 수식하고 있으므로 부사인 acutely는 적절하다.
③ that ~ younger people encounter more "turning points" than older people과 the fact가 동격이므로, 동격의 명사절을 이끄는 접속사 that은 적절하다.
④ '~일 것 같다'라는 의미의 〈be+likely+to-v〉 구문으로 to graduate는 적절하다.

10 the absence of frequent life-changing events

문제해설

고령자들이 만년의 수십 년이 매우 빨리 지나가는 것처럼 느끼는 이유를 설명하는 문장은 The absence of frequent life-changing events may partly explain why older people feel that the later decades seem to pass so quickly.에 나와 있다.

11 (A) is referred to (B) implying (C) what

문제해설

(A) Social mobility between generations가 '불리는' 것이므로 수동태로 써야 하는데, 핵심 주어가 Social mobility로 단수 명사이므로 is referred to로 고쳐야 한다.
(B) 앞 절의 내용을 부가적으로 설명하는 분사구문이고 능동의 의미이므로 implies를 현재분사 implying으로 고쳐야 한다.
(C) 등위접속사 and에 의해 what people believe와 병렬 연결되었으므로 which를 what으로 고쳐야 한다.

12 pulling oneself out of poverty

문제해설

밑줄 친 it은 앞부분에서 언급된 pulling oneself out of poverty(자신이 가난에서 벗어나는 것)를 가리킨다.

13 magic was an activity capable of results, they grew concerned about those who practiced harmful magic

문제해설

'성과를 낼 수 있는 활동'은 형용사구가 뒤에서 an activity를 꾸며주도록 하여 an activity capable of results로 나타낼 수 있다. '~에 대해 걱정하게 되었다'는 grew concerned about을 쓰고, '~하는 사람들'은 those who를 사용해서 문장을 완성한다.

14 condemned

문제해설

'누군가 또는 어떤 것에 대한 강하고 분명한 반감을 나타내다'라는 의미의 단어는 condemn(비난하다, 규탄하다)인데, 등위접속사 and에 의해 held에 병렬 연결되었으므로 과거분사 condemned로 쓴다.

15 (A) fearless (B) fearful

문제해설

새로운 자극에 대한 반응으로 분류된 아이들을 대상으로 한 연구에서, 유아의 초기 기질이 나중에도 크게 변하지 않았다는 것이 글의 핵심 내용이므로, 각각 fearless(두려움이 없는)와 fearful(두려워하는)이 알맞다.

16 depending upon their responses to an unfamiliar stimulus

문제해설

'~에 따라'는 depending upon을 사용하고, '~에 대한 그들의 반응'은 their responses to ~ 형태를 사용하여 쓴다.

18강

1-2번 — p.301

Word Test

1 얻다　2 동인(動因)　3 말하다, 관찰하다　4 ~이 아니라
5 ~이 …을 주리라고 기대하다　6 둔한 사람　7 창시자
8 경계선, 분수령　9 말로　10 means　11 evolutionary
12 primary　13 separate　14 speech　15 vast
16 ignorance　17 signal　18 awareness

유형 1
① from　② Unlike　③ indicate
④ who　⑤ comfortable

유형 2
① is　② are designed　③ directed
④ is　⑤ has been known
⑥ using

유형 3
① the ability to question　② so that
③ as opposed to　④ tend to be aware of

3-4번 — p.304

Word Test

1 (씨를) 뿌리다　2 깊이 배게 하다　3 기본의
4 예금 계좌, 적금 계좌　5 부정적인, 냉소적인　6 범죄를 저지르다
7 반영, 반사　8 결국, 언젠가는　9 숙고하다, 곰곰이 생각하다
10 ~을 상쇄하다　11 prosperity　12 confusing
13 with respect to　14 corrupt　15 occurrence
16 rotten　17 unconscious　18 blossom
19 attract　20 appetite

유형 1
① whatever　② reflection　③ which
④ ingrained　⑤ seed　⑥ while
⑦ commit

유형 2
① pondering　② remains　③ cancels
④ is shaped　⑤ to fall

유형 3
① This holds true for
② seem a bit confusing
③ with respect to money　④ as the direct result of
⑤ due to a chance occurrence

5-6번 — p.307

Word Test

1 절박한, 필사적인　2 묶, 부분　3 기여하다　4 친족이 아닌
5 협력적인　6 공감　7 위반하는 사람
8 친척, (공통의 계통을 갖는) 동물[식물]　9 동기를 부여하다

10 못된, 고약한　　11 in part　　12 opposing
13 preference　　14 collaborator　　15 charity
16 beg　　17 exposure　　18 welfare　　19 norm
20 aggression

유형 1

❶ others　　❷ were studied　　❸ the other
❹ Although　　❺ either　　❻ unrelated

유형 2

❶ comfort　　❷ had lived　　❸ was given
❹ was dispensed　　❺ be noted　　❻ was

유형 3

❶ at least in part　　❷ at no cost to
❸ in opposing enclosures
❹ exactly the same portion
❺ about equally frequently

7-8번
p.311

• Word Test

1 ~에 주의를 기울이다　　2 겉보기에는, 외관상으로　　3 잘못된
4 순간적으로, 순식간에　　5 지속되다　　6 잘못되게, 틀리게
7 인식하지 못함　　8 목격자　　9 오도하다
10 automatically　　11 humble　　12 limitation
13 convince　　14 change blindness　　15 critical
16 obvious　　17 intersection　　18 phenomenon

유형 1

❶ Despite　　❷ erroneous　　❸ that
❹ unawareness　　❺ that　　❻ incorrectly
❼ humble

유형 2

❶ to perceive　　❷ heading
❸ have missed　　❹ believing　　❺ misleading

유형 3

❶ draw their attention　　❷ few people believe
❸ Perhaps out of a desire to help
❹ they were attending to
❺ the limitations of attention

p.314

01 ②　　02 ④　　03 ①　　04 ③　　05 ④　　06 ③
07 ⑤　　08 ④　　09 ① → separates　④ → what
10 우리 인간은 다른 영장류와 달리 어린 사람이 연장자가 문화적
정보를 주리라고 기대하도록 설계되어 있는 것　　11 holds true
for both your conscious and unconscious thoughts,
which may seem　　12 unconsciously
13 (A) were　(B) eating　(C) whether
14 (A) empathy　(B) preferences　　15 자신이 항상 큰
변화를 알아차릴 것이라고, 즉 중요한 사건이 자동으로 자신의 주의를
끈다고 믿는 것　　16 change blindness, humble attitude,
incorrect perceptions

01 ②

문제해설

인류가 질문하기를 통해 필요한 정보를 얻고, 특히 훌륭한 질문자들이 자신들의 무지를 인식해서 질문하기를 통해 끊임없이 무지를 조사하고 공격한다는 내용이므로 글의 제목으로 가장 적절한 것은 ② '질문하기: 무지의 영역을 탐구하는 열쇠'이다.

오답노트

① 교실에서 질문하기의 교육적 효과
③ 질문의 수준: 지적 능력의 척도
④ 진화적 경계: 인간과 하등 영장류
⑤ 무지의 인식: 메타 학습의 본질

02 ④

문제해설

질문하기의 동인이 우리가 모르는 것에 대한 인식이며 그것이 똑똑하고 호기심 많은 사람을 모르거나 무심한 사람과 구별 짓는 것이라는 내용과 훌륭한 질문자들은 질문이라는 손전등을 사용하여 그 방대한 무지를 끊임없이 조사하는 사람들이라는 설명으로 미루어 보아 훌륭한 질문자들은 자신들의 무지를 (d) unaware(인식하지 못한)하는 것이 아니라 aware(인식하는) 해야 한다.

03 ①

문제해설

내면 세계의 방향, 즉 사고의 방향을 긍정적으로 하기 위해 지속적인 노력을 하면 우리 환경의 외부세계도 풍성해지는 삶을 살 수 있다는 내용이므로 글의 제목으로 가장 적절한 것은 '① 실재: 정신의 반영'이다.

오답노트

② 반복된 행동이 습관이 된다
③ 성취를 위한 필수: 숙고
④ 무의식적인 행동의 예상치 못한 결과
⑤ 부를 쌓는 비밀: 가난을 두려워하지 마라

04 ③

문제해설

비록 부를 늘리기 위해 노력을 해 왔더라도, 돈에 관한 비관적인 생각이 매우 뿌리 깊어 그것이 실제로 긍정적인 조치를 상쇄한다는 맥락이 자연스러우므로 (c) optimistic(낙관적인)이 아니라 pessimistic(비관적인)이 되어야 한다.

05 ④

문제해설

인간과 가장 비슷하다고 하는 침팬지들이 보여 주는 협력적 사냥이나 공격의 희생자를 향한 위로, 그리고 다른 집단 활동이 과연 인간이 보여 주는 타인의 행복에 대한 공감과 유사한 것인지 대조 실험을 통해 알아보는 내용이므로 글의 제목으로 가장 적절한 것은 ④ '침팬지가 공감의 측면에서 인간과 가까운가?'이다.

오답노트

① 대조 실험의 효과와 한계

② 침팬지가 보여 주는 깊고 진정성있는 공감
③ 인간과 침팬지의 생물학적 유사성
⑤ 침팬지가 행하는 공감적 행동의 감동

06 ③

문제해설

다른 침팬지가 절박하게 구걸하는 몸짓을 보이거나, 또는 음식이 제공될 때 행복하게 먹는 것을 분명히 봤음에도 불구하고 전혀 공감하는 기색을 보이지 않았다고 했으므로 침팬지들이 착한 선택권을 더 자주 선택하지 않는다는 게 자연스러우므로 (c) nasty(못된)가 아니라 nice(착한)로 바꿔야 한다.

07 ⑤

문제해설

변화를 인식하지 못할 수 있다는 주의의 한계를 인식하는 것이 우리가 우리의 인식을 오도하지 못하게 하는데 도움이 될 수도 있다고 했으므로 글의 제목으로 가장 적절한 것은 ⑤ '변화맹을 보지 못하는 것을 인정하기'이다.

오답노트

① 목격자들의 진술에 대한 갑론을박
② 위급 상황에서의 인간 감각의 한계
③ 실수를 범할 가능성을 인정하는 것의 어려움
④ 주의를 끄는 사건에 집중하게 하는 특성

08 ④

문제해설

우리가 항상 우리의 시계에서 큰 변화를 알아차린다고 생각하는 것이 결국 우리가 어떤 일이 일어났거나 일어나지 않았다고 잘못 믿는 경우처럼 사물을 잘못 인식하게 할 수도 있다는 문맥이므로 (d) correctly(올바르게)가 아니라 incorrectly(부정확하게)로 바꿔야 한다.

09 ① → separates ④ → what

문제해설

① 선행사가 〈one of+복수 명사〉의 형태로 쓰였으므로 복수 동사 separate를 단수 동사 separates로 고쳐야 한다.
④ 선행사가 없고 전치사 of의 목적절을 이끄는 역할을 해야 하므로 선행사를 포함하는 관계대명사 what으로 고쳐야 한다.

오답노트

② '기대하도록'이라는 의미이므로 목적을 나타내는 〈so that〉은 적절하다.
③ a look or gesture를 설명하는 분사구문이고 directed at은 '~으로 향해진'이라는 의미를 가지므로 directed는 적절하다.
⑤ '~을 사용하여'라는 능동의 의미이므로 현재분사 using은 적절하다.

10 우리 인간은 다른 영장류와 달리 어린 사람이 연장자가 문화적 정보를 주리라고 기대하도록 설계되어 있는 것

문제해설

밑줄 친 this가 가리키는 것은 앞 문장 "Unlike other primates, we humans ~ for cultural information."에 나타나 있다.

11 holds true for both your conscious and unconscious thoughts, which may seem

문제해설

주어가 This이므로 '~에 들어맞다'는 hold true for를 활용해서 This holds true for로 나타내고, 'A와 B 둘 다'는 〈both A and B〉 구문을 사용해서 나타낸다. '이것은' 이후의 내용은 앞 절의 내용을 부연 설명하는 계속적 용법의 관계대명사 which를 사용해서 문장을 연결하여 쓴다.

12 unconsciously

문제해설

의식적으로 부를 원하지만 예금 계좌가 계속 비어 있는 것은 자신이 부자가 될 것으로 생각하지 않는다고 무의식적으로 부정적인 생각을 하기 때문이라는 내용이고 동사를 수식하는 부사 자리이므로 빈칸에는 unconscious(무의식적인)의 부사 unconsciously(무의식적으로)가 알맞다.

13 (A) were (B) eating (C) whether

문제해설

(A) 〈if+주어+동사의 과거형, 주어+조동사의 과거형(would)+동사원형〉의 형태인 가정법 과거 구문이므로 are를 were로 고쳐야 한다.
(B) 등위접속사 or에 의해 displaying과 병렬 연결되었으므로 eat을 현재분사 eating으로 고쳐야 한다.
(C) 뒤에 완전한 절이 이어지고 있고, was의 보어 역할을 하는 명사절을 이끄는 접속사가 필요한데 의미상 '~인지'를 묻는 것이므로 what을 whether로 고쳐야 한다.

14 (A) empathy (B) preferences

문제해설

인간과 달리 침팬지는 다른 집단 구성원에 대한 공감이나 관심의 미덕이 없다는 내용의 글이므로, '인간은 타인의 행복에 대한 (A) 공감에 의해 동기 부여를 받는 반면, 인간과 가까운 침팬지는 다른 침팬지의 행복에 대해 신경을 쓰지 않고 단지 자신의 (B) 선호도에 따라 선택을 한다는 것이 실험을 통해 판명되었다.'와 같이 요약하는 것이 가장 적절하다.

15 자신이 항상 큰 변화를 알아차릴 것이라고, 즉 중요한 사건이 자동으로 자신의 주의를 끈다고 믿는 것

문제해설

밑줄 친 This erroneous belief가 가리키는 것은 앞 문장의 most people believe ~ automatically draw their attention.에 나타나 있다.

16 change blindness, humble attitude, incorrect perceptions

문제해설

우리가 변화맹을 보지 못하는 것을 인식하는 것은 그것이 실제로 우리가 보고 기억하는 것에 관해 우리로 하여금 겸손한 태도를 갖게 하고 사건에 대해 잘못된 인식을 갖는 것을 막아 주기 때문에 중요한 사고 기술이라는 내용의 글이므로, 순서대로 change blindness, humble attitude, incorrect perceptions가 각각 알맞다.

1-3번 _____ p.320

• Word Test

1 보아하니, 언뜻 보기에　2 주의가 산만한　3 여전히
4 촉발하다　5 떠맡다　6 잡종, (두 가지 다른 것, 동식물의) 혼합, 이종 교배　7 나누다, 구분 짓다　8 보증, 굳은 약속
9 공격적이지 않은　10 horror　11 thoroughly
12 well-behaved　13 assure　14 wander
15 attractive　16 chew　17 contentedly
18 escort

유형 1

❶ thoroughly　❷ where　❸ yell
❹ Apparently　❺ waving

유형 2

❶ being　❷ dividing　❸ was given
❹ bending　❺ following　❻ Thinking

유형 3

❶ well-behaved and non-aggressive
❷ settled down
❸ Not having time to do anything
❹ what might happen next
❺ all the same　❻ so long as

4-6번 _____ p.324

• Word Test

1 무역 회사　2 (손짓으로) 신호하다　3 (탁송된) 화물
4 부족한　5 ~하기로 되어 있다　6 염려, 관심사
7 물품 목록, 재고(품)　8 amount　9 significant
10 inform　11 confirm　12 replace　13 displeased
14 warehouse

유형 1

❶ motioned　❷ what　❸ significant
❹ nothing　❺ whether　❻ replacing

유형 2

❶ to go　❷ have been
❸ have arrived　❹ knew　❺ had arrived
❻ to know

유형 3

❶ seemed to be somewhat displeased
❷ make different amounts of money
❸ was supposed to　❹ at least knew of
❺ did inventory on it

7-9번 _____ p.328

• Word Test

1 ~에서 삐져나오다　2 우연히 듣다　3 말을 걸다
4 간절히 ~하고 싶어 하다　5 ~을 내밀다

6 그만해, 그것으로 됐어　7 구두닦이　8 보석(류)
9 앞으로 넘어지다　10 ~에게 …을 수여하다
11 lose one's temper　12 beard
13 bravery　14 passerby　15 struggle　16 polish
17 catch hold of　18 glance　19 count　20 theft

유형 1

❶ overheard　❷ though　❸ temper
❹ The other　❺ sticking　❻ bravery

유형 2

❶ counting　❷ saying　❸ looking
❹ have lost　❺ was found　❻ was taken

유형 3

❶ for a living　❷ has just escaped from
❸ managed to run away
❹ Through the corner of his eye
❺ concentrated his attention on
❻ They caught hold of him

10-12번 _____ p.332

• Word Test

1 이중으로　2 상관관계　3 ~과 연관된　4 당당하게 걷다
5 잠재적인　6 임무, 과제　7 결정하다　8 낙농의　9 내륙의
10 받아들여지다　11 발생하다　12 temperature
13 management　14 statistics　15 ban
16 agency　17 generous　18 calculate
19 impress　20 dismiss　21 consumption
22 present

유형 1

❶ that　❷ determine　❸ what
❹ though　❺ no　❻ banning
❼ dismissed

유형 2

❶ working　❷ was told　❸ to impress
❹ receiving　❺ be　❻ is

유형 3

❶ the large number of　❷ associated with
❸ generous in sharing data　❹ Just one short week
❺ To make doubly sure　❻ did not go over well

_____ p.336

01 ④　02 ⑤　03 ⑤　04 ⑤　05 ⑤　06 ⑤
07 ③　08 ②　09 ⑤　10 ①　11 ④　12 ③
13 (1) ③ → horror (2) ④ → constant
14 she didn't[did not] have time to do anything more than yell out of the window　15 it would be easier to show him why there was a significant difference in the salaries　16 gets paid differently, attitudes towards work　17 (A) to run (B) approaching / approach (C) was rewarded

18 was about to shine it with a cloth, he found something sticking out of it at the back
19 (1) ②, him → for him (2) ③, what → that
(3) ⑤, are → (should) be
20 (A) 주에서의 뱃놀이 사고 수를 줄이기 위한 몇 가지 방법을 결정하는 데 도움을 주는 일 (B) 어떤 미시간주의 호수라도 그 호수의 2마일 내에 있는 모든 상점에서 아이스크림 판매를 금지할 것

01 ④

문제해설

필자의 집으로 처음 온 Sally가 얼마나 말을 잘 듣고 공격적이지 않을까 필자가 시험하게 될 것이라는 내용의 주어진 글 (A) 다음에, 필자의 엄마가 부엌에서 창밖을 보았을 때 필자가 Sally의 입에서 뼈를 움켜쥐기 위해 허리를 숙였다는 내용의 (D)로 이어진 후, 엄마는 그 광경을 보고 소리를 지르지 못한 채 있었는데, 필자에게는 아무 일이 없었고, 이를 통해 둘의 평생의 우정이 시작되어 그 이후 Sally는 필자의 호위대원이자 보호자였다는 내용의 (B)가 와야 한다. 끝으로 삼촌의 팔을 물고 늘어진 일화가 소개되면서 Sally가 12년 동안 놀이 친구이자 가장 친한 친구였다는 내용의 (C)가 마지막에 오는 것이 글의 순서로 가장 적절하다.

02 ⑤

문제해설

밑줄 친 (a), (b), (c), (d)는 모두 Sally를 가리키지만, (e)는 필자의 엄마를 가리킨다.

03 ⑤

문제해설

(C)에 나오는 Phil 삼촌과의 일화는 Sally가 집에 온 다음 날의 일화가 아니라 한참 뒤의 시기에 일어난 일을 회상하는 것이므로 글에 관한 내용으로 적절하지 않은 것은 ⑤이다

04 ⑤

문제해설

Johnson씨가 세 아들이 근무하는 무역 회사의 부장과 이야기를 나누기 위해 그 회사로 가서 부장을 만나는 내용이 언급된 주어진 글 (A) 다음에, Johnson씨가 세 아들이 모두 직위가 같고 근무량이 같은데도 봉급 액수가 서로 다른 것을 이해하지 못하겠다고 말하는 내용의 (D)로 이어진 후, 부장이 Johnson 씨의 말을 듣고 그의 염려를 이해하고 나서, 봉급 액수에 차이가 있는 이유를 보여주기 위해 첫째 아들에게 전화를 걸어 그의 근무 태도를 제시함으로써 세 아들의 비교하기 시작하는 내용의 (C)가 오고, 둘째 아들과 셋째 아들의 근무 태도를 추가로 제시한 후, 세 아들의 봉급 액수에 차이가 나는 이유를 밝히는 내용의 (B)가 마지막에 오는 것이 글의 순서로 가장 적절하다.

05 ⑤

문제해설

밑줄 친 (a), (b), (c), (d)는 모두 부장을 가리키지만, (e)는 Johnson 씨를 가리킨다.

06 ⑤

문제해설

(D)에서 Johnson씨가 세 아들이 모두 직위가 같고 근무량이 같은데도 봉급 액수가 서로 다른 것을 이해하지 못하겠다고 말하는 내용이 있으므로, 글에 관한 내용으로 적절하지 않은 것은 ⑤이다.

07 ③

문제해설

구두닦이 소년인 Dhira가 어느 날 한 행인에게 도둑이 방금 보석상에서 도망쳤다는 이야기를 듣게 되는 내용의 주어진 글 (A) 다음에, Dhira는 한 손님이 구두를 닦으러 왔지만, 그 절도 사건을 계속 궁금해 했고, 마침 경찰관들이 왔다는 내용의 (C)로 이어진 후, 그 경찰관들을 본 손님이 Dhira를 갑자기 재촉하여 Dhira가 구두를 열심히 닦던 중 그의 구두 뒤쪽에서 무언가를 발견하는 내용의 (D)가 와야 한다. Dhira가 그 무언가를 자세히 본 후, 신발의 끈을 묶고 경찰관에게 신고하여 포상을 받았다는 내용의 (B)가 마지막에 오는 것이 글의 순서로 가장 적절하다.

08 ②

문제해설

밑줄 친 (a), (c), (d), (e)는 모두 Dhira을 가리키지만, (b)는 손님을 가리킨다.

09 ⑤

문제해설

(D)에서 Dhira가 도둑에 대해 경찰들에게 물어보고 싶었다고 말하는 내용이 있으므로, 글에 관한 내용으로 적절하지 않은 것은 ⑤이다.

10 ①

문제해설

Rob이 자신의 상사로부터 뱃놀이 사고를 줄이는 방법에 관한 임무를 맡게 되었다는 내용의 주어진 글 (A) 다음에, 많은 자료와 통계 지식을 통해 아이스크림 소비와 뱃놀이 사고 사이에 상관관계가 있음을 알게 되었다는 내용의 (B)로 이어진 후, 뱃놀이 사고를 줄이기 위해서는 아이스크림 소비를 통제해야 한다는 결론과 계획을 가지고 상사에게 갔다는 내용의 (D)가 오고, 아이스크림 소비를 줄이기 위한 구체적인 방안을 상사에게 제시하지만, 그 제안이 받아들여지지 않았고 상사가 Rob을 자기 사무실에서 내보냈다는 내용의 (C)가 마지막에 오는 것이 글의 순서로 가장 적절하다.

11 ④

문제해설

밑줄 친 (a), (b), (c), (e)는 모두 Rob을 가리키지만, (d)는 상사를 가리킨다.

12 ③

문제해설

(C)에서 Rob이 미시간 주의 호수라도 그 호수의 2마일 내에 있는 모든 상점에서 아이스크림 판매를 금지할 것을 제안했고, 그 제안의 잠재적 영향

은 컸는데, 왜냐하면 미시간에서는 어떤 사람도 내륙호수로부터 6마일이 넘는 거리에 있지 않기 때문이라는 내용이 있으므로, 글에 관한 내용으로 적절하지 않은 것은 ③이다.

13 (1) ③ → horror (2) ④ → constant

문제해설

(1) 자신의 두 살배기 아기가 잔디밭을 가로질러 개에게로 걸어가 개의 입에서 뼈를 움켜쥐기 위해 허리를 숙이는 것을 보았다는 내용이 이어지고 있으므로, 엄마의 감정은 '경악스럽게도'로 표현하는 것이 자연스럽다. 따라서 ③ delight(기쁨)를 horror(공포, 경악) 등으로 고쳐야 한다.
(2) 두 살 때부터 반려견 Sally와 내가 함께 자랐으며, 12년 동안 가장 친한 친구였고, 어디든 함께 다녔다고 했으므로, 반려견이 변함 없는 호위대원이자 보호자였다라는 내용이 문맥상 자연스럽다. 따라서 ④ occasional(가끔의)를 constant(변함 없는, 일정한) 등으로 고쳐야 한다.

14 she didn't[did not] have time to do anything more than yell out of the window

문제해설

양보를 나타내는 분사구문으로 〈양보의 접속사 + 주어 + 동사 ~〉 구조로 바꿔 쓸 수 있다. 주어가 my mother이므로 접속사 뒤에 주어를 she로 쓴다. 단순 분사 구문의 부정형이므로 주절의 시제와 같은 과거시제의 부정형인 didn't[did not]을 쓰고, 동사 have 이하를 연결하여 쓴다.

15 it would be easier to show him why there was a significant difference in the salaries

문제해설

'그에게 보여 주는 것이 더 쉽다'는 〈가주어 - 진주어 to부정사구〉 구문을 사용해서 it would be easier to show him이라고 쓰고, '왜 ~ 있는지'는 의문사절 〈why there be동사 + 주어〉 구문의 어순으로 나타낸다.

16 gets paid differently, attitudes towards work

문제해설

Johnson 씨의 세 아들의 봉급이 차이나는 이유를 보여 주는 글로, 'Johnson 씨의 세 아들 모두 같은 기간 동안 어느 무역 회사에서 일해 왔고, 직위가 같으며 같은 시간 일을 하는 데도 불구하고, 그들 각각이 다르게 돈을 받는 이유는 그들이 일에 대한 다른 태도를 갖고 있기 때문이다.'와 같이 요약하는 것이 적절하다.

17 (A) to run (B) approaching / approach (C) was rewarded

문제해설

(A) 동사 manage는 목적어로 to부정사를 취하므로 run을 to run으로 고쳐야 한다.
(B) 지각동사의 목적격 보어 자리로 동사원형과 현재분사를 쓸 수 있으므로 approached를 approach 또는 approaching으로 고쳐야 한다. 지금 진행중인 상황에는 주로 현재분사가 많이 쓰인다.
(C) 주어 Dhira가 '포상을 받았다'라는 수동의 의미를 나타내야 하므로 rewarded를 과거시제의 수동태인 was rewarded로 고쳐야 한다.

18 was about to shine it with a cloth, he found something sticking out of it at the back

문제해설

'막 천으로 광을 내다'는 〈be about to + 동사원형〉 구문을 사용해서 was about to shine it with a cloth로 쓰고, '무언가 삐져나와 있는 것을 발견했다'는 5형식인 〈주어 + found + 목적어 + 목적격 보어〉 구조로 나타낸다. 목적어로 something을 목적격 보어로 현재분사인 sticking을 쓴다.

19 (1) ②, him → for him (2) ③, what → that (3) ⑤, are → (should) be

문제해설

② 명사 a chance를 수식하는 형용사적 용법의 to부정사 to impress의 의미상의 주어로 〈for + 목적격〉의 형태가 되어야 하므로 him을 for him으로 고쳐야 한다.
③ 보어 자리에 명사절이 쓰인 문장으로, 의문사 what 뒤에 완전한 문장이 이어졌으므로 what을 명사절 접속사 that으로 고쳐야 한다.
⑤ 주절의 동사 proposed는 제안을 나타내므로 목적어 자리에 that절을 취할 경우 that 절의 동사는 〈should + 동사원형〉 또는 should가 생략된 동사원형이 쓰여야 한다. 따라서 are를 should be 또는 be로 고쳐야 한다.

20 (A) 주에서의 뱃놀이 사고 수를 줄이기 위한 몇 가지 방법을 결정하는 데 도움을 주는 일
   (B) 어떤 미시간주의 호수라도 그 호수의 2마일 내에 있는 모든 상점에서 아이스크림 판매를 금지할 것

문제해설

(A) 밑줄 친 this assignment가 가리키는 내용은 바로 앞 문장의 The boss asked him to help ~ in the state.에 나타나 있다.
(B) 밑줄 친 the proposal이 가리키는 내용은 앞의 he proposed banning ice-cream sales ~ two miles of any Michigan lake에 나타나 있다.

MEMO

MEMO

MEMO

엔이튜터 Ch

10분 만에 끝내는 영어 수업 준비!

NE Tutor

NE Tutor는 NE능률이 만든 대한민국 대표 영어 티칭 플랫폼으로
영어 수업에 필요한 모든 콘텐츠와 서비스를 제공합니다.

www.netutor.co.kr

NE Tutor
- 커리큘럼
- 스마트 문제뱅크
- 수업자료
- E-BOOK
- 레벨테스트
- 스마트 클래스
- 세미나

• 전국 영어 학원 선생님들이 뽑은 NE Tutor 서비스 TOP 3! •

 1st. 스마트 문제뱅크 1분이면 맞춤형 어휘, 문법 테스트지 완성!!
문법, 독해, 어휘 추가 문제 출제 가능

 2nd. 레벨테스트 학부모 상담 시 필수 아이템!!
초등 1학년부터 중등 3학년까지 9단계 학생 수준 진단

 3rd. E-Book 이젠 연구용 교재 없이도 모든 책 내용을 볼 수 있다!!
ELT부터 중고등까지 온라인 수업 교재로 활용

NE_Tutor

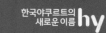

학생 여러분,
쉼 없는 일상에 지치시죠?

이제 스트레스로 인한 긴장
쉼으로 잠시 내려놓으세요

스트레스케어
쉼으로
시작하지

제조/판매 : (주)에치와이, 건강기능식품

하루 한 병으로 관리하는 스트레스케어 쉼

스트레스로 인해 긴장되는 일상을 쉼 없이 이어 나가는 학생 여러분께
hy 스트레스케어 쉼이 달콤한 휴식을 선사합니다.

스트레스로 인한 긴장 완화에 도움을 줄 수 있는 L-테아닌과 (일일 최대 섭취량 250mg 함유)
특허 프로바이오틱스 100억을 한 병에! 캐모마일, 레몬, 베르가못 향으로 상큼 달콤하게 섭취하세요.

마시는 스트레스케어 쉼